INTERNATIONAL ACCLAIM FOR

JOHN JULIUS NORWICH's

A Short History of Byzantium

"Magnificent. . . . This history brims with humanity, historical understanding and unrelenting drama." —*Publishers Weekly*

"Norwich is brilliant. . . . He writes like the most cultivated modern diplomat attached by a freak of time to the Byzantine court." —*The Independent*

"Vivid and entertaining. . . . This . . . is history expounded like the first-class conversation of a sprightly raconteur who responds to his enthusiasms as they seize him with each fresh turn of the story." —*The Sunday Times* (London)

"The best narrative history available today of an empire as fascinating as it was important." —*The Spectator*

"It is human even when contemplating humanity; it is witty; and it tells a remarkable story with boundless zest." —*Daily Telegraph* (London)

"Superbly enjoyable. In brilliantly colorful prose, enlivened by his gift for droll understatement, Norwich brings a complex subject to vivid life." —*Kirkus Reviews*

JOHN JULIUS NORWICH

A Short History of Byzantium

John Julius Norwich was born in 1929. He was educated in Canada, at Eton, at the University of Strasbourg and at Oxford, where he took a degree in French and Russian. In 1952, he joined the Foreign Service, serving at the embassies in Belgrade and Beirut, among other posts. In 1964, he resigned from the service in order to write. He has also published *A History of Venice, A Taste for Travel* and two volumes on the medieval Norman kingdom of Sicily. Lord Norwich, Chairman of the Venice in Peril Fund, is an active member of the House of Lords.

A Short History of
BYZANTIUM

JOHN JULIUS NORWICH

VINTAGE BOOKS

A Division of Random House, Inc.

New York

For Moll

FIRST VINTAGE BOOKS EDITION, JANUARY 1999

Copyright © 1997 by John Julius Norwich

This work is an abridgement of three volumes published
originally by Alfred A. Knopf, Inc., as *Byzantium: The Early
Centuries*, copyright © 1988 by John Julius Norwich; *Byzantium:
The Apogee*, copyright © 1991 by John Julius Norwich; and
Byzantium: The Decline and Fall, copyright © 1995 by
John Julius Norwich.

The Library of Congress has cataloged the Knopf edition as follows:
Norwich, John Julius.
A short history of Byzantium / John Julius Norwich.
p.   cm.
ISBN 0-679-45088-2 (hardcover)
1. Byzantine Empire—Civilization.   I. Title.
DF553.N68   1997
949.5'02—dc21   96-44458
CIP

Vintage ISBN: 0-679-77269-3

Author photograph © Jerry Bauer

www.randomhouse.com

Printed in the United States of America
10 9 8 7 6 5 4

Contents

PART III: THE DECLINE AND FALL

List of Illustrations

Illuminations from *The Chronicle of Manasses*, c. 1345: Basil II at Cimbalongus, 1014; blinded Bulgar prisoners return to Tsar Samuel, who dies of sorrow [*Vatican Library*]

The First Crusade: the army of Peter the Hermit is massacred by the Seljuk Turks [*Bibliothèque Nationale/Bridgeman Art Library*]

The Anastasis (The Harrowing of Hell), apse fresco in the south *parecclesion*, the Church of St Saviour in Chora (Kariye Camii), Istanbul [*Sonia Halliday Photographs*]

The siege of Constantinople, 1453. On the left, the Sultan's ships are being rolled down to the Golden Horn [*Bibliothèque Nationale/Bridgeman Art Library*]

Mehmet II, by Gentile Bellini [*National Gallery, London*]

Third section of black-and-white plates

The Virgin and Child: ivory statuette, eleventh or twelfth century [*Victoria & Albert Museum, London*]

The Western Emperor Otto III enthroned: from a Gospel Book painted at Reichenau or at the imperial court, c. 998 [*Bayerische Staatsbibliothek, Munich/Hirmer Fotoarchiv*]

St Sophia today, Istanbul [*Sonia Halliday Photographs*]

Mosaic of Christ Pantocrator, c. 1150, Cefalù Cathedral, Sicily [*Scala*]

The monastery of the Peribleptos, Mistra, late fourteenth century [*Sonia Halliday Photographs*]

The Emperor Frederick Barbarossa [*Vatican Library/Sonia Halliday Photographs*]

A Turkish Janissary, by Gentile Bellini, late fifteenth century [*British Museum*]

The Fortress of Rumeli Hisar on the Bosphorus, built by the Sultan Mehmet II in 1452, photographed c. 1914 [*AKG London*]

Maps

Family Trees

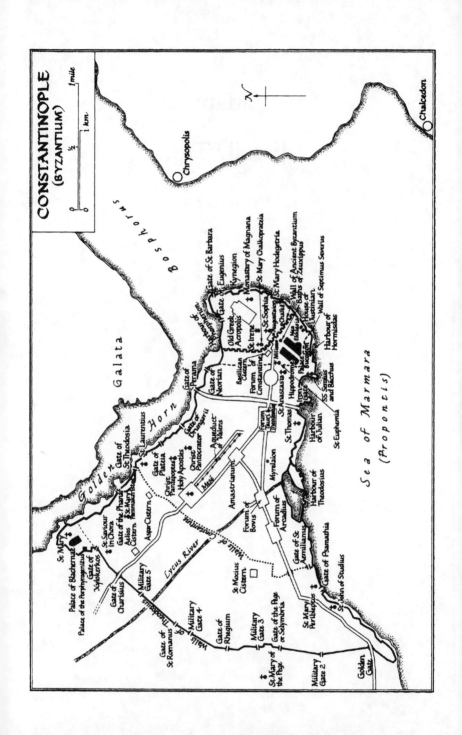

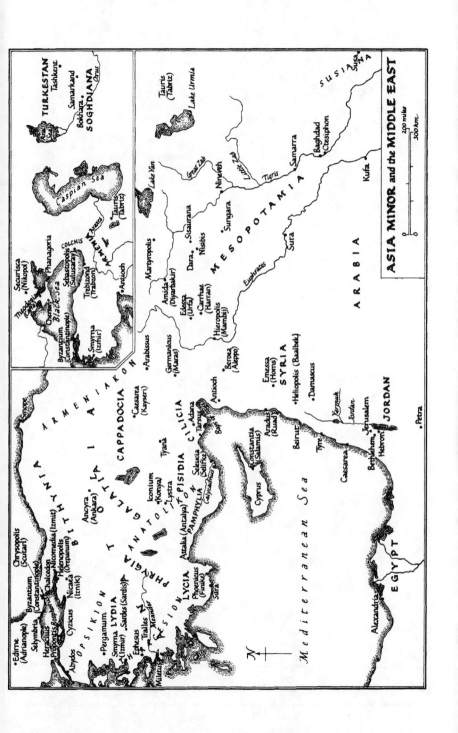

ASIA MINOR and the MIDDLE EAST

200 miles
300 km.

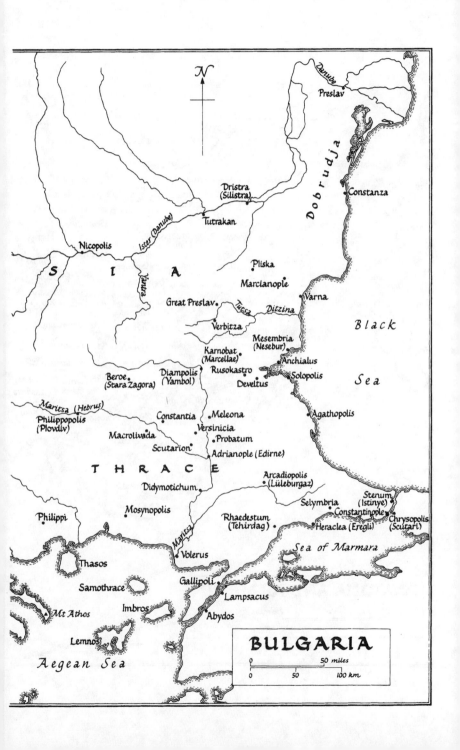

ANATOLIA AND ARMENIA

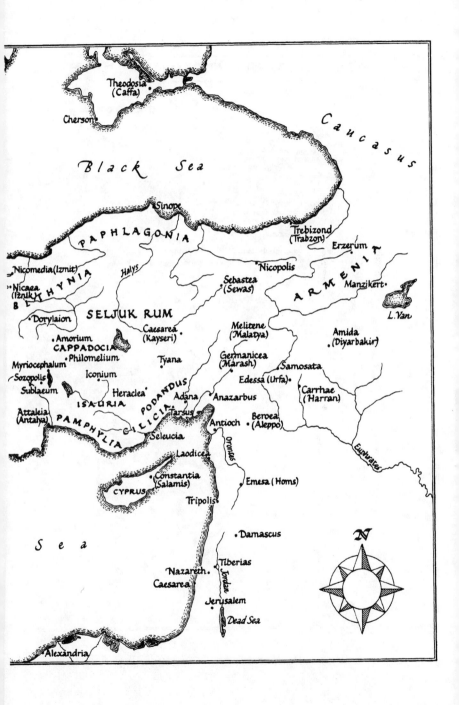

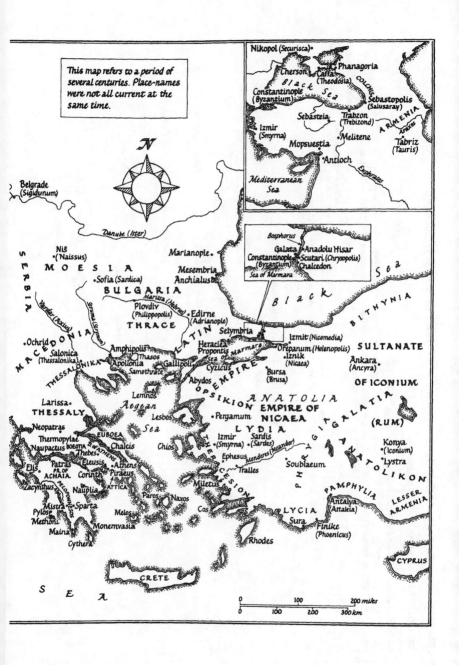

This map refers to a period of several centuries. Place-names were not all current at the same time.

THE FAMILIES OF DIOCLETIAN, CONSTANTINE THE GREAT, VALENTINIAN AND THEODOSIUS

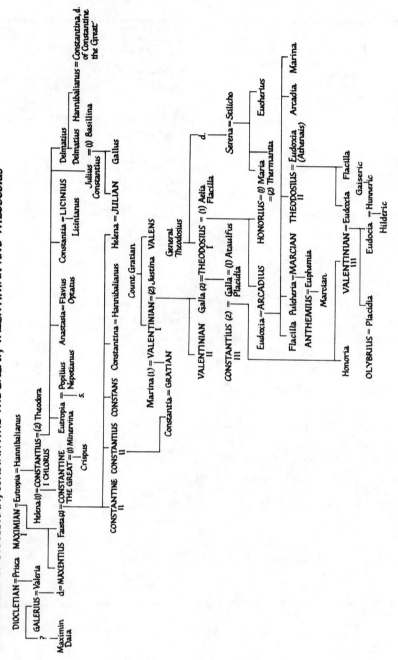

THE FAMILY OF LEO I

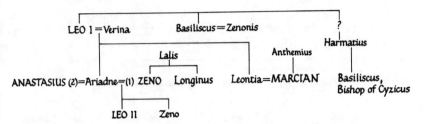

THE FAMILY OF LEO III

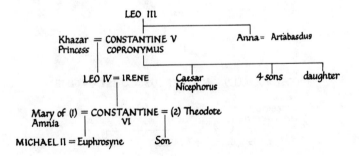

THE FAMILIES OF JUSTINIAN AND THEODORIC

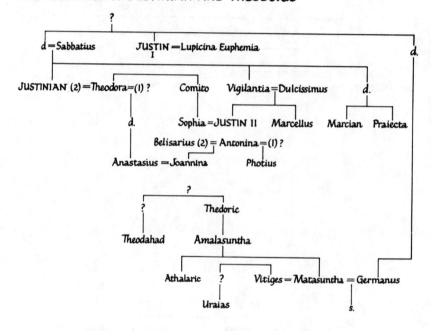

THE FAMILY OF TIBERIUS CONSTANTINE

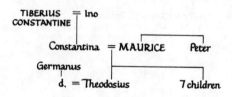

THE FAMILY OF HERACLIUS

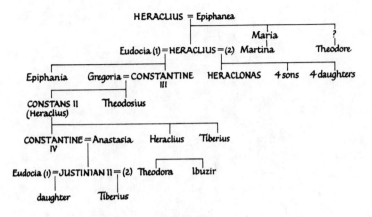

THE AMORIAN DYNASTY

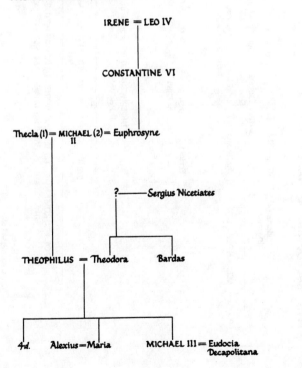

THE MACEDONIAN DYNASTY

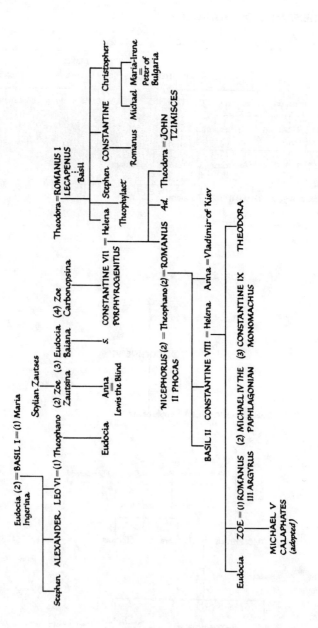

THE BULGARIAN KHANS

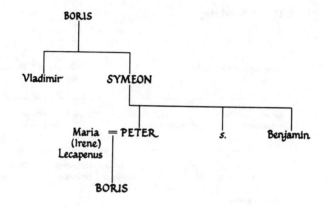

THE PRINCES OF KIEV

Rurik
Grand Prince of Kiev
|
Igor = Olga
|
Svyatoslav
|
Vladimir = Anna

THE COMNENI

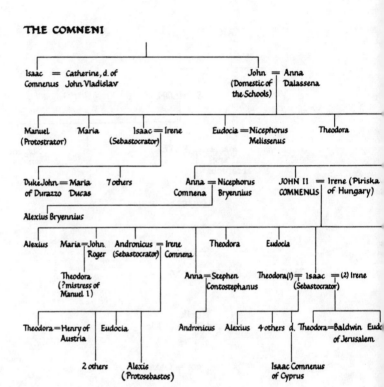

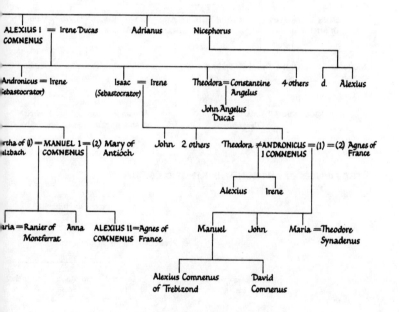

ALEXIUS I = Irene Ducas   Adrianus   Nicephorus
COMNENUS

Andronicus = Irene   Isaac = Irene   Theodora = Constantine   4 others   d.   Alexius
(Sebastocrator)   (Sebastocrator)   Angelus

John Angelus
Ducas

...rtha of (1) = MANUEL 1 = (2) Mary of   John   2 others   Theodora ≠ ANDRONICUS = (1) = (2) Agnes of
...lzbach   COMNENUS   Antioch   I COMNENUS   France

Alexius   Irene

...aria = Ranier of   Anna   ALEXIUS II = Agnes of   Manuel   John   Maria = Theodore
    Montferrat   COMNENUS   France   Synadenus

Alexius Comnenus   David
of Trebizond   Comnenus

THE DYNASTY OF ANGELUS AND THE DESPOTATE OF EPIRUS

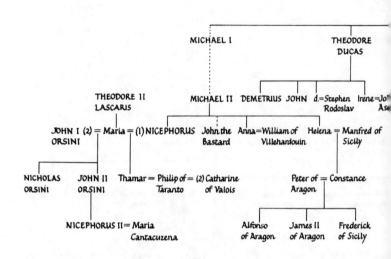

THE PRINCES OF ANTIOCH AND KINGS OF SICILY

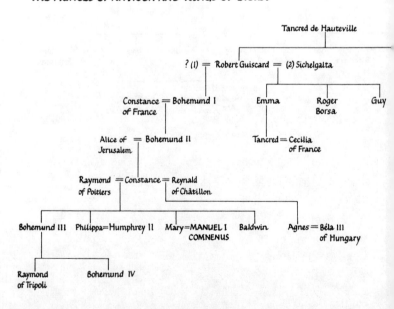

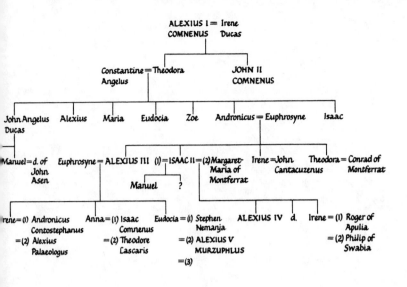

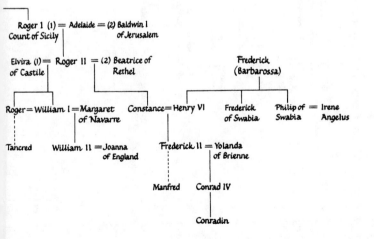

THE LASCARIS DYNASTY OF NICAEA

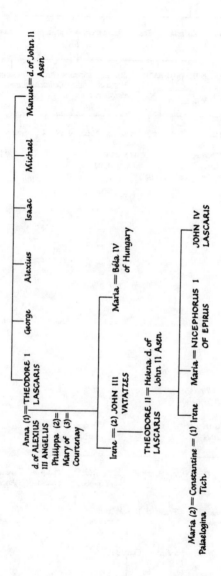

THE LATIN EMPERORS AT CONSTANTINOPLE

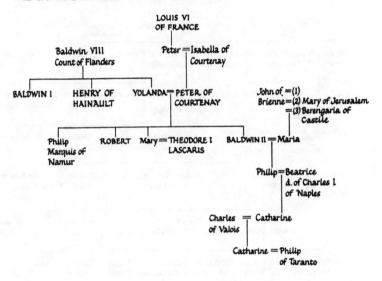

THE CANTACUZENI

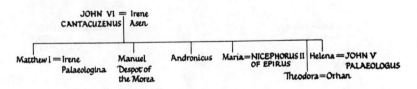

THE PALAEOLOGI

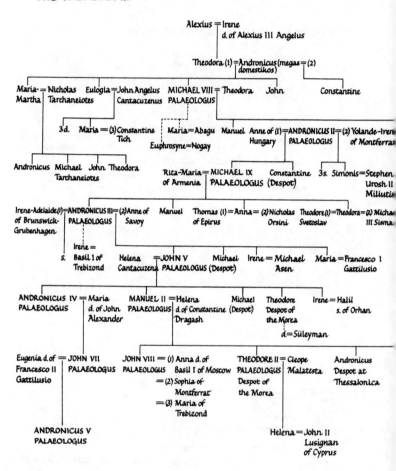

Alexius = Irene
d. of Alexius III Angelus

Theodora (1) = Andronicus (megas = (2)
domestikos)

Maria- = Nicholas   Eulogia = John Angelus   MICHAEL VIII = Theodora   John   Constantine
Martha   Tarchaneiotes   Cantacuzenus   PALAEOLOGUS

3 d.   Maria = (3) Constantine   Maria = Abagu   Manuel   Anne of (1) = ANDRONICUS II = (2) Yolande-Irene
                    Tich   Euphrosyne = Nogay   Hungary   PALAEOLOGUS   of Montferrat

Andronicus Michael John Theodora   Rita-Maria = MICHAEL IX   Constantine 3 s. Simonis = Stephen
            Tarchaneiotes   of Armenia   PALAEOLOGUS (Despot)   Urosh II
                                                                                                 Miliutin

Irene-Adelaide (1) = ANDRONICUS III = (2) Anne of   Manuel   Thomas (1) = Anna = (2) Nicholas   Theodore (1) = Theodora = 2) Michael
of Brunswick-   PALAEOLOGUS   Savoy   of Epirus   Orsini   Svetoslav   III Sisman
Grubenhagen

            Irene =
        s. Basil I of   Helena   = JOHN V   Michael   Irene = Michael   Maria = Francesco I
            Trebizond   Cantacuzena   PALAEOLOGUS (Despot)   Asen   Gattilusio

ANDRONICUS IV = Maria   MANUEL II = Helena   Michael   Theodore   Irene = Halil
PALAEOLOGUS   d. of John   PALAEOLOGUS d. of Constantine (Despot) Despot of   s. of Orhan
                Alexander   Dragash   the Morea
                                                                         d = Süleyman

Eugenia d. of = JOHN VII   JOHN VIII = (1) Anna d. of   THEODORE II = Cleope   Andronicus
Francesco II   PALAEOLOGUS   PALAEOLOGUS   Basil I of Moscow PALAEOLOGUS   Malatesta   Despot at
Gattilusio   = (2) Sophia of   Despot of   Thessalonica
                                             Montferrat   the Morea
                                         = (3) Maria of
                                             Trebizond

        ANDRONICUS V   Helena = John II
        PALAEOLOGUS   Lusignan
                                                                        of Cyprus

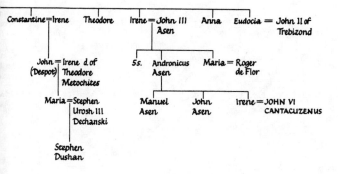

Constantine=Irene Theodore   Irene=John III   Anna   Eudocia = John II of
                                    Asen   Trebizond

        John = Irene d. of   5s. Andronicus   Maria = Roger
      (Despot) Theodore   Asen   de Flor
               Metochites

      Maria=Stephen   Manuel   John   Irene=JOHN VI
            Urosh III   Asen   Asen   CANTACUZENUS
            Dechanski

         Stephen
         Dushan

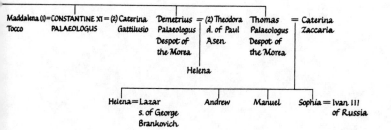

Maddalena (1)=CONSTANTINE XI = (2) Caterina   Demetrius = (2) Theodora   Thomas   = Caterina
Tocco   PALAEOLOGUS   Gattilusio   Palaeologus d. of Paul   Palaeologus Zaccaria
                                               Despot of   Asen   Despot of
                                               the Morea   the Morea

                                                    Helena

         Helena=Lazar   Andrew   Manuel   Sophia = Ivan III
               s. of George   of Russia
               Brankovich

Preface

The Byzantine Empire, from its foundation by Constantine the Great on Monday, 11 May 330, to its conquest by the Ottoman Sultan Mehmet II on Tuesday, 29 May 1453, lasted for a total of 1,123 years and 18 days – a period of time comfortably longer than that which separates us from the Norman Conquest of England in 1066. For everyone except astronomers and geologists, such a period must be considered a long time; and if anyone thinks me foolhardy to have attempted to cover it in a single volume, I can say only that I agree. When, a dozen years ago, I began to write the history of Byzantium, I had no such idea in mind; I simply followed, as I always had, the admirable advice of the King of Hearts in *Alice in Wonderland* 'Begin at the beginning, and go on until you come to the end: then stop.' The result was three volumes, published between 1988 and 1995, totalling some twelve hundred pages: an average – since for the sake of clarity the curtain had to rise some time before the beginning and for that of tidiness it had to fall a few years after the end – of almost exactly a page a year.

Of those volumes, the first told the story of the Empire from its foundation to the establishment of its western rival, the Holy Roman Empire, with the coronation of Charlemagne in Rome on Christmas Day 800. The second followed its fortunes through the dazzling dynasty on the Macedonians to the apogee of its power under the terrible Basil II *Bulgaroctonus*, the Bulgar-Slayer, but ended on a note of ill omen: the first of the three great defeats of Byzantine history, suffered at the hands of the Seljuk Turks at Manzikert in 1071. The third and last volume showed just how fateful that defeat proved to be, robbing the Empire of most of Asia Minor – the principal source of its manpower – weakening it and impoverishing it to the point where, rather more than a hundred years later, it was powerless to resist the onslaught of the grotesquely misnamed Fourth Crusade. That obscenity, and the fifty-six years of Latin rule that followed it, proved to be the second blow from which Byzantium never recovered. The story of the Empire's last two centuries, shadowed against the rising sun of the Turkish House of Othman, makes painful reading. Only the final chapter, tragic as it is, once again lifts the spirit – as all tales of heroism must inevitably do.

But twelve hundred pages, nowadays, is a lot to ask of the general reader; and it was suggested to me that many people who might be discouraged by the idea of a trilogy might welcome the same story if compressed between the covers of a single volume. The result, this time, has been the book that you now hold in your hand. To reduce the history to one third of its original length has been a long and painful task, one that has often seemed to savour less of pruning than of infanticide: many of my favourite brainchildren – anecdotes, digressions and pen-portraits, to say nothing of any number of rather good jokes – have found their quietus on the cutting-room floor. But at least the abridgement can claim, even more than the original version, the virtue of concision; and if it succeeds in awakening the interest – or, better still, the enthusiasm – of a few readers for the strange, savage, yet endlessly fascinating world of Byzantium, it will have been well worth while.

As I have been careful to point out in the Introduction, this book makes no claims to scholarship. I describe myself there as skating over the surface of the subject; in preparing the present condensation, I feel I have exchanged my skates for a hovercraft. But even here the story has been told in full, with nothing of primary importance omitted; and if at times you find the pace a little breakneck, or the facts coming rather too thick and fast – well, the trilogy awaits you.

John Julius Norwich
Castle Combe, October 1996

Introduction

Of that Byzantine Empire the universal verdict of history is that it constitutes, without a single exception, the most thoroughly base and despicable form that civilization has yet assumed ... There has been no other enduring civilization so absolutely destitute of all the forms and elements of greatness ... Its vices were the vices of men who had ceased to be brave without learning to be virtuous ... Slaves, and willing slaves, in both their actions and their thoughts, immersed in sensuality and in the most frivolous pleasures, the people only emerged from their listlessness when some theological subtlety, or some chivalry in the chariot race, stimulated them to frantic riots ... The history of the Empire is a monotonous story of the intrigues of priests, eunuchs and women, of poisonings, of conspiracies, of uniform ingratitude, of perpetual fratricides.

This somewhat startling diatribe is taken from W. E. H. Lecky's *History of European Morals*, published in 1869; and although to modern ears it is perhaps not quite so effective as the author meant it to be – his last sentence makes Byzantine history sound not so much monotonous as distinctly entertaining – the fact remains that, for the past 200 years and more, what used to be known as the Later Roman Empire has had an atrocious press. The long campaign of denigration seems to have been given its initial impetus in the eighteenth century by Edward Gibbon, who, like all classically educated Englishmen of his day, saw Byzantium as the betrayal of all that was best in ancient Greece and Rome; it was only after the Second World War, when the ease, speed and relative comfort of travel in the Levant made Byzantine monuments at last generally accessible, that the Empire began to come into its own again and to be recognized, in its own very different way, as a worthy successor to the two might civilizations which had gone before. The trouble was, for most of us, that we knew so little about it. The old attitudes died hard. During my five years at one of England's oldest and finest public schools, Byzantium seemed to be the victim of a conspiracy of silence. I cannot honestly remember its being mentioned, far less studied; and so complete was my ignorance that I should have been hard put to define it even in general terms until I went to Oxford. Many people, I suspect, feel similarly vague today; and it is for them that this book has been written.

The idea originated many years ago, not with me at all but with my friend Bob Gottlieb, some time before he left my American publishers to edit the *New Yorker*, and though I remember feeling a little daunted by the magnitude of the task before me, I don't think there was any real hesitation. For over a quarter of a century already I had been captivated by the Byzantine world; and my years in the British Foreign Service, during which I spent two and a half years in Belgrade and three in Beirut – when it was still one of the most enchanting places in the world to live in – had only deepened my affection for the eastern Mediterranean and all it stood for. It was no coincidence, when I finally left the Service in 1964 to try to earn my living by my pen, that I turned for my first book to the one place which, more than any other, still breathes the very spirit of Byzantium: Mount Athos.

Subsequently I spent several happy years writing about Venice, which was first a province and later an offshoot of the Empire, and where both the Basilica of St Mark – designed, incidentally, on the model of Constantine's Church of the Holy Apostles – and the Cathedral of Torcello both contain Byzantine mosaics worthy to rank with those of Constantinople itself. But how astonishingly different the two cities were! Throughout her history Venice, protected from the *terra firma* by the still, shallow waters of her lagoon, radiated security; until her very end she was inviolate, and she knew it. Constantinople, on the other hand, lived under almost perpetual threat of attack. Siege followed siege; again and again the city was saved only by the heroism of the Emperor and his subjects. The inhabitants, too, could scarcely have been more dissimilar. The Venetians were cynics: hard-faced, commercially-minded men of the world. The Byzantines were mystics, for whom Christ, his Mother and the Saints were as real as members of their own families. Finally and perhaps most important of all, Venice was governed by faceless committees – elected groups of black-robed men, working in secret, their composition constantly changing, taking their decisions collectively, avoiding all individual prominence. Byzantium was an autocracy, ruled by an Emperor half-way to heaven, Equal of the Apostles, God's Vice-Gerent on Earth, who held the life of every one of his subjects in the hollow of his hand. Some of these Emperors were heroes, others were monsters; but they were never, never dull.

For that reason alone, this book has been a constant pleasure to write; but it is also, in its modest way, a tribute. Our civilization has never adequately acknowledged the debt it owes to the Empire of the East. Were it not for that great oriental bastion of Christendom, what chance would Europe have had against the armies of the King of Persia in the seventh century, or those of the Caliph of Baghdad in the eighth? What language would we be speaking today, and what god would we worship? In the cultural field, too, our indebtedness is great. After the barbarian invasions and the fall of the Emperor in Rome, the lights of learning were almost extinguished in western Europe, apart from a few fitful monastic flickers; it was on the banks of the Bosphorus that they continued to blaze, and that the old classical heritage was preserved. Much of what we know of antiquity – especially of Greek and Roman literature and of Roman law – would have been lost for ever but for the scholars and scribes and copyists of Constantinople.

These tremendous services, however, have long since been taken for granted and forgotten. In our own day there remains to us only one continual reminder of the genius of the Byzantines: the splendour of their art. Never in the history of Christianity – or, one is tempted to add, of any other of the world's religions – has any school of artists contrived to infuse so deep a degree of spirituality into its work. Byzantine theologians used to insist that religious painters and mosaicists should seek to reflect the image of God. It was no small demand; but in the churches and monasteries of the Empire we see it, again and again, triumphantly accomplished.

Finally, let me emphasize that this book makes no claim to academic scholarship. Any professional Byzantinist perusing its pages will find little indeed that he does not already know – though there will probably be many a statement or opinion with which he will disagree. So be it. The four years of ancient Greek that constituted an important part of that public-school education I have already mentioned have not enabled me to read the simplest of Greek texts without a lexicon at my elbow; among primary authorities, I have consequently been obliged to rely almost entirely on those whose work exists in translations or summaries. But this has been less of a hindrance than I expected: particularly for the later centuries, the secondary sources are so copious that the difficulty has been less one of obtaining information than of selecting it. Since at all costs the story must be kept moving, I make no pretence of doing more than skating over the surface of my subject – an activity which is, by its very definition, a negation of scholarship.

But I am unrepentant. I have never presumed to cast a new light on Byzantium. All I have tried to do is to make some small amends for that con-spiracy of silence which has left so many of us with virtually no knowledge of the longest-lived – and, arguably, the most continuously inspired – Christian Empire in the history of the world; and, in the process, to tell a good story as interestingly and as accurately as I could. I cannot hope that the reader will lay down the book with the same regret that I have felt on the completion of a long yet wholly enjoyable task; but he will, I trust, at least agree with me that the tale was worth the telling.

PART I

The Early Centuries

I

Constantine the Great

[to 337]

In the beginning was the word – surely one of the most magically resonant place-names in all history. Even had its Empire never existed, Byzantium would surely have impressed itself upon our minds and memories by the music of its name alone, conjuring up those same visions that it evokes today: visions of gold and malachite and porphyry, of stately and solemn ceremonial, of brocades heavy with rubies and emeralds, of sumptuous mosaics dimly glowing through halls cloudy with incense.

Next, the site; and this too was supreme. Standing on the very threshold of Asia and occupying the easternmost tip of a broad, triangular promontory, its south side washed by the Sea of Marmara and its north-east by that deep and navigable inlet, some five miles long, known since remotest antiquity as the Golden Horn, it had been moulded by nature into a magnificent harbour and an impregnable stronghold, needing as it did major fortification only on its landward side. Even an attack from the sea was difficult enough, the Marmara itself being protected by two long and narrow straits – the Bosphorus to the east and the Hellespont (or Dardanelles) to the west.

Finally, the man: Constantine I, Emperor of Rome. No ruler in all history has ever more fully merited his title of 'the Great'; for within the short space of some fifteen years he took two decisions, either of which alone would have changed the future of the civilized world. The first was to adopt Christianity as the official religion of the Roman Empire. The second was to transfer the capital of that Empire from Rome to the new city which he was building on the site of old Byzantium and which was to be known, for the next sixteen centuries, by his name: Constantinople. Together, these two decisions and their consequences have given him a serious claim to be considered – excepting only Jesus Christ, the Buddha and the Prophet Mohammed – the most influential man in all history; and with him our story begins.

He was born around AD 274. His father Constantius – nicknamed 'Chlorus', the Pale – was already one of the most brilliant and successful generals in the Empire; his mother Helena was a humble innkeeper's daughter from Bithynia. Some historians have suggested that as a girl she had been one of the supplementary amenities of her father's establishment, regularly available to his clients at a small extra charge. Only later in her life, when her son had acceded to the supreme power, did she become the most venerated woman in the Empire; only in 327, when she was already over seventy, did this passionately enthusiastic Christian convert make her celebrated pilgrimage to the Holy Land, there miraculously to unearth the True Cross and so to achieve sainthood.

In 293 the Emperor Diocletian decided to split the imperial power into four, keeping the East for himself and entrusting the other three regions to an old comrade-in-arms, Maximian; to a rough, brutal professional soldier from Thrace named Galerius; and to Constantius Chlorus. Even at the time, the drawbacks of such an arrangement must have been obvious. However much Diocletian might emphasize that the Empire still remained single and undivided, sooner or later splits were inevitable. For some years all went smoothly enough – years which the young Constantine spent at Diocletian's court; but then, in 305, there occurred an event unparalleled in this history of the Roman Empire: the voluntary abdication of the Emperor. After twenty years on the imperial throne, Diocletian withdrew from the world, forcing an intensely unwilling Maximian to abdicate with him.

Galerius and Constantius Chlorus – who had by now abandoned Helena to marry Maximian's adopted stepdaughter Theodora – were proclaimed Augusti (the two senior Emperors), but the appointment of their successors, the two new Caesars, was disputed; and Constantine, finding himself passed over and fearing for his life, fled at night from Galerius's court at Nicomedia to join his father at Boulogne, where he was preparing a new expedition to Britain. Father and son crossed the Channel together; shortly afterwards, however, on 25 July 306, Constantius died at York; there and then the local legions clasped the imperial purple toga around Constantine's shoulders, raised him on their shields and cheered him to the echo.

Still needing official recognition, Constantine now sent to Galerius at Nicomedia, together with the official notification of his father's death, a portrait of himself with the attributes of Augustus of the West. Galerius, however, refused point-blank to recognize the young rebel – for such, in fact, Constantine unquestionably was – as an Augustus. He was prepared, reluctantly, to acknowledge him as Caesar; but that was all. For Constantine, it was enough – for the present. He remained in Gaul and Britain for the next six years, governing those provinces on the whole wisely and well. This rectitude did not, however, prevent him from putting aside his first wife in 307 in order to make an infinitely more distinguished alliance – with Fausta, the daughter of the old Emperor Maximian. The latter had by now revoked his involuntary

4

abdication of two years before, had resumed the purple and made common cause with his son Maxentius; together the two had won over the whole of Italy to their cause. The marriage was therefore diplomatically advantageous to both sides: for Maximian and Maxentius it meant that they could probably count on Constantine's alliance, while the latter for his part could now claim family links with two Emperors instead of one.

How long Constantine would have been content to rule this relatively remote corner of the Empire we cannot tell; for in April 311 Galerius, the senior Augustus, died at Sirmium on the river Sava. His death left three men sharing the supreme power: Licinius, one of the late Emperor's old drinking companions, who was now ruling Illyria, Thrace and the Danube provinces; his nephew Maximin Daia, whom he had named Caesar in 305 and who now took over the eastern part of the Empire; and Constantine himself. But there was a fourth who, though not technically of imperial rank, had long felt himself to be unjustly deprived of his rightful throne: this was Galerius's son-in-law Maxentius. As the son of the old Emperor Maximian, Maxentius had long hated his brilliant young brother-in-law. He was now as powerful as any of his three rivals – powerful enough, indeed, to take his father's death as a pretext for branding Constantine a murderer and a rebel. War, clearly, was unavoidable; but before marching against his adversary Constantine had to come to an agreement with Licinius. Fortunately for him, Licinius – already fully occupied with Maximin Daia in the East – was only too happy for him to undertake the reconquest of Italy on his behalf. The agreement was sealed by another betrothal – this time of Licinius himself to Constantine's half-sister Constantia.

Throughout Constantine's long advance, Maxentius had remained in Rome. Only when his brother-in-law's army was approaching the city did he march out to meet it. The two armies met on 28 October 312 at Saxa Rubra, the 'red rocks' on the Via Flaminia, some seven or eight miles north-east of Rome. It was here, as later legend has it, just before or perhaps even during the battle, that Constantine experienced his famous vision. As Eusebius describes it:

... a most marvellous sign appeared to him from heaven ... He said that at about midday, when the sun was beginning to decline, he saw with his own eyes the trophy of a cross of light in the heavens, above the sun, and bearing the inscription Conquer by This (*Hoc Vince*). He himself was struck with amazement, and his whole army also.

Inspired by so unmistakable an indication of divine favour, Constantine routed the army of Maxentius, driving it southward to where the Tiber is crossed by the old Milvian Bridge. Next to this bridge Maxentius had constructed another on pontoons, by which he could if necessary make an orderly retreat and which could then be broken in the middle to prevent pursuit. Over this his shattered army stampeded, the soldiers now fleeing for their lives. They might have escaped, had not the engineers lost their heads and drawn the bolts too early. The whole structure collapsed, throwing hundreds of men into the fast-flowing water. Those who had not yet crossed made blindly for the old stone bridge, now their only chance of safety; but, as Maxentius had known, it was too narrow. Many were crushed to death, others fell and were trampled underfoot, still others were flung down by their own comrades into the river below. Among the last was the usurper himself, whose body was later found washed up on the bank.

The battle of the Milvian Bridge made Constantine absolute master of all Europe. It also marked, if not his actual conversion to Christianity, at least the moment when he set himself up as a protector and patron of his Christian subjects. On his departure from Rome he presented Pope Melchiades with the old palace of the Laterani family which the Empress Fausta – who had joined him soon after his arrival – had occupied during her stay. It was to remain a papal palace for another thousand years. Next to it he ordered the building, at his own expense, of the first of Rome's Constantinian basilicas, St John Lateran, still today the Cathedral Church of the city. Significantly, it was given an immense free-standing circular baptistery: there was to be a formidable increase in the rate of conversions during the years to come.

To what extent did the vision of the Cross that the Emperor is said to have experienced near the Milvian Bridge constitute not only one of the decisive turning-points of his life but also a watershed of world history? Before we can answer that question, we must ask ourselves another: what actually happened? According to the Christian scholar and rhetorician Lactantius, tutor to Constantine's son Crispus,

Constantine was directed in a dream to cause *the heavenly sign* to be delineated on the shields of his soldiers, and so to proceed to battle. He did as he had been commanded, and he marked on their shields the letter X, with a perpendicular line drawn through it and turned round the top, thus ☧, being the cypher of Christ.

He says no more. We have no mention of a vision, only of a dream. There is not even any suggestion that the Saviour or the Cross ever appeared to the Emperor at all. As for 'the heavenly sign', it was simply a monogram of *chi* (X) and *rho* (P), the first two Greek letters in the name of Christ, that had long been a familiar symbol in Christian inscriptions. And perhaps more significant still is the fact that our other valuable source, Eusebius, makes no reference to either a dream or a vision in the account of the battle which he gives in his *Ecclesiastical History* of about 325. It is only in his *Life of Constantine*, written many years later, that he produces the passage quoted above.

What conclusions are we to draw from all this? Firstly, surely, that there was no vision. Had there been one, it is unthinkable that there should be no single reference to it until the *Life of Constantine*. The Emperor himself never seems to have spoken of it – except to Eusebius – even on those occasions when he might have been expected to do so. Then there is Eusebius's specific statement that 'the whole army . . . witnessed the miracle'. If that were true, 98,000 men kept the secret remarkably well.

There can be little doubt, on the other hand, that at a certain moment before the battle the Emperor underwent some profound spiritual experience. There are indications that he was already in a state of grave religious un-certainty, and was increasingly tending towards monotheism: after 310 his coins depict one god only – *Sol Invictus*, the Unconquered Sun – of whom Constantine also claimed to have had a vision some years before. Yet this faith too seems to have left him unsatisfied. No man, in short, was readier for conversion during that late summer of 312; and it is hardly surprising that, up to a point at least, his prayers were answered. If we accept this hypothesis Eusebius's story becomes a good deal easier to understand. Constantine had always cherished a strongly developed sense of divine mission. What could be more natural than that, looking back on his life, he should have allowed his memory to add a gentle gloss here and there? In his day the existence of miracles and heavenly portents was universally accepted; if he could have had a vision and if, in the circumstances, he should have had a vision, then a vision he had had.

Early in January 313, Constantine left Rome for Milan, where he had arranged to meet Licinius. Their talks passed off amicably enough. Licinius seems to have agreed that Constantine should keep the territories that he had conquered, and was duly married to Constantia. Where the Christians were concerned, the new brothers-in-law settled the final text of a further edict, granting Christianity full legal recognition throughout the Empire:

I, Constantine Augustus, and I, Licinius Augustus, resolved to secure respect and reverence for the Deity, grant to Christians and to all others the right freely to follow whatever form of worship they please, that whatsoever Divinity dwells in heaven may be favourable to us and to all those under our authority.

At the time of the Edict of Milan, the two Emperors were friends; but they did not remain so for long. For some time already Constantine had been determined to put an end to Diocletian's disastrous division of the Empire and to rule it alone. Open warfare broke out in 314, and again nine years later, when the two armies fought a furious battle outside Adrianople in Thrace. On both occasions Constantine emerged the victor; towards the end of 323 Licinius was captured and summarily put to death.

During the civil war Constantine had turned more and more exclusively towards the God of the Christians. For some years he had been legislating in their favour. The clergy were exempted from municipal obligations, while episcopal courts were given the right to act as courts of appeal for civil cases. Other laws, too, suggest a degree of Christian inspiration, such as that of 319 prohibiting the murder of slaves and – most celebrated of all – the law of 321 proclaiming Sunday, 'the venerable day of the Sun', as a day of rest. But in none of this legislation is the name of Christ himself mentioned or the Christian faith in any way professed. Now at last, with the Empire safely reunited under his authority, Constantine could afford to come into the open. There must be no coercion: pagans must be allowed to continue in the old faith if they chose to do so. On the other hand, there must be no heresy. If the Church were to stand as the spiritual arm of an indivisible Empire, how could it be divided? Unfortunately it was. For years Constantine had battled in vain against two schismatic groups, the Donatists in North Africa and the Meletians in Egypt. Now there had emerged a third faction which threatened to sow more discord than the other two put together.

This group had formed itself around a certain Arius of Alexandria, a man of immense learning and splendid physical presence. His message was simple enough: that Jesus Christ was not co-eternal and of one substance with God the Father, but had been created by Him as his Instrument for the salvation of the world. Thus, although a perfect man, the Son was subordinate to the Father, his nature being human rather than divine. Here, in the eyes of Arius's archbishop, Alexander, was a dangerous doctrine indeed; in 320 its propagator was arraigned before nearly a hundred bishops and excommunicated as a heretic. The damage, however, was done: the teaching spread like wildfire. Those were the days, it must be remembered, in which theological arguments were of passionate interest, not just to churchmen and scholars but to the whole Greek world. Broadsheets were distributed; rabble-rousing speeches were made in the market place; slogans were chalked on walls.

Towards the end of 324, Constantine decided on the solution to the problem. There would be no more synods of local bishops; instead, there would be a universal Council of the Church, to be held at Nicaea, of such authority that both Arius and Alexander would be bound to accept its rulings. Nicaea too boasted an imperial palace; and it was here that the great Council was held, between 20 May and 19 June 325. There were few delegates from the West, where the controversy aroused little interest. From the East, on the other hand, the delegates arrived in force: probably 300 or more, many of them with impressive records of persecution for their faith. The proceedings were opened by Constantine in person, like some heavenly Angel of God, clothed in a garment which glittered as though radiant with light, reflecting the glow of a purple robe and adorned with the brilliant splendour of gold and precious stones. When a low chair of wrought gold had been set for him, he waited to sit down until the bishops had signalled to him to do so. After him the whole assembly did the same.

The doctrinal point at issue interested Constantine not at all: his military cast of mind had little patience with theological niceties. He was, however, determined to put an end to the controversy. He therefore played a prominent part in the ensuing debate, forever urging the importance of unity and the virtues of compromise, and even on occasion switching from Latin into halting Greek in his efforts to convince his hearers. It was he who proposed the insertion, into the draft statement of belief, of the key word that was to settle, at least temporarily, the fate of Arius and his doctrine. This was the word *homooùsios* – meaning con-substantial, or 'of one substance', to describe the relation of the Son to the Father. Its inclusion in the draft was almost tantamount to a condemnation of Arianism, and it says much for Constantine's powers of persuasion that he was able to secure its acceptance, pointing out that the word was of course to be interpreted only 'in its divine and mystical sense' – in other words, that it could mean precisely what anyone chose it to mean. By the time he had finished, nearly all the pro-Arians had agreed to sign the final document; only two maintained their opposition. Arius, with his remaining adherents, was formally condemned, his writings placed under anathema and ordered to be burnt. He was also forbidden to return to Alexandria. His exile to Illyricum, however, did not last long; thanks to persistent appeals by the Arian bishops, he was soon back in Nicomedia, where events were to prove that his stormy career was by no means over.

For Constantine, the first Ecumenical Council of the Christian Church had been a triumph. He had succeeded in getting every major issue settled almost unanimously in the way he had wished. He had established both a great confederacy of the Eastern and the Western Churches and his own moral supremacy over it. He had, in short, good reason to congratulate himself. When at last the bishops left, each carried with him a personal present, placed in his hands by the Emperor himself. They were, Eusebius tells us, deeply impressed – just as Constantine had intended them to be.

Early in January 326, the Emperor left for Rome. The Romans had been deeply offended by his decision to hold his *vicennalia* at Nicaea; he had therefore agreed to repeat the celebration among them, as a means of smoothing their feelings and of showing them that they had not, after all, been entirely ignored. He was accompanied on the journey by several members of his family: his mother Helena, his wife the Empress Fausta, his half-sister Constantia, her stepson Licinianus and his own first-born, the Caesar Crispus. The party, however, was not a happy one, for relations among these individuals could hardly have been worse.

Helena, for a start, never forgot that Fausta was the daughter of the Emperor Maximian, the adoptive father of that Theodora who had stolen her husband Constantius Chlorus nearly forty years before; while Fausta for her part fiercely resented Constantine's recent elevation of his mother to the rank of Augusta like herself. For Constantia there was the memory of her husband Licinius, less than two years dead; for her stepson, the knowledge that his own hopes of power had been extinguished and that he was now obliged to stand by while Crispus enjoyed those honours which should equally have been his. As for Crispus himself, for some time he had been conscious of his father's growing jealousy – jealousy aroused by his popularity with the army and citizenry, which by now comfortably exceeded the Emperor's own. None of these reasons alone, however, could altogether account for the train of events that began when the imperial party reached Serdica some time in February. Suddenly and without warning, Crispus and Licinianus were arrested; a few days later they were put to death. Shortly afterwards they were followed by the Empress Fausta herself, who met her fate in the *calidarium* of the bath-house – though whether by scalding, stabbing or suffocation by steam we shall never know.

What, we may ask, launched Constantine into this sudden frenzy of slaughter – which was subsequently extended to many of his friends as well? One possibility must be that Crispus and Licinianus had plotted together for the Emperor's overthrow. The plot would have been discovered in time, and Constantine would have acted with his usual decisiveness. The later executions would have occurred as other members of his entourage were found to have been implicated. But such a solution fails to explain the fate of Fausta. She too might have been involved in an intrigue against her husband; after all, her father Maximian had also met his death at Constantine's hands. But that had been sixteen years before, and he had richly deserved it; besides, she had since borne her husband five children. Clearly, we must look for another solution to the problem.

Unfortunately for Fausta's reputation, at least four ancient historians associate her in one way or another with the fate of her stepson; and one,

Zosimus – writing admittedly in the following century – introduces a new element altogether. 'Crispus,' he writes, 'was suspected of having adulterous relations with his stepmother Fausta, and was therefore executed.' If this theory is correct, there are three possibilities. The first is that Crispus and Fausta were indeed having an affair; but why then, were they not executed at the same time? The second is that Crispus made proposals to Fausta, who angrily rejected them and informed his father; but if so, why was she executed at all? We are left with a third hypothesis: that Crispus had no designs of any kind on Fausta and was unjustly accused by her – perhaps as Gibbon suggests, because *he* rejected *her* advances – and that Constantine, discovering the false-ness of her allegations only after his son's death, ordered that she too must suffer a similar fate.

News of the family upheavals had preceded the Emperor to Rome, and had done nothing to diminish the sense of mistrust that he had long inspired there, particularly among the people. As Romans, they were increasingly concerned by the reports reaching them of his splendid new city on the Bosphorus; as republicans – or at least inheritors of the republican tradition – they were scandalized at the sight of a ruler who appeared less like a Roman *imperator* than an Oriental potentate; and as staunch upholders of the traditional religion, they deplored his desertion of the old gods and his adoption of the despised Christian faith, which they associated with the rabble of the streets and the lowest dregs of Roman society. They received him with all due ceremony, but made little effort to disguise their true feelings, just as he scarcely troubled to conceal his own.

He proved, however, still more assiduous in his determination to make Rome a Christian city. He endowed another great basilica, now known as S. Paolo fuori le Mura – dedicated this time to St Paul, at the site of the saint's tomb on the road to Ostia; and another – now S. Sebastiano – in honour of the Holy Apostles on the Appian Way. His most important creation of all, however, was the basilica that he commanded to be built above the traditional resting-place of St Peter on the Vatican Hill.

Constantine's frenetic building activity in Rome proves beyond all doubt that he saw the city as the chief shrine of the Christian faith, excepting only Jerusalem itself; and he was determined to do all he could to ensure that it would be architecturally worthy of its dignity. Personally, on the other hand, he never liked it, or stayed in it a moment longer than he could help. His heart was in the East. He had business in Byzantium.

When Constantine first set eyes on Byzantium, the city was already nearly a thousand years old: a small settlement was already flourishing on the site by about 600 BC, with its acropolis on the high ground where the Church of St Sophia and the Palace of Topkapi stand today. Inevitably, when his new city of Constantinople became the centre of the late Roman world, stories were to grow up about the supernatural circumstances attending its foundation: how he personally traced out the line of the walls with his spear – replying, when his companions showed astonishment at its length, with the words: 'I shall continue until he who walks ahead of me bids me stop.' In fact, however, at that time the Emperor was merely planning a commemorative city bearing his name and serving as a perpetual reminder of his greatness and glory. What decided him to make it the capital of his Empire was, almost certainly, his second visit to Rome, whose republican and pagan traditions could clearly have no place in his new Christian Empire. Intellectually and culturally, it was growing more and more out of touch with the new and progressive thinking of the Hellenistic world. The Roman academies and libraries were no longer any match for those of Alexandria, Antioch or Pergamum. In the economic field, too, a similar trend was apparent. In Rome and throughout much of the Italian peninsula, malaria was on the increase and populations were dwindling; the incomparably greater economic resources of what was known as the *pars orientalis* constituted an attraction which no government could afford to ignore.

Strategically, the disadvantages of the old capital were more serious still. The principal dangers to imperial security were now concentrated along the Empire's eastern borders: the Sarmatians around the lower Danube, the Ostrogoths to the north of the Black Sea and – most menacing of all – the Persians, whose great Sassanian Empire by now extended from the former Roman provinces of Armenia and Mesopotamia as far as the Hindu Kush. The centre of the Empire – indeed, of the whole civilized world – had shifted irrevocably to the East. Italy had become a backwater.

The focal point of Constantine's new city was the *Milion*, or First Milestone. It consisted of four triumphal arches forming a square and supporting a cupola, above which was set the most venerable Christian relic of all – the True Cross itself, sent back by the Empress Helena from Jerusalem a year or two before. From it all the distances in the Empire were measured; it was, in effect, the centre of the world. A little to the east of it, on a site occupied in former times by a shrine of Aphrodite, rose the first great Christian church of the new capital, dedicated not to any saint or martyr but to the Holy Peace of God, St Eirene. A few years later this church was to be joined – and somewhat overshadowed – by a larger and still more splendid neighbour, St Sophia, the Church of the Holy Wisdom; but for the time being it had no rival. A quarter of a mile or so away from it towards the Marmara stood Constantine's huge

Hippodrome, in the central *spina* of which was erected one of the most ancient classical trophies in the city – the so-called 'Serpent Column' brought by Constantine from Delphi, where it had been erected in the Temple of Apollo by thirty-one Greek cities in gratitude for their victory over the Persians at the battle of Plataea in 479 BC.[1] Half-way along its eastern side, the imperial box gave direct access by a spiral staircase to that vast complex of reception halls, government offices, domestic apartments, baths, barracks and parade grounds that was the palace.

Directly westward from the Milion ran a broad thoroughfare, already begun by Severus, known as the *Mesē*; some way along it, the Emperor laid out a magnificent new forum, oval in shape and paved entirely in marble. At its centre stood a hundred-foot column of porphyry, brought from Heliopolis in Egypt, on a twenty-foot marble plinth. Within this had been deposited a number of remarkable relics, including the hatchet with which Noah had built the ark, the baskets and remains of the loaves with which Christ had fed the multitude, St Mary Magdalen's jar of ointment and the figure of Athene brought back by Aeneas from Troy. On the summit stood a statue. The body was that of an Apollo by Phidias; but the head, which was surrounded by a metal halo with representations of the sun's beams radiating from it, was that of Constantine himself. The right hand carried a sceptre, while in the left was an orb in which had been placed a fragment of the True Cross. Once again, Christian and pagan elements are combined; but this time all are subordinated to a new supreme being – the Emperor Constantine.[2]

Around the palace, the church and the Hippodrome, tens of thousands of labourers and artisans worked day and night; and, thanks to the wholesale plunder by which the towns of Europe and Asia were deprived of their finest statues, trophies and works of art, it was already a fine and noble city – though not yet a very large one – that was dedicated, as Constantine had determined that it should be, in a special ceremony that marked the climax of his silver jubilee. The Emperor attended High Mass in St Eirene, while the pagan population prayed for his prosperity and that of the city in such temples as he had authorized for their use. It is with this Mass, at which the city was formally dedicated to the Holy Virgin, that the history of Constantinople really begins – and, with it, that of the Byzantine Empire. The date was 11 May 330. It was, we are credibly informed, a Monday.

*

1 The heads of the three intertwined bronze serpents are believed to have been chopped off by a drunken member of the Polish Embassy to the Sublime Porte in 1700.

2 The Column of Constantine still stands – but only just. After an accident in 416 it was bound together with iron hoops; in 1106 the Emperor's statue was blown down in a gale. It is a pitiful sight today.

Only half a dozen years before, Byzantium had been just another small Greek town; now, reborn and renamed, it was the 'New Rome' – its official appellation proudly carved on a stone pillar in the recently completed law courts. In the old Rome, to be sure, the people kept all their ancient privileges. Trade, too, went on as before; the port of Ostia remained busy. But several of the old Roman senatorial families were already beginning to trickle away to the Bosphorus, lured by the promise of magnificent palaces in the city and extensive estates in Thrace, Bithynia and Pontus; and a larger and infinitely more sumptuous Senate House had risen in the new capital to accommodate them. Meanwhile all the cities of the Empire were ransacked for works of art with which the growing city was to be adorned – preference being normally given to temple statues of the ancient gods, since by removing them from their traditional shrines and setting them up in public, unconsecrated places for aesthetic rather than religious purposes, Constantine could strike a telling blow at the old pagan faith.

In 327 his mother the Empress Helena had set off at the age of seventy-two for the Holy Land, where Bishop Macarius of Jerusalem took her on a tour of the principal shrines and where, according to tradition, she found the True Cross – distinguishing it from those of the two thieves by laying it on a dying woman, who was miraculously restored to health. Soon after it arrived in his new capital, Constantine sent a piece of it to Rome, to be placed in the old palace which his mother had always occupied during her visits to the city and which he now ordered to be converted into a church. Still known as S. Croce in Gerusalemme, the building has been indissolubly associated with St Helena ever since. Meanwhile, in the Church of the Holy Sepulchre at Jerusalem, the rock surrounding the Tomb was levelled to form a vast courtyard. At one end was the Tomb itself; to the east stood Constantine's new basilica. Its outer walls were of finely polished stone, while those of the interior were covered with revetments of polychrome marble, rising to a gilded and coffered roof. Little of these splendid edifices remains today. Fires and earthquakes have taken their toll, and the passage of sixteen and a half centuries has done the rest. Yet if few of these shrines nowadays possess a single stone dating from the time of Constantine, there remain, nevertheless, a remarkable number whose very existence is due to him – and to his mother. Her journey to the Holy Places caught the imagination of all Christendom. We do not know the length of her stay in the Levant, nor the circumstances of her death. She probably died in the Holy Land – the first recorded Christian pilgrim.

Throughout the triumphal ceremonies by which Constantine inaugurated his new capital – and a new era for the Roman Empire – he was uncomfortably aware that, in one vital respect, he had failed. Despite all that he had done to bind together the Christian Church, it remained as divided as ever it had been. The greater part of the blame lay with the Christian leaders themselves. Obviously, they believed that the vital issues were at stake – issues for which, as many had already proved, they were ready to face exile and even martyrdom; none the less, by their eternal bickering and squabbling, by their hatred and bigotry, intolerance and malice, they set a sad example to their flocks – an example which countless generations of their successors have been all too ready to follow.

Archbishop Alexander died in 328, and was succeeded in Alexandria by his former chaplain, Athanasius. The two had been together at the Council of Nicaea, where Athanasius had proved even more skilled and quick-witted than his master. In the years to come, he was to show himself to be something more: the leading churchman of his time, one of the towering figures in the whole history of the Christian Church, and a saint. (He was long erroneously believed to have been the author of the Athanasian Creed, which still bears his name.) Arius and his adherents were to have no more redoubtable adversary. For the moment, however, their star was once again in the ascendant. Arius had never lost the support of the Emperor's family – in particular that of his mother and his half-sister Constantia – while the Asian bishops were also overwhelmingly pro-Arian in their sympathies. Already in 327 they had persuaded Constantine to recall Arius from exile and to receive him in audience; the Emperor, impressed as much by the brilliance and obvious sincerity of the man as by his assurance that he accepted all the points of faith approved at Nicaea, had written personal letters to Archbishop Alexander urging that he should be allowed to return to Egypt. He seems to have been genuinely surprised when the archbishop proved reluctant to comply.

Thus the Emperor gradually concluded that Athanasius, rather than Arius, was now the chief impediment to Church unity. By now he was making plans for celebrating, in 335, the thirtieth year of his reign by the consecration of the rebuilt Church of the Holy Sepulchre in Jerusalem. Here he proposed to summon a vast convocation of bishops from all over the Empire; and he was determined that doctrinal harmony should prevail among them. He accordingly gave orders that the bishops on their way to Jerusalem should hold a synod at Tyre, in order – as he disarmingly put it – to 'free the Church from blasphemy and to lighten my cares'. The synod was called for July; but, as soon became clear, it was to be attended almost exclusively by Arian bishops and was thus less a gathering of distinguished churchmen than a trial of Athanasius. All the old charges were revived, and new ones introduced; hosts of new witnesses were called, each prepared to swear that the archbishop had committed every crime in the statute book. At this point Anastasius, believing – probably rightly – that his life was in danger, slipped away to Constantinople. He was deposed in his absence, after which the synod broke up and its members continued their journey to Jerusalem. Once arrived in the capital, Athanasius went straight to the palace – only to be refused an audience. Instead, he was banished by a furious Constantine to Augusta Treverorum – the modern Trier. The Emperor then returned to the interrupted task of getting Arius reaccepted in Alexandria.

In this, however, he failed. Every attempt by Arius to return brought new outbreaks of rioting in the city – led by the great St Anthony himself, now aged eighty-six, who had left his desert hermitage to champion the cause of orthodoxy. At length Constantine was persuaded to summon Arius back to Constantinople for a further investigation of his beliefs; and it was during this last inquiry – so Athanasius later wrote to his Egyptian flock – that 'Arius, made bold by the protection of his followers, engaged in light-hearted and foolish conversation, until he was suddenly compelled by a call of nature to retire; and immediately, falling headlong, he burst asunder in the midst and gave up the ghost'.

This story, to be sure, comes from the pen of Arius's arch-enemy; but although there are several different versions of what occurred, the unattractive circumstances of his demise are too well attested to be open to serious question. Inevitably, it was interpreted by those who hated him as divine retribution: it did not, however, put an end to the controversy – nor even to the exile of Athanasius, which lasted until after Constantine's own death in 337. The Emperor's dream of spiritual harmony throughout Christendom was not to be achieved in his lifetime; indeed, we are still awaiting it today.

One would like to hear more about the *tricennalia* celebrations in Jerusalem; in Constantinople – in contrast to those that had marked the city's dedication – they were exclusively Christian. (Between 331 and 334 Constantine had closed down all pagan temples in the Empire.) In the course of the festivities, however, he took the opportunity of announcing the promotion of his two nephews to key positions in the State. The elder, Delmatius, was proclaimed Caesar; the younger, Hannibalianus, was given the hand of his first cousin, the Emperor's daughter Constantina, in marriage. He was then sent off with his bride to rule in Pontus, that wild, mountainous region that extends back from the rainswept southern shore of the Black Sea.

The elevation of these two youths brought the number of reigning Caesars effectively to five, Constantine's three sons by Fausta having already been raised to similar rank – the youngest, Constans, only two years previously, at the age of ten. By multiplying their number the Emperor was deliberately attempting to reduce the Caesars' prestige: with advancing age he was becoming ever more convinced of a divine dispensation that singled him out from his fellow-men. But his very reluctance to delegate authority in the capital imposed on him a workload of almost Herculean proportions. He had spent the first months of 337 in Asia Minor, mobilizing his army against the young King Shapur of Persia, and showing all the energy, stamina and endurance that had made him a legend among his subjects. Shortly before Easter he returned to Constantinople – there to put the finishing touches to the Great Church of the Holy Apostles which he had begun a few years before. Perhaps he already suspected that he was ill, for it was at this time that he gave orders for his tomb to be prepared in the church; but only after Easter did his health begin seriously to fail. He sought a cure with the baths at Helenopolis, the city that he had rebuilt in honour of his mother; and it was there, so Eusebius tells us, that, 'kneeling on the pavement of the church, he for the first time received the imposition of hands in prayer' – becoming, in short, a catechumen. Then he started back to the capital, but when he reached the suburbs of Nicomedia found that he could go no further; nor could the momentous step that he had so long considered be any further delayed.

And so at last Constantine the Great, for years a self-styled bishop of the Christian Church, was baptized by Bishop Eusebius of Nicomedia; and when it was done, 'he arrayed himself in imperial vestments white and radiant as light, and lay himself down on a couch of the purest white, refusing ever to clothe himself in purple again'.

Why – the question has been asked all through history – why did Constantine delay his baptism until he was on his deathbed? The most obvious answer – and the most likely – is Gibbon's:

The sacrament of baptism was supposed to contain a full and absolute expiation of sin; and the soul was instantly restored to its original purity, and entitled to the promise of external salvation. Among the proselytes of Christianity, there were many who judged it imprudent to precipitate a salutary rite, which could not be repeated; to throw away an inestimable privilege, which could never be recovered.

After a reign of thirty-one years, Constantine died at noon on Whit Sunday, 22 May 337. His body was placed in a golden coffin draped in purple and brought to Constantinople, where it lay in state on a high platform in the main hall of the palace. There it remained for some three and a half months, during which – for no one was yet sure which of the five young Caesars was to assume the vacant throne – the court ceremonial was carried on in

Constantine's name precisely as if his death had never occurred. Where the succession was concerned, the army was the first to make its wishes known. Although the title of Augustus continued, in theory at least, to be elective, the soldiers everywhere proclaimed that they would accept no one but Constantine's sons, reigning jointly. With Crispus dead, that left the three sons born to Fausta: the Caesar in Gaul Constantine II, the Caesar in the East Constantius, and the Caesar in Italy Constans;[1] and of these it was naturally Constantius, now a young man of twenty, who hastened to the capital after his father's death and presided over his funeral.

This was an extraordinary occasion, as Constantine had intended that it should be. The funeral procession was led by Constantius, with detachments of soldiers in full battle array; then came the body itself in its golden coffin, surrounded by companies of spearmen and heavy-armed infantry. From the Great Palace it wound its way round the north-eastern end of the Hippodrome to the Milion, and thence along the Mesē to the newly-completed Church of the Holy Apostles. 'He had in fact chosen this place,' Eusebius tells us,

in the prospect of his own death, anticipating that his body would share their title with the Apostles themselves. He accordingly caused twelve sarcophagi to be set up in this church, like sacred pillars, in honour and memory of the number of the Apostles, in the centre of which was placed his own, having six of theirs on either side of it.

For the last few years of his life Constantine had regularly used the title *Isapostolos*, 'Equal of the Apostles'; now at his death he gave, as it were, physical substance to that claim. His choice of his own position in the midst of his peers, with six of them on each hand, strongly suggests that he saw himself as yet greater than they – a symbol, perhaps of the Saviour in person: God's Vice-Gerent on Earth.

But he was not to occupy his resting-place for long. In his capital, as in so many cities of the Empire, he had tried to build too much, too quickly. There was thus a chronic shortage of skilled workmen, and a general tendency to skimp on foundations, wall thicknesses and buttressing. Within a quarter of a century of its completion, the fabric of the Church of the Holy Apostles began giving cause for alarm. Before long the great golden dome was in imminent danger of collapse, and the unpopular Patriarch Macedonius gave orders for the Emperor's body to be removed to safety in the nearby

---

1 The distressing lack of imagination shown by Constantine in the naming of his children has caused much confusion among past historians, to say nothing of their readers. The latter can take comfort in the knowledge that it lasts for a single generation only.

Church of St Acacius the Martyr. The building did not, however, collapse as the Patriarch had feared it would; it stood – if somewhat unsteadily – for two centuries until, in 550, it was completely rebuilt by Justinian. Of those twelve apostolic sarcophagi, and the great tomb of the Emperor among them, not a trace remains.

2

Julian the Apostate

[337-63]

Young Constantius had behaved impeccably during those first few weeks in Constantinople after the Emperor's death. Once his father had been laid safely away in his huge apostolic tomb, however, and he and his two brothers had jointly received their acclamation as Augusti, he abruptly shed his mild-mannered mask. A rumour was deliberately put about to the effect that, after Constantine's death, a scrap of parchment had been found clenched in his fist – accusing his two half-brothers, Julius Constantius and Delmatius, of having poisoned him and calling on his three sons to take their revenge.

The story seems improbable, to say the least; but its effect was horrendous. Julius Constantius was butchered, with his eldest son; so too was Delmatius, together with both his sons, the Caesars Delmatius and Hannibalianus, King of Pontus. Soon afterwards, Constantine's two brothers-in-law met similar fates. Apart from three little boys – the two sons of Julius Constantius and the single offspring of Nepotianus and Eutropia – the three reigning Augusti, when they met in the early summer of 338 to divide up their huge patrimony, were the only male members of the imperial family still alive. To Constantius went the East, including Asia Minor and Egypt. His elder brother Constantine II was to remain in charge of Gaul, Britain and Spain, while to the younger brother, Constans – though he was still only fifteen – went the largest area of all: Africa, Italy, the Danube, Macedonia and Thrace. This theoretically gave Constans authority over the capital itself; but as in 339 he was voluntarily to surrender the city to his brother in return for his support against Constantine II, the point proved of little significance.

It was perhaps inevitable that the three Augusti should sooner or later start quarrelling among themselves. The initial blame seems to have been Constantine's. The eldest of the three, he found it impossible to look on his co-Emperors as equals and was forever trying to assert his authority. It was Constans's refusal to submit to his will that led him, in 340, to invade Italy from Gaul; but Constans was too clever for him, and ambushed him with his army just outside Aquileia. Constantine was struck down and killed, and his body thrown into the river Alsa. From that time onward there were two

Augusti only, and Constans, aged just seventeen, held supreme power in the West.

Unfortunately, the character of Constans was no better than that of his surviving brother. Sextus Aurelius Victor, the Roman Governor of Pannonia, described him as 'a minister of unspeakable depravity'; he certainly neglected the all-important legions along the Rhine and upper Danube, preferring to take his pleasures with certain of his blond German prisoners. By 350 the army was on the brink of revolt, and matters came to a head when during a banquet given by one of his chief ministers, a pagan officer named Magnentius suddenly donned the imperial purple and was acclaimed Emperor by his fellow-guests. On hearing the news Constans took flight, but was quickly captured and put to death. The usurper did not last long. Constantius immediately marched against him with a large army. In September 351 Magnentius was soundly defeated and two years later fell on his sword.

Constantius was now the undisputed sole ruler of the Roman Empire. The German confederations beyond the Rhine, however, were making themselves increasingly troublesome. Among his own army, too, several minor conspiracies had been brought to light. On the other hand the Persian War was by no means over, and he could not stay in the West indefinitely. By the autumn of 355 he realized that he would have to appoint another Caesar; and on the assumption that any new Caesar was to be chosen from within the Emperor's immediate family, there was only one possible candidate. A philosopher and a scholar, he had no military or even administrative experience; but he was intelligent, serious-minded and a hard worker, and his loyalty had never been in question. Messengers were accordingly dispatched posthaste to Athens to fetch him: the Emperor's twenty-three-year-old cousin Flavius Claudius Julianus, better known to posterity as Julian the Apostate.

Julian's father, Julius Constantius, was the younger of the two sons born to the Emperor Constantius Chlorus by his second wife Theodora – a branch of the imperial family that had been obliged to keep an extremely low profile after Constantine's elevation of Theodora's predecessor Helena to Augustan rank. Julius Constantius had thus spent much of his life in exile when, soon after Helena's death, Constantine had invited him, with his second wife and his young family, back to Constantinople; and it was there that his third son Julian was born, in 332. The baby's mother died a few weeks later; and the little boy, together with his two considerably older stepbrothers and a stepsister, was brought up by a succession of nurses and tutors under his father's somewhat distant supervision. Then, when he was still only five, his father was murdered – the first victim of that family blood-bath that followed his nephew's accession. Whether Julian actually witnessed the murder is not recorded; but the experience left a permanent scar, and as he gradually came to understand who was responsible, his early respect for his cousin turned to an undying hatred.

To Constantius, on the other hand, young Julian was no more than a minor irritation. The Emperor sent him first to Eusebius at Nicomedia and then, when he was eleven, to distant Cappadocia, with only books for company. In 349, by now formidably well read in both classical and Christian literature, he obtained permission to apply himself to serious study. The next six years were the happiest in his life, spent wandering across the Greek world from one philosophical school to another, sitting at the feet of the greatest thinkers, scholars and rhetoricians of the day. The teacher who attracted him most was Libanius, who rejected Christianity and remained a proud and self-confessed pagan; and before long Julian too had decided to renounce Christianity in favour of the pagan gods of antiquity – though it was to be another ten years before he could avow his new faith openly.

His fellow-student in Athens, St Gregory Nazianzen, remembered him:

There was no evidence of a sound character in that oddly disjointed neck, those hunched and twitching shoulders, that wild, darting eye, that swaying walk, that haughty way of breathing down that prominent nose, those ridiculous facial expressions, that nervous and uncontrolled laughter, that ever-nodding head and that halting speech.

As one of the Empire's leading Christian theologians, Gregory was admittedly *parti pris*; and yet the portrait he paints has an authentic ring, and it is at least partly corroborated by other descriptions that have come down to us. Julian was not a handsome man. Burly and stocky, he had fine, dark eyes under straight brows; but their effect was spoiled by the huge mouth and sagging lower lip. Utterly devoid of ambition, he asked no more than to be allowed to remain at Athens with his teachers and his books; but the Emperor's summons to Milan could not be disobeyed. After an agonizing wait of several days, he was duly received by Constantius and informed that he was now a Caesar. His hair was trimmed, his beard shaved, his ungainly body squeezed into military uniform; and on 6 November he received his formal acclamation from the assembled troops.

Julian learned fast. It was he, rather than his cautious generals, who led the whirlwind campaign in the summer of 356 that took his army from Vienne to Cologne, which he recaptured for the Empire. The following year near Strasbourg, his 13,000 legionaries smashed a Frankish enemy of 30,000 or more, leaving some 6,000 dead on the field at a cost of just 247 of their own men. Further victories followed, and by the end of the decade the imperial rule had been re-established for the whole length of the frontier. In the East, on the other hand – to which Constantius, after a brief visit to Rome, had long since returned – the situation was a good deal less happy. In 359 the Emperor had received a letter from the Persian King:

Shapur, King of Kings, brother of the Sun and Moon, sends salutation ...

Your own authors are witness that the entire territory within the river Strymon and the borders of Macedon was once held by my forefathers; but because I take delight in moderation I shall be content to receive Mesopotamia and Armenia, which was fraudulently extorted from my grandfather. I give you warning that if my ambassador returns empty-handed I shall take the field against you, with all my armies, as soon as the winter is past.

Constantius, aware that he now faced the greatest challenge of his reign, in January 360 sent a tribune to Paris demanding huge reinforcements. Julian was faced with the prospect of losing at a stroke well over half his army; he had moreover promised his Gallic detachments that they would never be sent to the East. They for their part knew that, if they went, they would never again see their wives and families. These would be left destitute, easy prey for the barbarian bands who would once again come swarming into imperial territory.

We shall never know for certain just what took place at Julian's head-quarters in Paris during those fateful days. According to his own account, he was determined that the Emperor's orders should be obeyed, however unwelcome they might be to him personally; but the legionaries would have none of it. He soon saw that he was faced with open mutiny. Yet even then – he called upon all the gods to witness – he had no idea what was in his soldiers' minds. Were they planning to proclaim him as their Augustus, or to tear him to pieces? Soon a trembling chamberlain came to report that the army was marching on the palace. 'Then,' wrote Julian,

peering through a window, I prayed to Zeus. And as the tumult spread to the palace itself I entreated him to give me a sign; and he did so, bidding me cede to the will of the army. Even then I resisted as long as I could, refusing to accept either the ac-clamation or the diadem. But since I alone could not control so many, and since moreover the gods, whose will it was, sapped my resolution, somewhere about the third hour some soldier or other gave me a collar; and I put it on my head and returned to the palace.

Does Julian, perhaps, protest a little too much? His four and a half years in Gaul had given him courage, confidence and, perhaps, ambition. By now, too, he seems to have believed himself divinely appointed to restore the old religion to the Empire: once he had received – or thought he had received – the sign from Zeus, he was, one suspects, not over-reluctant to accept the diadem. The only difficulty was that no diadem existed. Ammianus Marcellinus – a member of the imperial bodyguard and probably an eye-witness – writes that the soldiers first proposed to crown Julian with his wife's necklace and then the frontlet of a horse, but both he refused. At last a soldier took the great gold chain from his neck and placed it on Julian's head. The die was cast. There could be no going back.

Julian was in no hurry to march to the East. First he must inform his cousin of what had occurred and suggest some kind of accommodation between them. His envoys found Constantius at Caesarea in Cappadocia. On receiving their message he flew into such a rage that they feared for their lives. For the moment, tied down as he was in the East, all he could do openly was to send Julian a stern warning; in secret, he began encouraging the barbarian tribes to renew their offensive along the Rhine. It was only four years later, taking advantage of a lull in the Persian campaign, that he could prepare an all-out offensive against his cousin. Julian was profoundly uncertain about how best to react: whether to meet him half-way, securing as best he could the allegiance of the troops stationed along the Danube, or whether to wait for him in Gaul, on his own home ground, where he could be sure of his troops. Once again, we are told, the gods gave him a sign. Pausing only to make a ritual sacrifice of a bull to Bellona, goddess of war, he assembled his army at Vienne and set out for the East. He had advanced no further than Naissus (Nish) in modern Serbia when messengers arrived from the capital to report that Constantius was dead: he, Julian, had already been acclaimed Emperor by the massed armies of the East. Constantius, it appeared, had been stricken by a low fever at Tarsus, and had died, on 3 November 361, at the age of forty-four.

Julian, showing no sign of relief or jubilation, hurried on to Constantinople. When the body of his predecessor reached the capital, he dressed in the deep mourning that he had ordered for the whole city, and stood on the quayside to supervise the unloading of the coffin. Later he led the funeral procession to the Church of the Holy Apostles, weeping unashamedly as his father's murderer was laid to rest. Only after the ceremony was over did he assume the attributes of Empire. He never entered a Christian church again.

Within days of Julian's accession to the imperial throne, it was plain to all in Constantinople that the new regime was going to provide a marked contrast to the old. A military tribunal was established to try certain of Constantius's chief ministers and advisers suspected of having abused their powers. Several were condemned to death – including two who were sentenced to be buried alive. In the palace itself, the new broom was even more dramatically apparent. Thousands were summarily dismissed without compensation, until the Emperor was left with only the skeleton staff required to meet his own needs – those of a single man (his wife Helena was by now dead), ascetic and celibate, to whom food and drink were of little interest and creature comforts of none. Similarly radical reforms were made in the government and administration – usually in the direction of the old republican traditions.

But these measures were of a kind that any strong ruler might enforce. Where Julian stands alone is in his convinced and dedicated paganism. During his years as Caesar, he had been obliged to pay lip-service to the Christian faith, but from the moment he heard of Constantius's death he made no more pretence. It was as a professed pagan that he settled down to frame the laws which, he was convinced, would ultimately eliminate Christianity and re-establish the worship of the ancient gods throughout the Roman Empire. There would, he believed, be no need for persecution. Martyrs always seemed to have a tonic effect on the Christian Church. The first thing to do was to repeal the decrees closing the pagan temples. An amnesty would then be proclaimed for all those orthodox churchmen whom the pro-Arian government of Constantius had sent into exile. Orthodox and Arian would soon be at each other's throats again, for, as Ammianus notes, 'he had found by experience that no wild beasts are so hostile to men as are Christian sects in general to one another'. After that it would be only a question of time before the Christians saw the error of their ways.

Julian was that unique combination – a Roman Emperor, a Greek philosopher and a mystic. As Emperor, he knew that his Empire was sick. The army had lost its morale and was now barely able to keep the peace along the frontier. The government was plagued by corruption. The old Roman virtues of reason and duty, honour and integrity were gone. His immediate predecessors had been sensualists and sybarites, still just capable of leading their forces into battle, but happier by far to recline in their palaces, surrounded by women and eunuchs. All this, clearly, was the result of moral degradation. As a philosopher, however, Julian was determined to discover the cause of the decline; and he concluded that this all-important question could be answered in a single word – Christianity. It had ridden roughshod over all the old virtues, emphasizing instead such effete, feminine qualities as gentleness, meekness and the turning of the other cheek. It had emasculated the Empire, robbing it of its strength and manhood and substituting a fecklessness whose effects were everywhere apparent.

Dearly as he loved philosophical and theological debate, Julian's approach to religion was always emotional rather than intellectual. Never for a single second did it occur to him that he might be wrong, that the old religion might not, after all, prevail. It appeared, on the other hand, in no great hurry to do so. In the summer of 362 he transferred his capital to Antioch, in readiness for the Persian expedition that he was preparing for the following year; and as he marched through the heartland of Asia Minor he was concerned to note that the Christian communities were showing no sign whatever of tearing each other to bits; nor were the pagans noticeably stronger or more cohesive than in Constantine's day. In vain did he move from temple to temple, personally officiating at one sacrifice after another until he was nicknamed 'the butcher' by his subjects. The prevailing apathy was unshakeable.

If the pagans could not be galvanized into life, there was no alternative but to increase the pressure on the Christians; and on 17 June 362 Julian published an edict which struck them a body-blow. No teacher, it declared, would henceforth be permitted to follow his calling without first obtaining the approval of his local city council and, through it, of the Emperor himself. In a circular Julian explained that no Christian who professed to teach the classical authors – who in those days occupied virtually all the school curriculum – could possibly be of the required moral standard, since he would be teaching subjects in which he did not himself believe. He must consequently abjure either his livelihood or his faith. Christian demonstrations were held in protest, and on 26 October the temple of Apollo at Daphne was burnt to the ground. Julian retaliated by closing down the Great Church of Antioch, confiscating all its gold plate. Tension was now rising fast and, as the situation began to escalate, more than one hot-blooded young Christian achieved martyrdom. It was a blessed day indeed for the Christians when, on 5 March 363, Julian set off for the East at the head of some 90,000 men, never to return alive.

There was nothing new about the war with Persia. The two vast Empires had been fighting for the best part of two and a half centuries. Shapur II was at the time fifty-four years old, and had occupied the Persian throne for the same period – technically, indeed, a little longer, since he is perhaps the only monarch in all history to have been crowned *in utero*. As Gibbon explains:

A royal bed, on which the queen lay in state, was exhibited in the midst of the palace; the diadem was placed on the spot which might be supposed to conceal the future heir of Artaxerxes, and the prostrate satraps adored the majesty of their invisible and insensible sovereign.

The most recent climax in the war had come in 359 when Shapur captured the key fortress of Amida – the present Turkish city of Diyarbekir – which controlled both the headwaters of the Tigris and the approaches to Asia Minor from the East. After this a major Roman offensive was essential if the situation were not to get seriously out of hand; and Julian, believing, there is reason to suspect, that he might be the incarnation of Alexander the Great himself – was impatient to achieve similar glory. At Beroea – the modern Aleppo – he slaughtered a white bull on the acropolis as a tribute to Zeus. Further sacrifices followed at all the principal pagan shrines along the route until, after a few minor sieges and skirmishes but no real difficulties, he found himself on the west bank of the Tigris, gazing up at the walls of Ctesiphon, the Persian capital. On the opposite shore was a Persian army, already drawn up and ready for battle; and the Roman generals were concerned to note that it numbered, besides the normal cavalry, a quantity of elephants – always a powerful weapon, not just because their men had no experience of dealing with them but because their smell terrified their horses to the point of panic. None the less, Julian gave the order to advance across the river, and battle was joined. It ended – to the surprise of many on both sides – in an overwhelming victory for Roman arms. According to Ammianus, who took part in the fighting, 2,500 Persians were killed at the cost of a mere seventy Roman lives.

The date was 29 May; already by the next day, however, the situation had changed. For the Emperor had realized that Ctesiphon was virtually impregnable, and that Shapur's main army – larger by far than that which had just been defeated – was rapidly approaching. Moreover, morale in the Roman army was dangerously low. Food was short; the rivers were all in flood; the heat was murderous; and the flies, Ammianus tells us, were so thick that they blotted out the light of the sun. Julian, he goes on, was still in favour of advancing further into Persian territory; but his generals refused. On 16 June the retreat began. Ten days later, near Samarra, the army suddenly came under heavy attack. Once again the dreaded elephants were brought into action, once again the air was thick with spears and arrows. Without pausing to strap on his breastplate, Julian plunged into the thick of the fray, shouting encouragement to his men as he fought in their midst; and just as the Persians were beginning to retreat, a flying spear struck him in the side. It was extracted from deep in his liver, but the damage was done. He died just before midnight, according to legend, scooping up a handful of the blood that was flowing from his wound and murmuring the words, 'Thou hast conquered, Galilean!'

Julian was thirty-one at the time of his death, and had occupied the imperial throne for just nineteen and a half months. As an Emperor he was a failure. He wasted his time and energy on a hopelessly quixotic attempt to revive an ill-defined and moribund religion, to the detriment of that which was to give the Empire its binding force for a thousand years to come; he made himself thoroughly unpopular with his subjects, Christian and pagan alike, who hated his puritanism and his ceaseless sermonizing; and he came close to destroying the entire imperial army in a campaign which ended in near catastrophe. And yet, of all the eighty-eight Emperors of Byzantium, it is Julian, perhaps more than any other, who has caught the imagination of posterity.

His real tragedy lies not in his misguided policies or in his early death, but in the hairsbreadth by which he failed to achieve the greatness which he in so many ways deserved. Few monarchs have possessed his intelligence, his education and culture, his energy and industry, his courage and leadership, his integrity and incorruptibility, his astonishing ability to sublimate himself in the service of his Empire and, above all, of his gods. Sadly, however, he also possessed two faults, which made any lasting achievement impossible: first, his religious fanaticism; second, a lack of sharpness and definition in his thinking. He could on occasion be curiously indecisive. Again and again we find him asking the gods for guidance, when he should have been taking decisions for himself. Perhaps, had he lived, he would have overcome both these faults and proved himself one of the greatest of Roman Emperors. But he did not live. He died, in the most characteristic way he could have died, bravely but unnecessarily, leaving nothing but the memory of a misguided young visionary who attempted to change the world – and failed.

3
The Empire at Bay
[363-95]

Finding itself on Julian's death without a leader, the Roman army assembled *en masse* early the following morning to nominate his successor. What seems to have been a relatively small group of soldiers started shouting the name of Jovian, the commander of the imperial guard. He was thirty-two, a bluff, genial soldier, popular with his men; he was also, perhaps significantly, a Christian – a persuasion which in no way diminished his well-known *penchant* for wine and women. But he was in no sense distinguished, and certainly not of imperial calibre.

It was under this new and deeply uninspiring leader that the sad and weary retreat continued along the Tigris, still under constant harassment from the Persians. At the beginning of July, after the Roman army had succeeded in making a forced crossing of the river despite all that he could do to prevent it, Shapur decided to offer terms; and, humiliating as they were, Jovian accepted them. The resulting treaty provided for thirty years of peace, together with the restitution to Persia of five frontier provinces and eighteen important fortresses. Further, the Romans bound themselves not to assist Armenia against Persian attack – a promise tantamount to renouncing all their claims over that country. Jovian had made a disastrous beginning to his reign.

At Nisibis Julian's embalmed body was sent to Tarsus for burial. Jovian meanwhile led the army on to Antioch, where he immediately issued an edict of religious toleration, restoring full rights and privileges to Christians throughout the Empire. He left in mid-October, moving with his army in easy stages through Anatolia, and was generally acclaimed with enthusiasm. Only at Ancyra where he assumed the Consulship with his infant son Varronianus, did the deafening howls of the latter during the ceremony lead the more credulous of those present to fear an evil omen.

As well they might have. A few days later, on 16 February 364, Jovian was found dead in his bedroom. 'By some,' writes Gibbon, his death 'was ascribed to the consequences of an indigestion ... According to others, he was suffocated in his sleep by the vapour of charcoal, which extracted from the walls of the apartment the unwholesome moisture of the fresh plaster.' Surprisingly enough, foul play was not suspected.

The choice of Jovian as Emperor had marked not only the restitution of Christianity, but the end of the dynasty which had ruled the Empire for over half a century. The diadem was once again a prize open to all. And there could be no clearer indication of this changed state of affairs than the virtual unanimity with which the army now acclaimed Valentinian as his successor. At first sight the new Emperor seemed still more unfitted for the purple. Uncouth, almost illiterate and possessed of a quite uncontrollable temper, he was the son of a Pannonian rope-maker who had himself risen from the ranks to positions of high authority. Like his father, Valentinian made no attempt to conceal his peasant origins; but at forty-two he still boasted a magnificent physique and a commanding presence. He was a devout Christian and a superb soldier, though capable of unspeakable cruelty. When, after his acclamation, he was pressed to nominate a co-Augustus, he refused to be hurried: only after the army reached Constantinople did he name – to the general dismay – his younger brother Valens. It was a curious choice. Valens was an Arian and, in appearance, little short of grotesque – bandy-legged and pot-bellied, with a ferocious squint. Seven years younger than his brother, he equalled him only in brutality; he was, however, precisely what Valentinian wanted: a faithful lieutenant who could be trusted to provoke no difficulties or quarrels. Valens, the Emperor rather surprisingly announced, would be responsible for the East while he, Valentinian, would rule the West from his capital at Milan.

For the next decade we find the two Emperors caught up in their respective struggles: Valens engaged first with the Gothic tribes along the Danubian frontier, and then in 371 setting out on his long-delayed journey to the East, where Shapur had reduced Armenia to the status of a Persian satellite; Valentinian dealing with the repeated incursions of the barbarians into Gaul. Not till 373 could he leave it in safety; almost immediately, however, new troubles broke out along the Danube, where a normally law-abiding tribe, the Quadi, invaded imperial territory and laid waste a certain amount of land along the frontier. They then sent an embassy, explaining why they had done so and claiming that the real aggressors were the Romans themselves.

To Valentinian, such an accusation was an insult to Rome. The anger welled up within him as he listened, his face turning a deeper and deeper purple until he suddenly fell forward in a fit of apoplexy and died, on 17 November 375. He had worked, as few Emperors had ever worked, for the integrity of the imperial frontiers. As a Christian he had shown tolerance for those who did not share his own strongly-held Nicene faith; as a ruler he had dispensed justice with an impartial hand; if his punishments were severe, at least they were visited only on the guilty. But his harshness and austerity had won him little love from his subjects; and few were heartbroken to see him go.

Already as early as 367, Valentinian had persuaded his troops to recognize his seven-year-old son Gratian as co-Augustus. As he lay on his deathbed, however, knowing that Gratian was far away at Trier and Valens a good deal further at Antioch, he sent for his son by his second marriage, also called Valentinian, and still only four, and had him proclaimed co-Emperor with his half-brother. Thus the Empire theoretically had three rulers to carry on the government: a malformed, middle-aged sadist devoid of wisdom or judgement, a delightful boy of sixteen and a child scarcely out of its cradle. On those three the future of the Empire depended at one of the critical moments of its history; for only a year later it found itself confronting the most formidable invaders it had ever encountered. The Huns were, by any standards, savages – a vast, undisciplined, heathen horde, Mongolian in origin, who had swept down from the Central Asian steppe, destroying everything in their path. The Ostrogoths tried to resist, but in vain: and the greater number sought permission from Valens to settle within the Empire, on the plains of Thrace.

Their request was granted, the Emperor giving express orders to his local representatives to provide the refugees with food and shelter. Alas, his instructions were ignored: Lupicinus, Count of Thrace, robbed them of all they possessed and reduced them to the brink of starvation. The settlers, desperate, were driven to active resistance, and by the late summer all the Goths of Thrace were up in arms, to be joined by the Visigoths and even the Huns in a full-scale barbarian attack on the Roman Empire. The war raged throughout the winter following, and in the spring of 378, Valens himself headed for the Balkans. The ensuing battle, fought on 9 August 378, was a *débâcle*. The Emperor was killed by an arrow and two-thirds of the Roman army perished with him.

Everything now depended on Gratian, still only nineteen. Unable yet to leave the West, he turned to a certain Theodosius, son of one of his father's leading generals, who within a few months proved himself a leader of such distinction that, in January 379, Gratian raised him to be his co-Augustus. Establishing his headquarters at Thessalonica, Theodosius devoted the next two years to restoring order in Thrace and confidence among the Gothic rebels, vast numbers of whom were recruited into the legions. By the summer of 380, thanks to his quiet, patient diplomacy, the Goths were happily settled in their new homes and Thrace was once again at peace; and on

24 November he made his formal entry into Constantinople. 'Now that the wounds of strife are healed,' declared the court orator Themistius, 'Rome's most courageous enemies will become her truest and most loyal friends.'

Gratian's elevation of Theodosius to the supreme power was perhaps the most lasting benefit that he conferred on the Empire. And yet, ironically, the very year that saw the conclusion of his final peace treaty with the Goths also witnessed his downfall. Few had ever shown greater promise; but, at the age of twenty-four, he was already growing lazy. More dangerous still, he no longer attempted to conceal the predilection he felt for the barbarian element in the army (and particularly for his own personal guard of tall, blond Alani) whom he openly favoured at the expense of their Roman colleagues. Matters came to a head when one of the imperial generals serving in Britain, Magnus Clemens Maximus, was suddenly acclaimed Augustus by his men; a few days later he landed in Gaul, where his army met Gratian's just outside Paris. The Emperor would probably have won the day had not his Moorish cavalry unexpectedly defected. He fled, but was taken prisoner at Lyons and there, on 25 August, was murdered while attending a banquet – under a promise of safe conduct – with his captors. In Constantinople, Theodosius received the news with horror. For the moment, however, he was powerless. The new Persian King Shapur III was an unknown quantity who needed watching; meanwhile the Huns were still causing trouble along the northern frontier. This was no time to embark on a long punitive expedition. Reluctantly, Emperor acknowledged usurper – as did most of the provinces of the West.

Except Italy – where Gratian's co-Emperor Valentinian II, now twelve years old, maintained his somewhat precarious authority from Milan. His life cannot have been made happier by the machinations of Justina, his fanatically Arian mother, who feared the growing influence over her son of Ambrose, the great Bishop of Milan, and was forever intriguing against him; but Ambrose gave as good as he got, and outmanoeuvred her every time. Unfortunately during Justina's lifetime he never managed to persuade Valentinian to accept the Nicene faith; Maximus was thus given precisely the excuse he needed. In 387 he crossed the Alps, ostensibly to deliver the Empire from heresy. Justina and Valentinian fled to Thessalonica, where Theodosius was able to join them – Justina was now his mother-in-law, since his recent marriage *en secondes noces* to her daughter Galla – and to prepare for war. In June 388 he and Valentinian pressed up through the mountain passes of Macedonia and Bosnia. The campaign proved to be largely a matter of pursuit, and Maximus was finally driven to surrender at Aquileia. He was brought before Theodosius, and for a moment it looked as if the Emperor was about to spare his life; but the soldiers dragged him away before he could do so. They knew Theodosius's reputation for clemency, and preferred to take no chances.

Appointing the Frankish general Arbogast as *Comes* – effectively Governor – of Gaul, in 389 Theodosius and Valentinian moved on with the former's four-year-old son Honorius to Rome. The senior Emperor's energetic efforts to weaken the hold of paganism cannot have endeared him to members of the old regime; but his easy approachability and charm of manner won him a personal popularity such as no Emperor had enjoyed for a century or more. The two Augusti then returned to Milan, remaining there through the year of that famous confrontation between Theodosius and Ambrose for which both of them, perhaps unfairly, are best remembered.

The incident that set the two on a collision course was one at which neither was personally present: the murder, at Thessalonica, of the captain of the imperial garrison. Resentment had long been increasing among the citizens over the billeting of troops; and flash-point was reached when the captain – himself a Goth, by the name of Botheric – imprisoned the city's most popular charioteer. The mob attacked the garrison headquarters, smashed its way into the building and cut down Botheric where he stood. When the incident was reported to Theodosius in Milan, his anger was terrible. In vain Ambrose pleaded with him not to take vengeance on the many for the crimes of a few; he ordered the troops in the city to reassert their authority in whatever way they saw fit. Later he countermanded the order, but it had already been received, and the soldiers were only too eager to obey. They deliberately waited until the people were gathered in the Hippodrome for the games; then, at a given signal, they fell on them. Seven thousand were dead by nightfall.

Reports of the massacre at Thessalonica spread rapidly through the Empire. The guilt moreover fell on the Emperor himself, and Ambrose of Milan was not the man to overlook it. At this time he was the most influential churchman in Christendom – more so by far than the Pope in Rome. Member of one of the most ancient Christian families of the Roman aristocracy, he had never intended to enter the priesthood; only when it finally emerged that he alone, although a layman, possessed sufficient prestige to prevent open strife between the Orthodox and Arian factions in the city did he reluctantly allow his name to go forward. In a single week he was successively catechumen, priest and bishop. Once enthroned, he distributed his entire fortune among the poor and adopted an extreme asceticism in his private life. Since first hearing of the murder of Botheric he had done everything in his power to urge Theodosius towards moderation; when he saw that he had failed, he wrote the Emperor a letter in his own hand, telling him that, despite his continuing high regard, he must regretfully withhold communion from him until he should perform public penance for his crime.

And Theodosius submitted. His handling of the affair had been not only unworthy of him; it had also been uncharacteristic. Almost certainly, he had allowed himself to be persuaded by his military entourage. It seems to have been an immense relief to his spirit when, bare-headed and dressed in sack-cloth, he presented himself in the cathedral of Milan humbly to beg forgive-ness. But it was also something more. It was a turning-point in the history of Christendom – the first time that a Churchman had had the courage to assert the rights of the spiritual power over the temporal, and the first time that a Christian prince had publicly submitted to judgement, condemnation and punishment by an authority which he recognized as higher than his own.

Early in 391 the two Emperors left Milan – Theodosius to return to Constantinople, Valentinian to accept the transference of power in Gaul, where Arbogast the Frank had been ruling in his absence. On his arrival at Vienne, however, it soon became clear to him that Arbogast had no intention of handing over the reins. Determined to assert his authority, Valentinian handed the Frank a written order, demanding his immediate resignation. Arbogast looked at it for a moment and then, slowly and contemptuously, tore it to pieces. At that moment war between the two was declared; and a few days later, on 15 May 392, the young Emperor, now just twenty-one, was found dead in his apartment.

Arbogast, a pagan Frank, could not assume the diadem himself; but he was perfectly content with the role of kingmaker. He therefore named his hench-man Eugenius, a middle-aged Christian who had formerly served as head of the imperial chancery, as the new Augustus. Ambassadors were sent to Theodosius; but for Theodosius the right of designating his fellow-Emperor belonged to him and to him alone. He sent an evasive reply and began to make his preparations. Throughout 393 those preparations continued, while Arbogast succeeded, despite the vehement opposition of Ambrose, in having his protégé acclaimed in Italy also. For his principal support he relied on the pagan old guard, happy to welcome an Emperor who willingly permitted the re-erection of the ancient altars. By the middle of the year, Rome was under-going a full-scale pagan revival. The sky was cloudy with the smoke of sacrifice, while aged augurs peered anxiously into the entrails of their still-steaming victims. When in the early summer of 394 Theodosius marched for the second time against an upstart pretender, he was aware that he was fight-ing not just for legitimacy but also for his faith. He was well equipped to do so since, apart from the Roman legionaries, his army contained some 20,000 Goths – many of them serving under their own chieftains, among whom there was included a brilliant young leader named Alaric. As second-in-command he had appointed a Vandal, Stilicho, who had recently married his niece Serena. But his heart was heavy: on the eve of his departure his beloved second wife, Galla, had died in childbirth.

The two forces met on 5 September a little north of Trieste. The following day a violent tempest blew up from the east, accompanied by winds of hurricane force. While Theodosius and his men had these winds behind them, the soldiers of Arbogast found themselves blinded by dust and barely able to stand upright. Eugenius was beheaded as he grovelled at the Emperor's feet; Arbogast escaped, but after a few days' wandering found the old Roman solution for his troubles and fell on his sword.

Theodosius now turned his mind to the question of the succession. Valentinian having died unmarried and childless, the obvious course was to divide the Empire between his own two sons, giving to the elder, Arcadius, the East and to the younger, Honorius, the West. Both were in Constantinople, and Honorius was now summoned to Milan; but the call came too late. On 17 January 395 Theodosius died in his fiftieth year.

Had he earned his title 'the Great'? Not perhaps in the way that Constantine had done. But, if not ultimately great himself, he had surely come very close to greatness. Had he reigned longer, he might even have saved the Western Empire. It would be nearly a century and a half before the Romans would look upon his like again.

4
The Fall of the West

Theodosius the Great was the last Emperor to rule over a united Roman Empire before the final collapse of the West. From the moment of his death the Western Empire embarks on its eighty-year decline, until the ironically-named young Romulus Augustulus makes his final submission to a barbarian king. But the Empire of the East survives, gradually acquiring a personality of its own. Latin gives way to Greek, the world of the intellect to that of the spirit; yet the classical tradition remains unbroken.

When Theodosius died his elder son, Arcadius, was seventeen, Honorius ten. Both he entrusted to his nephew-by-marriage Stilicho, whose star was now rising fast. The son of a Vandal chieftain, he had somehow attracted the attention of Theodosius: for he was now married to Serena – the Emperor's niece, adopted daughter and favourite.

Though technically responsible for both young Emperors, his principal charge was Honorius; Arcadius, far away in Constantinople, fell under less desirable influences – the most pernicious of which was that of the Praetorian Prefect Rufinus. It was Rufinus, almost certainly, who had incited Theodosius to order the Thessalonica massacre. His avarice and corruption were renowned throughout Constantinople; above all he was ambitious, and his ambitions were centred on the throne. Arcadius was slow in speech and movement; and his character was as weak as his intellect. One thing only prevented him from being a puppet in Rufinus's hands: the influence of an elderly eunuch named Eutropius. With his egg-bald head and wrinkled yellow face, Eutropius was even uglier than his master; but, like Rufinus, he was intelligent, unscrupulous and ambitious; and he was determined to thwart his enemy in every way he could. Rufinus, he knew, planned to marry his daughter to Arcadius. After such a marriage it would be but a short step to the throne itself, and Eutropius's own chances of survival would be slim. He therefore picked on a young girl of startling beauty named Eudoxia and introduced her in Rufinus's absence into the palace. By the time Rufinus returned, Arcadius and Eudoxia were betrothed.

In 395, at just about the time of the wedding, the Goths within the Empire rose again in revolt. They had adopted as their leader the twenty-five-year-old Alaric, and in a few weeks had advanced to only a few miles from Constantinople. Here, however, they turned back – probably bribed by Rufinus – and headed west again towards Macedonia and Thessaly. It had been an uncomfortable moment; and Arcadius sent an urgent message to Stilicho in Milan, ordering him to bring back the eastern army with all possible speed. Stilicho started as soon as he could, but instead of heading directly for Constantinople he marched to confront Alaric in Thessaly – where, however, he received another order from the Emperor. The army was to come at once to the capital; he himself was to return to the West. Stilicho did as he was bid. The eastern army he dispatched to Constantinople; then, taking the western with him, he started for home.

Alaric was once again free to continue his advance unimpeded. Southward he marched through Thessaly into Attica. The port of Piraeus was completely destroyed; Athens was saved only by its walls. He and his army then crossed the isthmus of Corinth into the Peloponnese, sacking Sparta and the central plain. But early in 396, there was a surprise: Stilicho was back, with a new army brought by the sea from Italy. Suddenly the Goths found themselves surrounded. At last, it seemed, Stilicho had them at his mercy. But now, just as he was on the point of victory, he deliberately allowed them to escape. Why? Obviously, he had struck some bargain. Later we shall have to speculate on its nature; for the moment we must let the story unfold.

And what of the great army of the East, so hastily summoned by Arcadius? Its commander Gainas led it as instructed to Constantinople, halting just outside the Golden Gate. Here Arcadius duly appeared, accompanied by Rufinus, who began mingling with the troops, insidiously soliciting their support. At first he did not notice that they were slowly closing in around him; when he did so it was already too late. A moment later he was dead.

Now that Eutropius alone had the Emperor's ear, corruption became more widespread than ever. In 399 he managed to get himself nominated Consul. Although the title had long been purely honorary, it remained the highest distinction that the Empire could bestow. To see it now assumed by an erstwhile slave and emasculated male prostitute was more than the Constantinopolitans could stand. Matters were brought to a head by Gainas, whose soldiers had cut down Rufinus four years before. In the spring of 399, dispatched to Phrygia to deal with a new revolt, he sent a message to Arcadius that the insurgents were making only a few most reasonable demands which could be easily granted. The first of these proved to be the surrender of Eutropius. Arcadius hesitated. But now another voice was heard – that of the Empress herself.

Eudoxia is the first in that long line of Byzantine Empresses whose names were to become bywords for luxury and sensuality – she was said to flaunt her depravity by wearing a fringe low over the forehead, the trademark of a courtesan. She owed her position entirely to Eutropius; but he had reminded her of the fact once too often. With Arcadius, her relations had deteriorated to the point of mutual loathing. And so the Emperor gave the order; and Eutropius fled in terror to seek asylum in St Sophia, flinging himself at the feet of the bishop, St John Chrysostom. This lugubrious cleric had no more affection for him than did Eudoxia; but he could not deny the right of sanctuary. When the soldiers arrived he stood implacably before them and turned them away, while the trembling eunuch cowered beneath the high altar.

Eutropius was safe in St Sophia; but he was also trapped there. Finally he was persuaded to surrender, on condition that his life were spared. He was exiled to Cyprus, but was shortly afterwards brought back and executed.

The fourth century had been a fateful one indeed for the Roman Empire. It had seen the birth of a new capital, and the adoption of Christianity as the official religion of the Empire. It ended, however, on a note of bathos: in the West with silence and inertia in the face of the barbarian menace, in the East with a whimper – the only possible description for the reactions of a feckless Emperor as his vicious wife held him up to public ridicule as a fool, an incompetent and a cuckold. The new century, on the other hand, began with a bang. In the early summer of 401, Alaric the Goth invaded Italy.

Greatest of all the Gothic leaders, Alaric dominates the early fifth century. Before it opened, he had already spread terror from Constantinople to the Peloponnese; but, by accepting the title of *magister militum*, he had also shown that he was not fundamentally hostile to the Roman Empire. Alaric fought not to overthrow the Empire, but to establish a permanent home for his people within it. If only the Western Emperor and the Roman Senate could have understood this simple fact, the final catastrophe might have been averted. By their lack of comprehension they made it inevitable. In the four years since Alaric had withdrawn with his army into Illyricum, the Empire might have been expected to take some measures to avert the coming onslaught; it was typical of Honorius – whose only interest seems to have been the raising of poultry – that nothing had been done. Thus, as news of the invasion spread, blind panic spread with it. Slowly and irresistibly the huge Gothic host lumbered down the Isonzo valley, their wives and families trailing behind: this was not just an army but an entire nation on the march. West they headed towards Milan, the young Emperor fleeing before them; and it was just a few miles from Asti that they found the Roman army awaiting them, the familiar figure of Stilicho at its head. The resulting battle, fought on Easter Sunday, 402, was inconclusive; but the Goths advanced no further, retiring instead to the East. On their way, Alaric made a surprise attack on Verona, where he sustained an indisputable defeat at the hands of Stilicho. Once again, however, the Vandal captain allowed him to withdraw, his army still intact.

Stilicho had now had Alaric at least twice at his mercy, only to let him escape. From the start, his attitude towards the Gothic leader seems to have been strangely ambiguous. Did the two have some secret understanding? Whatever the truth, it seems clear that Stilicho saw the Goths as being potentially useful allies, and had no desire either to break their strength or to sacrifice their goodwill.

Meanwhile relations between East and West had steadily deteriorated, largely owing to the Bishop of Constantinople, St John Chrysostom. This saintly but insufferable prelate, by his scorching castigations of the Empress, had made himself dangerously unpopular at court; and in 403 he was deposed and exiled to Bithynia. He enjoyed, however, considerable support among the people: and furious fighting broke out in the streets. That night there was an earthquake, which so frightened the superstitious Empress that the exiled prelate was recalled and reinstated.

John had won the first round; if only he had moderated his tone, all might have been well. Only a few weeks later however he protested when a silver statue of Eudoxia was erected just outside St Sophia: the noise of the inauguration ceremony, he claimed, interrupted his services. Thereafter the breach was complete, Eudoxia refusing to allow her husband any communication at all with the leading ecclesiastic of the Empire. Early the following spring Chrysostom was again condemned. On this occasion Arcadius debarred the bishop from his church, and on 24 June John was exiled for the second time; but once again disaster overtook Constantinople. That same evening St Sophia was destroyed by fire, the flames being blown by a strong north wind on to the Senate House nearby. Less than four months later, on 6 October, came the final, unmistakable sign of divine displeasure: the Empress had a miscarriage, which proved fatal.

Shortly before his departure Chrysostom had appealed to Pope Innocent I, protesting against his unjust sentence and demanding a formal trial; and the Pope had summoned a synod of Latin bishops, which unanimously called for the bishop's restitution. Meanwhile Honorius had addressed a stern letter to his brother; but when in 406 he and Innocent sent a delegation to Constantinople, the envoys were imprisoned, interrogated and sent back to Italy. Thus, when St John Chrysostom died in exile in 407, he left the Empire split; and Stilicho decided to put his long-cherished plans into effect. Alaric, he knew, was standing by to help him. His first step was to order a blockade on the Eastern Empire. It was in effect a declaration of war; but he himself was still in Ravenna when a messenger arrived from Honorius. Alaric, it appeared, was dead. Meanwhile the Roman Governor of Britain, Constantius, had crossed to Gaul and raised the standard of revolt. Leaving the army at Ravenna, Stilicho hastened to Rome. On his arrival, he found that the first half of the message had been based on a false rumour. Alaric was alive and well but greatly displeased at the postponement, for which he expected compensation. The Senate, to whom his demands were addressed, was horrified; but Stilicho finally succeeded in persuading them.

Early in May 408, the Emperor Arcadius died aged thirty-one, leaving the throne to his seven-year-old son, named Theodosius after his grandfather. Stilicho hoped that he would now be able to realize his plans in the East without bloodshed or even expense, while Alaric would be left free to deal with the usurper in Gaul. But those plans came to nothing. Perhaps Stilicho's personal ambition was too obvious; perhaps the old jealousies were stirring again: he was, after all, a Vandal, and Vandals were expected to know their place. At the court of Ravenna, his chief enemy was a certain minister named Olympius; and it was he who persuaded Honorius that his father-in-law was plotting against him. We do not know the nature of the accusations, nor whether they had any foundation. The one certain fact is that Stilicho was tried, found guilty and, at Ravenna on 23 August 408, put to death.

With the execution of Stilicho, all the pent-up hatred of Roman for barbarian suddenly found its release. In garrisons throughout the Empire, the Roman legionaries fell upon their Gothic, Hunnish or Vandal auxiliaries and their families – with disastrous consequences. The survivors wandered through the countryside, looting and pillaging, and finally found their way to Alaric. Previously loyal to the Empire, they had now become its enemies, bent on vengeance. The Romans found, at this critical moment, that they lacked a commander. Whatever dark designs Stilicho may have harboured against the Eastern Empire, he had always remained a faithful servant of the West. He was one of those barbarians who believed in the Empire; and for all his severity and occasional deviousness, he was a fine leader of men. Only when he had gone did the Romans realize just how irreplaceable he was.

Alaric too believed in the Empire – in his fashion. But he did not believe in Honorius. Still less did he trust the Roman Senate, which was still prevaricating over compensation. This, as it should have understood, was virtually an open invitation to invade; yet even now the army – which had been stood down after Stilicho's death – remained unmobilized. So Alaric invaded;

and in September 408 he drew up his Gothic host before the walls of Rome.

A few days were all that he needed to establish a stranglehold. Every road, bridge and footpath, every inch of the walls was kept under constant watch; boats constantly patrolled the Tiber. Inside the city, strict rationing was introduced. Soon cases of cannibalism were reported. As the weather worsened, cold and undernourishment brought disease. Gradually it became clear that no help from Ravenna could be expected: Honorius was not lifting a finger to save the old capital. Shortly before Christmas, a ransom was agreed: 5,000 pounds of gold, 30,000 of silver, 4,000 silken tunics, 3,000 hides dyed scarlet and 3,000 pounds of pepper. The first two items involved the stripping of statues and their adornments from churches and temples alike, and the melting down of countless works of art.

But Alaric still wanted a home for his people; and he now made Honorius a new proposal. Venetia, Dalmatia and Noricum – now Slovenia and south Austria – while remaining part of the Empire, would be allotted to the Goths as their permanent home, in return for which Alaric undertook to be the effective defender and champion of Rome and the Empire against any enemy whatever. The offer seemed not unreasonable; Honorius, however, would have none of it. It was the first time he had shown a trace of spirit, but he could hardly have chosen a worse moment to do so. His army, demoralized and rudderless, would not stand the faintest chance when the Goths renewed their attack. The Eastern Empire was in a state of turmoil after the accession of a child of seven; Gaul, Britain and Spain were in the hands of a usurper who could at any moment march into Italy. If he did so, Alaric and his Goths might well prove an invaluable bulwark.

Thus Honorius, defenceless, insisted on defiance; while Alaric, who could easily have crushed him, still sought peace. He now reduced his requirements to Noricum alone. Again Honorius refused. Alaric's patience was finally exhausted. For the second time in twelve months, he marched on Rome; but this time, he told the Romans he had one purpose only: to overthrow Honorius, the single obstacle to peace in Italy. If they would now declare him deposed and elect a more reasonable successor, he would raise the siege forthwith.

The Roman Senate did not take long to decide. Another siege was unthinkable. Honorius had shown no concern for his people; so long as he personally was safe in Ravenna, he seemed oblivious to their fate. So the gates were opened, and Alaric entered Rome in peace; Honorius was declared deposed, and it was agreed that he should be succeeded as Augustus by the Prefect of the City, a Greek named Priscus Attalus. It was not a bad choice. Attalus was an intelligent and cultivated Christian, acceptable to the pagans on account of his tolerant views and his love of antique literature. Appointing Alaric his *magister militum*, he prepared to march on Ravenna; but there was one major problem to be settled. Heraclian, Governor of the province of Africa (roughly corresponding to northern Tunisia) on which Rome was entirely dependent for its corn, was expected to remain loyal to Honorius; so Attalus sent over a young man named Constans with instructions to take over the province peaceably in his name. This done, he set off with Alaric for Ravenna.

Honorius had finally abandoned his sang-froid. Panic-stricken, he sent messages to Attalus, agreeing to his rule in Rome if he himself might continue as Augustus in Ravenna; meanwhile he ordered ships to be prepared to take him to safety in Constantinople. At that point, however, there arrived six Byzantine legions from young Theodosius II, responding at last to his uncle's appeal. These reinforcements restored the Emperor's courage. He would, he declared, hold out in Ravenna, at least until he heard the news from Africa: if Heraclian had stood firm, all might not be lost.

Nor was it; a few days later there came a report that the unfortunate Constans had been executed, and Heraclian was cutting off the grain supply. To Alaric, this was a serious blow. It meant that he could no longer hope to oust the Emperor from Ravenna; moreover it pointed to a serious lack of political acumen on the part of Attalus. In the early summer of 410 he publicly stripped Attalus of the purple. He then returned to Rome and besieged it for the third time. With food already short, the city did not hold out for long. Some time towards the end of August, the Goths burst in. After the capture, there were the traditional three days of pillage; but this early sack of Rome seems to have been less savage than history-books suggest. Alaric, himself a devout Christian, had ordered that no churches or religious buildings were to be touched, and that the right of asylum was to be respected. Yet a sack, however decorous, remains a sack; there is probably all too much truth in the accounts of the splendid edifices burnt, innocents slain, matrons ravished and virgins deflowered.

When the three days were over, Alaric moved on to the south, intending to deal once and for all with Heraclian and deliver Italy from famine. But in Cosenza he was attacked by a sudden violent fever, and within a few days he was dead. He was still only forty. His followers carried his body to the river Busento, which they dammed. There, in the stream's dry bed, they buried their leader; then they broke the dam, and the waters came surging back and covered him.

No one, surely, can ever forget that first astonishing sight of the Land Walls of Constantinople. Running just over four miles from the Marmara to the upper reaches of the Golden Horn, they close off the city by land, and are still known as the Theodosian Walls after Theodosius II, in whose reign they were first built. In fact, however, Theodosius can take little of the credit. Begun in 413, when he was still a boy of twelve, the walls were conceived and built by his Praetorian Prefect Anthemius, at that time his guardian and the effective Regent of the East. Anthemius was the first highly-placed layman at Constantinople since the days of Theodosius the Great to combine ability with high principle; but he did not last long. After 414 he disappears, to be succeeded as the power behind the throne by the Emperor's own sister, the princess Pulcheria; and with her there is inaugurated a period of thirty-six years – the remainder of her brother's reign – during which virtually all effective power was concentrated in female hands.

Pulcheria had been born only two years before Theodosius; she was thus barely fifteen when she was proclaimed Augusta and took over the reins of government. By now it must have been apparent that her brother, as a ruler, would be little improvement on Arcadius. She herself was strong and determined, with a love of power for its own sake; she was also excessively pious. Under her influence, her two younger sisters developed similar inclinations: the prevailing mood in the imperial palace, it was said, was more that of a cloister than a court, thronged with priests and monks while the virgin princesses stitched away at their altar-cloths to the sound of psalmodies and muttered prayers. It was all a far cry, people somewhat wistfully observed, from what it had been in Eudoxia's day.

Born in the purple,[1] from his earliest childhood Theodosius had been obliged to live in that stultifying seclusion from his fellows that was considered appropriate for God's Vice-Gerent on Earth. He was certainly far from stupid: his tastes however lay less in religion than in the classical authors, in mathematics and the natural sciences, and above all in the art of illustrating and illuminating manuscripts. He also had a passion for hunting, and it was probably he who introduced to Constantinople the Persian game of polo. He therefore had no objection to leaving affairs of state to his sister, long after he had reached the age when he should have taken them over himself. Only in 420, when he was nineteen, did he send for Pulcheria on a matter of state importance. It was time, he told her, that she found him a wife.

At about this time there presented herself at the palace a young Greek girl of startling beauty named Athenais. Pulcheria, who saw her first, was immensely impressed – not only by her beauty but by her exquisite Greek. As

---

1 *Porphyrogenitus*, or born in the purple, was a title used exclusively of a prince who was born in the Purple Chamber of the Great Palace, after his father had become Emperor.

for Theodosius, he fell passionately in love. The potential difficulty of the girl's paganism was quickly overcome: she was baptized into the Christian faith, changing her name to Eudocia, her future sister-in-law standing as godmother. On 7 June 421, she and Theodosius were married. Into the insufferable atmosphere of the palace, Athenais arrived like a fresh breeze. Steeped from childhood in the Hellenistic tradition, her mind possessed a whole extra dimension compared to those of the three dismal princesses. Her star rose still higher when, the year after her marriage, she presented her husband with a baby daughter – to whom he gave the confusing name Eudoxia. In 423, he raised his wife to the rank of Augusta.

Nothing, one would have thought, could be more natural; but her sister-in-law did not take it well. Now, suddenly, her *protégée* was of equal rank. More beautiful, better educated and infinitely better liked, she also exerted a far greater influence over Theodosius than his sister could ever hope to do. And so Pulcheria determined to cut her down to size.

That same summer the imperial couple received at the palace the Empire's third Augusta: Galla Placidia, daughter of Theodosius the Great and half-sister of Honorius, who arrived in Constantinople with her two small children. Though still only in her early thirties, Placidia could already look back on an extraordinary life. After surviving all three sieges of Rome, she had married Alaric's brother-in-law and successor; on his death, she had taken as a husband Honorius's chief adviser Constantius, becoming Augusta when, in 421, he was raised to be co-Emperor; and when he too died six months later she was left in her second widowhood at her half-brother's court. Honorius was now becoming progressively more unbalanced. First he displayed embarrassing signs of falling in love with his half-sister; then, finding that his affection was not reciprocated, he became suspicious, jealous and at last openly hostile. Finally Placidia decided that she could stand no more. Early in 423 she sought refuge with her nephew in Constantinople, taking her children by Constantius, Honoria and Valentinian, with her.

There is no telling how long Placidia and her family might have remained on the Bosphorus had she not received news that must have caused both her and her hosts considerable relief: on 26 August Honorius had died of dropsy, in his fortieth year. Unfortunately this report was immediately followed by another: the empty throne had been seized by a certain Johannes, Chief of the Notaries. Theodosius had no intention of seeing the Empire of the West appropriated by a relatively unimportant member of the Civil Service. There and then he confirmed Placidia in the rank of Augusta, invested Valentinian as Caesar and gave orders for the preparation of an army to escort them back to Italy and to their rightful thrones. The expedition proved triumphantly successful, taking the defenders by surprise and capturing Ravenna early in 425 with scarcely a casualty. Johannes was captured and brought in chains to Aquileia, where he was led around the city on a donkey and finally put to death. Meanwhile the Byzantine soldiery were allowed a three-day sack of Ravenna – to punish the inhabitants for having supported a usurper – and Valentinian, now six, was carried off to Rome for his coronation.

In Constantinople, Athenais's Hellenism was now making itself felt far beyond the confines of the imperial palace. She and the Praetorian Prefect of the City, Cyrus of Panopolis – a poet, philosopher and art-lover, and a Greek through and through – transformed the relatively modest educational establishment instituted by Constantine into a large and distinguished university, thus providing a Christian counterpart to the essentially pagan university of Athens. A by-product of the university was the compilation of the Theodosian Codex, a rationalization of all the laws enacted in both East and West since the days of Constantine. Promulgated on 15 February 438, jointly by both Emperors, it was obviously intended to emphasize the unity of the Empire, following as it did only a few months after the marriage of Valentinian and the fifteen-year-old Eudoxia. That unity, however, was a good deal more apparent than real. Almost immediately the two halves of the Empire began to diverge once again, the legislation of the one being seldom if ever adopted by the other. By now, too, another rift had appeared within the framework of Byzantine life. The essentially Greek passion for theological speculation had been if anything intensified by such charismatic figures as St John Chrysostom, whose misfortunes could easily cause riots and demonstrations. And of all the issues most likely to inflame tempers to flash-point and beyond, the most contentious concerned the relation of Jesus Christ to God the Father.

This obviously unanswerable question had lain at the root of the Arian heresy; it had been condemned in 325 at Nicaea, but had smouldered on throughout the fourth century. Now it became polarized, with two opposing schools of thought, one each side of Nicaean orthodoxy. The first to cause concern was that of a certain Nestorius, an impassioned fanatic who in 427 had been appointed Bishop of Constantinople. Refusing to attribute the frailties of humanity to a member of the Trinity, he preached that Christ was not, as the Nicaeans believed, a single person but that he possessed two distinct persons, one human and the other divine.

Thanks in large measure to the power of his oratory, Nestorius's teachings rapidly gained ground; they found a worthy opponent, however, in Cyril, Bishop of Alexandria. As the dispute grew ever more bitter the Emperor, who always tended to believe those who were nearest him and was consequently a convinced Nestorian, decided in 430 to summon another Council of the Church. In doing so, however, he seriously underestimated the Alexandrians. When the Council met on 22 June 431 at Ephesus Cyril, who had beggared his own diocese to find sufficient funds for the bribing of civil servants and ecclesiastics as necessary, carried all before him. Effortlessly assuming the presidency of the Council, he commanded Nestorius to answer the charges of heresy levelled against him. Nestorius refused. He was, he pointed out, a delegate, not a defendant; he would attend the Council only when all the delegates had arrived. But Cyril was not disposed to wait; soon afterwards all 198 delegates cried anathema on Nestorius, who was thereupon dismissed from his episcopate. He retired into private life; and in 435 the Emperor – no longer a Nestorian – banished him, first to Petra in Arabia and later to a distant Libyan oasis, where he died.

Many years before – perhaps even while Galla Placidia and her children were still at Constantinople – Athenais had vowed that, if her daughter became Empress of the West, she would make a pilgrimage to Jerusalem. The marriage to Valentinian duly took place in the summer of 437; and in 438 she set out for the Holy Land. She remained in Jerusalem a whole year, returning with a profusion of relics – in which the bishop plied a profitable trade – including the bones of St Stephen and the fetters of St Peter. Her husband welcomed her warmly, and for a time all went on as before. But not, alas, for long. The likeliest explanation is to be found in the machinations of Pulcheria; but whatever the reason, Athenais somehow fell from her husband's favour. She returned to Jerusalem, where she lived on till 460, sad, lonely and em-bittered, a pathetic shadow of the brilliant, talented girl who had swept a young Emperor off his feet.

Athenais's son-in-law, the young Western Emperor Valentinian III, had proved a weak and ineffectual figure, utterly dominated by his mother Placidia, who had continued to govern in his name long after he had reached manhood – indeed, until her own death in 450, after which she was given the tomb in Ravenna that is the monument of the age. As for his sister Honoria, she deserves at least a footnote in any account of her time. Few princesses in history would, after all, have offered themselves in marriage to Attila the Hun. As Gibbon explains:

The daughter of Placidia sacrificed every duty and every prejudice, and offered to deliver her person into the arms of a barbarian of whose language she was ignorant, whose figure was scarcely human, and whose religion and manners she abhorred ... [Her] indecent advances were received, however, with coldness and disdain; and the King of the Huns continued to multiply the number of his wives till his love was awakened by the more forcible passions of ambition and avarice.

Attila – 'the Scourge of God' – had succeeded to the throne of the Huns in 434. After over half a century's contact with the Romans, his people had become perhaps one degree less bestial than at their first arrival; but they still lived and slept in the open, disdaining all agriculture and even cooked foods, softening raw meat by putting it between their thighs and their horses' flanks as they rode. Their clothes were made, rather surprisingly, from the skins of field-mice, crudely stitched together; these they wore continuously, without ever removing them, until they dropped off of their own accord. They practically lived on their horses, eating, trading, holding their councils, even sleeping in the saddle. Attila himself was typical of his race: short, swarthy and snub-nosed, with tiny beady eyes set in a head too big for his body and a thin, straggling beard. Within seven years of his succession he had built up a vast barbaric dominion of his own, stretching from the Balkans to the Caucasus and beyond; but thanks to the annual tribute paid him by Theodosius, it was not until 447 that he gave the Empire serious cause for alarm. His army now advanced in two directions at once: southward into Thessaly, and eastward to Constantinople. The Theodosian Walls had, it seemed, been built just in time: the Huns soon turned away in search of more accessible plunder. But they inflicted a crushing defeat on the Byzantine army at Gallipoli, withdrawing only after the Emperor had agreed to treble the annual tribute. From this time forward, embassies passed constantly between Attila and Theodosius. Attila believed, rightly, that the Emperor was now terrified of him; as for Theodosius, his only policy was one of appeasement, for which he was perfectly ready not only to exhaust his own treasury but to bleed his subjects white into the bargain. One of his embassies, sent to Attila in 448, has been described in detail by a certain Priscus, a member of it. Thanks to him we have an un-forgettable picture of the Hunnish court, as well as of its King:

While for us there were lavishly prepared dishes served on silver platters, for Attila there was only meat on a wooden plate ... Gold and silver goblets were handed to the men at the feast, whereas his cup was of wood. His clothing was plain, and differed not at all from that of the rest, except that it was clean. Neither the sword that hung at his side nor the fastenings of his barbarian boots nor his horse's bridle were adorned, like those of the other Scythians, with gold or precious stones or anything else of value.

There is no telling how much longer Attila would have continued to drain away the wealth of the Eastern Empire had not Theodosius been killed, on 28 July 450, by a fall from his horse. He had no male heir, but the problem of the succession was solved by Pulcheria. Despite her vow of virginity, she was able to contract a nominal marriage to a Thracian senator and ex-soldier named

Marcian, whom she promptly named Augustus and placed, with herself, on the throne – claiming that he had been nominated by Theodosius on his deathbed.

One of Marcian's first acts was to refuse the King of the Huns his annual tribute. Knowing that Attila was preparing a vast operation against the Western Empire, he doubtless gambled on his unwillingness to delay this by a punitive expedition to the East. The gamble paid off; and there was rejoicing in Constantinople when the news arrived that the Hunnish army had started upon its march into Italy and Gaul. But, as the immediate danger passed, Marcian found himself faced with another threat: the ever-deepening split in Byzantine society occasioned this time by the monophysite heresy.

It was rooted in the same old enigma: the precise relation of the Father and the Son within the Trinity. The error of the Nestorians, who upheld the principle of the two distinct persons in Christ, the human and the divine, had been dealt with at Ephesus in 431; now the pendulum had swung to the opposite extreme, and in 448 an elderly archimandrite named Eutyches was accused of preaching, equally subversively, that the Incarnate Christ possessed but a single nature, and that that nature was divine. Found guilty and degraded, Eutyches appealed to Pope Leo (the Great), to the Emperor and to the monks of Constantinople; and in doing so he unleashed a storm of unimaginable ferocity. At last, in October 451, the Fourth Ecumenical Council was held at Chalcedon to put an end to the chaos. Numbering as it did some five to six hundred bishops, representing the whole breadth of the Christological spectrum, it is astonishing that this Council should have reached any decisions at all; in fact, it achieved everything it set out to do and more. Eutyches was once again condemned; and a new statement of faith was drawn up, according to which his doctrines and those of Nestorius were alike repudiated. Christ was established as the possessor of one person with two natures: perfect God and perfect man.

But the Council of Chalcedon laid up a greater store of future trouble than it knew. Monophysitism was by no means dead. In the years to come, both in Egypt and Syria, bishop after bishop was to reject the findings of the Council; and when these provinces began their struggle for independence, the Single Nature of Christ was to be their rallying-cry. With the West also, the seeds of discord were sown – notably by the Council's bestowal on the Bishop of Constantinople of the title of Patriarch, with the clear implication that the Pope's supremacy would henceforth be purely titular, and that in every other respect there would be complete equality between the sees of Rome and Constantinople. The eastern provinces in particular would be responsible to the Patriarch alone. From this moment was born the ecclesiastical rivalry between the Old Rome and the New, which was to grow increasingly bitter over the centuries.

The details of Attila's western campaigns need not concern us here; yet it should never be forgotten that, in 451 and 452, the whole fate of Western civilization hung in the balance. Had the Hunnish leader toppled Valentinian from his throne and set up his own capital in Ravenna or Rome, there is little doubt that both Gaul and Italy would have been reduced to spiritual and cultural deserts. In 451 Attila penetrated Western Europe as far as the walls of Orléans; and early in 452 he launched his army upon Italy. Here the King of the Huns carried all before him. There was, it seemed, nothing to prevent him from marching on Rome. And yet, at the very point of departure for his advance down the peninsula, he suddenly halted; and historians have been speculating ever since as to precisely why he did so. Traditionally, the credit has always been given to Pope Leo the Great, who travelled from Rome to meet him on the banks of the Mincio and somehow persuaded him to advance no further. Attila, like all his race, was incorrigibly superstitious, and the Pope may well have reminded him of how Alaric had died almost immediately after the sack of Rome, pointing out that a similar fate was known to befall every invader who raised his hand against the holy city. The Huns themselves were far from enthusiastic: they were beginning to suffer from a serious shortage of food, and disease had broken out. Marcian's troops, too, were beginning to arrive from Constantinople. A march on Rome, it began to appear, might not prove quite so straightforward as had first been thought.

For some or all of these reasons Attila decided to turn back. A year later, during the night following his marriage to yet another of his innumerable wives, his exertions brought on a sudden haemorrhage; and, as his life-blood flowed away, all Europe breathed again. His body was encased in three coffins – of gold, silver and iron. Then, when it had been lowered into the earth and covered over, all those involved in the burial ceremonies were put to death, so that the King's last resting-place might remain for ever secret and inviolate. And so it has done, to this day.

Some time in the middle of March 455 the Emperor Valentinian III, who had moved his residence to Rome, rode out to the Campus Martius for archery practice. Suddenly, two soldiers of barbarian origin stepped out from behind some bushes and ran him through with their swords. He left no son; and the choice of the army fell on an elderly senator, Petronius Maximus, who attempted to take the widowed Empress Eudoxia as his wife. Eudoxia, horrified at the prospect of a marriage to a man nearly twice her age, decided on a desperate course of action: like her sister-in-law Honoria some years before, she invoked the assistance of a barbarian King – or so at least runs the traditional story. More probably, she proved well able to look after herself. The reputation of Rome provided motive enough for the subsequent invasion by Gaiseric, King of the Vandals. This Germanic tribe, in creed fanatically Arian, had fled westward from the Huns and, in 409, had settled in Spain. There they had remained until 428, when the newly-crowned Gaiseric led his entire people – probably some 160,000 men, women and children – across to North Africa, where in 439 he declared an independent autocracy. Having then conquered Sicily and established his capital at Carthage, he was soon master of the entire western Mediterranean.

Valentinian had been less than three months in his grave when the Vandal fleet put to sea. In Rome, the reaction was one of panic, the terrified Romans sending their wives and daughters away to safety, and the roads to the north and east choked with carts as the more well-to-do families poured out of the city. Petronius Maximus too had resolved upon flight; but his subjects, who held him responsible, were determined that he should not escape. On 31 May the palace guard mutinied, fell upon their hopeless master and flung his dismembered body into the Tiber. He had reigned for just seventy days. For the fourth time in half a century, a barbarian army stood at the gates of Rome.

Once again Pope Leo set out for the barbarian camp to plead for his city; but this time he was on far weaker ground: Gaiseric was already on the threshold of his objective, his men were healthy, and he had no enemy in his rear. On the other hand he was a Christian, with some respect for papal dignity. Leo's mission was not a total failure. The Vandal promised at least that there would be no killing or torturing, and no destruction of buildings. And so the gates were opened, and the barbarian horde passed into the city. For fourteen days they stripped it of its wealth: the gold and silver from the churches, the statues from the palaces, even the gilded copper roof from the Temple of Jupiter. Everything was loaded into the waiting ships at Ostia and taken off to Carthage. Gaiseric then departed, forcing Eudoxia and her two daughters to accompany him. True to his word, he had left the people and the buildings unharmed.

With the death of the Eastern Emperor Marcian early in 457, the male Theodosian line – of which, through his marriage to Pulcheria, he must be counted an honorary member – came to an end. Such moments of dynastic exhaustion were always dangerous for the Roman Empire. Pulcheria had died in 453, her two younger sisters having predeceased her; and so, to fill the empty throne, the people of Constantinople looked to the chief of the army – the *magister militum per orientem*, Aspar. After a brilliant military career Aspar now bore the title 'First of the Patricians', and would almost certainly have succeeded but for two things: first, he was an Alan – a member of a Germanic tribe driven by the Huns from its homeland beyond the Black Sea – and second, like nearly all the Christian barbarians, he was an Arian. He was, however, quite content to be a kingmaker, and his choice fell on the steward of his own household, an orthodox Christian named Leo. The legions obediently acclaimed their new Emperor and raised him on their shields according to tradition; but now, for the first time, a second ceremony was instituted. On 7 February 457 Leo was formally crowned by the Patriarch in the Church of the Holy Wisdom – a sign that the old order was beginning to change: away from the old military traditions and towards a new, mystical concept of sovereignty.

If Aspar had thought that he was placing a puppet on the throne of Byzantium, he was mistaken. A furious dispute between the two immediately broke out over Leo's determination to clip the wings of the powerful Germanic element led by Aspar, reconstructing the army around a nucleus of Isaurians, a tough mountain folk hailing from a wild region of the Taurus around the basin of the Calycadnus river. Aspar fought back; and their differences soon became the principal leitmotiv of Leo's reign. On the Emperor's side the leading influence was that of an Isaurian chieftain named Zeno, who had married Leo's daughter Ariadne. Aspar's chief adherent within the palace was Basiliscus, the brother of the Emperor's wife Verina. The two could scarcely have been more different. Aspar was without culture; as a convinced Arian, he came near to denying the godhead of Christ; as a leader of men, he was the finest general of his time. Basiliscus was a Hellenized, well-educated Roman; a fanatical monophysite, for whom Christ was divine rather than human; and a man totally unfitted for any sort of command. They were flung together, however, by their common hatred for the Isaurians; and when the Emperor decided in 468 to launch a long-overdue expedition against King Gaiseric, he was persuaded by his wife and Aspar to put Basiliscus at its head.

Thirteen years had passed since Gaiseric's sack of Rome; there could be no justification for leaving the Vandals still unpunished. Moreover, the Arian Gaiseric had initiated a savage persecution of the orthodox Christians. Leo's long-awaited announcement of his proposed expedition was therefore greeted with relief and satisfaction, and preparations began. Over a thousand ships, we are told, were collected from all over the eastern Mediterranean, and a hundred thousand men. Such a force should have destroyed the Vandals completely, and under any other commander would certainly have done so. Not, however, under Basiliscus. On his arrival at the port of Mercurion, and before he began his advance, Gaiseric sent envoys to say that he would accept any terms, asking only five days' grace to make the necessary arrangements; and Basiliscus agreed. It was the greatest mistake of his life. Gaiseric spent the time preparing his war fleet, and on the fifth day his ships sailed into Mercurion, towing a number of empty hulks behind them. As they entered the harbour they were set ablaze and bore down on to the densely-packed Byzantine fleet. The flames spread rapidly from one vessel to the next, and within hours it was all over. Basiliscus returned to Constantinople, where he was obliged to seek refuge in St Sophia. Only after impassioned entreaties by his sister did Leo agree to spare his life.

Leo was generally accounted the most fortunate and successful of all the Emperors that had preceded him; if not loved, he was at least respected by his subjects. Although he hardly deserved his title of 'the Great' – bestowed on him, apparently, for his religious orthodoxy rather than for any other qualities – he was on the whole a just and merciful ruler, and when he died on 3 February 474 he had, by the standards of the time, remarkably little blood on his hands. Five months previously, he had nominated his successor: not, as everyone had expected, his son-in-law Zeno but the latter's seven-year-old son, called Leo like his grandfather. Why he did so we cannot tell; in the event, however, Ariadne had instructed her son, when his father came to make his formal obeisance, to crown him co-Emperor on the spot. It was as well that she did. Nine months later young Leo was dead, and one of Zeno's first acts on his succession was to put an end to the Vandal War. Peace was signed before the end of the year; never again were the Vandals to cause the Empire concern.

But already the storm-clouds were gathering. By now the Isaurians had made themselves thoroughly unpopular. As imperial subjects they could not technically be called barbarians; they proved, however, more objectionable than the Germans had ever been: they were arrogant and noisy, with a propensity for violence. Inevitably, much of the hostility that they aroused now became focused on their most distinguished representative, the Emperor himself – who also had to face the implacable hatred of two powerful enemies within his own household: Verina the Empress Mother, and her brother Basiliscus.

Basiliscus, despite the African fiasco, wished to secure the diadem for himself; the Empress wanted it for her recently-acquired lover Patricius, Master of the Offices at the palace. Both, however, were determined to get rid of Zeno; and with the aid of an Isaurian general, Illus, they recruited a number of adherents to their cause. In November 475, as the Emperor was presiding in the Hippodrome, he received an urgent message from his mother-in-law: army, Senate and people were united against him, he must flee at once.

A fourth-century porphyry group believed to represent
Diocletian's Tetrarchs; incorporated into the south-west corner
of the Basilica of St Mark, Venice

St John Chrysostom.
A ninth-century mosaic from the north tympanum in St Sophia

The Church of St Eirene, Istanbul

The interior of the Church of St Eirene

Theodosius the Great or Valentinian I –
a late fourth-century bronze statue outside
the Church of S. Sepolero, Barletta

The Theodosian Walls

The sixth-century apse of S. Apollinaire in Classe, Ravenna

The Barberini Ivory; probably the Emperor Anastasius, who is
known to have received an embassy from India in 496 (see lower panel).
The right-hand panel (which presumably portrayed another
warrior bearing a statuette of Victory) is missing

opposite: Sixth-century mosaics from the Church of S. Vitale, Ravenna

above: The Emperor Justinian and his court

below: The Empress Theodora and her retinue

Charlemagne: reliquary bust, *c.* 1350

That night he slipped away with his wife and mother, to seek refuge in his native Isauria, and Basiliscus was proclaimed Emperor. He did not last long. He lost the sympathy of his sister by having her lover assassinated; he antagonized his subjects by vicious taxation; and he incurred the enmity of the Church, by his ham-fisted attempts to impose monophysitism throughout the Empire, even trying to abolish the Patriarchate of Constantinople. Patriarch Acacius draped the high altar of St Sophia in black; while Daniel, the famous stylite of the city, actually descended from his pillar for the first time in fifteen years, terrifying Basiliscus into the withdrawal of his edict. After all this it came as no great surprise when Illus, disgusted with the ruler whom he had helped to put on the throne, joined Zeno in his mountain retreat and began to plan his restoration. But the person directly responsible for the downfall of Basiliscus was, however, his own nephew Harmatius. This dandified young fop was promoted by his uncle to the rank of *magister militum*, whereat he took to parading around the Hippodrome dressed as Achilles. Sent with an army against Zeno and Illus, he was easily persuaded by the promise of the Praetorian Prefecture to declare himself in their favour. Thus, in July 477, Zeno returned to his capital unopposed. Basiliscus surrendered, on the undertaking that his blood would not be shed; he was exiled with his family to the wilds of Cappadocia where, the following winter, cold and hunger did for the lot of them.

There had been several developments during Zeno's absence that demanded his attention – among them, the final collapse of the Empire of the West. The sequence of events leading up to that collapse is too long and involved to be recounted here. Suffice it to say that in 476 a barbarian general named Odoacer deposed the boy-Emperor Romulus Augustulus, provided him with a generous pension and sent him off to live in peaceful obscurity with relatives in Campania. Then, as soon as Odoacer heard that Zeno had been reinstated, he sent ambassadors to Constantinople to inform him of the new dispensation and to hand over to him the imperial insignia of the West as a sign that he, Odoacer, made no claim to sovereignty for himself. All he asked was the title of Patrician, in which rank he proposed to take over the administration of Italy in the Emperor's name.

Did the abdication of Romulus Augustulus on 4 September 476 really mark the end of the Roman Empire in the West? The Empire, surely, was one and indivisible; whether it was ruled at any given moment by a single Augustus, or two, or even three or four, was purely a matter of administrative convenience. And was not Odoacer always at pains to emphasize the Emperor's continued sovereignty over Italy? Was he, in fact, any different from any of those other barbarian generals at the seat of power – Arbogast, Stilicho and the rest? The answer is that he was – for he had refused to accept a Western Emperor. In the past those Emperors, puppets as they may have been, bore the title of Augustus, being thus both symbols and constant reminders of the imperial authority. Without them, that authority was soon forgotten. Odoacer had requested the rank of Patrician; but the title that he preferred to use was *Rex*. In less than sixty years, Italy would be so far lost as to need a full-scale re-conquest by Justinian. It would be over three centuries before another Emperor appeared in the West; when he did, his capital would be in Germany rather than in Italy, and he would be a rival rather than a colleague – not a Roman, but a Frank. Odoacer's decision also created a political vacuum in the old capital. Instinctively, men looked for another father figure. And so they raised up the Bishop of Rome, already Primate of Christendom, investing him with temporal authority as well as spiritual and surrounding him with much of the pomp and semi-mystical ceremonial formerly reserved for the Emperors. The age of the medieval Papacy had begun.

In Constantinople, the elimination of Basiliscus had done little to restore harmony within the State. The arrogance and narcissism of Harmatius had reached the point where there were fears for his sanity; what chance was there that he would remain loyal to his Emperor? After a long and agonizing struggle with his conscience, Zeno finally decided that he must be removed. A willing assassin was found among his many enemies, and the deed was soon accomplished.

A serious insurrection broke out in 483, the central figure of which was Illus. He acted, admittedly, under considerable provocation. First, one of the imperial slaves had been found lying in wait for him, drawn sword in hand. Then, in 478, the palace guards had discovered another would-be assassin who confessed that he had been acting for the Prefect Epinicus and the Empress Verina. Realizing that his life was now in serious danger, Illus retired for a while to his Isaurian homeland. In September 479 an earthquake severely weakened the city walls and Zeno, fearing that the Goths might seize the opportunity to attack, recalled him to the capital; but the general refused to enter the city until Verina was surrendered into his charge. Zeno had no love for his mother-in-law and was only too happy to comply; the Dowager Empress was immured in an Isaurian fortress. After that, Illus was appointed Master of the Offices, a sign of high favour; but one day in 482, as he was entering the Hippodrome, he was attacked without warning by a member of the imperial guard. His armour-bearer managed to deflect the blow, but the blade sliced off his right ear. This time the instigator of the crime proved to be the Empress Ariadne herself, taking her revenge on Illus for his treatment of her mother.

At this point the Master of the Offices prudently retired again to Anatolia. Almost immediately, however, a revolt broke out in Syria, where a certain Leontius was attempting to restore the old pagan religion; and Illus was ordered to take command of the eastern armies and restore imperial rule. Probably grateful for this opportunity to prove himself once again in the eyes of his sovereign, he hurried at once to Syria; only on his arrival did he discover the local commander to be the Emperor's incompetent and profligate brother Longinus, who deeply resented this usurpation of his authority. A violent quarrel ensued, and Illus had Longinus arrested and imprisoned.

It was a high-handed action to take against so powerful a rival; but the Emperor's reaction was still more ill-judged. He ordered his brother's immediate release, denounced Illus as a public enemy and confiscated his property, thereby driving him into the opposing camp. Illus now made common cause with the rebel, and the two of them together released the old Empress Verina; she triumphantly crowned Leontius at Tarsus and accompanied him to Antioch, where on 27 June 484 he established a rival court.

He and Illus seem to have been content for the time to remain where they were – giving Zeno plenty of time to find new allies, among them a young barbarian named Theodoric, Prince of the Ostrogoths, who now agreed to lead an army of his subjects against the rebels. These were soon driven back into the Isaurian heartland. Here Verina died, lamented by no one; and here, in 488, Illus and Leontius were obliged to surrender. Their heads were cut off and sent to Constantinople. The rebellion was at an end.

The success had been largely due to Theodoric. Born around 454, he had spent ten years of his boyhood as a hostage in Constantinople; and though he may have gained little intellectually from the experience – all his life he signed his name by stencilling it through a perforated gold plate – he had acquired an understanding of the Byzantines and their ways which served him in good stead when, in 471, he succeeded his father as leader of the Eastern Goths. The main purpose of his early life was to secure a permanent home for his people. To this end he had spent the better part of twenty years fighting, sometimes for and sometimes against Zeno; and both must have welcomed the agreement, made in 487 or early 488, that Theodoric should lead his entire people into Italy, overthrow Odoacer and rule the land as an Ostrogothic Kingdom under imperial sovereignty. Early in 488 the great exodus took place: men, women and children, with their horses and pack-animals, their cattle and sheep, lumbering slowly across the plains of central Europe in search of greener and more peaceful pastures. Predictably, Odoacer fought back; but in February 493 an armistice was arranged, Theodoric agreeing to remarkably generous terms: that Italy should be ruled by him and Odoacer jointly, both of them sharing the palace of Ravenna.

Theodoric, however, had no intention of keeping his word. On 15 March, only ten days after his formal entry into Ravenna, he invited Odoacer, his brother, his son and his chief officers to a banquet in his wing of the palace. As Odoacer took his place in the seat of honour, Theodoric stepped forward and, with one tremendous stroke of his sword, sliced him down from collar-bone to thigh. The effect surprised even him: 'The wretch cannot have had a bone in his body,' he is said to have laughed. Odoacer's followers were quickly dispatched by the guards, while his brother succumbed to an arrow as he tried to escape. His wife was thrown into prison, where she died of hunger; his son was executed. Theodoric the Ostrogoth laid aside the skins and furs of his race, robed himself in purple and settled down to rule in Italy. He did not, however, forget his earlier agreement with the Byzantines. He remained a vassal, who like all his subjects owed allegiance to the Emperor. Though his coins carried his monogram, the only portrait they bore was that of Zeno. Theodoric himself had no objection to this arrangement. The Roman citizens in Italy – easily outnumbering the Goths – were far happier with an imperial viceroy than with a foreign oppressor. He allowed them to live just as they always had, with all their estates intact.

Theodoric's reign began with perfidy and bloodshed; its close was also clouded, by the imprisonment and garrotting, which he afterwards bitterly regretted, of the philosopher Boethius in 524. With these exceptions, his thirty-three years on the throne were prosperous and peaceful; and the extra-ordinary mausoleum which he built – and which still stands in Ravenna – perfectly symbolizes, in its half-classical, half barbaric strength, a colossus who himself bestrode two cultures. When he died, on 30 August 526, Italy lost the greatest of her early medieval rulers, unequalled until the days of Charlemagne.

5

The Rise of Justinian

[493–540]

On 9 April 491 the Emperor Zeno died in Constantinople, having finally freed the Empire – or, at least, that part of it still controlled from the capital – of the Goths. The only major problem that he had failed to solve was the religious one: the monophysite heresy continued to gain ground. In 482 Zeno and Patriarch Acacius together had sought to paper over the differences by affirming that Christ was both God and man, avoiding the word 'nature' altogether; but had only aroused the hostility of both sides. Most outraged of all was Pope Felix III, especially after the appointment to the Patriarchate of Alexandria of Paul the Stammerer, a cleric whose utterances, when comprehensible at all, were violently monophysite in character. At a synod in 484, Pope Felix had actually excommunicated the Patriarch of Constantinople – a sentence which, in default of anyone courageous enough to pronounce it, had been transcribed on to a piece of parchment and pinned to the back of Acacius's cope during a service in St Sophia. The Patriarch, discovering it later, instantly excommunicated him back, thereby confirming an open schism between the Churches that was to last for the next thirty-five years.

By the end of the decade the Emperor was obviously declining, physically and mentally. His only son had predeceased him, worn out by homosexual excesses and venereal disease. His expected successor was therefore his reprobate brother Longinus, who by 490 was in effective control of the State; but Longinus was passed over, and the choice fell on a certain Flavius Anastasius – thanks largely to Ariadne, who married him soon afterwards. Now in his early sixties, he had a reputation for uprightness and integrity. 'Reign, Anastasius!' the people shouted when he first appeared before them in the imperial purple. 'Reign as you have lived!' Anastasius did so; and if his subjects found life under his rule more irksome than they had expected, they had only themselves to blame. His chief defect was parsimoniousness – a failing which, combined with a strong puritanical streak, made Constantinople a duller place to live in than ever before. Contests with wild beasts were forbidden; citizens were no longer permitted to hold nocturnal feasts, on the grounds that they led to unbridled licentiousness – which indeed they very often did. Meanwhile his campaign against unnecessary public expenditure was finally to leave the imperial treasury richer by 320,000 pounds of gold.

In his religious policy, Anastasius was less successful. Genuinely pious, during the previous reign he had held regular theological seminars in St Sophia. Later, however, he had gradually moved towards monophysitism, to the point where Patriarch Euphemius was obliged to refuse him coronation until he had signed a written declaration of orthodoxy. Anastasius, sincerely believing that he stood firmly in the Chalcedonian camp, signed without hesitation; but there were those who were quick to accuse him of sacrificing his principles on the altar of political expediency. They were led by Longinus, who had never forgiven Anastasius for occupying a throne which he considered his own. He soon gathered around him an unsavoury mob of troublemakers, largely Isaurian; and the consequent outbreaks of street fighting that ensued led to fires in which several more of the city's finest buildings were destroyed. The Emperor fought back. In 492 Longinus was arrested and exiled; but strife in the city soon escalated into civil war. Only with great difficulty was order restored, after which all Isaurians were banned from the capital, including Zeno's entire family. Now at last Constantinople was quiet, though in Anatolia the war continued for three more years.

Another major cause of unrest was the division of the populace into two rival factions, the Blues and the Greens. Their names originally referred to the colours worn by the two principal teams of charioteers; but their leaders were by now appointed by the government, who also entrusted them with important responsibilities, including guard duties and the maintenance of the defensive walls. Thus, in all the main cities of the Empire, they existed as two semi-political parties which combined on occasion to form a local militia. At this period the Blues tended to be the party of the big landowners and the old Graeco-Roman aristocracy, while the Greens represented trade, industry and the civil service. Many members of this last group came from the eastern provinces, where heresy was more widespread; thus the Blues had gradually come to be loosely associated with religious orthodoxy, the Greens with monophysitism. Anastasius himself at first tried to maintain impartiality; soon, however, his instinctive tendency towards the monophysites drew him to the Greens.

Hostility between the two demes (as they were called) increased steadily as his reign continued. Worst of all were the disturbances of 511, which came dangerously near to toppling the Emperor from his throne. He was now in his eighties, and his monophysite sympathies had become plain for all to see. Patriarch Euphemius, accused of supporting the Isaurians, had been banished;

his successor Macedonius, the gentlest of men, was beginning to find dealings with his sovereign impossible. Matters came to a head when he was accused of fomenting a riot in St Sophia, which in fact had been the result of deliberate monophysite provocation. The people of Constantinople, outraged by this transparently unfair attack on their Patriarch, marched threateningly on the palace. Fortunately Macedonius hurried to the Emperor's side, and the crowd dispersed; but it had been a narrow escape.

It should also have been a salutary lesson; but the Emperor was too old to change his ways. Macedonius was quietly exiled like his predecessor, and in November 512 still more serious rioting broke out, continuing for three full days. Then at last Anastasius acted. Presenting himself in the Circus before some 20,000 of his furious subjects, he slowly removed his diadem. He was ready, he told them, to lay down the burden of Empire; all he asked was that they should name his successor. Alternatively, if they preferred, he would continue in office, never again giving them cause for dissatisfaction. The tall, white-haired figure was still handsome, the voice firm and persuasive. Gradually, the clamour ceased; once more the situation had been saved. There had been plenty of other threats to the peace during the long reign of Anastasius; none, however, had important long-term effects. It has seemed worth describing the religious riots in some detail simply to emphasize that aspect of daily life in Byzantium the twentieth century finds hardest to comprehend: the involvement by all classes of society in what appear today to be impossibly abstruse doctrinal niceties.

Some time towards the end of his reign, old Anastasius – so the legend goes – was consumed with curiosity to know which of his three nephews would succeed him. Superstitious as always, he invited all three to dinner, and had three couches prepared on which they could afterwards take their rest. Under one pillow he slipped a piece of parchment, on which he had inscribed the word REGNUM; whichever nephew chose that particular couch would, he believed, assume the throne. Alas, two of the young men, whose mutual affection seems to have gone somewhat beyond family feeling, chose to share the same couch; the marked one remained unrumpled. After fervent prayers for a sign, it was revealed to the Emperor that his successor would be the man who first entered his bedchamber the next day: it chanced to be Justin, Commander of the Excubitors. Anastasius bowed his head. It was, he knew, the will of God.

Justin was a Thracian peasant in his mid-sixties, uneducated and illiterate. His wife, Lupicina, had even humbler origins; she was a slave, and had already been the concubine of the man from whom Justin had bought her. Despite his undoubted military abilities, the new ruler was thus scarcely of imperial calibre. He seems however to have possessed plenty of self-confidence and ambition, and not a little peasant cunning. He was also uncompromisingly orthodox, standing four-square against the Anastasian party with its monophysite leanings, and openly championing the Blues against the by now highly unpopular Greens. He was well-liked and respected by the army, and could be trusted to deal firmly with any renewed attempts at insurrection. But his greatest advantage was his nephew Justinian. It was Justinian who, quite probably, engineered his uncle's elevation; it was he who carried through the reconciliation with the Papacy after a thirty-five-year schism; and it was he who celebrated his own Consulship in 521 with the most lavish games and public spectacles in the Hippodrome that Constantinople had ever seen. The equivalent of 3,700 pounds of gold was spent on decorations, stage machinery and largesse to the people; and the chariot races aroused such excitement that the final contest had to be cancelled for fear of public disturbances. The contrast with the austere, penny-pinching days of the previous reign was dramatic, the message clear: the Empire stood on the threshold of a new and glorious age – an age in which, under a proud and dazzling Emperor, it would regain its lost territories and recapture its past greatness.

Justinian was born in 482, also in Thrace. He came to Constantinople almost certainly at Justin's behest, when he was still a child: his education and culture could not have been acquired anywhere outside the capital. At the time of Anastasius's death he was an officer in the *Scholae*, one of the palace regiments. By now it seems that Justin had formally adopted him as a son, on which occasion he had assumed, as a mark of gratitude, the name by which he is known to history. One of his uncle's first actions on assuming the purple was to raise Justinian to the rank of Patrician and appoint him Count of the Domestics, a position which gave him access to the innermost circles of power; and it was from this moment that his effective domination began. Justin immediately showed himself willing to be guided by him in all things, and for the rest of his life thereafter was content to be his puppet. To Justinian, then, belongs the credit for the most important achievement of his uncle's reign: the healing of the breach with Rome, which had begun with the pinning of the sentence of excommunication on to the robes of Patriarch Acacius in 484. That breach was, in his eyes, an affront to the essential unity that must at all costs be maintained: just as there was one God, so there must be one Empire, and one Church. On 25 March 519 a papal embassy arrived at Constantinople, having been met at the tenth milestone by Justinian himself. Two days later, in St Sophia, Patriarch John declared the Churches of the Old Rome and the New to be one and indivisible, and solemnly read a sentence of anathema on a whole string of heretics, including his own predecessor Acacius. Finally the names of Zeno and Anastasius were ceremonially struck from the diptychs.[1] The schism was at an end. The cost to Byzantium had been almost unconditional surrender; but to Justinian it was a small enough price to pay for a reunited Church.

Only a year or two after this came the second great turning-point in Justinian's life: his meeting with his future Empress. Theodora was not an ideal match. Her father had been a bear-keeper at the Hippodrome, her mother an acrobat – antecedents more than enough to debar her from polite society. But they were not all. While still a child Theodora had joined her elder sister on the stage, playing in farce and burlesque. Before long she had graduated to being Constantinople's most notorious courtesan. In surely one of the most outspoken pieces of vilification ever directed against a queen or empress in all history, her contemporary Procopius writes:

When Theodora was still too immature to sleep with a man or to have intercourse like a woman, she acted as might a male prostitute to satisfy those dregs of humanity who remained some considerable time in a brothel, given over to such unnatural traffic of the body ... But as soon as she reached maturity she became a harlot. Never was any woman so completely abandoned to pleasure. Many a time she would attend a banquet with ten young men or more, all with a passion for fornication and at the peak of their powers, and would lie with all her companions the whole night long; and when she had reduced them all to exhaustion she would go to their attendants – sometimes as many as thirty of them – and copulate with each in turn; and even then she could not satisfy her lust. And although she made use of three apertures in her body, she was wont to complain that Nature had not provided her with larger openings in her nipples, so that she might have contrived another form of intercourse there. Often in the theatre, too, in full view of all the people ... she would spread herself out and lie on her back on the ground. And certain slaves whose special task it was would sprinkle grains of barley over her private parts; and geese trained for the purpose would pick them off one by one with their beaks and swallow them.

But Theodora soon began to look around for better things, and so became the mistress of a moderately distinguished civil servant, whom she accompanied to North Africa. Dismissed after a violent quarrel, she worked her passage home in the only way she knew; but while in Alexandria she seems to have come into contact with some leading churchmen and perhaps even undergone a religious experience. She was certainly a changed woman when

---

1 These carried the lists of the orthodox faithful whose names were regularly remembered by the early Church during the celebration of the Eucharist.

she returned to Constantinople. One characteristic that remained constant, however, was her strong attachment to the Blue party. Justinian too favoured the Blues, and it was probably through them that he first met Theodora, by now in her middle thirties. He was at once captivated, and determined to make her his wife. Inevitably, there were obstacles, not least of which was the implacable opposition of the Empress. Lupicina was still essentially the peasant she had always been and, having finally found someone of still baser extraction than herself, she was determined to do her down in any way she could. While she lived the marriage was impossible; but in 524 she died, and in 525 the pair were married in St Sophia. Only two years later, on 4 April 527, they were crowned co-Emperor and Empress, and when on 1 August old Justin finally succumbed, they found themselves the sole and supreme rulers of the Byzantine Empire. The plural is important. Theodora was to be no Empress Consort. At Justinian's insistence she was to reign at his side, taking decisions and giving him the benefit of her counsel in all the highest affairs of state.

What the people of Constantinople thought of Justinian's marriage is not recorded. Many must have seen it as a disgrace to the Empire; to others, however, Justinian had always seemed somehow remote from his future subjects. Here at last was a sign that he was human, just like anyone else. But to be human is not necessarily to be popular. Justinian was never loved. His extravagances all had to be paid for. So did the war with Persia; so did the 'Everlasting Peace' of 532 with which it ended, which provided for the payment of an annual tribute – though it was never so described – of 11,000 pounds of gold. So too did the monumental construction programme, which Justinian had begun with the great church dedicated to Mary the Mother of God at Blachernae, where the Walls of Theodosius ran down to the Golden Horn, and which he had continued with the rebuilding of no less than seven others. This alone would have been an impressive achievement; but it proved to be only the beginning. In the first days after his succession he built, in memory of the two martyrs St Sergius and St Bacchus, a church which, in its originality and sumptuousness, today ranks in Constantinople second only to St Sophia itself.

For all these purposes and many others, the necessary funds were raised by a general streamlining of the system of tax collection. But such measures are never welcome, and popular discontent was further increased by a certain John of Cappadocia, appointed by the Emperor to put them into effect. As Praetorian Prefect, John instituted stringent economies in the provisioning of the army, launched a determined campaign against corruption, introduced new taxes which fell as much on the rich and powerful as on the poor, and dramatically reduced the power of the senior provincial officials. His moral depravity, however, aroused universal contempt. Those whom he believed to possess hidden riches he subjected to imprisonment, flogging or even torture; neither, according to the contemporary writer John of Lydia, was there 'any wife, any virgin, or any youth free of defilement'. Thus it is small wonder that by the beginning of 532 John was the most hated man in the Empire. One other official, however, ran him close; and that was the jurist Tribonian, who in 529 was appointed Quaestor, the highest law officer in the government. John was at least a Christian, and personally incorruptible; Tribonian was an unashamed pagan and venal to boot: Procopius remarks that 'he was always ready to sell justice for gain and every day, as a rule, he would repeal certain laws and propose others, according to the requirements of those who bought his services'. On the other hand he astonished all with whom he came into contact by the breadth of his learning; and in Tribonian Justinian found the one man capable of bringing a long-cherished dream to fruition. This was a complete recodification of the Roman law, removing all repetitions and contradictions, ensuring that there was nothing incompatible with Christian teaching, substituting clarity and concision for confusion and chaos. Under Tribonian's chairmanship, a special commission appointed by the Emperor set to work. On 8 April 529, less than fourteen months after work began, the new *Codex* was ready; and a week later it came into force, the supreme authority for every court in the Empire. In 530 a second commission under Tribonian began a collection of the writings of all the ancient Roman jurists. Known as the *Digest*, or *Pandects*, it was the first attempt ever made to bring these also into the framework of a methodical system. Finally in 533 there appeared the *Institutes*, a handbook of extracts from the two main books designed for use in the imperial law schools.

In comparison with the immense weight of Tribonian's contribution to the imperial law, the irregularities of his professional life seem insignificant enough; there is no doubt, however, that he and John of Cappadocia were together largely responsible for the growing disaffection during the opening years of Justinian's reign. On 13 January 532, as the Emperor took his place in the Hippodrome and gave the signal for the games to begin, his appearance was greeted by uproar. Suddenly, he realized that, for the first time, the Greens and the Blues were united; and that their clamour was directed not at each other but at him. '*Nika! Nika!*' they cried, using the normal word of encouragement – 'Win! Win!' – by which they cheered on the charioteers. In the past, however, each side had tried to shout down the other. Now, they were speaking with one voice; and that voice was not pleasant to hear.

The races were soon abandoned. The mob poured out of the great circus, hell-bent on destruction. Their first objective was the palace of the City Prefect, where they released all the prisoners before setting fire to the building. From there they passed on to the Praetorian Prefecture, then to the Senate House and even to the two Great Churches of St Eirene and St Sophia, leaving a trail of flame behind them. By the end of the day all these buildings and countless others had been reduced to ruins. For five days and nights the smoke lay thick over the city. On the second day the mob, returning to the Hippodrome, called for the immediate dismissal of John of Cappadocia, Tribonian and the City Prefect Eudaimon – a demand which Justinian, by now seriously alarmed, granted at once. By now, too, the rioters had found a new favourite. Hypatius, an elderly nephew of the former Emperor, had done his best to hide when the mob began calling his name; but they ran him to earth and carried him shoulder-high to the Hippodrome, where he was crowned with a bystander's gold necklet and seated on the throne. Meanwhile, in the palace behind, a desperate Justinian was conferring with his advisers. He had already ordered preparations to be made for himself and his court to flee the capital if the need arose, and he now argued that that moment could no longer be delayed. Suddenly, Theodora intervened. The possibility of flight was not to be considered for a moment. 'Every man', she continued,

who is born into the light of day must sooner or later die; and how could an Emperor ever allow himself to be a fugitive? May I myself never willingly shed my imperial robes, nor see the day when I am no longer addressed by my title. If you, my Lord, wish to save your skin, you will have no difficulty in doing so. As for me, I stand by the ancient saying: the purple is the noblest winding-sheet.

After that, there could be no question of departure; the crisis, it was agreed, must be resolved by force of arms. Fortunately, two of the Empire's best generals were present in the palace. The first, a Romanized Thracian named Belisarius, was still in his twenties. The second, Mundus, was an Illyrian who happened to have with him a sizeable force of Scandinavian mercenaries. Secretly the two slipped out of the palace, rallied their soldiers and, by separate routes, marched on the Hippodrome. Then they burst in simultaneously on the mob, taking it completely by surprise. No quarter was given: Greens and Blues were slaughtered indiscriminately. Meanwhile the commander of the imperial bodyguard, a deceptively frail-looking Armenian eunuch named Narses, had stationed his men at the principal exits with orders to cut down all who tried to escape. Within a few minutes, the angry shouts in the great amphitheatre had given place to the cries and groans of wounded and dying men; soon these too grew quiet. As the mercenaries picked their way among the 30,000 bodies relieving them of such valuables as they possessed, the trembling Hypatius was led before the Emperor. Justinian was inclined to be merciful; but Theodora stopped him. The man, she pointed out, had been crowned by the people; he might at any time serve as a focus for further rebellion. Her husband, as always, bowed to her will. On the very next day Hypatius and his brother were summarily executed and their bodies cast into the sea.

The Nika revolt (as it came to be called) taught Justinian a lesson. Within a few weeks he reinstated Tribonian and John of Cappadocia in their former positions, but thereafter he was more circumspect: taxation no longer exceeded the bounds of reason. His subjects, too, were chastened. Emperors, it now appeared, could not be made and unmade as easily as they had thought. Justinian had shown that he was not to be trifled with. Meanwhile, for Emperor and people alike, there was work to be done. Their capital lay in ruins around them; it must be rebuilt – where possible, on a yet grander and more impressive scale than before. The priority was St Sophia itself. This, Justinian resolved, was to be his own creation, and he lost no time. On 23 February 532, work began on the third and final Church of the Holy Wisdom.

Justinian's building was to bear no resemblance to its two predecessors. First, it was to be infinitely larger – far and away the largest religious building in the entire Christian world. It would also be square rather than rectangular, reaching its climax not with its apsed sanctuary at the eastern end but with its high central dome. So revolutionary was the concept, indeed, that it seems likely that the Emperor was already planning it with his two chosen architects, Anthemius of Tralles and Isidore of Miletus, long before the Nika rising made it necessary; for all their undoubted genius, they could hardly have prepared their working drawings in under six weeks.

From the outset Justinian seems to have given the two men *carte blanche*. His only stipulations were that the building should be of unparalleled magnificence, and that it should be erected in the shortest possible time. According to one authority, he set 5,000 men on the north side and 5,000 on the south, so that each of the two teams should compete against one another. All provincial governors were meanwhile ordered to send at once to the capital any surviving classical remains that might be suitable for incorporation in the new structure. In response, eight porphyry columns, once part of a temple of the Sun, were received from Rome and eight of green marble from Ephesus. There is no mention of figurative murals, but there can be no doubt but that virtually the whole surface of the interior above the marble revetments was covered with mosaic, either in uniform gold or in decorative patterns in which red, blue and green *tesserae* were added. The majority of this original work is still in place.

But the splendour of the church was not confined to its surface decoration: architecturally, too, it seemed to its earliest visitors little less than a miracle. To most observers the most magical feature of all was that extraordinary dome, 107 feet across and 160 above the pavement, several times broader and higher than any other previously attempted, a shallow saucer pierced around its rim with forty windows so that it appeared to be 'suspended from heaven by a golden chain'. And then there was the furniture: the fifty-foot iconostasis in solid silver; the altar, encrusted with gold and precious stones; the immense circular ambo for the preacher, ablaze with polychrome marble and mosaic; the gold lamps innumerable. The relics, too, were such as no other church could match, dominated as they were by the True Cross itself, brought back from Jerusalem by the Empress Helena with the other instruments of the Passion. There too were Christ's swaddling clothes and the table at which he and his Apostles had sat for the Last Supper. No wonder that Justinian, entering the completed building for the first time on 27 December 537 – just five years, ten months and four days after the laying of the first stone – stood for a long time in silence before being heard to murmur: 'Solomon, I have surpassed thee.'

In the period of domestic tranquillity that followed the Nika revolt and the Persian peace eight months later, Justinian was at last able to turn his mind to the recovery of the Empire of the West. Previously such a reconquest had been impossible: the Empire had been hard put to protect itself from the Germanic and Slavic tribes forever pressing on its frontiers, while the barbarian infiltration of the army itself made its loyalty uncertain. But these problems were now largely solved; moreover, as it happened, Justinian found in Belisarius the one man, he believed, to whom this sacred task could confidently be entrusted. His military gifts and physical courage were unquestioned, and he was a natural leader of men. He had but one liability: his wife. Antonina too had been brought up in the theatre and the circus; and her past, if not as lurid as Theodora's, was certainly far from stainless. At least twelve years older than her husband, she had already had several children, in and out of wedlock. Unlike the Empress, she had made no attempt to reform her character after her marriage, and in the years to come was to cause her husband both embarrassment and anguish; but Belisarius continued to love her, and took her with him on all his campaigns.

The first territory to be singled out for reconquest was the Vandal Kingdom in North Africa. King Gaiseric was long dead; and in 531 his grandson had been deposed by a distant cousin named Gelimer, who had replied to Justinian's formal protest with a letter pointing out that 'nothing was more desirable than that a monarch should mind his own business'. To the Emperor these were fighting words. Belisarius was given his orders; and on Midsummer Day 533 the expedition set off. It consisted of 5,000 cavalry and twice as many infantry – at least half of them barbarian mercenaries, mostly Huns. They travelled in a fleet of 500 transports, escorted by ninety-two *dromons*.[1]

After some days' delay during which 500 men recovered from severe poisoning by the mouldy biscuit provided by John of Cappadocia, the fleet arrived safely in North Africa. The army then set off northward towards Carthage, the ships keeping pace with it offshore. It was still ten miles from the capital when, on 13 September, the Vandal army struck. Gelimer had planned a threefold attack: his brother Ammatas would occupy the vanguard while his nephew Gibamund swept down on the centre and he himself dealt with the rear. Unfortunately his communications let him down. Ammatas moved too early; the Byzantines were ready and waiting for him. In the ensuing battle Ammatas was killed; his soldiers soon lost heart. Some were cut to pieces around him; the remainder fled. The flanking attack was no more successful. Gibamund was still drawing up his troops when Belisarius's cavalry charged. They were Huns, hideous, savage and implacable. The Vandals took one look at the advancing horde and ran. All now depended on Gelimer. He started well, but suddenly came upon the body of his brother – and the fight went out of him. Once again, Belisarius saw his chance and bore down upon the Vandal host. The battle was over. With the road to the north already under Byzantine control, the Vandals fled westward, into the deserts of Numidia. Carthage lay open, and two days later, on Sunday 15 September, Belisarius – with Antonina at his side – made his formal entry into the city. There was no swagger, no insolence or arrogance: everything bought was paid for, promptly and in full. Belisarius went straight to the palace where, seated on the throne of the Vandal King, he received the leading citizens and later dined in state with his officers.

Gelimer did not immediately give up the struggle. He and his surviving brother Tzazo regrouped their forces and returned to the attack; but on 15 December they suffered another crushing defeat and the King fled back into his Numidian fastness, his army pell-mell after him. This time it was the end. Belisarius advanced to the city of Hippo and took possession of the royal treasure. Then, with a train of Vandal prisoners behind him and his wagons loaded with plunder, he returned to Carthage. Only in March 534 did Gelimer finally surrender.

---

1 The *dromon* was the smallest type of Byzantine warship, designed for lightness and speed.

It was high summer when Belisarius was recalled to Constantinople; and it was typical of Justinian's love of ancient customs that he should have accorded his victorious general a triumph, the Roman populace cheering to the echo as Belisarius marched into the Hippodrome at the head of his soldiers, followed by Gelimer, his family, and the tallest and best looking of the Vandal prisoners. The procession continued with a succession of wagons carrying the spoils of war – including the *menorah*, that sacred seven-branched candlestick that had been brought by the Emperor Titus in AD 71 from the Temple in Jerusalem to Rome, whence in 455 Gaiseric had taken it to Carthage. (Later, after representations by the Jewish community, Justinian returned, together with the other Temple vessels, to Jerusalem.) The climax of the ceremony came when Belisarius and Gelimer prostrated themselves before the imperial box, where Justinian and Theodora sat in state. In a subsequent private conversation with the Emperor, the last King of the Vandals gratefully accepted his offer of rich estates in Galatia where he could live in quiet retirement.

Justinian's thoughts now turned to Italy. A Roman Empire that did not include Rome was an absurdity; an Ostrogothic and Arian Kingdom that did, an abomination. Now that Theodoric was dead, it could also be politically dangerous. Clearly, then, it must be destroyed; but how? Unlike Gaiseric and his successors, the Ostrogothic King ruled in the Emperor's name as his Viceroy. Where they had persecuted the orthodox church, he – though an Arian – took pains to cultivate the friendship and support of the Pope and the leading Romans. He enjoyed great popularity among the imperial citizens he governed; and Justinian was well aware that those citizens might well resent the increased regimentation – and far heavier taxes – that would follow Italy's reintegration in the Empire.

Shortly before his death in 526, Theodoric had named as his successor his eight-year-old grandson Athalaric. He was the son of the King's only daughter Amalasuntha, now a widow and as remarkable as Theodora herself, with the same love of power; but she was also an intellectual, fluent in Latin and Greek, enjoying a breadth of culture rare in the sixth century and unique among the Goths. All too soon a body of Gothic nobles, horrified by her insistence on giving Athalaric a thorough classical education, removed the young King from her control; almost immediately he fell victim to the drunkenness and dissipation that was to kill him before he was seventeen. Meanwhile his mother entered into secret correspondence with Justinian, and finally a plot was hatched: Amalasuntha would flee across the Adriatic to Dyrrachium, where she would seek asylum and call on the Emperor to restore to her the power that was rightfully hers. With Theodoric's daughter at his side,

Justinian knew that he would be able to count on considerable support from the Goths themselves; he might even regain Italy without bloodshed. But events moved too fast for him. On 2 October 534 young Athalaric died at Ravenna; and the throne passed to his cousin Theodahad, who took no interest in power, preferring to lead the life of a gentleman-scholar in one of his innumerable villas. Amalasuntha saw her chance and proposed a joint monarchy: Theodahad would enjoy all the pleasures and privileges of kingship, while she took over the regulation of affairs. Theodahad agreed, and the new dispensation was proclaimed; soon, however, he began to plot his cousin's overthrow. In April 535 Amalasuntha was seized and imprisoned in an island-castle in Lake Bolsena, where she was shortly afterwards strangled in her bath. The murder gave Justinian precisely the excuse he needed. As soon as the news reached him, he issued his orders and Belisarius, fresh from his triumph, was commanded to sail with an army of 7,500 men to Sicily. The expedition started well enough, Belisarius taking the island with scarcely a struggle; but he was then seriously delayed by a mutiny in Africa, and it was not until the late spring of 536 that his army finally landed on Italian soil. He met no resistance until he reached Naples, whose citizens defended the city stoutly for three weeks. Belisarius had warned them that if they resisted he would be unable to restrain his army – which, he reminded them, was largely composed of semi-savage barbarians – from the usual murder, rapine and pillage after the capture of the city. When it finally fell they paid the price of their heroism. It was many hours before Belisarius was able to persuade his hordes to put up their swords and spears and return to their camps.

The Byzantine capture of Naples dealt a severe blow to the morale of the Goths, who laid the blame on Theodahad and deposed him – he was executed soon afterwards – nominating as his successor an elderly general named Vitiges. Many, however, must have regretted their choice when Vitiges announced that he would not be defending Rome. Its people must look after themselves as best they could while he withdrew to Ravenna, there to consolidate his forces. Belisarius, however, was in no hurry. Only in December did he move northward, ostensibly in answer to an invitation from Pope Silverius to occupy the holy city; the intervening months may well have been passed in arranging for such an invitation – which greatly strengthened his diplomatic position – to be sent. Whatever the truth may be, on 9 December 536 Belisarius entered Rome as the Gothic garrison marched out.

But if Silverius and his flock imagined that by opening the gates to the imperial army they were avoiding the miseries of a siege, they were to be disappointed. Belisarius, for his part, was aware that the Goths would soon be back and that they would fight a hard battle. Immediately he set about repairing the walls, requisitioning corn from the countryside and ordering more from Sicily until the granaries overflowed. The coming siege, he knew, might be a long one. And so it was. Vitiges and his men took up their positions around the city in March 537. They were to hold them for a year – an agonizing time for besiegers and besieged alike, at the beginning of which the Goths cut all the aqueducts, dealing Rome a blow from which it was not to recover for a thousand years. Justinian's reinforcements arrived in April – some 1,600 Slavs and Huns, who broke through the blockade and made it possible to launch occasional sorties outside the walls; but as summer drew on the sufferings increased on both sides – for the Romans, famine; for the Goths, pestilence. Only in November did the balance begin to shift, when 5,000 cavalry and infantry arrived from the East under a general known simply as John. Soon afterwards the Goths asked for a three-month truce, submitting peace proposals which Belisarius was obliged to forward to Constantinople. While awaiting a reply, he dispatched John with 2,000 horsemen on a punitive campaign. Leaving a trail of devastation behind him, John advanced rapidly up the peninsula to Rimini, where he set up his advance headquarters.

Hearing that the invaders had now occupied a city 200 miles in his rear and only thirty-three from Ravenna, Vitiges raised the siege of Rome. Early one morning in March 538 his dispirited troops set fire to their camps and headed northwards. But even now their humiliation was not over: the Byzantines fell on them from behind and left several hundred more dead on the river banks or drowned, weighed down by their armour, in the Tiber. A few days later, leaving only a small garrison in Rome, Belisarius himself set out for the north. One thing only worried him: the knowledge that John was still dangerously exposed in Rimini. He therefore sent two of his trusted officers up the coast with orders to the general to leave at once with his men and rejoin him in Ancona. But John refused; and hardly had the two officers returned when the Goths appeared beneath the walls of Rimini. A few days later the siege began, and the prospects for those within looked grim indeed. Unlike Rome, well defended and provisioned, here was a small town in a dead-flat plain, ill-protected and unprepared. The fury of Belisarius when he heard the news can be imagined. The loss of John he could bear; but his 2,000 horsemen were less easily spared. Any relief expedition would be highly dangerous. Was he, for the sake of a single regiment of cavalry, to put his entire army in jeopardy?

He was still considering his next move when fresh troops arrived from Constantinople, headed by the most powerful figure at the imperial court: the Armenian eunuch Narses, who had played a decisive part during the

Nika revolt. He was, however, no soldier: most of his sixty years had been spent in the palace. Justinian had given him command of the expeditionary force for one reason only: he was beginning to worry about Belisarius. The general was too brilliant, too successful, and – being still only in his early thirties – too young. He was the stuff of which not only Emperors were made, but men who made themselves Emperors. He needed watching; and who better to watch him than Justinian's most trusted confidant, a man whose age and condition debarred him from any imperial ambitions of his own?

Immediately on his arrival Narses was called to a council of war to discuss the desirability of a relief expedition to Rimini. He himself was strongly in favour: the capture of so important a Byzantine force, he pointed out, would be seen by the Goths as a major victory, perhaps as the turning-point of the war. His counsels prevailed; and Belisarius – who seems to have kept silent so as not to be overruled – made his plans accordingly. A week or two later he put the besieging army to flight, entering the city just in time to save the defenders from starvation. His natural resentment of his new rival, however, increased when John ascribed his rescue exclusively to Narses. The seeds of dissension had been sown.

Belisarius was a supreme strategist and a superb commander; there was only one quality that he lacked: the ability to inspire the loyalty of his subordinates. After the relief of Rimini, a considerable portion of the army made it clear that, in the event of a split, they would follow Narses rather than himself. And now, suddenly and unexpectedly, the split occurred. The cause of it was the growing hostility of Belisarius and Narses; the place, Milan.

The previous spring, during the three-month truce in Rome, Archbishop Datius of Milan had appealed to Belisarius for troops to deliver his diocese from Gothic – and Arian – occupation; and the general had sent 1,000 men back with him. Not only Milan but several other large towns immediately opened their gates to them. Each, however, required a small garrison of imperial troops, reducing the force in Milan – a city considerably larger than Rome – to some 300 men. Vitiges immediately sent an army to recover the city. It was joined almost at once by some 10,000 Burgundians. Thus, by the summer of 538, Milan was besieged by an immense force, and defended by so few soldiers that all able-bodied male citizens were called to the ramparts. Belisarius unhesitatingly sent two of his best commanders to its relief, with as large a force as he could afford. These commanders, however, realizing that they would be hopelessly outnumbered, refused to advance beyond the Po without the support of the general John and the *magister militum* of Illyria, Justin; while John and Justin in their turn claimed that they now took orders from no one but Narses. By then it was too late. The garrison, who had been reduced to a diet of dogs and mice, gratefully accepted the terms offered them by the Gothic commander, who gave them his word that they might leave the city unharmed. And so they did; but the offer did not extend to the people of Milan, who in the eyes of the Goths had betrayed the city. All the male citizens were put to the sword, the women being reduced to slavery and presented to the Burgundians in gratitude for their alliance. As for the city itself, not a house was left standing.

Milan fell in the first months of 539. It was a catastrophe, but it had one useful consequence: Justinian recalled Narses to Constantinople. No longer troubled by dissension within his ranks, Belisarius was able to concentrate on the last few pockets of resistance; and by the end of the year all Italy south of Ravenna was back in Byzantine hands. For Vitiges, one hope only was left. Knowing that the Persian King Chosroes I was threatening invasion, he had sent him a letter by the hand of two secret agents. In it he pointed out to the King that if he were to strike at once, he would force the Byzantines to fight on two fronts simultaneously, immeasurably increasing his own chances of success. The two agents never returned to the West. Their Syrian interpreter, however, was captured, brought to Constantinople, interrogated, and revealed the whole story. Justinian was now seriously alarmed. If Chosroes was truly bent on war, the imperial army must be ready for him. There was nothing for it: he would have to come to terms with the Goths, in order to free the most brilliant of his generals for another period of service in the East.

By the time the Emperor's orders reached Italy, Belisarius had already surrounded Ravenna – to the landward side with his army, to the seaward with his fleet, which had set up a blockade. All that was required was patience, and the city would be his. Then, towards the end of 539, ambassadors arrived from Constantinople empowered to sign a treaty with the Goths by the terms of which, in return for capitulation, they would be allowed to retain half their royal treasure and all Italy north of the Po. The general was dumbfounded; but he could see no way of preventing the proposed agreement, and was just about to accept the inevitable when the Goths played straight into his hands. Fearing some sort of diplomatic trick, they declared that they would accept the treaty as valid only if it bore his own signature, together with those of the ambassadors. Belisarius seized his chance. He refused absolutely to sign the treaty unless personally commanded by the Emperor himself. Then, one night, a message arrived from the Gothic court: Vitiges would resign his throne if Belisarius would proclaim himself Emperor. Many an imperial general would have seized such an opportunity; but Belisarius did not waver in his loyalty. On the other hand, here was the ideal way to bring the war to an end. All he had to do was to accept the offer, and the gates of Ravenna would be opened to him. Summoning a few trusted colleagues, he sought their approval for one last effort – which promised to win back all Italy for the Empire and bring the whole Gothic nobility, with the royal treasure, captive to Constantinople. They instantly agreed, and messengers sped to Vitiges. Duly the gates were flung open, and the imperial army marched in.

As the Goths watched the Roman soldiery loading their treasure on the ships while Vitiges and the chief nobles were borne off into captivity, they must have cursed the general who had betrayed them; but there is no indication that Belisarius's conscience gave him any trouble. The Goths were rebels: their proposal had been perfidious. War was war, and he had saved untold bloodshed on both sides. One promise he kept to the letter: there was no looting of private houses, rapine or killing. As he himself took ship for the Bosphorus in May 540 he felt only elation and pride.

But alas – every victory that Belisarius won increased the Emperor's jealousy, together with his fears that one day his brilliant young general might usurp the throne. There was no feeling of victory in the air when Belisarius returned to Constantinople, and Justinian was in no mood for celebration. In June 540 the troops of King Chosroes had captured Antioch. The general's presence would be required, not for another triumph at the Hippodrome, but on the eastern front.

6

Justinian – The Last Years

[540–65]

The Great King Chosroes I of Persia had occupied the throne since 531. Of all the Sassanian Kings he was the most illustrious and is still the best remembered. And yet, progressive as he was in many ways, in others Chosroes was very much the child of his time. His wars with the Byzantine Empire, for example, were fought not for conquest but, unashamedly, for plunder. In March 540 he crossed the imperial frontier and in early June found himself before Antioch – politely drawing his army aside to allow the newly arrived garrison, 6,000 strong but panic-stricken, to flee for its life. The citizens, however, fought with determination and courage. Sheer force of numbers allowed Chosroes finally to carry the day; and the people of Antioch paid dearly for their resistance. The great cathedral was stripped, other churches similarly pillaged. Meanwhile the Persian soldiery satisfied its various lusts, to the point where at least two distinguished ladies are said to have flung themselves into the Orontes to escape its attentions. With all the wealth of Antioch on his baggage wagons, Chosroes could afford to be generous; he offered peace in return for a down payment of 5,000 pounds of gold, plus 500 more each year. The Emperor had no choice but to accept.

In the spring of 542, the Empire suffered an outbreak of bubonic plague, one of the worst in Byzantine history. Among those stricken was Justinian himself. For weeks during that nightmare summer he lay between life and death – leaving the supreme authority in the hands of his wife. Theodora knew that her whole future was at stake. She and Justinian were childless; if he were to die, her only chance of retaining her power lay in arranging for a successor of her own choice: a trusted courtier, perhaps, or some faithful old general with whom she could go through a ceremony of marriage. Traditionally, however, the choice of Emperor lay with the army, most of whose senior officers were away in the East. At a meeting in Mesopotamia they agreed to refuse recognition to any ruler chosen without their consent. Reports of this meeting were brought back to the capital, but not before Justinian was out of danger; and Theodora, feeling herself threatened, flew into a fury. Two generals in particular were believed to have instigated the meeting. One of them, Buzes, was flung into the notorious palace dungeons, where he languished in total darkness for twenty-eight months, emerging, it was said, more like a ghost than a man.

The other was Belisarius. He was too popular, and too powerful, to be similarly dealt with, and he was now accused of having enriched himself unduly with plunder that was properly the Emperor's. On his return to the capital after the 542 campaign, the general found himself relieved of his command; his magnificent household was disbanded, his accumulated treasure confiscated on Theodora's orders – by the simple expedient of sending round one of her personal attendants with instructions to bring everything of value straight to the palace.

It was not until 543 that Justinian recovered. Soon afterwards Belisarius was partially restored to favour; and the seal was set on the reconciliation by the betrothal of Joannina, his and Antonina's only child, to the Empress's grandson Anastasius. Theodora declared in a letter that she had forgiven him because of her friendship with his wife, but there was another reason too: in the outlying provinces, the situation was deteriorating fast. A Moorish insurrection was spreading with terrifying speed throughout the province of Africa; in Italy, the Goths under their brilliant young leader Totila were also striking back and had already recaptured Naples. In Armenia, the late summer brought disaster: an immense Byzantine army of some 30,000 men was annihilated by a far smaller Persian force. This was, in short, no time to keep the Empire's one general of genius dishonoured in Constantinople; and Belisarius, who asked nothing better, received the command of the imperial army in the West. But here again disappointment awaited him. Old scores had not yet been entirely settled. It was not with the rank of *magister militum* but merely with that of *comes stabuli*, Count of the Stable, that he returned in May 544, in his fortieth year, to Italy.

There is no more convincing testimony to the ability of Belisarius than the collapse of Byzantine power in Italy after his departure in 540. With his triumphal entry into Ravenna it was universally assumed that the whole peninsula had been recovered for the Empire. True, there were one or two small pockets of resistance where the Goths acclaimed a young chieftain named Hildebad as their new King; but Hildebad's effective army amounted to no more than 1,000 men, and it seemed inconceivable that he could hold out longer than a few more weeks at most. Nor would he have done so, if Justinian had kept Belisarius in Italy. Instead, he left five generals jointly to consolidate the Byzantine position, giving none of them authority over the rest. With the arguable exception of John, they were all distinctly second-rate and simply concentrated on plunder. Within weeks, the demoralization was complete. By the year's end Hildebad had built up a considerable force, including many Byzantine deserters, and controlled all Italy north of the Po.

Clearly, Justinian had been informed of the offer of the throne to Belisarius, and was terrified lest any successor might succumb to the same temptation. So compelling was this fear that it was two years before he brought himself to appoint a Praetorian Prefect, and then chose a nonentity who was incapable of rebellion but unfortunately of everything else as well. Two more years passed before he reluctantly restored to Belisarius the command that he should never have lost. Hildebad meanwhile had been murdered, as had his immediate successors; and so the way was clear for the rise to power of the greatest, as well as the most attractive, of all the Gothic rulers.

Totila was Hildebad's nephew, still in his middle twenties. Once in power he galvanized the Goths as none of his predecessors had done. He never forgot, however, that the vast majority of his subjects was not Goth but Italian. In Theodoric's day, relations between the two peoples had been cordial; but since Belisarius's victories the Italian aristocracy had rallied to the Empire, and so it was to the humbler echelons of Italian society that young Totila now appealed. They no longer felt any natural loyalty to an Empire which, though Roman in name, was by now almost entirely Greek; furthermore, they were already suffering from the attentions of Justinian's own tax-gatherers, high officials called Logothetes who were paid by results and bled the country white. Totila's call promised an end to oppression. The slaves would be liberated, the great estates broken up, the land redistributed. It was hardly surprising that the people listened to him – and followed.

So indeed did many of the imperial soldiery. Within months of his accession Totila was strong enough to drive back one imperial army of 12,000 men from the gates of Verona, and to annihilate another in pitched battle outside Faenza. In the spring of 542, some fifteen miles north of Florence, he completely routed John's army. By the late summer he had subjugated all Italy apart from Ravenna, Rome, Florence and a few coastal cities. Chief among the latter was Naples; and it was to Naples that he now laid siege. The Gothic blockade of the city was total; and in May the Neapolitans were starved into surrender. Totila's terms were characteristically generous: the Byzantine garrison was allowed to leave in peace with all its possessions, and was even promised safe conduct to Rome.

The fall of Naples, for the second time in seven years, dealt a further blow to Byzantine morale. In January 544 the Greek generals in their various redoubts wrote to Justinian that they could no longer defend the imperial cause in Italy; it was this letter, almost certainly, that decided the Emperor to send back Belisarius. Meanwhile, hoping that he might occupy the city without bloodshed, Totila appealed from Naples directly to the people of Rome. There was, however, no spontaneous uprising as he had hoped; and so, in the early summer of 544, he set off up the peninsula. He might have been one degree less confident had he known that at that moment Belisarius was already on his way to Italy.

Belisarius had known from the beginning that he would have to fight his second Italian campaign with one hand tied behind his back: Justinian had given him only a handful of inexperienced troops, little authority and no money. He did his best. Within a year of his arrival in the summer of 544, he had relieved Otranto and rebuilt the defences of Pesaro, which subsequently withstood a determined Gothic attack. During this time, however, he had understood all too clearly how the situation had changed during his absence. It was now no longer just the Goths who were actively hostile; it was virtually the whole population. With the forces at his command he might just succeed in maintaining an imperial presence in Italy; but he could never reconquer it. In May 545 he entrusted John with a letter to Justinian, telling him of his desperate need of men, horses, arms and money. This time the Emperor responded. In late autumn John returned with a considerable army, a mixed force of Romans and barbarians under the joint command of himself and an Armenian general named Isaac. Almost simultaneously, the army of Totila reached Rome and laid siege to the city.

The prospects looked bleak. Totila controlled all the territory between Rome and the sea, while his fleet was already drawn up at the mouth of the Tiber. The commander of the imperial garrison, Bessas, had failed to lay in any emergency food supplies. Belisarius saw that the only hope lay in sailing quickly to the mouth of the Tiber, running the gauntlet of the Gothic fleet, landing his men and falling on the besieging army from behind. While Bessas kept the Goths occupied with sorties, he would lead an amphibious attack against their rear, marching part of his army along the south bank of the river while the rest, embarked on 200 ships, would smash the enemy fleet and then sail upstream in support. During the entire operation, the Armenian general Isaac was to remain in charge at the river-mouth, looking after the reserves, the remaining vessels and – not least important – Antonina, who had recently arrived to join her husband.

In the event Bessas made not the slightest effort to help his chief, but Belisarius launched his expedition regardless. Firing streams of arrows from their decks, his ships slowly forced their way up the river. They smashed through the great iron chain that Totila had flung across it as an additional protection, and were approaching Rome itself when news came that Isaac had been taken prisoner. As Belisarius saw it, this could mean one thing only: the Goths had launched a surprise attack and cut him off from the sea. Moreover, if Isaac had been captured, so had Antonina. Calling off the attack he dashed back to the coast – only to discover that Isaac had attacked the Gothic garrison at Ostia in flagrant disobedience of his orders and had been overcome by his intended victims. Apart from himself and the few soldiers who had accompanied him, everything and everyone else – including Antonina – was safe.

The last chance had been lost: Rome's fate was sealed. Yet it never surrendered. On the night of 17 December 546 a group of four discontented soldiers of the garrison opened up the Asinarian Gate, and the Goths flooded in. Bessas took flight at once, and several of the Roman nobles rode off with him. The remainder sought refuge in the churches till Totila had brought his men under control, then slowly emerged to resume their search for food until supplies in the city returned to normal. Of the populace, Procopius tells us that only 500 were left. Although the fall of Rome was of little strategic significance, as a symbol it was all-important; and Totila immediately made an offer of peace on the basis of a return to the status quo of happier days. It was refused; but when, after a few more months of fighting, it became clear that a stalemate had been reached, Belisarius decided on one last appeal to his Emperor. His emissary was Antonina. With direct access to the Empress, and through her to Justinian himself, she would not be fobbed off with underlings. Around midsummer 548, she left for Constantinople – only to find the city plunged into deepest mourning. Theodora was dead. The Emperor, prostrated with grief, would see no one. All that Antonina managed to obtain was the recall of her husband; if failure in Italy was now inevitable, she was determined that he should not carry the blame.

Early in 549 Belisarius returned to the capital. His second campaign had brought him only five years of frustration and disappointment; but he had saved Italy, at least temporarily, for the Empire. Had it not been for him, the Byzantines would have been expelled in 544; thanks to him the foundations for the reconquest were laid, enabling his old rival Narses – with all the resources for which he, Belisarius, had appealed in vain – to win the victories and the acclaim that should have been his own.

Justinian greeted his general like a long-lost friend. For years the two men had been kept apart by Theodora, who had continually poisoned her husband's mind against him. The Emperor had never really believed her; but she had inspired him with a vague feeling of mistrust. With her death, this feeling was quickly dissipated. Even Belisarius, however, was unable to persuade the

Emperor to provide the wherewithal for a final attack on Totila. Justinian was once again preoccupied; and the problem was once again theological.

The trouble had begun in 543, when a certain fanatical monophysite named Jacob Baradaeus ('the Ragged'), who had been consecrated bishop by the exiled Patriarch of Alexandria, had embarked on a mission to revive monophysite sentiment throughout the East, travelling the length and breadth of Syria and Palestine, Mesopotamia and Asia Minor, consecrating some thirty bishops and ordaining several thousand priests. Justinian found himself in a quandary. He dared not act against the monophysites in their present mood; at the same time he was already being criticized in the West for inertia in the face of the new threat. He therefore decided on a public condemnation – not of the monophysites but of those who occupied the other end of the theological spectrum, the Nestorians. Since 431 and the Council of Ephesus, few if any remained within the imperial frontiers and it consequently mattered little whether they were attacked again or not; but they were detested by monophysites and orthodox alike, and such a pronouncement might defuse the situation. In 544 he published an edict, condemning three particular manifestations of the heresy known as the 'Three Chapters'. But the monophysites were unappeased, while in the West the bishops erupted in fury. Any attack on the Nestorians, they thundered, could only be a blow in favour of the monophysites. The Patriarch, Mennas, was excommunicated on the spot.

Justinian was now seriously alarmed. At a moment when he desperately needed its support against Totila, he had managed to antagonize the entire Roman Church. The sooner the whole thing were forgotten, the better. He remained silent when Pope Vigilius refused to condemn the Three Chapters, and settled down quietly to mend relations. Eighteen months later, however, Totila was at the gates of Rome. Were he to capture the city he might hold the Pope hostage, with disastrous consequences. Justinian acted quickly. On 22 November 545 a company of the imperial guard arrived in Rome, seized Vigilius and carried him off to Constantinople. Once there, the constant pressure exerted by the Emperor and Empress began to wear him down. On 29 June he was officially reconciled with the Patriarch, and on 11 April 548 he published his *Judicatum*, in which he solemnly anathematized the Three Chapters.

Justinian's anxieties over the Three Chapters had turned his mind away from his Italian problems; but on 16 January 550, history repeated itself and another group of disaffected Isaurians in the Roman garrison opened the gates to Totila's men. Whereas in 546 the Goths had entered the city as raiders, they now showed every sign of staying. Many of them appropriated empty houses and settled in with their families; refugees were encouraged to return;

damaged buildings were repaired and restored. The following summer Totila revived the games in the Circus Maximus, personally presiding over them from the imperial box. This last insult finally stung Justinian to action. He immediately looked for a new commander-in-chief for Italy, choosing not Belisarius but the eunuch Narses, now well into his seventies.

In the early summer of 552 Narses and his army of 35,000 men began their march into Italy. Advancing around the head of the Adriatic to Ravenna, they continued southward down the Via Flaminia, Totila meanwhile advancing up the same road to block their path. So it was that one day towards the end of June the Roman and Gothic armies met for the decisive encounter of the war. It was over quite quickly: the Gothic army was progressively outflanked and outfought until, as the sun was sinking, it fled in panic and disorder, the Byzantines in hot pursuit. Totila himself, mortally wounded, took flight with the rest and died a few hours later.

Under Teia, one of the bravest of Totila's generals, the Goths continued the struggle as Narses advanced southward. Rome itself fell after a brief siege – changing hands for the fifth time since the beginning of Justinian's reign – but the old eunuch marched on. It was in the valley of the river Sarno, a mile or two from Pompeii, that in October 552 Romans and Goths met for the *coup de grâce*. Teia was soon felled by a well-aimed javelin; and on the evening of the following day the few surviving Goths agreed to negotiate. By the terms of the subsequent treaty, they undertook to leave Italy and to engage in no further warfare against the Empire. That desperate battle beneath Vesuvius marked the defeat of the Goths in Italy. Justinian's grandest ambition was realized at last.

Pope Vigilius, meanwhile, was still in Constantinople, enmeshed in the dispute over the Three Chapters. He had revoked his *Judicatum* in 550, and in 551 his relations with the Emperor had become still more strained when Justinian published another violent condemnation of the Chapters. The Pope now summoned an assembly of all the bishops from East and West present in the city, which pronounced unanimously against this edict, declaring the Patriarch once again excommunicated.

Such was Justinian's wrath on hearing the news that the Pope sought refuge in the Church of St Peter and St Paul. Scarcely had he reached it, however, when a company of the imperial guard burst into the church with swords drawn. Vigilius, seeing them, made a dash for the high altar and a scuffle ensued. The soldiers seized hold of the Pope, by now clinging to the columns supporting the altar, and tried to drag him away by the legs, hair and beard. But the more they pulled, the tighter he clung – until at last the columns themselves came loose and the altar crashed to the ground, narrowly missing his head.

By this time a crowd had gathered, and was protesting vehemently against such treatment of the Vicar of Christ; and the soldiers withdrew, leaving a triumphant though badly shaken Vigilius to survey the damage. The next day there arrived a delegation led by Belisarius himself to express the Emperor's regrets and to assure the Pope that he could safely return to his residence. Vigilius did so, but soon found that he was virtually under house arrest. On the night of 23 December 551, he squeezed through a small window of the palace and took a boat across the Bosphorus to Chalcedon, whence he returned only the following spring for a new round of negotiations. Now at last it was agreed to annul all recent statements on both sides covering the Three Chapters, including the Emperor's edict. To the papal supporters it must have seemed like victory: but Justinian was not yet beaten. He now decreed a new Ecumenical Council to pronounce upon the matter once and for all, and invited Vigilius to preside.

In theory an Ecumenical Council of the Church was a convocation of bishops from every corner of Christendom, on which it was believed that the Holy Spirit would descend, bestowing a sort of infallibility. In practice, however, the outcome of a Council's deliberations depended on the number of bishops from each side in attendance; and since bishops were considerably thicker on the ground in the East than in the West and the meetings were held in Constantinople, the Easterners would command a substantial majority. Vigilius accordingly decided on a boycott. In consequence, when the Fifth Ecumenical Council met in St Sophia on 5 May 553, of the 168 bishops present only eleven were from the West, of whom nine were African. No one present could have doubted what was expected of him.

On 14 May, the Pope issued a so-called *Constitutum*, declaring the entire agitation to be unfounded and unnecessary and forbidding any ecclesiastic to venture any further opinion on it. He cannot have expected his paper to be well received; neither, however, had he reckoned with the changed situation in Italy. The Goths were defeated; the support of the Roman citizens in Italy was no longer required. Now at last Justinian could treat Vigilius as he deserved. On receipt of the *Constitutum* he sent the Council three documents. The first was the text of a secret declaration by the Pope of June 547, anathematizing the Three Chapters; the second was an oath to work for their general condemnation; and the third was a decree that his name should be struck from the diptychs – virtually a sentence of excommunication. On 26 May the Council formally endorsed the Emperor's decree and condemned the Pope in its turn, 'until he should repent his errors'. For Vigilius, it was the end of the road. After six months' banishment he admitted all his previous errors, and two months later he again formally condemned the Three Chapters. By now too ill to travel, he remained another year in Constantinople and only then started for home. On the way, however, his condition suddenly grew worse. He was obliged to interrupt his journey at Syracuse; and there, broken alike in body and spirit, he died.

If death had come to Justinian at the same time as it came to Pope Vigilius, he would have been genuinely mourned. He had restored to his Empire its former frontiers; he had made the Mediterranean once again a Roman lake; and he had brought at least a semblance of unity to the Christian Church. He was seventy-three years old, Theodora was dead and it was time for him to follow her to the grave. But death delayed its coming for another ten years, during which he persistently refused to delegate his authority, while possessing neither the ability nor the appetite to wield it himself. Money was shorter than ever; he left it to his ministers to do the best they could. The army, which had once numbered 645,000, shrank to 150,000, while his great frontier fortresses stood desolate and abandoned. He cared now only for the state of his Church and for the endless theological disputations in which, true Byzantine that he was, he found both stimulus and relaxation.

Once only was he aroused from his torpor: when, in 559, a Hunnish tribe known as the Kotrigurs swarmed into imperial territory, advancing eastward through Thrace to within twenty miles of the capital. Many of the people of Constantinople took flight with their families across the Bosphorus, but Justinian himself was not unduly alarmed. As so often in the past at moments of crisis, he sent for Belisarius – who was still only in his middle fifties and had lost none of his energy or tactical imagination. With a few hundred men he drew the Kotrigurs into a carefully planned ambush and left 400 dead, driving the remainder back to their camp. Given a slightly larger force, he could probably have destroyed them utterly. But the Emperor preferred diplomacy, and bought the Kotrigurs with a generous annual subsidy.

Such an outcome hardly merited the triumph which Justinian awarded himself in August. This extraordinary ceremony, in which Belisarius took no part, was apparently intended to suggest to his subjects a great and glorious victory for which the Emperor alone had been responsible; that old jealousy of his general had suddenly flared up again. Belisarius doubtless took note, and retreated once more into the background. Then, in the autumn of 562, some distinguished citizens accused him of plotting against the throne. Nothing was ever proved; but he was shorn of all his dignities, and lived for eight months in a state of disgrace until Justinian, finally persuaded of his innocence, reinstated him. It was presumably this incident that gave rise to the legend of the blind old Belisarius thrown out into the streets with a begging-bowl; but since the earliest version of this story dates from five centuries later it can safely be rejected. After his return to favour Belisarius lived out his life in tranquillity, dying in March 565 at about sixty.

That same month saw Justinian's last item of legislation. He continued to give audiences through the summer and early autumn; then, suddenly, on the night of 14 November, he died. The only official with him at the time reported that he had, with his last breath, designated his successor: his nephew Justin.

The following morning Justin and his wife Sophia rode in state to the Great Church and thence to the Hippodrome to receive the acclamation of their new subjects. Then came the funeral. The body was carried slowly from the palace and through the densely packed but silent streets, followed on foot by Justin and Sophia, the Senate, the Patriarch, the bishops and clergy and the Palace Guard. On arrival at the Church of the Holy Apostles it was borne up the nave to the tomb of Theodora, next to which stood a vast porphyry sarcophagus, empty and waiting. Into this it was gently lowered, while a Mass was said for the old Emperor's soul.

An age had ended. Justinian was the last truly Roman Emperor to occupy the throne of Byzantium. It was not simply that, if Procopius is to be believed, he spoke barbarous Greek all his life; it was that his mind was cast in a Latin mould, and that he thought in terms of the old Roman Empire. He never understood that that Empire was by now an anachronism; the days when one man could stand in undisputed universal authority were gone, and would not return. In the great contemporary mosaic of 546 in Ravenna, Justinian looks younger than his sixty-four years, but his face is neither fine nor strong; certainly it bears no comparison with that of Theodora on the opposite wall. No wonder, one feels, that her husband was easily led – if it was she who was doing the leading. And yet Justinian was – with everyone except his wife – an autocrat through and through. His energy, too, astonished all who knew him, while his capacity for hard work was apparently without limit. And no one knew better than he the importance of moving out among his people, dazzling them with a magnificence that reflected the glory of the Empire itself. Hence the sumptuous processions; hence also his passion for building. Justinian transformed Constantinople; and though many of his monuments have long since disappeared, the Great Churches of St Sophia and St Eirene and the little miracle of SS Sergius and Bacchus still catch the breath.

Not all his other endeavours were equally successful. In his desire for religious unity he succeeded only in deepening the rift between East and West. His immense efforts to reform the administration and to purge it of corruption were repeatedly sabotaged by his own extravagance. Even his conquests had disappointing results. But there were successes too. Constantinople was already the principal centre of the entrepôt trade between Europe and Asia. With the West now sadly impoverished it was to Cathay and the Indies that the Byzantines looked for their commercial prosperity – and for the silks, spices and precious stones by which they set so much store. The problem was Persia, where the Great King exercised a strict control over all caravan routes – often, in time of war, blocking them completely. The sea route presented the same difficulty, since all cargoes had to be landed in the Persian Gulf. Huge tolls were levied – especially on silk, the most sought-after item of all.

This was the stranglehold that Justinian had determined to break. First, he opened up new routes designed to bypass Persia altogether: a northern one via the Crimea and the Caucasus and a southern one which used the Red Sea rather than the Gulf. The first of these attempts was partially successful; the latter failed, owing to the firmness of the Persian grip on the Indian and Ceylonese ports. The real breakthrough came only in 552, when a party of orthodox monks offered to bring back from the East a quantity of silkworm eggs, together with enough technical knowledge to establish an industry. Justinian leapt at the chance; before long there were factories not only in Constantinople but in Antioch, Tyre and Beirut, and the imperial silk industry – always a state monopoly – became one of the most profitable in the Empire.

Economically, despite all his efforts, Justinian left the Empire prostrate: for that reason alone, he cannot be considered a truly great ruler. On the other hand, he also left it infinitely richer in amenities, services and public works, and incomparably more beautiful. He extended its frontiers, he simplified and streamlined its laws. He worked ceaselessly, indefatigably, as few rulers in history have ever worked, for what he believed to be the good of his subjects. More than any other monarch in the history of Byzantium, he stamped the Empire with his own character; centuries were to pass before it emerged from his shadow.

7
The First Crusader

[565–641]

Byzantium was beset by its enemies; but the Emperor Justin II, unshakeable in his self-confidence, believed that with wisdom and courage those enemies could be scattered. He gave proof of this belief within a week of his accession, when he received an embassy from the Avars, a race of probably Tartar origin that had first appeared in the West only a few years before. His uncle had characteristically agreed to pay them an annual subsidy in return for an under-taking to protect the frontiers; this payment Justin now refused. Over the following year he took a similar line with the other recipients of Justinian's bounty, including King Chosroes himself. Such firmness much increased his popularity; it soon revealed, however, that his uncle's money had been well-spent.

The race responsible for the worst disaster of Justin's reign was however one which had never received Byzantine protection money. The Lombards were a Germanic people who had slowly drifted southwards into what we should now call Austria. Entering Italy early in 568, they skirted Ravenna and encountered little resistance except at Pavia. Their King, Alboin, advanced no further than Tuscany, but many of his nobles pressed on further to set up independent duchies in Spoleto and Benevento. Thus the Lombards invaded Italy not as raiders but as permanent settlers. They intermarried with the Italians, adopted their language, absorbed their culture and doubtless intended to make the whole peninsula their own. Their avoidance of Ravenna and the cities of the Venetian lagoon was probably due to their lack of numbers; Naples, Calabria and Sicily also remained in imperial hands. They were thus in no sense destroyers of Justinian's achievement; they merely intro-duced a powerful new element into Italy.

Justin could take no action against the Lombard tide; he was fully occupied with the Avars. In 568 they had burst into Dalmatia in a frenzy of destruction; but after three years the Byzantines were obliged to seek a truce. The ensuing treaty cost Justin 80,000 pieces of silver, far more than the original subsidy. That same year, 571, saw a dangerous development in the East, when the Armenians rebelled against King Chosroes and appealed to Justin as a fellow-Christian for support – a request which he could not possibly ignore. Early in 572 the Persian War was resumed. The following year the Persians seized Dara on the Tigris, an important Christian bishopric, simultaneously ravaging Syria – whence they are said to have returned with no fewer than 292,000 captives. Of these, 2,000 exquisite Christian virgins had been personally selected by Chosroes; but the maidens, reaching a river, sought permission to bathe, distanced themselves from the soldiers on grounds of modesty and then, rather than face the loss of religion and virtue together, drowned themselves.

By this time the Emperor had begun an open persecution of the monophysites. There were no executions or tortures, but monks and nuns were driven from their monasteries and convents, and the monophysite clergy were no longer recognized. This may have been due to Justin's rapidly-growing insanity. Often subject to fits of violence, he would attack anyone who approached and try to hurl himself from the windows, which were fitted with bars for his protection. Sophia, now supreme, bought a year's truce with Chosroes; but at the end of 574, she persuaded her momentarily lucid husband to raise a general named Tiberius to the rank of Caesar; the two then acted as joint Regents; and when Justin died in 578 Tiberius was his uncontested successor. He had not had an easy Regency. The Turks – now making their first appearance in Western history – had seized a Byzantine stronghold in the Crimea; and in 577 a vast horde of Slavs – perhaps a hundred thousand – had poured into Thrace and Illyricum. A still more immediate problem was that of Sophia herself. Increasingly reluctant to share her authority with Tiberius, she insisted on personally holding the keys of the treasury, granting the Caesar a meagre allowance for himself and his family. Only after Justin's death did Tiberius finally dare assert himself: Sophia was placed under close surveillance, in which condition she remained for the rest of her life.

The new Emperor, who now assumed the additional name of Constantine, proved outstandingly popular. The monophysite persecution was stopped; the powers both of the Senate and of the demes – the Greens and the Blues – were increased; and the army was strengthened with a new élite corps of 15,000 barbarians which, centuries later, was to evolve into the famous Varangian Guard. If Tiberius Constantine ultimately fell short of greatness, this was largely due to his uncontrolled liberality. Not content with remitting one quarter of all taxes levied throughout the Empire, in his first year alone he gave away no less than 7,200 pounds of gold. The next three years saw similar distributions; and it was fortunate for the treasury that, on 13 August 582, he died – of poison, it was rumoured, taken in a dish of mulberries.

A week before, he had appointed as his successor a young Cappadocian named Maurice. 'Make your reign my finest epitaph,' were the last words of the dying Emperor; and for the next twenty years Maurice ruled with a firm and competent hand. He also gave serious thought to Justinian's remaining conquests in Italy and Africa. The result was his two great Exarchates, Ravenna and Carthage. Organized on strict military lines under an Exarch with absolute power over both military and civilian administration, they were henceforth the principal western outposts of imperial authority. There was good news, too, from Persia. Old Chosroes had died in 579 and had been succeeded by his son Hormisdas; but in 590 the latter was killed in a *coup d'état*, his son Chosroes II fleeing into Byzantine territory and appealing to Maurice for help. The Emperor seized his chance: he willingly granted the prince the assistance he needed, in return for a treaty of peace by the terms of which both Persian Armenia and eastern Mesopotamia would be restored to Byzantium. In 591, with his support, young Chosroes overthrew the opposition – and kept his promises to the letter.

Maurice's principal problem was lack of money. His predecessor's extravagance had virtually bankrupted the Empire; warfare and subsidies prevented his ever properly replenishing the imperial coffers. The result was a parsimoniousness which gradually became an obsession. Already in 588 his reduction by a quarter of all military rations had led to a mutiny in the East; in 599 he refused to ransom 12,000 prisoners taken by the Avars, who consequently put them all to death; and in 602, most disastrously of all, he decreed that the army should not return to base for the winter, but should remain in the inhospitable and barbarous lands beyond the Danube. After eight months' campaigning, the army was exhausted. Traditionally, soldiers always returned for the winter to their families. They must now face the intense cold and discomfort of a winter under canvas, living off the local populations and in constant danger from barbarians. Flatly refusing to march another step, they raised one of their own centurions, a certain Phocas, on their shields and proclaimed him their leader. But he was not, they emphasized, their Emperor. Maurice they would no longer tolerate, but they would willingly acclaim either his seventeen-year-old son Theodosius or his father-in-law Germanus as his successor.

Both men were immediately accused by Maurice of treason. Theodosius was flogged; Germanus fled to St Sophia, where he successfully resisted several attempts to remove him. By now riots had broken out all over the capital, and an angry crowd had gathered outside the palace. That night Maurice, his wife and their eight children slipped out of the palace and across the Marmara, landing at last near Nicomedia. Here the Emperor remained with his family; Theodosius, however, headed east to Persia. Chosroes owed his throne to Maurice; now was his opportunity to repay him.

In Constantinople, Germanus had meanwhile emerged from his refuge in St Sophia and made his bid for the throne. But Phocas too – despite his comrades' disclaimer – had imperial ambitions. He now sent a message to be read from the high pulpit of St Sophia, requiring Patriarch, Senate and people to come at once to the Church of St John the Baptist; and there, a few hours later, he was crowned Emperor of the Romans. The following morning he rode in triumph into his capital; the day after, with still greater pomp, he invested his wife Leontia with the rank and title of Augusta. Meanwhile a troop of soldiers quickly ran the fugitives to earth. The Emperor is said to have watched impassively as his four younger sons were butchered before his eyes; then he himself faced the executioner and was dispatched at a stroke. The bodies were cast into the sea; the commander returned with the five heads to Constantinople.

In many ways, Maurice had proved a wise and far-sighted statesman. He had redrawn the administrative map of the Empire, incorporating the scattered imperial possessions in both East and West into a much-improved provincial system. Ultimate responsibility was henceforth in the hands of the military rather than those of the civil authorities. Had such firm organization existed in Justinian's day, Italy would have been far more easily conquered. Thus, by a combination of determination, clear-sightedness and sheer hard work, Maurice left the Empire immeasurably stronger than he found it. Had he allowed his soldiers only a little more bread, or his people just a few more circuses, he would easily have escaped his fate. Even as things were, it was only a matter of weeks before his subjects were mourning his death.

The appearance of the Emperor Phocas was distinctly unprepossessing. Under a tangle of red hair, his thick, beetling eyebrows met across his nose; the rest of his face was deformed by a huge, angry scar that turned crimson when he was aroused, giving it a still more hideous aspect. He was not, however, as pleasant as he looked. Debauched, drunken and pathologically cruel, he loved nothing more than the sight of blood. Until his day, torture had been rare in the Empire; it was Phocas who introduced the rack, the blindings and the mutilations which were to cast so sinister a shadow over the centuries to come. His eight-year reign brought the Empire to the nadir of its fortunes. The deaths of Maurice and his sons proved only the beginning; executions and judicial murders followed thick and fast – among them that of the former Emperor's oldest son Theodosius. Of his remaining family the only survivors were Germanus, whose life was spared on condition that he became a priest, and the Empress Constantina, who was dispatched with her three daughters to a nunnery. All others suspected of loyalty to Maurice met their deaths by the axe, the bowstring or, more frequently, slow torture.

In 603, King Chosroes launched a huge army against Byzantium. The Empire had at that time only one first-rate general in the East, a certain Narses – no relation to his more famous namesake – at whose name, we are told, every Persian child cringed in terror. For Maurice, Narses would have sprung to arms; for Phocas he refused to budge. He rose in rebellion, seized Edessa and appealed to Chosroes for help. Secretly, the two met, and made their plans. Phocas flung the whole weight of his army against the advancing Persians, but it was of no avail. Narses was lured to Constantinople under a guarantee of safe conduct, ostensibly to discuss peace terms. If only the Emperor had acted in good faith, he might even have won his general's allegiance. Instead, Narses was seized and burnt alive. At a stroke, Phocas had deprived himself of his best commander. Over the next four years the Persians overran much of western Mesopotamia and Syria, Armenia and Cappadocia, Paphlagonia and Galatia in a relentless tide, until in 608 their advance guard was encamped at Chalcedon, within sight of the capital. Meanwhile the Slavs and the Avars continued to flood into the Balkan peninsula.

At this point the crisis might have aroused feelings of solidarity, which Phocas should have encouraged. Instead, he initiated an all-out campaign for the forcible conversion of the Jews. Most of his intended victims lived in the eastern provinces – in the front line, in face of the Persian attack; to alienate them at such a time was an act of barely credible folly. The Jews of Antioch rose in revolt and began in their turn to massacre the local Christians, inflicting a particularly obscene death on the Patriarch, Anastasius. Thousands of terrified citizens, Christian and Jewish alike, fled the butchery and sought refuge in Persian-held territory. As the Empire sank into anarchy, plot succeeded plot in swift succession. Among the countless executions were those of the ex-Empress Constantina and her three daughters. In the capital, the Greens revolted and set fire to several public buildings; in the eastern provinces there was chaos. Christians and Jews were now everywhere at each others' throats, the latter openly allying themselves with the Persians, who received them with open arms.

It was from Africa that deliverance came at last. Ruling as Exarch in Carthage was a former general named Heraclius. He and his brother Gregorius, his second-in-command, were both in their late middle age – too old to take any decisive action themselves beyond cutting off the grain supplies on which the capital depended; but in 608 they raised a considerable army and prepared a fleet of warships, which they placed under the command of their respective sons: the army under Gregorius's son Nicetas, the fleet under the son of Heraclius, who bore the same name as his father. Towards the end of the year, Nicetas set out overland for Egypt, where he captured Alexandria before continuing his advance; and in 609 young Heraclius sailed for Thessalonica, where he collected men and further ships and, in the summer of 610, set off for Constantinople.

On Saturday 3 October this formidable force advanced through the Marmara to the Golden Horn. Heraclius had been secretly assured that he would be welcomed in the city as its deliverer, and the information proved correct. Two days later the captive Emperor was rowed out to his ship.

'Is it thus,' asked Heraclius, 'that you have governed the Empire?'

'Will you,' replied Phocas, with unexpected spirit, 'govern it any better?'

It was a good question; but it was hardly calculated to incline Heraclius towards clemency. Phocas, his henchmen and cronies were all executed on the spot. That afternoon, in the Great Palace, Heraclius underwent two separate, though near-simultaneous, religious ceremonies. First he was married: his wife, formerly known as Fabia, now changed her name to Eudocia. Immediately afterwards, he was crowned Emperor.

Now about thirty-six, fair-haired and broad-chested, Heraclius must have appeared something of a demi-god when he stepped out of the palace, his young wife on his arm. Yet there were surely many of his subjects who feared that he might be the last Emperor of Byzantium. Never had any of his predecessors inherited so desperate a situation. To the west, the Avars and the Slavs had overrun the Balkans; to the east the Persian watch-fires were clearly visible at Chalcedon, immediately across the Bosphorus. True, the Theodosian Walls were in good repair, and the Persians had no ships by which to cross the straits; but though the capital was secure, the provinces were falling away. The year after Heraclius's accession, the Persian general Shahr-Baraz seized Antioch. In 613 he added Damascus, and in 614 Jerusalem, where hardly a Christian was left alive. The Church of the Holy Sepulchre was burnt to ashes, together with most other Christian shrines; the True Cross was seized, together with all the other relics of the Crucifixion, including the Holy Lance and Sponge, and carried away to Ctesiphon. No clearer mark of divine displeasure could be imagined. The Great King then turned his attention to Egypt; and before long the chief source of the Empire's corn had become a Persian province. Famine and pestilence followed.

The very day after his coronation, Heraclius had set to work. His first task was to prepare and protect his remaining dominions. Eastern Anatolia was lost; the Western part he now divided into four Themes, each under a *strategos*, or military governor. Considerable numbers of potential soldiers were settled in each, receiving inalienable grants of land on condition of hereditary military service. This new arrangement laid the foundations for a well-trained native army – a vast improvement on unreliable foreign mercenaries. Meanwhile, finances were restored, by taxation, forced loans, crippling fines for past corruption and – for the first time in its history – major contributions from the Orthodox Church. Despite Patriarch Sergius's disapproval of the Emperor's private life – after the death of Eudocia in 612 he had gone through a ceremony of marriage with his niece Martina – Sergius had unhesitatingly put all the ecclesiastical and monastic treasure at the disposal of the State.

His political position strengthened by a patched-up agreement with the Avars, by the spring of 622 Heraclius was ready for his Persian War. On Easter Monday he boarded his flagship – the first Emperor since Theodosius the Great to lead his forces into battle – and headed down the Ionian coast to Rhodes, then east along the southern shore of Anatolia to Issus, where Alexander had routed the Persians nearly a thousand years before. Here he spent the summer in an intensive programme of tactical training, testing his own generalship and building up the stamina of his men. Only as autumn approached did he begin his advance to the north; and it was somewhere in the Cappadocian highlands that the two armies came face to face. Heraclius had never commanded an army in the field; but the Persians under their foremost general, Shahr-Baraz, were put to flight. Heraclius then returned to Constantinople, leaving his army to pass the winter in Pontus. This time there were no protests from his men. They were, after all, soldiers of the Cross – and victorious ones at that.

Back again the following spring – this time with Martina – Heraclius advanced through Armenia and Azerbaijan to the Great King's magnificent palace at Ganzak, which he destroyed. Then, leaving a trail of burning cities behind him, he headed for the Persian capital at Ctesiphon. Cut off by Shahr-Baraz, he withdrew for the next winter to the western shore of the Caspian, where Martina was safely delivered of a child. Another summer of campaigning, another winter, this time on Lake Van; and then, on 1 March 625, the Emperor led his men away on the longest and hardest journey that they had yet undertaken, first through the foothills of Ararat, then 200 miles along the Arsanias river to Martyropolis and Amida, both of which he captured. Thence it was only another seventy-odd miles to the Euphrates, which he reached without, as yet, a glimpse of the enemy. Finally, just to the north of Adana, he found the Persian army drawn up on the opposite bank ready for battle. There was, as it happened, a modest bridge nearby and the Byzantines, despite the fatigues of their long march, immediately flung themselves into the attack; but Shahr-Baraz, feigning retreat, led them into a carefully-prepared ambush. Within minutes, the vanguard of the Emperor's army was shattered. The Persians, however, had allowed their attention to become distracted from the bridge; Heraclius spurred his horse forward and charged across, his rearguard close behind him, oblivious to the hail of Persian arrows. Not even Shahr-Baraz could conceal his admiration: 'See your Emperor!' he is said to have exclaimed to a renegade Greek. 'He fears these arrows and spears no more than would an anvil!'

By his courage alone, Heraclius had saved the day. But the war was not yet over. To the city of Trebizond, where the army wintered, came ominous reports from both east and west. Chosroes had ordered a mass conscription of all able-bodied men, including foreigners, within his dominions and had entrusted his general Shahin with 50,000 hardened troops; Shahr-Baraz was to march across Asia Minor to Chalcedon, there to assist the Avars in a projected attack, now imminent. Meanwhile the Avar Khagan, with a horde consisting of virtually all the barbarian tribes from the Vistula to the Urals, was already dragging his huge siege engines towards Constantinople.

Determined neither to leave his capital undefended, nor to abandon positions on which the whole containment of Chosroes depended – to say nothing of all hope of recovering the True Cross – Heraclius decided to divide his forces into three. The first left immediately for Constantinople; the second, under the command of his brother Theodore, he sent off to deal with Shahin in Mesopotamia; the third and smallest would remain with him, hold Armenia and the Caucasus and, he hoped, ultimately invade a relatively defenceless Persia. He meanwhile turned his attention to one of the principal tribes of the Caucasus, the Khazars, dazzling their Khagan, Ziebil, by the richness of his presents and promising him the hand of his daughter Epiphania in marriage. Ziebil, flattered beyond measure, offered 40,000 men in return. Fortunately for Epiphania, he was dead by the end of the year.

While Heraclius and his new Khazar army were ravaging Azerbaijan, Theodore scored a crushing victory over Shahin in Mesopotamia, after which the Persian commander fell into a deep depression and died. Chosroes ordered the body to be packed in salt and brought to him; on its arrival he watched grimly while it was stripped and scourged until it was no longer recognizable. For some time now, members of the Persian court had doubted the Great King's sanity. After this they doubted no longer.

On 29 June 626 the Persians and Avars were ready to mount their attack on Constantinople. The inhabitants of the suburbs sought refuge within the gates, which were closed and bolted behind them; and the long-threatened siege began. The barbarian host of some 80,000 extended along the walls from the Marmara to the Golden Horn. The walls were defended by rather more than 12,000 Byzantine cavalry; and these were supported by the entire population, worked up by Patriarch Sergius to a frenzy of religious enthusiasm. Day and night, catapults hurled rocks against the ramparts; but the walls held, and the defenders stood firm. All through a sweltering July the siege continued, Sergius making a daily procession with his clergy along the whole length of the walls, carrying above his head a miraculous icon of the Virgin. On 7 August a fleet of Persian rafts, about to pick up troops and ferry them over the Bosphorus, suddenly found itself surrounded by Greek ships. The crews were either killed outright or thrown overboard to drown. Almost immediately afterwards, a collection of similar craft which the Slavs had gathered in the upper reaches of the Golden Horn attempted to force its way through to the open sea. It ran straight into a Byzantine ambush and was similarly destroyed. After this second disaster the besiegers seem to have been overcome by panic. Their siege engines had proved useless, their subtlest stratagems thwarted. Now too the news reached them of Theodore's victory over Shahin and Heraclius's new alliance with the Khazars. There could be but one explanation: the Empire was under divine protection. The next morning they struck their camp; the day after, they were gone.

The year 626, so memorable for Constantinople, for the Emperor Heraclius had been boring in the extreme. Early in 627, therefore, he decided to march on the palace of the Great King himself – at Dastagird, near Ctesiphon. He moved with caution; a Persian army was not far away. But that too was biding its time. Its new commander, Razates, was determined not to meet Heraclius until he was ready. Only at the very end of the year, by the ruins of Nineveh, was battle joined. It continued for eleven hours without a break. At its height, Razates suddenly challenged Heraclius to single combat. The Emperor accepted, spurred on his charger and, we are told, struck off the general's head with a single thrust. He himself was wounded more than once, but refused to sheathe his sword. Only when the sun set did the Greeks realize that there was virtually no enemy left to oppose them.

Heraclius arrived at Dastagird to find the Great King fled, his sumptuous palace deserted. The Byzantines showed it no mercy, committing it, and everything within it, to the flames. From his refuge at Suziana, Chosroes now called on his subjects to rally to the defence of Ctesiphon. But the Persians had lost patience with their King; and for Heraclius, there was no purpose in overthrowing a ruler whose subjects were obviously about to do so themselves. A week or two later he and his army headed for home. Chosroes, meanwhile, was flung into prison by his son Siroes, being allowed only as much bread and water as would keep him alive and so prolong his agony. On the fifth day he was shot slowly to death with arrows. The news reached Heraclius at Tabriz. There followed a treaty of peace, whereby the Persians surrendered all their conquered territories and their captives, together with the True Cross and the other relics of the Passion.

On Whit Sunday, 15 May, Patriarch Sergius ascended the high ambo in St Sophia and read the Emperor's message to his people, more a hymn of thanksgiving than a proclamation of victory. Soon afterwards Heraclius arrived at his palace of Hiera, opposite Constantinople across the Bosphorus, to find the entire population of the capital waiting to greet him. In the palace was his family: his sixteen-year-old elder son Constantine; his daughter Epiphania; and Martina herself, with her younger son Heraclonas, now thirteen. The family might now have been expected to cross to Constantinople; the Emperor, however, had resolved not to enter his capital without the True Cross, which his brother had been charged to bring as quickly as possible. It was well into September before Theodore arrived at Chalcedon and arrangements could be made for the imperial home-coming.

On 14 September 628, Heraclius entered his capital in triumph. Before him went the True Cross; behind, four elephants – the first ever seen in Constantinople. Though still only in his middle fifties he looked old and ill; but if he had worn himself out, he had done so in the service of the Empire; thanks to him, Persia would never again threaten Byzantium. The procession threaded its way to St Sophia; during the thanksgiving service that followed, the True Cross was slowly raised up until it stood, vertical, before the high altar. It was, perhaps, the most moving moment in the history of the Great Church, and many saw it as a sign that a new golden age was about to dawn.

Alas, it proved to be nothing of the kind. Just six years before, in September 622 – the year Heraclius had launched his Persian expedition – the Prophet Mohammed had fled from hostile Mecca to friendly Medina, thereby initiating the Muslim era; and just five years afterwards, in 633, the armies of Islam would begin the advance that was to take them, in the course of a single century, to within 150 miles of Paris and to the very gates of Constantinople. Until the early seventh century, Arabia had been unknown to the West, while its inhabitants, where the Christian world was concerned, showed no interest, made no impact and certainly posed no threat. Then, in the twinkling of an eye, all was changed. In 633, they burst out of Arabia. After three years they had taken Damascus; after five, Jerusalem; after six, all Syria; within a decade, Egypt and Armenia; within twenty years, the Persian Empire; within thirty,

Afghanistan and most of the Punjab. Then, after a brief interval for consolidation, they turned their attention to the West. In 711, having occupied the entire coast of North Africa, they invaded Spain; and by 732, less than a century after their first eruption from their desert homeland, they had crossed the Pyrenees and driven north to the banks of the Loire – where they were checked at last.

Mohammed died of a fever on 8 June 632; and the leadership passed first to his most trusted lieutenant, Abu-Bakr, who assumed the title of Caliph – literally, 'representative' of the Prophet. In the year following, the Muslim armies marched; but Abu-Bakr died soon afterwards, and it was under the second Caliph, Omar, that the first historic victories were won. In one respect in particular, luck was on the side of the Arabs: the Byzantine-Persian war had left both Empires exhausted. The monophysite peoples of Syria and Palestine, moreover, felt no real loyalty towards Constantinople, which represented an alien Graeco-Roman culture. The Muslims, Semites and fervent monotheists like themselves, who furthermore promised toleration for all Christian beliefs, may well have seemed preferable.

The Arab invasion of Syria in 634 found Heraclius already back in the East. His newly-conquered provinces were still to be organized, doctrinal problems with the Eastern churches resolved. Most important of all, the True Cross must be returned to Jerusalem. In spring 629, accompanied by Martina and his eldest son Constantine, he had set off for Palestine. On reaching the Holy City, he personally carried the Cross along the Via Dolorosa to the rebuilt Church of the Holy Sepulchre, where the Patriarch was waiting to receive it. The Emperor spent the next seven years in his eastern provinces, improving and streamlining the administrative machine. Meanwhile, in the theological field, Patriarch Sergius propagated a new formula which it was hoped would prove acceptable to orthodox and monophysite communities alike. This proposal was that although Christ had two natures, the human and the divine, these natures possessed a single active force, or energy. All that the monophysites would now be asked to accept was that the unity which they perceived in the Saviour was one of energy rather than of nature. But although this doctrine was enthusiastically supported by Heraclius, there was strong opposition elsewhere – notably from a fanatically orthodox monk by the name of Sophronius. It was, he thundered, nothing but a bastard form of monophysitism, a betrayal of all that had been achieved at the Council of Chalcedon. When in 634 Sophronius was elected Patriarch of Jerusalem, support for the theory of the single energy suddenly fell away; and the Emperor watched powerless while his hopes for unity crumbled to dust.

Meanwhile, the armies of the Prophet had poured into Syria; a modest Byzantine force sent against them was annihilated. A few months later they had occupied Damascus and were laying siege to Jerusalem. Shattered as he was by these events, Heraclius at once began to raise a full-scale army; and a year later 80,000 men were drawn up outside Antioch. In face of this threat the Muslims fell back on the Yarmuk river, just south of Galilee. In May 636 the imperial army advanced to meet them – but, three months later, on 20 August, a violent sandstorm swept up from the south; the young Muslim general Khalid saw his chance and charged. The Byzantine troops, caught unawares and blinded by the sand blown full in their faces, gave way under the impact and were massacred. The struggle was over. Jerusalem resisted stoutly for a further year; but in the autumn of 637 the Patriarch agreed to capitulate, and in February 638 the Caliph Omar rode into the Holy City on a snow-white camel.

And what of Heraclius himself? Why did this stalwart defender of Christendom, recoverer of the True Cross, stand by inactive while Jerusalem itself fell into the hands of the infidel? Already stricken by mortal disease, Heraclius was approaching a state of both mental and spiritual collapse. After the battle of the Yarmuk, he had given up hope. Pausing only to slip into beleaguered Jerusalem, thence to remove once again the True Cross that he had so recently restored, he set off once more on the long road to Constantinople. By the time he reached the Bosphorus his mind was seriously affected. Somehow he had developed an unreasoning terror of the sea: once arrived at Hiera, nothing would induce him to cross the strait. Finally, according to one authority, a bridge of boats was thrown across the Bosphorus and fenced with green branches, preventing him from seeing the water; Heraclius then mounted his horse and rode across 'as if he were on land'. The last return of the Emperor to his capital was a pathetic contrast to that of nine years before. Clearly, his subjects whispered, he had incurred the wrath of God by his incestuous marriage to his niece. Of Martina's nine children, four had died in infancy, one had a twisted neck and another was deaf and dumb. The Empress, never popular, now found herself publicly reviled.

She, however, hardly noticed; for all her energies were now directed towards ensuring the succession of her own first-born, Heraclonas, as co-Emperor with Constantine, her husband's son by his first wife Eudocia – a sad and sickly young man, probably consumptive. Heraclius no longer possessed the strength to resist his wife; and thus it was that on 4 June 638, in the Palace of the Bosphorus, he tremulously lowered the imperial diadem on to the head of Heraclonas, while Martina and Constantine stood by.

Before he died, Heraclius made one last attempt to solve the monophysite problem. Patriarch Sergius had now slightly amended his formula: Christ, while possessing his two natures, had not so much a single energy as a single *will*. And so the principle of monothelitism, the doctrine of the Single Will, was circulated throughout Christendom, all four of the Eastern Patriarchs signifying their assent. Only two years later did the blow fall – when, in 641, the newly-elected Pope John IV condemned the formula categorically. An issue which had been virtually confined to the Eastern Church had suddenly been inflated into a major schism between East and West. It led, too, to the final humiliation of Heraclius. In December 640 he had been informed of the arrival of the Saracen army at the gates of Alexandria; and now, just two months later, came the news of the Pope's action. His body by now distended and near-paralysed with dropsy, he was too tired for courage: with his last breath he denied having ever really supported monotheism. Only at the Patriarch's request, he muttered, had he given it his unwilling approval. Thus, on 11 February 641, with a transparent lie on his lips, one of the greatest of Byzantine Emperors expired in misery and shame.

He had lived too long. Could he only have died in 629, with the Persian Empire on its knees and the Holy Cross restored to Jerusalem, his reign would have been the most glorious in the Empire's history. Without his leadership, Constantinople might well have fallen to the Persians, and would then inevitably have been engulfed by the Muslim tide, with consequences for Western Europe that can scarcely be imagined.

Culturally, too, his reign marked the beginning of a new era. If Justinian had been the last of the truly Roman Emperors, it was Heraclius who dealt the old Roman tradition its death-blow, for it was he who decreed that Greek, long the language of the people and the Church, should henceforth be the official language of the Empire, simultaneously abolishing the ancient Roman titles of imperial dignity. Like his predecessors, he had been formally hailed as *Imperator, Caesar* and *Augustus*; all these were now replaced by the old Greek word for 'King', *basileus*.

For three days after his death the body of the Emperor lay, grotesque and misshapen, on an open bier guarded by the palace eunuchs. It was then laid in a sarcophagus of white onyx and buried, near that of Constantine the Great, in the Church of the Holy Apostles.

8

The Heraclian Line

[641-711]

The death of Heraclius, long expected as it was, threw Byzantium into chaos; and the cause of all the trouble was Martina, who had forced him to make a will entrusting the Empire jointly to Constantine, Heraclonas and herself. Now, at a public rally in the Hippodrome, she made it clear that she proposed to exercise effective power. But the Byzantines, who had long mistrusted her, would have none of it. They might reluctantly accord her the respect due to an Empress Mother, but their obedience would be given only to her son and stepson. Then on 25 May 641, Constantine, long an invalid, died after a reign of only three months. Was he killed by Martina? He had certainly felt threatened: why, otherwise, should he have moved to Chalcedon and appealed to the army from his deathbed to protect his children? But he need not have worried. The people of Constantinople had had enough of Martina's ambition and arrogance – as well as her enthusiastic support of monothelitism. In the summer of 641, in response to increasingly insistent demonstrations, Constantine's eleven-year-old son Heraclius was crowned Emperor, and his name changed to Constans; and in September Martina and Heraclonas were arrested. Her tongue was cut out; his nose was slit;[1] and the two were exiled to Rhodes. If the Empress and her son were indeed regicides, they were lucky to have escaped so lightly.

The twenty-seven-year reign of Constans II – for the beginning of which the Senate assumed the Regency – was overshadowed by his constant struggle with the Saracens. In 642 Alexandria fell to the Muslim general Amr, who razed the walls and established his new capital at Fostat, now Cairo – the local population, like their Syrian and Palestinian neighbours, apparently finding their conquerors a welcome change from the Byzantines. Having thus deprived the Empire of its richest province, the conquerors then drove

---

1 The slitting – effectively the amputation – of the nose was an ancient oriental practice, introduced for the first time in Byzantium by Heraclius. Its purpose was to invalidate the victim's claim to the throne since the Byzantines maintained that their Emperor must be free of all obvious physical imperfections.

westward along the North African coast – in 647 inflicting a disastrous defeat on the Exarchate of Carthage.

With the accession of the new Caliph Othman in 644, they began building a fleet, entrusted to Muawiya, Governor of Syria. Its first objective was Cyprus, one of the Empire's chief naval bases; the capital Constantia was sacked, the harbour installations destroyed, the surrounding country ravaged. In 654 Muawiya launched a still more formidable expedition and captured the island of Rhodes; this finally persuaded Constans that he must take the initiative. The following year an imperial fleet sailed southward down the coast and met the Saracens off the modern Finike, in Lycia. It was the first of a whole millennium of sea fights between Christian and Muslim, and it was a catastrophe. The Byzantine navy was shattered, and Constans himself escaped only by changing clothes with one of his men.

The situation now looked grave indeed; but on 17 June 656 the Caliph Othman was assassinated in his house at Medina. Ali, the Prophet's son-in-law, was elected his successor on the spot; Muawiya, on the other hand, who had been simultaneously proclaimed in Syria, accused Ali of complicity in the murder and swore vengeance. The ensuing strife continued until 661, when Ali's own assassination left Muawiya supreme. For the next five years the Muslim world would be in ferment – and Byzantium could breathe again.

Why had Constans waited fourteen years before taking action against his enemy? Largely because the ill-feeling caused by the monothelite controversy and the intrigues of Martina had left Constantinople dangerously split. It was vital that before embarking on foreign adventures he should somehow re-establish religious and political unity. He himself had never had any time for theological speculation: but when in 647 the dispute reached the point where Pope Theodore I excommunicated Patriarch Paul of Constantinople, his reaction was so characteristic that it was surely his own initiative. Early in 648, aged eighteen, he published an edict which simply decreed that the whole dispute should be consigned to oblivion, and that the state of affairs that had prevailed before it began should continue 'as if the issue had never arisen'. If a bishop should dare even to raise the subject, he would be deposed; a private person doing so would be flogged and banished. It is hard not to sympathize with him; but the problem would not go away. In October 649 Theodore's successor Martin I summoned a Council in the Lateran Palace which again condemned monothelitism; he then sent the Emperor a full report of the Council's findings under cover of a letter in which he invited Constans to express his own abhorrence in similar terms. Little did the Pope know that before his letter was even written the Exarch of Ravenna was on his way to Italy with orders to arrest him – on the somewhat shaky grounds that his election had not been submitted to Constantinople for approval.

In June 653 the Exarch landed in Italy. Within days of his arrival, Pope Martin was duly arrested and taken – after a year's detention on Naxos – to Constantinople. There he was imprisoned for ninety-three days. Only then, half-starving, freezing cold (for it was now mid-winter) and unable to walk, was he brought before the tribunal. A new and graver charge had now been added: conspiracy against the Emperor. Martin naturally denied the allegation, but he was found guilty, sentenced to death and led out into an open court-yard where, before a dense crowd, his robes were torn from his shoulders, an iron chain was flung around his neck and he was marched through the streets to the imperial prison. There he was obliged to share a cell with murderers and common criminals, and was treated with such brutality that the floor of the cell was stained with his blood. Finally, after another eighty-five days in prison and a deathbed appeal by the Patriarch for clemency, his sentence was commuted to banishment. He died less than six months later, in the Crimea.

As the eastern provinces fell to the Arab invaders, Constans's thoughts turned increasingly to the West. In the Balkans, the Slav settlers were growing restive and making difficulties over their annual tribute; in Italy, not surprisingly, Byzantium was more unpopular than ever; Sicily, meanwhile, was under serious threat from the Saracens of North Africa. Without firm action, the western provinces might fall away just as those in the East had done. Thus, in 662, Constans took a momentous decision: to leave Constantinople for ever and establish his capital permanently in the West. There were those who attributed this decision to a desire to escape hideous visions of his brother Theodosius, whom he had murdered two years before; but the Emperor's primary purpose was indubitably to protect Italy, Sicily and what was left of his African province from Saracen conquest. Having left his family in Constantinople, early in 663 he landed with his army in south Italy and advanced via Naples – a Greek city, and therefore friendly – to Rome where, despite his treatment of Martin, he was accorded a formal welcome by Pope Vitalian. Here he somewhat imperiously began stripping the city of what few valuables it still possessed – including even the copper from the roof of the Pantheon – and sending them back to Constantinople. In the autumn, having marched south through Calabria, he crossed to Sicily; and for the next five years he kept his court at Syracuse. To the Sicilians, those five years were one protracted nightmare; fortunately for them, the Emperor unexpectedly came to a violent and somewhat humiliating end. On 15 September 668, while he was lathering himself in his bath, one of his Greek attendants, in a fit of uncontrollable nostalgia, felled him with the soap-dish.

During the Emperor's long absence from Constantinople, the remaining eastern provinces had been administered by the eldest of his three sons, who now succeeded him as Constantine IV. He proved a wise statesman and born leader of men, the first decade of whose reign marked a watershed in the history of Christendom: the moment when, for the first time, the armies of the Crescent were turned and put to flight by those of the Cross. The brief respite was over. In 661 the Caliph Ali had been assassinated; since then, Muawiya had reigned supreme, establishing his capital at Damascus and founding the Omayyad dynasty that was to endure for the next eighty years. With now vastly increased resources he had resumed his old tactics, his army in Anatolia and his fleet along the Ionian coast plucking off the imperial cities and islands one by one. Finally, in 672, his ships entered the Marmara, where they captured the peninsula of Cyzicus, only some fifty miles across the water from Constantinople itself. Two years later the siege began.

The Saracen ships carried heavy siege engines and huge catapults; but the fortifications along the Marmara and the Golden Horn were proof against their assaults. The Byzantines, moreover, possessed a secret weapon. To this day we are uncertain of the composition of 'Greek fire'. Whether it was sprayed over an enemy vessel or poured into long, narrow cartridges and catapulted against its objective, the results were almost invariably catastrophic: the flaming, oil-based liquid floated upon the surface of the sea, frequently igniting the wooden hulls of the ships and causing an additional hazard to those who tried to jump overboard. For long the Muslims refused to admit defeat; only after the fifth year did the battered remnants of the Saracen fleet turn about and head for home. In 679 Muawiya sulkily accepted Constantine's offer of peace, which demanded the evacuation of the newly-conquered Aegean islands and an annual tribute. A year later he was dead. Constantine, on the other hand, was at the height of his popularity. He had inspired his subjects with the morale to withstand five years of siege by a power hitherto considered irresistible, and in doing so he had saved Western civilization. Had the Saracens captured Constantinople in the seventh century rather than the fifteenth, all Europe – and America – might be Muslim today.

With the enemy finally in retreat, Constantine could turn his attention to another, lesser, enemy – the Bulgars, a race of warlike pagan tribesmen who had settled on the north bank of the Danube, whence more and more of them were trickling across into imperial territory. Here, however, he was less successful. An abortive naval expedition in 680 served only to facilitate and encourage further Bulgar penetration of the Empire. The invaders thus rapidly established a strong Bulgar state – which, in a somewhat different form, survives to this day – and even obliged the Emperor to agree to the annual payment of protection money to their King. It was more of a humiliation than a disaster, since it had the advantage of cementing a general peace which was to endure to the end of Constantine's reign and which allowed him to tackle the most stubborn of all his internal problems.

In 678 the Emperor had written to the Pope, proposing an Ecumenical Council of the Church to settle outstanding doctrinal issues once and for all; and the Pope had enthusiastically agreed. All through the early autumn of 680 the delegates poured into Constantinople – 174 of them, from every corner of Christendom; and in mid-November the Sixth Ecumenical Council held its first session in the Domed Hall of the imperial palace. There were to be eighteen altogether, spread out over the next ten months. Constantine himself presided over the first eleven of them and again over the last, when on 16 September 681 he formally endorsed the almost unanimous findings. The doctrine of the Single Will, the Council decided, was incompatible with that of the humanity of the Saviour – who possessed, on the contrary, 'two natural Wills and two natural Energies, without division, alteration, separation or confusion'. Those who had maintained otherwise were condemned and cursed.

After the Emperor's closing speech he was cheered to the echo; and when, four years later, he died of dysentery at the age of thirty-three, he could congratulate himself not only that he was leaving his Empire stronger and more united than at any time in the century, but that he had dealt monothelitism a blow from which it would never recover.

Constantine IV was barely seventeen when his wife Anastasia had given birth to their son. It was a mistake to name the baby Justinian, for the obstreperous youth who inherited the throne sixteen years later was determined to model himself on his namesake. In some respects he was to succeed; intelligent and energetic, he showed all the makings of a capable ruler. Unfortunately he had inherited that streak of insanity that had clouded the last years of Heraclius and was again apparent in the ageing Constans. Constantine IV had died before it could become manifest; in his son Justinian, however, it rapidly gained hold, transforming him into a monster whose only attributes were a pathological suspicion of all around him and an insatiable lust for blood.

The beginning of his reign was promising enough. Successful military expeditions to Armenia, Georgia and Syria led the fifth Caliph, Abdul-Malik, to seek a renewal of the earlier treaty concluded with Muawiya. Thus, in 688–9, the Emperor felt free to lead a major military expedition into the

Slav lands of the West. Having made a triumphal entry into Thessalonica, he transported vast numbers of Slav villagers and peasants to the Theme of Opsikion on the south coast of the Marmara. Several other shifts of population followed until, after five or six years, some quarter of a million new immigrants had been resettled in Asia Minor. Inevitably, such immense upheavals brought radical changes in social conditions. At the beginning of the century, the dominant influence was that of the great landowners; by the end, the emphasis is on the new class of free and independent peasants. The improvement in living conditions led to a rising birthrate and a steady increase in the amount of land under cultivation; and the growing population produced an ever-stronger provincial militia ready for action at short notice. The trouble came only when Justinian began to raise his taxation demands to extortionate levels, causing, after the resumption of the Muslim war in 691, some 20,000 Slav soldiers to desert to the enemy – thus ensuring the loss of Armenia to the Empire. Justinian in his anger is said to have ordered the massacre of all the Slav families in Bithynia, in which men, women and children by the thousand were slain in cold blood and flung into the sea.

The document that tells us most about life in Justinian II's day is the record of a synod of 165 Eastern bishops, summoned by the Emperor in 691 to regulate matters left outstanding after the Fifth and Sixth Ecumenical Councils and hence known as the *Quinisextum*. The delegates were compelled to spend much of their time on matters of quite astonishing triviality. We read, for example, that hermits who dress in black, wear their hair long and go about the towns visiting laymen and women must cut their hair and enter a monastery; that six years of penitence were to be imposed on all who consulted fortune-tellers, 'showed bears or other animals to deceive the simple', or sold lucky charms and amulets; that all dances by women were prohibited, as was any dancing by either sex in honour of pagan gods; this ban extending to all comic, tragic or satyrical masks, all transvestites, and all invocations to Bacchus during the grape harvest; and that the ban of the Church would fall on all those who 'curled their hair in a provocative or seductive manner'.

All might have been well had not Justinian – who had invited no representatives from Rome – sent the 102 approved Canons to Pope Sergius I, with peremptory instructions to endorse them. Since several were directly contrary to Roman usage, the Pope naturally refused; whereupon Justinian ordered Zacharias, Exarch of Ravenna, to arrest him and bring him to Constantinople for judgement. Unfortunately for him, Pope Sergius was a good deal more powerful, and more popular, than his predecessors Virgilius and Martin. The imperial militias of both Ravenna and Rome flatly refused to obey. Soon after

Zacharias reached the Lateran Palace, the building was surrounded; and the Exarch found himself a prisoner of the Roman populace. Only, we are told, after Sergius's personal intervention did he emerge from under the papal bed and slip away.

When the news reached Constantinople, Justinian flew into another of his rages; his subjects, however, felt no sympathy. At the age of twenty-three, he had already acquired a degree of unpopularity equalled only by Phocas. He had antagonized both the old aristocracy and the new peasantry; he had lost Armenia; meanwhile his tax-collectors – above all his Grand Logothete (and defrocked priest) Theodotus and his *sacellarius* Stephen of Persia, a huge and hideous eunuch never seen without a whip in his hand – thought nothing of torturing their victims (often by hanging them over a slow fire and smoking them into unconsciousness) if they could thereby extract a few additional pieces of gold for their master. Obviously, it was the rich aristocracy that suffered most. They bore the extortions till they could bear them no more; then they rose in revolt.

Their leader was a professional soldier named Leontius who had been disgraced and thrown into prison. While there a monk had told him that he would one day wear the imperial diadem – a prophecy that had so preyed on his mind that when he was freed in 695 he marched on the prison and released all the prisoners – many of them his old comrades-in-arms – who declared for him at once. Together they moved on to St Sophia, calling on all whom they passed to follow them. On their arrival the Patriarch, who had recently given the Emperor some offence and was fearing the worst, unhesitatingly declared in their favour. By morning, with the support of the Blues, Leontius had been proclaimed *basileus* and the revolution was over. Justinian was taken prisoner and led in chains round the Hippodrome. In token of Leontius's long friendship with his father, his life was spared; he suffered instead the by now usual mutilations to nose and tongue before being sent into exile in Cherson. His rapacious ministers were less fortunate: tied by the feet to heavy wagons, they were dragged from the Augusteum to the Forum Bovis and there burnt alive.

The deeply undistinguished reign of Leontius is notable for one thing only: the Muslim capture of Carthage which in 698 ended the Exarchate of Africa. The upstart Emperor had sent a sizeable fleet to its relief; ironically, it was this that overthrew him. Rather than return and report failure, its leaders decided to rebel, acclaiming as *basileus* one of their own number, whose Germanic name of Apsimar was hastily changed to Tiberius. When the fleet reached Constantinople, the Greens upheld the cause of the mutineers, and their support proved decisive. Leontius lost – all too predictably – his nose, together with as much of his hair as was necessary to provide him with a tonsure, and was packed off to a monastery.

Tiberius proved a good deal more effective. In 700 he actually invaded Muslim-held Syria, going on to regain (though unfortunately only briefly) parts of Armenia. But in 705 he too was overthrown. Justinian, after a decade in exile, had returned to the capital, with vengeance in his heart. The Emperor had escaped from Cherson in 693 and appealed for protection to the Khazar Khagan Ibuzir, who welcomed him and gave him his sister – whom he immediately renamed Theodora – as his bride. The two then settled in Phanagoria, at the entrance to the Sea of Azov, to await developments. At some point in 704, news came to them that an imperial envoy had arrived at the Khazar court, offering rich rewards for Justinian, dead or alive: a report which was confirmed a few days later with the arrival of a detachment of soldiers. Justinian soon singled out two officers as his potential assassins, and invited them separately to his house; as they entered, he leapt upon them and strangled them with his own hands. Returning the now-pregnant Theodora to her brother, he then took a fishing-boat back to Cherson, where he somehow managed to gather his supporters; and they all set sail across the Black Sea to the Bulgar-held lands around the Danube delta. The Bulgar King Tervel readily agreed to provide military assistance in return for the title of Caesar; and in the spring of 705 the exiled Emperor appeared, at the head of an army of Slavs and Bulgars, before the walls of Constantinople. For three days he waited, during which his scouts discovered an old conduit, long disused, running beneath the walls into the city. On the third night, accompanied by a few picked men, Justinian squeezed himself along it, emerging at the northern extremity of the walls outside the Palace of Blachernae. The sleeping guards were taken by surprise, and within minutes the building was his. Tiberius fled to Bithynia; and the citizens of Constantinople, faced with the alternatives of surrender or sack, very wisely chose the former. Tiberius himself was soon captured, and his predecessor Leontius was dragged from his monastery; the two were then led in chains to the Hippodrome, while the populace pelted them with ordure. Finally they were flung down before the Emperor, who symbolically planted one purple-booted foot on the neck of each before they were taken away to the place of execution.

Meanwhile the Bulgar army was waiting. Not without difficulty had Tervel restrained his men; he would not lead them home before claiming his reward. The following day, in an impressive ceremony before a vast concourse of spectators, Justinian draped a purple robe across the shoulders of the Bulgar King and proclaimed him Caesar. But now came the Terror: an orgy of blood-letting worse even than that of Phocas a century before. Tiberius's brother Heraclius, the best general in the Empire, was hanged with all his staff officers on a row of gibbets erected along the Land Walls; others were tied in sacks and thrown into the sea. Patriarch Callinicus, who had crowned both usurpers, was blinded and exiled to Rome. As for Justinian, he wanted only two things. The first was blood. The other was his wife. After a two-year absence, Theodora arrived safely in Constantinople with her little son Tiberius, the first foreign-born Empress to ascend the throne of Byzantium. Inevitably, there were those who shook their heads as the Emperor lowered the diadems on to the heads of his wife and son in St Sophia. The woman was, after all, not just a foreigner; she was a barbarian. *Mésalliances* of this kind, they whispered, would have been unthinkable in former times. But then, so would an Emperor without a nose. Such old-fashioned prejudices were no longer acceptable in Justinian's Constantinople. Now that Justinian had proved that Emperors did not need noses, the abominable practice of *rhinokopia* is hardly heard of again.

Justinian's neighbours had meanwhile realized that his wholesale purges had eliminated all his best officers, and they took full advantage. In 708 the Byzantines were defeated by the barbarian tribes near the mouth of the Danube; and in 709, more serious still, they lost the key stronghold of Tyana in Cappadocia to the Arabs. That same year, 709, saw Justinian's punitive expedition against Ravenna. His motives remain a mystery; all we know is that he sent a fleet under a certain Patrician named Theodore, with instructions to invite all the dignitaries of Ravenna to a banquet in his name. Unsuspectingly, they presented themselves on the appointed day; whereupon they found themselves seized, fettered, loaded on to a ship and carried off to Constantinople, while Theodore's men sacked and looted the city. On their arrival they were led before Justinian, who unhesitatingly sentenced them to death. The Archbishop's sentence alone was commuted to one of blinding, after which he was exiled to Pontus. Only after Justinian's death was he permitted to return.

In Ravenna, the Emperor's action provoked an open insurrection; in Rome, by contrast, there was no reaction. Any Pope worthy of his tiara would have protested at such treatment of his flock, and of a consecrated prelate; from Pope Constantine I there came not a word of remonstration. At long last, Emperor and Pope together were hoping to solve their outstanding differences. The 102 canons approved by Justinian's Synod were still without papal endorsement; and in 711 Pope Constantine, a Syrian, arrived himself in the capital to settle matters once and for all. He was met at the seventh milestone by an impressive delegation headed by the Patriarch and the co-Emperor Tiberius, Justinian's son, now aged six. He then made his formal entry into the city by the Golden Gate before proceeding to the Palace of Placidia. The Emperor, oddly enough, was away in Nicaea; the two eventually met at the half-way point of Nicomedia, where Justinian prostrated himself to kiss the Pope's foot; they then returned together to Constantinople, where their discussions began. Concessions were made on both sides, the Pope finally approving about half the Canons, the Emperor dropping the rest. In October the papal mission returned safely to Rome.

Early in 711 Justinian struck again, this time against his former place of exile, Cherson in the Crimea. If he was impelled solely by vengeance, he had certainly taken his time; but his brother-in-law the Khagan had recently advanced to Cherson and then established a Khazar *Tudun*, or Governor, and it may have been this technical infringement of the imperial frontier that caused the Emperor to act as he did. Whatever his motives, he achieved his object well enough. Seven of the leading citizens were roasted alive, countless others were drowned in the approved manner (with weights attached) and some thirty, including the Tudun, were sent in chains to Constantinople. But when the Emperor himself (who had taken no part in the operation) came to summon his army home, disaster struck: one of those famous Black Sea storms arose without warning and engulfed his entire fleet.

At this point Justinian, hearing of the catastrophe, is reported to have burst into peals of laughter: it is hard to escape the conclusion that he had fallen victim to the family madness. His plan to send out a second expedition was thwarted only by the news that a Khazar army had arrived in Cherson to defend the city from Byzantine attack, and that his garrison had deserted *en masse* to the enemy. Insane or not, he now took the only course left to him, releasing the Tudun and sending him back, with an escort of 300 soldiers, to resume his former position. With him went the Grand Logothete, George of Syria, with instructions to present the Emperor's apologies to the Khagan for all that had occurred.

But the citizens of Cherson were in no mood for conciliation. The Logothete and his entourage were put to death on their arrival; the Tudun, with his 300-strong escort, was dispatched to the Khagan. Unfortunately he died on the way; and the Khazars, taking the view that he would probably need his escort on his journey to the next world, killed the lot of them. Cherson and the other cities of the Crimea now formally announced that they no longer recognized Justinian as their Emperor. Instead, they gave their allegiance to a long-exiled Byzantine general named Bardanes – who, adopting the fine old Roman name of Philippicus, forthwith proclaimed himself *basileus*.

Justinian's anger at these developments was fearful to behold. At once he prepared a new armament under the Patrician Maurus, with orders to raze Cherson to the ground; but Maurus had destroyed only two of its defensive towers when a Khazar army arrived and he was obliged to make terms. Having done so, however, he knew that he could never return and report his failure to Justinian; brought before Philippicus, he fell on his knees before him. The die was cast. The Byzantine fleet and what remained of the army returned to Constantinople with the new Emperor at its head.

Justinian, meanwhile, was on his way to Armenia; but he never got there. 'Roaring like a lion', he turned and made all possible speed back to his capital. But he was too late. Philippicus arrived first, and was welcomed with open arms. Justinian was arrested at the twelfth milestone and executed on the spot, his head being sent to the new Emperor as a trophy. When the news of his death reached the capital his mother, the Empress Anastasia, hurried her little grandson Tiberius off to sanctuary in the Church of the Virgin at Blachernae. They were pursued, however, by two agents of Philippicus, demanding that the Prince be given into their custody. The old Empress pleaded in vain; one of them advanced upon the terrified child, who stood clinging to the altar with one hand and clutching a fragment of the True Cross in the other. Wrenching the fragment from Tiberius's grasp, he reverently laid it upon the altar. Only then did he drag his small prisoner to the porch of a neighbouring church where, a chronicler tells us, he 'slaughtered him like a sheep'. Thus, with the cold-blooded murder of a little boy of six, the Heraclian line was extinguished for ever. Running in direct succession through five Emperors, that line constitutes the first true dynasty in Byzantine history. It had begun magnificently; it ended in butchery and shame.

Justinian II was not an unmitigated disaster. In his first reign especially, he did much to strengthen the imperial defences; he strove to improve relations with the Arabs and the Bulgars; and he left the Empire on excellent terms with the Church of Rome, living to receive the Pope as an honoured guest in his capital – the last Emperor ever to do so.[1] Such a record is far from contemptible; yet no amount of pleading can excuse his atrocities. The violence of his nature has been attributed to the mutilation that he had suffered and the hideous face which he was thenceforth obliged to present to the world, and which can have been but little improved by the artificial nose of solid gold which he is said to have worn in later years. That may be an explanation; there can be no excuse. His subjects, in short, were well rid of him; and his death, on 4 November 711, came not a moment too soon.

---

[1] The next papal visit was that of Paul VI to Istanbul in 1967.

9
Iconoclasm

[711–802]

In Constantinople, morale was now dangerously low. Philippicus Bardanes proved a hopeless hedonist who, in his serious moments, seemed interested only in reviving the old theological disputes, even attempting to reimpose the monothelite compromise. Pope Constantine, already horrified by the fate of his friend Justinian, refused categorically to recognize him.

Meanwhile the murder of Justinian had given the Bulgar King Tervel just the opportunity he needed. He now invaded the Empire for the second time and advanced once again to the walls of Constantinople. If the invaders were to be driven back, the Emperor had no choice but to summon additional troops from the Opsikion Theme across the Marmara. The decision proved his undoing. The Opsikians felt no loyalty to an upstart who, having effectively usurped the throne, now treated it like a plaything. On 3 June 713, soon after he had retired for a siesta after a morning banquet with friends, a group of soldiers burst into his bed-chamber and hurried him away to the Hippodrome, where his eyes were put out. He had reigned just nineteen months.

The choice of Senate and people now fell on a certain Artemius, the former Emperor's Chief Secretary; and on the following day, Whit Sunday, he was crowned as the Emperor Anastasius II. Anastasius was a far abler ruler than his predecessor. The first problem was that of defence. The Bulgars had retreated back into their homeland; it was now the Arabs who, the Emperor's spies ominously reported, were preparing another full-scale attack. Anastasius at once began a major repair and reinforcement of the Land Walls; the state granaries were replenished to bursting point, every citizen being ordered to lay in enough food to last his family for three years; meanwhile the shipyards worked harder than ever before. The Empire would not again be caught unprepared. But could the attack not be prevented altogether? Early in 715 Anastasius decided to launch a pre-emptive strike against the Saracens, using Rhodes as his base. Alas, the Opsikion troops had developed a taste for rebellion. No sooner had they arrived in Rhodes than they turned on John, the General Logothete commanding the expedition, and clubbed him to death. They then marched on Constantinople, picking up *en route* an inoffensive tax-gatherer named Theodosius whom they had inexplicably decided to proclaim Emperor – an honour that was, to him, as undesirable as it was unexpected. Anastasius was deposed in his turn, withdrawing to a monastery in Thessalonica.

With the accession of Theodosius III, Byzantium could look back on no fewer than six Emperors in twenty years; five of their reigns had already ended violently. Never since the foundation of Constantinople had there been so prolonged a period of restless anarchy. But salvation was on the way; and its instrument was a certain Leo, often known as 'the Isaurian' although he was probably nothing of the sort. He was, however, a first-rate general, whom Anastasius had appointed *strategos* of the Anatolikon Theme, one of the largest and most important in the Empire.

Some months previously Leo had taken the precaution of obtaining the support of Artabasdus, *strategos* of the Armeniakon, promising him in return the hand of his daughter in marriage and the rank of *curopalates* – one of the three highest in the Empire. They in their turn now marched on Constantinople. At Nicomedia they easily defeated a small army under the command of Theodosius's son, taking him prisoner with his entire household. From there Leo opened negotiations with the Patriarch and Senate. They did not take much persuading. The Saracens would renew their offensive at any moment; if Constantinople were to face another siege, they were in little doubt as to whom they would rather have as their leader. Early in 717 Theodosius, armed with safe-conducts for himself and his son, retired to a monastery at Ephesus; and on 25 March, the greatest Emperor since Heraclius entered the city in triumph by the Golden Gate. He was just in time. In the high summer of 717, the Caliph's brother Maslama marched across Asia Minor with a huge army of 80,000 men; and on 15 August he stood before Constantinople. Just over a fortnight later, on 1 September, a general turned admiral named Suleiman entered the Marmara, at the head of a fleet which the chroniclers estimate at 1,800 ships; and the blockade of the city began.

Leo III was ready. During the five months since his coronation he had pressed on with defence measures and ensured that his subjects had all they needed to defend themselves. In the previous siege, the fighting had been limited to the summer months; now it continued throughout the cruellest winter that anyone could remember. Inevitably it was the besiegers who suffered most, having no protection but their flimsy tents. Soon, too, they were reduced to eating their horses, donkeys and camels and, finally, dead men's flesh. Famine, as always, brought disease; the frozen ground making burial impossible, hundreds of corpses were flung into the Marmara. Suleiman himself was among the victims. On the sea, meanwhile, Greek fire exacted a daily toll among the Saracen ships. It was, however, a Bulgarian army that delivered the *coup de grâce*. The Bulgars had no love for the Byzantines, but they were determined that, if Constantinople were to be taken, it should fall into Bulgar rather than Arab hands. As spring turned to summer they marched down from the north, fell on the sick and demoralized Saracens and killed, we are told, 22,000 of them. Now at last Maslama gave the signal to withdraw. What was left of the land army dragged itself back to Syria; but of the fleet, much of it by now dangerously unseaworthy, only five vessels returned home in safety.

With so decisive a victory, the Emperor had amply justified his bid for power. In just a dozen years – he cannot even now have been much over thirty – Leo had risen from the status of a simple peasant to that of Emperor of Byzantium; and in doing so he had saved his Empire from destruction. And yet, strangely enough, his chief claim to fame rests on neither of these achievements. The greatest and most fateful step of his career had yet to be taken. It concerned the age-old questions: is art the ally of religion, or its most insidious enemy? Is the visual depiction of the godhead possible? And, if so, should it be permitted?

The sudden appearance of iconoclasm – the word means, literally, 'the smashing of icons' – on the Byzantine religious scene has often been explained by the proximity of the world of Islam, to which the very idea of such depictions was abhorrent; and it would be hard indeed to argue that Leo – whose family almost certainly originated in the wilds of eastern Anatolia – was not influenced by Islamic principles. On the other hand, this new and revolutionary doctrine was an obvious corollary to the monophysite belief: if we accept only the divine nature of Christ we cannot logically approve of a two- or three-dimensional portrayal of him as a human being. In more practical respects, the iconoclasts had a strong case. For some time the cult of icons had been growing steadily more uncontrolled, to the point where holy images were openly worshipped in their own right and occasionally even served as godparents at baptisms. It was thus as a protest against what they considered flagrant idolatry that a number of bishops in Asia Minor had adopted an iconoclast manifesto.

Leo himself had given no early indication of similar tendencies. It seems that his change of heart was the result of a combination of Muslim and Jewish influences, together with others exerted by a number of his own Christian subjects. In 725 he preached a series of sermons in which he pointed out some of the more flagrant excesses of the iconodules – as the image-worshippers were called – which he held to be in open disobedience of the

Law of Moses as laid down in the Second Commandment. Then, in 726, he decided to set an example. Facing eastwards towards St Sophia was the principal gateway to the Imperial Palace, known as the Chalkē; and above the great bronze doors that gave the building its name there rose a vast golden icon of Christ. It was this, the largest and most prominent icon in the whole city, that Leo selected as the first to be destroyed. The popular reaction was immediate: the commander of the demolition party was set upon by a group of outraged women and killed on the spot. More demonstrations followed, with widespread mutinies in both the army and the fleet. The Emperor's European subjects – inheritors as they were of the old Graeco-Roman tradition – left their sovereign in no doubt of their own feelings. They loved and revered their images, and they were prepared to fight for them. In 727, the Exarchate of Ravenna rose in revolt, backed by the Pope who, quite apart from his natural feelings of revulsion at the destruction of the holy images, resented the Emperor's presumption in arrogating to himself the supreme authority in matters of doctrine. The Exarch was murdered, while the rebellious garrisons, all recruited locally, chose their own commanders and asserted their independence.[1]

These upheavals, it should be noted, were the consequence not of any imperial decree but of a single action by the Emperor: the destruction of the Chalkē icon. Seeing its effect, Leo might have been expected to call a halt; but his resolution never wavered. In 730 he finally issued his one and only edict against the images. All, he commanded, were to be destroyed forthwith. Those who disobeyed would be arrested and punished. In the East, the blow fell most heavily on the monasteries, many of which possessed superb collections of ancient icons – together with vast quantities of holy relics, now similarly condemned. Hundreds of monks fled secretly to Greece and Italy, taking with them such smaller treasures as could be concealed beneath their robes. Others sought refuge in the deserts of Cappadocia, whose contorted outcrops of soft and friable tufa had long offered troglodytic sanctuary for other Christian communities threatened by the advancing Saracen. Meanwhile in the West Pope Gregory II publicly condemned iconoclasm and wrote to Leo suggesting that he leave the task of defining Christian dogma to those best qualified to perform it. Leo's first reaction was to deal with Gregory as Constans II had dealt with Pope Martin; but the ships sent to arrest the Pontiff foundered in the Adriatic, and before anything further could be done the Pope was dead. His successor Gregory III took an equally determined line, decreeing excommunication for all who laid impious hands on sacred

---

1 Marking the birth, incidentally, of the Republic of Venice.

objects. Leo retaliated by transferring the Sicilian and Calabrian bishoprics, together with many others throughout the Balkans, from the see of Rome to that of Constantinople. Henceforth relations between the Eastern and Western Churches were marked by unconcealed hostility.

Of the last decade of Leo's reign we know little. Although the 730s were a relatively quiet time for Byzantium, they were certainly not happy. Leo III, like Heraclius before him, had saved the Western world; but whereas Heraclius had striven to end religious strife, Leo seems almost deliberately to have encouraged it. When he died, on 18 June 741, he left an Empire which, though secure against its Arab enemies, was more deeply and desperately divided than ever before.

Constantine V, his son and successor, was the last man to reunite it. Known by the unattractive nickname of Copronymus (the result, it appears, of an embarrassing accident at his baptism) from childhood he had been closely associated with iconoclasm. It was almost certainly for this reason that his much older brother-in-law Artabasdus in 742 launched a surprise attack on him and proclaimed himself *basileus*, immediately ordering the restoration of the icons, which reappeared in astonishing quantities. For sixteen months Constantinople looked itself again; but Constantine soon took his revenge. Artabasdus and his two sons were publicly blinded; Patriarch Anastasius, who had crowned him, was flogged, stripped and paraded backwards on a donkey round the Hippodrome, after which he was – surprisingly – reinstated. But Constantine was always anxious to reduce the influence of the hierarchy; a thoroughly discredited Patriarch was ideal for his purposes.

His hatred of iconodules was now inflamed still further, his persecutions crueller than ever. And yet in other respects the iconoclasts were far from puritanical: even in the visual arts, secular subjects remained welcome. In the palace church at Blachernae, for example, the mosaics portraying the life of Christ were replaced with landscapes; while the Patriarchal Palace was somewhat inappropriately embellished with scenes of horse-races and the chase. Constantine himself, shamelessly bisexual, filled his court with exquisite young favourites and was said to be an accomplished harpist. He remained, however, fundamentally religious and a monophysite – though it was another twelve years before he felt strong enough to summon a Council to give its formal approval to iconoclasm. When he finally did so, he took care not to invite representatives from the sees of Alexandria, Antioch and Jerusalem, whose Patriarchs had all declared in favour of images. Nor of course were any invitations sent to Rome. The modest assembly that gathered on 10 February 754 had thus no conceivable right to the title of 'Ecumenical' that it claimed. After seven months of debate, its findings were unsurprising. Christ's nature, it declared, was *aperigraptos*, not circumscribable, or therefore representable as a figure within a finite space. Images of the Virgin and saints smacked of heathen idolatry and were similarly to be condemned.

These conclusions were all that the Emperor needed. His decrees were reconfirmed, the iconodules excommunicated. And the persecutions continued, especially of the monasteries – 'the unmentionables', as he called them. His most celebrated victim was Stephen, Abbot of the monastery of St Auxentius. Accused of every kind of vice, he was stoned to death in the street; but he was only one of several thousands of intractable monks and nuns who suffered ridicule, mutilation or death in defence of the icons. The *strategos* of Thracesion commanded every monk and nun to marry or face transportation to Cyprus. He is also said to have set fire to the beards of the intractable monks and committed whole libraries to the flames.

The monasteries in the Empire had indeed multiplied to a dangerous degree. Huge areas of Asia Minor were still desperately underpopulated, particularly after the bubonic plague of 745-7 removed a third of the inhabitants. Manpower was urgently needed – to till the soil, to defend the frontiers and, above all, to reproduce. Instead, more and more of the population, male and female, were opting for a life utterly useless to the State. But Constantine lost the battle; soon after his death the monasteries were as full as before. For all their cultural contributions, they were to continue to drain the life blood of Byzantium.

The reign of Constantine Copronymus is so overshadowed by iconoclasm that his military achievements are all too often overlooked. He was a courageous fighter, a brilliant tactician and leader; of all his subjects, it was his soldiers who loved him the most. He was fortunate when, in 750, the Omayyad dynasty of Damascus came to an end. The Caliphate passed to the Abbasids of Baghdad, who were more interested in Persia and Afghanistan than in Europe, Africa or Asia Minor; and the Emperor in Constantinople was able to turn his attention to dangers nearer home.

Notably the Bulgars. Henceforth successive Bulgar campaigns became a regular feature of Byzantine life. Constantine himself was to lead no less than nine of them; in one battle, fought on 30 June 763, he utterly destroyed the invading army of King Teletz, celebrating with a triumphal entry into his capital. But in 775, as he was marching in the fierce heat of August, his legs grew so swollen that they could no longer support him. He did not live to complete his journey home, and died on 14 September. He was fifty-seven.

It was unfortunate that Constantine should never have cared for his Western dominions as he did for those of the East. Instead of resisting the advancing Lombards, he deliberately antagonized the Pope, and with him the vast majority of his Italian flock, by his attempts to enforce iconoclasm. Somehow the Exarchate survived the events of 727, but in 751 Ravenna was finally captured by the Lombard King Aistulf and the last imperial foothold in north Italy was lost. Rome, abandoned by the Emperor, was left naked to her enemies. But not for long. Beyond the Alps to the west, a new power was rapidly rising to greatness. The Frankish leader Pepin the Short had deposed the Merovingian King Childeric, and Pope Stephen II went in person to France, where in 754 he anointed him King of the Franks. In return Pepin promised to transfer all those formerly imperial territories captured by the Lombards to the Papacy. He proved as good as his word. Frankish troops swept into Italy, bringing Aistulf to his knees; and in 756 Pepin proclaimed the Pope sole ruler of the former Exarchate, snaking across central Italy to embrace Ravenna, Perugia and Rome itself. His authority to do any such thing is, to say the least, doubtful; but alliance with the Pope was to lead, less than half a century later, to the establishment of the only Christian polity, apart from the Papacy itself, ever to put forward claims equal to those of Byzantium: the Holy Roman Empire.

Despite his proclivities, Constantine Copronymus was three times married, fathering six sons and a daughter; and it was the eldest of those sons who on his death assumed the throne as Leo IV. If he proved to be less capable a ruler, allowance must be made for two cruel handicaps: one was the disease which was to kill him at thirty-one; the other was his wife Irene. Scheming and duplicitous, consumed by ambition and ever thirsty for power, she brought dissension and disaster to the Empire, being additionally guilty of one of the foulest murders that even Byzantine history records. Why Leo chose her is a mystery. True, she was startlingly beautiful; but the Empire was full of beautiful women. Her family and antecedents were obscure; her native Athens was now an insignificant provincial town. Like most Athenians, however, she was a fervent supporter of images, who constantly strove against iconoclasm and all it stood for. Thanks to her, exiled monks were allowed back into their monasteries, the Virgin Mary once again accepted as an object of veneration.

Then, in the summer of 780, Leo was stricken with a violent fever. He died on 8 September, leaving a son of ten. Irene immediately declared herself Regent, and for the next eleven years was the effective ruler of the Empire. Her position was not, however, undisputed. The army in Anatolia, overwhelmingly iconoclast, mutinied immediately in favour of one of Constantine's five hopelessly incompetent brothers. The insurrection was quickly put down and its ringleaders punished, the five brothers being tonsured and forcibly ordained. But every high office of Church and State, with most of the army, was still in iconoclast hands. Irene would have to pick her way with care. But despite further mutinies, insurrections and defections in the East and West, Irene pressed on with her policy. In 784 the iconoclast Patriarch resigned, his place being taken by her former secretary Tarasius. A civil servant and diplomat rather than a churchman, his approach to the iconoclast issue was that of a practical statesman. Much of the short-term success of the iconodule reaction was due to his wisdom and judgement.

The first priority, he decided, must be the restoration of relations with Rome. Irene and her son now invited Pope Hadrian I to send delegates to a new Council, which would repudiate the findings of its heretical predecessor. The Pope willingly agreed; and when the Council convened on 17 August 786 in the Church of the Holy Apostles, with delegates from Rome and all three Eastern Patriarchates, the cause of the icons seemed assured. Soon after the delegates had taken their seats, however, a detachment of soldiers suddenly burst in, and the meeting broke up in disorder. The papal legates, deeply shaken, left at once for Rome. Irene and Tarasius acted quickly. A few weeks later they announced a new expedition against the Saracens. The mutinous troops were carried across into Asia; once there they were disbanded, their place in the capital being taken by trustworthy units from Bithynia. The departed delegates were reassembled, and in September 787 the Seventh Ecumenical Council reconvened at the scene of the First, the Church of the Holy Wisdom at Nicaea, the two papal delegates being given precedence over all the rest. Iconoclasm was condemned as heresy; icons were however to be objects of veneration rather than adoration. For its last session the Council moved to Constantinople, where it met in the Palace of Magnaura under the joint presidency of Irene and her son. Its findings were solemnly signed by both, and the delegates dispersed to their homes.

The seventeen-year-old Emperor Constantine VI was obviously still a figurehead; but in 790 Irene overreached herself. Instead of associating him more closely with the government, she now decreed that she would always take precedence. Thenceforth Constantine found himself the rallying-point of all his mother's enemies, including many of the iconoclast old guard. Some soon formed a conspiracy against her; but she learned of it in time, punished those responsible, flung Constantine into prison and finally demanded that the entire army swear an oath of allegiance to her personally. In Constantinople and the European provinces, the soldiers swore willingly enough; but in Asia Minor there was point-blank refusal. The mutiny spread rapidly: within days, Constantine was being acclaimed as the Empire's sole legitimate ruler. Stauracius, Irene's chief lieutenant, was flogged, tonsured and banished. Irene herself was confined to her palace. Constantine, hastily released from prison, found his popularity greater than it had ever been, his supremacy undisputed. The future was his.

And he threw it away. When in 791 Caliph Harun al-Rashid's army invaded his eastern provinces, he immediately concluded a shameful peace, involving a tribute which the Empire could ill afford; when hostilities broke out with the Bulgars, he proved incapable of command and ignominiously fled the field. In 792 he restored his mother to her former power. For the secret iconoclasts in Constantinople this was the last straw. A new plot was hatched in favour of the Caesar Nicephorus – one of the five brothers of Leo IV – despite the holy orders that had been forced on him a dozen years before; but it too was discovered, and for the first time in his life Constantine acted with decision. He had Nicephorus blinded, and ordered that all four of his other uncles should have their tongues cut out.

By now, one group only was prepared to support him: the old monastic party, who had been gratified to find him still well-disposed. But in January 795 they learned to their horror that the Emperor had divorced his wife Mary of Amnia and was contemplating a second marriage. Mary had, admittedly, borne him a daughter; but there was no son and Constantine had long ago given his heart to Theodotē, one of the court ladies. Mary was packed off to a nunnery; Tarasius condoned the divorce; and the following August the Emperor and Theodotē were married. Fourteen months later she presented him with a son. The monks were scandalized. Constantine's association with Theodotē, they thundered, could not be tolerated; nor could their child be considered his heir. Almost as much fury was directed against Tarasius for having allowed the marriage to take place, although he had not officiated himself. Whether or not the Patriarch ever revealed that Constantine had threatened to espouse iconoclasm if the permission were refused, we do not know. But the controversy was soon seen to have a far wider significance. Its long-term effect was to deepen the split between the two groups of iconodules: on the one hand the fanatics, on the other the moderates who understood that the Empire was not just an outsize monastery, and that if Church and State were to work together there must be compromise on both sides.

Meanwhile, Constantine had forfeited his last remaining supporters and was now defenceless against his most formidable enemy – his mother. Irene was fully aware that his real sympathies lay with the iconoclasts, and vice versa. While he lived, another coup was always a possibility. In June she was ready to strike. One day, when Constantine was riding from the Hippodrome to Blachernae, a party of soldiers fell upon him. He managed to escape, was quickly recaptured and brought back to the palace; and there, on Tuesday, 15 August, his eyes were put out. The act was performed in a particularly brutal manner to ensure that he would not survive; and there can be no doubt that Irene was guilty of his murder.

Since Constantine's young son by Theodotē had died in infancy Irene was now not only the sole occupant of the throne but the first woman to preside in her own right over the Empire. It was a position for which she had long striven but one which she had little opportunity to enjoy. Her unpopularity increased sharply after the murder of her son, and she now attempted to redeem it by granting enormous remissions of taxes; but she could not long delay the inevitable. Her more thoughtful subjects despised her for supposing that their affections could be so easily bought. The largely iconoclast army of Asia, which had almost mutinied after the murder, was humiliated by the newly-increased tribute promised to Harun al-Rashid. The reactionaries throughout the Empire, horrified at the thought of a female *basileus*, saw their direst suspicions confirmed. Yet the inevitable *coup* finally occurred for none of these reasons. There was now another, which called still more urgently for action. On Christmas Day 800 at St Peter's in Rome, Charles, son of Pepin the Frank, had been crowned by Pope Leo III with the imperial crown and the title of Emperor of the Romans; and some time in the summer of 802 he sent ambassadors to Irene with a proposal of marriage.

Well before his coronation, Charles the Great – or, as he soon came to be called, Charlemagne – was an Emperor in all but name. He had become sole ruler of the Franks in 771; two years later he captured Pavia and proclaimed himself King of the Lombards. Over the following quarter-century he had transformed his kingdom from a minor, semi-tribal European state to a single political unit unparalleled since the days of imperial Rome. And he had done so with the enthusiastic approval of the Papacy. He and his father, Pepin, had in fact succeeded where Byzantium had failed; and although the rift between Rome and Constantinople had been theoretically healed at Nicaea, Pope Hadrian had been far from satisfied by the report he had received from his representatives on their return to Rome. Small wonder, then, that he and his successor Leo had remained loyal to their more reliable Western champion.

The King of the Franks had been to Rome once before: on a state visit in 774 when he had confirmed his father's donation of that central Italian territory which became the Papal State. In 800 he came on more serious business. Pope Leo, who had already been obliged on one occasion to seek refuge at Charles's court at Paderborn, had returned to find himself facing a number of serious charges fabricated by his enemies, including simony, perjury and adultery. Who, however, was qualified to pass judgement on the Vicar of Christ? Formerly, the only conceivable answer to that question would have been the Byzantine Emperor; but the throne was now occupied by a woman. The fact that she was also a murderess was, in the minds of both Leo and Charles, almost immaterial: the female sex was believed to be incapable of governing, and by the old Salic tradition was debarred from doing so. As far as Western Europe was concerned, the Throne of the Emperors was vacant.

Charles was fully aware that he had no more authority than Irene to sit in judgement at St Peter's; but he also knew that until the accusations were refuted Christendom lacked not only an Emperor but a Pope as well, and he was determined to clear Leo's name. We do not know the nature of his testimony; but on 23 December the Pope swore a solemn oath that he was innocent of all the charges levelled against him, and the assembled synod accepted his word. Two days later, as Charles rose from his knees at the conclusion of the Christmas Mass, Leo laid the imperial crown upon his head. That crown conferred a title only; but it meant that after more than 400 years there was once again an Emperor in Western Europe.

Why did the Pope act as he did? There was, so far as he was concerned, no living Emperor at that time. Very well, he would create one – the man who by his brilliant statesmanship and the vastness of his dominions, as well as by his prodigious physical stature, stood head and shoulders above his contemporaries. But Leo conferred a still greater benefit on himself: the right to appoint, and to invest with crown and sceptre, the Emperor of the Romans. No Pontiff had ever before claimed for himself such a privilege – establishing the imperial crown as his own personal gift and simultaneously granting himself implicit superiority over the Emperor he had created.

By what authority, then, was his extraordinary step taken? The answer to this question leads us to the most momentous – and the most successful – fraud of the Middle Ages: that known as the Donation of Constantine, according to which Constantine the Great diplomatically retired to the 'province' of Byzantium, leaving his imperial crown for the Pope to bestow on whomsoever he might select as temporal Emperor of the Romans. It was a totally spurious document, but it was to prove of inestimable value to papal claims for well over 600 years.

Charles, for his part, did not wish to owe any obligation to the Pope; at any other time in his career he would almost certainly have refused the crown. But now, at this one critical moment of history, he recognized an opportunity that might never be repeated. Irene, for all her faults, remained a marriageable widow – and, by all accounts, a beautiful one. If he could but persuade her to become his wife, all the imperial territories of East and West would be reunited under a single crown: his own.

The Byzantines, on the other hand, saw things rather differently. To them, Charles's coronation was an act not only of breathtaking arrogance, but of sacrilege. Their Empire was built on a dual foundation: on the one hand, the Roman power; on the other, the Christian faith. Thus, just as there was only one God in heaven, so there could be but one supreme ruler on earth. Moreover, unlike the princes of the West, they had no Salic Law. They detested their Empress, but they never questioned her fundamental right to occupy the throne. So much the greater, therefore, was their alarm when they realized that Irene, far from being repelled by the very idea of marriage with an illiterate barbarian, appeared on the contrary to be disposed to accept. She was a deeply selfish woman and a pragmatist. By 802, when Charles's ambassadors arrived in Constantinople, she had reduced the Empire to penury. Her subjects despised her, her advisers were at each other's throats, her exchequer was exhausted. Sooner or later a *coup* was inevitable. Now, suddenly, there came a chance of salvation. It mattered little to her that her suitor was a rival Emperor, nor that he was in her eyes an adventurer and a heretic; by marrying him she would preserve the unity of the Empire – and, incidentally, her own skin.

But it was not to be. Her subjects had no intention of welcoming this boorish Frank in his ridiculously cross-gartered scarlet leggings, speaking an incomprehensible language and unable even to sign his name except by stencilling it through a plate, like Theodoric three centuries before. On the last day of October 802 a group of high-ranking officials summoned an assembly in the Hippodrome and declared Irene deposed. Arrested and brought to the capital, she accepted the situation with dignity. She was exiled to Lesbos; and a year later she was dead. But, though the Empire had been saved from further humiliation, the unthinkable had occurred. A jumped-up barbarian chieftain was calling himself Emperor, and had been crowned as such by the Pope in Rome. Henceforth there would be two Empires, not one. The old order was gone. The Christian world would never be the same again.

PART II

The Apogee

10

The Images Restored

[802–56]

The new Emperor of Byzantium was the leader of the revolt that had deposed Irene: the former Logothete of the Treasury, who now assumed the title of Nicephorus I. Determined to set the Empire to rights, he was not unduly concerned about how this was to be done. Unfortunately he aroused the hatred of the monkish chronicler Theophanes, our only – and otherwise reliable – source for the period; thus, for many centuries, Nicephorus suffered a bad press. There were in fact few men better qualified to set Byzantium back on its feet. Irene's tax exemptions were countermanded; other levies were massively increased. Private loans to merchants were forbidden; shipowners were permitted to raise money only from the State, which charged interest at 17 per cent. The Emperor instructed his provincial officials to treat bishops and clergy 'like slaves'; to the monasteries he showed even more contempt (hence the wrath of Theophanes), quartering troops upon them, confiscating monastic properties without compensation and levying poll-tax on their tenants and employees. The economy was soon on a sounder footing than it had been for years.

Meanwhile Nicephorus had written to the Caliph, informing him that he would pay no further tribute. Harun al-Rashid's reply was to launch an immediate attack, which proved the more damaging when in 803 the Byzantine general, Bardanes Turcus, suddenly rebelled and proclaimed himself Emperor. The revolt was almost immediately crushed, but not before the Saracens had made considerable territorial gains. Harun died in 809, but by then Nicephorus was occupied on two other fronts. The first was the region which we now know as Greece. In the sixth century it had been occupied by the Slavs, and the Emperor's writ had largely ceased to run. Fortunately the immigrants had given little trouble: but the rise of the Bulgars presented new dangers. One huge Slavonic bloc, extending from the Danube to Cape Matapan, was not a pleasant prospect. In 805 Nicephorus therefore decided on a wholesale resettlement of the Peloponnese, to which he brought Greeks from all over the Empire. With them came the Christian religion, to which the Slavs had not yet been converted. Like most resettlement programmes, this one was achieved only by compulsion; but without it the history of the Balkans might have been different indeed.

It came, moreover, just in time; for this decade saw the rise of Krum, the most formidable leader the Bulgars had ever produced. First he annihilated the Avars; then in 807 he united the Bulgars of the Danube basin with those of Transylvania, welding them together to form a nation. In the late autumn of 808 he destroyed a Byzantine army near the river Strymon, and six months later tricked his way into Sofia, slaughtering the garrison. Such an atrocity could not go unpunished. Leaving the capital at once with the army, by dint of forced marches Nicephorus reached the Bulgar capital, Pliska, on Easter Sunday – finding it virtually undefended. The Khan's wooden palace was burnt to ashes. Passing on to Sofia, he paused to rebuild the fortress before returning in triumph to Constantinople.

All 810 the Emperor spent in preparing what he was determined would be his decisive campaign against Krum. Since the death of Harun the eastern frontier had been quiet; the armies of the Asian Themes were accordingly free to join their European colleagues; and in May 811 an immense host marched out through the Golden Gate, the Emperor and his son Stauracius at its head. Once again Pliska was devastated, Nicephorus sparing neither women nor children – babies, we are told, were hurled into threshing machines. Then, on 24 July, still in pursuit of his prey, he led his army through a rocky defile; and the Bulgars saw their chance: that night they blocked the gorge at each end with heavy wooden palisades. As dawn broke, Nicephorus realized that he had been drawn into a trap. Most of his army was cut to pieces; of the remainder, many were burnt to death when the Bulgars fired the palisades, others were crushed by artificially-induced landslides. A few managed to escape, chiefly cavalry; but these, pursued by the Bulgar horsemen, plunged in their panic into a nearby river. Many were drowned. Stauracius, his spinal cord severed, was carried back in unspeakable agony to Constantinople. As for Nicephorus, his body was retrieved where it fell and carried back to the Bulgar camp. There the head was cut off and impaled on a stake. Later, Krum had the skull mounted in silver, and for the rest of his life used it as his drinking cup.

On the Bosphorus, the news of the Emperor's death was received with horror. The people had never liked Nicephorus, but they had a deep sense of humiliation. What they now needed was another strong leader, capable of rebuilding the army and of negotiating with Charlemagne – whose demands for the recognition of his imperial claims were growing ever more insistent. Nothing of the kind could be hoped for from the pitiable figure of Stauracius, paralysed and in constant pain. Since he was childless, he must clearly abdicate in favour of the only other male member of his family: his brother-in-law Michael Rhangabe, whose almost miraculous escape from the fatal battle suggested some special divine favour. Accordingly, on 2 October 811, Michael was crowned *basileus*. Stauracius was tonsured and dispatched to a monastery, where he died three months later.

Michael I was not the Emperor for which his subjects had hoped. Weak-willed and easily led, he was a natural puppet who could be manipulated by anyone who seized the strings. His principal manipulators were the two leading churchmen of the day: Nicephorus, Patriarch of Constantinople, and Theodore, Abbot of the Studium. Nicephorus, like his predecessor Tarasius, had formerly been a civil servant. A man of considerable ability and utter integrity, a devout churchman and a staunch supporter of the holy images, he was nevertheless looked on by the extremist monastic party, led by Theodore of the Studium, with hatred and mistrust. To them he was an impostor: an ecclesiastic only in name, whose ordination had made a mockery of one of the most solemn sacraments of the Church. And their hostility was made more dangerous by the fact that Theodore, by his formidable energy and personal magnetism, quickly gained immense influence over the Emperor – who consulted him on all matters, religious or secular, and invariably followed his advice.

At the time of Michael's accession, imperial ambassadors had already been for some months at Charlemagne's court at Aachen; by the time of Nicephorus's death, agreement had been reached on all major issues. True, it was another year before new envoys – now representing Michael – went to acclaim Charlemagne as Emperor, and another three before the treaty was finally ratified; but there can be no doubt that the initial olive branch was extended by Nicephorus. The ensuing peace was not to be known as the *Pax Nicephori* for nothing.

Perhaps, on reflection, an Emperor of the West seemed not such a bad idea after all. Constantinople might be the New Rome; but it was Greek through and through. It had nothing in common with the new Europe that was emerging beyond the Adriatic; nor did it any longer wield any effective power in those regions. It was Aachen, not Byzantium, that had re-established the *Pax Romana* in the West. The Roman Empire must remain indivisible; but would two Emperors necessarily divide it? So long as they remained on good terms, might they not give it new strength? Meanwhile Charlemagne offered excellent terms. He would relinquish all claims to Venice and its province, together with Istria and the Dalmatian coast; all he asked was the recognition of his imperial status and the right to style himself *basileus* in official documents. In theory this meant that he and his heirs would be the equal of the Byzantine Emperor, with right of succession to his throne; though whether such an interpretation was ever wholly accepted by the Byzantines is open to doubt. In the event, it hardly mattered. Charlemagne's Empire was soon to disintegrate. But the *Pax Nicephori* is no less important for that. It marked the acceptance, for the first time, of two simultaneous Roman Emperors, genuinely independent of each other, each pursuing his own policies but at the same time recognizing and respecting the claims of his counterpart. In doing so, it created the mould in which later medieval Europe was to be formed.

The dying Stauracius had been right in opposing the succession of Michael Rhangabe. He was almost insanely prodigal with money, lavishing huge sums on churches and monasteries. In one department only did he refuse to loosen his purse-strings: that which concerned the defence of his Empire. And seldom had the Empire needed it more. In the spring of 812 Krum had seized Develtus, a Byzantine town on the Black Sea, and carried off all its inhabitants, including the local bishop. In June Michael set out to confront Krum; but his newly-recruited army mutinied and he was obliged to return. The Khan's next target was Mesembria, one of the richest ports in the Balkans. As the siege began, Patriarch Nicephorus held a service of intercession in the Church of the Holy Apostles in Constantinople. Half-way through there was a sudden commotion: part of the congregation surrounded the great marble tomb of Constantine V, beseeching the dead Emperor to rise up and lead them, as so often in the past, to victory. The conclusion was not hard to draw. Constantine had been an iconoclast; under his three icon-loving successors the Empire had, time and time again, been humiliated and brought low. The pendulum, in short, was once again ready to swing.

On 5 November 812 Mesembria fell. It was now clear to Michael that he must march once more against his adversary; and this time he must win. All that winter he spent gathering troops, from every corner of the Empire; and in May 813 he set out. The following month, on the field of Versinicia near Adrianople, the armies came face to face; and on 22 June John Aplakes, commander of the Macedonians on the left wing, led his men into the attack. The Bulgars fell back in confusion, and for a moment it looked as if the battle were over almost before it had begun. But then an astonishing thing happened: the Anatolian troops on the right, commanded by an Armenian named Leo, suddenly turned tail and fled from the field. At first, we are told, Krum stood incredulous; then he and his men fell on the luckless Macedonians and slaughtered them wholesale. Nothing now lay between them and Constantinople. On 17 July the Bulgars pitched their camp beneath the walls of the city. By this time, however, Michael Rhangabe was no longer Emperor. Escaping once again unscathed, he had hurried back to Constantinople and informed the Patriarch of his intention to abdicate. He, the Empress and their five children took refuge in a church until they had received assurances for their safety. Their lives were spared, though the three boys were castrated to prevent their making any bids for power; his wife Procopia and their daughters were immured in convents. Michael himself, under the monastic name of Athanasius, retired to a monastery on one of the Princes' Islands in the Marmara, where he died in 845; and Leo the Armenian, who had betrayed his Emperor and thrown away a decisive victory, entered Constantinople by the Golden Gate and rode in triumph to the Imperial Palace.

What had really happened? The only reasonable explanation is treachery. The Anatolians' apparent cowardice must have been deliberately feigned, intended to instil a genuine panic. As for their commander, by standing firm himself until the last moment he had saved his personal reputation and had won the crown of Byzantium. But what about Krum himself? The Bulgars invariably avoided pitched battles on an open plain; why should their wily Khan suddenly abandon the practice of a lifetime and draw up his men as he did before a vastly superior army? And was it really astonishment that kept him rooted to the spot as the Anatolians hurried from the field, allowing them to get clean away before he settled down to the massacre of the valiant Macedonians?

Krum could now look back on six years of unbroken success. He had been responsible for the deaths of two Roman Emperors, and the downfall of a third; and he had overwhelmingly defeated two imperial armies. For the moment, however, he had been brought to a halt: the walls of Constantinople could never, he knew, be taken by storm. And so, in the absence of any reaction from within the city, he demanded, as the price of his withdrawal, huge quantities of gold, chests full of sumptuous vestments and, finally, a selection of the most beautiful maidens that the Empire could provide. Leo in reply proposed a meeting between Krum and himself, to be held where the northern end of the walls ran down to the Golden Horn. He would arrive by water, Krum by land; they would carry no weapons, and would be accompanied only by a few similarly unarmed followers.

The Khan accepted the suggestion, and rode down to the appointed spot. Here he was joined by the Emperor and a court official named Hexabulios. All seemed to be going smoothly when Hexabulios made a sudden gesture. Krum, recognizing it as a prearranged signal, leapt on to his horse only just in time: at that moment three armed men burst out of a nearby hiding-place.

As he galloped away to safety, he was slightly wounded by darts fired by the attackers; but these merely increased his fury at so shameless a betrayal of trust.

His revenge began on the following day. The Bulgars could not penetrate the walls; but the suburbs beyond the Golden Horn, with all their churches, palaces and monasteries, were consumed in one mighty conflagration. Every living creature left unburnt was butchered. To the west of the city, as he set off homeward, the countryside suffered a similar fate. The Palace of Hebdomon was razed, Selymbria reduced to a smouldering heap of ashes; whole families were destroyed, the men put to the sword, the women and children sent off into slavery. Krum then turned north to Adrianople. For some weeks already the city had been under attack by his brother; food was running out, and the arrival of the Khan with the main body of his army finally broke its morale. All 10,000 inhabitants were carried off beyond the Danube where many, including the archbishop, found martyrdom.

But the Empire was fighting back; and Krum's fury was increased when reports reached him in the autumn of a surprise attack on a Bulgar army near Mesembria. It had been planned and carried out by the Emperor in person, who had taken his victims by surprise as they slept and massacred the lot of them. He had then advanced deep into enemy territory where, while sparing the adult populations, he had seized all the children he could find and dashed their heads against the rocks. The Khan's mind was now made up: however formidable the walls of Constantinople might appear, he would smash them – and, with them, Byzantium itself. By the early spring of 814 the capital was abuzz with rumours of his preparations: of scaling ladders and battering rams; of towering siege-engines and of catapults capable of hurling either huge boulders against the walls or flaming firebrands over them. The Byzantines worked furiously to strengthen the defences, but salvation came from another quarter. On 13 April 814, just as his new expeditionary force was ready to march, Krum suffered a sudden seizure; within minutes he was dead.

Peace descended on the Empire. Krum's son Omortag was young and inexperienced, fully occupied with a revolt of the Bulgar aristocracy. Similar upheavals in Baghdad paralysed the Caliph Mamun. In the West, the *Pax Nicephori* still held. Leo was free at last to take the decisive step for which, more than any other, he is remembered.

Of the personal appearance of the Emperor Leo V we know little; of his character we can deduce a good deal more. First of all there was his consuming ambition: he had made his way from humble beginnings, rising to power entirely through his own efforts. If we accept the explanation of his conduct at Versinicia given earlier, we have no cause to question his courage or powers of leadership; accounts of his Bulgarian expedition of 813, however, point to a streak of bestial cruelty, quick to burst forth when his anger was aroused. He was, moreover, an Armenian; a race noted for its keen and subtle intelligence, shot through with resourcefulness and guile.

This intelligence was plain to see when, in 814, Leo reimposed iconoclasm on the Empire. His reasons for taking such a step were very different from those which had prompted his namesake eighty-eight years before. Leo III had genuinely believed that he was obeying the will of God; Leo V's approach was purely practical. The city was by now full of destitute peasant smallholders, dispossessed and driven from their homes by Saracen incursions into the eastern provinces. During the Bulgarian war they had proved useful enough; with the coming of peace, however, they were once again begging for their daily bread. Being easterners, these men were nearly all iconoclasts; they tended, moreover, to blame Irene for their misfortunes, and through her the condemnation of iconoclasm which she had brought about.

Thus, by 814, there was an ominous ground-swell of iconoclast opinion which might have turned dangerous if ignored: among not only the dissatisfied ex-soldiers but also among the upper classes and the senior ranks of the army. It was thus as a means of preserving domestic peace rather than as an expression of religious conviction that Leo went ahead with his plan. His first step was to appoint a special commission with orders to examine the scriptures and patristic writings for evidence in favour of iconoclasm. As its chairman he nominated brilliant young Armenian known as John the Grammarian; as his deputy, Bishop Antony of Syllaeum, an agreeable old reprobate who spent most of his time telling dubious stories to the rest of the commission.

In December the Emperor, armed with their report, summoned Patriarch Nicephorus to the palace. He first proposed, 'to please the soldiers', the removal only of those icons hanging low on the walls; the Patriarch, however, would have none of it; and so, with typical disingenuousness, Leo laid his plans. His first target was the huge representation of Christ above the Chalkē, pulled down by Leo III in 726 and subsequently replaced by Irene. A detachment of soldiers would create a disturbance, in the course of which they would hurl imprecations and abuse at the holy image; the Emperor would then fortuitously arrive and order its removal to save it from any further desecration.

The operation went according to plan. Then, early on Christmas morning, the Patriarch had another audience with Leo. The Emperor smoothly assured him that he contemplated no doctrinal changes, and at Christmas Mass in St Sophia ostentatiously bowed down before a representation of the Nativity. At Epiphany less than two weeks later, however, it was noted that he made no such obeisance. A few days later he summoned Nicephorus again; but the Patriarch did not come alone. With him there appeared a large body of the faithful, including Abbot Theodore – formerly an enemy but now steadfast at his side. During the meeting Theodore openly defied the Emperor; soon afterwards Nicephorus was put under unofficial house arrest and effectively prevented from performing his official duties.

That Easter, what was called a General Synod – to which, however, a considerable number of iconodule bishops failed to receive invitations – was held in St Sophia. By this time the Patriarch had fallen ill; unable to attend the assembly, he was deposed *in absentia*. In his place the Emperor appointed – significantly – a relative of Constantine V named Theodotus Cassiteras. Iconoclast the new Patriarch undoubtedly was; but he proved totally incapable of managing the Synod. Nicephorus, one feels, would somehow have imposed his authority; but when certain Orthodox bishops were cross-examined and tempers became heated, Theodotus lost control. Only after the unfortunate prelates had been physically attacked, thrown to the ground, punched, kicked and spat upon, did the delegates dust themselves down, resume their places – and do as they were told.

With iconoclasm once again reinstated, the immediate dangers of civil disruption removed and peace established on all his frontiers, Leo V could congratulate himself on an excellent start to his reign. He took no stringent measures against most of the icon-worshippers who refused to submit. A few of its most vociferous opponents were punished for form's sake: Abbot Theodore, for example, the acknowledged leader of the iconodules, was thrown into three different prisons. But Theodore had asked for it: the previous Palm Sunday he had ordered his monks to parade round the monastery, carrying their most precious icons shoulder-high before them. Most iconodules found, however, that provided they kept a suitably low profile they could carry on as before. Leo's primary interests were State security and public order. For him, the doctrinal considerations so dear to Theodore were of secondary importance. And yet, inevitably, the edict of 815 unleashed a new wave of destruction. Any holy image could be smashed by anyone at any time, without fear of punishment. Vestments bearing representations of Christ, the Virgin or the Saints were torn to shreds or trampled underfoot; painted panels were smeared with ordure, attacked with axes or burnt in the public squares. The artistic loss from the two periods of iconoclasm must have been immense; and when we consider the breathtaking quality and pathetically small quantity of Byzantine art that has survived, it is a loss that we can still feel today.

From an early stage in his career Leo had enjoyed the close friendship of a brother-officer named Michael: a bluff, unlettered provincial from the Phrygian city of Amorium, of humble origins, with an impediment in his speech. When Leo had ridden in triumph to the Imperial Palace, the Amorian had followed immediately behind; and although, when the two dismounted, Michael had accidentally trodden on the Emperor's cloak and almost dragged it off, Leo had nevertheless appointed him Commander of the Excubitors – one of the crack palace regiments. Some time in the autumn of 820, however, word came to the Emperor that Michael was spreading sedition; and on Christmas Eve a conspiracy was uncovered of which he was unquestionably the ringleader. Leo instantly summoned the Amorian and confronted him with the evidence; Michael confessed his guilt; and the Emperor ordered him to be hurled into the huge furnace that heated the baths of the palace. This terrible sentence would have been immediately carried out had it not been for his wife Theodosia. How, she demanded, could he possibly accept the Sacrament on Christmas Day with such an act on his conscience? Moved by her words, Leo countermanded his order. The condemned man was put in irons and locked away in a distant corner of the palace, under constant guard. Leo himself took charge of the keys; then, deeply troubled, he retired to bed.

But he could not sleep. On a sudden impulse he got up again, seized a candle and hurried down the labyrinthine corridors to Michael's cell, where he found the gaoler sound asleep on the floor; the prisoner lay on a pallet bed, apparently sleeping too. Leo then quietly withdrew. What he did not know was that there was a third person in the room. Michael had contrived to bring with him one of his personal servants, who on hearing footsteps had hidden under the bed. He could not see the intruder's face; but the purple boots, worn only by the *basileus*, were sufficient identification. The moment Leo had gone, he woke up his master and the gaoler and the latter, realizing his own danger, readily agreed to help his prisoner. On the pretext that Michael was anxious to confess his sins before execution, he sent another of the Amorian's trusted servants into the city, ostensibly to find a priest but in fact to gather his fellow-conspirators for a last-minute rescue.

The plan was soon made. It was the custom, on great feasts of the Church, for a choir of monks to assemble in the early hours by the Ivory Gate of the palace before proceeding to the Chapel of St Stephen. Long before first light on that Christmas morning, the conspirators shrouded themselves in monks' robes and joined the choristers with whom, their faces hidden deep in their cowls, they moved into the palace. Once inside the chapel, they lost themselves among the shadows. The opening hymn was the signal for the arrival of the Emperor, who took his seat as usual and joined in the singing. The conspirators waited until the music reached a climax; then they struck. Strangely enough, both Leo and the officiating priest were wearing peaked fur caps to protect their heads from the bitter cold; and the first blows were directed against the priest. This brief delay allowed the Emperor to seize a heavy cross with which to defend himself; but a moment later a sword severed his right arm at the shoulder – sending it, the hand still clutching the cross, spinning across the floor. He fell to the ground, where another blow struck off his head. The assassins, hurrying to Michael's cell, now found to their dismay that they could not unlock his fetters: the new Emperor of Byzantium was carried to his throne and seated upon it with the heavy iron shackles still on his legs. Only around midday did a blacksmith arrive with a sledgehammer and chisel to set him free – just in time for him to limp into St Sophia for his coronation. Soon afterwards, what remained of Leo V was retrieved from a common privy and dragged naked to the Hippodrome, where it was exposed to the public gaze. Thence it was carried on muleback to the harbour, where the Empress and her four sons were waiting, and loaded on to the ship that was to take them to exile on the Princes' Islands. On their arrival, further grim news awaited them: to ensure that they should plan no retaliation, it was the wish of the new Emperor that all four boys should be castrated.

To say that Michael II ascended the Byzantine throne with blood on his hands is an understatement. Many other Emperors, to be sure, had done the same; none, however, had dispatched his predecessor more cold-bloodedly, or with less excuse. Leo had had his faults, but he had done much to restore imperial fortunes and, given the opportunity, would have continued to rule with firmness and confidence. Michael could not justify his murder on grounds of incapacity any more than he could on grounds of religion, since he shared Leo's views on iconoclasm. His motivation, in short, was ambition alone.

The people of Constantinople were perfectly aware of this. They laughed at Michael for his boorishness, but they feared him too. And yet he was to prove a better ruler than anyone had expected, and his reign was to be characterized less by stupidity or cruelty than by sound common sense. It was this, surely, that led him to crown his seventeen-year-old son Theophilus co-Emperor. He was deeply conscious that he was the seventh *basileus* in a quarter of a century, and that of his immediate predecessors two had been deposed, two killed in battle and two assassinated. The last three, moreover, had all been unrelated to each other, and to himself. More than anything the

Empire needed stability; and the coronation of Theophilus was the first step towards it. But he too must produce an heir: and the second step was to marry him to a Paphlagonian lady of startling beauty by the name of Theodora.

By now, however, the Empire was once again under threat, from a military adventurer known as Thomas the Slav. During the lifetime of Leo, who had entrusted him with a high military command, Thomas had caused no trouble; but as soon as the throne passed to his old rival Michael he began to stir up rebellion. In the East he claimed to be the Emperor Constantine VI (who had, he claimed, somehow miraculously escaped the blinding ordered by his mother Irene) and actually organized a ceremony of coronation in Muslim-held Antioch. In the West he took a violently anti-iconoclastic stand calculated to win him a large measure of support. Everywhere he set himself up as a champion of the poor, of all those oppressed by high taxation and the corruption of officials. Though relatively advanced in age there seems to have been something attractive about him: his courtesy and charm stood out in marked contrast with the incoherent coarseness of the Emperor. What his innumerable supporters did not know was that Thomas was enjoying considerable financial support from Caliph Mamun – to whom he may well have promised, if successful, to hold the Empire as a fief of the Caliphate.

This twisted, resentful yet charismatic figure invaded the Empire in the spring of 821; within a matter of months, only two Themes in all Asia Minor remained loyal to Michael. And so, aware that he had virtually the whole Empire behind him from Ararat to the Aegean, Thomas crossed to Thrace in December 821 and laid siege to Constantinople. But the people of the capital were unlike those of Anatolia. They resisted with their usual courage and their walls, as always, held firm. Thomas's siege-engines proved no match for the catapults and mangonels that Michael had ranged along the ramparts. At sea, too, though he had won over the fleet around the Anatolian coast, the raging winter winds prevented the ships from doing appreciable damage. By the second winter of the rebellion Thomas had still not achieved a single major victory; but the stalemate might have continued indefinitely had it not been for Krum's son Omortag who, having concluded a thirty-year truce with the Empire, now offered Michael armed assistance. In March 823 the Bulgar horde swept down and a few weeks later, on the plain of Keduktos near Heraclea, smashed the rebel army to pieces. It was consequently powerless to resist when, a few weeks later, the Emperor rode out of the capital with his own army, to settle the issue once and for all. Thomas attempted the time-honoured tactic of a pretended flight; but when the moment came to turn and charge the enemy his troops laid down their arms instead. Escaping with a handful of followers, he fled to Arcadiopolis and barricaded himself in.

Now the roles were reversed: Michael was the besieger, Thomas the besieged. The latter held out through the summer; but in October, by which time his men were reduced to eating the putrescent corpses of their horses, it became clear that they could resist no longer. The Emperor now sent a message to the soldiers in the city, promising a free pardon if they would deliver their leader into his hands. Unwilling to risk a general massacre, they agreed. Brought in chains into the Emperor's presence, Thomas was pushed roughly to the ground before him; and Michael, resting a purple-booted foot on the neck of his victim, pronounced his fate: the hands and feet were to be cut off, the body then to be impaled on a stake. The sentence was carried out on the spot. By the beginning of 824 the most serious rebellion in all Byzantine history was at an end.

The same could not be said, however, for the tribulations of Michael II. In 825 a huge Arab fleet appeared in imperial waters carrying 10,000 armed Muslim refugees, expelled from Andalusia some years before. They had captured Alexandria in 818; seven years later, forcibly expelled by the Caliph Mamun, they headed for Crete, founding the city of Candia which has ever since been the island's capital. From there they quickly spread across the island, forcibly imposing Islam and enslaving the inhabitants. Crete henceforth became a nest of pirates, from whom no island or harbour in the eastern Mediterranean could consider itself safe; Candia became the busiest slave market of its time. Michael II launched three separate expeditions against it between 827 and 829, but there were to be several more attempts by his successors before control was finally reimposed.

Within only two years of the capture of Crete another company of Arabs invaded Sicily. This time, however, they came by invitation – to support the cause of Euphemius, a former Byzantine admiral who had been dismissed from his post after eloping with a local nun and, on the theory that opposition was the best defence, had risen in revolt, appealing for assistance from the North African Emir of Kairouan. Accordingly, in June 827 a fleet of nearly 100 Arab ships crossed to Sicily. The invaders did not have things entirely their own way. Euphemius was soon killed, but the contest between Christian and Saracen – still fought nightly in the traditional puppet-shows of Palermo – was to continue for another half-century. Meanwhile, however, Sicily had proved itself an even better pirate stronghold than Crete: before long the armies of the Prophet had crossed the Straits of Messina, overrun Calabria and much of Apulia, and had even passed thence over the Adriatic to the southern Dalmatian coast. The Emperor and his successors did all they could, but their navy could not cope with Crete and Sicily simultaneously.

Like his predecessor, Michael II was uninterested in theological speculation. If anything he was an iconoclast; as he himself pointed out, he had never in his life worshipped a holy image. But he was no fanatic. On his accession he had freed or recalled all iconodules condemned to imprisonment or exile – including of course Theodore of Studium, who had immediately renewed his campaign for the restitution of the images; and though Michael remained firm on basic principles he was perfectly prepared to allow his subjects to do as they liked, so long as they refrained from preaching or proselytizing. Outside the capital, things were even easier. Professional icon-painters or fervent image-worshippers could retire to Greece or Asia Minor, and pursue their chosen activities undisturbed.

This moderation won the Emperor general popularity in ecclesiastical circles. His only serious differences with the Church concerned his own remarriage after the death of his beloved first wife Thecla. Among Orthodox theologians second marriages, especially by Emperors, were deplored; more unfortunate still, the lady concerned – Euphrosyne, daughter of Constantine VI – had long been a nun. How Michael managed to obtain her release from her vows we shall never know; but he did so, and this second marriage proved as happy as the first had been – Euphrosyne keeping vigil at her husband's bedside through his last illness and, in October 829, finally closing his eyes in death. He was the first Emperor for half a century to expire, while still a reigning monarch, in his bed; the first, too, to leave a strong and healthy son to succeed him.

At the time of his father's death, Theophilus had already been co-Emperor for eight years, during which time the chroniclers barely mention him. Now, with his assumption of power at the age of twenty-five, he came into his own – and at last revealed himself as being magnificently qualified to take on the responsibilities of Empire. In marked contrast to Michael, he was an intellectual, with the characteristically Byzantine passion for theology; but he had also acquired a thorough military training and was a highly competent leader in the field. Finally, he was an aesthete and a patron of the arts, with a particular love for the culture of Islam. Like his exemplar, the great Caliph Harun al-Rashid, he early adopted the habit of wandering incognito through the streets of Constantinople, listening to the grievances of the people and endlessly investigating prices – especially of food. Once a week, too, he would ride from the Great Palace to the Church of the Virgin at Blachernae – one end of the city to the other – in the course of which he could be approached by any of his subjects with complaints of unfair treatment.

Thus Theophilus became something of a legend in his own lifetime; and yet, for all his love of justice and his comparative accessibility, he had his own firmly-held ideas of Empire. However often he might descend from his pedestal, he knew that it must be of the finest gold. Here again he modelled himself on Harun: in a love of opulence and splendour unequalled in Byzantium since Justinian himself. After only a few months on the throne, he sent a diplomatic mission to Baghdad, led by John the Grammarian. Its ostensible object was to give the Caliph Mamun formal intimation of his succession, but its real purpose was to impress him with his wealth and generosity. John took with him, as presents to Mamun, works of art as sumptuous as any ever wrought by the jewellers and craftsmen of Constantinople. He had also been given 36,000 gold pieces to distribute as he liked, which he is said to have scattered 'like the sand of the sea'. Where all this wealth came from remains a mystery. Michael II had always practised a rigid economy; but he could never have saved a quarter of the amount that his son dispensed with such largesse. Yet Theophilus never ran into debt, and was to leave his treasury a good deal fuller than he found it. Some time towards the end of Michael's reign, therefore, the Empire must suddenly have had access to a new and seemingly inexhaustible source of wealth, possibly the opening of certain gold mines in Armenia; but we shall never know.

With expensive tastes and the means by which to indulge them, the new Emperor initiated a huge construction programme in the capital, understandably concentrating on the Great Palace. Originally established by Constantine at the time of his foundation of the city, it had been largely rebuilt by Justinian; but Theophilus totally transformed it, creating new buildings of marble and porphyry, their walls brilliant with mosaics. To the north-east of the Great Palace, next to the Church of St Sophia, was the Palace of the Magnaura, another of Constantine's foundations; it was here that Theophilus installed his most celebrated mechanical toy. An ambassador received here in audience would be astonished to find the imperial throne overshadowed by a golden plane tree, its branches full of jewelled birds – some of which appeared to have hopped off the tree and on to the throne itself. Around the trunk were lions and gryphons couchant, also of gold. Still greater would be the visitor's wonderment when, at a given signal, the animals would rise up, the lions would roar and all the birds would burst simultaneously into song. Suddenly the chorus would be interrupted by a peal of music from a golden organ, after which there would be silence to permit conversation. The moment the visitor rose to leave, the whole chorus would start up again and continue till he had left the chamber.

It is only fair to add that Theophilus also spent much time and money on the defences of Constantinople. The walls along the shore of the Golden Horn had caused some anxiety during Thomas's siege. An ambitious plan to heighten them along their entire length, initiated by Michael II, was almost wholly carried out by Theophilus. Extravagant and self-indulgent he may have been; but he was well aware of his responsibilities too, and he never shirked them.

By a sad stroke of irony, this most pro-Arab of all the Emperors passed almost the whole of his reign in warfare against Islam. For sixteen years the eastern frontier had been quiet. The Caliphate, beset with internal problems, had been obliged to cease its annual invasions. Then, in 829, hostilities flared up again. In the first campaigns fortune favoured Theophilus. He led a successful expedition into enemy territory in 830, and in the following year took the initiative by invading Muslim-held Cilicia – with such gratifying results that, on returning with his victorious army to Constantinople, he awarded himself a triumph. Alas, the festivities were premature. In the autumn of the same year the imperial army sustained a crushing defeat. Mamun's death in August 833 afforded a few years' respite, while his brother and successor Mutasim encountered the usual difficulties in confirming his authority; but in 837 the war was resumed. Once again Theophilus, who had done much in the interim to strengthen his army, started off well; expeditions into Mesopotamia and western Armenia were successful enough, at least in his eyes, to justify another triumph. But once again he celebrated too soon. In April 838 Mutasim rode out of his palace at Samarra at the head of an army estimated at 50,000, with an equal number of camels and 20,000 mules. On his banner was inscribed the single word AMORIUM – home of the Emperor's family and by now the second city of the Empire – which he made no secret of his intention of reducing to rubble. A week later Theophilus set out from Constantinople determined to block his path; his army met one wing of the Saracen host in pouring rain at Tokat. Before long the Emperor saw that his own opposite wing was in difficulties and led 2,000 men round to reinforce it; unfortunately he omitted to tell his junior commanders what he was doing, and his unexpected disappearance gave rise to a rumour that he had been killed. Panic broke out, followed – as always – by flight; and when the rain stopped Theophilus realized that he and his men were surrounded. Somehow – largely because the bowstrings of the enemy archers had been rendered useless by the rain – they fought their way out; but the battle was lost and the Caliph was already marching on Ankara, which surrendered a few days later without a struggle.

Amorium itself soon followed. Many of the inhabitants took refuge in a large church, in which they were promptly burnt alive by the conquerors; others, captured and led off into slavery, were slaughtered when the army's water supplies threatened to run low, or were left to die of thirst in the desert.

Only forty-two survived the journey back to Samarra; these, after seven years' captivity during which they had steadfastly refused to renounce their religion, were finally offered the choice: conversion or death. All of them chose without hesitation to die, and on 6 March 845 were decapitated on the banks of the Tigris – to go down in the history of the Greek Orthodox Church as the Forty-Two Martyrs of Amorium.

In Constantinople, the disaster was seen as a personal affront to the Emperor and his line. Theophilus himself, now seriously alarmed, immediately sent an impassioned appeal for aid to the Western Emperor Lewis the Pious, proposing a joint offensive. The alliance between the two Empires could, he suggested, be sealed by the marriage of one of his daughters to Lewis's grandson, the future Lewis II. The Byzantine envoys were warmly received at Lewis's court at Ingelheim in June 839, and the talks continued spasmodically for another four years, despite the deaths of both Emperors during that time. Had they proved fruitful, the age of the Crusades might have been brought forward by some two and a half centuries; but they came to nothing. The Caliph made no immediate attempt to follow up his victory until 842, when a huge fleet sailed against Constantinople from the Syrian ports. Victim of a sudden storm, all but seven vessels were smashed to pieces. But Mutasim never heard of this catastrophe. On 5 January he had died in Samarra; and just fifteen days later Theophilus followed him to the grave.

With his known admiration for Arabic art and learning, it is hardly surprising that Theophilus should have shared the iconoclast convictions of his immediate predecessors; but he was no fanatic. Lazarus, the leading icon-painter of the day, was admittedly – after repeated warnings – scourged and branded on the palms of his hands; but after his release he is known to have completed at least two more important commissions, including a new gigantic figure of Christ to replace the one removed by Leo V from the Chalkē; so his injuries cannot have been too severe.

All in all, it seems clear that the Emperor's motives, when he did take punitive measures, were more political than religious. Where he drew the line was at the public profession of the cult of icons in Constantinople. Elsewhere in the Empire, or within the privacy of their own homes in the capital, his subjects might do as they pleased. Perhaps he himself subconsciously understood that the forces of iconoclasm were almost spent. The times, too, were changing. There was a new humanism in the air, a revived awareness of the old classical spirit that stood for reason and clarity, and had no truck with the tortuous, introspective spiritualizings of the Oriental mind. At the same time a naturally artistic people, so long starved of visual beauty, was beginning to crave the old, familiar images that spoke of safer and more confident days.

And when, on 20 January 842, the Emperor Theophilus died of dysentery at thirty-eight, the age of iconoclasm died with him.

The Empress Theodora, who now found herself Regent on behalf of her two-year-old son, made her first concern the eradication of iconoclasm throughout the Empire. She moved with caution: John the Grammarian, a fervent iconoclast, was now firmly ensconced upon the patriarchal throne, and there must have been a few old men who could remember the fiasco of 786, when the last woman to wield the supreme power had had the same purpose in mind and had nearly started a riot. But Theodora was more intelligent than Irene had been; moreover she was lucky to have as her chief advisers three men of quite exceptional ability – her uncle Sergius Nicetiates, her brother Bardas and Theoctistus, Logothete of the Course. The first two shared her views: Theoctistus was emotionally an iconoclast but above all a statesman, and he realized that if the new regime did not take decisive action, the image-worshippers would take the law into their own hands. The four laid their plans with care, and then gave notice that a Council would be summoned early in March 843.

The Council passed off smoothly enough, the only major problem being presented by John the Grammarian, who refused to resign. Only after he had been forcibly deposed did he retire to his villa on the Bosphorus. A monk named Methodius was elected in his place, and the decrees of the Seventh Ecumenical Council – that which had put an end to the first period of iconoclasm in 787 – were confirmed. At Theodora's insistence, however, her dead husband's name was omitted from the lists of those prominent iconoclasts who were now anathematized as heretics. The story, assiduously circulated, that he had repented on his deathbed can safely be discounted; but it solved a potentially embarrassing problem and no serious objections were raised. The victory was won: a victory of clarity over mysticism, of Greek thought over Oriental metaphysics, of West over East. And, as with so many victories, it almost certainly owed its long-term success to the moderation and magnanimity shown by the victors. It was almost a quarter of a century before the first figurative mosaic was unveiled in the Great Church itself – that huge, haunting image of the Virgin and Child enthroned which still gazes impassively down on us today.

Nor, despite many sufferings in the cause of his beloved icons, did Patriarch Methodius show any desire for vengeance. Anathematized the iconoclast leaders might be; they were never ill-treated or imprisoned. Such expressions of indignation as there were came, on the contrary, from the monks of the Studium, whose attacks on the Patriarch when he passed them over for promotion to vacant sees finally obliged him to excommunicate them *en masse*. By this time, we are told, they had even tried to force him to resign by bribing a young woman to accuse him of seduction. At the ensuing inquiry Methodius is said to have proved his innocence by producing for inspection those parts which might have been thought most directly responsible for the alleged offence, explaining the shrivelled remnants of his manhood with a story of how, years before in Rome, a prayer to St Peter for deliverance from lustful thoughts had been answered with distressing efficiency. Not surprisingly, he won his case.

For the defeated image-haters, one small consolation remained. After this time Byzantine art restricted itself to two dimensions. Sculpture was set aside. This should not, perhaps, occasion us too much astonishment: the Second Commandment is clear enough. It is, none the less, a very real cause for regret. If Byzantium had gone on to produce sculptors and woodcarvers as talented as its painters and mosaicists, the world would have been enriched indeed.

Soon after the restoration of the icons, the Logothete Theoctistus succeeded in ousting his two colleagues; and for the next thirteen years he was, with Theodora, the effective ruler of Byzantium. He was that most unusual of combinations, a Patrician and a eunuch; but he was also highly cultured, and devoted much time and effort to the improvement of educational standards in the capital, already far ahead of anything known in the West. His financial policy in particular yielded excellent results: gold continued to flow into the imperial coffers, just as in Theophilus's day – and for no clearer reason. In the military sphere, too, he was unusually successful. His expedition against the Saracens of Crete recovered the island for Byzantium; while in May 853 a Byzantine fleet suddenly appeared off Damietta on the Nile delta, set fire to all the Saracen vessels in harbour, destroyed an arms magazine and returned with scores of prisoners.

Where Theoctistus and the Empress must stand condemned is in their persecution of the Paulicians. This fundamentally harmless Christian sect rejected not only holy images but also the institutions of baptism, marriage and the Eucharist, the sign of the cross, all the Old Testament and quite a lot of the New, and the entire hierarchy of the Church. A decree was now promulgated, calling on them to renounce their errors on pain of death; and a vast military expedition put the order into effect. The result was a massacre: 100,000 are reported to have perished – by hanging, drowning, the sword, even by crucifixion. All their property and lands were confiscated by the State. Those who escaped sought refuge across the imperial frontier with Omar ibn Abdullah, the Emir of Malatya, and his fellow Saracens. Left to themselves, these devout, disciplined men and women would have constituted a formidable bulwark against Saracen attacks; instead, they were driven into the arms of the Caliphate.

Michael III, meanwhile, was growing up, perhaps rather too fast. In 855 at the age of fifteen he took a mistress; but his mother forced him to cast her aside in favour of one Eudocia Decapolitana, in whom he took no interest whatever. He obeyed unquestioningly; but his suppressed resentment may well have made him sympathetic to the conspiracy which was soon to bring about Theodora's downfall. The Empress's brother, Bardas, had never forgiven Theoctistus for out-manoeuvring him in 843; and for twelve years he had waited for his chance. With the assistance of the High Chamberlain Damianus he easily persuaded Michael that his mother and Theoctistus were determined to cling to power, and that any attempt to assert himself might be fatal. Once assured of Michael's support, Bardas acted quickly. On 20 November 855 the Logothete was walking through the palace when he was set upon by Bardas and a group of his fellow-officers. Quickly overpowered, he was hustled to the Skyla – a small antechamber which led directly into the Hippodrome. It was Michael himself who gave the order to kill him. Dragging him out from under a chair, the guards held him fast while their captain ran him through.

With the death of Theoctistus, Theodora's power was ended; and in March 856 her son was proclaimed sole Emperor, in which capacity he was to reign for the next eleven years. But he was weak and irresponsible, and the effective power soon passed into the hands of his uncle Bardas, who proved more capable even than his predecessor, stamping his imprint indelibly on what was soon to become a golden age of Byzantium. The first of his many victories was won over Omar ibn Abdullah, Emir of Malatya, whose forces were now further strengthened by detachments of Paulician refugees. In a desperate battle near the Halys river, Omar himself was killed, as were almost all his men. The Emperor – who was present throughout – had not long returned to the capital before news reached him of yet another decisive victory – this time over the Saracen Governor of Armenia, who had also fallen in the fray. The disgrace of Amorium had been avenged. The tide was beginning to turn. No longer were the Byzantines fighting a defensive war; henceforth, they were to be increasingly on the attack. There was a new confidence in the air.

I I
Of Patriarchs and Plots

The wise old Patriarch Methodius had been succeeded in 847 by Ignatius, one of the three castrated sons of the deposed Emperor Michael I. Ignatius had other assets besides his imperial blood. He had never wavered in his support for the holy images, and had made his monastery on the island of Terebinthos in the Marmara a popular refuge for all who shared his views. But where Methodius had been moderate and conciliatory, Ignatius was a blinkered bigot who did not even wait for the end of his own consecration before ordering Gregory Asbestas, Archbishop of Syracuse – a moderate and therefore his arch-enemy – out of the church. Six years later he had him deposed and excommunicated.

Gregory appealed to two successive Popes for reinstatement; but Ignatius had always upheld papal supremacy and the Vatican had no wish to antagonize him. By now the former moderates were determined somehow to get rid of the Patriarch; and they found a more effective leader than Gregory could ever have been. His name was Photius. He too was an aristocrat, tenuously connected to the Emperor by marriage. He was also the most learned scholar of his day, capable of running rings round Ignatius, whose mind was too narrow to encompass any but the simplest doctrines. He was, however, not a churchman. He had chosen instead a career in the imperial chancery, and it was inevitable that when Bardas came to power Photius should become his closest friend and counsellor. To Patriarch Ignatius, few developments could have been more unwelcome. At this point Bardas had had the misfortune to fall in love with his own daughter-in-law, for whom he had abandoned his wife; the ensuing scandal was the talk of Constantinople. Ignatius excommunicated him and, on the Feast of the Epiphany 858, refused him the Sacrament. From that moment on, Bardas was waiting for his revenge. The opportunity came when the Emperor finally decided to send his mother, together with his unmarried sisters, to a convent. When, however, he called upon Ignatius to shave their heads, he met with a point-blank refusal. Bardas easily persuaded him that this could only mean that Patriarch and Empress were allied against him. Ignatius was put under arrest and banished, without trial, to his monastery.

As to his successor, Photius was the obvious candidate. Two obstacles, however, remained to be overcome. The first was that he was a layman; but that problem was easily solved. On 20 December he was tonsured; on the 21st he was ordained lector; on the 22nd, subdeacon, on the 23rd, deacon; on the 24th, priest; and on Christmas Day he was consecrated bishop by his friend Gregory Asbestas. His enthronement as Patriarch followed at once. The second obstacle was more serious. No amount of pressure would induce Ignatius to resign. Photius could occupy the patriarchal throne *de facto*; he could not hope to do so *de jure*, unless or until Ignatius changed his mind.

Meanwhile he wrote to the Pope, informing him of his elevation. The letter itself was a model of tactful diplomacy; but it was accompanied by another, ostensibly from the Emperor himself, in which Ignatius was said to have neglected his flock and to have been canonically deposed – both of which claims the Pope rightly suspected of being untrue. He was certainly not prepared to recognize Photius without further investigation. In his reply he proposed a council of inquiry, to be held the following year in Constantinople, to which he would send two commissioners who would report back personally to him. He also dropped a gentle reminder about the Sicilian and Calabrian bishoprics, the vicariate of Thessalonica and other Balkan dioceses which had been removed by Leo III from the jurisdiction of Rome and placed under that of Constantinople; was it not time that they were returned to papal control? There was naturally no overt suggestion of a *quid pro quo*; but the implication was clear enough.

In the high summer of the year 860, the people of Constantinople underwent as terrifying an experience as any of them could remember. Suddenly on the afternoon of 18 June, a fleet of some 200 ships from the Black Sea appeared at the mouth of the Bosphorus and made its way towards the city, plundering the monasteries that lined the banks, burning and pillaging every village it passed. Some of the vessels continued into the Marmara to ravage the Princes' Islands; the majority cast anchor at the entrance to the Golden Horn. It was the Byzantines' first real confrontation with the Russians. The leaders were probably not Slavs at all but Norsemen – representing that huge migration from Scandinavia which had begun towards the end of the eighth century. In about 830 they had established a khaganate around the upper Volga; a quarter of a century later they were using that mighty river, together with the Dnieper and the Don, to carry their longships southward against the great trading cities of the Black Sea. With them came their Slav subjects, by whom they were soon to be absorbed.

The situation was made more serious still by the absence in Asia of the Emperor, his commander-in-chief and the bulk of his army. The Prefect Oryphas, who had been left in command of the capital, sent messengers after them and Michael returned at once; but the raiders had already sailed back up the Bosphorus into the Black Sea. Why did they leave so soon? Photius, who preached two sermons on the raid, ascribes the deliverance to the miraculous robe of the Virgin, which was carried shoulder-high around the walls and provoked their immediate retreat. More probably the raiders, finding the city impregnable and having exhausted the possibilities of extramural plunder, simply decided to call it a day.

In any event, Photius emerged from the incident with increased prestige. Ignatius was less fortunate. First he had been removed to Hieria, where he was lodged in a goat-shed. Sent back to Constantinople, he was next thrown into a prison where he was beaten and two of his teeth were knocked out. He was then transferred to Lesbos, whence six months later he was allowed to return to his monastery. Now it was the turn of the Russians. Those who had continued into the Marmara fell on Terebinthos, plundering the monastic buildings and killing no fewer than twenty-two monks. Ignatius himself barely escaped with his life. This last catastrophe was widely interpreted as a further sign of divine displeasure; but the stubborn old eunuch held firm. He would bide his time – and would put his faith in Pope Nicholas, whose emissaries were expected the following spring.

The papal commissioners, Zachary of Anagni and Rodoald of Porto, reached Constantinople in April 861 and immediately found themselves under formidable pressure from Photius: swept up into a ceaseless round of Church ceremonies, banquets and entertainments of every kind, while the Patriarch himself alternately dazzled them with his erudition and captivated them with his charm. Their audiences with the Emperor, on the other hand, were less pleasant, he more than once hinting that their return home depended entirely on his benevolence. Thus, by a judicious combination of cajolery and veiled threats, it was made clear to the commissioners which side they should support. They were not allowed even a glimpse of Ignatius until he was led into the church to answer the charges. Then, in a simple monk's habit, he was obliged to listen while seventy-two witnesses testified that his former appointment was due to the Empress Theodora rather than to any canonical election. His deposition was confirmed by a formal document at the foot of which, prominent among the signatories, were the names of Zachary of Anagni and Rodoald of Porto.

Pope Nicholas was furious, and left the unfortunate prelates in no doubt of his displeasure. They had betrayed the interests of the entire Church, obtaining not a single concession in return. Had the wretched envoys even mentioned the Illyrian bishoprics in their conversations with Photius? They had not. At this point there arrived in Rome a certain Theognostus, the most vocal champion of the deposed Patriarch; and he now described in detail the unfairness of the inquiry, the perfidy of the witnesses, the iniquity of Photius, the loyalty of Ignatius to Rome and the tribulations he had been called upon to endure. In their efforts to force him into an abdication he had been arrested once again, subjected to further repeated beatings, starved for a fortnight and incarcerated in the Church of the Holy Apostles, where he had been stretched across the desecrated sarcophagus of the arch-iconoclast Constantine V, with heavy stones tied to his ankles. Finally, when he was barely conscious, a pen had been thrust into his hand and guided to form a signature, above which Photius had himself written an act of abdication. Despite the obvious wild exaggerations, the Pope hesitated no longer. A synod, meeting at the Lateran in April 863, divested Photius of all ecclesiastical status and restored Ignatius, and all who had lost office in his cause, to their former positions.

The Emperor and his Patriarch were no doubt intensely annoyed at the Pope's obduracy, but Michael in particular was in a bullish mood. The year 863 had proved, as we have seen, something of an *annus mirabilis* for Byzantine arms; while in the field of religion there had been developments compared with which the whole Photian dispute must have seemed insignificant indeed. At the very height of the quarrel between Nicholas and Photius envoys arrived in Constantinople from Rostislav, Prince of Moravia. Their master, they explained, wished with all his subjects to embrace Christianity, but such Christian teachers as they had previously heard had all expounded contradictory doctrines. Would the Emperor send trustworthy missionaries from whom the truth could be learned?

So, at least, runs the legend. There was indeed a Moravian mission; but mass conversions almost invariably have political undertones, and this was no exception. Early in 862, the Frankish King Lewis concluded a treaty of alliance with the Bulgar Khan Boris and Rostislav had found himself in desperate need of an ally: the main object of his mission was to alert the Emperor to the danger and to persuade him to take up arms against his Bulgar neighbours. His proposed adoption of Orthodox Christianity was merely an additional inducement, particularly since it seemed likely that Boris might at any moment announce a mass conversion of his own people, leading them almost certainly into the Roman fold.

To Photius, here was an opportunity not only of extending the influence of Orthodoxy to the far north-west but – still more satisfactory – of striking a major blow at the Papacy. He had, moreover, a perfect candidate for the job: a monk from Thessalonica who was to adopt the Slavonic name of Cyril. A brilliant scholar with a remarkable flair for languages, he had pursued his studies under Photius himself, who had made him his librarian. Subsequently he had undertaken a mission to the Khazars, preaching to them in their own tongue and making a number of conversions.

Where military intervention was concerned, the Emperor Michael was initially unenthusiastic, reluctant to interrupt spectacular progress on the eastern front in favour of a more problematical campaign in the west. But to allow Lewis a free hand in the Balkans would be to invite disaster. Several regiments were summoned back to Constantinople, and the Emperor and his army advanced across the frontier while the fleet made ready for war. In the summer of 863 it sailed up the Bosphorus into the Black Sea and dropped anchor off the Bulgarian coast. The timing was perfect. The Bulgar forces were away in the north, while the south was in the grip of the most severe famine of the century. Boris immediately sent envoys to Michael to ask for terms. They proved simple enough: the Khan must renounce the Frankish alliance and adopt Christianity according to the Orthodox rite. He agreed with almost unseemly haste. In September 865 he travelled to Constantinople, where he was baptized by the Patriarch and took the name of Michael, the Emperor himself standing sponsor.

Meanwhile, in the spring of 864, Cyril had set off on his Moravian mission, accompanied by his brother Methodius. They remained in Moravia for over three years. According to an ancient tradition, Cyril now invented a new alphabet with which to transcribe the hitherto unwritten Slavonic speech, and then proceeded to translate the Bible and parts of the liturgy. The language he chose, however, was Macedonian Slavonic; the Moravians could not have understood a word of it. It comes as no surprise therefore to learn that the Moravian experiment was to have extremely disappointing results; but it remains true that by providing the Slav peoples with an alphabet adapted to the phonetic peculiarities of their various tongues, Cyril and Methodius laid the foundations for their literary development; and it is above all for this that they are revered today.

While the two scholar-saints laboured in their Moravian vineyard, the Bulgar Khan was growing dangerously restive. Suddenly his Kingdom was overrun with Greek and Armenian priests, at loggerheads with each other over abstruse points of doctrine incomprehensible to his subjects, most of whom had been horrified to discover that they were expected not only to take instruction from these discordant strangers but to feed and lodge them as well. And there was something else. The magnificent ceremony of his own baptism in St Sophia had impressed him deeply, and he now wished to have similar ceremonies performed among – and by – his own people. He had accordingly written to Photius requesting the appointment of a Bulgarian Patriarch.

It was at this point that Photius made perhaps the worst mistake of his life. He not only refused Boris's request but dismissed it out of hand. The Khan had also listed various small points of Orthodox custom which conflicted with local traditions, suggesting that, if these traditions could be permitted to continue, much of the popular resistance to the new faith might be overcome; some of his proposals Photius rejected, the rest he simply ignored. The Khan was furious. He was happy to be the Emperor's godson, but he was not his vassal. Fully aware of the possibility of playing off Patriarch against Pope, in the summer of 866 he sent a delegation to Nicholas with a list of all the points that Photius had dismissed, adding a number of new ones and requesting the Pope's views on each.

Nicholas saw his chance. At once he dispatched two more bishops to the Bulgarian court with meticulous answers to every one of the 106 items in Boris's questionnaire, making all possible concessions permitted by canon law and, for those that could not be granted, explaining the reasons for his refusal. Trousers, he agreed, could certainly be worn, by men and women alike; turbans too, excepting only in church. When the Byzantines maintained that it was unlawful to wash on Wednesdays and Fridays, they were talking nonsense; nor was there any cause to abstain from milk or cheese during Lent. All pagan superstitions on the other hand were forbidden, as was the Greek practice of divination by the random opening of the Bible. Bigamy, too, was out.

The Bulgars were disappointed about the bigamy, but on the whole more than satisfied. Boris cheerfully swore perpetual allegiance to St Peter and, with every sign of relief, expelled all Orthodox missionaries from his Kingdom. Their Catholic counterparts were not slow in coming.

Michael III was not entirely without qualities: by his early twenties he was already a seasoned campaigner, and his physical courage in the field was never in question. What he lacked was will. Content to leave the responsibilities of government to others, he was unable to check his own moral decline which, in the last five years of his life, finally reduced him to a level of degradation that fully earned him his later sobriquet of 'the Sot'.

Fortunately there were statesmen of exceptional ability ready to take up the reins of power and to govern in his name: first, in the days of his mother's Regency, the eunuch Theoctistus; later her brother Bardas. In April 862, on the Sunday after Easter, Bardas was created Caesar. By this time Michael's chances of legitimate progeny were negligible. Bardas was universally accepted as the next Emperor, and nobody believed that his succession could be long delayed. Already he was *basileus* in all but name, and an excellent one. The ten years of his government saw a string of victories over the Saracens in the east and the conversion of the Bulgars, with major advances in the long-drawn-out struggle of the Byzantine Church for independence from Rome; he himself shared the interest of his brother-in-law Theophilus in the administration of justice, and that of Theoctistus in his encouragement of learning. The old University of Constantinople had long been allowed to decline until, during the days of the first iconoclasts, it had collapsed completely. Bardas revived it, establishing it this time in the Palace of the Magnaura under the direction of Leo the Philosopher – or, as he is sometimes called, Leo the Mathematician.

With Photius and Cyril, Leo was one of the three greatest scholars of his time. As a young man he had taught philosophy and mathematics in Constantinople; but he had become famous only after one of his pupils, taken off to Baghdad, had so impressed the Caliph Mamun that the latter had inquired who his master had been. Mamun, himself an intellectual, had then written to the Emperor, offering 2,000 pounds of gold and a treaty of eternal peace in return for the loan of Leo for a few months; but Theophilus had preferred to set him up in the capital, where he gave regular lectures. Under his direction at the Magnaura, Cyril had briefly occupied the chair of philosophy, while others of his pupils held those of geometry, astronomy and philology. There was no chair of religious studies; the university concerned itself solely with secular learning – which accounted for the hostility with which it was viewed by Ignatius and his followers.

Among Michael's many unattractive habits was that of surrounding himself with favourites and cronies who would accompany him in wild roisterings through the capital. One of these men was a rough and uneducated Armenian peasant named Basil. His family, like so many of their countrymen, had been settled in Thrace; but they had subsequently been taken prisoner by Krum and had been transported beyond the Danube to an area known as 'Macedonia' – probably because of the number of Macedonians who had suffered a similar fate. Here Basil had spent much of his childhood, and it is as 'the Macedonian' that he and his dynasty are most misleadingly known, despite the fact that he possessed not a drop of true Macedonian blood, spoke Armenian as his first language and Greek only with a heavy Armenian accent. Entirely illiterate, he could boast only two obvious assets: herculean physical strength and a remarkable way with horses. Indeed, it was his ability to control

Ravenna: two lunettes in the Mausoleum of Galla Placidia, fifth century

above: St Laurence the Martyr

below: Apostles in Veneration

The Archangel Gabriel, *c.* 861, mosaic on arch of
north bema, St Sophia, Istanbul

The Emperor Alexander (912-13):
contemporary mosaic, north gallery, St Sophia, Istanbul

Illuminations from the Chronicle of Manasses. *c.* 1345

above: Basil II at Cimbalongus, 1014

below: Blinded Bulgar prisoners return to King Samuel, who dies of sorrow

The First Crusade: the army of Peter the Hermit is massacred by the Seljuk Turks
(Paris, Bibliothèque Nationale)

The Church of St Saviour in Chora (Kariye Camii), Istanbul
the Anastasis (The Harrowing of Hell), apse fresco in the south *parecclesion*

The siege of Constantinople, 1453:
on the left, the Sultan's ships are being rolled down to the Golden Horn

Mehmet II, by Gentile Bellini
(London, National Gallery)

one of the Emperor's high-spirited stallions that had induced Michael to take him into his service.

Thenceforth Basil's promotion was swift. Appointed High Chamberlain, he soon became more Michael's friend than his servant. Thenceforth Emperor and chamberlain lived together on terms of close intimacy; suggestions of a homosexual relationship seem improbable only because of the unusual arrangements now made by Michael. In order to be able to introduce his long-time mistress Eudocia into the palace without provoking a scandal, he persuaded Basil to marry her. Does this mean that the baby boy, Leo, to whom she gave birth on 19 September 866 was not Basil's child but Michael's? If so, what we call the Macedonian dynasty was in fact simply a continuation of the Amorian; we shall never know.

As Basil's influence increased, so too did the mutual hostility between himself and Bardas. The Caesar had at first believed that Michael trusted him implicitly with the government of the Empire, and that, as long as his pleasures were not interrupted, he would continue to do so. But the speed with which Basil was tightening his hold soon caused him to revise his opinion. And Basil's ambition was still far from satisfied. By now his eyes were fixed on the throne. And so – just as Bardas had poisoned Michael's mind against Theoctistus – Basil began insidiously to arouse his suspicions of his uncle.

Bardas was now preparing a major expedition against the island of Crete, which, after its brief recovery by Theoctistus, was once more in Muslim hands. Some time during the winter of 865, however, word reached him of a plot against his life, in which both Michael and Basil appeared to be involved. He seems to have faced his nephew squarely with his suspicions, for on 25 March 866 we find Emperor and chamberlain putting their signatures – in Basil's case a simple cross – to a formal declaration swearing that they had no hostile intentions towards him. So solemn was this oath – it is said to have been signed in the blood of Jesus Christ, a small and diminishing quantity of which was kept among the most precious of the sacred relics in St Sophia – that the Caesar relented; and he was in his accustomed place beside the Emperor when the expedition left Constantinople soon after Easter.

On the day of the embarkation at Miletus, Bardas rode to the imperial pavilion, where he seated himself next to his nephew and listened with every show of attention while one of the Logothetes read out the morning report. When this was over, out of the corner of his eye, he saw the chamberlain make a surreptitious signal. His hand flew to his sword; but it was too late. With one tremendous blow Basil struck him to the ground, while other conspirators rushed forward to finish him off. The Emperor himself made no move; but there can be no doubt that he was aware of Basil's intention. He wrote at once to Photius informing him that Bardas had been found guilty of high treason and summarily executed. A few days later the army was back in Constantinople. The Cretan expedition was over before it had begun.

On Whit Sunday, 866, worshippers at the Church of St Sophia were intrigued to notice two similar thrones, set side by side. They were still more surprised when the Emperor arrived and instead of moving directly to his seat climbed to the top level of the ambo, the great three-decker pulpit of polychrome marble. Basil, in his robes of office, then mounted to the middle level, while one of the secretaries took his place on the lowest and began to read in the Emperor's name: 'It is my will that Basil, the High Chamberlain, who is loyal to me, who has delivered me from my enemy and who holds me in great affection, should be the guardian and manager of my Empire and should be proclaimed by all as *basileus*.'

Basil's ambition had been fulfilled. The transition from stable-boy to Emperor had taken him just nine years.

The shared monarchy, by contrast, was to last only sixteen months – principally occupied by religious affairs. As the western missionaries poured into Bulgaria in ever greater numbers, Photius realized that he had driven Boris into the Roman camp. To make matters worse these missionaries were spreading two dangerous heresies. One of these – that Constantinople was not the senior Patriarchate but the most recent and therefore the least venerable of the five – was nothing short of an insult. The other, to serious theologians like Photius, was still worse: a doctrine which Pope Nicholas had now endorsed for the first time and which was to become the cornerstone of the whole controversy between the Eastern and the Western Churches: that of the Double Procession of the Holy Ghost.

In the early days of Christian belief, the Third Person of the Trinity was held to proceed directly from God the Father. Then, towards the end of the sixth century, the fatal word *Filioque* – 'and the Son' – began to appear; and soon after 800, when it became the practice to recite the Nicene Creed during the course of the Mass, the formula 'that proceedeth from the Father and the Son' was generally adopted in the West. To the Eastern Church, on the other hand, it remained the vilest heresy; and the knowledge that accredited papal representatives were now disseminating this poison among the Bulgars was more than the Patriarch could bear. He resolved therefore to call a General Council. It would anathematize the Double Procession. It would snatch back the poor misguided Bulgars from the jaws of hell. Finally and most dramatically, it would depose the Pope.

But would this last be more than an empty gesture? Photius believed that it would. Nicholas was now almost as unpopular in the West as he was in Byzantium. By refusing to allow King Lothair II of Lorraine to divorce his wife and marry his mistress, he had dangerously antagonized not only Lothair himself but his elder brother, the Western Emperor Lewis II. Emissaries sped to Lewis's court, and an understanding was quickly reached. The General Council would declare Pope Nicholas deposed, and Lewis would send a military force to Rome to remove him physically. In return, the Byzantine government would recognize its ally as Emperor of the Franks. This was no small concession. Admittedly such recognition had been accorded to Lewis's great-grandfather in 812; but circumstances had been very different, and Charles had paid dearly for the privilege. Lewis, moreover, although he might call himself Emperor, was in fact only a relatively insignificant princeling in Italy; was he really to be raised to the same level as God's Vice-Gerent on Earth, the Elect of Heaven, Equal of the Apostles? Michael or Basil, whose personal supremacy was at stake, might have been expected to protest, but Photius did his work well; neither of them, so far as is known, breathed a word in opposition. They did, however, preside jointly at the Council, which performed just as the Patriarch had intended that it should. Heresies were condemned, the Pope was deposed and, for good measure, anathematized. Lewis and his wife Engelbertha were acclaimed in their most sonorous imperial titles. Photius was jubilant: this was his finest moment, the summit of his career.

But when Michael III and Basil I took their places side by side to inaugurate the Council of 869, few of those present could have guessed the true state of relations between them. Michael had raised his friend to the throne because he had no delusions about his own incapacity; but as he sank ever lower into dissipation, he became less an embarrassment than a serious liability. Bardas had been able to control him; but for Basil, not unnaturally, Michael never had the same respect; and he bitterly resented any attempt on the part of his co-Emperor to remonstrate with him. Once again, Basil the Macedonian made up his mind to act.

On 24 September 867, the two Emperors and Eudocia were dining together in the Palace of St Mamas. Towards the end of the meal Basil made an excuse to leave the room and hurried to Michael's chamber, where he bent back the bolts of the door in such a way that it could not be locked. He then returned to the table until his colleague, now as usual hopelessly drunk, staggered off to bed and immediately fell into a deep alcoholic slumber. Byzantine Emperors never slept alone; the official sharing the imperial bedchamber was the Patrician Basiliscianus, one of Michael's old drinking companions. He had noticed the condition of the bolt, and was still lying anxiously awake when he heard footsteps: there stood Basil, with eight of his friends. Basiliscianus was hurled aside and was seriously wounded by a sword-thrust as he fell to the floor. One of the conspirators approached the sleeping Emperor, but apparently had not the courage to kill him outright; it was left to Basil's cousin Asylaion to administer the *coup de grâce*.

Leaving Michael dying in a pool of his own blood, the assassins hurried down to the Golden Horn and rowed across to the Great Palace. One of the guards was expecting them, and the doors were immediately opened. The following morning, Basil's first act was to install Eudocia – his wife and his victim's mistress – in the imperial apartments. The news of the murder seems to have been received with little regret outside Michael's immediate family; but one of the court officials, sent the following morning to St Mamas to arrange for the funeral, found the horribly mutilated body wrapped in a horse-cloth, and the Empress Theodora with her daughters – all now released from their monastery – weeping uncontrollably over her son. He was buried with the minimum of ceremony at Chrysopolis, on the Asiatic shore.

The Macedonian and the Sage

Relieved at last of the dead weight of his co-ruler, Basil lost no time in setting the Empire on a radically different course. Michael's body was hardly cold before Photius was dismissed from the Patriarchate. He had not raised a finger in condemnation of the murder of Caesar Bardas, nor of the obscene cavortings of the pitiable Emperor – whom, it was rumoured, he had once challenged to a drinking-bout and had beaten by sixty cups to fifty; and many people had been shocked by his willingness to grant Lewis II imperial recognition in return for ephemeral advantage. The Patriarch's humiliation was further intensified by the reinstatement two months later of his despised old adversary Ignatius.

Why the volte-face? Simply because for Basil there were issues more important than choice of Patriarch; and foremost among these was the recovery of the Empire's western provinces. For the first time, effectively since Justinian, here was an Emperor who had thought long and hard about reconquest and was determined to achieve it. This could, however, be done only with papal support, and for such support the reinstatement of Ignatius was a small price to pay.

Whether or not Pope Nicholas would have been prepared to accept this sudden change of heart we cannot tell; he died on 13 November 867. His successor Hadrian II shared his views, but was of a less tempestuous character, willingly accepting Basil's invitation to send delegates to yet another Council, by which the Photian schism would be healed at last. But when this Council held its opening session at the beginning of October 869, the papal delegates found Basil neither contrite nor submissive. Their assumption that they would preside was firmly corrected; the *basileus* himself, or his representative, would take the chair. Later, when the Council came to discuss the fate of Photius, Basil insisted that the former Patriarch be permitted to speak in his own defence. In fact, Photius wisely refused to say a word, even when sentence of anathema was pronounced upon him; but this hardly mattered. For Basil, two important points of principle had been made: first, that Byzantine, not Roman, legal procedure had been complied with in every detail, leaving the accused no grounds on which to appeal; second, that he himself, not the papal legates, had delivered the verdict.

Shortly before the Council closed in February 870, two separate embassies arrived in Constantinople within a few days of each other. The first was from Boris of Bulgaria. Converting his people to Christianity was proving a good deal more troublesome than he had imagined. In the four years since his baptism he had been obliged to put down a rebellion that had almost cost him his throne; he had quarrelled with Byzantium; and it was gradually becoming clear to him that his honeymoon with Rome was likewise over: the Roman missionaries were every bit as unpopular as their Orthodox predecessors. And he had still not been allowed his Patriarch. His envoys had one question only to ask the Council, but that question could be guaranteed to sow maximum dissension among the delegates: if he were to have no Patriarch of his own, to which see did Bulgaria belong, Constantinople or Rome? Basil wisely referred the question to the theoretically neutral representatives of the other three Patriarchates: Alexandria, Antioch and Jerusalem. No one had any doubt what the answer would be. The papal legates, in a minority of two, protested with vehemence; but nobody took any notice. Furious, they took ship for Rome; and their tempers could hardly have been improved when Dalmatian pirates stripped them of all that they possessed and held them captive for nine months.

And so Bulgaria returned to the Orthodox fold, in which it still remains; and Boris had no difficulty in finally getting what he wanted. On 4 March, Ignatius consecrated a Bulgarian archbishop and several bishops. Technically subject to Constantinople, in effect they were autonomous. Basil gave his full approval; he was conscious, however, of the price he had had to pay: his recent *rapprochement* with Rome. Photius had been sacrificed in vain.

The second embassy to arrive on the Bosphorus that February carried a letter from Lewis II. The Emperor of the West had been insulted. Two years before, while he was besieging Muslim-held Bari, Basil had offered him the services of the Byzantine navy. Lewis had accepted, but the fleet had arrived only after the Franks had gone into their winter quarters, and the Byzantine admiral Nicetas had been horrified to find his new allies not only far fewer than he had been led to expect but roaring drunk into the bargain. He had immediately sought out the Emperor, whom he had addressed as *King* of the Franks. A furious argument had ensued, after which Nicetas had returned to Constantinople, the Frankish envoys following. They left Basil in no doubt of their master's wrath.

Thus, within a matter of weeks, Basil had antagonized both his prospective allies. Where the Pope was concerned, the recovery of Bulgaria had been a worthwhile *quid pro quo*; but the quarrel with Lewis brought no compensating advantage. Since the Franks were also rivals for the possession of south Italy, their relations might easily have deteriorated still further; soon afterwards, however, Lewis's strength began to fail and he retired to the north, where in 875 he died near Brescia, leaving no male heir.

While the Byzantine fleet was occupied – or, more accurately, unoccupied – in the Adriatic, the bulk of the army was engaged in the East. Here the Empire was fighting not just the Saracens but also the Paulicians, now spreading westward across Asia Minor. In two whirlwind campaigns Basil and his brother-in-law Christopher drove them back into the Anatolian heartland; they then turned their attention to the Saracens, for the next decade maintaining a continual pressure which won them several important strongholds in the Euphrates Valley. In Western Europe, Byzantine successes were on much the same scale. True, Basil failed in his attempts to drive the Saracens from Crete and Sicily, whose last Christian stronghold, Syracuse, was to fall in 878; but he was able to expel them from the Dalmatian coast, and in 873 established his suzerainty over Lombard Benevento. The same year saw the recovery of Otranto, and 876 that of Bari. This made possible a major offensive, as a result of which virtually the whole of south Italy was to be restored to Byzantine authority before the end of the century.

Missionary work too went on apace. One by one the Slav tribes of the Balkans embraced the Christian faith; and although Roman influence was to prevail in Croatia, the northern part of the Dalmatian coast and Moravia – where Cyril and Methodius had had to admit defeat – in Serbia, Macedonia and Greece the Orthodox rule and the supremacy of Constantinople were alike enthusiastically adopted. Paradoxically, it was precisely these triumphs which led to the return of Photius from exile. During his seven-year banishment the sudden expansion of the Orthodox faith had created huge problems with which the blundering old Ignatius was totally unfitted to deal. Gradually more and more self-confessed Photians were promoted to key positions; and in 874 or 875 their leader himself was recalled to the capital, given charge of the University of the Magnaura and entrusted with the education of the Emperor's sons. When Ignatius finally expired in 877 at the age of eighty, it was Photius who for the second time assumed the patriarchal throne and who three years later received official recognition from Pope John VIII.

There seems little doubt that – at least during the final decade of his reign – Basil began to see himself as another Justinian. He was reconquering Italy; he was revising the law; and he had also embarked on a vast building programme. There had been few important new constructions under the ninth-century iconoclasts: no new churches had been built, and many of the older ones had been culpably neglected. A number were in urgent need of repair – including St Sophia itself, which had been damaged in the earthquake of 9 January 869 and was now in imminent danger of collapse. Basil saved it in the nick of time. The old Church of the Holy Apostles was in a still sorrier state. Basil repaired it from top to bottom. Many other, humbler shrines were restored and in several cases re-roofed, the old wooden roofs – always a dangerous fire risk – being replaced by new ones of stone. But the Emperor's greatest architectural triumph was his new church, which was always called just that: the Nea. It stood within the precincts of the Great Palace, and no expense was spared on either its construction or its decoration. If Basil was the Justinian of his day, this was his St Sophia. Its cluster of gilded domes could be seen from all over the city and from far out at sea. Few Emperors did more to ensure that Constantinople remained the most opulent city in the world. It is a sad irony that, in the whole of that city, there now survives of Basil's work not one stone resting on another.

By the high summer of 879, the Emperor could look back on twelve years of quite remarkable success. His armed forces were stronger than they had ever been. The Saracens were in retreat. The Paulicians had been crushed. The Bulgars and the Serbs had been converted, and had entered the Orthodox fold. The Photian schism was over, having effectively proved to the Pope that Byzantium was not to be trifled with. The revision of the laws was well under way. The principal buildings of the capital had been restored and embellished, while his own great church, the Nea, rose tall and triumphant, a continuing reminder to the world of the majesty and magnificence of its founder. In little over a decade the illiterate Armenian peasant, who had reached the throne by way of two of the vilest murders that even Byzantium could recall, had proved himself the greatest Emperor since Justinian.

But Justinian had had no son to succeed him; Basil, truthfully or not, could claim four. For the three younger ones he cared little – his second, Leo, he loathed – but his eldest son, Constantine, the only child of his first wife, Maria, was the one human being, perhaps, whom he ever really loved. Outstandingly handsome, Constantine had been little more than a boy when he had first accompanied his father into battle. In 869 he had been crowned co-Emperor and had he married the daughter of Lewis II, would have united both Eastern and Western Empires under his sway. He showed every prospect of proving himself, in the fullness of time, as great a ruler as his father.

And then, suddenly, at the beginning of September 879, he was dead. The circumstances of his death are unknown, but Basil never recovered from the blow. He began to withdraw further and further into himself, lapsing into deep depressions and even bouts of insanity. At such times, one man only could hope to control him: Photius, who would humour the distracted Emperor by arranging ever more elaborate Masses for the soul of Constantine, whom he ultimately went so far as to canonize. All this he did for one reason: to prevent the succession of Basil's second son and heir apparent, Leo. We do not know why this should be: the boy was quick-tempered and perhaps over-fond of women, but he promised to make a fine *basileus*. However that may be, Photius did all he could to work on Basil's known dislike of his son – and to considerable effect.

When Leo was sixteen he had been married off against his will to an ill-favoured girl of asphyxiating piety named Theophano; he had, however, steadfastly refused to give up his first love, Zoe Zautsina. Theophano had complained to Basil, who had flown into a fury and flogged his son with his own hands, Zoe being banished from the capital and married off in her turn. Meanwhile the Patriarch continued his whispering campaign. Given his mental state, the old Emperor proved all too easily persuaded. Only a year later, Leo was arrested and imprisoned without trial, remaining a captive for three months.

In these last tormented years, Basil found some slight consolation in the chase; and it was while hunting in the summer of 886 that he met his end. Most of the chroniclers record that he died as a result of a hunting accident, and two give us a detailed account; but the story they tell is, at least, improbable. According to them Basil was riding alone when he surprised a huge stag drinking at a stream. It suddenly turned and charged him, somehow contriving to hook its antlers under his belt and pull him from his saddle. It then galloped off into the forest, dragging the helpless Emperor with it. The rest of the party knew nothing until they saw their master's riderless horse approaching; his bodyguard then pursued and finally caught up with the stag, closing in until one of them was able to cut Basil free with his sword. The Emperor fell senseless to the ground. On recovering consciousness he commanded that the distance should be measured from the place where the accident had occurred, later calculated to be sixteen miles. Only then would he allow himself to be carried back to the palace. After lingering nine days in agony, he died on 29 August. He was seventy-four.

What are we to make of this farrago? Why, first of all, was a mentally disturbed Emperor in his middle seventies left completely unattended? How did he allow such an accident to occur? Why did he not himself slash through his belt? Why did the stag not free itself from its burden before making its escape? And, having failed to do so, could it really have dragged a man famous for his colossal physique sixteen miles across rough forest country? All this sounds still more suspicious when we read that the rescue party was led by Stylian Zautses, father of young Leo's mistress.

And so we come to the last and most important question of all: was Basil the Macedonian murdered by Stylian – presumably with the knowledge and approval of Leo? Motives, certainly, would not have been lacking. The old man was increasingly unbalanced. Once already he had thrown Leo into prison; he was perfectly capable of ordering his execution. Stylian, as one of the closest associates of the young prince and father of his mistress, was in similar danger. But there is no evidence; we can only draw our own conclusions.

At the time of his consecration, Leo VI was just twenty years old. He had been only thirteen when the death of his brother had changed his father's feelings towards him from mild dislike to bitter loathing; less than three years later, there had been the enforced marriage, the banishment of his beloved mistress and his own incarceration – made a good deal more irksome by the presence of his wife Theophano, who had insisted on sharing it together with their infant daughter. So much adversity during his formative years might well have had a catastrophic effect on Leo's character. It is greatly to his credit that it did nothing of the sort. There is, admittedly, a suspicion – no more – of patricide; for the rest, he seems to have been possessed of considerable charm, a first-rate academic mind, and very considerable learning – more than could have been claimed by any of his predecessors on the Byzantine throne. His many sermons, personally delivered from the pulpit of St Sophia, occasionally reveal a somewhat disconcerting lack of self-consciousness: diatribes against those who 'instead of bathing in the pure waters of matrimony prefer to wallow in the mud of fornication' come strangely from the lips of a man who kept a regular mistress from the age of fifteen. The general tenor of his writings, however, leaves us in no doubt of the breadth of his scholarship, which was enough to earn him the sobriquet of *sophōtatos*, 'the most wise'; and it is as Leo the Wise that he is still known today.

It was only to be expected that when Leo succeeded to the throne – in theory he shared it with his brother Alexander, but Alexander was a pleasure-loving nonentity – he should have made radical changes in the administration, the chief beneficiary of which was Stylian Zautses, who now became Master of the Offices and Logothete of the Course, effectively the director of imperial policy at home and abroad. The chief casualty, equally predictably, was Photius. For the second time the Patriarch was obliged to sign an act of abdication; he was then permitted to retire to a remote monastery where he could continue his theological and literary work undisturbed, and where he died in obscurity a few years later. The choice of his successor showed clearly the way Leo's mind was working: on Christmas Day 886 he raised to the patriarchal throne his own youngest brother Stephen. Although at fifteen Stephen was the youngest Patriarch in history, his appointment aroused little opposition. There was no other obvious candidate for the post, and Stephen – a sickly youth, unlikely to last very long – may well have seemed a harmless stopgap. He proved every bit as cooperative as expected.

With Stylian Zautses as his political adviser and Stephen as his willing instrument in Church affairs, Leo was now admirably equipped to govern his Empire. There were no major domestic upheavals for the rest of the century, which was to end on a particularly happy note when an important synod – it may even have been a General Council – was summoned in 899 and did much to restore relations between the Eastern and Western Churches. The Emperor was consequently able to give his full attention to the tremendous work initiated by his father – the revision and recodification of the Roman law. He applied himself to the task with energy and enthusiasm. In the resulting books, published in series over the years, the laws were, first, systematically arranged: a given subject was treated *in extenso* in a given book, and nowhere else. Second, they were written in Greek rather than Latin, now a dead language in Constantinople, comprehensible only to scholars. Thus, from the reign of Leo VI onwards, the work of Justinian was effectively superseded.

This blessed period of domestic quiet was not, unfortunately, reflected by a similar degree of tranquillity abroad. The Arabs kept up the pressure: but a more immediate threat came from Bulgaria. After the conversion of King Boris the Byzantines had hoped that the two Christian peoples might hence-forth live together in peace; but Boris had abdicated in 889, leaving the throne to his son Vladimir, who had immediately identified himself with the boyar aristocracy which Boris had done his utmost to crush. The boyars were dyed-in-the-wool reactionaries who detested Christianity and sought a return to the bad old days of privilege and paganism; with their support Vladimir was rapidly undoing all his father's work. He had, however, reckoned without Boris. In an explosion of rage still almost audible down the centuries, the old King burst out of his monastery, seized back the government, deposed and blinded Vladimir and, summoning a great conference from every corner of his kingdom, bade the assembled delegates acclaim his younger son Symeon as their ruler. Unhesitatingly they did so, whereupon he returned to his cloister never to leave it again.

Symeon was now twenty-nine and himself a monk; but when the call came to assume the throne he was not slow to respond. In Byzantium the news of his accession was received with relief, and all might have gone well had not Stylian Zautses in 894 awarded the monopoly of trade with Bulgaria to two of his own protégés. They dramatically increased the customs dues payable on all goods imported into the Empire, simultaneously transferring the entrepôt from Constantinople to Thessalonica. Thus, at a stroke, the freight trade from the Black Sea down the Bosphorus to the Golden Horn had been destroyed; the Thessalonica road not only involved far greater distances but was frequently impassable. Symeon protested, but Leo supported his Logothete and nothing was done.

He had underestimated the young King; within weeks, a Bulgar army had invaded Thrace. The Empire's one outstanding general, Nicephorus Phocas, was urgently recalled from south Italy; he was able to hold the situation while the Emperor turned for assistance to the Magyars. These savage warrior people were the northern neighbours of the Bulgars, whom they greatly disliked. They needed little enough encouragement to swarm across the Danube into Bulgar territory. But if Leo could summon a barbarian tribe to his aid, so too could Symeon. Beyond the lands of the Magyars, in the plains of southern Russia, dwelt another nomadic tribe, the Pechenegs. Bribed with Bulgar gold, they fell on the Magyar rear. The Magyars hurried back to save their wives and children, only to find their way blocked by the Pecheneg host. Unable to remain in Bulgaria, where Symeon was now advancing against them, they had no choice but to continue their old westward migration into the great Pannonian plain – the land which we now call Hungary and which is still their home.

With the Magyars finally off his back, Symeon was able once again to devote his full attention to the Byzantines. Nicephorus Phocas had been unwisely recalled by Stylian to Constantinople; his successor Catacalon possessed little of his ability and Leo was obliged to sue for peace; and after five years of negotiation, with an undertaking to pay a large annual tribute, he got it. The Thessalonica staple was closed; Constantinople once again became the centre for Bulgarian trade. Symeon had shown that he was a force to be reckoned with. He had also dangerously reduced Byzantine power just when the Empire needed to mobilize all its resources against the Arabs. On 1 August 902 Taormina fell, the last imperial possession in Sicily; in the East, Armenia was left defenceless and the Muslim forces began a new advance into Cilicia. The situation in the Aegean was no better. The worst catastrophe of all, however, occurred in 904 when a Greek renegade, Leo of Tripoli, led a Saracen fleet up the Hellespont and into the Marmara. Finally driven back, he made straight for Thessalonica. The city resisted for three days, but on 29 July the defences crumbled and the Saracens poured through the breach. The bloodshed and butchery continued for a week; only then did the raiders re-embark with their plunder and – we are told – more than 30,000 prisoners, leaving the second city and port of the Empire a smouldering ruin.

It was more than a disaster; it was a disgrace. A plan was hastily prepared, acccording to which the admiral Himerius would sail round the coast to Antalya, embark a land army under the command of the local military governor, Andronicus Ducas, and then continue to Tarsus, a port almost as important as Thessalonica, which would now suffer a similar fate. Himerius duly arrived, only to find that Ducas had risen in open revolt. The admiral, ill-equipped as he was, pressed on regardless; and a few days later, having utterly destroyed a Saracen fleet dispatched to intercept him, reduced Tarsus to ashes. Ducas fled to Baghdad, where he died shortly afterwards. Byzantine honour had been saved.

On the domestic front, Leo's troubles had begun with his wife Theophano. He had never liked her at the best of times, but now – perhaps to compensate for the love he could never give her – she had turned all her thoughts to religion to the point where she became, even by Byzantine standards, mildly ridiculous. At night, we are told, she forsook her husband's bed, preferring a rough mat in a corner, from which every hour she rose to pray. A more un-satisfactory consort for a lusty young prince could hardly be imagined; moreover, Leo desperately wanted a son. It was a huge relief to him when she retired to the convent at Blachernae, where on 10 November 897 she died. He gave her a magnificent funeral and immediately summoned his beloved Zoe to Constantinople. There remained the problem of her husband; but fortunately – some people thought a little too fortunately – he chose this moment to die in his turn. With unseemly dispatch his widow was installed in the palace, and early in 898 the two lovers were married at last. To his delight Zoe soon found herself pregnant, and he eagerly awaited the son promised by the astrologers. Alas, the child proved to be another girl, who was given the name of Anna. But worse was to come: at the end of 899 Zoe succumbed to some mysterious disease. The long-awaited idyll had lasted just two years.

Leo's grief was deep and genuine; but so was his concern for the succession. His brother and co-Emperor Alexander was rapidly drinking him-self to death. A disputed succession was the fundamental evil from which all others sprang: the plots and intrigues, the palace revolutions and the *coups d'état*, the pointless and bewildering changes of policy. The conclusion was obvious: the Emperor must marry a third time, and have a son. But was such a thing permitted? Certainly, by the early Fathers of the West. Premature deaths from disease or childbirth were frequent, and for a man to take a second wife after the loss of his first, or even a third after his second, seemed to them pardonable enough. But in the East the code was more stringent. St Basil had reluctantly permitted second marriages; third marriages, however, were at best what he called 'moderated fornication', and carried the penalty of four years' denial of the Sacrament. As for those who attempted matrimony for the fourth time, their crime was polygamy, for which a penalty of no less than eight years was enjoined.

But Emperors were special cases, particularly when state interests were involved. Leo's brother Stephen had been succeeded as Patriarch by the equally easy-going Antony Cauleas, who was quite ready to grant the necessary dispensation. Leo selected a ravishing girl named Eudocia Baiana as his new consort, and on Easter Sunday, 12 April 901, she presented him with a son. Alas, she died while doing so, and the baby prince survived her by only a few days. But the Emperor refused to give up. He was, after all, still only thirty-five. A fourth marriage, on the other hand, would be harder to arrange than the third had been, and even if he succeeded would unquestionably be his last chance. He had to be sure of his ground. His first step was to take as his mistress the strikingly beautiful niece of the admiral Himerius, Zoe Carbonopsina – 'with eyes of coal'. He made no secret of this union which the Church, while not actually condoning it, infinitely preferred to a fourth marriage. Zoe's first child was a girl; but in September 905 she produced a son. The Emperor was overjoyed; the Patriarch, on the other hand, found himself in a quandary. He could not permit the Emperor to marry again; neither, however, could Leo and his mistress live indefinitely in sin. Finally agreement was reached: Zoe would leave the palace, after which the Patriarch would consent to baptize his son in St Sophia. And so it came about. On the Epiphany following, 6 January 906, the baptism took place, the baby prince being given the name of Constantine.

After just three days Zoe was back in the palace, where Leo was already contemplating his next step. His son was still a bastard and, as such, debarred from the throne. Somehow he must be legitimized. And so Leo did the only sensible thing. Quietly, almost secretly, in the private chapel of the palace and before a simple parish priest, he and Zoe went through a form of marriage. Only when the service was over did he make public what he had done and proclaim his new wife Empress. For eight years the storm had been gathering; now it broke. The Church exploded in fury. There could be no question of the ceremony being recognized: Leo himself had been joint signatory of the article in the civil code which read: 'If any shall dare to proceed to a fourth marriage, which is no marriage, not merely shall the offspring of it be illegitimate, but it shall be subject to the punishment prescribed for those who are soiled with the filth of fornication, it being understood that the persons who have indulged in it shall be separated from each other.'

Where the civil code was concerned, Leo could have claimed immunity, or even changed it. Against canon law, on the other hand, he was powerless. How could he obtain a special dispensation? Antony Cauleas was dead; his successor Nicholas, formerly the Emperor's private secretary, might if left to himself have agreed to the dispensation; but he was now confronted with Arethas, Bishop of Caesarea, henceforth to prove his most implacable enemy.

Although the two protagonists of the recent schism were long in their graves, the Photian and Ignatian factions were still very much alive. Arethas, for the first half-century of his life, had been a dedicated Photian. His writings had consequently given mortal offence to the Ignatians, who at Easter 900 had had him arraigned on a charge of atheism. He had been acquitted; but he never forgot an injury, and when his friend Nicholas was appointed Patriarch, had pressed him to take suitable steps against his enemies. Nicholas however had refused, having promised the Emperor that he would do everything in his power to heal the breach between the two sides; and Arethas, furious, had sworn revenge – for which the issue of the Emperor's fourth marriage gave him the perfect opportunity. Inevitably it had developed on factional lines, with the worldly-wise Photians inclined to allow Leo his dispensation while the Ignatians, bigoted to the last, remained inflexibly against it. Arethas would normally have stood squarely in the Photian camp; his vindictiveness alone drove him to the Ignatians, who welcomed him with open arms. They could never have hoped to hold their own in intellectual argument with the sophisticated Photians; now, suddenly, they had found a voice.

All through the year the debate continued; the Emperor, meanwhile, was losing patience. Then he had an idea. By now the Ignatians had the upper hand. They had admittedly set their faces firmly against any dispensation, but might they not be persuaded? Discreet inquiries were made of Euthymius, abbot of the monastery of Psamathia, the most widely respected member of the Ignatian party before the adherence of Arethas. Normally a stern moralist, he might have been expected to reject out of hand the proposal that was now made to him; but Leo knew his man. After a decent moment of hesitation Euthymius accepted the offer of the Patriarchate and pronounced himself ready to issue the required dispensation, provided only that some respectable pretext could be found. The Emperor was ready for this. He now revealed that he had recently submitted the whole question to Pope Sergius III, from whom he confidently expected a favourable reply. If the Supreme Pontiff were now to give his blessing, what better authority could Euthymius require? That he would give it, Leo was certain. No Pope worthy of his throne would let slip such an opportunity of seeming to impose his authority on Constantinople. Sergius was moreover in desperate need of military assistance in south Italy, where the Saracens were showing every sign of strengthening their hold; for such support he could not fail to consider a dispensation for the fourth marriage an acceptable *quid pro quo*.

Meanwhile, Leo was prepared to bide his time. While the question remained unresolved, he insisted that Zoe should be treated with all the honour due to an Empress; but when at Christmas 906 and on the Feast of Epiphany following, Patriarch Nicholas denied him entry into St Sophia, he turned back without protest to the palace. A month later he struck. Nicholas was accused of having been in secret communication with the rebel Andronicus Ducas, put under close arrest and forced to sign an act of abdication from the Patriarchate. Such an abdication would not have been valid without the approval of the other Patriarchs and, at least in theory, of the Pope in Rome; once again, however, Leo had made his preparations in good time. He had secretly brought to the capital accredited representatives of the three Eastern Patriarchates – Alexandria, Antioch and Jerusalem. Pope Sergius, too, had been apprised of Leo's intentions. It was gratifying enough to him to have been asked to pronounce on the fourth marriage; an additional appeal by an Emperor against his own Patriarch was an even more valuable testimonial to the respect in which the Papacy was held in the East, and was certainly not to be refused.

Sergius's reply justified the Emperor's highest hopes. Before the end of the month Euthymius, now enthroned as Patriarch, duly granted the long-awaited dispensation. Leo and Zoe, he insisted, would still be admitted to the Great Church only as penitents, debarred from the sanctuary and obliged to remain standing. But for the Emperor this was a small enough price to pay for a happy married life. Sinful as it might be, his marriage was now at least recognized. He and Zoe were man and wife, and the baby Constantine, now eighteen months old, was held to be *porphyrogenitus*, 'born in the purple'. Insofar as it ever could be in those uncertain times, the succession was assured.

It would have been better for Leo if he had died there and then. Instead, in the autumn of 911 he sent Himerius on a final attempt to recapture Crete. For six months the admiral maintained the siege; but the defenders held firm. Then, in April 912, there arrived an urgent message from the capital: the Emperor's health had taken a sudden turn for the worse: he was unlikely to live. Reluctantly, Himerius gave up the siege and set sail for the Bosphorus. His ships were just rounding the island of Chios when they found themselves surrounded by a Saracen fleet under the command of Leo of Tripoli – he who had practically annihilated Thessalonica eight years before. Nearly all the Byzantine ships were sent to the bottom, Himerius himself narrowly escaping to Mitylene whence he sadly made his way back to Constantinople.

Leo's life was now ebbing fast. He lived just long enough to hear the news, then turned his face to the wall. On the night of 11 May he died. He had proved himself, if not perhaps a great Emperor, at any rate an outstandingly good one. True, he had split the Church more deeply than ever; but this was the inevitable result of his fourth marriage, by which he had ensured both a recognized succession and the continuation of the Macedonian house, which was to survive for another 150 years – the greatest dynasty in the history of Byzantium. For the rest, he had ruled wisely and well; and had left the Empire, at least internally, in far better shape than when he inherited it. He was not an exhibitionist: no great churches or sumptuous palaces stand to his memory, and his mosaic portrait over the Imperial Door of St Sophia – which shows him, incidentally, in an attitude of prostration before Christ – dates almost certainly from several years after his death. His most enduring achievements – the codification of the law, the reorganization of the provincial administration, the restructuring of the armed forces – were unspectacular; but they were no less valuable for that. In his lifetime Leo was genuinely loved by his people; and after his death they had good cause to be grateful.

13
The Gentle Usurper

[912–48]

The only good thing that can be said of the reign of the Emperor Alexander is that it was short. Worn out at forty-one by dissipation, he was to occupy the throne for a little under thirteen months. His normal behaviour could be compared only to that of Michael the Sot at his worst: there were the same senseless cruelties, the same drunken roisterings, the same acts of wanton sacrilege. On one occasion he became convinced that the bronze boar in the Hippodrome was his other self, and had it provided with new teeth and genitals in an attempt to remedy the extraordinary wear and tear that he had inflicted on his own.

He had always hated his brother, and in 903 had been involved in a plot to assassinate him in church. Once in power he reversed all Leo's policies, countermanded all his orders. The Empress Zoe was unceremoniously evicted from the palace; her uncle Himerius, who had given such sterling service to the Empire, was disgraced and thrown into prison, where he died soon afterwards. Meanwhile a Bulgarian embassy had arrived in Constantinople, sent by Symeon to suggest a renewal of the peace treaty of 901. To Alexander, the treaty had been the work of his brother and for that reason alone must be abrogated. He shouted at the ambassadors that he wanted no more treaties and, moreover, that Byzantium would be paying no further tribute. Then he dismissed them. Symeon, confident in the strength of his army and realizing that he had nothing to fear from so pathetic a figure, began preparations for war.

By this time, too, for no other apparent reason than to go against his brother, Alexander had recalled Patriarch Nicholas from banishment and restored him to his throne. The Patriarch had spent his five-year exile brooding over the injustice he had suffered and, in particular, over his betrayal by the Ignatians; he now thought only of revenge. Euthymius was arraigned before a tribunal in the Palace of the Magnaura where, we read, he was publicly stripped of his robes, which were trampled into the dust by all those present. He was then thrown to the ground, kicked and spat upon, and beaten until he lost several teeth and was on the point of collapse. Had not a nobleman named Petronas caught hold of him, writes the chronicler, he would quickly have died a martyr's death.

Having banished Euthymius to the monastery of Agathon, Patriarch Nicholas now initiated a major purge of the entire hierarchy, aimed at the elimination of all bishops and clergy with Ignatian sympathies. How he expected the Church to function after such drastic surgery – where the episcopal bench alone was concerned, the Ignatians represented some two-thirds of the total – was never explained; but those dismissed flatly refused to go. Arethas of Caesarea announced that he would leave his see only when removed by force. Many others followed his example; meanwhile several Photian bishops who had tried to get rid of their Ignatian clergy found themselves besieged in their palaces by their mutinous flocks. When the panic-stricken Patriarch countermanded his former orders, only four bishops had accepted their dismissal.

By this time the Emperor Alexander was dead. He collapsed, we are told, in the course of various pagan sacrifices in the Hippodrome – including, presumably, one to the boar – in the hopes of curing his impotence; he died two days later, on Sunday 6 June 913. His mosaic portrait in the north gallery of St Sophia must unquestionably date from his reign; after his death, his subjects wished only to forget him. His sister-in-law Zoe had meanwhile forced her way back into the palace, desperately worried for the future of her son Constantine. Alexander, she knew, had planned to castrate him; with the return of the Patriarch, her anxieties were increased. Nicholas had never accepted the dispensation given by his enemy Euthymius; she knew that he would do everything in his power to keep Constantine from the throne, and she was determined to frustrate his efforts. Her suspicions were well founded: the Patriarch did indeed have an alternative candidate. It was Constantine Ducas, Domestic of the Schools,[1] son of the traitor Andronicus, a man who felt absolutely no loyalty to the Macedonian house. He could however rely on the support of much of the army, and had connections with most of the leading aristocratic families; if he were to attempt a *coup* his chances of success would be high. For some time already he and Nicholas had been in secret correspondence; when the moment came, they would be ready.

Zoe was still battling to regain her old position when the dying Emperor recovered sufficient consciousness to nominate his successor – which was indeed Constantine. Unfortunately he went on to appoint a Council of Regency. Its president was to be Nicholas; she herself was not included. She protested vigorously: never in the history of Byzantium had the mother of an

1 i.e. Commander-in-chief of the land forces of the Empire.

Emperor and a crowned Augusta been denied a place on such a council. But Nicholas knew that he could take no chances. One of his first actions as Regent was to have her arrested, shorn of her hair and dispatched to a distant convent. Even her name was no longer her own: henceforth she would be known as Sister Anna, and nothing more. For the moment at least, her seven-year-old son was sole Emperor; but, with a Regent who denied him any legal right to the throne, how long could he be expected to survive? The first threat came within days of his accession, with the attempted *coup* of Constantine Ducas. Marching eastward from his Thracian camp, he entered the city by night, expecting the palace gates to be opened to him from within; but the *magister* John Eladas, forewarned, was waiting for him with a company of militia. Several of Ducas's men were killed in the fighting; and just as he was trying to escape his horse slipped on the wet pavement. He fell heavily to the ground, where one of the defenders quickly dispatched him. The Patriarch, instantly disclaiming any association with the plot, instituted a reign of terror against all those whose complicity was even suspected. Whole companies were massacred, others were flogged or blinded. Only when the Regency Council itself began to protest at the relentless bloodshed did he reluctantly call a halt.

Less than two months after the Ducas fiasco, Symeon of Bulgaria appeared before Constantinople with an army so immense that its camp occupied the entire four-mile stretch of the walls from the Marmara to the Golden Horn. Once there, however, he discovered what his great-great-grandfather Krum had discovered before him: that the fortifications were impregnable. But he made no move to retire. The threat of a blockade, combined with the systematic devastation of the surrounding countryside, might still enable him to make favourable terms without the loss of any of his men. From the Palace of the Hebdomon he sent messengers to the Regency Council, announcing that he was ready to negotiate a settlement. Nicholas was only too pleased to agree. War, after all, would be virtually certain to lead to the breaking away of the Bulgarian Church – still part of his Patriarchate – and might even drive it back to Rome. He paid a secret visit to Symeon at the Hebdomon; in the discussions that followed, the Bulgar King insisted only that he be paid the arrears of tribute and that young Constantine should take one of his daughters to wife. Then, loaded with gifts, he returned to his homeland.

Why did he not drive a harder bargain? Simply because his policy had changed. His ambitions where Byzantium was concerned were now focused on the crown itself – which, once he was the Emperor's father-in-law, would be within his grasp. But his examination of the walls had convinced him that it could be won only by diplomacy, while his discussions with Nicholas had revealed to him a hitherto unsuspected ally. It was not just that the Patriarch obviously felt no loyalty to the Macedonians; his obvious terror at the thought of losing control of the Bulgarian Church gave Symeon immense bargaining strength. An aggressive attitude at this juncture would have been disastrous. Symeon in short had played his hand beautifully; Patriarch Nicholas had badly overplayed his. His fellow-members of the Council were as irritated by his arrogance as they had been revolted by his cruelty. They were also appalled by his treatment of Zoe, and they could not but be moved at the sight of the pale little Emperor, wandering around the palace crying for his mother. The news that the Patriarch had been in secret negotiations with the Bulgar King was the last straw. In February 914 Sister Anna was recalled from her nunnery and, once again an Empress, took over the Regency.

The new government was contemptuously described by Symeon as a 'council of eunuchs'. But eunuchs in the Byzantine Empire were neither the mincing male sopranos of later Western Europe nor the overweight harem-keepers of the Oriental tradition. For at least four centuries they had been highly-respected members of society and holders of many of the most distinguished offices of Church and State. By the tenth century to be a eunuch was, for a promising youth about to enter the imperial service, a virtual guarantee of advancement; many an ambitious parent would have a younger son castrated as a matter of course, for eunuchs, with no families to support, tended to be far more industrious and dedicated than their more completely-endowed colleagues. Since they left no sons, posts could be awarded on merit alone. Finally, they were safe. A eunuch might engage in a little mild intrigue on behalf of a nephew; but never could he make a bid for the throne. Small wonder, then, that the Empress and her eunuchs soon showed themselves far better administrators of the Empire. The old Patriarch himself, on the other hand, presented them with a problem. Zoe's first intention had been to recall Euthymius; but Euthymius had had enough. With some reluctance, therefore, she allowed Nicholas to continue as Patriarch – though with dire warnings as to what he could expect if he meddled any further in affairs which did not concern him. Her luck, it seemed, had indeed turned. Over the next eighteen months she was able to regain Armenia from the Caliph and place the firmly pro-Byzantine Prince Ashot on the throne; defeat another Muslim army that had launched a major raid on imperial territory from its base at Tarsus; and totally destroy yet a third army just outside the city of Capua, thereby restoring Byzantine prestige in the Italian peninsula. By the end of 915, in the minds of the large majority of her subjects, the Empress Zoe could do no wrong.

Even Symeon of Bulgaria suffered a reverse, if only a temporary one. To him Patriarch Nicholas's fall from power and the return of Zoe had been a severe blow: the Empress, he knew, would never countenance the marriage on which he had set his heart. It would have to be war after all. In September he appeared with his army before Adrianople, which surrendered without even a show of resistance. He seems to have been genuinely astonished when the Empress sent a massive force to recover the city, and he in his turn was obliged to withdraw. But in 917 he was back again in Thrace, and Zoe decided on a pre-emptive strike. Her *strategos* at Cherson in the Crimea, a certain John Bogas, had bribed the notoriously venal Pechenegs to invade Bulgaria from the north; and the Byzantine fleet had been enlisted to carry them across the Danube. Meanwhile the army was to march up from Constantinople to the southern frontier. Trapped in a gigantic pincer movement, Symeon would have no alternative but to come to terms.

But Symeon, we must assume, had also exercised his remarkable talent for bribery. John Bogas arrived with his Pechenegs on the banks of the Danube to keep his rendezvous with the fleet, which was commanded by an Armenian named Romanus Lecapenus; the moment they met, however, the two men became involved in a furious argument, each denying the authority of the other. The upshot was that Romanus categorically refused to transport the invaders across the river; and the Pechenegs, tired of waiting, drifted away to their homes. The army meanwhile, under the command of the Domesticus Leo Phocas, had advanced from the capital along the Black Sea coast; dawn on 20 August found it encamped outside the little port of Anchialus. It was then that Symeon, who had been monitoring its progress, saw his chance. Sweeping down on it from the western hills, he showed it no mercy. Virtually the entire army was massacred. Leo Phocas escaped; few others were as lucky. The anger of the Empress can easily be imagined. Romanus Lecapenus was sentenced to be blinded; it was fortunate for him that influential friends were able to win him a last-minute reprieve. Strangely enough, her confidence in Leo Phocas remained apparently unshaken; but that same winter she entrusted him with another army which was destroyed almost as completely as his first had been.

In the capital, the year 918 opened in growing chaos. After two annihilating defeats, Zoe's reputation was in ruins, her regime in serious danger. There was no chance of any accommodation with Symeon: he continued to insist on the marriage between Constantine and his daughter as the condition of any settlement, and the Empress still could not contemplate the idea of a barbarian daughter-in-law. She must somehow find supporters within the Empire. But where? There were only two possibilities. The first was Leo Phocas, discredited as he was. His family now headed the rich landed aristocracy; he was moreover a widower, with whom the Empress may have been contemplating marriage – which would have immeasurably strengthened her own and her son's position. The other alternative was Romanus Lecapenus. Unlike Leo, he was a man of neither birth nor breeding, an Armenian peasant's son who had risen entirely by merit. On the other hand, although he had scarcely distinguished himself during the recent hostilities, he was undefeated: his great flagship was even now riding at anchor in the Golden Horn, surrounded by the imperial fleet. Of the two, the Empress not surprisingly preferred the handsome, aristocratic general to the jumped-up foreign parvenu, and Leo soon became one of her most trusted advisers. The people of Constantinople, however, had always mistrusted the Anatolian aristocracy. Their traditional loyalties were to the established imperial dynasty. Young Constantine was now thirteen years old; although his health remained poor, he was clearly a child of unusual intelligence who appeared to have the makings of a first-class Emperor. But what chance would he stand against the ambitions of a Phocas, when not even his own mother seemed aware of the danger?

It was at this moment that Theodore, Constantine's personal tutor, took matters into his own hands and wrote a letter in his pupil's name appealing to Romanus Lecapenus; and Romanus unhesitatingly proclaimed his readiness to serve the young Emperor as his champion. He can have had no delusions as to the effect that this would have on the Empress. Encouraged by Phocas, she commanded Romanus to pay off his sailors and disband the fleet. The admiral agreed with the utmost courtesy, inviting her court chamberlain aboard the flagship to see for himself how conscientiously the order was being obeyed. All unsuspecting, the chamberlain did so – only to be arrested; and when Zoe sent envoys to demand an explanation they were greeted by a hail of stones. Now seriously alarmed, she called a meeting of her ministers; but they too had turned against her. She was obliged to listen in silence while young Constantine read from a prepared script, informing his mother that her Regency was at an end.

Leo Phocas and Romanus Lecapenus were now locked in an open struggle for supremacy. Finally, on 25 March 919, Romanus appeared with his fleet, entered the palace and announced that he had taken over the government of the Empire; and only a month later, in St Sophia, he gave away his exquisite young daughter Helena to Constantine in marriage, taking for himself the title of *basileopator*. For the second time in just over half a century, an Armenian upstart stood but one short step from the throne of Byzantium.

Meanwhile Leo Phocas had returned to the army across the Bosphorus and raised the standard of revolt, with the object – as he put it – of freeing the

Emperor from the clutches of the usurping Romanus. Romanus countered this by using two undercover agents, a priest and a prostitute, to disseminate copies of a letter signed by the boy Emperor himself, confirming that his father-in-law enjoyed his complete confidence and trust. The priest was arrested, but the prostitute did her work admirably and Leo's men laid down their arms. He himself was caught in a Bithynian village, where his eyes were put out before he was brought back in chains to Constantinople.

When he heard of the blinding, Romanus is said to have flown into a fury. But Leo Phocas was now a spent force; a far more important consideration in the mind of Romanus was to smooth his own path to the throne – an objective which could be achieved only by undermining the claims of Constantine. Thus, with the enthusiastic cooperation of the Patriarch, a formal synod was summoned to Constantinople in the summer of 920; and on 9 July this synod published, finally and authoritatively, the revised canon law on remarriage. Fourth marriages, it declared, were absolutely forbidden, and would be punished by excommunication until the partner was permanently repudiated. The decree was not retrospective, but Leo VI's last two marriages were condemned in the strongest possible terms, and the legitimacy of his son accepted only reluctantly and on sufferance. Barely a month later, Zoe was accused by Romanus of attempting to poison him. It was enough to settle her fate once and for all. Again her hair was shorn; again she was obliged to don the coarse nun's habit that she detested; and again the great doors of St Euphemia slammed shut behind the reluctant Sister Anna.

There remained one last adversary. Constantine's tutor Theodore, who had played a crucial part in Romanus's rise to power, now saw that his intrigues had placed Constantine in precisely the position that he had most wished to avoid: Romanus had shown himself every bit as self-seeking as Leo Phocas. Theodore's attitude to him abruptly changed, and Romanus soon realized that his former accomplice had become his enemy. Theodore was arrested on a charge of conspiracy, and exiled to his north-west Anatolian homeland. With his departure, Constantine lost his last true friend. He was now nothing but a pawn in the hands of his father-in-law, whom a few days after his fifteenth birthday he dutifully appointed Caesar. Less than three months later, on 17 December 920, he marked the culmination of the astonishing career of Romanus Lecapenus by laying on his head the imperial diadem. Theoretically, of course, he – Constantine – still remained the senior Emperor; but within a year it was Romanus whose portrait began to appear in the place of honour on the coinage. To the vast majority of his subjects, the demise of the young Porphyrogenitus must have seemed only a matter of time.

*

Of the early history of Romanus Lecapenus – or, as we must now call him, the Emperor Romanus I – all too little has come down to us. His father, known universally to contemporaries as Theophylact the Unbearable, was an Armenian peasant whose good fortune it was to have once rescued Basil I from the Saracens. This earned him a place in the imperial guard, but he left his son to make his own way in the world. Born around 870, Romanus had entered the imperial service and was probably still in his thirties when he was appointed *strategos* of the Samian Theme. In 912 he succeeded Himerius as *drungarius*, or High Admiral.

At the time of his accession his wife Theodora had borne him at least six children, and before her death in 923 she was to present him with two more. Of their four sons, no fewer than three were to be crowned co-Emperor by the end of 924; the youngest, Theophylact, was a eunuch intended for the Patriarchate. Clearly, like his fellow-Armenian Basil I, the new Emperor intended to found a dynasty. Where he differed from his predecessor was in the comparative gentleness of his character. Romanus Lecapenus had employed trickery and deceit in plenty, but he was neither violent nor brutal. While the Porphyrogenitus lived, there could be little long-term future for the house of Lecapenus, and given the boy's fragility it would have been easy to poison him: Basil would not have hesitated. Romanus might do all he could to displace the young Emperor, but never did he lay a finger upon him.

For Constantine it must nevertheless have been a miserable childhood: a father dead, a mother reviled as a concubine and twice exiled, he himself facing constant accusations of bastardy and forced to accept in silence the gradual removal of everyone in whom he could put his trust. Amid a huge and fundamentally hostile family he was alone, unwanted and unloved. Fortunately his physical weakness was offset by a lively mind, and a wide range of artistic interests: he seems to have been a talented painter, and his intellectual curiosity was boundless. He would also spend hours at a time studying the intricacies of Byzantine court ceremonial, on which his exhaustive survey, *De Ceremoniis Aulae Byzantinae*, remains our most valuable authority.

But he made no attempt to assert himself. When his father-in-law elbowed him aside as senior Emperor; when in May 921 Romanus elevated his eldest son Christopher to be another co-ruler; when, four years later, he elevated two more sons, thus producing a ridiculous total of five simultaneous Emperors; even when in 927 he proclaimed Christopher second only to himself, relegating the Porphyrogenitus to third position – on none of these occasions, though he felt each one deeply, did Constantine utter a word of protest. He knew that he had one duty that took precedence over all the others: to survive.

Beyond the imperial frontiers, Romanus's chief problem was Bulgaria. From the moment of his accession, he had done everything in his power to restore good relations; but Symeon would accept no terms that did not begin with Romanus's abdication, and so hostilities continued. In 919 the King pushed south as far as the Hellespont; in 921 he was within sight of the Land Walls; in 922 he advanced to the European shore of the Bosphorus, sacked the whole area around Istinye and burnt one of Romanus's favourite palaces at Pegae; while 923 saw his recapture of Adrianople. But none of these small triumphs brought him any nearer to his goal. From the land, Constantinople remained impregnable. In 924 he resolved on a final onslaught, this time from the sea. He himself had no fleet; but he had negotiated for the assistance of that belonging to the Fatimid Caliph in North Africa. What he did not know was that the Byzantines had secretly bribed the Caliph to take no action; and when in the high summer of 924 he led his army for at least the tenth time into Thrace he was surprised to find no trace of the Fatimids in the Marmara. Instead of launching another campaign of devastation in the surrounding country, he therefore sent to the city with a request for a meeting with his old friend the Patriarch.

Once again the aged Nicholas made his way to the Land Walls, where one of the gates was unbarred to allow him to slip out to the Bulgar camp. This time, however, he found the King in a less amenable mood. Symeon was no longer prepared to negotiate with inferiors. Curtly, he informed Nicholas that he would discuss peace only with Romanus himself. The Emperor had no objection. He always preferred talking to fighting. But neither he nor Symeon had forgotten what had happened with Krum and Leo V a century before. And so a great pier was constructed at Cosmidium at the northern end of the Golden Horn, with a fence extending transversely across it. Symeon was to approach from the landward side, Romanus by water; the barrier would remain between them.

The meeting took place on Thursday, 9 September. Symeon rode up in considerable state; the Emperor, accompanied by the Patriarch and carrying with him the city's holiest relic, the mantle of the Blessed Virgin, seemed thoughtful and subdued. The discussion was dominated by Romanus who, in typical Byzantine fashion, treated his adversary to a sermon: instead of begging for peace he appealed to Symeon's better nature as a Christian and pressed him earnestly to mend his ways. It was by all accounts a masterly performance; and it succeeded. Romanus spoke from a position of weakness. It was he who was suing for peace. He was the son of an Armenian peasant, while Symeon could boast a proud ancestry going back at least to the great Krum, and probably further. But he spoke with the authority of the thousand-year-old Roman Empire, compared with which Bulgaria was a parvenu principality of semi-civilized barbarians. And Symeon knew it.

Details of the terms that Romanus himself had proposed were soon settled. Apart from an increased tribute, they were to include an annual gift of 100 richly embroidered silken robes, in return for which Symeon agreed to withdraw from imperial territory and from his captured fortresses on the Black Sea coast. Then he turned in silence from the fence and rode back to his homeland. He never invaded the Empire again. He was now over sixty, and had occupied the throne for more than thirty years. No longer did he dream of reigning in Constantinople; and his assumption in 925 of the title of *Basileus of the Romans and the Bulgars* was, in its way, an admission of defeat: the action not of a statesman but of a petulant child. As Romanus somewhat icily remarked, Symeon could call himself the Caliph of Baghdad if he wished. In the following year Symeon finally declared the independence of the Bulgarian Church, elevating its archbishop to Patriarch. Nicholas would have been horrified; but Nicholas was now dead and nobody else seemed to care. Symeon himself died soon afterwards, on 27 May 927, aged sixty-nine.

He left behind him clear orders: the Bulgarian crown should go to his son Peter, during whose minority his maternal uncle George Sursubul should act as Regent. George set his heart on a formal treaty of peace, cemented by a marriage alliance. Romanus responded with alacrity; and George led a delegation to Constantinople, where he was presented to – and enchanted by – the young Maria, daughter of Romanus's eldest son Christopher. He wasted no time and sent for his nephew. The imperial wedding was held in the palace at Pegae on 8 October, only four and a half months after Symeon's death. The pair were duly blessed by Patriarch Stephen II, who had succeeded Nicholas in 925, the Emperor's son Theophylact being considered, at the age of eight, still a little too young for office. Then, tearfully – because she was hardly more than a child – the princess, now rechristened Irene, set off to the northwest.

Of the peace treaty signed at the same time we know little. Romanus agreed to recognize the independence of the Bulgarian Patriarchate and Peter's imperial title of Tsar – or, in Greek, *basileus*. The first of these obligations did not worry him unduly: the independence of the Patriarchate effectively deprived the Bulgars of one of their favourite blackmailing threats, secession to Rome. The second he simply ignored. He was above all a realist. In the interests of a quick agreement, with a marriage alliance as a further guarantee, he was quite prepared to make a few minor concessions. In the first four years of his reign he could never have afforded such a luxury; but now every key post was in the hands of one of his own supporters. The navy and most of the army were behind him. The Church, under a subservient Patriarch, gave no further trouble. His only possible rival was completely under his control and, incidentally, his son-in-law. At last he was secure. Moreover, it soon became clear that Bulgaria was a spent force. She could never have become great until she had conquered Byzantium, and Byzantium had proved unconquerable. Young Peter, in any case, possessed none of his father's aggressiveness. In a reign of forty-two years he never learned to hold his kingdom together. Thus, for half a century, Bulgaria was to give the Empire no further cause for concern.

The same could not be said of the Empire's eastern frontier. At the time of Leo's death in 912, it had remained substantially as it had been for the past two centuries. Then, in 923, and over the following quarter-century, under the brilliant general John Curcuas, the whole complexion of the age-long and hitherto indecisive struggle in the East was to be changed. The pirate Leo of Tripoli was finally defeated; imperial authority in Armenia was confirmed and consolidated; and in 934 the important Arab Emirate of Melitene was incorporated into the Empire. Trouble now came neither from the west nor from the south, but from the north-east.

In the year 941 there may have been old men and women still alive in Constantinople who remembered their parents' stories of the terrible Russian raid of eighty-one years before; in the intervening period, however, the Russians had come a long way. In 882 or thereabouts the Viking Oleg had captured Kiev, and made it the capital of a new state. He had been succeeded on his death by Igor, son of Rurik, as Grand Prince of Kiev; and it was Igor who, at the beginning of June 941, dispatched a massive armada against Byzantium. When Romanus first heard of its approach, his heart sank: his army was away on the eastern frontier, his navy divided between the Mediterranean and the Black Sea. The only craft that could be quickly mobilized were fifteen pathetic hulks, long destined for the scrapyard. These were loaded to the gunwales with Greek fire and dispatched, under a certain Theophanes, to block the Bosphorus at its northern end. Theophanes arrived only just in time: on the morning of 11 June the Russian fleet appeared on the horizon. He attacked at once.

It is impossible to exaggerate the importance of Greek fire in Byzantine history. To the Saracens it was all too familiar; to the Russians, a total surprise. As the first of their ships was engulfed in flames, the remainder turned abruptly away from the mouth of the Bosphorus and headed east along the Black Sea coast of Bithynia, where they landed in strength, perpetrating unspeakable horrors on the local populations. For many weeks the terror continued; but the *strategos* of the Armeniakon, Bardas Phocas, hurried to the scene with his local levies and kept the marauders occupied pending the arrival of Curcuas. The fleet too was on its way, and as each new squadron arrived it went straight into the attack. Soon it was the Russians who were on the defensive: autumn was approaching and they were anxious to sail for home. But it was too late. The Byzantine fleet was between them and the open sea, and slowly closing in. Early in September they made a desperate attempt to slip through the blockade; but suddenly the whole sea was aflame. As the Russian ships went up like matchwood their crews leapt overboard; the lucky ones were dragged down by the weight of their armour, while the rest met their deaths in the oil-covered water, which blazed as fiercely as the ships. In Constantinople Theophanes was given a hero's welcome.

Only three years later Igor tried again – this time with an amphibious operation. Romanus, however, had no intention of fighting if he could avoid it. His ambassadors met the Grand Prince on the Danube and, quite simply, bought him off. The following spring a Russian delegation arrived to conclude a political and commercial treaty, and for the next quarter of a century relations between Russia and Byzantium were unruffled.

John Curcuas, meanwhile, had led his army back to the East. To his relief, he had found all his old positions intact: his chief enemy Saïf ed-Daula – 'Sword of the Empire', the Hamdanid Emir of Mosul – was detained elsewhere and all seemed set fair for a continuation of the interrupted offensive: the late autumn of 942 found him, after a long and arduous campaign, in Edessa. This city, though it had fallen to Islam as early as 641, could boast a long and venerable Christian tradition. It was above all famous for its two priceless possessions: a letter from Jesus Christ, and the Saviour's own portrait, miraculously imprinted on a cloth. Both these objects were known to be spurious, but their legends refused to die. The portrait in particular had caught Curcuas's imagination, and he was determined to have it. He therefore offered the Edessans peace and the return of all his prisoners in return for the famous image. The Edessans first consulted the Caliph, who gave his permission since there was no other way of saving the city; and only then surrendered their treasure. With much ceremony Curcuas immediately forwarded it to Constantinople where, at the Golden Gate, it was formally received by the Patriarch and the three young co-Emperors still surviving. It was then borne in triumph through the streets to St Sophia.

Romanus himself was not present. By now well into his seventies, he was spending more of his time with monks than with ministers, gradually losing his grip on the state as he sank into morbid religiosity. His conscience was troubled, for he had acquired the throne by perjury and deceit, depriving the legitimate Emperor of power and promoting his own worthless sons to imperial rank. Christopher had admittedly shown some degree of promise; but the two younger brothers, Stephen and Constantine, were notorious for their immorality, and the readiness with which Romanus submitted to their demands was a clear indication of his own decline. Almost the only sensible action of his last sad years was to make a new will in which he confirmed the seniority of Constantine Porphyrogenitus, thus eliminating them from power after his death. His mistake was to make his decision public; for he left his sons in no doubt that unless they acted quickly they were lost. If Constantine became senior Emperor, what was there for them to hope for? Banishment? Castration? Exile? Even worse fates were not impossible. And so, five days before Christmas 944, the two young Lecapeni and their supporters made their way to their father's chamber. He offered no resistance when they carried him down to the little harbour of Bucoleon; and a few minutes later he was on his way to the Princes' Islands. There he was tonsured and obliged to take monastic vows – which, one suspects, he was only too happy to do.

By the time the sons returned to the mainland, Constantinople was agog. Nobody minded much about Romanus; the name now on everyone's lips was that of Constantine. Before long, angry and suspicious crowds had gathered at the gates of the palace. Only after the young Emperor had shown himself at a window did they agree to disperse. Here was something that nobody had suspected: Constantine was loved by his people. He had never set out to win their affection; on the contrary, he had deliberately remained in the background. But he possessed the great virtue of legitimacy. Grandson of the great Basil himself, born in the purple, he and he alone was the rightful Emperor of Byzantium. The Lecapeni were upstarts. Their so-called subjects had had enough of them.

The brothers, seeing that they had miscalculated, took the only course open to them: with ill grace, they formally recognized Constantine as senior Emperor. It was an uneasy partnership, and the gentle, retiring Constantine if left to himself would probably have allowed the situation to drag on. But Helena his wife, daughter of Romanus, was made of sterner stuff. For twenty-five years she had loyally defended her husband's interests against her own family, and now she urged him to act while there was still time. On 27 January 945 the two co-Emperors were arrested, tonsured in their turn and sent off to separate places of exile. Of the remaining Lecapeni, only the Patriarch Theophylact – and, away in Bulgaria, the Tsaritsa Maria – still occupied positions of power.

As for the old Emperor, he lived on in his monastery, his conscience still allowing him no rest. On Holy Thursday 946, before an assembly of 300 monks from all over the Empire – even, we are told, from Rome itself – he listed all his sins one by one, asking absolution for each. Then, before the high altar, he was scourged by a young novice before returning to his cell. He died on 15 June 948. His body was carried back to Constantinople and was buried in the monastery of the Myrelaeum beside that of his wife.

He had been a good Emperor – perhaps even a great one. He had wielded his ill-gotten power with wisdom and moderation and had given the Empire new direction. His immediate predecessors had had to cope with two principal problems: the Church and Bulgaria. Romanus had solved them both, by allowing his enemies their head, exhausting them and then making sure that they were not replaced. Only in the East did his quiet diplomacy prove useless. There armed force was the only argument understood, and there – since he had lost not a single fighting man to the Bulgars – he was able to throw his entire strength against his Saracen foes. Luck, admittedly, was on his side – first in John Curcuas, who proved a general of quite exceptional merit, and secondly in the state of the Abbasid Caliphate, which was no longer capable of exercising any real authority; but it remains a fact that, for the first time since the rise of Islam, it was the Christian forces that were on the offensive.

Why was Romanus not better loved by his subjects? Was it simply that they disliked usurpers? The fact is that his virtues and qualities were not such as to seize the popular imagination. He was not a great soldier, nor a great legislator. He appeared rarely in public and never made much of a show at the Hippodrome. In short, although he did his utmost to see his people properly provided with bread, he was distinctly short on circuses. They consequently tended, when they thought of him at all, to remember the only memorable thing in the life of this able, quiet and surprisingly colourless man: his path to the throne. And he remembered it too: so vividly, so remorsefully, that his last few years were passed in unremitting torment. It is pleasant to reflect that he died at last with his spirit at peace, and his sins forgiven.

14

The Scholar Emperor

[945–63]

By the time Constantine Porphyrogenitus assumed sole power in the Byzantine state at the beginning of 945, he had long outgrown the sickliness of his youth. Tall and broad-shouldered, his ruddy complexion half-hidden by a thick black beard above which shone eyes of a brilliant pale blue, he looked at the age of thirty-nine as if he had never known a day's illness in his life. From his father Leo the Wise he had inherited a passion for books and scholarship which he had had plenty of time to indulge; and the body of work he left behind him is impressive by any standards. No other Emperors have contributed so much to our knowledge of their time.

Apart from his biography of his grandfather, Constantine is known above all for two major works. The first, *De Ceremoniis Aulae Byzantinae*, is an encyclopedia of Byzantine ritual and court protocol; the second, written for his son Romanus, is a practical textbook on the art of government which we now know as *De Administrando Imperio*. It covers a vast range of subjects; among other pieces of advice, Romanus is recommended to refuse all suggestions for marriage alliances, for Constantine the Great himself had decreed that the imperial family should never marry outside the Empire except on occasion to the Franks. At this point all Constantine VII's pent-up resentment of his father-in-law suddenly comes boiling up to the surface:

If they point out that the Lord Emperor Romanus himself made such an alliance when he gave the hand of his own granddaughter to the Bulgarian Tsar Peter, you should reply that the Lord Romanus was a vulgar illiterate who had been neither educated in the palace nor initiated in the Roman traditions. His family was not imperial or even noble, and tended accordingly to be arrogant and headstrong.

Most of this was written in the Emperor's own hand; with the help of countless scribes and copyists he also compiled digests of all the available manuals and treatises on military strategy, history, diplomacy, jurisprudence, hagiography, medicine, agriculture, natural science, even veterinary surgery. The result was a reference work which must have been of immense value to the imperial civil service for many years to come. He was, we are told, a passionate collector – not only of books and manuscripts but of works of art of every kind; more remarkable still for a man of his class, he seems to have been an excellent painter. He was the most generous of patrons – to writers and scholars, artists and craftsmen. Finally, he was an excellent Emperor: a competent, conscientious and hard-working administrator and an inspired picker of men, whose appointments to military, naval, ecclesiastical, civil and academic posts were both imaginative and successful. He did much to develop higher education and took a special interest in the administration of justice. That he ate and drank more than was good for him all our authorities seem to agree; but there is unanimity, too, on his constant good humour: he was unfailingly courteous to everyone and was never known to lose his temper.

It is easily understandable that Constantine should have looked with instinctive favour on the family of Phocas: they had been arch-enemies of the Lecapeni ever since Romanus's original *coup*, and had made no secret of their sympathy for his own position. As successor to John Curcuas in command of the armies of the East he now named Leo's brother Bardas Phocas, giving his sons Nicephorus and Leo the military governorships of the Anatolikon and Cappadocian Themes respectively. Of the Lecapeni, on the other hand, only one (apart from the Empress Helena herself) enjoyed his complete trust – though not until after he had been castrated. This was Romanus's natural son Basil, whom he appointed his chamberlain.

Meanwhile both foreign and domestic policy continued unchanged. Bardas Phocas, after being seriously wounded in 953, was succeeded by his son Nicephorus, who four years later gained one of the two greatest victories of the reign by capturing the city of Adata in Pamphylia. The second triumph came in 958, when Samosata on the Euphrates fell to another brilliant young general, John Tzimisces. In the West, the German King, Otto the Saxon, was building up the kingdom he had inherited in 936, pushing out its eastern frontiers against the Slav tribes and simultaneously extending his influence into neighbouring states. Constantine instinctively recognized the ability of this dynamic young prince, with whom he had opened up relations as soon as he assumed power; though he could not know that less than three years after his own death, Otto would be crowned Western Emperor in Rome.

By then, of course, he would have made himself master of Italy; but in the early years of Constantine's reign the Italian peninsula was still in semi-chaos, as it had been since the collapse of Charlemagne's Empire in 888. Its crown was a prize open to anyone with the strength, ambition and unscrupulousness to snatch it; and since that crown had by now become the surest stepping-stone to that of the Western Empire itself, the struggle for it was frequently joined by the kings and princes of neighbouring lands. Meanwhile in Rome the local aristocracy had made the Papacy their plaything: Nicholas I was virtually the last Pontiff of any ability or integrity to occupy the chair of St Peter for a century and a half. His second successor, John VIII, had been hammered to death by jealous relations, while in 896 the dead body of Pope Formosus had been exhumed, brought to trial before a synod of bishops, stripped, mutilated and thrown into the Tiber. As recently as 928 the infamous Marozia, Senatrix of Rome – mistress, mother and grandmother of Popes – had had her mother's lover, Pope John X, strangled in the Castel Sant'Angelo in order ultimately to install her son by her own former paramour, Pope Sergius III. In 932 she had taken as her second husband Hugh of Arles (who had murdered his wife and blinded his brother to marry her) and the two would unquestionably have become Emperor and Empress of the West had not her son engineered a popular revolt against them.

It was from this somewhat lurid background that there sprang one of the most valuable and colourful of our sources of tenth-century history. Liudprand, Bishop of Cremona, had been born in 920 into a well-to-do Lombard family. He had served some years as a singing pageboy at King Hugh's court at Pavia, after which he entered the Church and soon afterwards became chancellor to Hugh's effective successor, Berengar of Ivrea; and it was on Berengar's behalf, on 1 August 949, that he set off on a diplomatic mission to the Bosphorus. He arrived on 17 September and was soon afterwards received by the Emperor in audience. There was an early moment of embarrassment when he discovered that whereas other ambassadors had brought magnificent presents, his own master had sent nothing but a letter – 'and that was full of lies'. Fortunately he had with him a number of gifts that he had intended to offer Constantine on his own account; and these, most reluctantly, he now pretended had come from Berengar. Rather surprisingly, they included 'four *carzimasia* – young eunuchs who had been deprived not only of their testicles but of their penises as well, an operation performed by merchants at Verdun, who export them to Spain at huge profit to themselves'.

On the domestic front, too, Constantine continued the policies that Romanus had initiated. Much of his predecessor's legislation had been concerned with the protection of the small-holding peasant militia against the rich feudal aristocracy, now universally known as 'the powerful'. It was inevitable that Constantine, as an aristocrat himself, should have felt a good deal more sympathetic to this group than did his Armenian parvenu father-in-law; as we have seen, he made no secret of his particular friendship for the family of Phocas. Yet from the first he steadfastly continued the agrarian policy of Romanus – in 947 even ordering the immediate restitution, without compensation, of all peasant lands that had been acquired by 'the powerful' since his effective accession. Thus, by the end of the reign, the condition of the landed peasantry – which formed the foundation of the whole economic and military strength of the Empire – was better off than it had been for a century.

In September 959 the Emperor crossed over to Asia to see his old friend the Bishop of Cyzicus. From Cyzicus he travelled to Bursa, in the hopes that its celebrated hot springs would cure him of a persistent fever; and when this treatment failed he passed on to a monastery high on the mountain some twenty miles outside the town. By this time, however, it was plain that he was mortally ill: the monks bade him prepare for death. He returned hurriedly to the capital where, on 9 November 959, he died aged fifty-four, surrounded by his sorrowing family: his wife Helena, his five daughters and his twenty-year-old son Romanus, now Emperor of Byzantium.

No reign ever opened more auspiciously than that of Romanus II. The Empire's economic and military strength was greater than it had been for centuries; intellectually and artistically the Macedonian Renaissance was at its height. The legitimate son of a much-loved Emperor, born like his father in the purple, Romanus had inherited both his magnificent physique and his charm of manner. He was devastatingly attractive to women; and, not surprisingly, he himself fell in love. As a child he had been married off to Bertha, one of the countless natural progeny of Hugh of Arles; but she had died soon afterwards and in 958 he had unwisely rejected his father's next choice for him in favour of a Peloponnesian innkeeper's daughter who had taken the name of Theophano. History offers no more striking example of the *femme fatale*. Her beauty, for a start, was breathtaking. She was also intensely ambitious and utterly devoid of moral scruple; and although barely eighteen at the time of her husband's accession, she dominated him completely. Almost her first action as Empress was to deal with her mother-in-law and her five daughters. Helena was relegated to a distant corner of the palace, where she was to die, alone, in September 961; all five princesses – one of whom, Agatha, had for years been her father's confidential secretary and, more recently, his nurse – were obliged to take the veil. In vain did their brother plead for them; the young Empress stood by grimly as Patriarch Polyeuctus himself sheared off their hair and, as a final blow, dispatched them to five different convents.

Thanks to Theophano, many senior officials of government and court also lost their posts; two of the most important, however, remained in power. Basil, the former chamberlain, was given the new title of *proedrus*, which effectively made him the Emperor's right-hand man, while his previous post was inherited by the eunuch Joseph Bringas, who had combined the duties of chief minister and High Admiral (*drungarius*) during the last years of Constantine's reign. Bringas emerges from the chronicles as an able yet somewhat sinister figure. Highly intelligent and energetic, with a limitless capacity for hard work, he was also greedy, self-seeking and cruel. Constantine's dying wish had been that he should continue in charge of the government; with the accession of Romanus his power became virtually absolute.

Before the young Romanus had been more than a few weeks on the throne preparations were begun for a new expedition to Crete, conceived on a scale infinitely more ambitious than any of its predecessors. The army's total strength – including regiments of Russian mercenaries and Varangian axemen from Scandinavia – was well in excess of 50,000. The fleet consisted of 1,000 heavy transports, 308 supply ships and no fewer than 2,000 carriers of Greek fire. Command of this tremendous armament was entrusted to an ugly, austere and deeply religious man of forty-seven who was to prove himself one of the greatest generals in all Byzantine history. His name was Nicephorus Phocas. His grandfather and namesake had been responsible for the re-conquest of south Italy during Basil I's reign; his uncle, Leo, had led the resistance to Romanus Lecapenus; his father, Bardas, had commanded the imperial armies against the Saracens of the East until a hideous wound in the face put an end to his military career. Nicephorus himself had immediately taken over the command. He was a superb soldier of enormous strength, fearless in battle, quick to seize an opportunity and unfailingly considerate of his soldiers, who would follow him anywhere. Outside the army he had no interests save his religion, leading a life of almost monastic austerity and spending hours in conversation or correspondence with holy men. (Of these his particular favourite was the future St Athanasius, then a hermit on Mount Athos.) He had absolutely no social graces. He was in short a cold fish.

In the last days of June 960 the great fleet set sail; Nicephorus advanced directly on the city of Candia. It was the island's largest town; once it were taken there might well be no further serious resistance. A day or two later the siege began. It continued for eight months, and as winter came – the longest and harshest for many years – the citizens' morale began to flag. Their only consolation was the sight of their half-frozen enemies huddling round their fires and the knowledge that winters were often a good deal more uncomfortable for the besiegers than for the besieged. But Nicephorus on his daily rounds somehow managed to imbue his men with strength, hope and courage – being himself inspired by his friend Athanasius, whom he had urgently summoned from Mount Athos to join him. It was – Nicephorus was convinced – entirely through Athanasius's intercession that around the middle of February the long-awaited relief fleet arrived with supplies from Constantinople; Byzantine morale was restored, the city fell and on 7 March 961, for the first time in 136 years, the imperial standard flew again over Crete. The usual massacre followed; and the victorious fleet headed back to the Bosphorus, laden to the gunwales with the results of more than a century's plunder of one of the richest cities of the eastern Mediterranean.

The fall of Candia, and the consequent collapse of Saracen power in Crete, was a victory for the Byzantines unparalleled since the days of Heraclius. When the news reached Constantinople an all-night service of thanksgiving was held in St Sophia in the presence of the Emperor and Empress. Among the whole vast congregation there was one man only whose overriding emotion was not jubilation but anxiety. The eunuch Joseph Bringas had always hated the house of Phocas. Overnight Nicephorus had become the Empire's hero. Victorious generals were dangerous at the best of times; if his ambition was to be contained, he must be carefully watched; there would be difficult weeks ahead. And so it came about that when Nicephorus Phocas sailed proudly back into the Golden Horn, to be greeted by Romanus and Theophano and publicly congratulated on his historic achievement, he was not offered the full imperial triumph that he expected and deserved. Instead, it was made clear to him that he must not remain in the capital any longer than necessary: the Empire must quickly follow up its advantage; he was needed in the East.

When Nicephorus had left his eastern command to prepare the Cretan expedition, he had been succeeded by his younger brother Leo, who had almost immediately been faced with a major challenge from the Empire's old enemy, the Emir of Mosul, Saïf ed-Daula. In 944 Saïf had captured Aleppo, which he had made his headquarters and from which he had rapidly extended his domains to embrace the greater part of Syria and northern Mesopotamia, including Damascus, Emesa and Antioch. Well before the age of thirty-five he had become the *beau idéal* of the Arab Emir of the early Middle Ages: cruel and pitiless in war but chivalrous and merciful in peace, poet and scholar, patron of literature and the arts, possessor of the largest stable, the most extensive library and the most sumptuously stocked harem in the Muslim world. Every year without fail, he had led at least one major raid into imperial territory. None, however, had been so ambitious as that of 960. The moment was perfectly chosen. The Byzantine army of the East was seriously depleted by the demands of the Cretan expedition; Leo Phocas was several days' march away. At almost exactly the time that Nicephorus sailed for Crete Saïf crossed the border at the head of an army estimated at 30,000 men. Leo pursued him, but his army was exhausted after an arduous campaign. He advanced only as far as the mountains, where he carefully disposed his men to command the principal passes. Then he settled down to wait.

It was early November before Saïf returned with his army. His expedition had been a triumph. Long trains of captives shuffled behind him, carts groaned with the weight of his plunder; he himself rode proudly at the head of his men on a magnificent Arab mare. Then, just as he entered a pass, there rang out the blast of a hidden trumpet. Within seconds, immense boulders came spinning down the mountainside on top of the defenceless column. Saïf at first stood his ground; only when he saw that the day was lost did he wheel round and gallop away, with some 300 of his cavalry. Of the rest, nearly half lay dead; the survivors were secured with the same ropes and fetters that had formerly held the Christian captives.

The victory showed that Leo Phocas, even with diminished forces, was well able to defend the eastern frontier; this alone is enough to cast doubt on the real motives for the hasty dispatch of Nicephorus to join him. Inevitably, however, the renewed presence of both brothers, at the head of an army restored to its former size, had a dramatic effect. In the space of just three weeks early in 962, the Byzantines regained no fewer than fifty-five walled towns in Cilicia; then, after a brief pause at Easter, they advanced slowly and methodically southward, burning and plundering as they went. A few months later they were beneath the walls of Aleppo. The city was now for the first time the capital of an independent state; and Saïf's palace was one of the most beautiful and lavishly-appointed buildings of the Muslim world. It had only one disadvantage: a cruelly exposed position outside the walls. On the very night of their arrival Nicephorus's men fell on it, emptied it of all its treasures and burnt it to the ground. Only then did they turn their attention to Aleppo itself. Saïf, caught outside the walls, had once again to flee; without him the local garrison lacked stomach for the fight; and two days before Christmas the triumphant Byzantines swarmed into the city. As at Candia, no mercy was shown: the carnage, writes an Arab historian, ceased only when the conquerors were too exhausted to go on.

Aleppo, though occupied, had not quite fallen. A handful of soldiers in the citadel had dug themselves in and refused to surrender. Nicephorus ignored them: the city was no longer a force to be reckoned with. He gave the order to retire, and the victorious army began the long journey home. It had advanced no further than Cappadocia when a message arrived from Constantinople. Romanus II was dead.

15
The Tale of Two Generals
[963–76]

Romanus had died on 15 March 963; and already by the next morning the rumour was circulating that Theophano had poisoned him. The beautiful young Empress, in the forty months since Romanus's accession, had acquired a fearsome reputation. Few doubted that she was capable of such a crime; but it is hard indeed to see how her position might have been improved by widowhood, self-inflicted or not. There is every reason to believe that she loved her husband, to whom she had already given four children – the youngest, a daughter, born only two days before his death. While he lived she was all-powerful, with her own future and that of her children assured. Now that he was gone, they were in grave danger. She herself still lay in childbed; her two sons, the co-Emperors Basil and Constantine, were six and three years old respectively. The example of her own father-in-law had illustrated the perils of a long minority, especially when there were ambitious generals in the offing; and of these there were now three – the two Phocas brothers and John Tzimisces – who would be sure to see the present situation as a possible path to the throne. In short she needed a protector, and a strong one. Secretly she sent an urgent appeal to Nicephorus Phocas, begging him to return at once. Nicephorus did not hesitate, and some time in early April reached the capital. Bringas had protested violently when he heard of the Empress's summons, claiming that the general had become a public danger who deserved immediate arrest. But he had found no support, and the crowds in front of the palace were loudly demanding that Nicephorus be awarded the triumph of which he had been so unjustly deprived.

And so the triumph was held, and given additional sanctity by the tattered tunic of John the Baptist, recently snatched from its long-time resting-place in Aleppo and now carried before Nicephorus – 'the White Death of the Saracens' – as he rode to the Hippodrome. In the face of his popularity, Bringas was powerless; he was also afraid. The general was in daily consultation with the Empress; if he were now to make a bid for the throne, what would be his own fate? Nicephorus, it was true, lost no opportunity of proclaiming his indifference to worldly power and his eagerness to retire to the monastery that Athanasius was already building on the Holy Mountain. But Bringas was not deceived. Quietly he made his plans, and when all was in readiness he summoned his enemy to the palace.

Nicephorus too was on his guard. Instead of obeying the summons he went straight to St Sophia, where he publicly accused Bringas of plotting to murder him. An indignant crowd collected, which was soon joined by Patriarch Polyeuctus himself. Polyeuctus was a narrow-minded bigot, but this austere, devout general was a man after his own heart: he had no hesitation in lending his own voice to that of the crowd. Bringas could only watch, fuming, while the Senate confirmed Nicephorus in his command and undertook to make no major decision of policy without his consent. The general thanked them for their confidence and immediately after the Easter celebrations returned to Anatolia. But not for long. Those secret discussions with the Empress had ended in a mutually advantageous agreement. Nicephorus would protect the rights of the two child-Emperors; in return, he would himself be proclaimed co-Emperor and join them on the throne.

Bringas, now desperate, played his last card. He sent letters to two of Nicephorus's senior commanders, Romanus Curcuas and John Tzimisces, offering them the supreme commands of East and West respectively in return for the betrayal of their chief. 'First accept the command in Anatolia,' he wrote to Tzimisces, 'then be patient a little and before long you will be *basileus* of the Romans.' His confidence was misplaced: Tzimisces went at once to Nicephorus and showed him the letter. It was enough. At dawn on 3 July 963, before the entire army drawn up on a great plain just outside the walls of Caesarea, Nicephorus Phocas was raised by his generals on a great shield in the ancient manner and proclaimed Emperor of the Romans. Then, after a short service in the cathedral, he set off for his capital.

Even now Bringas refused to admit defeat. From Macedonia he had summoned large numbers of European troops who traditionally mistrusted the Anatolians; a number of these were dispatched to the Asiatic shore of the Bosphorus, there to commandeer all the vessels they could find and sail them over to Europe. Thus it was that when Nicephorus and his army arrived at Chrysopolis on 9 August they were unable to cross the strait. The new Emperor was not unduly disturbed; he knew that some at least of his supporters would join him under cover of darkness, and so they did. But one of the first to arrive, his own brother Leo, brought disturbing news. Their father, old Bardas Phocas, now well into his eighties, was being held by Bringas as a hostage.

In fact, events were moving a good deal faster than Leo realized. Old Bardas had escaped and sought asylum in St Sophia; and Bringas had sent a detachment of militia after him. He had forgotten, however, that it was a Sunday: the Great Church was thronged. Bardas was a popular figure, and the soldiers found themselves surrounded by a hostile crowd who drove them forcibly from the building. Bringas, however, whatever his other faults, was no coward. He rode to St Sophia, pushed his way through the crowd, mounted the ambo and tried to address them. Once again he had underestimated his opposition. A few words of conciliation might yet have saved the day; instead he blustered, threatening to cut off all the city's supplies of food. It was an empty threat, and his listeners knew it. Bringas waited, fuming, until at noon the people began to stream from St Sophia. Then, sending for the two child-Emperors, he took them firmly by the hand and led them to the old general, sitting quietly in the sanctuary. The subsequent conversation is unrecorded – though the presence of the two children suggests that they too might have become hostages. All we know is that Bardas allowed himself to be led away.

For the third time the eunuch had misjudged. When St Sophia began once again to fill with people for vespers, their first thought was for Bardas; and when they failed to find him their mood grew uglier than ever, their anger being now principally directed against the Patriarch, who had failed to protect the fugitive. A terrified Polyeuctus hurried to the palace, found the old general, seized him by the arm and returned with him to the church, where his appearance produced an immediate hush; and when Bringas arrived a few minutes later with a platoon of Macedonians the people decided that they had had enough. While some took charge of the bewildered old man, carried him back to his house and mounted guard over him, the remainder seized bricks, stones and anything else – even church furniture – that might serve them as a weapon and flung themselves on the soldiers.

The riot spread like wildfire through the city, and as it gathered momentum it began to reveal a guiding hand: that of Basil, the natural son of Romanus Lecapenus. Presumably to protect the interests of his elder, legitimate, sons Romanus had had him castrated in infancy; but Basil was able and intelligent and had long played an important part in affairs of state. At the first sign of the insurrection, he had gathered together all his retainers and led them down to the Forum, where he quickly assumed control. First he sent men to every corner of the city to proclaim the imminent arrival of the new Emperor; next he led the mob to Bringas's palace, which was plundered of everything of value and burnt to the ground. After this the burning and looting became general. Only after three days could Basil lead his men down to the Golden Horn, take possession of all the vessels there and sail the vast flotilla across the Bosphorus to the Hieria, where Nicephorus was still patiently waiting.

At last, on Sunday, 16 August 963, Nicephorus Phocas was ready to enter his capital. With Basil at his side he boarded the imperial *dromond* and was rowed across the strait and westward to the Palace of the Hebdomon, just outside the Land Walls at their southern end. Here he changed into ceremonial attire, strapped on his golden breastplate and mounted the huge white charger, caparisoned in purple and gold, that was to bear him through the city to St Sophia where, in the presence of the two child-Emperors, Polyeuctus laid the diadem on his head.

Nicephorus Phocas, we are told, was short and squat, with broad shoulders and barrel chest; his face swarthy and weather-beaten with small, dark eyes under heavy brows. His black, curly hair was unusually long. He was a man of total moral integrity, intelligent but narrow-minded, incorruptible, impervious to flattery and hard as nails; but he could also be pitiless and cruel, and his meanness and avarice were notorious. It is difficult to feel much affection for a man who for years had eaten no meat, who abhorred women, who slept in a hair shirt and spent several hours of each day in prayer; but Nicephorus had never courted popularity. Though now over fifty, his energies were unabated, and he flung himself into his new role with every appearance of enthusiasm.

His first concern was Bringas, whom he banished to his wild Paphlagonian homeland. On old Bardas, his father, he conferred the title of Caesar; his brother Leo became *curopalates*, or Marshal of the Imperial Court; while John Tzimisces was confirmed as Domestic of the Schools, commander-in-chief of the army in Anatolia. There remained Theophano, without whom he would have probably spent the rest of his active life in Syria, fighting the Saracen. The Emperor's first action where she was concerned was surprising: he moved her from the palace to the old fortress of the Petrion, on the upper reaches of the Golden Horn. She remained there over a month, while Nicephorus occupied the imperial apartments; then, on 20 September in the Palatine Church of the Nea, he married her.

The purpose of Theophano's temporary banishment was clearly to preserve the proprieties – though Nicephorus could hardly have found her a more uncomfortable residence. It was suggested at the time that, dazzled by the Empress's beauty, he had fallen passionately in love with her; and it is not hard to see why. The picture of a rough, unbending old general suddenly losing his head and heart to the loveliest – and most vicious – woman of her day is difficult to resist. But is it likely? Nicephorus was, after all, a deeply religious ascetic, who after the death of his first wife had taken a vow of chastity; would he really have proved so susceptible? Was this not, quite simply, part of the contract agreed between the two of them? For her it could have been nothing else. This exquisite young Empress, after a happy if short-lived marriage with the outstandingly attractive Romanus, could have felt nothing but repugnance for a sanctimonious and unattractive old puritan more than twice her age. As for Nicephorus, we cannot be so sure. He would not have been the first confirmed bachelor to have been swept unexpectedly off his feet; and his conduct when the legality of the union was called in question suggests that he loved his young wife to distraction.

For there were others less ready to overcome their scruples, and among them was Polyeuctus the Patriarch. He had, so far as we know, voiced no prior objections to the marriage; but when, towards the end of the service, Nicephorus advanced alone towards the middle door of the iconostasis to implant the traditional kiss upon the high altar behind it, the Patriarch stepped forward, hand upraised. Was the Emperor unaware, he asked, of the penance imposed by the Church on all who contracted a second marriage? After one full year he might once again be permitted within the sanctuary; until then it would remain closed to him. Nicephorus accepted the ruling; but he never forgave Polyeuctus for the insult. Neither was this the end of his tribulations. Some days later the palace chaplain Stylianus was foolish enough to mention that the Emperor was godfather to one of Theophano's children. By another law of the Church, this put them within the proscribed degrees and would, if upheld, render the marriage null and void. Once again, the Patriarch did not hesitate. The law was the law, and must be obeyed. He now offered Nicephorus a simple choice: he must either repudiate Theophano or suffer the ban of the Church in perpetuity.

At this point, had he cared nothing for his wife, Nicephorus might have given in. To have submitted with a good grace, simultaneously consigning Theophano to a nunnery, would have reinstated him in divine favour while also enabling him to escape a tiresome responsibility. But he did not submit. Instead, he called a meeting of all the bishops who chanced to be in Constantinople, several of whom had fortunately come to seek favours from him. They obediently ruled that the law in question had been promulgated during the reign – and thus in the name – of Constantine V, a condemned heretic. The decree was consequently without validity. The marriage stood.

Not, however, in the eyes of the Patriarch, who simply repeated his ultimatum. And yet, though he was now excommunicate, the breach between Church and State complete, Nicephorus still refused to submit. His soul might be in jeopardy, but he refused to leave Theophano. Finally, he himself hit upon a solution. A few days later Stylianus testified that he had never made the statement attributed to him or, if he had, that his memory had played him false. Old Bardas was then brought in, and quaveringly confirmed that neither he nor his son had stood sponsor to any of Theophano's children. Polyeuctus, confronted with two bare-faced perjuries one after the other, saw that he was beaten. The aged Caesar, who enjoyed not only the reverence due to the Emperor's father but also that popularity exclusively reserved for those with one foot in the grave, was beyond his reach. He gave in.

For Nicephorus II, the war against the Saracens was a crusade. Even his love for Theophano could not keep him from his duty; and in 964 he returned to the attack. The summer of 965 saw the recapture of Tarsus, the Muslims' springboard for their annual incursions into Cilicia. From Tarsus it was but a short sail across to Cyprus. Since 668, when the island had been the subject of a treaty between Constantine IV and the Caliph Abdul-Malik, it had been ruled jointly by Emperor and Caliph. The same summer of 965 imperial troops occupied it in strength, and Cyprus became a Byzantine Theme. As the Abbasid Caliphate crumbled, so its subjects grew ever more demoralized. Saïf ed-Daula of Aleppo had never recovered from the destruction of his palace and the effective conquest of his capital; partially paralysed after a stroke, he died in 967 aged only fifty-one. Nicephorus encountered no more serious obstacles to his progress; Aleppo became an imperial vassal and protectorate. And in 969, after 332 years, the ancient patriarchal city of Antioch returned once more to Christian hands.

Where the West was concerned, there is a less happy story to tell; in dealing with Europe diplomacy was required, and there were few worse diplomats than Nicephorus Phocas. Power had gone to his head: as his reign continued he became ever more arrogant and overbearing. He provided an excellent example of this boorishness as early as 965, when an embassy arrived from Bulgaria to collect the annual subsidy agreed at the time of Tsar Peter's marriage in 927. Bulgaria was an invaluable buffer state, protecting the Empire from both Magyars and Russians, and the modest subsidy – which had been paid unquestioningly for thirty-eight years – was a small price for its friendship. Nicephorus however turned on the ambassadors, abusing their countrymen as a race of hideous and filthy beggars, ruled by a prince dressed only in the skins of animals. Then he had them scourged before sending them back empty-handed to Preslav. Such conduct was paralleled only by that of the Emperor Alexander over half a century before. But Alexander had been a drunken boor; Nicephorus was in deadly earnest. He advanced to the frontier and captured several border strongholds, and in other circumstances he would doubtless have penetrated further; but he had no wish to weaken the army of the East. He therefore concluded an agreement with Prince Svyatoslav of Kiev whereby Svyatoslav, in return for a handsome fee, undertook to subdue the Bulgars on his behalf; here, so far as he was concerned, was a heaven-sent opportunity to push forward his already extensive frontiers as far as the Danube. The Bulgars could put up no effective resistance: too late, the Emperor saw that he had succeeded only in replacing a weak and peace-loving neighbour with an ambitious and aggressive enemy.

In his dealings with Western Europe, Nicephorus's diplomacy was equally calamitous, and his chief adversary still more formidable. Otto the Saxon had come a long way since the time of his first appearance in this story, some fifteen years before. Titular King of Italy since 952, he had at first been largely occupied in Germany, while the peninsula had been effectively ruled by the Marquis Berengar of Ivrea. In 961, however, in response to an appeal by the unspeakable John XII, he had swept down into Italy, taken Berengar prisoner and ridden on to Rome, where in February 962 the Pope had crowned him Emperor. Otto had been greatly displeased by the rejection of his niece Hedwig by Romanus II, in favour of the lovely Theophano; and when in 959 Romanus succeeded his father on the throne relations between the two became chillier still; but Otto continued to dream of a dynastic union, and in the early summer of 968 he dispatched a mission to Constantinople, under an experienced ambassador: our old friend Liudprand of Cremona.

Liudprand's report of this second visit is incontestably the most enjoyable account ever written of a diplomatic mission to the court of Byzantium; and it is hardly surprising if he has little good to say of it. First of all there was the abrasive personality of the Emperor himself. To Nicephorus, Liudprand was everything he most hated: a smooth-tongued trickster, made still more dangerous by his fluent Greek, and a heretic to boot. On top of this he represented a German adventurer who called himself Emperor: a pretender to his throne and a usurper of his title. Liudprand was nevertheless deeply wounded by the manner of his reception:

The palace in which we were confined neither kept out the cold nor afforded protection from the heat; furthermore we were placed under armed guards ... It was so far from the residence of the Emperor that when we walked there we arrived exhausted. To make matters worse, the Greek wine was quite undrinkable, having been mixed with pitch, resin and plaster ...

We arrived at Constantinople and waited in heavy rain outside the Carian Gate until the eleventh hour. Only then did Nicephorus order us to be admitted on foot, for he did not deem us worthy to ride, and we were escorted to the aforesaid loath-some, waterless and draughty stone house. On the sixth of June I was brought before the Emperor's brother Leo, marshal of the court and Logothete; and we wore our-selves out in a fierce argument over your title. He called you not 'Emperor', which is *basileus* in his tongue, but – most insultingly – *rex*, which is 'King' in ours ...

On the following day Liudprand had his first audience of the Emperor – who came, he tells us, straight to the point. Nicephorus regretted not having received his guest more courteously, but in view of his master's conduct, he said, he had no choice. Liudprand gave as good as he got. His master, he pointed out, had liberated Rome from a tyranny of libertines and harlots; if Nicephorus and his predecessors were the Roman Emperors they claimed to be, why had they allowed this state of affairs? If however Nicephorus would give the hand in marriage of one of Romanus's daughters to Otto's son, the younger Otto – now co-Emperor with his father – several important concessions could be expected. Six days later, Liudprand was informed that a princess born in the purple might indeed be available – but only if the Western Empire were prepared to cede to Byzantium Rome, Ravenna and all eastern Italy, together with Istria and the northern part of the Dalmatian coast.

Nicephorus cannot have imagined for a moment that Otto would consider such terms, nor would Liudprand have had the authority to accept them; there was consequently no good reason for him to remain in Constantinople, and his alarm was all the greater when, instead of being sent on his way, he found himself confined even more closely to his detested lodgings, from which he was allowed to emerge only when the Emperor occasionally invited him to dinner. Even these functions were less agreeable than they might have been, owing first to the disgusting food, and second to Nicephorus, who saw them only as opportunities to bully his guest. Not until 2 October, after four months of misery, sickness and almost constant vilification, was he allowed to leave.

Even that was not the end of Liudprand's tribulations. He was delayed at Naupactus, deserted by his ship's crew at Patras, unkindly received by a eunuch bishop and half-starved on Leucas, and subjected to three consecutive earthquakes on Corfu, where he subsequently fell among thieves. He was conscious, too, that it had all been in vain. The imperial marriage was no nearer, relations between East and West more strained than ever: indeed, before he was back in Cremona war had erupted in south Italy. Poor Liudprand – he could not have known that his account of his journey would still be read a thousand years after his death. A pity: it would have cheered him up.

It was only to be expected, in view of the character, manners and appearance of Nicephorus Phocas, that he should have been incapable of maintaining the affections of his subjects. They hated the shameless favouritism which he showed to the only two sections of society that represented his own background: the army and the Anatolian aristocracy. The imperial garrison in the capital could, in his eyes, do no wrong: at night the streets were loud with the carousings of drunken soldiery, to the point where honest citizens feared to leave their homes. The fortunes of 'the powerful' underwent an even more dramatic change. Formerly, if a holding came up for sale, first refusal was given to the owners of the immediately adjoining land; henceforth it was to be available to the highest bidder – almost inevitably a landed nobleman bent on increasing his estates. Thus the rich became richer and the poor poorer; and the people of Constantinople did not attempt to conceal their displeasure.

Another source of opposition was the Church. The Emperor's puritanical sensibilities were profoundly shocked by the enormous wealth of the monasteries; vast tracts of superb agricultural land were lying fallow under their mismanagement. His approach was characteristically uncompromising: all further transfers of land to the Church were forbidden, whatever the circumstances. The edict called forth a storm of protest from monks and clergy alike, but worse was to follow: there now came a decree that no new bishop might be appointed without the Emperor's personal approval.

Finally, affecting rich and poor, cleric and layman, soldier and civilian alike, was the crippling taxation that Nicephorus had increased to unprecedented levels to finance his endless warfare. And so dissatisfaction grew. On Easter Sunday 967, as the games were about to begin, a rumour spread to the effect that the Emperor intended to order random killings among the crowd. Nicephorus surely had no such intention; but later, in an interval between the races, he gave the signal for certain companies of armed guards to descend into the arena. It may have been a warning; but mock battles were common enough in the games. The immediate reaction, in any event, was panic. Only after many had been crushed to death or trampled underfoot was it noticed that the soldiers had made no move against anyone and that the Emperor was still in his box. Two months later, on Ascension Day, as Nicephorus was proceeding in state through the city after matins, abusive shouts were heard from the crowd; within moments he was surrounded by a hostile mob. As always when in physical danger, he betrayed no trace of emotion, continuing his measured progress and looking neither to right nor left; but had it not been for his personal guard he might never have returned to the palace alive.

The next morning Nicephorus gave orders for the fortification of the Great Palace, sealing it off completely. Within this huge enclave he built what seems to have been a private citadel, for the use of himself and his family. By now it was clear to all of them that – perhaps for the first time in his life – the Emperor was afraid. His aspect grew still more sombre, his religious observances ever more morbid and morose. He no longer slept in a bed, but on a panther-skin laid on the floor in the corner of the imperial bedchamber. What ultimately brought matters to a head was the fate of Bulgaria. On 30 January 969 King Peter died, to be succeeded by his elder son Boris, un-remarkable except for an enormous red beard. Six months or so later Peter was followed to the grave by Princess Olga of Kiev, the only restraining influence on her headstrong son Svyatoslav, who in the early autumn swept down into the Bulgarian heartland. Preslav fell, and Boris with his entire family was taken off into captivity. Philippopolis put up a heroic resistance; but it too surrendered in the end, and paid dearly for its heroism when Svyatoslav impaled 20,000 of its citizens. By the onset of winter the Russians were ranged along the whole Thracian border.

At this point the spotlight returns to the Empress Theophano. Whatever her feelings for Nicephorus, there can be little doubt that she had by now fallen passionately in love with his old companion-in-arms, the outstandingly good-looking John Tzimisces. The degree to which this tiny but irresistible Armenian returned her love is somewhat less certain: there were plenty of other considerations that might have impelled him to act as he did. But Theophano at twenty-eight was still as beautiful as ever: her embraces cannot have been altogether distasteful. Her first task was to convince her husband that he had been unjust towards his former friend – to whom, after all, he probably owed his crown. Nicephorus readily agreed to recall Tzimisces, on the condition that he remained in his house at Chalcedon, coming over to Constantinople only with specific permission. Obviously, from the lovers' point of view, the situation was still less than ideal; but before long the little general was slipping nightly across the strait to the corner of the palace where the Empress was waiting – and where, among other less reprehensible occupations, the two of them cold-bloodedly planned her husband's murder. By now accomplices were not hard to find. The date of the assassination was fixed for 10 December. On the afternoon of that day the leading conspirators, disguised as women, entered the *gynaeceum* of the palace ostensibly on a visit to the Empress, who distributed them among various small rooms in which they could wait unobserved until the signal was given.

Darkness came early during those December days, and as night fell a blizzard began. The conspirators dared not act without John Tzimisces – but would he be able, in such weather, to make his journey across the Bosphorus? Meanwhile it was for Theophano to allay her husband's suspicions. She had decided, she told him, to pay a quick visit to two little Bulgar princesses recently arrived in the city. She would not be gone for long, so he must not shut her out. Nicephorus raised no objection. For some time he continued to read a devotional work and to pray. At last he wrapped himself up in his uncle's hair shirt and stretched himself out on the floor to sleep. Outside, the storm continued. It was snowing hard and John Tzimisces, making his way from Chalcedon in an unlit boat, had a long and perilous crossing. It was nearly midnight when his accomplices heard the low whistle announcing his arrival. Silently a rope was let down from a window, and one by one the conspirators were drawn up into the building. A eunuch was waiting to lead them straight to the Emperor's bedchamber. There was a moment of alarm when the bed was found to be empty, but the man quietly pointed to the far corner of the room where their victim lay on his panther-skin, fast asleep.

Awoken by the noise, Nicephorus tried to rise; at the same time one Leo Balantes struck him a violent blow with his sword. It was aimed at the neck, but he deflected it and received its full force diagonally across the face. Streaming with blood, he called upon the Holy Virgin for aid while he was dragged to the foot of his bed, on which John Tzimisces was sitting. There he lay motionless as his former companion-in-arms cursed him for his ingratitude, kicking him savagely and tearing out handfuls of his hair and beard. After Tzimisces had finished it was the turn of the others, each with his own private score to settle. At last he was run through with a sword.

Minutes after the deed was done Tzimisces's men were out in the snow-covered streets of the city, shouting 'John, Augustus and Emperor of the Romans!' at every corner. Meanwhile the duty guard of Varangian Vikings, axes in hand, hurried up just in time to see the head of Nicephorus, held triumphantly aloft at a window. At once they were still. Alive, they would have defended him to the last breath; dead, there was no point in avenging him. They had a new master now.

Throughout the next day the city lay silent and apparently deserted: Basil had proclaimed a curfew. The storm had been succeeded by an eerie stillness, the fog hung thick over the Marmara – and the body of Nicephorus lay below the window from which it had been flung, an obscene bundle on the blood-stained snow. When night had fallen, it was thrown on to a makeshift wooden bier and carried to the Church of the Holy Apostles, where it was laid in one of the marble sarcophagi ordered by Constantine the Great six centuries before. It was an honourable resting-place; but Nicephorus Phocas, the White Death of the Saracens, saintly and hideous, magnificent and insufferable, had deserved a better end.

For the second time in ten years the throne of Byzantium had been snatched by a member of the Anatolian aristocracy. On both occasions the usurping

Emperor, a spectacularly successful general, had succeeded through the machinations of the Empress Theophano, of whose sons he had proclaimed himself protector. Between Nicephorus Phocas and John Tzimisces there was, however, one crucial difference. Though neither had any legitimate claim to the imperial diadem, Nicephorus had accepted it by invitation of the Empress; John had acquired it by violence. The ever-inflexible Patriarch could not reject the new claimant, but he did impose conditions which John was compelled to accept; and the first of these concerned Theophano. There could be no question of John's coronation until the Empress were put away, never again to show her face in Constantinople.

John did not hesitate. The Empress, humiliated and heartbroken, was unceremoniously packed off to that favourite repository of imperial waste, the island of Proti in the Marmara. Polyeuctus next demanded that the Emperor should do public penance, denounce all those who had been his accomplices in the crime and abrogate all his predecessor's decrees against the Church. These conditions too were accepted without hesitation; and on Christmas Day 969, just two weeks after the murder, the new Emperor proceeded to his coronation.

When we compare John Tzimisces with Nicephorus, he emerges surprisingly well; indeed, it is hard to reconcile the brutal murderer with the *chevalier sans peur et sans reproche* depicted by the chroniclers. They emphasize not only his valour but his kindness and generosity, his integrity and intelligence, his dash and panache. They speak of his good looks – darkish-blond hair, red beard, a clear and direct gaze from startlingly blue eyes – and, despite his small stature, extraordinary agility and strength. He possessed, too, an easy-going charm that won all hearts. He too was a widower; but his way with women was still irresistible. He presented, in short, an astonishing contrast to his predecessor, against whose sombre asceticism his own *joie de vivre* stood out in even greater relief. But the virtue that most endeared him to his subjects was his generosity. The larger part of his fortune he distributed among those who had suffered the most from the recent disastrous harvests; another major beneficiary was the leper hospital at Chrysopolis, which he visited regularly, occasionally bathing the patients' sores with his own hands. No wonder that the perpetrator of one of the foulest murders in Byzantine history became one of its best-loved rulers.

It was fortunate that he did, for Prince Svyatoslav of Kiev was already on the march. John tried to negotiate, but it soon became clear that war was inevitable. The citizens of Constantinople had faced many similar dangers in the past; but most recent threats had been from the Bulgars, whose numbers were at least finite. They were now confronted by a nation whose frontiers extended from Balkans to Baltic, comprising whole races of whose names they had scarcely heard – all capable, it was said, of hideous savagery.

But the Byzantine army was ready. This time John knew that he must stay in the capital: his position there was not yet sufficiently secure to allow any campaigning. But he had every confidence in his commanders. One was his brother-in-law and close friend Bardas Sclerus, the other the eunuch Peter Phocas, a hero like Sclerus of the Saracen wars. Nephew of the murdered Nicephorus, Peter was the only one of his immediate family to have escaped exile. Both generals had orders not to engage in battle unnecessarily; perhaps the sight of the Byzantine army *en masse* might persuade Svyatoslav to retreat. But the Prince of Kiev was determined to fight. The armies met near Arcadiopolis. The engagement began when Svyatoslav's regiment of Pechenegs was enticed into an ambush and effectively wiped out; and this was followed a few days later by a pitched battle near Arcadiopolis – the first ever fought on open ground between Byzantines and Russians. For the Byzantines, it proved a triumph; for the Russians, a massacre. It was a shamed and shattered army that Svyatoslav led back to Bulgaria – and a full year before he showed his face again.

By the early spring of 971 John was ready for the second round. His army was in first-class condition, and this time he would lead it himself. Then, just before he was due to leave, news arrived from the East: Bardas Phocas, nephew of Nicephorus, had escaped from exile and returned to Caesarea, his Cappadocian power base, where a large assembly had proclaimed him *basileus*. Soon afterwards came another report, informing him that Leo Phocas and his son, away in exile on Lesbos, had somehow contrived to spread the news of this rebellion through Thrace, announcing their own imminent arrival and calling upon the people to rise against the new usurper.

The Emperor acted with his usual speed. Leo and his son were given a summary trial and condemned to death. Almost at once, however, John had second thoughts. He commuted the death sentence to one of blinding, with perpetual exile; and then, stretching his compassion further still, sent secret instructions to Lesbos that the red-hot iron should at the last moment be withdrawn, leaving the two men their sight. To the pretender himself John sent a promise to spare his life and property if he would submit; but Bardas Phocas was already marching on the capital. The Emperor now had only one course open to him: to send his best general, with his best men, from Thrace. A few days later Bardas Sclerus too was on the march. The eastern threat was more immediate than the western, and the risk had to be taken.

Even now John enjoined his brother-in-law to make every effort to avoid bloodshed, and to offer all those who submitted a guarantee that they would go unpunished. Sclerus was only too happy to obey. He was an old friend and companion-in-arms of Phocas and the whole affair was little to his taste. Thus, when his scouts reported a sighting of Phocas's camp, he made no attempt to attack; instead, he sent a number of secret agents, disguised as wandering beggars, to suborn the rebels. They were extraordinarily successful. Every night more and more of Phocas's adherents dropped away. The pretender soon found his army reduced to a few hundred men. Finally he took refuge with his family in a nearby fortress. But Sclerus had followed him, and immediately put the castle under siege. He held out as long as he could, then – after confirmation that all their lives would be spared – made his submission. John Tzimisces was as good as his word. He ordered Bardas Phocas to be tonsured and exiled with his family to Chios, one of the most delightful of the Aegean islands. Few rulers anywhere would have dealt so leniently with a rebel pretender.

Tzimisces was to encounter no further threats to his throne; but he could claim no legitimate right to it unless he could make himself part of the imperial family. Marriage with Theophano was now out of the question, but fortunately there were the five sisters of Romanus II whom she had packed off to convents; and it was to one of these, Theodora, that he announced his betrothal in the autumn of 971. Twelve years of seclusion had done little to improve her appearance, but John was not interested in her looks; he was marrying her because she was the great-granddaughter, granddaughter, daughter and sister of Emperors. Through her he became at last a member of the Macedonian dynasty. The wedding took place in November, the ceremony being performed by Polyeuctus's successor, an unworldly ascetic named Basil. The celebrations continued until well after Christmas – by which time, however, there was another imperial marriage in the air: one intended to settle the five-year quarrel with Otto the Saxon and to forge an indissoluble link between the Eastern and the Western Empires. To Nicephorus Phocas the very idea had been repugnant; John Tzimisces supported it for all he was worth, and it was at his invitation that the Archbishop of Cologne arrived in late December to collect the bride-to-be.

This bridegroom was the seventeen-year-old Otto, son and heir of the Emperor of the West. The bride's name was Theophano. She seems to have been a niece of Tzimisces and there was some consternation when she arrived in Rome and proved not to be the *porphyrogenita* that had been expected; but she was finally accepted, and she and Otto were married by Pope John XIII in St Peter's on 14 April 972. Theophano was lucky: the marriage proved a surprisingly happy one. She was treated with kindness and consideration and allowed to maintain all her Byzantine customs – to the point where her son, the future Otto III, was to grow up more of a Greek than a Saxon. None the less, for a girl of just sixteen, those first four months of 972 must have been little short of a nightmare; and it is only right that we should spare a thought for her loneliness before we return to her uncle – who was having the time of his life.

Just before Holy Week, 972, John left Constantinople for Thrace. He was in buoyant mood: the Prince of Kiev had failed to launch his major attack and was still skulking in Bulgaria. The time had now come to deal with him. He reviewed the fleet in the Golden Horn, then gave it the signal to sail to the mouth of the Danube, there to prevent any attempt by Svyatoslav to escape by sea. As soon as the first ships were under way he himself headed westward, his troops behind him. At Adrianople he picked up the rump of the army that Bardas Sclerus had left in Thrace the year before; the sight of the Emperor in his gilded armour put new life into his men as they headed into the Bulgarian heartland. To John's relief, the Balkan defiles were found to be unguarded: the Prince of Kiev, expecting him to celebrate Easter in Constantinople, had as yet made no defensive arrangements. On the Wednesday of Holy Week John emerged from the mountains above the old Bulgarian capital of Preslav and found himself looking down on the Russian camp. He attacked at once.

The battle was furious, and for a long time indecisive. It was only after John had loosed the regiment of 'Immortals', which he had raised and trained himself, in a murderous charge against their flank that the Russians suddenly broke up in disorder, fleeing towards Preslav with the imperial cavalry in hot pursuit. Few reached the city alive. The siege of Preslav began the following day, the Byzantine catapults hurling flaming bolts of Greek fire over the walls. The city was soon overrun. Among those who delivered themselves up to the conquerors was the deposed Tsar Boris – he of the red beard – who had been held for two years by Svyatoslav as his prisoner. The Emperor received him with courtesy; his mission, he told Boris, was not to conquer Bulgaria but to set it free – an assurance which, in view of his later actions, he had better not have made.

Easter was celebrated amid the ruins, while John considered the problem of Svyatoslav himself. The Prince, he learned, was at Dristra, Bulgaria's chief port on the Danube. John set off at once. It was a long and arduous march, but at last on St George's Day he drew up his army before Dristra. This time the siege continued for three months, until on 24 July Svyatoslav burst out of the main gate with the remainder of his army. The day was eventually won by means of John's favourite trick, a feigned retreat, and at nightfall the Prince sued for peace, offering to evacuate the whole country and deliver over every prisoner. All he asked in return was safe conduct across the Danube, and a little food for his few surviving men. The Emperor was only too happy to agree.

Now at last the two rulers met, at Svyatoslav's request, face to face. John rode down on his charger to the meeting-place on the river bank; the Prince arrived by boat, rowing alongside his men and distinguishable from them only by his clean white robe, his jewelled earring and the two long strands of fair hair – badges of rank and evidence of his Viking forebears – that fell from his otherwise shaven head. He briefly expressed the hope that the old commercial treaty might be renewed; then, with a dignified bow, he returned to his boat and rowed away.

As for John Tzimisces, he had regained Bulgaria for the Empire; for, whatever he might have said to Boris at Preslav, he had no intention of reinstating him on his throne. Anyone witnessing his triumphal entry into Constantinople that August might have been forgiven for supposing that it was the Bulgars who had been defeated. Place of honour in the procession – in the gilded chariot, drawn by four white horses, that had been intended for his own use – he had accorded to the most revered of all Bulgarian icons, a portrait of the Virgin which he had brought back with him among the spoils. He himself rode behind it in his gleaming armour. At the rear of the procession, on foot, walked Tsar Boris, his wife and children. In St Sophia, John laid upon the high altar not only the icon but the crown of the Bulgar state. Shortly afterwards he forced the young Tsar into formal abdication. Henceforth Bulgaria was an imperial province. The Bulgar Patriarchate was abolished, its dependent bishoprics subjected once again to Constantinople. Characteristically, John gave Boris the honorary rank of *magister*; his younger brother Romanus, less fortunate, was castrated. It was an inglorious end to the house of Krum, which had more than once caused Byzantium itself to tremble.

John Tzimisces now turned his attention to the East. Only three years before, in 969, the Caliphate of the Fatimids had embarked on a new policy of expansion. Advancing eastward from their capital at Mahdiya in what is now Tunisia, Fatimid troops had swept through the Nile Valley and on across Sinai into Palestine and Syria. In 971 they had attacked Antioch; and in July 973, before the walls of Amida, they almost annihilated a Byzantine army. By the spring of 974 John was ready. His army supplemented by some 10,000 Armenians made available by King Ashot, he headed south to the plains of Mesopotamia, nowhere meeting any opposition worthy of the name. Why he did not press on to Baghdad is a mystery; demoralized as it was, the city could hardly have resisted any major offensive. Instead he retraced his steps to

Antioch, leaving the army in its winter quarters while he himself returned hurriedly to Constantinople – to meet the Pope.

In the early summer of 974 the Cardinal Deacon Franco had staged a *coup* against Otto's puppet Pope Benedict VI. Franco had then mounted the throne himself under the name of Boniface VII; but a counter-revolution had obliged him almost immediately to flee for his life to Constantinople. Meanwhile the young Emperor had appointed in his stead the Bishop of Sutri, one of whose first actions as Pope Benedict VII was to excommunicate his predecessor. The arrival of Boniface on the Bosphorus put the Byzantines in a quandary. His long opposition to the Western Empire had led him to forge strong links with Constantinople, and he had steadfastly supported Nicephorus Phocas in all the latter's differences with Otto I. The palace had consequently decided that relations with Rome must be broken off. Patriarch Basil, on the other hand, who had never questioned the essential unity of the Church or the supremacy of the legitimate Pontiff, was determined to uphold the excommunication.

It was nearly always the worldly Patriarchs of Constantinople who challenged the status of the Pope; the spiritual ascetics had no such doubts. Basil himself was almost too holy, living on a diet of berries and water, wearing the same filthy robe until it disintegrated, sleeping on the bare earth. He had never been popular, and when the decision was taken to replace him with someone more amenable there was no shortage of bishops ready to testify against him. He himself insisted that he could be deposed only by an Ecumenical Council, on which the Pope would be properly represented. An imperial tribunal, meeting soon after the Emperor's return, was only too happy to prove him wrong.

So Basil was exiled, Benedict was refused recognition and Boniface remained in Constantinople until April 984 when, with Byzantine help, he managed to depose his rival's successor John XIV and regain the pontifical throne. This time he held it for fifteen months – until his death, almost certainly by poison, in the following year. His corpse, we are told, was dragged naked through the city and eventually left on the Capitol, where it lay until a passing group of priests recovered it and arranged for its burial.

In the early spring of 975 John Tzimisces returned to the East and set off on the last and the most successful of all his campaigns. By the end of the summer most of Palestine, Syria and the Lebanon – regions where no Emperor had set foot since the days of Heraclius – were under Byzantine control. But when he returned to Constantinople towards the end of the year he was a dying man. Our three most authoritative sources all accuse Basil the Chamberlain. They tell us that the Emperor, hearing that every one of the most prosperous estates through which he passed belonged to Basil, made no secret of his intention of confronting him and demanding an explanation. His words were reported to Basil, who made his dispositions accordingly. A week or two later, when John was dining with one of his vassals in Bithynia, a slow-acting poison was slipped into his cup; he awoke the next morning scarcely able to move his limbs. By the time he reached the Bosphorus he was breathing with difficulty. Somehow he managed to attend the service at which the two principal prizes gained in the East – Christ's sandals and the hair of John the Baptist – were installed in St Sophia; then he took to his bed. All his wealth he left to the poor and the sick; then, calling repeatedly on the Holy Virgin to intercede for him, he died on 10 January 976, after a reign of six years and a month. He was fifty-one.

What are we to make of this poisoning story? Foul play was invariably suspected on such occasions. If Basil were guilty would he have remained in power as he did, acting as Regent for the two young Emperors? And what was this mysterious poison, so slow-acting and yet so grimly effective? Is it not far likelier that John died – as thousands of humbler soldiers must have died during those eastern wars – of typhoid, or malaria, or dysentery?

Yes – but we can never be sure. John Tzimisces is a mystery in his death, just as he was in his life. In his short reign he proved himself one of the very greatest of Byzantine Emperors. He had conquered the Russians, the Bulgars and the Caliphs of both Baghdad and Cairo; he had regained the greater part of Syria and the Lebanon, of Mesopotamia and Palestine. He had been admired by allies and enemies alike for his courage, his chivalry, his compassion. His radiant personality, like his golden armour, leaves us dazzled. Yet it can never quite blind us to another, darker vision: that of a pitiful, misshapen heap lying huddled on a palace floor, while another figure – spare, sinewy and immensely strong – gazes contemptuously down, and kicks.

16
The Bulgar-Slayer

[976–1025]

With the death of the childless John Tzimisces, the way seemed clear for the assumption of power by the two young sons of Romanus II, the eighteen-year-old Basil and his brother Constantine, two years his junior. The two could scarcely have been more dissimilar. Constantine never displayed the slightest interest in public affairs; Basil impressed everyone by his quickness of mind and inexhaustible energy. He was in no sense an intellectual like Leo the Wise or Constantine Porphyrogenitus; he showed no inclination towards scholarship or literature. Leo and Constantine had emphasized their power by dazzling panoply; Basil cut state ceremonial to a minimum and wore workaday clothes quite unbefitting an Emperor and, it was noted, none too clean. Physically, also, he bore little resemblance to his father and grandfather: he was short and stocky, with a heavy beard and pale blue eyes. When not in the saddle, we are told, his appearance was undistinguished; it was only when mounted – for he was a superb horseman – that he came fully into his own. In one other respect, too, did Basil differ from his father. Romanus had been a voluptuary; Basil led a life of quite exceptional austerity, eating and drinking sparingly and avoiding women altogether. Almost alone among Byzantine Emperors he never married.

From the moment that he found himself senior Emperor he was determined to rule as well as reign; and with a brother only too grateful to be relieved of responsibility this should have presented no problem. Two obstacles, however, stood in his path. The first was his great-uncle and namesake, Basil the Chamberlain. It was now some thirty years since this natural son of Lecapenus had been raised to the highest office in the state after the Emperor himself; he had no intention of letting go without a struggle. The second obstacle was the nature of the throne itself. The first Roman Emperors had gained power by the acclamation of their army; and although the hereditary principle had long been generally accepted, it had never been legally recognized. Now, after the seizure of power by three generals in less than sixty years, it was – especially in the minds of the Anatolian military aristocracy – wearing thin: should not the imperial diadem be the preserve of mature men proved in battle, rather than of callow youths whose only recommendation was their birth?

Thus the first nine years of Basil's theoretically autocratic reign were largely overshadowed by his formidable Chamberlain, and the first thirteen occupied in defending his throne against the attacks of two generals determined to wrest it from him. One was Bardas Sclerus, domestic of the armies of the East; the other was Bardas Phocas, nephew of the Emperor Nicephorus, who having failed in his first rebellion was resolved to launch a second at the earliest opportunity. Sclerus was the first to act. Only a month or two after his brother-in-law's death he had himself proclaimed *basileus* by his troops; by the autumn of 977 he had won two decisive battles and gained the support of the southern fleet; and a few months later, having captured Nicaea, he settled down to an amphibious siege of the capital.

At sea the issue was quickly settled. The home fleet, loyal to the Emperor, made short work of the rebel ships. On land, however, the situation seemed grave; and so it might have continued had not the Chamberlain surprisingly entrusted the command of the army to Bardas Phocas. Phocas's loyalty was scarcely more certain than that of Sclerus himself; indeed, he was still in exile on Chios. But whatever dreams of power he might cherish, he would still have to deal with Sclerus first.

So Bardas Phocas flung off his monastic habit, swore an oath of loyalty and made his way back to his own power base in Cappadocian Caesarea, where it was an easy matter for him to raise an army. The civil war that followed lasted nearly three years. During their last battle in the spring of 979, Bardas Phocas, seeing the tide turning against him, challenged the rebel to single combat. Courageously – for Phocas was a giant – Sclerus accepted; and, in a scene straight out of the *Iliad*, the contest began. Suddenly Sclerus pitched forward and slid to the ground, blood streaming from his head. A few of his men carried him, unconscious, to a nearby stream to bathe the wound; the remainder fled from the field. The war was over.

For the moment, at least: but Basil's grip on the throne remained uncertain, since both his rivals were very much alive. Sclerus had quickly recovered from his blow on the head and had sought refuge with the Saracens in Baghdad; while Phocas, stronger than ever, was equally certain to make another bid for power. Here, nevertheless, was a much-needed respite, giving the Emperor time to prepare himself for the tasks ahead: to familiarize himself with the innermost workings of the army, the navy, the Church, the monasteries and every department of state. In 985 he was ready; only his great-uncle and namesake stood in his way. At first he was genuinely attached to the young Emperor; his mistake was to treat him like the child he no longer was. Basil, frustrated at every step, knew that he must get rid of him. Fortunately there were grounds in plenty for doing so. The Chamberlain's corruption was notorious, and had brought him enormous wealth. More serious still, he had recently been discovered to be in secret correspondence with Bardas Phocas. The capital awoke one morning to the news that the most feared man in the Empire had been arrested and exiled, his property confiscated.

At last Basil was master in his own house. But less than a year later his Empire was facing a new threat: Samuel, self-proclaimed Tsar of the Bulgarian Empire, had invaded Thessaly. Of his origins we know little. His father, the *comes* Nicholas, seems to have been Governor of western Bulgaria around the time of Svyatoslav's invasion; and when he died his influence, if not his position, passed to his four sons. These young men thus became the natural leaders of an insurrection which broke out soon after the death of John Tzimisces and developed into a full-blown war of independence. When the news reached Constantinople, the captive Tsar Boris escaped with his brother Romanus to join the insurgents; but Boris was accidentally killed at the frontier by his own subjects while Romanus, a eunuch, was debarred from the throne. The leadership therefore remained with the sons of the *comes* – known collectively as the *Cometopuli* – and, in particular, with the youngest and ablest of the four, Samuel.

During the Sclerus revolt, Samuel had been free to extend his dominions without opposition. He had assumed the title of Tsar and simultaneously revived the Bulgarian Patriarchate. Thus, with the close association of Prince Romanus, his new state came to be seen by its citizens as simply the continuation of its predecessor. From 980 every summer saw one or more Bulgar incursions into Thessaly; and in 986 Samuel captured its chief city, Larissa. On hearing the news, Basil personally assumed the supreme command and marched on Sardica; but just short of his objective he stopped to await his rearguard: a disastrous mistake, since it allowed Samuel to occupy the surrounding mountains. On Tuesday, 17 August, as the Byzantine troops went through the pass known as Trajan's Gate, they marched straight into Samuel's carefully-prepared ambush. The vast majority were cut down where they stood. Basil, who had schooled himself to be the most efficient ruler Byzantium had ever known, was bitterly ashamed; but he was also angry. When he arrived back in Constantinople, he swore a solemn oath that he would have his revenge on the entire Bulgar nation. He was, as we shall see, as good as his word.

The news of the battle persuaded Bardas Sclerus in Baghdad that the Empire was at last his for the taking. With men, money and provisions supplied by the Caliph, he returned to Asia Minor and for the second time proclaimed himself *basileus*. He found the Anatolian barons already on the point of revolt. The imperial army, they firmly believed, was their own special preserve; without one of their own number in command, Trajan's Gate had been inevitable, conclusive proof that they should never have allowed the crown out of their own hands. But whose should it be? Sclerus soon found that many of them favoured Bardas Phocas rather than himself: so many in fact that on 15 August 987 Phocas formally claimed the Empire on his own account. Of the two pretenders he was now substantially the stronger; but he did not dare to leave Sclerus in his rear. He therefore proposed a partition of the Empire, whereby he would be satisfied with the European part – including, of course, Constantinople – leaving Sclerus all Anatolia from the Marmara to the eastern frontier. Sclerus accepted – and walked straight into the trap. Soon afterwards he was arrested, and spent the next two years in the same fortress from which he had starved out Phocas sixteen years before. Meanwhile his rival made a final bid for power. When he reached the Marmara he divided his army, sending half of it west to Abydos on the Hellespont while the other half dug itself in at Chrysopolis; then he began to prepare his two-pronged attack on the capital.

Basil kept his head. He desperately needed foreign help; and that help could come from one quarter only: Svyatoslav's son Vladimir, Prince of Kiev. Even before Phocas's arrival ambassadors were on their way. Vladimir, they reported on their return, considered himself bound by his father's agreement with John Tzimisces. A force of 6,000 fully-equipped Varangians would be dispatched as soon as possible. In return, the Prince asked the hand in marriage of the Emperor's sister, the *porphyrogenita* Anna.

The effect of this demand on the Byzantine court can hardly be imagined. No princess born in the purple had ever been given in marriage to a foreigner; and Vladimir was not only a foreigner but a heathen, who had killed his own brother and who already boasted at least four wives and 800 concubines: a fact which in no way discouraged him from creating havoc among the matrons and maidens of any town he happened to visit. He possessed only one redeeming feature: he was said to be seeking, for himself and his people, a respectable religion. Already he had made searching inquiries of Muslims, Jews and Roman Catholics – none of whom, however, had impressed him. Finally he had sent emissaries to Constantinople where a special service had been held in their honour in St Sophia, of such beauty that, as they subsequently reported, they had not known whether they were on earth or in heaven. It seemed likely therefore that Vladimir might soon be forswearing his pagan gods and, perhaps, some of his more reprehensible habits; and Basil accordingly gave his consent to the match, providing only that the Prince of Kiev were to embrace the Orthodox faith. Then he settled down to wait.

He waited for the best part of a year, during which only the constant patrols of the imperial navy prevented Bardas Phocas and his men from crossing over into Europe. Finally in late December 988 the Black Sea lookouts espied the first of a great fleet of Viking ships on the northern horizon; early in 989 the whole of that fleet was safely anchored in the Golden Horn and 6,000 burly giants disembarked. A few weeks later the Norsemen, led by Basil himself, crossed the straits under cover of darkness and took up their positions a few hundred yards from the rebel camp. At first light they attacked, while a squadron of imperial flame-throwers sprayed the shore with Greek fire. Phocas's men, roused from sleep, were powerless: their assailants swung their swords and battle-axes without mercy until they stood ankle-deep in blood. Few of the victims escaped with their lives. Three subordinate commanders, delivered into the hands of the Emperor, were respectively hanged, impaled and crucified.

Bardas Phocas, who had remained with his reserves some distance away, now hastened to join the rest of his army outside Abydos and immediately laid siege to the city; but the town put up a determined resistance, and the imperial navy in the straits made a blockade impossible. Meanwhile the Emperor set about preparing a relief expedition, and in March 989 sent off an advance contingent under the command – rather surprisingly – of his brother and co-Emperor Constantine: the only time in his long life that this unsatisfactory prince led an army in the field. Basil himself embarked a few days later, landed near Lampsacus and immediately set off for the besieged city, his gigantic Varangians following behind.

The next morning saw the two armies drawn up facing each other on the open plain beside Abydos. There, at dawn on Saturday 13 April, the Emperor gave the order to attack. The rebel troops scattered: many were cut down, others simply turned and ran. Only with the greatest difficulty did Phocas manage to restore order and regroup the survivors. Then, we are told, as he gazed across the plain, he caught sight of Basil himself, riding up and down the lines of Norsemen, with young Constantine at his side; and he remembered how, during his last encounter with Bardas Sclerus, he had turned defeat into victory. Suddenly he spurred his horse to a gallop and, as both armies watched in silence, thundered towards the imperial lines, his sword pointing directly at the Emperor. Basil stood his ground, his own sword clasped in his right hand, while in his left he clutched an icon of the Virgin, well known for its miraculous powers. Nearer and nearer came his assailant; then, suddenly, he seemed to falter. Swaying as if in a fit of dizziness, he reined in his horse, slipped slowly from the saddle and lay motionless on the ground. When Basil, Constantine and their followers rode up they found that he was already dead of a sudden stroke. His surviving troops panicked and fled; but they were no match for the Norsemen, who pursued them and cheerfully hacked them to pieces.

Bardas Sclerus was left the only pretender to the throne of Byzantium. During his two years' captivity his gaoler had been none other than Phocas's wife; with her husband's death, however, she immediately set him free to raise a new army. But it was too late. He was getting old, and his sight was rapidly failing. Basil had already offered him almost unbelievably generous terms; Sclerus accepted them; and on one of the imperial estates in Bithynia, for the first time in thirteen years, the young Emperor and the old general met face to face. The Emperor opened the conversation by seeking the general's advice. How, he asked him, could he best guard against any further rebellions by the 'powerful'? Sclerus recommended that they should be kept on the tightest of reins, taxed to the hilt, financially persecuted, even deliberately and unfairly victimized; they would then be far too preoccupied to pursue any schemes of personal ambition. Basil remembered those words for the rest of his life.

In view of all the momentous events of the past two years, it is understandable that Basil should have given little time to the question of his sister's promised marriage to the Prince of Kiev. It was by way of reminding him of his responsibilities that in the summer of 989 Vladimir suddenly seized the imperial colony of Cherson, the last Byzantine outpost on the northern Black Sea coast, simultaneously informing him that if his forgetfulness continued, Constantinople itself would suffer a similar fate. Basil could not risk the withdrawal of Russian support while Bardas Sclerus was still at large and Tsar Samuel was still building up his kingdom. The 6,000 Varangians were still in Constantinople: a word from their sovereign would change their present benevolence to open hostility. There was nothing for it: the agreement must be honoured. The twenty-five-year-old Anna tearfully accepted the inevitable, and reluctantly embarked on the ship that was to take her to Cherson, where her betrothed awaited her. There she and Vladimir were duly married, the colony being immediately returned to her brother as the traditional gift from the bridegroom; there too, immediately before the ceremony, the Prince of Kiev was baptized by the local bishop in the most fateful religious ceremony in Russian history.

The conversion of Vladimir marked the entry of Russia into the Christian fold. After their marriage, he and his bride were escorted to Kiev by the local clergy of Cherson, who immediately set about proselytizing and converting

towns and villages *en masse*. The new Russian Church was thus from the outset subordinated to the Patriarchate of Constantinople, and there is some
reason to hope that poor Anna may have found her new life a degree or two
less intolerable than she had feared it might be. Her husband became, after his
baptism, a changed man. Away went the previous wives and the concubines;
henceforth he was to spend his time supervising conversions, standing
godfather at baptisms and building churches and monasteries wherever he
went. Saints can never be the easiest of husbands, and St Vladimir of Kiev
is unlikely to have been an exception; but for a girl who had expected to
share her bed with an ogre it must, all the same, have been something of a
relief.

By 989 Basil had been Emperor for twenty-nine of his thirty-one years. For
sixteen he had been a minor; for nine a puppet; while for the last four he had
seen a succession of disasters ending with his submission to a piece of shameless blackmail on the part of the Prince of Kiev. That year itself had seen misfortunes enough: there had been the struggles with Phocas and Sclerus; the
loss of Cherson; and serious disturbances in Antioch. On 25 October an
earthquake destroyed or damaged over forty churches in the capital alone –
including St Sophia itself, whose dome was split across while the apse subsided altogether. Yet the year was to close with the Empire enjoying internal
peace for the first time since the death of John Tzimisces in 976, and its
Emperor at last on the threshold of glory, free to concentrate on the task to
which he had dedicated his life: the annihilation of the Bulgar Empire.

In the early spring of 991 he set off for Thessalonica. For the next four
years he never relaxed the pressure. The new army, trained and toughened by
the Emperor in person, was as impervious to January snow as to August sun.
Many cities were recaptured. Some were garrisoned; others, less lucky, razed
flat. There were no dramatic advances, no great victories. Success for Basil
depended on faultless organization. The army must act as a single, perfectly
coordinated body. When battle began, he forbade any soldier to break ranks.
Heroics were punished with instant dismissal. His men complained about
their master's endless inspections; but they gave him their trust because they
knew that he never undertook an operation until he was certain of victory. In
such circumstances progress might be sure; but it was also slow, and it comes
as no surprise to find that when the Emperor was summoned urgently to Syria
early in 995 he had achieved relatively little. Samuel too had moved with
caution. He had one great advantage: he was on home ground. Sooner or later
Basil would be called away, and Samuel's turn would come. He kept his
powder dry, and played a waiting game.

But though the Emperor preferred to move slowly, he was also capable of astonishing speed, as he showed during his whirlwind Syrian expedition of 995, mounted in response to an appeal by the Emir of Aleppo, now a Byzantine protectorate: Antioch itself, as well as his own Emirate, was being seriously threatened by the Fatimid Caliph. Basil knew that in such an emergency he could trust no one but himself. Hurrying back to the capital with as many troops as he dared, he collected all available reserves until he could boast a new army of some 40,000 men. There remained, however, the problem of getting them to Syria: by the time they arrived, in all probability, both Antioch and Aleppo would be lost.

Basil's solution was unprecedented in all Byzantine history. He mounted his entire army. Every soldier was provided with two mules, one for himself and one for his equipment. Towards the end of April 995, he drew up the first 17,000 of his troops beneath the walls of Aleppo. They had taken just sixteen days. The city was already under siege; a week more and it would have fallen, with much of northern Syria. Now it was saved. Caught unawares and hopelessly outnumbered, the Fatimid army fled back to Damascus. A few days later the Emperor himself headed south, sacking Emesa and sowing a trail of devastation as far as Tripoli. Then he started back to his capital. On his return journey, he had time to observe the countryside through which he rode. This was his first visit to Asia since he was a child; and he was horrified by the splendour of the estates built up by the 'powerful' on what was legally either imperial property or that of the local village communes. Several of these noblemen made the mistake of receiving him in style: mindless displays of wealth which aroused his fury. On 1 January 996 an imperial edict decreed that any territorial claim, to be valid, must go back at least sixty-one years, to the reign of Romanus I. All property acquired since that time was to be restored immediately to its previous owner or his family, without compensation or payment for any improvements. Even imperial *chrysobuls* – including those signed by Basil himself – were to be inadmissible as a defence, while all grants made by Basil the Chamberlain were automatically null and void unless specially revalidated in the Emperor's own hand. The results, to the Anatolian aristocracy, were calamitous. The Phocas lost virtually all their vast estates. Some noble families were reduced to beggary, others to the level of the peasants around them. But for those peasants, and for the local smallholders – the traditional backbone of imperial armies for hundreds of years – the way was open to regain the lands of their forefathers.

The Emperor did not at once return to Bulgaria. There was, inevitably, serious disaffection in Anatolia, and it was important that he should be at hand in Constantinople. He was still in the capital four months later when there arrived an embassy from the court of the seventeen-year-old Otto III. Otto wanted a Byzantine wife; and he was now making a formal request for the hand of one of Basil's three nieces, Eudocia, Zoe or Theodora – he did not greatly mind which. The request was surprising. Admittedly Otto II had married the Greek princess Theophano, who had done much for the spread of Byzantine culture in the West; but he had unfortunately claimed all the Byzantine lands in Italy as part of her dowry, and war had been the inevitable result. Then in 981 he had marched into Apulia, his wrath on this occasion directed principally against the occupying Saracens, who – with Byzantine assistance – soon afterwards cut his army to pieces near Stilo in Calabria. He never recovered from the humiliation and died in Rome the following year, aged twenty-eight.

His son by Theophano, Otto III, combined the ambitions of his line with a romantic mysticism inherited from his mother, forever dreaming of a great Byzantinesque theocracy that would embrace Germans and Greeks, Italians and Slavs alike, with God at its head and himself and the Pope – in that order – his twin Viceroys. What better foundation could there be for the realization of this dream than another marriage alliance between the two Empires? As his emissary for this delicate mission, Otto chose John Philagathus, Archbishop of Piacenza, a Greek from Calabria who had been the close friend and chaplain of his mother.

Basil for his part asked nothing better than a marriage which might preserve the peace in south Italy and when Philagathus returned to Rome he took with him Byzantine ambassadors to negotiate the details with Otto in person. Unfortunately, however, they arrived only to find that Otto had left some weeks before, with consequences that would be unhappy for him, unpleasant for them and, for John Philagathus, nothing short of catastrophic. These consequences were too involved to be described in detail; suffice it to say that in Otto's absence the Patrician Crescentius, head of the most influential family in Rome, seized Basil's ambassadors and threw them into prison – more, it seems, to spite Otto by spoiling his marriage plans than for any other reason. The newly-crowned Pope Gregory V, Otto's cousin and appointee, fled to Pavia, whereupon Crescentius appointed in his place none other than the Archbishop of Piacenza, John Philagathus.

Why one of the Emperor's most trusted servants should have lent himself to such villainy is hard to understand; but the immediate prospect of the papal throne, even if he were to occupy it only as Anti-Pope, seems to have been more than he could resist. He soon had cause to regret his decision. Towards the end of the year the Emperor of the West marched into the peninsula for the second time, joined Pope Gregory at Pavia and advanced on Rome.

Crescentius was publicly beheaded on the Castel Sant'Angelo, where he had sought refuge; John Philagathus was taken prisoner. His captors cut off his ears, nose and hands, put out his eyes and tore out his tongue. He survived his subsequent trial and lived, after a fashion, till 1013. For Basil II, news of these developments could hardly have been more unwelcome: it would have suited him to have a Greek on the papal throne almost as much as to have a niece as Empress of the West. His ambassadors, after nearly two years, had finally been released; but they had not yet made contact with Otto – whose pro-Greek sympathies might well have faded.

He had another concern too: the past three years had seen an alarming increase in the power of Tsar Samuel. Having seized the important Adriatic harbour of Dyrrachium, Samuel had now begun a long, triumphant advance through the Dalmatian hinterland into Bosnia. The Byzantine lands along the Adriatic shore were now seriously at risk. They were no further from Constantinople than was Syria; but the terrain was mountainous, the roads and populations unfriendly. There was, as Basil saw it, only one solution: the Republic of Venice. Why should the Republic not now take over responsibility for the entire Dalmatian coast, ruling it as a protectorate under Byzantine suzerainty? For Doge Pietro Orseolo II, here was an offer of an invaluable new source of corn, and of timber for ship-building. It would also give him a free hand to deal with the Croatian pirates who were plaguing the Venetian merchantmen. On Ascension Day, AD 1000, Orseolo – newly dubbed *Dux Dalmatiae* – boarded his flagship and set sail at the head of a huge fleet to receive the homage of his new subjects. Tsar Samuel might control the Bosnian fastness; but the Greek-speaking cities of the coast were henceforth in safe hands.

In 1001 Otto III, his determination unshaken, sent a second embassy to Constantinople to bring him back his bride. At its head was Archbishop Arnulf of Milan, the most magnificent ecclesiastic in the West, who appeared on a superbly caparisoned steed whose very horseshoes were of gold, secured with silver nails. Basil made no difficulties: the sooner the marriage were over, the sooner he could return to Bulgaria. Of his three nieces, two was villainously plain: the middle sister, Zoe, was however a good-looking girl of twenty-three. The archbishop was delighted with her, and she herself showed no reluctance. In January 1002, accompanied by a retinue appropriate to a *porphyrogenita* and an Empress, she set sail for her new home. Alas, it was not to be. At Bari, tragic news awaited her. Her betrothed, stricken by a sudden fever, had died on 24 January aged twenty-two. Poor Zoe: if she and Otto had had a son, he might have inherited not only the Western Empire but – in the absence of any other male heir – the Eastern as well, uniting them at last and ruling from France to Persia; and the history of the world would have been changed.

Campaigning almost continuously between 1000 and 1004, Basil II regained virtually all the eastern half of the Balkan peninsula. Samuel was now struggling against an enemy who could move through rough country as quickly as he could himself, who never gave him an opportunity for ambush or surprise attack and who was impervious to wind and weather alike. Throughout the next decade the advance continued, though our sources give us infuriatingly little detail. It is only in 1014 that the mists clear sufficiently to allow a glimpse of a battle which put the eventual outcome of the war beyond reasonable doubt. That battle was fought in the narrow defile of Cimbalongus, leading from Serrae into the valley of the Upper Struma. It ended suddenly when the Bulgars, taken by surprise, panicked and fled; some 15,000 were captured. It was now that Basil meted out the punishment for which he is chiefly remembered. Of each hundred prisoners, ninety-nine were blinded; to one man a single eye was left, that he might conduct the remainder to the presence of their king. At the beginning of October the dreadful procession shuffled into the Tsar's castle at Prespa. At the sight of his once-splendid army Samuel, already a sick man, collapsed in a fit of apoplexy, dying two days later. The Bulgars fought on until February 1018, and soon afterwards Basil made his formal entry into their capital. He was now sixty: after thirty-two years his task was accomplished. For the first time since the arrival of the Slavs the entire Balkan peninsula was under Byzantine control.

In war Basil II – called *Bulgaroctonus*, the Bulgar-Slayer – had been merciless and brutal; with the coming of peace he proved moderate and understanding. The Bulgars were no longer his enemies; they were his subjects, and as such they deserved every consideration. Taxes were kept deliberately low, and payable not in gold but in kind. The Patriarchate was downgraded to the status of an archbishopric, but the Bulgarian Church continued to be autocephalous in every respect save one: the appointment of the archbishop was kept by the Emperor in his own hands. Certain areas in the west – notably Croatia and Bosnia – continued to be ruled by their native princes under imperial suzerainty. The Bulgar aristocracy was integrated into the Byzantine social and official hierarchy, several of its numbers being given high office; the rest gave no trouble. Meanwhile in the East, after the Emperor's last expedition in 1023, he had established no fewer than eight new Themes, running in a huge arc north-eastward from Antioch. He now reigned supreme from the Adriatic to Azerbaijan. Yet his energies were still undiminished, and he was actively planning an invasion of Sicily when, ten days before Christmas 1025, he died suddenly in Constantinople, aged sixty-seven.

He had been a phenomenon: effortlessly dominating Church and State and – by virtue of his ability to combine the strategic vision of a commander-in-chief with the meticulous attention to detail of a drill-sergeant – showing himself one of the most brilliant generals that the Empire had ever seen. More remarkable still is the fact that, apart from what must inevitably surround the figure of an Emperor, he was utterly devoid of glamour. His campaigns generated no thunder or lightning. Under him the imperial army was more like a flood of volcanic lava, advancing slowly but inexorably. After his youthful humiliation at Trajan's Gate – which he never forgot, and for which the entire Bulgarian war was, in a sense, an act of revenge – he took few risks, and suffered few casualties. But although he was trusted by his troops, they never loved him.

No one ever did. No lonelier man ever occupied the Byzantine throne. And it is hardly surprising: Basil was ugly, dirty, coarse, boorish, philistine and almost pathologically mean. He was in short deeply un-Byzantine. He cared only for the greatness of his Empire. No wonder that in his hands it reached its apogee. In one respect only did he fail; he left no children. Although his attitude to women remains a mystery, could he not have forced himself to take a wife and engender a son or two, for the Empire's sake? Dying without issue, he virtually ensured its decline.

He died on 15 December. By the 16th, that decline had already begun.

17
The Decline Begins

[1025–55]

Constantine VIII, the sixty-five-year-old widower who now found himself sole Emperor of Byzantium, was as different from his brother as it is possible to be. Physically, he was magnificent. Once a superb horseman and athlete, he still remained an impressive figure. Though he had received little formal schooling, a lively intellectual curiosity had given him a modicum of culture which enabled him to hold his own with foreign ambassadors. Those whom he received in audience were invariably impressed by his eloquence and his beautiful speaking voice. He could thus have made a perfectly adequate Emperor; but he was devoid of any semblance of moral fibre, reacting to every challenge with mindless cruelty, ordering executions and mutilations by the hundreds. His tendency to indulge later in an orgy of remorse, tearfully flinging his arms around his sightless victims and imploring their forgiveness, did little to increase his popularity. Only one class of Byzantines welcomed the weakness of the new regime: the Anatolian aristocracy. The Emperor was quite unable to resist their demands, and within months Basil's detested land laws were buried. Once again the 'powerful' descended on their erstwhile properties, snapping up every available acre while the poor peasant small-holders were left to survive as best they might. Once more Asia Minor became a country of vast estates, owned more often than not by absentee landlords and worked by serfs.

Meanwhile Constantine VIII carried on as he always had: carousing with his cronies, cavorting with his concubines, watching obscene performances in his private theatre and avoiding whenever possible the affairs of state. But in November 1028 he fell mortally ill. Who was to succeed him? He had no sons; of his three daughters, the eldest had long been a nun. The second, Zoe, since her thwarted marriage, had spent twenty-six years in the imperial *gynaeceum*, in the company of her more intelligent but less attractive sister Theodora, whom she detested. Theodora had now become distinctly spinsterish; but Zoe, though now approaching fifty, still dreamed voluptuously of the marriage that she had never had and longed for liberation. This must, she knew, come sooner or later; for she was her father's heir, and it was through her that the crown would be transmitted to her husband. But who was he to be? After protracted discussions by the bedside of the dying Emperor, the bureaucracy proposed a sexagenarian senator and aristocrat named Romanus Argyrus. As it happened, he was already happily married; but Constantine's mind was made up: either Romanus divorced his wife and married Zoe or he would be blinded. He agonized, but his wife did not hesitate. Cutting off her hair, she immediately entered a convent. On 10 November Romanus married Zoe in the imperial chapel of the palace; on the 11th he stood at his new father-in-law's bedside as he breathed his last; and on the 12th he found himself Romanus III, seated beside his beaming wife on the imperial throne. His next duty, despite his wife's advanced age, was to found a dynasty. To increase his chances, he made himself easy game for all the charlatans in Constantinople, swallowing their aphrodisiacs, applying their ointments and performing extraordinary exercises that would, he was promised, restore to him the vigour of his youth. Zoe, meanwhile, did much the same in her determination, somehow, to conceive – though no one was much surprised when she failed to do so.

His subjects discovered that their Emperor was no soldier when, in 1030, against the advice of all his generals, he decided to lead a campaign in Syria and took precipitately to flight at the first engagement. Thenceforth, he wisely forsook military matters and devoted himself to the cares of government; but as time went on he proved no more successful as an administrator than as anything else. It was perhaps inevitable, therefore, that he should have turned his attention to church-building: like Justinian, he was determined to leave some lasting memorial behind him. The result of this decision was a vast church dedicated to the Virgin *Peribleptos* or All-Seeing, with an even more enormous dependent monastery. Together, these two monuments to imperial megalomania are said to have brought the people of Constantinople to the verge of rebellion.

What, meanwhile, of Zoe? Frustrated and dissatisfied, she was also furious with her husband: first because, having finally given up hope of posterity, he had refused to share her bed and taken a mistress; and secondly because he had denied her access to the treasury. Zoe was intensely proud; she had also, for fifty years, been thoroughly spoilt by a father who had denied her nothing. At first she had vented her anger on her sister, whom in 1031 she ordered into a convent. Soon, however, she took more direct action, and it is at this moment that there enters upon the scene the strange and sinister figure of John the Orphanotrophus – a Paphlagonian eunuch who had risen from obscure and humble origins to become director of the city's principal orphanage, whence he took his name. Of his four younger brothers, the two eldest were eunuchs like himself; the youngest, Michael, an outstandingly handsome – though unfortunately epileptic – youth still in his teens, was one day in 1033 brought by John to the palace and presented to Romanus and Zoe in formal audience. Zoe, after one look, fell – precisely as John had intended her to fall – instantly and besottedly in love.

From that moment she thought of nothing but the young Paphlagonian. Michael, though flattered, remained far from enthusiastic; but he received careful instruction from his brother, and his own ambition did the rest. The Emperor, warned by his sister Pulcheria of what was going on, was only too pleased when Michael assured him that the rumours were unfounded. At this point, however, he fell seriously ill. Was he being poisoned by his wife? Zoe had motive and opportunity, and would certainly have been fully capable of the crime. Death finally came to him on the Thursday before Good Friday 1034, in the palace baths; though whether it was caused by a sudden seizure or by his head being firmly held under the water was never established.

At dawn on Good Friday, 12 April, Patriarch Alexis was summoned urgently to the palace, where he was horrified to see the near-naked body of Romanus. Before he had recovered from the shock, a pair of enormous doors opened – and there, in the great Coronation Hall, sat the Empress enthroned in state. On her head was the imperial diadem, in her hand the sceptre, over her shoulders the gold brocade robe of the Emperors, heavy with jewels. And there at her side, to the astonishment of the Patriarch, sat young Michael, similarly robed and crowned. Zoe spoke firmly and steadily; Alexis could not refuse. There and then he joined the hand of the fifty-six-year-old Empress – widowed only a few hours before – with that of her paramour and probable fellow-murderer, an epileptic young Paphlagonian nearly forty years her junior; and consecrated him *basileus*, Equal of the Apostles.

If the Empress had hoped for a second husband who would be little more than a crowned slave, she was soon to be disappointed. Long before the end of the year Michael was showing signs of impatience. It had quickly become clear to him that he could govern the Empire very much better than his wife: and not long afterwards Zoe once again found herself confined to the *gynaeceum*, her liberty – and her spending – even more curtailed than in the days of Romanus. There were other reasons too why Michael should wish to keep his distance. His epileptic fits were becoming ever more frequent, and since on these occasions he minded the presence of Zoe more than that of anyone else, he preferred to avoid her altogether. He was also becoming dropsical – a disability which quickly led to impotence. Finally there was his conscience. He owed everything to the Empress, and he could not bear to meet her eye. But he knew too that this betrayal was as nothing compared to his treatment of Romanus, and the rest of his life was one desperate attempt to save his soul. He spent hours a day in church; he established monasteries and convents by the dozen; he set up a vast refuge for reformed prostitutes; and he sought out holy men from every corner of the Empire.

At those times when he was not preoccupied with spiritual matters the Emperor devoted himself to the business of government – at which he proved surprisingly adept. He made no dramatic changes. Questions of finance and taxation he left to his brother the Orphanotrophus; everything else he kept firmly in his own hands, paying particular attention to local administration, foreign affairs and the army, whose shattered morale he managed in large measure to restore. Although he had had little formal education, he learned fast. Within months of his assumption of power he was ruling the Empire with a sure and steady hand. His advisers marvelled at his industry, his quickness of perception, his political instinct and, despite his epilepsy, his emotional balance; while those who knew him well had nothing but admiration for the courage with which he struggled against his two cruellest handicaps – his health and his family.

Of his four elder brothers, three were parasites: the eldest, the Orphan-otrophus, was a formidable figure. He lacked Michael's new-found self-lessness and high moral principle; where intelligence and industry were concerned, however, he was cast in a similar mould. He thought only of the advancement of his family. He would go to any length to keep the Emperor in ignorance of his brothers' misdeeds: which explains why Michael never took firm action against them. More serious still, he extended this family feel-ing to his brother-in-law Stephen, a former ships' caulker in the harbour of Constantinople, arranging for him to be given command of the transport fleet for the most ambitious military undertaking of Michael's reign: the long-delayed Sicilian expedition.

Originally planned by Basil II for 1026 but postponed as a result of his death, this expedition was now more necessary than ever. The continual raids on Byzantine south Italy by the Sicilian-based Saracens were rapidly becom-ing a threat to imperial security. The Mediterranean was alive with pirates, prices of imports were rising and the level of foreign trade was beginning to decline. To every Byzantine, Sicily remained part of the imperial birthright; it also continued to boast a considerable Greek population. That it should still be occupied by the heathen after more than two centuries was an affront not only to security but also to national pride. Furthermore civil war had broken out among the Arab Emirs of the island. Revolt was now spreading throughout Sicily; and the Saracens, more and more hopelessly divided, seemed unlikely to be able to offer much resistance to a concerted Byzantine attack.

The expedition sailed in the early summer of 1038. It had been put under the command of George Maniakes, who after a long and distinguished career in the East was by now the foremost general of the Empire. The strongest element in his army was an impressive Varangian contingent which included the celebrated Norse hero Harald Hardrada, returning from a pilgrimage to Jerusalem; the weakest a body of grumbling Lombards from Apulia who made no secret of their disgust at having been forced into service. Landing in the late summer, the army at first carried all before it; the Saracens could do little to stem the tide. Messina fell almost at once, and there seems to have been a slow but steady advance on Syracuse, which fell to Maniakes in 1040. But the collapse of the Byzantine forces after the victory at Syracuse was sudden and complete. The fault seems to have lain partly with Maniakes and partly with Stephen, for whom the general had never bothered to hide his contempt and upon whom, after some worse-than-usual ineptitude, he launched a violent attack. Stephen then accused him of treason. Maniakes was called back to the capital and imprisoned, to be succeeded first by Stephen – with predictable results – and then, on his death, by a eunuch named Basil who proved very little better. Meanwhile dissatisfaction had been growing in Apulia, where the Lombard separatists had had little difficulty in working up the local populations; and in 1040 the signal was given for revolt. The Byzantine governor was assassinated, and all the local militias along the coast rose up in mutiny. The army was hastily summoned from Sicily; and within a few months the entire island apart from Messina was once again in Saracen hands.

By now, too, it was clear that the Emperor was dying. No longer capable of dealing with affairs of state, he thought only of appeasing the divine anger which had reduced him, while still in his twenties, to a bloated travesty of what he had been only a few years before when his beauty had won him the heart of an Empress. The government was now in the hands of his brother, who was obsessed by the idea of founding a dynasty. Michael would soon die, leaving no issue; how would the succession be assured? Their two surviving brothers were eunuchs like himself; his brother-in-law Stephen was dead. There remained only Stephen's son Michael, nicknamed *Calaphates*, 'the caulker', after his father's early profession. He was a compulsive liar and inveterate schemer, but John's mind was made up. He had little difficulty in persuading the Emperor and soon afterwards, in the Church of St Mary at Blachernae, his nephew's succession was assured. The old Empress declared her formal adoption of Michael the Caulker as her son.

In the summer of 1040 a revolt broke out in Bulgaria. The leaders were one Peter Deljan, the bastard grandson of Tsar Samuel, and his cousin Alusian. They drove out the Byzantines, invaded northern Greece, and by the end of the year had stormed Dyrrachium – thus giving them an outlet on the Adriatic – penetrating as far south as the Gulf of Lepanto; and at this point an astonishing thing happened. The Emperor Michael, speaking from his palace in Thessalonica, suddenly announced his intention of leading his army in person against the enemy. He was by now semi-paralysed, his monstrously swollen legs having been attacked by gangrene; the slightest movement was an agony. But this was not the old story of a mortally sick man seeking a glorious death on the battlefield. The campaign was meticulously planned before the dying *basileus* led his army across the frontier to war.

The defeat of the rebels was due, not alas to the Emperor's courage, but to their own lack of discipline. Soon too a serious quarrel broke out between Deljan and his cousin, whom he accused of treachery. Alusian responded by removing Deljan's eyes and nose with a carving knife; soon afterwards he surrendered. And so, early in 1041, Michael returned to his capital in triumph, followed by his army and a host of captives including the eyeless and noseless Deljan. It was his last public appearance. On 10 December he had himself carried to his own monastery of St Cosmas and St Damian, where he donned a monk's robe and died the same evening. Few Emperors had risen from more lowly origins, or by more questionable methods; none suffered a more agonizing end. And yet, had he lived, Michael might have reversed his Empire's decline. He possessed wisdom, vision and courage. He was a tragic figure; and, in the reigns that followed, there would be many who regretted his loss.

Where the succession was concerned, John the Orphanotrophus insisted on one point above all others: that nothing must be done without the consent of the Empress. She alone represented the legitimate succession; her support was essential. And so to Zoe they went, Michael flinging himself at the feet of his adoptive mother, promising to be her slave. Old, weak, stupid and gullible, with no one to advise her, Zoe was easily persuaded. And so, with her blessing, Michael V proceeded to his consecration. No Emperor ever had less title to the throne. His birth was lowly, his military record non-existent. He owed his elevation to the machinations of a self-seeking minister and to the weakness of a foolish old woman. During the first weeks of his reign he maintained an appropriate humility; but within weeks John saw that Michael's attitude was beginning to change and that his own brother Constantine, now Grand Domestic, was encouraging his hostility. Some days later a vessel flying the imperial standard appeared at the landing-stage of John's estate with a summons to present himself at once at the palace. The Orphanotrophus had his misgivings, but decided to obey. As he approached the Great Palace the Emperor, watching from the topmost terrace, gave a pre-arranged signal. The boat swung about; then another, larger vessel came alongside, took John on board and carried him off to exile. He never saw Constantinople again.

Michael Calaphates could now put into effect the ideas which had been germinating in his mind. He moved first against the court aristocracy, who had always treated him with barely-concealed contempt, depriving them one after the other of their privileges until they trembled for their lives. He next replaced his Varangian Guard with a company of 'Scythians' whose loyalty he ensured by disproportionate rewards. Meanwhile he gave ever more liberty to the masses, on the grounds that his authority must be based on the love of his people. Not surprisingly, the masses responded. All too soon, he began to see himself as universally beloved, the father of his people. He was ready now to pass on to the next stage of his plan – the elimination of Zoe. To be sure, she had done him no harm; but she represented everything he hated most: the old aristocracy, the Macedonian line, the ossified traditions of the court. It was not enough that she was old, and living in relative obscurity; into exile she must go. On the Sunday after Easter, 18 April 1042, Zoe was arrested on a charge of attempted regicide. Witnesses were suborned and she was not even permitted to speak in her own defence. Her hair was cut off and taken straight to the Emperor as he had commanded; she herself was then borne away that very night to a convent on the Marmara island of Prinkipo.

The next morning the Emperor called a meeting of the Senate. Its members, fully aware of the consequences of any protest, obediently signified their approval. A public proclamation was accordingly read out by the City Prefect to a large crowd assembled in the Forum of Constantine, in which Zoe was accused of having brought her punishment on herself by her repeated attempts to murder her co-Emperor. Scarcely had the Prefect finished his reading when a voice was heard from the crowd, calling for the overthrow of the blasphemer Michael and his replacement by Zoe, the rightful Empress. Immediately the crowd took up the cry. Strangely enough, it was she whom the people of Constantinople had taken to their hearts. She was the daughter, granddaughter and great-granddaughter of Emperors, and the niece of the greatest that Byzantium had ever known. She had been Empress since before most of them were born; almost without being aware of it, she had become an institution. Within hours the whole population was up in arms. Their first target was the Emperor's family, all of whose magnificent mansions were looted and destroyed. Meanwhile, in the palace, the terrified Michael and his family realized that their one chance of survival was to bring Zoe back at once from exile, and a boat was hurriedly sent to fetch her. Pending her arrival they defended the building as best they could, firing volley after volley of arrows and bolts from the towers and upper windows. They were well-nigh exhausted by the time the old Empress appeared, and she herself was in little better state; but she readily agreed to show herself to the people as their lawful ruler. Her coarse woollen habit was hastily replaced with a robe of purple, while the imperial diadem was arranged in such a way as to cover, as far as possible, the few wisps that were all that remained of her hair. So arrayed, she and Michael advanced tremblingly to the imperial box of the Hippodrome, to which there was direct access from the palace.

The insurgent leaders, however, would have none of them. The presence of the Emperor at Zoe's side convinced them that she was still effectively his prisoner; there could be no solution to the crisis while he remained on the throne. Then, suddenly, a new thought struck them: what about Theodora? It was now fifteen years since Zoe had had her younger sister immured in her convent. Theodora had never re-emerged, but she was still very much alive and still an Empress, with as much claim to the throne as Zoe and without her obvious disadvantages. The two must reign jointly. That same afternoon a deputation was sent off with orders to bring Theodora back immediately to Constantinople. It was not an easy task, but she was eventually dragged forcibly into the street. Then, having changed her monastic habit for an imperial robe, she was borne in triumph to St Sophia. And so it was late in the evening of Monday 19 April, that the furious old lady received with the greatest possible reluctance the crown of Byzantium. Michael Calaphates was declared deposed. The congregation then left the Great Church, and marched towards the palace.

Michael's position was now desperate. For hours he and his uncle had tried to make themselves heard above the angry tumult in the Hippodrome, pushing the miserable Zoe in front of them; but when the mob began throwing stones, and even firing arrows, in their direction they had been forced to retreat once again into the palace, where the news was brought to them of Theodora's coronation. Tuesday, 20 April 1042, was one of the bloodiest days that Constantinople had seen in all its history. In that one day over 3,000 perished. In the early hours of Wednesday morning the palace fell, and the whole vast complex of buildings was overrun by a frenzied mob, pillaging and looting wherever it went but with one supreme objective in mind: to find the Emperor and kill him.

Shortly before dawn Michael and the Grand Domestic Constantine together sailed along the coast to the Studium, where they submitted to immediate tonsure and were accepted as members of the monastic community. Zoe, meanwhile, left in the palace to fend for herself, was soon found by the insurgents, who raised her on to their shoulders and set her upon the imperial throne. Her satisfaction, however, soon changed to fury when she was informed of the coronation of Theodora, whom she had hoped never to see again. Her first reaction was to order her immediate return to the convent; only when she was told that the cheering outside St Sophia was for her sister did she begin to understand. This lugubrious elderly virgin had suddenly and inexplicably become the idol of the populace. Reluctantly Zoe agreed to the partnership. It was better to reign as joint Empress than not to reign at all.

The scene now shifts to the Studium. The Emperor and his uncle had underestimated the strength of the popular feeling. As soon as their place of refuge became known, the mob headed straight for the monastery, bellowing for their blood. Michael Psellus, an eye-witness, reports:

We found the monastery already surrounded by huge crowds, many of whom were trying to smash down the building in their eagerness to get inside. We had appalling difficulty in forcing our way through the hysterical throng, all shouting abuse and threatening the miserable fugitives with unspeakable atrocities. When I arrived in the chapel and saw the Emperor on his knees, clutching the altar, the *nobilissimus* standing on his left, both of them scarcely recognizable in their sordid rags, their very faces transformed by mortal fear, my eyes filled with tears.

All that afternoon the two men cowered at the altar while the mob held back. At dusk there arrived the new City Prefect, claiming that he had orders from Theodora herself to take charge of the fugitives and promising them safe conduct back to the palace; and Michael and Constantine were dragged, shouting and struggling, from the building. They were then mounted on donkeys and – still surrounded by the mob – were borne along the Mesē towards the palace; but they had not gone far when they were met by the platoon of soldiers commanded by Theodora to blind them. The sentence was carried out on the spot.

And so the reign of Michael V came to a close, and with it the Paphlagonian dynasty. What are we to make of him? Professor Bury, doyen of British Byzantinists, sees him, rather surprisingly, as a far-sighted ruler who aimed at nothing less than a radical reform of the administration. Now this may be perfectly true so far as it goes. Whatever we may think of his treatment of Zoe, Michael's elimination of the Orphanotrophus was probably necessary. There remains, however, the fact that he was deposed by a popular insurrection after only four months and eleven days on the throne. The story of his last days is scarcely edifying, and neither he nor his subjects emerge from it with credit; but they were right to get rid of him, and we too can be glad to see him go.

When Michael V met his fate on Tuesday evening, 20 April 1042, the Empress Theodora had been in St Sophia for well over twenty-four hours, refusing to proceed to the palace until she received word from her sister. Only the following morning did Zoe, swallowing her pride, send the long-awaited invitation. Then, before a large assembly of nobles and senators, the two old ladies marked their reconciliation with a somewhat chilly embrace and settled down to govern the Roman Empire. From the outset Zoe was accorded precedence. Her throne was placed slightly in advance of Theodora's, who seemed perfectly content with her inferior status.

In personal appearance, Psellus tells us, there were marked differences between the two. The prodigal, emotional Zoe was short and plump. Her hair was still golden, her skin very white and unwrinkled. Theodora was taller and thinner, with a disproportionately small head. Once she had overcome her timidity she was cheerful, smiling and talkative. Together, apart from Zoe's extravagance, they seem to have governed respectably enough: there were decrees against the buying and selling of offices, improvements to the civil and military administration and several admirable high appointments. A tribunal was appointed to inquire into the abuses of the previous reign: Constantine was dragged from his monk's cell for interrogation, and revealed the existence of a secret hiding-place in which were found 5,300 pounds of gold missing from the treasury.

What the regime lacked was stability. As the two sisters' mutual dislike increased, officials had inevitably to side with one or the other; and the government thus began to polarize. Clearly it needed a firm male hand at the helm; and this could be achieved only by a marriage. Theodora, after over half a century of virginity, refused to contemplate such a step; Zoe, on the other hand, asked nothing better. Despite the horror with which third marriages were viewed by the Eastern Church, hope sprang eternal in her sixty-four-year-old breast; and her thoughts now returned to a man she had long admired: a third Constantine, member of the ancient family of Monomachus: elegant, sophisticated and rich, with a formidable reputation as a ladies' man. Michael IV and the Orphanotrophus, uneasy about his increasingly close relationship with Zoe, had exiled him seven years before to Lesbos, whence he was now summoned. He arrived in the capital in the second week of June 1042, and on the 11th he and Zoe were married in the chapel of the Nea. The service of coronation was held on the following day.

The Emperor Constantine IX was more confident than Constantine VIII, more of a realist than Romanus III, healthier than Michael IV and less headstrong than Michael V. Politically, however, through sheer irresponsibility, he did the Empire more harm than the rest of them put together. By his death in 1055 the Normans of south Italy were well on the way to finally eliminating the Byzantine presence in Apulia, Calabria and Sicily; the Seljuk Turks were already contemplating their irruption into the Anatolian heartland; the Danube frontier had been smashed by invading tribes; the Eastern and Western Churches were effectively in schism; while within the Empire itself the army had declined to the worst state it had known for a century. Constantine scarcely seemed to notice, imitating rather than restraining his wife's wild prodigality. Zoe, for her part, proved equally tolerant, and made no objection to Constantine's continued association with his second wife's niece, the granddaughter of old Bardas Sclerus, a lady of unusual charm who had uncomplainingly shared her lover's exile. When Monomachus had received his summons she had at first remained tactfully on Lesbos; great must have been her surprise when a letter arrived from the Empress, assuring her of her good will and encouraging her to return. The affair, at first carried on with seemly discretion, gradually became more and more flagrant; finally the Emperor made a public admission. In the course of a ceremony attended by the entire Senate, Monomachus and the Sclerina (as she is always called) were formally linked by means of a 'loving-cup', after which she joined him and Zoe in an apparently harmonious *ménage à trois*.

Sadly, these warm feelings were not shared by the populace. On 9 March 1044 an imperial procession was interrupted by catcalls of 'Down with the Sclerina! Long live our beloved mothers, Zoe and Theodora, whose very lives she threatens!' The accusation was certainly baseless; and in fact it was not the Empresses who died; it was the Sclerina herself, attacked by some pulmonary disease. On her death the Emperor wept like a child, and buried her in the convent of St George at Manganes alongside the grave that he had reserved for himself.

It is impossible not to feel sympathy for the Sclerina. She was a woman of rare qualities, and her love for Constantine was deep and true. But their association had one disastrous consequence, which was to have a profound effect on Byzantine Italy. George Maniakes had returned to the peninsula in April 1042. Since his recall to Constantinople two years before, the situation there had gone from bad to worse. In Sicily, only Messina remained in Byzantine hands; on the mainland the Normans were rapidly mopping up the whole of south Italy. Maniakes landed to find that virtually all Apulia north of the Taranto–Brindisi line was in open revolt. He wasted no time. The horrors of that summer were long remembered as he engulfed the land in a fury of destruction. Men and women, monks and nuns, young and old – some were hanged, some beheaded; many children were buried alive. Then, for the second time in two years, George Maniakes fell victim to palace intrigue. His enemy on this occasion was the Sclerina's brother Romanus. The two possessed adjoining Anatolian estates, and relations between them had long been poisoned by territorial disputes. Now, finding himself a member of the Emperor's intimate circle, Romanus engineered Maniakes's recall. Meanwhile, profiting by the latter's absence, he looted his house, laid waste his estate and finally seduced his wife.

The rage of George Maniakes was terrible to behold. When his successor arrived at Otranto in September he seized him, stuffed his ears, nose and mouth with horse dung and tortured him to death. He then had himself proclaimed Emperor by his men and led them back across the Adriatic with the intention of advancing to Constantinople. On his way he met and defeated an imperial army sent to intercept him but fell, mortally wounded, at the very moment of victory. Thus, but for a single well-aimed lance, Constantinople might have found itself in the power of the most terrifying ruler in all its history.

For the progressive weakening of the Empire's military strength, Constantine Monomachus must take the lion's share of the responsibility; for the greatest tragedy of his reign he can, on the other hand, be largely absolved from blame. For centuries, the Eastern and Western Churches had been growing apart. There were many reasons, but one of them was a fundamental difference in their approach to Christianity itself. The Byzantines, for whom matters of doctrine could be settled only by an Ecumenical Council, were scandalized by the presumption of the Pope – who was, in their view, merely *primus inter pares* among the Patriarchs – in formulating dogma and claiming both spiritual and temporal supremacy; while to the legalistic and disciplined minds of Rome the old Greek love of theological speculation was repugnant and occasionally shocking. Since the Photian schism two centuries before, friendly relations had been outwardly restored; but the basic problems remained unsolved.

The resurgence of the quarrel was largely due to the Patriarch of Constantinople, Michael Cerularius. A mediocre theologian with only a sketchy knowledge of Church history, Cerularius was a bureaucrat through and through; but he was an able and efficient administrator, with a will of iron;

and he enjoyed considerable popularity in Constantinople. If he was the instrument of the dispute, its occasion was the alarming advance of the Normans in south Italy. In 1053 Pope Leo IX had himself led an army against them near the little town of Civitate; but he had been defeated and imprisoned, returning to Rome only just in time to die. The Byzantines were every bit as apprehensive of the Norman menace as was the Papacy itself, and it was plain enough that the only hope of saving the province lay in a strengthening of the alliance of the two. But Michael Cerularius distrusted the Latins; he loathed the idea of papal supremacy, and he knew that such an alliance would effectively prevent the return of the disputed territories to the jurisdiction of Constantinople. Even before Civitate he had inspired a document, to be passed on 'to all the bishops of the Franks and to the most venerable Pope himself' – violently condemning certain practices of the Roman Church as sinful and Judaistic. From this sprang an increasingly acrimonious correspondence between Pope and Patriarch, which in turn resulted in Leo's sending an official legation to Constantinople. Its composition was, to say the least, unfortunate. It consisted of his principal secretary, Cardinal Humbert of Mourmoutiers – narrow-minded, opinionated and rabidly anti-Greek – and two others, Cardinal Frederick of Lorraine (later Pope Stephen IX) and Archbishop Peter of Amalfi, both of whom had fought at Civitate and bore a bitter grudge against the Byzantines, who had not turned up on the battlefield and by whom they felt betrayed.

The three prelates arrived in Constantinople at the beginning of April 1054. From the outset, everything went wrong. Calling on the Patriarch, they immediately took offence at the manner in which they were received and stalked away in a huff, leaving the papal letter behind them. Cerularius, examining it, not only found it offensive, but noticed that the seals on it had been tampered with. These so-called legates, he decided, were not only discourteous; they were downright dishonest. He announced forthwith that he refused to accept their legatine authority or to receive from them any further communications.

It was lucky for the Patriarch that shortly afterwards came the news that the Pope had died in Rome. Humbert and his colleagues had been Leo's personal representatives; his death deprived them of all official standing. They on the other hand seemed in no way discomfited but remained in Constantinople, growing more high-handed with every day that passed. Finally Humbert lost the last shreds of his patience. At three o'clock in the afternoon of Saturday, 16 July 1054, in the presence of all the clergy assembled for the Eucharist, the three ex-legates of Rome, two cardinals and an archbishop, strode into St Sophia and up to the high altar, on which they formally laid their solemn Bull of Excommunication. This done, they marched out of the building, pausing only to shake the dust symbolically from their feet. Two days later they left for Rome.

Such in brief is the sequence of events that resulted in the lasting separation of the Eastern and Western Churches. However inevitable the breach may have been, those events themselves should never – and need never – have occurred. More strength of will on the part of the dying Pope or the pleasure-loving Emperor, less bigotry on the part of the narrow-minded Patriarch or the pig-headed cardinal, and the situation could have been saved. The fatal blow was struck by the disempowered legates of a dead Pope, representing a headless Church – since the new Pontiff had not yet been elected. Both the Latin and Greek excommunications were directed personally at the offending dignitaries rather than at the Churches for which they stood; neither was at the time recognized as introducing a permanent schism. Technically indeed they did not do so, since twice in succeeding centuries did the Eastern Church acknowledge the supremacy of Rome. But though a temporary bandage may cover an open lesion it cannot heal it; and the wound which was jointly inflicted nine centuries ago on the Christian Church by Cardinal Humbert and Patriarch Cerularius still bleeds today.

Despite the successive disasters that marked the reign of Constantine Monomachus, life for the leisured classes in the capital must have been more agreeable than it had been for many years. The Emperor, for all his faults, possessed a sense of style. He actively encouraged the arts and sciences and liked to surround himself with men of genuine learning and ability. Of these the most remarkable was Michael Psellus: historian, politician, philosopher and by far the most distinguished classical scholar of his time. (The pity is that he should also have been self-seeking, conceited, sanctimonious and untrustworthy.) His fellow-intellectuals in the inner circle around the Emperor were his friend the lawyer John Xiphilinus, who was said to carry the whole legal code of the Empire in his head; his old teacher, the poet and scholar John Mauropous; and the chief minister, Constantine Likhoudes. It was to them that the cultural renaissance of the mid-eleventh century was chiefly due, they above all who were responsible for the revival in 1045 of the University of Constantinople. Their first concern was the Law School; entirely reconstituted by Mauropous, it had at its head Xiphilinus, now named *nomophylax*, 'Guardian of the Law'. Courses at the new Faculty of Philosophy, entrusted to Psellus, opened with the ancient *trivium* of grammar, rhetoric and dialectic, continued with the *quadrivium* of arithmetic, geometry, astronomy and music and ended with philosophy itself, the ultimate synthesis of all knowledge.

Within a very few years, the university had become once again famous throughout Christendom and even beyond. For the past two centuries it had been the Arabs, rather than the Greeks, who dominated the intellectual world; now Byzantium regained its old reputation and became once again a meeting-point for the scholars of Europe and Asia. The greatest benefit, however, was to be felt at home. By the end of Constantine's reign the new university was producing a steady stream of highly educated young men on which the government could draw for its senior administrators. Their expertise would be more than ever necessary in the years to come.

Constantine IX never recovered his prestige after the departure of Humbert and his friends. He continued to be suspected (with good reason) of pro-Latin sympathies, and his grovelling excuses to the Patriarch impressed nobody. His health, too, was rapidly giving way. Soon afterwards he retired to his monastery of Manganes, where his tomb, next to the Sclerina's, was already awaiting him. The monastery was perhaps the most sumptuous religious foundation that even Constantinople had seen. Psellus writes: 'The building was decorated throughout with golden stars, like the vault of heaven ... There were fountains which filled basins of water; gardens, some of them hanging, others sloping down to the level ground; and a bath that was beautiful beyond description.'

In this bath the Emperor would lie for several hours every day in an attempt to find some relief from his constant pain; but some time in the autumn of 1054, with the air already growing chill, he stayed in it too long. Pleurisy resulted. He lingered on until the new year; then, on 11 January 1055, he died.

18
Manzikert

[1055–81]

Constantine IX died a widower. Some time in 1050 his wife Zoe had pre-deceased him. Surprisingly perhaps, he had been devastated. Admittedly he owed her a lot: not only his crown, but also his quasi-conjugal life with his mistress, which would have been impossible had the old Empress not looked kindly on it. To many people, nevertheless, his grief seemed somewhat over-done. Since he had no legitimate issue the imperial crown devolved once again on Theodora. Her imperial presence had heretofore been shadowy; but now, refusing as always to contemplate marriage, she elected to govern on her own behalf. This she did with quiet efficiency: promulgating laws, receiving ambassadors and stubbornly resisting repeated attempts by the Patriarch to take over. She was however in her seventy-seventh year: who was to succeed her?

The problem was still unresolved when, in the last days of August 1056, it became evident that the end was near. Anxiously, her counsellors conferred together on whose name they would submit for her approval. Their choice finally fell on an elderly patrician named Michael Bringas, who had formerly held the rank of *stratioticus*, a civil service post concerned with military ad-ministration. 'He was,' sniffs Psellus, 'less qualified to rule than to be ruled by others,' but this was seen by those around the throne as a distinct advantage. By now the old Empress was sinking fast. She could no longer speak, but those closest to her insisted that they had distinctly seen her head nodding in consent. A few hours later she was dead, and Michael VI 'Stratioticus' reigned supreme over the Empire.

Michael was a collateral descendant of Joseph Bringas, chief minister to Romanus II; but he showed tragically little of his forebear's political acumen. Wise government in mid-eleventh-century Byzantium consisted above all in striking a balance between the administration and the military aristocracy: Michael indulged the one and victimized the other. In the spring of 1057 – during the annual Holy Week ceremony at which the Emperor traditionally distributed largesse – the entire Senate, together with all the senior magistrates and civil servants, was astonished to receive huge bonuses and automatic promotion, some by two or even three ranks. Then came the turn of the army; but instead of complimenting the leading generals on their dedicated service to his predecessors, he turned on the commander-in-chief Isaac Comnenus with a torrent of abuse, accusing him of having all but lost Antioch, corrupted the army, shown no signs of leadership and embezzled public money.

This groundless attack seems to have been purely the result of pique. For forty years Michael had been patronized by the military aristocracy; now at last he could tell them what he thought of them. From that moment, his downfall was assured. The outraged generals had had enough of government by bureaucrats, who feathered their nests while the army atrophied and the enemies of the Empire advanced; the time had come, they believed, to get rid of this long succession of good-for-nothing Emperors, superannuated Empresses and the epicene eunuchs who manipulated them, and to return to the old Roman tradition of the *imperator*, the Emperor-general who would personally lead his armies to victory. Isaac Comnenus was the obvious choice, but he refused and retired to his estates in Paphlagonia. His colleagues, however, remained in the capital to take soundings, and soon found that they had an unexpected ally: the Patriarch Michael Cerularius, who opened the doors of St Sophia secretly to the conspirators.

That night, in the darkness of the Great Church, the military leaders of Byzantium met to discuss the overthrow of Michael Stratioticus; and it was soon agreed that Isaac Comnenus was the only possible choice as his successor. And so it was that on 8 June 1057, on his Paphlagonian estate, Isaac allowed himself to be proclaimed Emperor of the Romans. The movement he now led was no mere insurrection. It was a full-scale civil war, in which virtually the whole of the army of Asia was on the march, supported by vast numbers of Byzantines from all social classes and walks of life. Isaac, proclaimed by his soldiers and raised on a shield according to the old imperial tradition, had a far more legitimate claim to the throne than Michael; he came not as a pretender but as one who, in the eyes of his followers as well as his own, was already the rightful *basileus*. As for Michael, he had suspected nothing until he received the news of his rival's proclamation. He had then summoned the army of Europe, supplemented by such few Asian detachments as remained loyal. Its command was entrusted to Theodore, Domestic of the Schools, and – a rather more curious choice – the *magister* Aaron, a member of a princely Bulgarian family who happened to be Isaac Comnenus's brother-in-law.

Arriving in Constantinople in early August, Theodore and Aaron crossed to Asia and established their headquarters in Nicomedia. It was a catastrophic mistake. Had they continued to Nicaea, whose tremendous walls commanded the only road round the Marmara, Isaac – who had no ships – would have been hard put to advance any further; instead, Nicaea surrendered to him without a struggle. For a few weeks the two armies remained encamped within some five miles of each other, between the two cities; then, on 20 August, battle was joined. There were heavy casualties on both sides; but the ultimate outcome was inevitable, and Michael's defeated army fled in disorder back to Constantinople. For the old Emperor the only hope now lay in diplomacy. A day or two later a delegation under Michael Psellus set off for Isaac's camp. The proposal was simple enough: that Isaac should come in peace to Constantinople, where he would be crowned Caesar, on the under-standing that he would automatically succeed on Michael's death. Psellus describes his reception on 25 August:

[Isaac] was seated on a couch, raised on a high platform and overlaid with gold. A magnificent robe gave him an air of high distinction; a far-away look in his eyes suggested that he was sunk in profoundest thought ... Around him were circles upon circles of warriors. There were Italians, and Scyths from the Taurus, men of fearful aspect in outlandish garb, glaring fiercely about them. Some had plucked their eyebrows and had covered themselves in war-paint ... Finally there were warriors armed with long spears and carrying their single-edged battle-axes on their shoulders.

Alarming as it was, the interview proved a success. Isaac confirmed that he would be perfectly content with the title of Caesar, on certain easily-acceptable conditions. That same evening, however, further news came from the capital: a *coup d'état*, abetted by the Patriarch, had deposed Michael and obliged him to take refuge in St Sophia. On 1 September 1057, accompanied by thousands of Constantinopolitans who had sailed across the Marmara to greet him, Isaac I Comnenus entered his capital in triumph. Michael VI Stratioticus had enjoyed one year of power. To his successor's eternal credit, he suffered no blinding, no exile. Abdication was enough. He died soon afterwards, a private citizen.

Isaac Comnenus assumed the throne of Byzantium with one object only in mind: to recover for the Empire the greatness it had known half a century before. Psellus tells us that he settled down to work on the very same evening that he entered the palace, before he had taken a bath or even changed his clothes. His object was a complete military reform, and he pursued it with military efficiency. He ensured that the army should once again receive proper financial support, and rapidly restored the firm military rule in which lay the only long-term hope of security. But all this needed money; and Isaac immediately embarked on a programme of large-scale territorial confiscation. Vast tracts of land recently conferred on favourites and time-servers were seized without compensation. His moves against Church property, on the other hand, proved more difficult. Michael Cerularius was by now almost as powerful as the *basileus* himself, and even more popular. Having been substantially responsible for Michael VI's overthrow, he expected recognition. Isaac, perfectly prepared to be accommodating where imperial interests were not directly threatened, willingly handed over the administration of St Sophia – formerly an imperial responsibility – and agreed not to trespass on the Patriarch's ecclesiastical preserves, while Cerularius gave a similar undertaking with regard to secular affairs. The difficulty was to know exactly where the line was to be drawn between them. Here the Patriarch had his own very definite ideas, in the expression of which he did not hesitate to threaten Isaac with deposition.

This, for the Emperor, was going too far. On 8 November 1058 Cerularius was arrested and exiled. Even then, however, he refused to resign his office; Isaac was obliged to arrange for a formal sentence of dethronement. The necessary synod was held, prudently, in a provincial city. Cerularius would in former days have put up a spirited defence; but he was by now an old man and the strain was too much for him. He died, of rage and a broken heart, before sentence could be passed. But the battle was far from over. The populace saw their beloved Patriarch as a martyr, and the Emperor never regained his popularity. Thus, little more than a year after his accession, he found the Church, the aristocracy and the people of Constantinople ranged implacably against him. Only the soldiers supported him to a man; thanks to them he defended the eastern frontiers and beat off several attacks by Magyars and Pechenegs. Meanwhile he astonished everyone by his seemingly superhuman energy: he seemed to need scarcely any sleep or even rest. His only recreation was the chase, into which he flung himself with the same tireless determination; and it was while hunting that, towards the end of 1059, he contracted the fever that was to bring about his early death.

Back at Blachernae, the dying Emperor nominated as his successor – almost certainly at the instigation of Psellus – Constantine Ducas, the most aristocratic of that group of intellectuals who had been responsible for reviving the university a few years before. Then he had himself carried to the Studium, where he adopted the monk's habit and where, a few days later, he died.

If Psellus was indeed responsible for the choice, his burden of guilt must be heavy indeed; for there is no Emperor in history whose accession had more disastrous consequences. Had Isaac Comnenus reigned for twenty years instead of two, he would have built up the strength of the army to the level it had known under Basil II and would have been able to bequeath his Empire, undefeated and undiminished, directly to his nephew Alexius. But it was not to be. Isaac's tragically premature death, and his choice of successor, rendered inevitable the first of the two great catastrophes that were ultimately to bring about the downfall of Byzantium.

Within weeks of Isaac's death it had become clear that his brief reign had marked only a momentary pause in the imperial decline. Now, under Constantine X Ducas, that decline reached its nadir. There was nothing evil about him; he was a scholar and an intellectual, a scion of one of the oldest and richest families of the military aristocracy. Had he but remained true to his background and continued Isaac's work during his eight-year reign, building up the army in preparation for the challenge ahead, the situation might have been saved. But he preferred the comforts of Constantinople, passing his time in learned discussions and the drafting of interminable dissertations on the finer points of law. And the price that the Empire paid was heavy indeed.

Once again the bureaucracy was all-powerful; for the Byzantine Empire, absolute monarchy though it might be, ran its economy on socialist lines. Private enterprise was rigidly controlled: production, labour, consumption, foreign trade, public welfare, even the movement of population were all in the hands of the State. The consequence was a vast horde of civil servants, imbued by the Emperor with one overriding principle: to curb – if not actually to destroy – the power of the army. It must be starved of funds, the authority of the generals limited, the former peasant-soldiers progressively replaced by foreign mercenaries. What Constantine and his government of intellectuals could never understand was, first, that these were the very measures most likely to provoke further *coups*; second, that mercenaries were by definition unreliable; and finally that the enemy – the most formidable enemy that Byzantium had seen for four centuries – was at the gates.

The Seljuk Turks first appear in the later tenth century, as a nomadic tribe in Transoxiana, where they adopted the prevailing faith of Islam. By 1045 they had spread across Persia; ten years later they were masters of Baghdad, establishing a protectorate over the moribund Abbasid Caliphate. This, however, had never been their ultimate objective; nor indeed was Byzantium. Their eyes were fixed upon Fatimid Egypt, whose Empire now extended as far as Aleppo. As orthodox Sunni Muslims they detested these Shi'ite upstarts, who represented in their eyes not only unspeakable heresy but a rupture in the fundamental unity of Islam. They knew that the Fatimids would not rest until they had taken Baghdad; and they were determined to destroy them before they had the opportunity to do so.

From 1063 the Seljuk Sultan was Alp Arslan, then in his early thirties, whose moustaches were apparently so long that they had to be tied behind when he went hunting. In the spring of 1064 he led a huge expedition against Armenia and captured its capital, Ani, from where he was able to advance unimpeded through Anatolia as far as the Cappadocian Caesarea, which was subjected to another merciless sack, and to within a hundred miles of Ancyra. That same year saw the death of Constantine X. Even on his deathbed he had done his best to perpetuate his catastrophic policies, obliging his young wife Eudocia to swear that she would not remarry and demanding from his ministers written commitments that they would recognize only a member of his own family as his successor. But by this time the fate of Caesarea was known and alarm was widespread. Even among the bureaucracy there were many who saw the necessity of a radical change of policy. Short of a *coup d'état*, however, the only way to ensure an effectively legitimate Emperor was for Eudocia to marry him – which she had sworn not to do.

The Empress herself was perfectly ready to remarry if she could be absolved from her oath, but for this she needed a dispensation from both the Patriarch and the Senate. Unfortunately, since the former was John Xiphilinus, one of Constantine's closest friends and supporters, while the latter was almost entirely composed of his appointees, her chances appeared slim. She, however, ingeniously suggested that she was considering marriage to the Patriarch's brother; Xiphilinus believed her, and persuaded the Senators to give their consent. Only then did Eudocia announce that she would marry, not the Patriarch's brother, but an outstandingly handsome man who seemed to personify the military aristocracy. His name was Romanus Diogenes, and on 1 January 1068 he was crowned Emperor.

It is impossible not to feel sorry for him. An able administrator and a brave soldier who fully recognized the gravity of the Seljuk menace, he set to with spirit to restore imperial fortunes – and it was not his fault that he failed. In Constantinople, he had to contend with Psellus and the Ducas family, who bitterly resented him and were resolved to bring about his destruction; in the field he found a demoralized, largely mercenary army, ill-fed, ill-equipped and frequently on the point of mutiny. Both 1068 and 1069 saw him leading expeditions to the East, where he appreciably strengthened the Byzantine position; his courage and determination are the only bright spots in a saga of frustration and disorganization, of cowardice and chaos.

Knowing as he did that the existing army of the East could never ensure the safety of Anatolia, Romanus devoted his time in Constantinople to settling arrears of pay, producing new equipment and recruiting new forces. Meanwhile he laid careful plans for a new campaign in which he would be able to throw some 60,000 to 70,000 men into the fray; and in the second week of March 1071 that expedition crossed the Bosphorus and headed eastward to Erzurum, where he split his army into two. The greater part he dispatched under the command of his general Joseph Tarchaniotes to Khelat, a few miles from the northern shore of Lake Van, while he himself – together with his other principal commander, Nicephorus Bryennius – set off for the little fortress-town of Manzikert, which gave in without a struggle. Tarchaniotes was less fortunate. We do not know precisely what happened. Muslim historians refer to a battle in which Alp Arslan scored a decisive victory, but there is no mention of such an engagement in any Byzantine source – the most trustworthy, Attaleiates, simply reporting that the news of the Sultan's arrival was alone sufficient to send 'the scoundrel' Tarchaniotes into headlong flight, his men after him. But it cannot have been as simple as that. Tarchaniotes was a highly respected general, in command of a force of perhaps 30,000 to 40,000 – larger, very probably, than the entire Seljuk army. If we reject the Muslim version we are left with various other possibilities: that he was angry with Romanus, whom he had advised not to split the army, and determined to prove him wrong; that Alp Arslan had taken his army by surprise, and that a general *sauve-qui-peut* was the only answer; or that Tarchaniotes was a tool of the Ducas, who deliberately abandoned his Emperor when the moment came. Such a theory might also explain why no word was sent to Romanus, thirty miles away at Manzikert. One thing is sure: that by the time the Emperor finally met the Seljuks more than half his army had deserted him.

Romanus Diogenes had captured Manzikert; he did not have long, however, to savour his triumph. On the very next day his army suffered serious harassment from bands of Seljuk bowmen, in the course of which Bryennius received three unpleasant but fortunately superficial wounds. That night there was no moon – and little sleep for the Byzantine army. The Seljuks kept up their pressure, causing such tumult in the darkness that again and again they were thought to have overrun the camp. It was a pleasant surprise to everyone the next morning to find that the palisades had held – but a disagreeable shock to learn that a large contingent of Uz mercenaries had defected to the Seljuks; there were several other Turkic units in the army, any or all of which might at any moment follow their example. In such circumstances, and with half his army and one of his best generals vanished without trace, one might have expected the Emperor to welcome the delegation that arrived a day or two later proposing a truce.

But why did the Sultan want one? Probably because he was far from sure of victory. The Seljuks had always preferred irregular warfare to pitched battles, which they avoided whenever possible. Besides, was there any real reason to fight? The only serious difference of opinion concerned Armenia, which had considerable strategic value for both him and Romanus. If the two of them could agree on a mutually acceptable division of Armenian territory, both armies could remain intact – and Alp Arslan could turn his attention back to what really interested him: the Fatimids.

But the Emperor's determination remained firm. This was his only chance of finally freeing his Empire from the Turkish menace. Alp Arslan was only a few miles away; he himself still commanded a force larger than he was ever likely to muster again. Moreover, if he were to return to Constantinople without a fight, what chance would he have of saving his throne – or indeed his life – against the intrigues of the Ducas? Dismissing the embassy with the minimum of courtesy, he prepared for the fray.

Oddly enough, the battle of Manzikert was until its very final stages hardly a battle at all. Romanus had formed up his army in one long line several ranks deep, with the cavalry on the flanks. He himself took the centre, with Bryennius on the left and, on the right, a Cappadocian general named Alyattes. Behind was a substantial rearguard composed, we are told, of the 'levies of the nobility' under the command, somewhat surprisingly, of Andronicus Ducas, a nephew of the late Emperor. This young man seems to have made little secret of his contempt for Romanus, and the wonder is that he should ever have been allowed to participate in the campaign at all. Throughout the afternoon the imperial army advanced across the steppe, but the Seljuks withdrew in a wide crescent, leaving the initiative to their mounted archers who galloped up and down on the Byzantine flanks, showering them with arrows; but for the increasingly frustrated Emperor in the centre there remained, where the enemy should have been, an empty void. On and on he rode, always hoping that he could somehow force his antagonists to turn and fight; then, suddenly, he realized that the sun was fast declining and that he had left his camp virtually undefended. He gave the signal for turning back – and wheeled his horse.

This was the moment for which Alp Arslan had been waiting. From the hills above he had watched Romanus's every move; now he gave the order for the attack. The Byzantine line broke in confusion; some of the mercenary units, thinking the Emperor had been killed, took to their heels. Meanwhile the Seljuks cut across immediately behind the broken line, separating it from the rearguard. At this point that rearguard should have moved forward, squeezing the enemy between it and the forward line and preventing its escape. Instead, Ducas deliberately spread the word among his troops that the Emperor was defeated and the battle lost. He and they thereupon fled from the field and, as the panic spread, more and more contingents followed them. Only those on the left wing, seeing the Emperor in difficulties, rode to his rescue; but the Seljuks bore down upon them swiftly from the rear and they too had to flee.

Meanwhile Romanus stood his ground, calling in vain on his troops to rally. But the chaos and confusion were too great. As Michael Attaleiates, an eye-witness, describes it:

It was like an earthquake: the shouting, the sweat, the swift rushes of fear, the clouds of dust, and not least the hordes of Turks riding all around us. It was a tragic sight, beyond any mourning or lamenting. What indeed could be more pitiable than to see the entire imperial army in flight, the Emperor defenceless, the whole Roman state overturned – and knowing that the Empire itself was on the verge of collapse?

Who survived? Effectively, those who took flight in time. The mercenaries behaved as mercenaries all too often did: nevertheless they were under contract, their wages had been paid, and they might have shown a little more spirit. The real villains were the 'levies of the nobility' who formed the rear-guard, and their commander Andronicus Ducas. Their shameful flight was probably due to treachery rather than cowardice, but it was not a jot the more excusable for that.

There was another survivor too: Romanus Diogenes himself. Left almost alone, he had refused to flee. Only when his horse was killed under him and a wound in his hand made it no longer possible for him to hold his sword did he allow himself to be taken prisoner. His captors gave him no special treatment. All night he lay among the wounded and dying. Only the following morning, dressed as a common soldier, and in chains, was he brought before the Sultan. At first Alp Arslan refused to believe that the exhausted captive who was flung at his feet was indeed the Emperor of the Romans; only when he had been formally identified by former Turkish envoys and by a fellow-prisoner did the Sultan rise from his throne and, ordering Romanus to kiss the ground before him, plant his foot on his victim's neck. It was a symbolic gesture, nothing more. He then helped Romanus to his feet and assured him that he would be treated with all due respect. For the next week the Emperor remained the Sultan's guest, eating at his table; never once did Alp Arslan show him anything but friendliness and courtesy. All this was, of course, in the highest tradition of Islamic chivalry; but it was also sound policy on the part of the Sultan. How much better, after all, that a friendly Romanus should return safely to Constantinople and resume the throne than that it should be taken over by some inexperienced and headstrong young man who would think only of revenge.

The peace terms were both merciful and moderate. The Sultan demanded no extensive territories; all he asked was the surrender of Manzikert, Antioch, Edessa and Hieropolis, together with one of the Emperor's daughters as a bride for one of his own sons. There remained the question of a ransom. Alp Arslan first suggested 10 million gold pieces; but when Romanus objected that the imperial treasury simply did not possess such a sum, he willingly reduced his demand to a million and a half, with a further 360,000 in annual tribute. It was agreed that the Emperor should return to Constantinople at the earliest possible moment, lest he be dethroned in his absence. And so, just a week after the battle, Romanus set out on his homeward journey. The Sultan rode with him on the first stage, and for the remainder granted him an escort of two Emirs and a hundred Mamelukes.

In Constantinople, the news of the defeat had come as the second shattering blow in this most catastrophic of years. The previous April – just a month after Romanus had left for the East – the Normans under Robert Guiscard had captured Bari. It was the end, after more than five centuries, of Byzantine Italy. But the reports from Bari had at least been clear; from Manzikert, they were hopelessly confused. On one point only was everyone in agreement: Romanus could not continue as *basileus*. But who was to take his place? Some called for Eudocia; others favoured Michael, her son by Constantine X; yet others saw in Constantine's brother, the Caesar John Ducas, the best hope for the Empire. In the event, it was John who acted – though not, ostensibly, on his own behalf. Fortunately he had the Varangian Guard behind him. This he now divided into two groups. One, under the command of his recently-returned son Andronicus, charged through the palace proclaiming Michael Emperor; with the other he marched straight to the Empress's apartments and arrested her. It was all over quite quickly. The terrified Eudocia was exiled, tonsured and compelled to take the veil. Michael VII Ducas was crowned with due ceremony by the Patriarch in St Sophia. It remained only to deal with Romanus Diogenes.

Romanus's movements after his departure from the Seljuk camp are hard to trace. He certainly tried to reassemble what remained of his once-great army, with the intention of marching on the capital. The Caesar John was, however, ready for him. After two defeats the ex-Emperor finally gave himself up to Andronicus Ducas, agreeing to renounce all claims to the throne and to retire to a monastery, and receiving in return a guarantee from his successor that no harm would come to him. Andronicus might perhaps have argued that his decision to mount him on a mule and to parade him in his degradation the 500-odd miles from Adana to Cotiaeum was not actually harmful, though it seems a curious interpretation of the terms of his undertaking. In the light of what happened afterwards, however, the question seems academic. John Scylitzes writes: 'Carried forth on a cheap beast of burden like a decaying corpse, his eyes gouged out and his face and head alive with worms, he lived on a few days in pain with a foul stench all about him until he gave up the ghost, being buried on the island of Proti where he had built a monastery.'

Nor was that the last insult. A few days before his death in the summer of 1072, Romanus received a letter from his old enemy Psellus, congratulating him on his good fortune in losing his eyes – a sure sign that the Almighty had found him worthy of a higher light. As he lay in his final agony, the thought must have given him profound comfort.

The battle of Manzikert was the greatest disaster suffered by the Empire in the seven and a half centuries of its existence. The humiliation was bad enough, the performance of the imperial army having been characterized by a combination of treachery, panic and ignominious flight. The fate of the Emperor, too, was unparalleled since the capture of Valerian by the Persian King Shapur I in AD 260. The real tragedy, however, lay not in the battle itself but in its epilogue. Had Romanus been permitted to retain his throne, he would have respected the treaty he had made with Alp Arslan, who would have resumed his expedition against Fatimid Egypt. Even had he been succeeded by an Emperor worthy of the name, the damage could have been contained: a Nicephorus Phocas or a John Tzimisces – let alone a Basil II – would have restored the situation in a matter of months, and the Seljuks did not begin any systematic move into Anatolia until the summer of 1073 – two years after the battle. By then they can hardly be blamed for doing so. Michael VII's refusal to accept the obligations of the treaty signed with Romanus gave them a legitimate motive, while the chaos within the Empire and the collapse of the old defensive system based on military holdings ensured that they met with no resistance.

Thus it came about that tens of thousands of Turkoman tribesmen swarmed into Anatolia, and that by 1080 or thereabouts Alp Arslan's son Malik-Shah controlled an area of some 30,000 square miles, which, in recognition of its former inclusion in the Roman Empire, he named the Sultanate of Rum. The Empire still retained western Asia Minor and its former Mediterranean and Black Sea coasts; but it had lost at a single stroke the source of much of its grain and more than half its manpower. The battle through which it had suffered that loss need never have been fought and could easily have been won. Even after defeat, its consequences might have been avoided. But those in power in Constantinople, blinkered by smug intellectualism and obsessive ambition, threw away every opportunity offered to them. In doing so they martyred a courageous and upright man who was worth more than all of them put together and could, with their loyalty and support, have saved the situation; and they dealt the Empire a blow from which it would never recover.

The reign of Michael VII continued as disastrously as it had begun. The Church of Rome was steadily extending its influence beyond the Adriatic, in the lands over which Basil II had formerly claimed suzerainty. As the imperial hold weakened, the Pechenegs and Magyars became increasingly troublesome. Within half a century of Basil's death, his whole magnificent achievement in the Balkans was already crumbling away. At home the situation was very little better. Inflation was rising, to the point where a gold *nomisma* lost a quarter of its value. Before long the Emperor became known as Michael Parapinaces, or 'Minus-a-quarter', a nickname which stuck with him until his death. Then there were the military insurrections. The first of these was inspired by a Norman soldier of fortune named Roussel of Bailleul, who had been sent with a mixed force of Norman and Frankish cavalry against Seljuk marauders in Anatolia. Once deep in Turkish-controlled territory he had betrayed his trust and, with 300 followers, had set up a self-declared independent Norman state. Had Michael VII thought for a moment, he would have realized that compared with the Turkish tide Roussel was little more than a mild irritant; instead, he turned to the Seljuks for aid, offering in return the formal cession of already-occupied territories and thus immeasurably strengthening the Turkish hold. Even then Roussel managed to escape; only when an army was sent out under the command of the ablest of the Empire's younger generals, Alexius Comnenus, was he hunted down.

But Alexius could not be everywhere at once and experienced generals were in short supply; thus a year or two later, when the Empire was faced with two new and far more serious insurrections, Roussel was suddenly released from his captivity and found himself fighting with Alexius against two new pretenders to the imperial throne. The first of these was Nicephorus Bryennius who, having fought loyally at Manzikert and being no longer prepared to accept the incompetence of Michael Parapinaces and his government, raised the standard of revolt in November 1077 and marched to Adrianople, where he was acclaimed *basileus*. A week later he and his army were beneath the walls of the capital. His insurrection might well have succeeded had it not been for another, almost simultaneous, rising in the East. Its leader was the *strategos* of the Anatolikon Theme, Nicephorus Botaneiates.

He too, like Bryennius, had taken up arms against the Emperor from the highest motives.

Of the two rival claimants, Bryennius was first in the field; Botaneiates was, however, of nobler birth, being a member of the old military aristocracy; he was also the stronger, since he had managed to suborn the Seljuk forces hired by Michael to oppose him. Neither made a direct attack on Constantinople, knowing full well from secret contacts within the capital that popular discontent over rising prices would soon bring matters to a head – which, in March 1078, it did. Riots broke out in every corner of the city. Many government buildings were burnt to the ground. Michael, lucky to escape with his life, abdicated and withdrew to the Studium, and on 24 March Nicephorus Botaneiates entered Constantinople in triumph. His rival Bryennius was captured and blinded.

It was an inauspicious start. Botaneiates, though a competent general, knew nothing of politics; besides, he was already well into his seventies and his bid for the throne had used up much of his remaining strength. Incapable of coping with the crisis, he could do little but preside over the further disintegration of the Empire. The old party of the civil bureaucracy had collapsed, and with it the authority of the Senate; all that the Byzantines could now do was pray that of the several military commanders struggling for power, one might prove himself capable of putting an end to the chaos.

Three years later their prayer was answered. Botaneiates abdicated in his turn in favour of an aristocratic young general who, coming to the throne on Easter Day 1081, was to reign for the next thirty-seven years, giving the Empire the stability that it so desperately needed and governing it with a firm and steady hand. That general was Alexius Comnenus, nephew of Isaac I. Not even he could undo the damage done by the battle of Manzikert; but he could, and did, restore to Byzantium its good name among nations.

PART III

The Decline and Fall

19
Alexius Comnenus

[1081–1118]

On Easter Sunday, 4 April 1081, in the Great Church of St Sophia at Constantinople, the twenty-four-year-old Alexius Comnenus ascended the throne of a sad and shattered Empire. He had first seen action against the Seljuk Turks at the age of fourteen; since then he had never lost a battle. He was a superb general, whose soldiers loved and trusted him. He came of imperial stock, his uncle Isaac Comnenus having occupied the throne some twenty years before; moreover his marriage to the fifteen-year-old Irene Ducas assured him the support not only of the most influential family in the Empire but of the clergy and most of the aristocracy as well.

For these very reasons, however, Alexius had enemies at court; and it was here that he found an invaluable champion in the Empress herself. Mary of Alania – the beautiful widow of Michael VII, whom Nicephorus Botaneiates had married on his accession – had no love for a husband old enough to be her grandfather. Her first loyalty was to the Ducas family. She may even have fallen in love with Alexius; all we know is that in 1080 she adopted him as her son. Botaneiates, now clearly senile, made no protest. Indeed, towards the end of the year he approved Alexius's appointment as commander of a new campaign against the Turks, thereby giving him his opportunity. The doddering old Emperor must, Alexius knew, be removed; the problem had been to rally the necessary forces. That problem was now solved. A rendezvous with his new army was quickly arranged, and in the early hours of Sunday, 14 February 1081, he and his brother Isaac made their way to the imperial stables. There they took the horses they needed, hamstrung the rest and galloped away to the monastery of SS. Cosmas and Damian, where they enlisted the help of Irene's mother Maria Traiana Ducas, and of her influential brother-in-law George Palaeologus. They then hurried on to their appointed meeting-place and sent an appeal to her grandfather, the Caesar John Ducas, for support. The Caesar was now living in retirement on his estate some miles away. He was asleep when the messenger arrived, but was roused by his little grandson. At first he refused to believe the news and boxed the boy's ears; then he called for a horse and set off for the camp.

After two or three more days Alexius gave the order to march. Until now there seems to have been no suggestion of his assuming the throne; only when the army stopped for the night was it consulted, and then in the form of a choice: whom would it prefer as *basileus*, Alexius or Isaac? Isaac himself was happy to defer to his brother, and the influence of the Ducas carried the day. Alexius was acclaimed with the imperial titles and formally shod with the purple buskins, embroidered in gold with the double-headed eagles of Byzantium – which, we can only assume, he had brought with him from the palace.

He was still uncertain of his next step. There could be no question of taking the capital by force. Careful reconnaissance, however, suggested that although certain regiments like the Varangian Guard would fight to the death for the reigning Emperor, others – including the Germanic tribesmen who guarded the Adrianople Gate – might be suborned. George Palaeologus made secret contact with their leader, and the matter was soon settled. One evening, just as darkness was falling, George and a few followers put ladders against one of the German-held towers and slipped over the bastion; Alexius then concentrated his entire force at the foot of the tower. At daybreak Palaeologus gave the signal; the gates were opened from within and Alexius's army poured into Constantinople.

The citizens had little respect for their old Emperor; most of them were delighted to see him replaced by a popular young general. What they did not expect was to be treated like a conquered enemy; but the barbarian element in Alexius's army was too strong, and quickly infected the rest. No sooner were the soldiers inside the walls than they scattered in all directions, looting, pillaging and raping, and confusion quickly spread throughout the city, to the point where the success of the whole operation seemed in doubt. Botaneiates himself, on the other hand, knew that he was beaten. Crossing the square from the palace to St Sophia, he declared his formal abdication. He was consigned to the monastery of the Peribleptos, the huge and hideous building on the Seventh Hill endowed by Romanus Argyrus half a century before.

The young man who now found himself seventy-sixth Emperor of Byzantium was short and stocky, deep-chested and broad-shouldered, with a heavy beard. To his daughter Anna 'he reminded one of a fiery whirlwind ... radiating beauty, grace and dignity and an unapproachable majesty'. When she writes of her father, Anna's testimony must be treated with caution; there can however have been little doubt that for the first time in over half a century the Empire was in capable hands. On his arrival at the Great Palace Alexius went immediately to work. After twenty-four hours he had rounded up all his soldiers and confined them to their barracks to cool off. But his conscience still troubled him. He confessed his anxieties to the Patriarch, who set up an official inquiry. There was, it was concluded, evidence of guilt. The Emperor, his family and all who had participated in the *coup* were sentenced to a period of fasting and to various other acts of penance. For forty days and nights Alexius wore sackcloth beneath the imperial purple, sleeping on the ground with a stone for a pillow.

Meanwhile a breach was already appearing between his own followers and the family of Ducas, who objected to his relationship with the Empress Mary of Alania. She might have been expected to leave the palace on his arrival; she did not do so. True, she was the new Emperor's adoptive mother; but that hardly explained his decision to remain with her, settling his wife and her family in another, smaller palace on lower ground. The rumours spread quickly. Some whispered that Alexius was planning to divorce Irene to become Mary's third husband; others, that the real force behind these developments was his mother, the formidable Anna Dalassena, who hated the Ducas and was determined to remove them from power and influence. The first of these rumours may well have been true; the second certainly was. A few days later on Easter Sunday, fuel was added to the flames when Alexius excluded his wife from his coronation.

To the Ducas, this was a gratuitous insult. The Empress was not one of their own; she was the holder of a recognized rank, which carried considerable power. She had her own court and exercised control over her own revenues; and she played an indispensable part in the imperial ceremonial. Alexius himself was certainly uneasy about the decision. He owed the Ducas an enormous debt; and it was folly to antagonize the most powerful family of the Empire. For the moment, he allowed his mother to persuade him; but he soon realized that he had seriously overstepped the mark.

Matters were finally brought to a head by the Patriarch. He spoke seriously to the Emperor, and a few days later the young Empress was duly crowned in St Sophia. The Ducas family knew that they had won; and Alexius had learnt his first lesson. Any emotional ties between himself and his adoptive mother were now broken: Mary agreed to leave the Bucoleon, on condition only that Constantine, her son by Michael VII, should be made co-Emperor with Alexius. The request was granted; whereupon she and Constantine retired to the sumptuous mansion built by Constantine IX for the Sclerina some thirty-five years before. They were accompanied by Isaac Comnenus, to whom Alexius had awarded the newly-invented rank of *sebastocrator*, second only to the two co-Emperors themselves. He himself brought Irene back to the Bucoleon, where their married life proved unexpectedly happy, ultimately resulting in nine children.

On the political horizon, however, the clouds were gathering fast. Within a month of Alexius's coronation, Robert Guiscard, Duke of Apulia, launched his grand offensive against the Roman Empire.

The story of the Normans in south Italy begins around 1015, with a group of young Norman pilgrims who were persuaded by certain Lombard leaders to serve as mercenaries against the Byzantines. Word soon got back to Normandy, and the initial trickle of footloose younger sons in search of wealth and adventure rapidly grew to the point where it became a steady immigration. Soon they began to exact payment for their services in land, and in 1053, at Civitate in Apulia, they defeated a vastly superior army raised and led against them by Pope Leo IX in person.

By this time supremacy had been assumed by the family of one Tancred de Hauteville, an obscure knight in the service of the Duke of Normandy. Of his twelve sons, eight settled in Italy, five became leaders of the front rank and one – Robert, nicknamed Guiscard ('the crafty') – possessed something very like genius. After Civitate papal policy changed: and in 1059 Robert was invested by Pope Nicholas II with the previously non-existent dukedoms of Apulia, Calabria and Sicily. Two years later he and his youngest brother Roger invaded the island, and for the next decade they kept up the pressure both there and on the mainland. Bari had fallen in 1071, and with it the last remnants of Byzantine power in Italy; early the next year Palermo had followed, and the Saracen hold on Sicily was broken for ever. Four years later it was the turn of Salerno, the last independent Lombard principality. In all Italy south of the Garigliano river, Robert Guiscard and his Normans now reigned supreme.

For many centuries already this land had been known as Magna Graecia, and at this time it was still in spirit far more Greek than Italian. The vast majority of its inhabitants spoke Greek as their native language; the Greek rite prevailed in almost all the churches and in most of the monasteries. No wonder that the Guiscard should begin to harbour designs on the imperial throne – designs which were unwittingly encouraged by the Byzantines themselves. In 1074 Michael VII had suggested his own son Constantine as the prospective bridegroom for the most beautiful – he had been careful to specify – of Robert's daughters. The Guiscard had not hesitated: the opportunity of becoming father-in-law to the Emperor of Byzantium was too good to miss. He had accepted the proposal, and shortly afterwards had bundled his daughter Helena off to Constantinople, there to pursue her studies in the imperial *gynaeceum* until her infant fiancé should be of marriageable age.

The overthrow of Michael VII in 1078 put paid to all Helena's chances of attaining the imperial throne. The hapless princess found herself immured in a convent, with which she was doubtless far from pleased. Her father received the news with mixed feelings. His immediate hopes of an imperial son-in-law had been dashed; on the other hand the treatment accorded to his daughter gave him a perfect pretext for intervention. In the summer of 1080 he began his preparations. The Empire was slipping deeper and deeper into chaos: in its present condition, a well-planned Norman offensive would have every chance of success.

All through the autumn and winter the work went on. The fleet was re-fitted, the army increased in size and re-equipped. In an effort to stir up enthusiasm among his Greek subjects, the Guiscard had even managed to produce a disreputable and transparently bogus Orthodox monk, who appeared in Salerno at the height of the preparations and gave himself out to be none other than Michael VII in person, escaped from exile and trusting in his gallant Norman allies to replace him on his throne. Nobody believed him much; but Robert, professing to be entirely convinced by his claims, persisted in treating him with exaggerated deference throughout the months that followed.

On hearing of Alexius's *coup*, he refused to change his plans. He had by now lost all interest in the imperial marriage, but the last thing he wanted was his daughter's return; he had six others, and she was serving a far more useful purpose where she was. So far as he was concerned the disreputable pretender was still the Emperor Michael, and Michael was still the legitimate Emperor. The important thing now was to embark before Alexius returned Helena to him. He had already sent his eldest son Bohemund with an advance party across the Adriatic. The sooner he could join him the better.

The fleet sailed towards the end of May 1081. With some thirteen hundred Norman knights, supported by a large body of Saracens, some rather dubious Greeks and several thousand foot-soldiers, it moved slowly down the coast to Corfu, where the imperial garrison surrendered at once. His bridgehead now secured, Robert's next target was Durazzo across the Adriatic, from which the old Via Egnatia ran east across the Balkan peninsula to Constantinople. Soon, however, it became clear that progress was not going to be so easy. Several ships were lost in a sudden tempest, and several more were destroyed by a fleet from Venice – no keener than Constantinople to see the straits of Otranto under Norman control.

But it took more than this to discourage the Duke of Apulia, whose army was still unimpaired and who now settled down to besiege Durazzo. Here too the task proved harder than expected; the garrison, knowing that the Emperor was himself on the way with a large relief force, resisted stoutly. Finally, on 15 October, Alexius appeared, and three days later he attacked. By this time Robert had moved a little to the north of the city and had drawn up his line of battle. He himself commanded the centre, with Bohemund on his left, inland, flank and on his right his wife, the Lombard princess Sichelgaita of Salerno.

Sichelgaita needs some explanation. She was cast in a Wagnerian mould, the closest approximation in history to a Valkyrie. A woman of immense build, she hardly ever left her husband's side – least of all in battle, one of her favourite occupations. At such moments, charging into the fray, her long blonde hair streaming from beneath her helmet, deafening friend and foe alike with huge shouts of encouragement or imprecation, she must have looked – even if she did not altogether sound – worthy to take her place beside Brünnhilde herself.

As always when the Emperor took the field in person, his Varangian Guard was present in strength. It now consisted largely of Englishmen, Anglo-Saxons who had left their country in disgust after Hastings and had taken service with Byzantium. Longing to avenge themselves on the detested Normans, swinging their huge two-handed battle-axes round their heads and then slamming them into horses and riders alike, they struck terror in the hearts of the Apulian knights. The horses too began to panic, and before long the Norman right had turned in confusion. But now, if contemporary reports are to be believed, the day was saved by Sichelgaita. The story is best told by Anna Comnena:

Directly she saw the soldiers running away, she called out to them in a powerful voice an equivalent to Homer's words: 'How far will ye flee? Stand, and acquit yourselves like men!' And when they continued to run, she grasped a long spear and at full gallop rushed after the fugitives; and on seeing this they recovered themselves and returned to the fight.

Now, too, Bohemund's left flank had wheeled to the rescue, with a detachment of crossbowmen against whom the Varangians found themselves defenceless. Their retreat was cut off; they could fight only where they stood. At last the few remaining alive turned and sought refuge in a nearby chapel; but the Normans fired it and most of them perished in the flames.

The Emperor himself was still fighting bravely; but the cream of his army had been destroyed at Manzikert and when he found himself betrayed by a whole regiment of 7,000 Turkish auxiliaries, lent to him by the Seljuk Sultan, he knew that the battle was lost. Weak from loss of blood and in considerable pain from a wound in his forehead, he rode slowly back over the mountains to Ochrid, there to regroup what he could of his shattered forces.

Somehow, Durazzo was to hold out till February 1082; from there on, however, there was little resistance; Robert marched east to Kastoria, by which time he was probably congratulating himself that Constantinople was as good as won. But it was nothing of the kind. In April, messengers arrived from Italy: Apulia and Calabria were up in arms, and much of Campania as well. They also brought a letter from Pope Gregory VII. His enemy Henry IV, King of the Romans,[1] was at the gates of Rome, demanding to be crowned Emperor of the West. The Duke's presence was urgently required at home. Leaving the command of the expedition to Bohemund, Robert hurried back to the coast and took ship across the Adriatic.

Neither of these crises were as fortuitous as they seemed. Robert's own nephew Abelard, whom he had dispossessed and who had later sought refuge in Constantinople, had needed little persuading to return to Italy and, with the aid of much Byzantine gold, to raise the revolt. Meanwhile Alexius Comnenus had sent an embassy to Henry IV, pointing out the dangers of allowing the Duke of Apulia to continue unchecked; and Henry, in return for 360,000 gold pieces and a quantity of priceless treasure, had been happy to conclude a treaty of alliance.

Alexius had spent the winter in Thessalonica raising troops; Bohemund and his army were steadily extending their power through the Empire's western provinces, and Robert himself would probably be back before long. By now money was running seriously short; Isaac the *sebastocrator* was obliged to summon a synod at St Sophia, where he announced the confiscation of all church treasures. The hierarchy, while making little attempt to conceal its displeasure, had no choice but to submit.

For a year Bohemund continued to advance, until all Macedonia and much of Thessaly lay under his control. Not until the spring of 1083, at Larissa, did Alexius succeed in turning the tide. Bohemund was obliged to raise the siege and to withdraw to Kastoria, and from that moment on he was lost. Dispirited and homesick, with its pay long overdue, the Norman army fell away. When Bohemund took ship for Italy to raise more money, his principal lieutenants instantly surrendered; a Venetian fleet recaptured Durazzo and Corfu; and by the end of 1083 Norman-held territory was once again confined to one or two offshore islands and a short strip of the coast.

Across the Adriatic, on the other hand, Robert Guiscard was doing splendidly. By mid-summer the last pockets of Apulian resistance had been eliminated. He had then set about the rescue of Pope Gregory, who had

---

1 A purely honorary title, normally adopted by the elected Emperor of the West until he could be properly crowned by the Pope in Rome.

barricaded himself into the Castel Sant'Angelo; and on 24 May 1084 he pitched his camp beneath the walls of Rome. Henry IV, however – who had deposed Gregory and had had himself crowned by a puppet anti-Pope – had not waited for him. Three days before the Normans appeared at the gates he had retired to Lombardy. At dawn on 28 May the first of Robert's shock-troops burst through the Flaminian Gate; and it was not long before they had released the Pope from his fortress and borne him back in triumph to the Lateran. Then, and only then, came the tragedy. The entire city now fell victim to an orgy of pillage and destruction. For three days this continued – until the inhabitants, able to bear it no longer, rose against their oppressors; and the Normans set fire to the city. The Capitol and the Palatine were gutted; churches, palaces and temples were left empty shells. Between the Colosseum and the Lateran, hardly a building escaped the flames.

A few weeks later, in the autumn of 1084, Robert Guiscard returned to Greece with Bohemund and a new fleet of 150 ships. At the outset, things could hardly have gone worse: on their way to Corfu, they were set upon by a Venetian fleet and soundly beaten twice in three days. After the second defeat the Venetians sent back messengers to the lagoon with news of the victory; but they had underestimated the Guiscard. Seeing the pinnaces disappear over the horizon and recognizing the chance of taking the enemy by surprise, he rallied his few vessels still afloat and flung them forward in a last onslaught. He had calculated it perfectly. Anna Comnena reports 13,000 Venetian dead, together with 2,500 prisoners. Corfu fell; and it was a much happier army that settled down into winter quarters on the mainland.

But in the course of the winter a new enemy appeared: an epidemic – probably typhoid – that struck without mercy. By spring 1085 five hundred Norman knights were dead, and a large proportion of the army incapacitated. Robert himself remained cheerful and confident; but in mid-summer, sailing to occupy Cephalonia, he felt the dreaded sickness upon him. The vessel put in at the first safe anchorage, a bay still known as Phiscardo. Here he died on 17 July 1085, Sichelgaita beside him. He was sixty-eight. The past four years had seen both the Eastern and Western Emperors fleeing at his approach, and one of the greatest of medieval Popes rescued and restored by his hand. Had he lived another few months, Alexius Comnenus might have proved one of the more transitory – possibly even the last – of the Emperors of Byzantium.

The Empire was now delivered from immediate danger; but it was never safe for long. With the temporary disappearance of the Normans from the scene, it was the turn of the Pechenegs. For more than two hundred years they had proved themselves the most grasping (as well as the cruellest) of the barbarian tribes. In the spring of 1087 a huge Pecheneg army invaded the Empire; three years later it stood within reach of Constantinople. Alexius was obliged to fall back on one of the oldest diplomatic tricks: enlisting the help of one tribe against another. He now appealed to the Cumans. They had no fundamental quarrel with the Pechenegs, but they willingly answered his call. They arrived in the late spring; and on Monday, 28 April 1091, the two armies faced each other at Levunium, near the mouth of the Maritsa river.

In the battle the next day the Pechenegs – whose women and children, as was the barbarian custom, had followed them to war – were almost exterminated. A few prisoners survived and were taken into imperial service; the vast majority perished in a general massacre. Neither the imperial army nor the Cumans emerge with much credit; Levunium was, however, the most decisive victory to have been won by a Byzantine army since the days of Basil II. Not only did it deliver the Empire for the next thirty years from the Pechenegs; it provided a healthy example for other tribes as well. More important still, it secured the Emperor's own position. Now at last he had proved himself capable of restoring to Byzantium at least part of her former greatness. The *basileus* who, a few days after the battle, rode proudly through the streets of Constantinople to St Sophia could look to the future, as never before in the ten years since his accession, with confidence and hope.

Some time towards the end of 1094, Alexius Comnenus received an embassy from Rome. Urban II had now been seven years on the pontifical throne, working hard to improve relations between Constantinople and the Holy See. There was indeed room for improvement: on his accession Alexius had been excommunicated by Gregory VII, and the Emperor's esteem for the Pope had sunk still further when he heard of his alliance with the hated Duke of Apulia. The Pope, meanwhile, had been similarly appalled to learn that Henry IV was in the pay of Alexius, and by the time of his death in 1085 the situation was as bad as it had ever been. When Urban had succeeded to the papal throne three years later he had started the reconciliation by lifting the excommunication; and Alexius, who had previously closed all the Latin churches in Constantinople, had responded by opening them again. Letters were exchanged, and the breach was gradually healed, until by the time the papal embassy reached Constantinople Emperor and Pope were once again on friendly terms.

The legates carried with them an invitation to send representatives to a Great Council of the Church, to be held in Piacenza the following March; and Alexius accepted at once, sensing a perfect opportunity to appeal for Western aid against the Turks. The situation in Anatolia was in fact a good deal more promising than it had been at any time since Manzikert, and the reconquest of Asia Minor seemed a distinct possibility; but this was impossible without military assistance from the West, and Piacenza promised to be just the place to say so. The Byzantine spokesmen did their work well, emphasizing not the prizes to be won but the religious aspects of the appeal: the sufferings of the Christian communities of the East, the submergence of Asia Minor beneath the Turkish tide, the presence of the infidel armies at the very gates of Constantinople and the imminence of the threat, not only to their Empire but to all Christendom. Urban in particular was impressed. As he travelled home to France, a scheme gradually took shape in his mind more ambitious than Alexius had ever contemplated: a Holy War, in which the combined forces of Europe would march against the Saracen. He therefore called another council, to meet at Clermont on 18 November, at which he promised to make a statement of immense significance to all Christendom. When that day came, so vast were the crowds assembled to hear him speak that the cathedral was abandoned, and the papal throne was erected instead on a high platform outside the eastern gate of the city.

The text of Urban's speech has not come down to us, but the substance is certain enough. It was, he declared, the duty of Western Christendom to march to the rescue of the Christian East. All those who agreed to do so 'from devotion only, not from advantage of honour or gain', would die absolved, their sins remitted. The great Crusading army must be ready to march by the Feast of the Assumption, 15 August 1096. The response to his words was electric. Led by Bishop Adhemar of Le Puy, several hundred people – priests and monks, noblemen and peasants together – pledged themselves to take the Cross. The First Crusade was under way.

Alexius Comnenus was appalled. This was the last thing he wanted. Just when there was a real chance of regaining his lost territory, he was to have hundreds of thousands of undisciplined brigands pouring across his borders, constantly demanding food but recognizing no authority whatever. He took what precautions he could, establishing stocks of provisions and police escorts at Durazzo and regular points along the Via Egnatia. Then he settled down to wait; and the arrival of the first Crusaders confirmed his direst fears.

Peter the Hermit was not a hermit at all, but a malodorous monk from Amiens. Preaching the Crusade throughout northern France and Germany, he had quickly attracted a following of some forty thousand, composed principally of local peasants and including large numbers of women and children. Somehow this straggling company made its way across Europe to the Hungarian town of Semlin, on the Sava river, where they stormed the citadel and killed four thousand Hungarians. Crossing to Belgrade, they pillaged and set fire to the city. At Nish they attempted the same, but this time the local Byzantine governor sent in his own troops. Many Crusaders were killed, many more taken prisoner. Of the forty thousand who had started out, a good quarter were lost by the time the party reached Constantinople on 1 August. A single conversation with Peter, and a glance at his followers, was enough to convince Alexius that this so-called army would not stand a chance against the Seljuks. But it clearly could not remain in the city – complaints were already pouring in of robberies, rapes and lootings – and it refused to turn back. On 6 August, therefore, it was ferried across the Bosphorus and left to look after itself.

The end of the story can be quickly told. The Crusaders advanced to the village of Cibotus, between Nicomedia and Nicaea, whence they terrorized the countryside, killing, raping and occasionally torturing the Greek Christian inhabitants. Soon, however, came reports that the Turks were approaching. On 21 October, the entire Crusading army of some twenty thousand men marched out of Cibotus – straight into a Turkish ambush; and within a few minutes the whole host was in headlong flight back to the camp, the Seljuks in pursuit. A few lucky ones managed to save their lives, as did a number of young girls and boys whom the Turks appropriated for their own purposes. The rest were slaughtered. The People's Crusade was over.

Peter's rabble army was in no way typical of the armies of the First Crusade. Over the next nine months Alexius was to find himself the unwilling host to perhaps another 70,000 men, and a fair number of women, led by some of the most powerful feudal princes of the West. The economic, logistic, military and diplomatic challenges presented by this horde were unparalleled in Byzantine history, the basic problem being one of trust. Alexius was understandably sceptical about the high Christian motives so glibly professed. The Normans at least, as he well knew, were out for what they could get – if not the Empire itself, then their own independent principalities in the East. This latter objective did not worry him: a few Christian buffer-states between himself and the Saracen might be no bad thing. But such principalities must not be founded on imperial territory and their princes must acknowledge him as their suzerain. Feudalism in Western Europe, he understood was based on solemn oaths of fealty; very well, he would demand just such an oath from all the leaders in respect of any future conquests.

The first of these leaders, Hugh of Vermandois, younger brother of King Philip I of France, willingly swore the required oath. The next two – Godfrey of Bouillon, Duke of Lower Lorraine, and his brother Baldwin of Boulogne –

proved rather less tractable. At first, indeed, they categorically refused; only after Alexius had sent his crack regiments, obviously ready to fight, did the brothers finally capitulate. On Easter Sunday they and their leading knights swore their oaths at last. Immediately, amicable relations were restored. Alexius showered them with presents and entertained them all to a banquet. The next day he shipped the lot of them over the Bosphorus.

Of all the leaders of the First Crusade, there was one whom Alexius Comnenus mistrusted more than any other. Bohemund, now Prince of Taranto, was the eldest son of Robert Guiscard who, had he not succumbed to that most fortunate epidemic twelve years before, might well have displaced Alexius on the Byzantine throne. The fact that Robert had divorced Bohemund's mother to marry the formidable Sichelgaita, and that he had subsequently left his Italian dominions to the latter's son Roger Borsa, made Bohemund more dangerous than ever: having nothing to hope for in Italy, he could be expected to cause still greater havoc in the East. Moreover, his military reputation was unmatched in Europe.

When the Emperor received him the day after his arrival, Bohemund cheerfully admitted his former hostility; this time, however, he had come of his own free will, as a friend. He instantly agreed to take the oath of allegiance. He knew and understood the Greeks and spoke their language; unlike the other Crusaders, he was well aware that success would depend on having the *basileus* on his side. With this thought in mind he had specifically forbidden his soldiers, on pain of instant execution, any marauding or other misbehaviour on their way to Constantinople. A fortnight later he and his army were conveyed in their turn across the Bosphorus, while Alexius dealt with his next guest.

Raymond IV of Saint-Gilles, Count of Toulouse and Marquis of Provence, was the oldest, richest and most distinguished of the Crusaders. His was almost certainly the largest of the properly-organized Crusading armies – perhaps some ten thousand strong. Though already in his late fifties, he had been the first nobleman to take the Cross at Clermont and had publicly vowed never to return to the West; his wife and his son Alfonso had accompanied him, together with his friend Bishop Adhemar of Le Puy, to whom Pope Urban had entrusted the spiritual well-being of the Crusade. There can be little doubt that, like Bohemund, he coveted the military leadership for himself. Unlike the Prince of Taranto, however, Raymond seems to have made little attempt to control his men, whose taste for indiscriminate rape and pillage had brought them into repeated confrontation with their imperial escort. From the outset, he made it clear that he had no intention of taking the oath. All he would say was that if the *basileus* himself were to assume personal command of the Crusading army, then he, Raymond, would be happy to serve under him – to which Alexius could only reply that much as he might wish to do so, in present conditions he could not leave the Empire. Finally, a compromise was reached: the Count agreed to swear an oath promising to respect the life and honour of the Emperor; and Alexius, realizing that this was the best he could hope for, very sensibly accepted.

The fourth and last expedition of the Crusade was that of Robert, Duke of Normandy, eldest son of William the Conqueror, who set out in September 1096. With him rode his brother-in-law Count Stephen of Blois and his cousin Count Robert II of Flanders, the three of them heading an army which included many distinguished noblemen and knights from Normandy, Brittany and England. They made no difficulties over the oath of allegiance, and were enchanted by the Emperor's generosity, as well as by the quality of the food, horses and silken robes that he pressed on them. The rank and file were less lavishly indulged; as usual, however, all those who wished to do so were allowed to enter Constantinople in groups of half a dozen at a time, to see the sights and worship at the principal shrines. After a fortnight they followed the other armies over the Bosphorus and joined them at Nicaea.

The relief of Alexius Comnenus, as he watched the last of the Crusaders embark, may well be imagined. Inevitably, there had been a few unfortunate incidents; on the whole, however, thanks to his preparations and precautions, the armies had caused remarkably little trouble. All the commanders except Raymond – with whom he had come to a private understanding – had sworn allegiance; even if they were later to break their oaths, his own moral position could only be strengthened.

On this last score he had no delusions. There was no telling what ambitions the Crusaders might cherish. They had no love for the Byzantines. In the Balkans and Thrace they had been received with suspicion and mistrust. In Constantinople itself, the carefully-shepherded groups of sightseers had been thoroughly shaken by what they had seen. For a French peasant or the burgher of a small medieval German town, the first sight of the richest and most luxurious city in the world, of its extravagantly dressed noblemen with their retinues of slaves and eunuchs, and of its great ladies borne along on gilded palanquins, their faces brilliant with enamel, must have appeared both incredible and profoundly shocking; while such religious services as they attended would have seemed unfamiliar, incomprehensible and deeply heretical into the bargain.

The Byzantines felt no more warmly disposed to the Crusaders. Foreign armies are never welcome guests; and these ill-mannered barbarians were surely worse than most. They had ravaged their lands, ravished their women, plundered their towns and villages. Fellow-Christians they might be; but there must have been a number of the Emperor's subjects who devoutly hoped for the success of Saracen arms in the encounters that were to come.

Contrary to the expectations of many, the First Crusade turned out to be a resounding, if undeserved, success. Nicaea was besieged and captured, with the consequent restoration of Byzantine sovereignty in western Asia Minor. The Seljuk Turks were smashed at Dorylaeum in Anatolia; Antioch fell to Crusader arms; and finally on 15 July 1099, amid scenes of hideous carnage, the soldiers of Christ battered their way into Jerusalem, slaughtering all the Muslims in the city and burning all the Jews alive in the main synagogue. Two of their former leaders, however, were no longer among them: Baldwin of Boulogne had made himself Count of Edessa on the middle Euphrates, while Bohemund had established himself as Prince of Antioch.

To Alexius Comnenus, the news of the recovery of Jerusalem could only have been welcome. The situation in Antioch, on the other hand, caused him grave anxiety. This ancient city and patriarchate, after centuries of Muslim occupation, had been reconquered in 969 by the Empire, of which it had thereafter remained a part until 1078. Its inhabitants were overwhelmingly Greek-speaking and Orthodox, and in the eyes of Alexius it was Byzantine through and through. It had now been seized by a Norman adventurer who, despite his oath, clearly had no intention of surrendering it. He had even gone so far as to expel the Greek Patriarch and replace him with a Latin. Alexius's satisfaction can therefore well be imagined when in the summer of 1100 Bohemund was captured by local Turks and carried off in chains to a far-away castle in Pontus. There he remained for three years until he was finally ransomed by Baldwin, who had become King of Jerusalem in succession to his brother Godfrey.

During these first years following the Crusaders' triumph, it became ever more clear that Bohemund was not alone in his attitude to Byzantium. After the capture of Jerusalem, the genuine pilgrims had begun to trickle home; the Franks who remained in Outremer (as the Crusader lands in the Middle East had come to be called) were military adventurers, now out for what they could get. Of all the leaders of the First Crusade, only Raymond of Toulouse – who, ironically, had alone refused to swear the oath of fealty – had acted in good faith and had returned to the Emperor certain conquests of what had formerly been imperial territory. By the time Bohemund was released in 1103, the Crusaders were fighting Arabs, Turks and Byzantines more or less indiscriminately, with occasional brief truces; and in the early summer of 1104 they suffered a crushing defeat by the Turks at Harran, near Edessa. Bohemund's army escaped but the forces of Edessa were massacred almost to a man. Both Baldwin and his cousin, Joscelin of Courtenay, were captured.

This catastrophe dealt the early Crusaders a blow from which they never recovered. It virtually closed the crucial overland supply line from the West, and enabled Alexius to recapture several important fortresses and coastal cities. Bohemund, now dangerously threatened, left in the late autumn for Europe to raise reinforcements. Arriving in Apulia early in 1105, he moved on to Rome in September to see Pope Paschal II, whom he effortlessly convinced that the enemy of the Crusader states was neither the Arab nor the Turk, but the Byzantine Emperor. Continuing to France, he was accompanied by a papal legate with instructions to preach a Holy War against Byzantium.

In a lifetime spent fighting the Eastern Empire, Bohemund never did it – or indeed, the whole Christian cause – so much harm as in those conversations with Pope Paschal. Henceforth his own narrow, predatory policy became the official policy of Christendom. Those Crusaders who for whatever reason disliked the Byzantines, now found their prejudices endorsed by the highest authority. To Alexius and his subjects, the entire Crusade was now revealed as nothing more than a monstrous exercise in hypocrisy.

By the autumn of 1107 Bohemund was back in Apulia, his new army ready to sail. His plan was basically the same as that of Robert Guiscard a quarter of a century before; this time, however, Alexius was ready for him. The mercenaries he had hired from the Seljuk Sultan stoutly resisted every attempt to take Durazzo by storm, and no sooner had Bohemund settled down to a siege than he found himself blockaded by a Byzantine fleet, cutting off his communications with Italy throughout the winter. As spring approached, so did Alexius with the main body of his army. The invaders, now surrounded, fell prey to famine and malaria, and by September the Prince of Antioch was forced to surrender. Brought before Alexius in his camp on the bank of the Devol river, he signed a humiliating treaty of peace, in which he expressed regret at having broken his oath, swore fealty to the Emperor and recognized him as his suzerain for the Principality of Antioch. Finally he agreed that the Latin Patriarch he had appointed should be replaced by a Greek.

His career was over. He returned to Apulia, leaving Antioch in the hands of his nephew Tancred. He had been a charismatic leader of men; but his ambition had betrayed him and brought him low. He died three years later in relative obscurity, never again having dared to show his face in Outremer.

The first decade of Alexius's reign had been hard indeed. Once the supreme power was in his hands, his magic had quickly faded and he was generally accounted a failure. People were beginning to wonder whether Byzantine

Europe, under almost constant pressure from Normans, Pechenegs and the rest, was not going the same way as Byzantine Asia. The Patriarch of Antioch, John the Oxite, went further and, in the course of two bitter diatribes against the Emperor referred to this whittling away of the Empire as a *fait accompli*. The people, he continued, were depressed and disillusioned. The only exceptions to the general misery were the members of the imperial family, 'who have become the greatest scourge upon the Empire and upon us all'.

The accusations of nepotism are difficult to answer. It is true that in the early years Alexius had few people that he could trust outside his immediate family. Without the support of powerful relations, he would not have remained *basileus* for long. Was he not justified, therefore, in raising them to key positions, and rewarding them accordingly? Perhaps he was; unfortunately, he did not stop at remunerative offices and titles; he gave them regional power as well. In former times, public lands were the direct responsibility of the imperial government; Alexius now granted to his relatives the administration of large tracts of such lands, together with their revenues. These grants were admittedly only temporary; but they were a dangerous precedent, and a further drain on his hard-pressured treasury.

Already for a good half-century before his accession, the Byzantine economy had been in steady decline. For a quarter-century after, this decline continued, to the point where six different *nomismata*, of as many metals, were in circulation. In 1092 Alexius introduced the gold *hyperpyron* ('highly refined') which became the standard coin for the next two centuries; but not until 1109 did he finally manage to establish a proper rate for the whole coinage. The situation was still unsatisfactory; but at least it allowed an effective operation of the fiscal system – and that, for Alexius, was the most important consideration. If Byzantium were to survive, the army had to be reorganized and strengthened, the fleet rebuilt virtually from scratch; and neither of these objectives could be achieved without considerable cost. Alexius had set to work at once; for him, it had been a labour of love. He was never happier than when taking part in military exercises, transforming his soldiers from ill-disciplined barbarians into trained fighting men. And once he had moulded his army as he wanted it, he was determined to keep it to himself: he had no intention of allowing any of his generals to topple him as he had toppled his predecessor. He therefore assumed personal command whenever possible, proving himself the greatest Byzantine military commander since Basil II.

Given the huge expenditure on defence, it is understandable that Alexius's fiscal policy should have been harsh; and the aristocracy, the senatorial families and the monasteries suffered greatly from his extortions. For the

Emperor's more humble subjects, too, times were hard. Compulsory military service, in particular, was bitterly resented. The peasantry, even more than the townsmen, lived under constant dread of the imperial recruiting sergeants, for ever scouring the Empire for able-bodied young men. Not only did they desperately need the labour to restore their own ravaged fields; there was also the danger that those recruited, when their period of service was over, would settle in Constantinople or elsewhere and never return to their old homes. It might well be argued that it was better for a family to provide a soldier for the Empire than to have its house destroyed, its sons slaughtered and its daughters violated by foreign invaders; the truth was that the Emperor, held responsible for all these tribulations, was hated by the vast majority of his people. And he knew it.

What steps did Alexius take to brighten his image? From the outset of his reign he had struggled hard to win at least his subjects' respect. Since the death of Basil II the Empire had had an average of one ruler every four years; his first task had been to show that he was not just such another. The entire system must be reformed, and spiritually purified. Therefore, while his mother tackled the Augean stables of the palace *gynaeceum*, he himself launched a campaign to rid the Empire of heresy. There can be no doubt of his genuine religious faith. He was also deeply concerned with Church affairs, and in 1107 instituted a general reform of the clergy with the foundation of a special order of preachers, each serving also as a one-man guardian of public morals in his allotted parish. A more welcome benefaction was the vast hospital and refuge which he established on the site of the present Topkapi Palace. His daughter describes it as 'a city within a city': 'All around were two-storeyed dwellings for the poor and disabled. All their needs of food and clothing were provided by the Emperor's generosity.'

The peace that had begun in 1108 with the Treaty of Devol continued for three years; then the wars began again and continued for the rest of the reign. That autumn, indeed, Alexius narrowly avoided having to fight simultaneously on two fronts, when a new outbreak of hostilities against the Turks coincided with the arrival of a fleet of Genoese and Pisan ships which threatened to ravage the Ionian coast. Fortunately he was able to buy them off by concluding a treaty with the Pisans, whom he allowed to maintain a permanent trading colony in Constantinople. The Turks were less easily dealt with. Since they still had more than enough territory in Asia Minor, their invasions were more raids than anything else: they avoided pitched battles, attacking over a wide front at several points simultaneously and then making a quick getaway with as much plunder and as many prisoners as they could. In

1111 they crossed into Thrace; in 1113 they laid siege to Nicaea, but were defeated; and in 1115, they were once again on the march, this time beneath the banners of Malik-Shah, Seljuk Sultan of Iconium.

But the Emperor was slowing down. By now nearly sixty – or sixty-eight if we are to believe one chronicler – and already prey to the disease that was to destroy him, not until the autumn of 1116 did he set off with his army against the Sultan. He advanced as far as the city of Philomelion; then, for reasons unclear, he decided to return, and it was only when he was on the way home that Malik-Shah decided to attack. Of the ensuing battle we know little. The Emperor seems to have been victorious; but it was his last victory. He returned to Constantinople a sick man, to find himself in the centre of bitter domestic strife, caused largely by his wife Irene. His daughter Anna describes her thus:

Most of her time was devoted to household duties and her own pursuits – reading the books of the saints, or turning her mind to good works and acts of charity. She was however forced to accompany the Emperor on his frequent expeditions. The disease which attacked his feet required the most careful attention, and my mother's touch was what he most valued, for by gentle massage she could relieve him to some extent of his agony.

But there was another consideration which caused Alexius to insist so firmly on Irene's presence. He knew that she and her daughter Anna had conceived a bitter hatred for her eldest son, the heir apparent John Comnenus, and were for ever plotting to eliminate him in favour of Anna's husband, the Caesar Nicephorus Bryennius. Irene never let slip an opportunity to blacken John in his father's eyes, but Alexius refused to listen. He loved and trusted John; besides, he was determined to found a dynasty. If his achievements were to endure, the crown must be handed down in orderly succession to his first-born son and, God willing, to his son after him.

By the summer of 1118 it was clear that death could not be far away. By this time the Emperor was in constant pain and was obliged to sit upright in order to breathe. His stomach and feet were hideously swollen, while his mouth, tongue and throat became so inflamed that he could no longer swallow. Irene had him carried to her own Palace of the Mangana, spending hours a day by his bedside and ordering prayers said throughout the Empire for his recovery; but it was clear that he was sinking fast.

Some time in the afternoon of 15 August the dying Alexius summoned John Comnenus to his bedside, gave him his imperial ring and ordered him to lose no time in having himself proclaimed *basileus*. John hurried to St Sophia where, in the briefest of ceremonies, the Patriarch crowned him. Returning to the palace, he was at first – presumably on Irene's orders – denied admittance by the Varangian Guard; only when he showed them the ring and told them of his father's imminent death did they let him through.

Where was Irene? She would not willingly have absented herself from her husband's last conversation with his son; and yet, somehow, he had contrived to remove her, and by the time she returned it was too late. Even now she made one last attempt on behalf of their son-in-law; but Alexius only smiled, raising his hands as if in thanksgiving. That evening he died. He was buried the next day in the monastery of Christ Philanthropos, founded by Irene some fifteen years before.

His subjects owed him more than they knew. First of all, he had given the Empire a new stability. After fifty-six years during which it had been mis-governed by thirteen different monarchs, he alone had reigned for thirty-seven; his son was to continue for another twenty-five before his accidental death, his grandson for another thirty-seven. Next there was his military record: no Emperor had defended his people more courageously, against a greater number of enemies; nor had any done more to build up the imperial forces. Thirdly, there was his brilliant handling of the Crusade. Had those Crusading armies marched a quarter of a century earlier than they did, the consequences for them – and for Byzantium – might have been grave indeed.

Inevitably, he had had his failures: the restoration of the economy, the healing of the rift with Rome, the recovery of south Italy. But of these the last two were little more than dreams. He had his failings, too – among them his nepotism and his susceptibility to women. Even on the matter of the succession he had not trusted himself to impose his will upon Irene, preferring to achieve his ends by trickery rather than by firm command.

Did he regret that – except among his soldiers, by whom he was idolized – personal popularity should always have remained beyond his grasp? Not, probably, very much. He had never compromised his principles for the plaudits of the crowd. Instead he had ruled conscientiously, energetically and to the very best of his ability; and he left his son an Empire incomparably stronger and better organized than it had been for a century. He died content – as well he might.

20

John the Beautiful

[1118–43]

Anna Comnena's hatred for her brother John, which lasted all her life, was a simple matter of jealousy. She had been betrothed in her infancy to Michael VII's son Constantine, and had thus, for five years, been heiress-presumptive to the throne of Byzantium. Then the Empress Irene had produced a son, John, and Anna's dreams were shattered. But not for long. On the premature death of Constantine she had married in 1097 Nicephorus Bryennius, son of that Nicephorus who had made his unsuccessful bid for the throne twenty years before. On Nicephorus, in 1111 or thereabouts, Alexius had conferred the title of Caesar; and all Anna's ambitions were resurrected. Even after her father's death she did not give up. She was almost certainly behind a plot to murder John at Alexius's funeral, and shortly afterwards she and her husband organized another conspiracy. Unfortunately, Bryennius's courage failed and he never turned up at the rendezvous; his fellow-conspirators were caught in the palace and immediately arrested. The new Emperor showed himself surprisingly merciful. Bryennius escaped scot-free and served the Emperor loyally for another twenty years until his death, occupying his idle hours in the composition of a remarkably boring history. His wife was not so lucky. Her property was confiscated and she was barred in perpetuity from the imperial court. Abandoned and humiliated, she withdrew to a convent where she lived for the next thirty-five years, writing the life of her father.

At the time of his accession, John Comnenus was a month short of his thirtieth birthday. Even his admirers admitted that he was physically ill-favoured, with hair and complexion so dark that he was known as 'the Moor'. He had, however, another nickname too: *Kaloiannis,* 'John the Beautiful'. This was not intended ironically; it referred not to his body, but to his soul. Levity he hated: luxury he frowned upon. Today, most of us would find him an insufferable companion; in twelfth-century Byzantium he was loved. First of all he was no hypocrite. His piety was genuine, his integrity complete. Second, there was a gentle, merciful side to his nature that in his day was rare indeed. He was generous, too: no Emperor ever dispensed charity with a more lavish hand. Unlike his father, he deliberately kept his family at arm's length. Most trusted of all his close advisers was a certain John Axuch, a Turk who had been captured in infancy by the Crusaders, given as a present to Alexius Comnenus and brought up in the imperial household, where he soon became John's boon companion. On his accession John at once took him into his service, and before long he had been appointed Grand Domestic, commander-in-chief of the armies.

John Comnenus was a soldier, like his father. He too saw the Empire as a sacred trust; but whereas Alexius had been largely content to defend it, John saw his duty in more positive terms – to liberate all territories occupied by the infidel, and to restore to Byzantium its ancient glory. To his subjects it seemed as though his life were one long campaign; he certainly spent more time in the field than in Constantinople, as did his four sons when they were old enough to accompany him. He was more fortunate than Alexius in that for several years after his accession Europe presented few problems. One lightning campaign subdued the Pechenegs; the Cumans were quiet; the Serbs were too divided to make trouble; the Hungarians were fully occupied with the Dalmatian coast which, though technically Byzantine, had long been abandoned to the Venetians. Pope and Holy Roman Emperor were still locked in their long struggle for supremacy. The dukedom of Robert Guiscard's pathetic son Roger Borsa and Roger's equally feckless son William was subsiding into chaos. True, their cousin Count Roger of Sicily was rapidly making a name for himself; but for the moment he presented no threat. John could thus focus his attention on Asia Minor, where the Empire controlled the northern, western and southern coasts and all the land north-west of a jagged line from the mouth of the Meander to the south-eastern corner of the Black Sea. South-east of that line were the Turks, most of them subject to the Seljuk Sultan of Iconium; but recent years had seen the rise of another tribe, the Danishmends, whose Emir Ghazi II now ruled from the Halys river to the Euphrates. There were also large numbers of nomadic Turcoman tribesmen who effectively did as they wished and had already cut off the Byzantine port of Attaleia, now accessible only by sea. It was they, as much as the Seljuks themselves, who were the target of John's first campaign; by late autumn the vital land links with Attaleia had been re-established; John and Axuch returned to the Bosphorus well satisfied with what they had done.

Then, in 1122, came trouble with Venice; and for this John was responsible. In Alexius's day the Republic had been the Empire's closest ally; to keep the Venetians well-disposed, the Emperor had not hesitated in 1082 to remit their customs dues and to grant them trading privileges enjoyed by no other foreigners. Their colony on the Golden Horn had thus grown to the point where it had aroused the resentment of the Byzantines; and when the newly-elected Doge Domenico Michiel requested the confirmation of all the old privileges, John refused point-blank. The Venetians were furious, and on 8 August 1122 the Doge's flagship sailed out of the lagoon with seventy-one men-of-war in its wake. The objective was Corfu, which successfully resisted a six-month siege; but over the next three years the Venetians continued to be active in the eastern Mediterranean, capturing Rhodes, Chios, Samos, Lesbos and Andros, and when, early in 1126, they sent troops to occupy Cephalonia, John had had enough. The aggression was costing him far more than the commercial privileges he had withheld. In August he swallowed his pride and restored them.

By 1130, when the Emperor turned his attention once again to the East, the situation had changed for the worse. The Danishmend Emir Ghazi was now the most formidable power in Asia Minor, and between 1130 and 1135 John led five separate expeditions against him. Such was his success that on his return to the capital in 1133 he made a triumphal entry in the traditional manner. As befitted the troubled times, his ceremonial chariot with its four snow-white horses was trimmed with silver rather than with gold; but the streets were decorated, as always on such occasions, with damasks and brocades, and rich carpets hung from the windows. The whole route from the Land Walls to St Sophia was lined with stands, where the populace stood cheering as the procession passed by, the Emperor on foot and carrying a cross. Like Tzimisces before him, he had refused to mount the chariot, preferring to give pride of place to the icon of the Virgin that had accompanied him throughout his campaigns.

The following year saw him back in the field where, towards the end of the summer, there came news of the death of the Emir Ghazi, and early in 1135 the Emperor returned to his capital. In five years he had regained territories that had been lost for over half a century. The Turks were not beaten; but it would be some time before they could return to the offensive. He himself was now almost free to march against the two Christian states at that time occupying what he considered to be imperial territory: the Armenian Kingdom of Cilicia and its close ally, the Norman Principality of Antioch.

Almost, but not quite. He had one other potential enemy to deal with first. In 1130 the Count of Sicily had been crowned as King Roger II; since that time he had gained steadily in power and influence, and he too dreamed of foreign conquest. In particular he was known to have his eye on the Crusader states. As the cousin of Bohemund he had a strong claim to Antioch, while the marriage of his mother Adelaide to Baldwin I in 1113 had been solemnized with the clear understanding that if it proved childless – which, given their ages, it almost certainly would – the Crown of Jerusalem was to pass to him. Baldwin's subsequent behaviour when, having spent Adelaide's immense dowry, he had the marriage annulled and sent her home to Sicily, was an insult that Roger never forgave. Admittedly he had no similar claim to Constantinople, but such considerations had inhibited neither Robert Guiscard nor Bohemund. And so, early in 1135, John sent ambassadors to the Western Emperor Lothair; and by autumn agreement had been reached. In return for financial support from Byzantium, Lothair undertook to launch a major campaign in the spring of 1137 to crush the King of Sicily. With his rear now satisfactorily protected, John could at last set off for the East.

The story of the Armenian settlement of Cilicia – the region extending between the southern coast of Anatolia and the Taurus mountains, from near Alanya to the Gulf of Alexandretta – goes back to the eleventh century when Basil II and his successors offered to certain Armenian princes extensive territories running from Sebasteia to the Euphrates; thus, by 1070 or so, there was a steady emigration from the harsh Armenian uplands to the warmer and more luxuriant country to the south. After Manzikert this became a flood, giving rise to a number of semi-independent principalities; but they did not last. Most were liquidated by the Frankish Crusader states; one family only was cunning enough to survive – that of a certain Ruben, who had established himself in the Taurus in 1071. His grandson, Leo, had succeeded to the throne of what was by now known as Lesser Armenia in 1129, and three years later had embarked on an ambitious programme of conquest. He it was who, in the early spring of 1137, received the news that John Comnenus was marching against him.

The Emperor had brought with him not only his old, well-tried army but several new regiments, Pecheneg, Turkish and perhaps even Armenian – for the Rubenids were no more popular among their own countrymen than were the Crusaders. Leo did not surrender, but withdrew with his two sons deep into the Taurus; John did not bother to pursue him. He pressed on via Issus and Alexandretta, and on 29 August drew up his army before Antioch.

The city had been passing through a time of crisis. Young Bohemund II, arriving from Apulia at the age of eighteen in 1126, had been killed less than four years later, leaving a two-year-old daughter, Constance. His widow Alice, daughter of Baldwin of Jerusalem, should properly have waited for her father, as her nominal suzerain, to appoint a successor. Instead, she had assumed the Regency herself; and when Baldwin arrived in Antioch to settle matters as he thought fit he found the gates shut in his face. When he finally forced his way in, he exiled her to Laodicea and himself assumed the Regency – which, after his death in 1131, passed to his son-in-law and successor, Fulk of Anjou, husband of his eldest daughter Mélisende. Four years later Fulk had allowed Alice to return, and she had immediately sent an envoy to Constantinople with a proposal of marriage between her daughter Constance (now aged seven) and the Emperor's youngest son Manuel.

Such an alliance would have been excellent for Antioch; but the local Franks refused to contemplate Constance's marriage to a Greek, and Fulk had a candidate of his own: Raymond of Poitiers, younger son of Duke William IX of Aquitaine, who arrived at Antioch in April 1136. The problem of obtaining Alice's consent was neatly avoided by the Patriarch, Radulf, who told her that this handsome young prince had come to ask for her own hand in marriage. Alice, still under thirty, was delighted and withdrew to her palace to prepare for his arrival. Meanwhile Constance was carried off to the cathedral, where the Patriarch married her to Raymond on the spot. Faced with a *fait accompli*, her mother returned disconsolately to Laodicea where she died shortly afterwards.

When the Byzantine siege engines began their bombardment of Antioch, many of its inhabitants must have regretted that the marriage to Manuel Comnenus had not taken place; and Raymond probably felt much the same. His new principality possessed none of the sophistication that he had known in Europe. He was bored and lonely, and his child wife had nothing to offer a husband almost thirty years her senior. After a few days he sent John a message: if he were to recognize the Emperor as his overlord, would John in return allow him to remain as his Viceroy? When John insisted on unconditional surrender, Raymond replied that he must first consult the King of Jerusalem. Fulk's answer was careful. The Atabeg of Mosul, Imadeddin Zengi, was growing stronger every day and was by now a serious threat to the Crusader states; why antagonize the only Christian power capable of holding him in check? Besides, if the sacrifice of Antioch would prevent his further advance to the south, should Antioch not be sacrificed? In any event, his reaction was better than Raymond – or John – can have dared to hope: Antioch, he declared, was historically part of the Empire; the claims made by the Emperor were accordingly correct. And so Antioch capitulated, and John showed his usual generosity. Raymond swore allegiance, giving him free access to the city and the citadel. He further undertook that, if the *basileus* were successful in his coming campaign and were to return to him Aleppo, Shaizar, Emessa and Hama in perpetual fief, he would surrender Antioch in exchange.

In the first half of September the victorious army struck camp, John having decided to complete his unfinished business with the Armenians. A few weeks later all the Rubenid princes were safely in prison in Constantinople. The Emperor was now free to embark on the next stage of his plan: to join forces with his Crusader vassals against the Arabs of Syria. In March 1138 he was back in Antioch, where he and Raymond were joined by a regiment of Knights Templar and a force commanded by Joscelin II of Courtenay, Count of Edessa. Joscelin, now twenty-four, inspired neither liking nor trust. Deceitful and lascivious, he was the antithesis of the popular image of a Crusader. It was thus with two most unsatisfactory allies that John set off on the new campaign. Avoiding Aleppo, he pressed on to Shaizar, a stronghold which controlled the valley of the middle Orontes and would be invaluable in blocking Zengi's advance. The army surrounded it and the siege began.

Alas, neither Raymond nor Joscelin had stomach for the fight. Raymond knew that if the Emperor made too many conquests he would, by the terms of the recent agreement, exchange them for Antioch; and he dreaded having to move into the front line. Joscelin, who hated Raymond, lost no opportunity of stirring up his suspicions and mistrust. Meanwhile Zengi of Mosul was approaching. Left to himself, John Comnenus could almost certainly have defeated him; but he could not leave his siege engines undefended, nor could he trust the Franks. Just in time a message arrived from the Emir of Shaizar, offering recognition of the Emperor as his overlord, an annual tribute and presents which included a cross that had been taken from Romanus Diogenes at Manzikert. John raised the siege and headed back towards Antioch.

On his arrival he made a solemn entry into the city together with his sons. Received at the gates by the Patriarch, he rode through the decorated streets, while the surly-looking Prince of Antioch and Count of Edessa escorted him on foot. After Mass in the cathedral he passed on to the palace, where he took up his residence. Then he sent for Raymond, Joscelin and the leading Latin barons. The war, he told them, was not ended; future campaigns, however, must be planned in Antioch. He must therefore require Raymond to surrender the citadel.

The Prince's reply is unrecorded; Joscelin, however, requested time for Raymond and his advisers to consider what they had just heard. Then, slipping out of the palace unobserved, he told his men to spread the rumour among the Latins that the Emperor had ordered their immediate expulsion, urging them to attack their Greek fellow-citizens. Within the hour the rioting had begun; Joscelin then rode back at full gallop to the palace, claiming that he had narrowly escaped death at the hands of a furious mob. By this time the tumult outside was clearly audible in the palace. John was anxious at all costs to prevent bloodshed; he was also aware that his army was encamped a mile or more away across the river, leaving him dangerously exposed. He told Raymond and Joscelin that for the moment he would be satisfied with the renewal of their oaths, and returned to Constantinople.

The story of his last Syrian campaign of 1142 can be quickly told. In the four years since his departure the Latin princes had missed every opportunity. Not only had they made no further progress against the Saracens; they had failed even to preserve John's earlier conquests, nearly all of which had been retaken and were back in Muslim hands. The situation must be saved, while there was still time. He set off in the spring, once again with his four sons, heading for Attaleia on the south coast. There tragedy struck. His eldest son Alexius, the recognized heir to the Empire, died of a fever. The Emperor, who had loved him dearly, ordered his second and third sons, Andronicus and Isaac, to escort their brother's body by sea back to Constantinople; and on the voyage Andronicus – infected, presumably, by the same virus – died in his turn. This double blow left John heartbroken; but he pressed on through Cilicia and yet further east. On 25 September he sent a message to Raymond demanding the immediate surrender of Antioch.

This was the moment that Raymond had dreaded. He replied that he must consult his vassals, which he immediately did; and the vassals refused. Raymond, they pointed out, had no right to dispose of his wife's property. Any attempt to surrender Antioch would result in the immediate dethronement of both himself and Constance. To the Emperor, this could only mean war. But winter was coming and he decided to postpone the offensive until the spring. He returned to Cilicia, where he could spend the coming months making proper preparations for a campaign that promised to be the most decisive of his life. Alas, those preparations were in vain. In March 1143, when all was ready, he set off on a brief hunting expedition, in the course of which an arrow accidentally wounded him in the hand. Septicaemia set in, and before long he knew he was dying. Quietly competent as ever, he began to make provision for the succession. Of his two surviving sons the elder, Isaac, was still in Constantinople; the younger, Manuel, was at his side.

On Easter Monday, 5 April, the dying Emperor called a council to announce his successor. Both his sons, he said, were fine young men; he loved them both. Isaac, however, was prone to anger, while Manuel possessed a singular gentleness which enabled him to listen carefully to advice. It was therefore Manuel – the youngest of his children – who should succeed him. Turning to his son, who knelt at his bedside, he took the imperial diadem and lowered it on the young man's head, then draped the purple robe across his shoulders.

He lived on for three more days. His death, on 8 April 1143, was pious, efficient and well-ordered, like his life. Had he been granted just a few more years, he would surely have extended Byzantine power deep into Syria and might indeed have gone a long way towards undoing the damage sustained at Manzikert. Dying as he did at only fifty-three, he was obliged to leave his work unfinished; yet he could take comfort in the knowledge that his son Manuel would prove a worthy successor.

21

Manuel Comnenus

Manuel Comnenus had been proclaimed *basileus* by his father; but his succession was by no means assured. Emperors were made in Constantinople: he was still in the wilds of Cilicia. Clearly he must return to the capital as soon as possible; on the other hand, he had filial duties to perform. There was the funeral service to be arranged, and a monastery to be founded where John had died; the body must then be brought back for burial. He immediately sent Axuch ahead of him to Constantinople, with the title of Regent and instructions to arrest his most dangerous rival: his brother Isaac, passed over by his father but living in the Great Palace, with instant access to the treasure and the regalia.

Axuch reached the capital even before the news of the Emperor's death. He seized Isaac and, for good measure, also ordered the arrest of another Isaac, John's brother, already exiled after previous conspiracies. The only other possible source of trouble was the Patriarchate, at that moment vacant. Axuch therefore summoned the hierarchy to the palace and presented them with a diploma providing for an annual grant to St Sophia of two hundred pieces of silver. They accepted it with gratitude, assuring him that there would be no difficulties over the coronation. (Little did they know that concealed in his robe Axuch had another, emergency document offering two hundred pieces of gold.) When Manuel finally arrived around the middle of August, his priority was to appoint a new Patriarch, Michael Curcuas; and the first task of the new Patriarch was to crown the Emperor. A few days later Manuel ordered the release of the two Isaacs: there was nothing more to fear from either of them. At last his position was secure.

The first thing people noticed about Manuel Comnenus was his height; and in two other respects at least he differed from his father. First, he was outstandingly handsome; secondly, there was a charm of manner, a love of pleasure and an enjoyment of life that stood out in refreshing contrast to John's high-principled austerity. Yet there was nothing shallow about him. A fine soldier and superb horseman, he was, perhaps, too headstrong to be quite the general that his father had been, but there could be no doubting his energy and courage. A skilful diplomat and a born statesman, he remained the typical Byzantine intellectual, cultivated in both the arts and the sciences, a man who loved to immerse himself in doctrinal issues, arguing not so much to establish the truth as for the love of the debate itself. No wonder that he became increasingly unpopular with the Church – which mistrusted his continued overtures towards Rome, deplored his frequent tactical alliances with the Saracen and was scandalized when he not only invited the Seljuk Sultan to Constantinople but included him in a solemn procession to St Sophia.

Most of all, perhaps, it deplored his private life. Manuel's appetite for women was prodigious, his way with them irresistible. His natural proclivities were doubtless given additional impetus by the appearance and character of his first wife, Bertha of Sulzbach, sister-in-law of the Western Emperor-elect Conrad. Bertha, who changed her name to Irene before her marriage, was, we are told, 'less concerned with the embellishment of her body than with that of her spirit; rejecting powder and paint, she sought only that solid beauty which proceeds from the splendour of virtue'. Not surprisingly, she never endeared herself either to Manuel or his subjects, to whom she appeared stiff and inelegant. Only in the diplomatic field did she prove her worth, playing a valuable part in the alliance concluded between Manuel and Conrad on the latter's visit to Constantinople in 1148. For the rest, she spent her life quietly in the palace, occupying herself with pious works and the education of her two daughters.

Manuel Comnenus had ascended the throne of Byzantium with anger in his heart. He could not forgive the alacrity with which Raymond of Antioch had moved to reconquer the captured castles the moment he had started back to Constantinople after his father's death. Early in 1144 he dispatched an amphibious expedition to the south-east. The lost castles were regained, the land around Antioch devastated. The fleet, meanwhile, swept the entire coast-line of the principality, destroying all the ships it found drawn up on the beaches and taking many of the local inhabitants into captivity.

But before the year was out the whole situation in Outremer had changed: on Christmas Eve Zengi captured the Crusader Principality of Edessa. Antioch, it seemed, would be next on the list. Raymond could only swallow his pride and seek help from Manuel. At first the Emperor ignored him; only after he had knelt at John's tomb was he reluctantly promised a regular subsidy. Direct military assistance was refused.

The following year Zengi was murdered by a drunken eunuch, and the Crusader states were rid of their most formidable enemy. The fall of Edessa, however, had horrified all Christendom. How could it have occurred? Could it be, perhaps, that the Franks of Outremer, degenerate as they were said to be, were no longer worthy in the eyes of the Almighty to guard the Holy Places? The Franks themselves understood the true cause perfectly well. The first great wave of Crusading enthusiasm was now spent. Immigration had slowed to a trickle; of the pilgrims, many still arrived unarmed, and even those prepared to wield a sword normally found a single summer's campaign more than enough. An embassy was accordingly sent to the Pope appealing, with all possible urgency, for a Crusade.

Pope Eugenius III was in none too strong a position himself. In the usual turmoil of medieval Rome he had been obliged to flee from the city three days after his election, to take refuge in Viterbo. He was happy to give his blessing to a second Crusade, but who would lead it? King Conrad was still beset with difficulties in Germany; Stephen of England had a civil war on his hands; Roger of Sicily was out of the question. That left King Louis VII of France. Though still only twenty-four, Louis had about him an aura of lugubrious piety which irritated to distraction his beautiful, high-spirited young wife, Eleanor of Aquitaine. He was one of Nature's pilgrims; the Crusade was his duty as a Christian – and was not Eleanor the niece of the Prince of Antioch? At Christmas 1145 he announced his intention of taking the Cross, and sent for Bernard, Abbot of Clairvaux.

St Bernard, now fifty-five, was the most powerful spiritual force in Europe. Tall and haggard, his features clouded by constant pain after a lifetime of exaggerated austerities, he was consumed by a blazing zeal that left no room for tolerance or moderation. Constantly on the move, preaching, persuading, arguing, debating, writing innumerable letters and compulsively plunging into the thick of every controversy, he saw in the proposed Crusade a venture after his own heart. Willingly he agreed to launch it – at the assembly summoned by the King for the following Palm Sunday at Vézelay in Burgundy.

The magic of Bernard's name never failed: as the day approached men and women from every corner of France began to pour into the little town. And there, on 31 March 1146, from a great wooden platform erected on the hillside, Bernard made the most fateful speech of his life. As he spoke the crowd, silent at first, began to cry out for crosses to sew on their clothes. Bundles of these had already been prepared; when the supply was exhausted, the Abbot flung off his own robe and began tearing it into strips to make more. He and his helpers were still stitching as night fell.

Manuel Comnenus, who fully understood the nightmare that the First Crusade had caused his grandfather half a century before, had no wish to see it repeated. He undertook to provide food and supplies for the Crusading

The Virgin and Child: ivory statuette, eleventh or twelfth century,
one of the very rare examples of post-iconoclastic sculpture in the round

The Western Emperor Otto III enthroned; from a Gospel Book
painted at Reichenau or at the imperial court, *c.* 998

Istanbul: St Sophia (with minarets added after the Turkish conquest)

Cefalù Cathedral, Sicily: apse mosaic of Christ Pantocrator, *c.* 1150

Mistra: the monastery of the Peribleptos, late fourteenth century

The Emperor Frederick Barbarossa
(Rome, Vatican Library)

A Turkish Janissary, by Gentile Bellini, late fourteenth century
(London, British Museum)

Istanbul: the Fortress of Rumeli Hisar on the Bosphorus,
built by the Sultan Mehmet II in 1452, photographed *c.* 1914

armies, but emphasized that everything would have to be paid for. And all the leaders would be required once again to take an oath of fealty to him. Meanwhile any faint hopes that he might have entertained about the quality of the new Crusaders were soon dashed. The German army that set off from Ratisbon in May 1147 seems to have ranged from the religious fanatics to the rabble of footloose ne'er-do-wells and fugitives from justice, attracted as always by the promise of absolution. Hardly had they entered Byzantine territory than they began pillaging, ravaging, raping and even murdering as the mood took them. Fighting became ever more frequent between the Crusaders and the military escort which Manuel had been careful to provide, and when the army reached Constantinople in mid-September relations between German and Greek could hardly have been worse.

The French army was smaller and more seemly. The presence of many distinguished ladies accompanying their husbands, including Queen Eleanor herself, exercised a moderating influence. The Balkan peasantry, however, was by now frankly hostile, and asked ridiculous prices for what little food the Germans had left. Mistrust soon became mutual, and led to sharp practices on both sides. Thus the French had quickly begun to feel considerable resentment against Germans and Greeks alike; and when they arrived on 4 October they were scandalized to hear that the Emperor had concluded a truce with the Turks.

He had of course been perfectly right. The Crusading armies constituted a far greater danger. He was well aware that both French and German extremists were proposing a combined attack on Constantinople; only by deliberately spreading reports of a huge Turkish army massing in Anatolia, and implying that if the Franks did not make haste to pass through Anatolia they might never do so at all, could he save the situation. Besides, it was in their own interest. If attacked, they would stand little chance. He had provided food and guides; he had warned them about the scarcity of water; and he had advised them to keep to the coast, still under Byzantine control. He could do no more.

Within days of bidding them farewell the Emperor received two reports. The first informed him that the German army had been surprised by the Turks near Dorylaeum and virtually annihilated; the second that the fleet of King Roger of Sicily was at that very moment sailing against his Empire. It was, he learnt, commanded by George of Antioch, a renegade Greek who had risen to the proudest title his country had to offer: Emir of Emirs, Chief Minister of the realm. Having effortlessly captured and garrisoned Corfu, it had raided Athens and Corinth and penetrated inland as far as Thebes, centre of all Byzantine silk manufacture. There, together with countless bales of brocades, George had seized the skilled women workers and taken them triumphantly back to Palermo.

The news of these depredations stung Manuel to a fury, and the knowledge that the admiral was a Greek can hardly have assuaged his wrath. Roger must be driven for ever from the Mediterranean. The problem was to find suitable allies. With France and Germany out of the running, Manuel's thoughts turned to Venice. In March 1148, in return for increased trading privileges, he was promised the full support of the Venetian fleet for six months. By April his huge expeditionary force was ready to leave, with himself in command. Then, suddenly, everything went wrong. The Cumans swept down into Byzantine territory; the Venetian fleet was delayed by the death of the Doge; and storms disrupted shipping. It was autumn before the two navies began a blockade of Corfu. Manuel meanwhile rode on to Thessalonica, where an important guest was awaiting him. Conrad of Hohenstaufen had just returned from the Holy Land.

The Second Crusade had been a fiasco. Conrad, with the few survivors of Dorylaeum, had continued in the company of the French to Ephesus, where he had fallen ill. Manuel had sailed down from Constantinople and brought him back to the palace, where he had personally nursed him back to health. Then, in March 1148, he had provided ships to carry him to Palestine. The French, meanwhile, had had an agonizing passage through Anatolia. Although Louis had ignored the Emperor's warnings to keep to the coast, he persisted in attributing every hostile encounter to Byzantine treachery and rapidly developed an almost psychopathic resentment against the Greeks. Finally he had taken ship from Attaleia, leaving his followers to struggle on as best they might. Only around Easter 1148 had the last remnant of the great host reached Antioch.

And that was only the beginning. Aleppo, the chief focus of Muslim strength now ruled by Zengi's still greater son Nureddin, should have been the Crusaders' first objective, and Louis had been pressed by Raymond to mount an immediate attack. He had pleaded that he must first pray at the Holy Sepulchre; whereat Queen Eleanor — with whom Raymond's relations were already suspected of going somewhat beyond the avuncular — had announced her intention of remaining at Antioch and suing for divorce. Louis dragged her off to Jerusalem regardless, and arrived in May, soon after Conrad, his tight-lipped queen in tow. There they remained until on 24 June a general meeting decided on a concerted attack on Damascus. The only major Arab state to continue hostile to Nureddin, it was their one potential ally. By attacking it they forced it into the arms of Nureddin, thus ensuring their own destruction. They arrived to find the walls of Damascus strong, its defenders determined. On 28 July, just five days after the opening of the campaign, they withdrew. The once-glorious army had given up the whole enterprise after four days' fighting, having regained not one inch of Muslim territory.

Louis was in no hurry to return to France. His wife was now determined on divorce, and he dreaded the attendant difficulties and embarrassments. Conrad left on 8 September on a ship bound for Thessalonica, whence the Emperor for the second time bore him back to Constantinople. The pair were by now close friends. Manuel remained fascinated by Western culture and customs, while Conrad for his part had totally succumbed to his host's charm. That Christmas, Manuel's niece Theodora was married to Conrad's brother, Duke Henry of Austria, and the two rulers agreed on a joint south Italian campaign later in the year. It was in fact to achieve little, but it remained the only positive result of the Second Crusade, in all other respects a disgrace to Christendom.

The moment Manuel had bidden his friend goodbye he set off to rejoin his forces at Corfu, where the siege had continued throughout the winter. Not till September 1149 did the Sicilian garrison surrender. The Emperor now proposed to keep his rendezvous with Conrad in Italy; but he was still waiting for fine weather when reports came of a major insurrection by the Serbs. He also heard to his fury that George of Antioch had taken a fleet of forty ships up to the very walls of Constantinople, sailing some distance up the Bosphorus, pillaging several rich villas along the shore, and even firing a few impudent arrows into the grounds of the palace. Here was another insult that the Emperor would not forget; but the Serbian uprising was a good deal more serious – particularly if, as he suspected, the King of Sicily were behind it. What Manuel did not know was that Roger had engineered a similar *coup* against Conrad by financing a league of German princes led by Count Welf of Bavaria, his still-hopeful rival for the imperial throne. Thus it was that the King of Sicily, facing the two Empires acting together, had effectively immobilized both of them. The unprincipled adventurer was at least a worthy adversary.

On 29 July 1149, Louis and Eleanor landed in Calabria from Palestine and rode to Potenza, where Roger awaited them. Louis had recently lost several of his household and nearly all his baggage to Greek pirates, and had already persuaded himself that Manuel Comnenus was solely responsible for the failure of the Crusade. He was only too ready to listen to the King of Sicily's proposal for a league against the Byzantine Empire. Roger fully shared his opinion that Manuel had kept the Turks fully informed about the Crusade: it had been doomed before it started. The first priority was to eliminate him altogether. Then and only then could they launch a victorious Third Crusade to wipe out the humiliation of the Second.

The proposal was deeply disingenuous. The King of Sicily cared nothing for the Christians of Outremer. He infinitely preferred the Arabs, who constituted much of his Sicilian population, who ran most of his civil service, and whose language he spoke perfectly. There were however his claims on Antioch and Jerusalem; besides, if he did not take the offensive against Manuel, the Emperor would do so against him. When Louis passed on to Tivoli to sound out the Pope, Eugenius was lukewarm; he had no wish to see Roger any stronger than he was already. But other leading churchmen – including St Bernard – were enthusiastic; and so, after the King returned to Paris, was Suger, Abbot of Saint-Denis, who became the leading champion of the projected new Crusade.

The plan foundered because of Conrad. He bitterly resented this usurpation of his imperial prerogatives; he strongly suspected, too, that Roger was financing Welf of Bavaria. Manuel was his trusted friend; he had no intention of breaking their alliance. And so the great league came to nothing; and soon the pendulum swung back. Welf was defeated in 1150 and in the following year the Serbs and the Hungarians were similarly crushed. At last the forces of the two Empires were free to march into south Italy. Venice had pledged her support. Even Pope Eugenius had finally been won over. For Roger, the future looked black. Then, on 15 February 1152, Conrad died at Bamberg, aged fifty-nine. His last injunction to his nephew and successor, Frederick of Swabia, was to continue the struggle. Frederick asked nothing better: but the succession brought its own problems, and he soon had to accept an indefinite postponement. Where he parted with his uncle was on the matter of Byzantium. The very thought of a rival Emperor was bad enough; the idea of sharing, let alone making over, the disputed south Italian provinces was anathema to him. Barely a year after his accession he had signed a treaty with the Pope, by the terms of which it was agreed that Byzantium would be allowed no concessions on Italian territory.

On 8 July 1153 Pope Eugenius died suddenly at Tivoli, and was deeply mourned. The same cannot be said of Bernard of Clairvaux, who six weeks later followed him to his grave. His launching of the Second Crusade had led to the most shameful Christian humiliation of the Middle Ages. Many believed him to be a great man; few would have called him a lovable one. Next, on 26 February 1154, King Roger died at Palermo. His son and successor – generally known as William the Bad – did not altogether deserve his nickname; but he was lazy and pleasure-loving, with little of his father's intelligence and finesse. The last in this series of deaths was that of Pope

Eugenius's successor Anastasius IV, who was succeeded by a man of a very different calibre: Adrian (or Hadrian) IV, the only Englishman ever to wear the Triple Crown. Born around 1115, Nicholas Breakspear while still a student had travelled to Rome, where his eloquence and ability had caught the attention of Pope Eugenius; thereafter his rise had been swift. His election came not a moment too soon: within six months Frederick Barbarossa arrived in Italy and demanded his imperial coronation.

Frederick was now thirty-two. Tall and broad-shouldered, attractive rather than handsome, his eyes twinkled so brightly under his reddish-brown hair that he always seemed on the point of laughter. But beneath this breezy exterior lurked a will of steel, dedicated to a single objective: to restore his Empire to its ancient greatness. Arriving in north Italy in early 1155, he had been infuriated by the republican feeling everywhere and had decided upon a show of strength. Milan had proved too strong for him; but he had made an example of her ally Tortona, which he had captured after a two-month siege and of which he left not one stone on another.

After celebrating Easter at Pavia Frederick had descended through Tuscany at such a speed as to cause the Roman Curia serious alarm. Adrian therefore decided to ride up to meet him; and on 9 June the two met near Sutri. The encounter was not a success. According to custom, the King should have advanced towards the Pope on foot and led his horse the last few yards by the bridle, finally holding the stirrup while Adrian dismounted; but he did not do so, and Adrian in return refused to bestow on him the traditional kiss of peace. Frederick objected that he was not a papal groom; but Adrian held firm. This was not a minor point of protocol; it was a public act of defiance that struck at the very root of the relationship between Empire and Papacy. It was Frederick who finally gave in: two days later the ceremony was restaged, and he did all that was expected of him. Adrian settled himself on the waiting throne; Frederick knelt and kissed his feet, and the kiss of peace was duly bestowed.

But the way was not yet clear. Since the last coronation the Roman people had revived their Senate; and the delegation of senators which now appeared at the imperial camp insisted that before receiving his crown Frederick should make an *ex gratia* payment of five thousand pounds of gold. Frederick refused, and the senators withdrew; but it was clear that serious trouble was to be expected. Both Pope and Emperor-to-be would have to move swiftly. So it was that at dawn on Saturday, 17 June Frederick entered Rome and went straight to St Peter's where the Pope, who had arrived an hour or two before, was awaiting him. After a quick Mass Adrian hurriedly girded the sword of St Peter to Frederick's side and laid the imperial crown on his head. The

Emperor, still wearing the crown, then rode back to his camp outside the walls, while the Pope retired hastily to the Vatican.

It was not yet nine; and the senators were assembling to decide how best to prevent the coronation when they heard that it was already over. Furious, they gave the call to arms. In their camp above the city, the German soldiers too received the order to prepare for battle. For the second time that day Frederick entered Rome; but this time he had his armour on. Night had fallen before his troops had driven the insurgents back across the bridges. Among the Romans almost a thousand are said to have been slain, another six hundred captured. The Senate had paid a high price for its arrogance; but the Emperor too had bought his crown dearly. The only sensible course was to withdraw, and to take Pope and Curia with him. A month later he was heading back towards Germany, leaving Adrian, isolated and powerless, at Tivoli.

For Manuel Comnenus, the whole situation was now changed. He could no longer expect any help from the Western Empire. Any Italian partition would have to be fought for. If the Germans did march against William of Sicily, it was essential that Byzantium should be represented, to defend its legitimate rights; if they did not, he himself would have to take the initiative. The good news was that the Norman barons in Apulia were once again on the point of revolt. They had always resented the house of Hauteville; Roger's death had encouraged them to make yet another effort to shake off their Sicilian shackles; now that Frederick had let them down, they were perfectly ready to accept help from Manuel instead. And Manuel was ready to give it. As a first step he sent two of his senior generals, Michael Palaeologus and John Ducas, across to Italy to contact the principal centres of resistance and to coordinate a general rising. If, however, Frederick was still in Italy they were to make one last effort to persuade him to join forces. On their arrival inquiries soon revealed the Emperor to be in Ancona, where he willingly received them.

Frederick had marched northward in a fury. He longed to lead his army immediately against King William but his ailing German barons would not hear of it. They had had enough of sun, insects and disease. Sadly, he had to inform the Byzantine envoys that they would have to launch their campaign alone.

Manuel was not unduly worried by the news. He would have no shortage of allies. The revolt was now spreading rapidly under a new leader, Count Robert of Loritello. In the late summer of 1155, Robert met Michael Palaeologus at Viesti. Agreement was quickly reached; then the two allies struck. Their first objective was Bari. The Greek majority of its citizens resented the government of Palermo, and the city fell almost at once. When

King William's army finally appeared it was largely destroyed outside the walls of Andria, where the local population surrendered on the spot. For those still faithful to the Sicilian crown, the future looked grim.

From Tivoli and later from Tusculum, Pope Adrian had followed these developments with satisfaction. He greatly preferred the Greeks to the Sicilians; the time had clearly come to ally himself with them. Discussions were held in the late summer, Adrian undertaking to raise a body of mercenary troops from Campania. On 29 September he marched south. Thus, only a century after the great schism, an Emperor of Byzantium was allied with the Pope of Rome. The exiled Apulian vassals joyfully agreed to recognize him as their suzerain in return for his support, and before the end of 1156 all Campania and most of Apulia was in Greek or papal hands. At this rate it might not be long before all south Italy acknowledged the dominion of Constantinople. William would be annihilated; Adrian, seeing the Greeks succeed where the Germans had failed, would acknowledge the superiority of Byzantine arms; and Manuel's great dream, the reunification of the Roman Empire under Constantinople, would be realized at last.

But William was not yet ready for annihilation. He had lost the first round, but he had now shaken off his habitual lassitude and his blood was up. Early in 1156 his army and navy met at Messina; the Greeks, the papalists and the rebels were to be attacked simultaneously from land and sea. In April, his army crossed to the mainland while the fleet sailed down through the straits and then turned north-east towards Brindisi, then under siege by the Byzantines. Now, with William's advance, the Greeks saw their rebel allies begin to fall away. The mercenaries predictably chose the moment of supreme crisis to demand impossible increases in their pay; meeting with a refusal, they disappeared *en masse*. Robert of Loritello deserted and many of his compatriots followed him. Michael Palaeologus was dead; John Ducas found himself hopelessly outnumbered. With the other Byzantine survivors and the few Norman rebels who had not already fled, he was taken prisoner. The Greek ships were seized, together with large sums of gold and silver. On that one day, 28 May 1156, all the previous year's achievements in Italy were wiped out. William treated his Greek captives according to the rules of war; but to his own rebellious subjects he showed no mercy. Brindisi, which had resisted valiantly, was spared; Bari, which had capitulated, paid the price. The inhabitants were given two clear days to salvage their belongings; on the third day the city was destroyed, including the cathedral. Only the Great Church of St Nicholas was left standing.

The time had come, it was now clear, for a radical change in imperial policy. If Manuel could not recover the lost Italian provinces by force of arms, neither could Frederick Barbarossa; but Frederick would certainly launch another expedition, and might even topple William from his throne. In such an event, given his determination to unite the two Empires, would he not make Byzantium his next objective? The conclusion was plain. William, upstart as he was, was a good deal preferable to Frederick. Some form of agreement with him would have to be reached. And so in the summer of 1157, Manuel sent a new emissary to Italy: Alexis, the brilliant young son of his Grand Domestic Axuch. Alexis's orders, like those given earlier to Michael Palaeologus, were ostensibly to make contact with potential rebels, to hire mercenaries and generally to stir up disaffection; but he also had a second task – to establish secret contact with William and discuss terms for a peace. The two objectives were not as self-contradictory as might appear: the fiercer the preliminary fighting, the more favourable to Byzantium William's conditions were likely to be.

Alexis discharged both parts of his mission with equal success. Within a month or two of his arrival he had Robert of Loritello once again ravaging Sicilian territory in the north and another rebel band driving down through the Capuan lands and seriously threatening Monte Cassino – beneath which, in January 1158, it even defeated a royalist army in pitched battle. Meanwhile, some time in the early spring, a secret agreement was concluded and a peace treaty duly signed. The Norman barons, suddenly bereft of funds, had no course but to abandon their new conquests and seek a more reliable champion.

At the time of the signing of the Sicilian peace treaty, Manuel Comnenus had occupied the throne of Byzantium for fifteen years, during which he had been involved in every corner of his Empire. The only region to which he had been able to pay relatively little attention was that in which he had begun his reign – Cilicia, and the Crusader states of Outremer; and in the autumn of 1158 he set out from Constantinople to make good the omission.

He was furious, and with good reason. The first object of his wrath was Thoros, the eldest surviving son of Leo the Rubenid. He had escaped from prison in Constantinople in 1143, and in 1151 had killed the imperial governor at Mamistra. After seven years, he was still unpunished. More serious, however, was Reynald of Châtillon, Prince of Antioch. The younger son of a minor French nobleman, Reynald had joined the Second Crusade and then decided to stay on in the East. There he might have lived out his life in obscurity but for the death of Raymond of Antioch, who in 1149 had allowed himself and his army to be surrounded by the forces of the Emir Nureddin. The consequence was a massacre, after which Raymond's skull, set in a silver case, was sent by Nureddin as a present to the Caliph in Baghdad. Although the Emir did not follow up his victory with a march on Antioch, it was clear that his widow Constance must find herself another husband as soon as possible. She herself asked nothing better – despite her four children, she was still only twenty-one – but it was not until 1153 that her eye fell on Reynald.

From the beginning Reynald proved faithless and irresponsible. He had promised Manuel, in return for recognition, to bring Thoros to justice; instead he prepared an expedition, with Thoros, against the peaceful and prosperous island of Cyprus, where the Franks and Armenians together abandoned themselves to an orgy of devastation and desecration such as the island had never before known. No wonder, then, that the Emperor marched his army to Cilicia with vengeance in his heart. But if Manuel was angry, Reynald was panic-stricken. The imperial army was far too strong to be resisted; his only hope lay in abject submission, and he accordingly presented himself in sackcloth at the Emperor's camp. When the Emperor finally deigned to hear his submission he made three conditions. The citadel of Antioch must be surrendered immediately on demand; the city must provide a contingent for his army; and a Greek Patriarch was to be installed in place of the Latin. Only when Reynald took his oath on all three was he pardoned and dismissed.

A few days later King Baldwin III arrived from Jerusalem. Though he and Manuel had never met, he had recently married the Emperor's thirteen-year-old niece Theodora. He was now thirty, intelligent and cultivated and possessed of more than a little of Manuel's famous charm; he and Manuel took to each other at once, and he was delighted to participate in the Emperor's ceremonial entry into Antioch on Easter Sunday, 12 April 1159. The celebrations continued for eight days. As a gesture to the Franks, Manuel even organized a tournament – something unknown in the East – during which he himself, to the horror of his older subjects, took part in the jousting. Meanwhile he and Baldwin became firm friends, and when Baldwin broke his arm in a hunting accident Manuel insisted on treating it himself, just as he had previously treated Conrad.

By the time the Emperor left Antioch, relations between Byzantium and Outremer were better than they had ever been; and so they might have remained had he now moved against Aleppo. As soon as he reached the frontier, however, he was met by Nureddin's ambassadors: in return for a truce, the Emir would release all his six thousand Christian prisoners and send a military expedition against the Turks. Manuel accepted and set off for Constantinople, his army behind him. The reaction of the Franks can well be imagined. Why had the Emperor brought a vast army across Asia Minor, only to return without engaging the enemy? They had welcomed him with all honours, believing that he would destroy the enemy who threatened their existence. Instead, he had made a separate peace and was now leaving them to their fate.

But however vital Syria might be to the Franks, to Manuel it was only one of his many outlying provinces. He could not afford to linger several hundred miles from his capital. Already there were reports of conspiracy in Constantinople and trouble on the European frontier. Besides, Nureddin was most satisfactorily frightening the Franks, who remained loyal only when they were afraid. The Seljuks were a far greater danger than the Atabeg, whose offer of an alliance he consequently could not refuse. Subsequent events proved him right. Thanks to that alliance, in 1162 the Seljuk Sultan Kilij Arslan II was obliged to agree to a treaty whereby he returned all the Greek cities recently captured, forbade all further raiding, and agreed to provide a regiment for the imperial army whenever called upon to do so. To seal the agreement, he paid a state visit to Constantinople.

From the outset, the Emperor was determined to dazzle him. He received his guest seated on a throne plated with gold, set with carbuncles and sapphires and surrounded with pearls. From his neck hung a ruby the size of an apple. Twice each day during his twelve-week stay, the Sultan's food and drink were brought in vessels of gold and silver, all of which immediately became his property. There were banquets, tournaments, circuses, even a water pageant, at which the wonders of Greek fire were displayed to remarkable effect. A performance arranged by the Sultan was unfortunately less successful, when one of his suite proposed to give a demonstration of flying. Swathed in a garment consisting entirely of pockets, in which the air was intended to support him, he climbed to a high platform and launched himself into space. When the body was carried away a moment later the populace, we are told, could not contain its laughter.

The Byzantine position in the East was now stronger than at any time since Manzikert. The Sultan had been brought low, the Atabeg badly frightened. The land route to Palestine was once again open to pilgrims. Among Christians, only those of Outremer continued to grumble. Meanwhile, however, at the end of 1159 the Empress Irene had died, leaving only two daughters. Manuel still desperately needed a son. Accordingly at Christmas 1161 he married Mary, the ravishing daughter of Constance of Antioch by Raymond of Poitiers. Six months later, her cousin King Baldwin of Jerusalem died in Beirut. Manuel wept at the news. Baldwin had been a good King; he might even have proved a great one. The two had also been firm personal friends, no small consideration where ruling monarchs are concerned.

Another royal death, however, was of greater political importance: that of King Geza II of Hungary. This led to a disputed succession, which in turn led to war; and the fighting continued until 1167, when a major victory left the Emperor in possession of Dalmatia, Bosnia and the greater part of Croatia. In the West, the principal loser was Venice, whose reaction to the Byzantine annexation of the entire Dalmatian coast can well be imagined. Not that the Venetians were particularly surprised: they had long been concerned by the way Genoa, Pisa and Amalfi were all consolidating their positions in Constantinople – formerly, so far as foreign merchants were concerned, their own exclusive preserve.

But Manuel also had a case. There were by now some 80,000 Latins resident in Constantinople, all enjoying special privileges. Of these, the Venetians were the most numerous, the most favoured and the most objectionable. He was able to teach them a further lesson when, early in 1171, the new Genoese settlement at Galata was attacked and largely destroyed. Those responsible were never identified; but Manuel cast the blame squarely on the Venetians and ordered that all citizens of the Serenissima anywhere on Byzantine soil should be placed under immediate arrest, with confiscation of their ships and property. In the capital alone ten thousand were seized.

The reaction on the Rialto was one of fury. The smoothness and efficiency of the arrests, on the same day throughout the Empire, showed careful advance planning, and the Republic was now bent on war. A forced loan was ordered; Venetians living abroad were recalled and pressed into service; and in September Doge Vitale Michiel led a fleet of over 120 sail against the Eastern Empire. At Euboea, however, imperial ambassadors greeted him. Let him only send a peace mission to Constantinople; he would find that all differences could be resolved.

Vitale Michiel accepted. It was the worst mistake of his life. While his emissaries continued to the Bosphorus he awaited developments at Chios, and it was there that disaster struck. Plague broke out in the overcrowded ships and spread with terrible speed. By spring thousands were dead, the survivors weakened and totally demoralized. Now the ambassadors arrived from Constantinople to report complete failure. The Emperor had no intention of changing his attitude. He had summoned them only to gain time. Michiel could only return to face his subjects; but he would have been better advised to remain in the East. In their eyes he had shown criminal gullibility by falling into a typically Byzantine trap; and now he had brought the plague back to Venice. They rose against him, while a mob gathered outside calling for his blood. Slipping out of the palace, he sought asylum in the convent of S. Zaccaria, but never reached it. Before he had gone more than a hundred yards he was set upon and stabbed to death.

It was to be fourteen years before diplomatic relations were restored between Byzantium and Venice, and thirty-two before the Venetians took their revenge; but only five years after the murder of the Doge, the Republic became the centre of attention of all Christendom. On 24 July 1177 Michiel's successor, Sebastiano Ziani, masterminded the most important political ceremony of the twelfth century: the reconciliation of Pope Alexander III and the Western Emperor Frederick Barbarossa. Ever since his ill-fated corona-tion, Frederick's relations with the Papacy had steadily deteriorated. On the death of Pope Adrian in 1159 he had deliberately engineered a schism within the Curia, so that the chaotic political scene was further bedevilled, for the next eighteen years, by a disputed Papacy.

To Manuel Comnenus, the quarrel between Barbarossa and the Pope seemed a perfect opportunity to re-establish the supremacy of Byzantium. When therefore two papal legates had arrived in Constantinople early in 1160 to request the Emperor's support for Pope Alexander III against Frederick's candidate he had received them warmly; and in 1166 he decided to put to Alexander a firm proposition. He would make such doctrinal concessions as were necessary to end the schism, while providing the Pope with vast subsidies; in return, Alexander would award him the imperial crown and restore the old unity of the Empire. It was, however, no use. The Churches were too far apart, while Manuel himself was too unpopular in the West, being generally believed to harbour sinister designs on Syria and Palestine, including the elimination of the Franks and the reintroduction of the Eastern rite.

Nevertheless, the first five years of the 1170s saw Manuel Comnenus at the pinnacle of his career. In the East, he had imposed his suzerainty over the Crusader states of Outremer, consolidated it with a dynastic marriage and brought the Seljuk Sultan to heel. In the West, he had made huge territorial gains at Hungarian expense and had broken the power of Venice within his Empire, to his own enormous profit. But the East and the West were well over a thousand miles apart; Manuel could not be everywhere at once, and after his treaty with Kilij Arslan he had turned his back on Asia Minor for more than a decade. Then, on 15 May 1174, Nureddin died in his turn, leaving the Danishmends – whom he had always protected – defenceless against Seljuk strength. Kilij Arslan unhesitatingly annexed their territories, and two refugee Danishmend princes appealed to Constantinople. In the summer of 1176, the Emperor marched on Iconium, but was met on the way by envoys from the Sultan, with an offer of peace on generous terms. Most of his senior officers favoured its acceptance; unfortunately the army also contained a number of young noblemen eager for battle. They pressed hard for a continuation of the campaign, and the Emperor foolishly heeded them.

Just beyond the fortress of Myriocephalum, Manuel's route led through a long and narrow pass; here the Seljuks struck, sweeping down from the mountains to each side and concentrating their fire on the beasts of burden, whose dead bodies soon blocked the road in both directions. For some time it looked as though a general massacre was inevitable. Then there was a sudden lull; and a Turkish emissary arrived at the imperial camp. The Sultan, he reported, had no desire for further bloodshed; if the Emperor would agree to destroy the fortifications of Dorylaeum and Sublaeum – two fortresses which he had strengthened only a year or two before – Kilij Arslan would be happy to conclude a treaty of peace. Manuel accepted; and the two armies withdrew.

Why did the Sultan act as he did? We shall never know. Perhaps he felt he might well need the Empire's support in the future. In any case, the dismantling of the two fortresses, enabling his subjects to spread themselves without let or hindrance through two major valleys, would be no small reward; and Myriocephalum had unquestionably destroyed Manuel's hopes of reimposing his rule across Asia Minor. What then did Manuel Comnenus achieve in the East? Where the Saracens were concerned, absolutely nothing – owing to a single mistake. Relying on the treaty of 1162, he had left Kilij Arslan for eleven years to his own devices. This *détente* had allowed the Sultan to eliminate his Muslim rivals and establish himself as the only important force in eastern Anatolia. Thus Manuel had succeeded only in replacing a number of small and mutually hostile rulers with a single determined one.

In the West, one last diplomatic success awaited him: the marriage in March 1180 between his son by Mary of Antioch, Alexius, and Princess Agnes of France – Louis's daughter by his third wife Alix of Champagne. The bride was nine years old, her husband ten. Within a month or two of the wedding Manuel fell seriously ill, and by mid-September he could no longer doubt the approach of death. It came to him on 24 September, and he was buried in the Church of the Pantocrator.

It is impossible not to feel sorry for him. Of the five Comnenus Emperors, he was the most brilliant and imaginative; and these very qualities were perhaps his undoing. His father and grandfather had worked slowly and patiently to restore the damage done by Manzikert. His own quicksilver mind saw possibilities everywhere; and once seen they were immediately pursued.

Had he concentrated on the situation in the East, he might have re-established Byzantine power throughout Anatolia. But he remained fascinated by the West, and allowed his attention to be taken up in turn by Italy and Hungary, Serbia and Venice, the Western Emperor and the Pope. He gained many victories, but he consolidated none of them; and he left the Empire in a worse state than he found it.

Even in Constantinople he seems to have had few real friends. The trouble was, once again, the attraction that he always felt for Western Europe: its art, its customs, its institutions. His subjects resented the way Western visitors always received a warmer welcome than those from the East, and in particular his preference for Western architects. They were shocked by the informality of his manners – by his light-hearted participation, for example, in Western-style tournaments, competing on equal terms with Frankish knights. He had told them once too often how old-fashioned they were, still sticking to outdated concepts and outmoded traditions. They were glad to see him go.

Fortunately for him, he went just in time, leaving his successors to reap the wild wind. The fact remains, however, that of the many misfortunes that were soon to descend upon Byzantium, many – perhaps most – were indirectly of his making. He left behind him a heavy heritage: one that would have defeated better men by far than those who were, alas, to succeed him.

22

The Fourth Crusade

Alexius II Comnenus was an unimpressive child. He passed, we are told, 'his entire life at play or the chase, and contracted several habits of pronounced viciousness'. Meanwhile his mother, Mary of Antioch, governed in his stead. The first Latin ever to rule in Constantinople, she started off at a grave disadvantage. The Byzantines now feared – and with good reason – still further extensions to Western merchants of their trading rights and privileges; and they were more worried still when Mary took as her chief adviser another character of extreme pro-Western sympathies, Manuel's nephew, the *protosebastus* Alexius: 'He was accustomed to spend the greater part of the day in bed ... Whenever the sun appeared he would seek the darkness, like a wild beast; he took much pleasure in rubbing his decaying teeth, putting new ones in the place of those that had fallen out through old age.'

As dissatisfaction grew, various conspiracies were discovered, the chief of which was the work of Andronicus Comnenus, the Emperor's first cousin. In 1182 Andronicus was already sixty-four years old, but looked nearer forty. Over six feet tall, he had preserved the good looks, intellect, charm, elegance and panache that, together with the fame of his almost legendary exploits in the bed and on the battlefield, had won him an unrivalled reputation. The list of his conquests of both kinds seemed endless. Three in particular had roused Manuel to fury. The first was the Emperor's own niece, the Princess Eudocia; the second was his sister-in-law, Philippa of Antioch; the third Queen Theodora, the twenty-one-year-old widow of King Baldwin III. She became the love of his life.

Andronicus had always had his eye on the imperial crown; and when, after Manuel's death, he learnt of the growing dissatisfaction with the Empress Regent, he needed little persuading that his opportunity had come at last. He, unlike Mary of Antioch, was a true Comnenus. He had energy, ability and determination; his romantic past lent him a popular appeal unmatched in the Empire. In August 1182 he marched on the capital. The old magic was as strong as ever. Army and navy hastened to join him. Even before he crossed the straits, rebellion had broken out in Constantinople, and with it exploded all the city's long-pent-up xenophobia. What followed was the massacre of virtually every Latin in the city: women and children, the old and infirm, even the sick from the hospitals. The *protosebastos* was thrown into the dungeons and later blinded; the young Emperor and his mother were taken to the imperial villa of the Philopation, there to await their cousin's pleasure.

Their fate was worse than either could have feared. Andronicus's triumph had brought out a degree of brutality that none had suspected. He now set about eliminating everyone who stood between himself and the throne. Manuel's daughter Maria and her husband were the first to go; no one doubted poison. The Empress herself was strangled in her cell. In September 1183 Andronicus was crowned co-Emperor; two months later the boy Alexius met his own death by the bowstring. For the last three and a half years of his short life, he had been married to Agnes of France, now re-baptized in the more seemly Byzantine name of Anna. Scarcely was she widowed when the new Emperor, now sixty-four, had married the twelve-year-old Empress and, it seems, consummated the marriage.

In one way Andronicus did more good to the Empire than Manuel had ever done. He attacked all administrative abuses, wherever he found them and in whatever form. The tragedy was that as he eliminated corruption from the government, so he himself grew more and more corrupt. Violence and brute force seemed to be his only weapons. Before long, however, his popularity was gone. Once again the air was thick with sedition; traitors were everywhere. Those who fell into the hands of the Emperor were tortured to death, often in his presence, occasionally by his own hand; but many others escaped to the West, where they could be sure of a ready welcome. As early as 1181 King Béla III of Hungary had seized back Dalmatia and much of Croatia. In 1183, he invaded the Empire: Belgrade, Branichevo, Nish and Sardica were all sacked. There was trouble, too, in Asia, from the landowning aristocracy against which Andronicus nurtured a particular hatred. Indeed, one of his distant cousins, Manuel's great-nephew Isaac Comnenus, formally established himself in Cyprus, declaring its political independence. The paramount threat, however, came from Byzantium's oldest and most determined enemy: Norman Sicily.

Throughout the winter of 1184–5 William II 'the Good' of Sicily – son of William the Bad, on whom he was no improvement – was at Messina. He was out for the crown of Byzantium; and he was determined that the force he sent out to attain it should be stronger, both on land and sea, than any other ever to have sailed from Sicilian shores. By the time it was ready to start, his fleet is said to have comprised between two and three hundred vessels and to have carried some eighty thousand men. The expedition sailed from Messina on

11 June 1185 and headed straight for Durazzo. Andronicus seems to have been caught unprepared. The garrison, totally without provisions for a siege, surrendered without a struggle. As the army marched across the Balkan peninsula, not a single attempt was made to block its progress. On 6 August the entire land force was encamped outside the walls of Thessalonica; on the 15th the fleet took up its position in the roadstead; and the siege began.

Thessalonica was a thriving and prosperous city, with a Christian tradition going back to St Paul. As a naval base it dominated the Aegean; as a commercial centre it vied with Constantinople itself. Yet even had it been adequately prepared and defended, it could not have held out very long against the furious attack that the Sicilians now launched. The garrison resisted bravely, but before long the eastern bastions began to crumble; meanwhile, on the western side, a group of German mercenaries within the walls was bribed to open the gates. Early on 24 August the Sicilian troops poured into the second city of the Byzantine Empire, giving themselves up to an orgy of savagery and violence unparalleled in Thessalonica since Theodosius the Great had massacred seven thousand of its citizens eight centuries before. Women and children were seized and violated, houses fired and pillaged, churches desecrated and destroyed. 'These barbarians,' wrote a contemporary chronicler, 'carried their violence to the very foot of the altars. It was thought strange that they should wish to destroy our icons, using them as fuel for the fires on which they cooked. More criminal still, they would dance upon the altars, before which the angels trembled, and sing profane songs. Then they would piss all over the church, flooding the floors with their urine.'

Within a week or two, the Thessalonians began to discover that there was money to be made out of these foreigners who had so little understanding of real prices and values, and the Archbishop was lamenting the ease with which the ladies of Thessalonica yielded to the Sicilian soldiers. But the atmosphere remained explosive, and to Greek and Sicilian alike it must have been a relief when, leaving only a small garrison, the army headed off to the East. Its vanguard had advanced as far as Mosynopolis, nearly half-way to Constantinople, when there occurred an event that changed the entire situation – completely and, so far as the invaders were concerned, disastrously. His subjects rose up against Andronicus Comnenus and murdered him.

In Constantinople as elsewhere, the news from Thessalonica had brought the inhabitants to the verge of panic. Andronicus's reactions were typical of his contradictory nature. On the one hand he took firm action to repair and strengthen the city's defences, while a fleet of a hundred ships was hastily mobilized and victualled; but there were other times when he seemed totally indifferent to the emergency, drawing back still further into his private world of pleasure. In the three years since his accession he had developed a persecution mania that led him to new extremes of cruelty. The spark of revolution was fired when the Emperor's cousin Isaac Angelus, who had incurred his wrath when a soothsayer had identified him as successor to the throne, leaped on the imperial henchman sent to arrest him and ran him through with his sword. Galloping to St Sophia, he there proudly announced to all present what he had done. And the people responded. Every householder was called to arms; the prisons were broken open, the prisoners joining forces with their deliverers. Meanwhile, in the Great Church, Isaac Angelus was proclaimed *basileus*.

When the news of the revolution reached Andronicus, he was initially confident in his ability to reassert control; but when he reached the Great Palace and found his guards unwilling to obey him, he suddenly understood. Throwing off his purple cloak and boots, he hastily embarked his child-wife and his favourite concubine on to a waiting galley and fled with them up the Bosphorus. Emperor, Empress and concubine were soon caught. The ladies were spared; but Andronicus, bound and fettered, was brought before Isaac for punishment. His right hand was cut off and he was thrown into prison; then, after several days without food or water, he was blinded in one eye and brought forth on a scrawny camel to face the fury of his erstwhile subjects. Nicetas Choniates reports:

They beat him, stoned him, goaded him with spikes, pelted him with filth. A woman of the streets poured a bucket of boiling water on his head ... Then, dragging him from the camel, they hung him up by his feet. At last, after much agony, he died, carrying his remaining hand to his mouth; which he did, in the opinion of some, that he might suck the blood that flowed from one of his wounds.

Isaac Angelus, when at last he accepted the crown, inherited a desperate situation. The Sicilians were less than two hundred miles from Constantinople; their fleet was already in the Marmara. He appointed the ablest of his generals, Alexius Branas, to the supreme command of the army, sending with him the most massive reinforcements that the Empire could provide. The effect was instantaneous: the Greeks were infused with a new spirit. They saw too their enemy grown overconfident; no longer expecting resistance, the Sicilian soldiers had relaxed their discipline. Branas swooped down upon them and pursued them all the way back to Amphipolis. There at last they consented to discuss peace. Their defeat had not affected the main body of the army; they still held Thessalonica. But winter was approaching, and the autumn rains in Thrace fall heavy and chill. To an army that had counted on spending Christmas in Constantinople, the battle of Mosynopolis had probably proved more demoralizing than its strategic importance warranted.

But the Greeks, suspecting a darker purpose, resolved to strike first; and on 7 November they did so. The Sicilians turned and fled. Some were cut down as they ran; many more were drowned in the swollen river Strymon; others still were taken prisoner. Those who escaped found their way back to Thessalonica, where a few managed to pick up ships in which to return to Sicily; but since the bulk of the Sicilian fleet was still lying off Constantinople the majority were not so lucky. The Thessalonians rose up against them, taking a full and bloody revenge.

Byzantium was saved. Nevertheless, its people would have done well to take the Sicilian invasion as a warning. Other Western eyes were fixed covetously on their Empire. Only twenty years later Constantinople was again to face attack. Next time it would succeed.

Of all the families that reigned over Byzantium, the Angeli were the worst. Their supremacy was mercifully short: the three Angelus Emperors – Isaac II, Alexius III and Alexius IV – altogether reigned only nineteen years. But each was disastrous, and together they were responsible for Constantinople's greatest catastrophe until its final fall.

It was regrettable that Isaac found it necessary to blind both the surviving sons of his predecessor, but for most of his subjects the beginning of his reign was 'like a gentle spring after a bitter winter, or a peaceful calm after a furious tempest'. They were soon to be disillusioned. Andronicus, for all his faults, had stamped out corruption; Isaac 'sold government offices like vegetables in a market'. Meanwhile the Theme system, which had been the backbone of administration and defence, effectively disintegrated; and the feudal aristocracy grew steadily more obstreperous.

Not that the Emperor was entirely inactive. He showed considerable energy in the putting down of rebellions and the protection of his frontiers; but he was unable to prevent the formation of the Second Bulgarian Empire, and a Balkan campaign in 1190 was to end in catastrophe when his army was ambushed and he himself narrowly escaped with his life. By now it was clear to everyone that the days of Byzantine supremacy in Eastern Europe were over. They would not return.

Meanwhile, in October 1187, there had come dreadful news: the Saracens had taken Jerusalem. It had caused no real surprise. On the Muslim side there had been the rise of Saladin, a leader of genius who had vowed to recover the Holy City for his faith; on the Christian, nothing but the three declining Frankish states of Jerusalem, Tripoli and Antioch, governed by mediocrities and torn apart by internal struggles for power. For Jerusalem there had been the further tragedy of its leper King, Baldwin IV. When he succeeded at the age of thirteen in 1174, the disease was already upon him; eleven years later he was dead. At the one moment when resolute leadership was essential, the kingdom devolved upon a child of eight; and when he in turn died the following year the throne passed to his stepfather, Guy of Lusignan, whose record of incapacity fully merited the scorn in which he was universally held. Jerusalem was thus in a parlous state when in May 1187 Saladin crossed the Jordan into Frankish territory. On 3 July Guy led the largest army his kingdom had ever assembled towards Tiberias, where Saladin was laying siege to the castle. After a long day's march in the hottest season, this army was obliged to camp on a waterless plateau; and the next day, half-mad with thirst, beneath a little double-summited hill known as the Horns of Hattin, it was surrounded by the Muslim army and cut to pieces.

It remained only for the Saracens to mop up the isolated Christian fortresses one by one. When they came to Jerusalem, its defenders resisted heroically for twelve days; but by 2 October they knew the end was near and sought peace terms. Saladin's magnanimity was already celebrated. Every Christian, he decreed, would be allowed to redeem himself by payment of a suitable ransom. Of the twenty thousand poor who had no means of raising the money, seven thousand would be freed on payment of a lump sum by the various Christian authorities. That same day he led his army into the city; and for the first time in eighty-eight years the green banner of the Prophet flew over Jerusalem. Everywhere, order was preserved. There was no murder, no bloodshed, no looting. Few Christians ultimately found their way to slavery.

When the news of the fall of Jerusalem reached the West, Pope Urban III died of shock; but his successor Gregory VIII lost no time in calling upon Christendom to arms. It soon became plain to Isaac that the coming Crusade would prove a more dangerous threat than either of its predecessors. At its head would be Byzantium's old enemy, Frederick Barbarossa. Scarcely more friendly was William of Sicily, who had also declared his intention of taking the Cross. Fortunately for Byzantium William died in November 1189, leaving no issue; but the marriage of his aunt Constance, to whom his crown now passed, to Barbarossa's eldest son Henry was a clear enough indication that Sicilian foreign policy would remain unchanged. Of the two other Western sovereigns participating, Richard Coeur-de-Lion of England was William's brother-in-law, while Philip Augustus of France, remembering the recent sufferings inflicted on his sister Agnes, was unlikely to be any better disposed.

Richard and Philip elected to travel to the Holy Land by sea, bypassing the

Empire altogether. They consequently play little part in this narrative – though it should be recorded that in May 1191 Richard seized Cyprus from Isaac Comnenus, passing it first to the Templars and then in 1191 to Guy of Lusignan, the deposed King of Jerusalem. Frederick on the other hand preferred the land route, setting out in May 1189 with between a hundred and a hundred and fifty thousand – the largest Crusading army ever seen. He had naturally informed the Emperor of his intentions but Isaac was well aware of his intrigues with the Balkan princes, and his misgivings were only strengthened when it was reported to him that both the Serbs and the Bulgars had offered to swear him allegiance against Byzantium. He next sent Constantine Cantacuzenus and John Ducas to await the great army at the frontier; but instead of greeting Barbarossa as instructed they too actively encouraged him to attack their master. By this time Isaac was close to panic; and when Frederick's envoys arrived to discuss the transport of his army to Asia he flung them into prison. The enraged Emperor immediately ordered his eldest son Henry, who had remained in Germany, to secure papal blessing for a Crusade against the schismatic Greeks, to collect a fleet and to bring it with all speed to Constantinople. Isaac then capitulated, promising to provide the necessary transport in return for an undertaking by Frederick to cross by the Dardanelles rather than the Bosphorus, thereby avoiding Constantinople altogether.

On 10 June 1190, after a long and exhausting journey across Anatolia, Frederick Barbarossa led his troops out on to the flat Cilician coastal plain. The heat was savage, and the little river Calycadnus that ran past Seleucia to the sea must have been a welcome sight. Frederick, riding alone a short distance ahead of the army, spurred his horse towards it. Whether he dismounted to drink and was swept off his feet by the current, whether his horse slipped and threw him, whether the shock of the icy mountain water was too much for his tired old body – he was nearing seventy – we shall never know. His followers reached the river to find their Emperor lying dead on the bank.

Immediately, his army began to disintegrate. His younger son, the Duke of Swabia, assumed command, but he was no substitute for his father. The army, carrying with it the Emperor's body not very successfully preserved in vinegar, marched grimly on, losing many more of its men in an ambush as it entered Syria. The survivors who finally limped into Antioch had no more fight left in them. The Emperor's rapidly decomposing remains were hastily buried in the cathedral, where they remained until in 1268 a Mameluke army burnt the whole building to the ground.

Richard and Philip Augustus arrived, by contrast with their armies essentially intact; and it was thanks to them that the Third Crusade, though it failed to recapture Jerusalem, was marginally less humiliating than the Second. Acre was recovered, to become capital of the Kingdom of Jerusalem for another century until the Mameluke conquest; but that Kingdom, now reduced to the short coastal strip between Tyre and Jaffa, was a pale reflection of what Crusader Palestine had once been.

On Christmas Day, 1194, by virtue of his marriage to Roger II's daughter Constance, Frederick Barbarossa's son Henry VI had received the royal crown of Sicily in Palermo Cathedral. His wife was not with him. Pregnant for the first time at the age of forty, she was travelling more slowly and in her own time; and she had got no further than Jesi, some twenty miles west of Ancona, when she felt the pains of childbirth upon her. There on the day after her husband's coronation, in a large tent erected in the main square to which free entrance was allowed to any matron of the town, she brought forth her only son whom, a day or two later, she presented in the same square, proudly suckling him at her breast. Of that son, Frederick – later to be known as *Stupor Mundi*, the Astonishment of the World – we shall hear more as our story continues.

At the time of Frederick's birth, his father was already contemplating a new Crusade. Barbarossa, had he lived, would surely have recovered Jerusalem; it was plainly his duty to retrieve the family honour. In Easter week of 1195 he took the Cross; and a few days later he wrote a firm letter to the Emperor Isaac, making a number of quite unrealistic demands. The letter was a typical piece of imperial bluster; but it missed its target. On 8 April 1195 Isaac Angelus fell victim to a *coup* engineered by his elder brother Alexius, who deposed him, blinded him and seized the throne.

If Isaac had been a poor Emperor, it can only be said that Alexius III was a good deal worse, and still more easily manipulated. Thus, when Henry demanded a huge tribute to pay for his mercenary troops, the terrified Emperor immediately instituted a special tax, which he supplemented by stripping the precious ornaments from the imperial tombs in the Church of the Holy Apostles. Two years later he was obliged to stand impotently by while his niece Irene, daughter of the blinded Isaac, was married off by Henry to his younger brother, Philip of Swabia.

But what became of the great expedition proclaimed by Henry in 1195? Many of the foremost names in Germany had responded to his call: two archbishops, nine bishops, five dukes and countless lesser nobles. They had sailed from Messina and had immediately advanced against the Saracen foe. By the end of October, however, the news reached them that Henry had died of a fever at Messina. Many of the nobles decided to return at once to protect their interests in the ensuing power struggle, and when civil war broke out in

Germany most of the others followed. Thus it was that when in February 1198 the German rank and file were preparing to confront an Egyptian army, they suddenly realized that their leaders had deserted them. There followed a headlong flight to Tyre, where their ships were waiting. The second German expedition had been, if anything, a still greater fiasco than the first.

The end of the twelfth century found Europe in confusion. The Empires of both East and West were rudderless; Norman Sicily was gone; Germany was torn apart by civil war; and both England and France were occupied with inheritance problems following the death of Richard Coeur-de-Lion in 1199. Of the luminaries of Christendom, one only was firmly in control: Pope Innocent III, who had ascended the papal throne in 1198 and had immediately proclaimed yet another Crusade. The lack of crowned heads to lead it did not worry him; they were more trouble than they were worth. A few great nobles would suit his purpose admirably; and he was still seeking suitable candidates when he received a letter from Count Tibald of Champagne. Tibald was the younger brother of Henry of Champagne, who had been effective ruler of the Kingdom of Jerusalem from 1192 until his accidental fall from a window in 1197. As the grandson of Louis VII and the nephew of both Philip Augustus and Coeur-de-Lion, he had the Crusades in his blood. Once he had informed Innocent that he had taken the Cross, there could be no other leader.

Major problems, however, lay ahead. Coeur-de-Lion had declared that the Achilles' heel of the Muslim East, to which all future expeditions should be directed, was Egypt; it followed that the new Crusade must travel by sea, and would need ships in a quantity that could be obtained from one source only: the Venetian Republic. Thus it was that, early in 1201, a party of six knights led by Geoffrey de Villehardouin, Marshal of Champagne, arrived in Venice, which agreed to provide transport for 4,500 knights with their horses, 9,000 squires and 20,000 foot-soldiers, with food for nine months. The cost would be 84,000 silver marks. In addition the Republic would produce fifty fully-equipped galleys at her own expense, on condition that she received half the territories conquered.

This decision was conveyed to the Crusaders by the Doge, Enrico Dandolo. In all Venetian history there is no more astonishing figure. At this time he was well into his eighties, and stone blind to boot. Villehardouin, who knew him well, assures us that he could not see a hand in front of his face. Fortunately for posterity, Geoffrey has left a superb record not only of the Crusade itself but also of these preliminary negotiations. He notes in passing that the agreement did not mention Egypt as the immediate objective; such news would have appalled the rank and file, for whom Jerusalem was the only legitimate goal. The Venetians would have been happy to cooperate in the deception: at that very moment their ambassadors were in Cairo, discussing a highly profitable trade agreement. Such considerations, however, could not be allowed to affect plans for the Crusade; and it was agreed that the Crusaders should all foregather in Venice a year later, on the feast of St John, 24 June 1202, when the fleet would be ready for them.

But alas: when that day came, the army that gathered on the Lido numbered less than one-third of what had been expected. For its leaders, the situation was embarrassing in the extreme. Venice had kept her promise: there lay the fleet, war galleys as well as transports, sufficient for an army three times the size of that assembled. In such circumstances the Crusaders could not hope to pay the Venetians the money they had promised. When their commander-in-chief, the Marquis Boniface of Montferrat – Tibald of Champagne having died the previous year – arrived in Venice, he found the whole expedition in jeopardy. The Venetians were refusing to allow a single ship to leave port till their money was forthcoming; they were even talking of cutting off food for the waiting army, which was confined to the Lido and forbidden to set foot in the city itself. Boniface emptied his own coffers, many of his colleagues did likewise, and every man in the army was pressed to give what he could; but the total raised still fell short by 34,000 marks of what was owing.

For as long as the contributions trickled in, old Dandolo kept the Crusaders in suspense. Then, when he knew there was no more to be got, he came forward with an offer. The Venetian city of Zara had recently fallen to Hungary. If the Franks would agree to assist Venice in its recapture, settlement of their debt might perhaps be postponed. There followed another of those ceremonies in St Mark's that Dandolo, despite his years, handled so beautifully. Before a congregation that included all the leading Franks, he addressed his subjects. '"Signors, I myself am old and feeble; but if you will allow me to take the Cross while my son remains in my place to guard the Republic, I am ready to live and to die with you." So he came down from the pulpit and moved up to the altar, and knelt there, weeping; and he had the cross sewn on to his great cotton hat, so determined was he that all men should see it.'

On 8 November 1202 the army of the Fourth Crusade set sail from Venice. Its 480 ships were however bound neither for Egypt nor for Palestine. A week later, Zara was taken and sacked. The Pope, outraged, excommunicated the entire expedition. The Crusade could hardly be said to have got off to a good start. But worse was to follow. Early in the new year a messenger arrived with a letter from Philip of Swabia – not only the brother of Emperor Henry VI but also the son-in-law of the deposed and blinded Isaac Angelus. In the previous year Isaac's young son, another Alexius, had escaped from prison, and Philip's court had been his obvious place of refuge. If the Crusade would enthrone the young Alexius in place of his usurper uncle, he would finance its subsequent conquest of Egypt, supplying ten thousand soldiers of his own and maintaining five hundred knights in the Holy Land at his own expense. Finally, he would submit the Church of Constantinople to the authority of Rome. The old Doge accepted the idea with enthusiasm. He had little love for Byzantium. Genoese and Pisan competition was becoming ever fiercer; if Venice were to retain her hold on the Eastern markets, decisive action would be required. The Crusading army, too, was happy to accept the change of plan, which would strengthen and enrich the Crusade and restore the unity of Christendom. Thus, on 24 June 1203, a year to the day after the rendezvous in Venice, the fleet dropped anchor off Constantinople.

Alexius III had characteristically made no preparations for the city's defence; the dockyards had lain idle since his brother had entrusted the whole shipbuilding programme to Venice sixteen years before; his admiral, meanwhile, had sold off the anchors, sails and rigging of the few remaining vessels, now reduced to useless hulks in the inner harbour. He and his subjects watched, half-stunned, as, soon after sunrise on the morning of 5 July, the Crusading army crossed the Bosphorus and landed below Galata, on the north-eastern side of the Golden Horn. Being a commercial settlement largely occupied by foreign merchants, Galata was unwalled; its only major fortification was a single round tower, in which stood the huge windlass for the raising and lowering of the chain that barred the entrance to the Horn.[1] Its garrison held out for a full twenty-four hours; but by the following morning it had to surrender. The Venetian sailors unshackled the windlass, and the great iron chain that had stretched over five hundred yards across the mouth of the Golden Horn subsided thunderously into the water. The fleet swept in, destroying such few Byzantine vessels as it found in the inner harbour. The naval victory was complete.

The assault, when it came, was directed against the weakest point in the Byzantine defences: the sea frontage of the Palace of Blachernae, which occupied the angle formed by the Land Walls and those following the line of the Horn, at the extreme north-west corner of the city. It was launched simultaneously from land and sea, with the Venetian ships riding low in the water under the weight of their siege machinery: catapults and mangonels on

---

1 The tower was demolished in 1261. The present Galata Tower is a fourteenth-century replacement on a different site.

the forecastles, covered gangplanks and scaling-ladders suspended by rope tackles between the yard-arms. The Frankish army, attacking from land, was initially beaten back by the axe-swinging Englishmen and Danes of the Varangian Guard; it was the Venetians who decided the day – and, to a considerable degree, Enrico Dandolo in person.

Villehardouin reports that although the Venetian assault craft had approached so close in-shore that those in the bows were fighting hand-to-hand with the defenders, the sailors still hesitated to effect a proper landing:

The Duke of Venice, an old man and stone-blind, stood on the prow of his galley with the banner of St Mark and ordered his men to drive the ship ashore. And so they did, and he leaped down and planted the banner before him in the ground. And when the others saw the standard of St Mark and the Doge's galley beached, they were ashamed and followed him ashore.

Before long twenty-five towers along the wall were in Venetian hands. By this time too, the Crusaders were pouring into the city, setting fire to the wooden houses until the whole district was ablaze. That evening Alexius III fled.

Byzantium, at this gravest crisis in its history, was left without an Emperor; and old Isaac Angelus was hurriedly retrieved from his prison and replaced on the imperial throne. Though now even blinder than Dandolo he remained the legitimate Emperor, and by restoring him the Byzantines had theoretically removed all grounds for further intervention by the Crusaders, apart from the undertakings made by young Alexius. These Isaac was now obliged to ratify, agreeing at the same time to make his son co-Emperor. Only then did the Crusaders accord him formal recognition, after which they withdrew to Galata to await their promised rewards.

On 1 August 1203, Alexius IV Angelus was crowned alongside his father. Immediately he regretted the offers he had made in the spring. The treasury was empty; the new taxes that he was obliged to introduce were openly resented by his subjects, who knew full well where their money was going. The clergy were scandalized when he seized and melted down their church plate, and furious at his plans to subordinate them to Rome. So his unpopularity steadily grew; and the ubiquitous Franks increased the tension still further. One night a group of them came upon a little mosque in the Saracen quarter behind the Church of St Eirene and burnt it to ashes. The flames spread, and for the next forty-eight hours Constantinople was engulfed in its worst fire since the days of Justinian.

When, a few days later, a delegation of three Crusaders and three Venetians came to the Emperor to demand immediate payment of the sum owing to them, there was nothing he could do; and so the war began. Neither the Crusaders nor the Greeks wanted it. The people of Constantinople wished only to be rid of these Western thugs who were destroying their city and bleeding them white into the bargain. The Franks resented their enforced stay among an effete and effeminate people when they should have been getting to grips with the infidel. Even if the Greek debt were to be paid in full, they would not benefit materially; it would only enable them to settle their own outstanding account with the Venetians.

The key to it all lay with Enrico Dandolo. He, at any moment, could give his fleet the order to sail: the Crusaders would have been relieved and the Byzantines overjoyed. Formerly, he had refused on the grounds that the Franks would never be able to pay him their debt until they received the money from Alexius. He had now almost forgotten that debt. His mind was now fixed on a far greater objective: the overthrow of the Byzantine Empire. And so his advice took on a different tone. Nothing more could be expected of the Angeli: if the Crusaders were ever to obtain their due, they would have to take Constantinople by force. Once inside the city, with one of their own leaders on the throne, they could settle the debt and finance the Crusade. This was their opportunity; it would not recur.

Within Constantinople too, it was generally agreed that Alexius IV must go; and in January 1204 the only really effective figure on the Byzantine stage took the law into his own hands. Alexius Ducas – nicknamed Murzuphlus on account of his eyebrows, which met in the middle – was a nobleman who now occupied the court position of *protovestarius*, which carried rights of un-restricted access to the imperial apartments. Late at night he burst into the Emperor's chamber and woke him with the news that his subjects had risen against him; muffling him in a long cloak, he led him by a side door out of the palace to where the fellow-conspirators were waiting. The unhappy youth was then clapped into irons and eventually succumbed to the bowstring. His blind father died soon afterwards; Villehardouin suggests a natural death; it does not seem to have struck him that it might have been artificially induced.

His rivals eliminated, Murzuphlus was crowned in St Sophia as Alexius V and immediately began to show the leadership that the Empire had lacked. The walls and towers were properly manned, strengthened and heightened. There were to be no more negotiations, no further payments on a debt for which the new Emperor bore no responsibility. For the Crusaders, one chance only remained: an all-out attempt on the city. It was exactly what Dandolo had been advocating for months, and the old Doge, who was by now recognized by Venetians and Franks alike as the leader of the entire expedition, called a series of council meetings in the camp at Galata. They were concerned less with the plan of attack than with the administration of the Empire after its conquest. It was agreed that the Franks and the Venetians should each appoint six delegates to an electoral committee, and that this should choose the new Emperor. If it decided on a Frank, then the Patriarch should be a Venetian; otherwise vice versa. The Emperor would receive a quarter of the city and of the Empire, including the two chief palaces – Blachernae on the Golden Horn and the old palace on the Marmara. The remaining three-quarters should be divided equally, half going to Venice and half in fief to the Crusading knights. For the Venetian portion, the Doge was specifically absolved from the need to do the Emperor homage.

The attack began on Friday morning, 9 April, against that same stretch of sea wall where Dandolo and his men had distinguished themselves nine months before. The new, higher walls and towers were no longer accessible from the Venetian mastheads; but after several initial failures the Venetians lashed their ships together in pairs, thus throwing twice as much weight as before against each tower. Before long, two of these were overwhelmed and occupied. Almost simultaneously, the Franks broke open one of the gates in the wall and surged into the city. Murzuphlus, who had been commanding the defenders with courage and determination, galloped through the streets in a last desperate attempt to rally his subjects; then, seeing that he had failed, he fled with Euphrosyne, wife of Alexius III, and her daughter Eudocia to join Alexius in Thrace. On arrival there, he married Eudocia and began to gather his forces for a counter-offensive.

Once the walls were breached the carnage was dreadful. Only at nightfall did the conquerors call a truce and withdraw to their camp in one of the great squares of the city. The next morning they awoke to find all resistance at an end. But for the people of Constantinople the tragedy had scarcely begun. Not for nothing had the Franks waited so long outside the world's richest capital. Now that the customary three days' looting was allowed them, they fell on it like locusts. Never since the barbarian invasions had Europe witnessed such an orgy of brutality and vandalism; never in history had so much beauty, so much superb craftsmanship, been wantonly destroyed in so short a space of time. Among the witnesses was Nicetas Choniates:

They smashed the holy images and hurled the sacred relics of the Martyrs into places I am ashamed to mention, scattering everywhere the body and blood of the Saviour ... As for their profanation of the Great Church, they destroyed the high altar and shared out the pieces among themselves ... And they brought horses and mules into the Church, the better to carry off the holy vessels, and the pulpit, and the doors, and the furniture wherever it was to be found; and when some of these beasts slipped and fell, they ran them through with their swords, fouling the Church with their blood and ordure.

A common harlot was enthroned in the Patriarch's chair, to hurl insults at Jesus Christ; and she sang bawdy songs, and danced immodestly in the holy place ... nor was there mercy shown to virtuous matrons, innocent maids or even virgins consecrated to God ...

And these men, he continues, carried the Cross on their shoulders, the Cross upon which they had sworn to abstain from the pleasures of the flesh until their holy task was done.

It was Constantinople's darkest hour – even darker, perhaps, than that which was to see the city's final fall to the Ottoman Sultan. But not all its treasures perished. While the Franks abandoned themselves to a frenzy of destruction, the Venetians kept their heads. They too looted – but they did not destroy. They knew beauty when they saw it. All that they could lay their hands on they sent back to Venice – beginning with the four great bronze horses which, from their high platform above the main door of St Mark's, were to dominate the Piazza for the next eight centuries.

After three days of terror, order was restored. Then all the spoils were gathered together and careful distribution made: a quarter for the Emperor when elected, the remainder to be split equally between the Franks and Venetians. As soon as it was done, the Crusaders paid their debt to Enrico Dandolo. Both parties then applied themselves to the next task: the election of the new Emperor. Dandolo had no difficulty in steering the electors towards the easy-going and tractable Count Baldwin of Flanders, who on 16 May received his coronation in St Sophia – the third Emperor to be crowned there in less than a year. In return, Venice appropriated the best for her own. She was entitled to three-eighths of the city and the Empire, together with free trade throughout the imperial dominions, from which both her principal rivals, Genoa and Pisa were to be rigorously excluded. In Constantinople itself, the Doge demanded the entire district surrounding St Sophia and the Patriarchate, reaching right down to the shore of the Golden Horn; for the rest, he took for Venice all those regions that promised to give her an unbroken chain of colonies and ports from the lagoon to the Black Sea, including the Peloponnese and the all-important island of Crete.

Thus it was the Venetians who were the real beneficiaries of the Fourth Crusade; and their success was due, almost exclusively, to Enrico Dandolo. Refusing the Byzantine crown for himself – to have accepted it would have created insuperable constitutional problems at home and might well have destroyed the Republic – he nevertheless secured a Venetian majority and the success of his own candidate. Furthermore, while encouraging the Franks to feudalize the Empire he had kept Venice outside the feudal framework, holding her new dominions not as an imperial fief but by her own right of conquest. For a blind man not far short of ninety it was a remarkable achievement. Yet even now he did not rest. Murzuphlus was to cause no further trouble: captured by the Franks, he was brought back to Constantinople and flung to his death from the column of Theodosius in the centre of the city. But on all sides the erstwhile Crusaders had to fight hard to establish themselves, nowhere more fiercely than in Venice's newly-acquired city of Adrianople where, just after Easter, 1205, the Emperor Baldwin fell into the hands of the Bulgars and the old Doge, who had fought determinedly at his side, was left to lead a shattered army back to Constantinople. Six weeks later he was dead. His body was not returned to Venice but was buried in St Sophia – where, in the gallery above the south aisle, his tombstone may still be seen.

He had deserved well of his city, but in the wider context of world events he was a disaster. The Fourth Crusade – if indeed it can be so described – surpassed even its predecessors in faithlessness and duplicity, in brutality and greed. By the sack of Constantinople, Western civilization suffered a loss greater than the sack of Rome in the fifth century or the burning of the library of Alexandria in the seventh – perhaps the most catastrophic single loss in all history. Politically, too, the damage done was incalculable. Byzantium never recovered any considerable part of its lost dominion. Instead, the Empire was left powerless to defend itself against the Ottoman tide. There are few greater ironies in history than the fact that the fate of Eastern Christendom should have been sealed by men who fought under the banner of the Cross. Those men were transported, inspired, encouraged and ultimately led by Enrico Dandolo in the name of the Venetian Republic; and, just as Venice derived the major advantage from the tragedy, so she and her magnificent old Doge must accept the major responsibility for the havoc that they wrought upon the world.

23
Exile and Homecoming

[1205–61]

In contrast to Doge Dandolo, who now proudly styled himself 'Lord of a Quarter and Half a Quarter of the Roman Empire', the Emperor Baldwin cut a sorry figure. He was left with just a quarter of the territory that had been ruled by his immediate predecessors; and even this was contested. Boniface of Montferrat, furious at having been passed over, refused the Anatolian lands he was offered and seized Thessalonica, where he established a kingdom extending over a large part of Macedonia and Thessaly.

The new rulers were, not surprisingly, detested. The Franks, staunch upholders of the Church of Rome, unhesitatingly imposed the Latin rite wherever they could. Many Greeks left their ancestral lands and moved to the Byzantine successor states in which the national spirit and the Orthodox faith were still preserved. Of these states, the largest and by far the most important was the so-called Empire of Nicaea, where Alexius III's son-in-law Theodore Lascaris was crowned in 1208. It occupied a broad strip of land in western Anatolia, extending from the Aegean to the Black Sea. Although the official capital remained Nicaea – the seat of the Patriarch, where the imperial coronations took place – Theodore's successor John III was to establish his residence in the Lydian city of Nymphaeum; and for most of the fifty-seven-year period of exile from Constantinople this was the seat of government. The two other successor states, situated one on the Adriatic coast and the other at the south-eastern extremity of the Black Sea, were too remote to exert much influence. The Despotate of Epirus was founded soon after the capture of Constantinople by a certain Michael Comnenus Ducas, great-grandson of Alexius I Comnenus. From his capital at Arta he controlled the north-west coast of Greece and part of Thessaly – a domain substantially increased in 1224 by his half-brother Theodore who captured Thessalonica from the Latins and was crowned Emperor as a rival to John III in Nicaea. Unlike Nicaea and Epirus, the Empire of Trebizond was not the result of the fall of Constantinople. It had been founded in April 1204 by Alexius and David Comnenus, grandsons of the Emperor Andronicus through his son Manuel, who had married a Georgian princess. After the fall of Andronicus in 1185 the young brothers had been brought up at the Georgian royal court. Determined to continue the Comnenus dynasty, they had captured Trebizond in April 1204. For the greater part of its 257-year history the Trapezuntine Empire was confined to a coastal strip between the Pontic mountains and the sea.

As ruler of Byzantium in exile, Theodore I Lascaris of Nicaea faced a multitude of problems. Even within his own borders, petty Greek principalities were declaring themselves; then, in autumn 1204, a Frankish army led by Baldwin himself began to move against him. Theodore was still hopelessly unprepared; and on 6 December a calamitous defeat at Poimanenon gave the Franks control of the whole Bithynian coast as far as Brusa. But Baldwin's arrogance soon caught up with him. The Greek landowners in Thrace offered the imperial crown to the Bulgarian Tsar Kalojan in return for driving the Latins from Constantinople. Earlier in 1204 Kalojan had been crowned King (though not Emperor) by Innocent III's envoy and had accepted the jurisdiction of Rome; but he was as anxious to get rid of the Crusaders as were the Byzantines themselves. On 14 April 1205 he destroyed the Frankish army outside Adrianople, taking prisoner Baldwin himself, who died soon afterwards. Just a year after the capture of Constantinople, the power of the Latins was broken. In all Asia Minor, only Pegae on the Marmara remained in Frankish hands.

Now at last Theodore could forge his new state, never for a moment doubting that his subjects would be back, sooner or later, in their rightful capital. He followed the old Byzantine pattern in every detail; thus, after his coronation in 1208, there were two Eastern Emperors and two Patriarchs, the Latin in Constantinople and the Greek in Nicaea, each initially determined to destroy the other. In the following year Baldwin's brother and successor Henry of Hainault, swallowing his Crusader scruples, concluded a military alliance with the Seljuks, who also saw the new Greek state in Asia Minor as a threat; and in 1211 he inflicted a serious defeat on Theodore, pressing on to Pergamum and Nymphaeum; but he was too hard pressed by the Bulgars in his rear to be able to pursue his advantage. In late 1214 the two Emperors agreed to a treaty of peace: Henry would keep the north-west coast of Asia Minor as far south as Atramyttion; the remainder as far as the Seljuk frontier would go to Theodore.

The young Empire had finally obtained formal recognition by the Crusaders of its right to exist. Almost simultaneously, the Latin Empire began once again to decline; in June 1216 Henry died at Thessalonica. In barely a decade, by respecting the rights and religion of his Greek subjects and achieving a balance of power with Nicaea, he had saved an apparently lost cause. He died childless; and to succeed him the Frankish barons elected Peter of Courtenay, husband of his sister Yolanda. Peter, who was then in France, set out for the East in the first weeks of 1217. Unfortunately he stopped at Durazzo to recover the city from the Despot of Epirus, but his attempt ended in fiasco. He was captured, thrown into prison and never heard of again.

The Empress Yolanda, who had wisely decided to travel out with her children by sea, meanwhile arrived without mishap in Constantinople, where she gave birth to a son, Baldwin. She then governed as Regent until her death in 1219, confirming her brother's conciliatory policy by giving her daughter Mary to Theodore Lascaris as his third wife. News of this step, however, was received with horror in Epirus, where the star of the Despot Theodore was rising fast. He had never accepted the treaty of 1214; here, he claimed, was a further betrayal. The truth was that Theodore could never be satisfied with Epirus. As the legitimate great-grandson of Alexius I, he could boast a far stronger claim to the imperial throne than Lascaris. His immediate ambitions were now focused on Thessalonica; but Thessalonica was, in the eyes of Theodore Angelus Ducas Comnenus, little more than a stepping-stone to Constantinople itself.

Since the death of Boniface of Montferrat in 1207, Thessalonica had been governed by his widow, acting as Regent for her son Demetrius; but after the arrival of the Empress Yolanda it could no longer rely on firm support from Constantinople. It was already plain that its days as an independent state were numbered; and in the autumn of 1224 it fell. Theodore of Epirus now ruled supreme from the Adriatic to the Aegean. Soon afterwards, in open defiance of Lascaris, he was crowned by the Bishop of Ochrid as Emperor of the Romans. Thus it was that, in place of the single Empire that had existed little more than a generation before, there were now four – three Greek and one Latin. And not far away there loomed a fifth: for the Second Bulgarian Empire was growing rapidly. Tsar Kalojan had already extended his rule over much of Thrace and Macedonia; his second successor, John II Asen, also coveted Constantinople. By far the weakest of the powers was the Latin Empire itself, by 1225 reduced to the capital itself, the region immediately to the north and west, and a small area of Asia Minor south of the Marmara. Yolanda had died in 1219; her son Robert was a feckless youth, totally outclassed by Theodore, John Asen and John Vatatzes, who had inherited the Empire of Nicaea from his father-in-law Theodore Lascaris in 1222. After a punishing defeat by Vatatzes, the capture of Thessalonica was too much for him. From that moment on he gave himself up to a life of pleasure and dissipation, dying in January 1228.

Robert left no legitimate children; and since his brother and successor Baldwin II was still only eleven the barons therefore turned for a Regent to the most distinguished of living Crusaders: the former King of Jerusalem, John of Brienne. Though now nearly eighty years old, he was still remarkably spry – he had a daughter of four – and no one else could match his record. He made, however, a number of conditions. The young Emperor must immediately marry Maria, his own four-year-old daughter, who must receive a suitable territorial dowry; he himself must be recognized as *basileus* in his own right, with Baldwin succeeding him on his death; and at the age of twenty Baldwin, if not yet Emperor, should be invested with the Empire of Nicaea, together with all Frankish possessions in Asia Minor. He was still in no hurry: only in the autumn of 1231 did he finally appear off the Golden Horn. A few days later he was crowned Emperor in St Sophia.

During this three-year interregnum, the balance of power in the Balkans suffered a radical change. In April 1230 the Emperor Theodore Comnenus had been defeated and captured by John Asen. To be sure, his brother Manuel was allowed to stay on in Thessalonica with the title of Despot; but this was only because he was married to Asen's daughter. He was a puppet of his father-in-law and made little pretence of being anything else. The Latins had been saved from almost certain destruction – and by a nation that they had previously spurned. But they now had to watch John Asen advance un-opposed across the Balkans, from the Adriatic to the Black Sea.

The effective elimination of the fourth participant in the struggle for supremacy led inevitably to a radical realignment among the other three. To John Asen, Vatatzes now seemed a far more useful ally than the Latins, particularly since he was about to abandon the Church of Rome. Western Christianity had never really taken root among the Bulgars; besides, any future offensive against the Latin Empire would be a lot easier to justify if the Tsar were seen to be acting against heretics. In 1232 the break was made. A Bulgarian Orthodox Patriarchate was once again established; and three years later John Asen signed a treaty of alliance with Nicaea, which was subsequently sealed by the marriage of his daughter Helena to the son of John Vatatzes, Theodore II Lascaris. In the late summer of 1235 the combined forces of Orthodoxy were besieging Constantinople by land and sea.

Old John of Brienne fought like a tiger for the defence of his Empire, and Venetian ships provided invaluable support; but Constantinople was saved only by a change of heart on the part of John Asen, who suddenly realized that an energetic Greek Empire would constitute a far more serious threat to Bulgaria than an exhausted Latin one and called off the attack. Almost at once, however, disaster struck. His own capital fell victim to a furious epidemic, which carried off his wife, one of his sons and the recently-installed Patriarch. To John Asen, this was the judgement of heaven; immediately he made his peace with Vatatzes. Soon, however, he began to look for a new wife; and somehow his prisoner Theodore of Thessalonica managed to persuade him to marry his daughter Irene. As the Tsar's father-in-law, Theodore was then released from his captivity and returned to Thessalonica, where he deposed his brother Manuel and enthroned instead his own son John, restoring to him the title of Emperor.

The year 1241 proved a watershed. Before it was over, three of the protagonists were in their graves: John Asen of Bulgaria, Manuel of Thessalonica and Pope Gregory IX, one of the most redoubtable champions of the Latin Empire. That same year also saw a Mongol horde sweep through Hungary into the Danube basin, leaving the Bulgars little opportunity to undertake further adventures to the East: another once formidable nation was thus effectively eliminated. The power of Thessalonica had already been broken. The Latin Empire, which now consisted of little more than the city of Constantinople itself, had survived only thanks to dissension among its enemies. Of those enemies, there remained but one: the Empire of Nicaea, whose ruler John Vatatzes continued to prepare for its reconquest. He still had the problem of Thessalonica to settle. Its Emperor John was a weak and pious figurehead; the real power was back in the hands of Theodore, as ambitious as he had ever been. Thus it was Theodore whom in 1241 John Vatatzes invited to Nicaea as his guest. The old man accepted, and was received with every courtesy; only when he came to leave was it politely explained to him that his departure would unfortunately not be possible. He remained a prisoner until the following summer, when Vatatzes escorted him back to Thessalonica and then sent him as an envoy to his son to negotiate a treaty. The result was that John exchanged the title of Emperor for that of Despot, and acknowledged the supremacy of Nicaea.

While Vatatzes was still in Thessalonica, the Mongols invaded Asia Minor. In June 1243 they defeated the Sultan Kaikosru II at the battle of Kösedağ; the Emperor of Trebizond, who had been a vassal of the Sultan, suffered much the same fate. Fortunately the Mongols moved away again, leaving a broken Sultanate behind them but the Nicaean lands untouched. The Bulgar Empire too had been crippled by this most recent of the barbarian invasions; while the death in 1246 of Coloman, John Asen's twelve-year-old son, and the succession of his still younger half-brother Michael, further troubled the waters in which Vatatzes cheerfully intended to fish. By the autumn of that year he had occupied a good deal of western Macedonia. He was still encamped there when a group of Thessalonians arrived with a proposal. If he would guarantee to the city the continuation of its ancient rights and privileges, it would be surrendered without a struggle. Vatatzes agreed at once. In December he entered Thessalonica unopposed, exiled old Theodore and left as his Viceroy his distant kinsman Andronicus Palaeologus.

One more enemy was left for him to conquer before he could concentrate on Constantinople. Some nine years before, Epirus had separated from Thessalonica and set itself up once again under Michael II, an illegitimate son of its original founder Michael I. John Vatatzes did not attack it: instead, in 1249 he concluded a treaty of friendship with Michael, sealing it by betrothing his granddaughter Maria to Michael's son Nicephorus. Theodore, still unreconciled, persuaded his nephew to take up arms once again against the Nicaean Empire; but John Vatatzes was taking no more chances. Early in 1253 he forced the Despot's surrender. Michael ceded much of his territory; his son Nicephorus was carried off to Vatatzes's court as a hostage for his future good behaviour. As for the old, blind, insufferable Theodore, he was shipped off to end his days in the prison he so richly deserved.

The Latin Empire was tottering. Already in 1236 the young Emperor Baldwin, now nineteen, had left for Italy in a desperate attempt to raise men and money; it was not until early 1240 that he returned to the Bosphorus. This chronic shortage was also responsible for another decision, deeply demoralizing to Greeks and Latins alike: the pawning to Venice of Constantinople's most hallowed possession, the Crown of Thorns that Christ had worn on the Cross. The Emperor being unable to redeem it, the opportunity was seized by St Louis of France, who built the Sainte-Chapelle to receive it.

For Baldwin, even cap in hand, the courts of Europe must have been vastly preferable to life in gloomy, beleaguered Constantinople. In 1244 he was off again – to Frederick II; to Count Raymond in Toulouse; to Innocent IV in Lyon; to St Louis in Paris; and even to London, where King Henry III made a small and grudging contribution to his funds. But he returned in October 1248 to find himself in such straits that he was obliged even to sell off the lead from the roof of the imperial palace. He would never have reigned for another thirteen years if his enemy in Nicaea had survived; but on 3 November 1254 John Vatatzes died at Nymphaeum. During the last ten years of his life his worsening epilepsy had seriously unbalanced him: it was clear to everyone at court that he was rapidly losing his grip.

He had, nevertheless, been a great ruler. He had inherited from his predecessor a small but viable state; when, thirty-two years later, he left it to his son Theodore II, its dominions extended over most of the Balkan peninsula and much of the Aegean, its rivals were crippled or annihilated, and it stood poised to achieve the purpose for which it had been established. At home, John continually reminded his subjects that they lived in a state of emergency, and that sacrifices were required of them until Constantinople should be theirs. Foreign imports were forbidden; self-sufficiency was now the watchword, and he himself set an example by running a profitable farm, using the profits from his sales of eggs to buy his wife Irene her 'egg crown' – a jewelled coronet, which he publicly presented to her as proof of what could be achieved by efficient husbandry. The gift was well-deserved. Thanks to the two of them hospitals and orphanages were established, art and literature encouraged, and the foundations laid for the spectacular cultural revival which was to occur in the reign of their son Theodore, under whom Nicaea would become a dazzling centre for Byzantine culture. In consequence John and Irene were genuinely loved by their subjects.

John knew as he lay on his deathbed that the day towards which he had worked all his adult life could not be long delayed, despite some doubts that he may have entertained about his only son and successor. Not that the young Theodore II Lascaris was altogether unworthy of the throne. He was an intellectual who produced in the course of his short life a whole corpus of literary, theological and scientific works; and he never allowed these interests to deflect him from the business of government. Unfortunately he had inherited his father's epilepsy in an even more serious form. This was dangerous enough in Constantinople; when he was with his army in the field it was potentially disastrous. He ruled, nevertheless, with a strong hand. Instinctively distrustful of the aristocracy, he relied on a small group of bureaucrats, chief among them being his *protovestiarius* George Muzalon and George's two brothers, Theodore and Andronicus; and he enraged the clergy by appointing as Patriarch a bigoted ascetic named Arsenius, annihilating at a stroke his father's old dream of union with Rome.

Theodore signed a peace treaty with Bulgaria in 1256, and relations were further improved when the Tsar Michael Asen was murdered shortly afterwards and succeeded by a boyar named Constantine Tich, who married Theodore's daughter Irene. Another dynastic marriage was that of John's daughter Maria to Nicephorus, son of the Despot Michael II of Epirus. This unfortunately proved counter-productive, Theodore having unwisely made a last-minute demand for Durazzo and the Macedonian city of Servia as a condition of the marriage. The bridegroom's mother, who had accompanied her son to the imperial camp on the Maritsa, was intimidated into agreement; but when she returned to tell her husband that she had given away two of his most important cities, he immediately launched a furious campaign against Thessalonica, encouraging the Serbs and the Albanians to support him. Within days, Macedonia was up in arms.

The man best qualified to handle the situation was a young general named Michael Palaeologus; the Emperor, however, had always been jealous of this handsome young aristocrat, who seemed to possess all the gifts he himself lacked. He also mistrusted him. Earlier that year he had accused him – quite unjustifiably – of high treason, threatening him to the point where the young general had been obliged to take refuge with the Seljuks. Michael had since sworn fidelity to the Emperor; nevertheless Theodore had decided only hesitantly to entrust him with the new command. Fearing, presumably, that his general might turn against him, he also gave him too small an army to be of any real use. Michael and his men fought bravely, penetrating as far as Durazzo; but they were unable to stem the tide. By summer the Despot was at the gates of Thessalonica, and Michael Palaeologus, disgraced and shortly afterwards excommunicated, was languishing in a Nicaean prison. This shameful treatment of the Empire's outstanding general confirmed the people of Nicaea in their conviction that their *basileus* was no longer capable of responsible government; and there would surely have been a military revolt had not Theodore suddenly and conveniently succumbed to his disease in August 1258, aged thirty-six. His eldest son John being a child, he had appointed the hated George Muzalon as Regent. On his deathbed he had forced the leading members of the aristocracy to swear allegiance to John and George together, but in the course of a memorial service held nine days later they murdered Muzalon at the high altar and hacked the body to pieces. A palace revolution ensued, the result of which was to nominate the hastily-liberated Michael Palaeologus – who had probably instigated the plot – in his stead.

Michael, now thirty-four, was in many respects the obvious choice. He could claim kinship with the houses of Ducas, Angelus and Comnenus, while his wife Theodora was a great-niece of John Vatatzes. His complicity in Muzalon's murder should have been seen as a stain on his character; but the *protovestiarius* had been so hated that it was overlooked. He remained immensely popular with the army and was well thought of by the clergy. He was awarded the title of Grand Duke (*megas dux*) and soon afterwards that of Despot. Finally in November 1258 he was raised on a shield and proclaimed co-Emperor, his coronation taking place at Nicaea on Christmas Day. He and Theodora were crowned first, with imperial diadems heavy with jewels; only afterwards was a narrow string of pearls laid upon the head of his young colleague, John IV.

Few of the congregation doubted that it was Michael VIII Palaeologus who would lead his subjects back into their capital. First, however, there was one more enemy to be faced. Early in 1258 Manfred of Sicily, bastard son of Frederick II, had invaded Epirus and occupied Corfu. The Despot Michael had joined with him against Nicaea, offering him the hand of his eldest daughter Helena. Manfred had accepted and had sent his new father-in-law four hundred mounted knights from Germany. Soon afterwards the new alliance was joined by William of Villehardouin, the Latin Prince of Achaia, who married Michael's second daughter Anna. The ultimate object of the expedition was Constantinople, but this would clearly involve the capture of Thessalonica on the way.

Thus, at the time of the accession of Michael Palaeologus, virtually the whole of the Greek mainland was ranged against him. Fortunately he had dispatched a large expeditionary force to the Balkans, commanded by his brother, the *sebastocrator* John Palaeologus, and the Grand Domestic Alexius Strategopulus; and early in 1259 he ordered them to advance against the enemy. The two armies met at Pelagonia; and almost immediately the coalition fell apart. The Despot Michael and his son Nicephorus, wrongly suspecting that their allies were planning to betray them to the enemy, deserted the camp and fled. Another son, John the Bastard, taunted by Villehardouin over his illegitimacy, joined the Nicene forces out of pique. By the time the battle began John Palaeologus found only the cavalry of Villehardouin and Manfred ranged against him; and they proved defenceless in the face of his Cuman archers. Manfred's knights surrendered and were taken prisoner, as – subsequently – was Villehardouin himself, who was found hiding in a haystack near Castoria and was recognized only by his protruding teeth. John then advanced through Thessaly, while Alexius marched straight to Epirus and captured its capital, Arta. The victory was complete.

It was by now plain that the recapture of the city could only be a question of time, and a short time at that. Of all Baldwin's allies, there remained only the Papacy and Venice. Pope Alexander IV was uninterested; that left the Venetians, who had been largely responsible for the Latin Empire, and whose fleet of thirty ships still patrolled the Bosphorus. But soon the value of even Venetian support began to appear problematical, for on 13 March 1261 Michael Palaeologus, desperate for a navy, signed a treaty with Genoa whereby, in return for their help, the Genoese were promised all the concessions hitherto enjoyed by Venice, with their own quarter in Constantinople and the other principal ports of the Empire and free access to those of the Black Sea. For Genoa it was a historic agreement, laying as it did the foundations for her commercial empire in the East.

The recovery of Constantinople eventually came about almost by accident. In the summer of 1261, Michael VIII had sent Alexius Strategopulus to Thrace with a small army to indulge in a little mild sabre-rattling, sounding out the city's defences at the same time. At Selymbria, Alexius learned that the Latin garrison was absent, having been carried off by the Venetians to attack the Nicaean island of Daphnusia, a harbour controlling the entrance to the Bosphorus from the Black Sea. They also told him of a postern gate in the walls, through which a handful of men could easily pass into the city. The opportunity seemed too good to miss. That night a detachment slipped into the city, surprised the guards and threw them from the ramparts. They then quietly opened one of the gates. At dawn on 25 July 1261 the army poured in.

Baldwin, awakened by the tumult, fled for his life. Making his way on foot to the little harbour of the Bucoleon, he escaped on a Venetian merchantman to the Latin-held island of Euboea. Meanwhile Alexius and his men set fire to the entire Venetian quarter so that the sailors returning from Daphnusia, finding their houses destroyed and their terrified families huddled on the quayside, would have no real choice but to sail back to their lagoon. Among the remaining Franks – perhaps a thousand all told – there was widespread panic. Some hid; some fled to monasteries; a few even resorted to the sewers; but there was no massacre. Gradually they emerged from their various refuges and made their way down to the harbour where the thirty Venetian ships were waiting. These too sailed for Euboea – not, apparently, even pausing to take on provisions, since it is recorded that many of the refugees died of hunger before reaching their destination.

The Emperor Michael was two hundred miles away, asleep in his camp at Meteorium in Anatolia, when the messengers arrived. His sister Eulogia woke him and told him the news; but only when he was handed Baldwin's abandoned regalia did he believe her. Immediately he began his preparations; and on 15 August 1261 he made his entry into the capital. Entering by the Golden Gate and preceded by the great icon of the Virgin Hodegetria – 'She who points the way' – painted, as everyone knew, by St Luke himself, he proceeded on foot along the traditional route through the city as far as St Sophia, where a second coronation ceremony was performed by Patriarch Arsenius. This time, however, he and his wife were crowned alone, their baby son Andronicus being proclaimed as heir presumptive. As for John Lascaris, Michael's ten-year-old co-Emperor, he had been left behind in

Nicaea, ignored and forgotten. A little over four months later, on Christmas Day, his eyes were put out. It was, as it happened, his eleventh birthday.[1]

From the start, the Latin Empire of Constantinople had been a monstrosity. In the fifty-seven years of its existence it had achieved nothing, contributed nothing, enjoyed not a moment of distinction or glory. After 1204 it had made no territorial conquests, and before long it had shrunk to the immediate surroundings of the ruined and ravaged city. The only wonder is that it lasted as long as it did. Of its seven rulers, not one made the slightest attempt to understand his Greek subjects, let alone to learn their language. Meanwhile its knights trickled back to the West, its allies turned away, its treasury lay empty. And its fall was, if anything, even more ignominious than its beginning – overpowered by a handful of soldiers in a single night.

But the dark legacy that it left behind affected all Christendom – perhaps all the world. For the Greek Empire never recovered from the damage, spiritual as well as material, of those fateful years. Nor, with its loveliest buildings reduced to rubble and its finest works of art looted or destroyed, did it ever succeed in recovering its morale. Before the Latin conquest the Empire had been one and indivisible, under a single *basileus*, Equal of the Apostles. Now that unity was gone. There were the Emperors of Trebizond, still stubbornly independent on the Black Sea shore. There were the Despots of Epirus, always ready to welcome the enemies of Constantinople. How, fragmented as it was, could the Greek Empire continue as the last great eastern bulwark of Christendom against the Islamic tide?

But Christendom too was changed. Long divided, it was now polarized. For centuries before and after the Great Schism, the differences between the Churches had been essentially theological. After the sack of Constantinople this was no longer true. To the Byzantines the barbarians who had desecrated their altars, plundered their homes and violated their women could not be considered, in any real sense, Christians at all. Future attempts to force them into union could never succeed for long, simply because anything appeared to them preferable to the idea of submission to Rome. 'Better the Sultan's turban than the cardinal's hat,' they used to say; and they meant it.

---

1 He was confined in a fortress on the southern shore of the Marmara, where he remained until his death nearly half a century later.

24

The Angevin Threat

[1261–82]

The *basileus* was back in his capital. The bells of the city pealed in jubilation and every church held its service of thanksgiving. Michael Palaeologus, however, took no part in these festivities. His first sight of the city had affected him profoundly. Everywhere was desolation: churches in ruins, palaces razed, whole districts reduced to piles of blackened timber. Much of the debris still lay where it had fallen over half a century before. After his coronation he had quietly withdrawn to the old palace – Blachernae he felt to be tainted by the Latins – to ponder the problems that faced him.

The most immediate was defence. Much of Greece was still under Frankish domination; Epirus and Thessaly, though Greek, remained hostile, as did Serbia and Bulgaria. Venice and Genoa controlled Byzantine waters and much of the eastern Mediterranean. Pope Urban IV, a former Latin Patriarch of Jerusalem, refused to accept the collapse of the Crusader Empire; and Manfred, now back in Sicily, would welcome any excuse to return to the offensive. An alliance of some or all of these could kill the newly-restored Empire at its birth. Among the Emperor's priorities, therefore, was a thorough restoration of the land and sea walls, together with a renewal of the great iron chain across the Golden Horn. Meanwhile he had no alternative but to put his faith in the Genoese, his only Western allies, and to set to work on the rebuilding of the city. Living accommodation was a primary need, but Michael did not forget the ravaged churches and monasteries, realizing their vital importance to popular morale; the reawakening of his subjects' religious life simultaneously revived their feelings of patriotism and national pride – while ensuring ecclesiastical support for his policies. Finally he erected before the Church of the Holy Apostles a column bearing a statue of his patron, St Michael, with, at its foot, another statue representing himself, holding in his hands a model of Constantinople and offering it in the traditional manner to the Archangel.

As for Pope Urban, Michael had been right in his assessment. Of two envoys sent to the Holy See with notification of his accession, one, we are somewhat implausibly told, was flayed alive; the other barely escaped with his life. Urban, meanwhile – encouraged by Baldwin – was pressing for a new Crusade to recover Constantinople for the West. The Venetians were predictably giving him their fullest support; but elsewhere, to his disappointment, there was little enthusiasm. In France, St Louis sensibly maintained that the purpose of Crusades was to fight the infidel and not fellow-Christians. Germany had been in confusion ever since the death of Frederick II in 1250. Frederick's son Manfred would have asked nothing better; an alliance with Rome would almost certainly have achieved his long-desired papal recognition. But to Urban such an alliance was unthinkable. The King of Sicily, he knew, had ambitions of his own; and even if Baldwin were to be reinstated, the prospect of owing his return to Manfred was too ghastly to be contemplated.

Nothing was to be expected from the Genoese, whom the Pope had recently excommunicated for their support of the Eastern Empire. Their *rapprochement* with Constantinople, however, did not last long. In the summer of 1263, off the island of Spetsai, a mixed fleet of forty-eight imperial and Genoese ships encountered a Venetian force of thirty-two. The engagement ended in humiliation for the Genoese, whose fleet was ignominiously scattered. It was years before they were once again a force in the eastern Mediterranean; more important still, they surrendered the respect of Michael Palaeologus, who paid for their patrols and demanded better returns for his money. A few weeks later, Michael abruptly dismissed their remaining fleet of some sixty galleys and ordered it to return home.

He had other reasons, too, for dissatisfaction. The Genoese were now flooding into Constantinople in such numbers – and trading so aggressively – as to threaten the native merchant community; and they were becoming dangerously unpopular. In the following year a conspiracy was discovered on the part of the Genoese *podestà* in Constantinople, Guglielmo Guercio, to betray Constantinople to King Manfred of Sicily. Confronted by the Emperor with incontrovertible evidence, Guercio immediately confessed, whereupon all Genoese were banished from the city. Just three years after the Treaty of Nymphaeum, the Genoese alliance had ended in disaster.

More than ever now, Michael Palaeologus needed friends. Manfred had ignored him; King Louis was fully occupied with his own campaigns. There remained the Pope himself, whose hostility sprang not from personal animosity but simply from a natural desire to see Constantinople once again subject to Rome. On the other hand he would, as Michael well knew, infinitely prefer a heretic Greek Emperor on the Bosphorus to the King of Sicily. In the spring of 1263 a Greek named Nicholas, the Latin Bishop of Crotona in Calabria, left Constantinople for Rome with a letter to the Pope, hinting at the possibility of Church unity.

Urban rose to the bait. The Emperor's letter suggested fidelity and obedience; in such circumstances Manfred would have to renounce his dreams of Constantinople. The papal reply, addressed 'to Palaeologus, Illustrious Emperor of the Greeks', was drafted in almost unctuous terms. It too was entrusted to Bishop Nicholas; but on his return to Constantinople he was left in no doubt that the questions at issue could be decided only by a full council. He had no choice but to agree; but before such a council could be convened Urban died suddenly at Perugia, on 2 October 1264.

The chief preoccupation of Pope Urban during the last year of his life had been Manfred of Sicily. Their quarrel was not just a personal one: by now the age-old rivalry between the Papacy and the Western Empire – which, in the continuing interregnum, Manfred effectively represented – had cut a great rift across the Italian political scene, polarizing itself into two opposite camps: the Guelfs – who were, roughly speaking, the papal party – and the Ghibellines, who supported and were supported by the Hohenstaufen Emperors. Urban particularly resented Manfred's seizure in 1258 of the Kingdom of Sicily (the so-called *Regno*, which included much of south Italy and now had its capital at Naples) from his six-year-old nephew Conradin, thus bringing his dominions up to the southern frontier of the Papal State. The Regno was, by tradition, under papal suzerainty; and from the moment of Manfred's *coup* the Papacy had been seeking another, friendlier prince with whom to replace him. The choice had finally fallen on Charles, Count of Anjou and Provence, the younger brother of King Louis of France.

Charles was the very archetype of the younger son who cannot forgive fate for the accident of his birth. Cold and cruel, ambitious and self-seeking, he asked nothing better than to take over Manfred's kingdom in the papal name. The new Pope, Clement IV – another Frenchman – completed the arrangements; and at Whitsun 1265 Charles arrived in Rome. Against his army of thirty thousand Manfred stood little chance. On 26 February 1266, outside Benevento, he went down fighting. His wife and three young children were captured. Of the four, three never appeared again; one son was still in prison forty-three years later. Charles was not a man to take chances. In 1268 he proved it more conclusively still, when Conradin made a last attempt to save his family's inheritance. On 23 August Charles shattered his army at Tagliacozzo; Conradin himself was captured and beheaded in the market square of Naples. He was just sixteen, and the last of the Hohenstaufen.

Tagliacozzo marked the supplanting of the Germans by the French in south Italy. To Michael Palaeologus, watching developments from Constantinople, the change was distinctly unwelcome. Manfred had been trouble enough;

Charles, he strongly suspected, would be far worse – and events were soon to prove him right.

Charles started as he meant to continue. He had not been a year on the throne before he had acquired Corfu and part of the coast of Epirus; and in May 1267 he put his seal on two treaties which made his long-term intentions clearer still. The first provided for the marriage of Isabella, daughter of William of Achaia, to Charles's son Philip, and their inheritance of the principality on William's death. In the second, Charles undertook that, within seven years, he or his heirs would provide two thousand cavalry to replace Baldwin on his throne. In return, Baldwin would cede suzerainty over the principality of Achaia; most of the Aegean islands; one-third of the expected conquests excluding Constantinople; the Kingdom of Thessalonica under certain conditions; and, finally, the imperial throne itself in the event of Baldwin and his son Philip of Courtenay dying without legal heirs. Meanwhile Venice would regain all her former rights in the Empire and, to seal the new alliance, Philip would marry Charles's daughter Beatrice as soon as she reached marriageable age. It was an astonishing document. In return for the vague promise of insignificant reinforcements a long time in the future, it secured for Charles a small empire, allowing him to move against Constantinople equally easily by land and sea. No wonder Michael Palaeologus felt anxious.

Now more than ever, it was plain to him that he must improve his relations with the Papacy; Clement IV, however, categorically rejected a council since, as he put it, 'the purity of the faith could not be put in doubt'. Thus there could be no discussion of the *Filioque* clause, nor of any of the theological differences between the Churches. Instead, Clement sent the Emperor the text of a 'confession of faith', to be accepted unconditionally before any further progress could be made. His letter ended: '... we proclaim that neither are we wanting in justice towards those who complain of oppression by your Magnificence, nor shall we desist from pursuing this matter in other ways which the Lord may provide'. The implied threat was clear enough. Equally clear was the fact that in such circumstances union was out of the question. When Clement died in November 1268 the two sides were as far apart as ever they had been.

Even an uncooperative Pope, however, was better than no Pope at all. For the next three years Charles succeeded in keeping vacant the pontifical throne, thus enabling himself to act as he liked without any restraint from Rome. By now, fortunately, Michael had acquired two allies. At the end of 1267 he had signed a new agreement with Genoa, ceding to it the whole district of

Galata; then, in April of 1268, he signed another – with Venice, now gravely concerned at Charles's acquisition of Corfu and part of Epirus, from which he could blockade the entire Adriatic if he chose. The Venetians promised not to attack the Empire, and to withhold all help to its enemies; in return, the Emperor undertook to allow Venetian merchants freedom to reside, travel and trade throughout his dominions – although the Genoese would retain their existing rights. Henceforward there would be free competition between the two republics.

Meanwhile Charles of Anjou, freed of papal constraints, was preparing for war. Dockyards throughout the Regno were working overtime; food, money and troops were sent urgently to the Morea, which was to be the principal bridgehead of the expedition. Charles was also busy negotiating alliances with the princes of Europe and even with the Seljuk Sultan, the King of Armenia and the Mongol Khan; and in August 1269 he succeeded in concluding a commercial treaty with Genoa, thus confirming the furious Michael in his frequently-expressed opinion that the Genoese were not to be trusted. Against such forces, the future of Byzantium looked bleak indeed.

Henceforth the Emperor would have to rely on diplomacy. One last hope remained. As a devout Catholic and the elder brother of Charles of Anjou, King Louis would not normally have seemed a probable source of salvation; but he was preparing for another Crusade and could think of nothing else. Byzantine envoys hastened to Paris: the *basileus*, they explained, would willingly have joined the King's expedition, contributing a strong military contingent; unfortunately, he faced attack by His Majesty's brother – an eventuality which would prevent both parties from lending the Crusade the assistance it deserved. A second embassy in 1270 confirmed his readiness to return to the Roman obedience and, where his conflict with Charles was concerned, to submit himself unconditionally to Louis's personal decision.

The King replied at once. He would immediately inform the Curia, recommending the dispatch of a senior prelate to Constantinople. Soon afterwards the Bishop of Albano arrived on the Bosphorus with the Curia's conditions: the 'confession of faith' enclosed in Pope Clement's earlier letter was to be circulated for signature by all the leading churchmen of the Empire. Meanwhile a council was to be held in Constantinople at which that same confession would be read out and publicly accepted by Emperor, Patriarch, clergy and people. Michael, desperate, dispatched a third embassy to King Louis, who had by now departed for Tunis. The envoys arrived in early August, to find Louis gravely ill with typhoid fever; and on 25 August he died. They could only return home – just as Charles of Anjou was arriving with his navy.

Why, finding his brother dead, did Charles not renounce the Crusade and set off immediately for Constantinople? Probably the campaign was too far advanced; with excellent prospects of success, it would have been foolish not to have seen it through. Soon afterwards he inflicted an overwhelming defeat on the Emir of Tunis. Then he sailed to Sicily for the winter. His army and navy in full readiness, his morale boosted by a triumphant victory, Charles of Anjou had never been more dangerous, Michael Palaeologus never more threatened. Only a miracle, it seemed, could save him now.

And then that miracle happened. Scarcely had Charles reached Trapani than on 22 November there arose one of the worst storms ever to have struck western Sicily. All eighteen of his largest men-of-war were splintered to matchwood, together with innumerable smaller vessels. Men and horses, most of whom were still on board, perished by the thousand. Within a few hours, both army and navy were effectively destroyed. Michael Palaeologus wept when he heard the news. Once again the Blessed Virgin, Protectress of Constantinople, had saved the city.

By 1271, Western Christendom had been without a Pope for nearly three years, the longest interregnum in papal history; at last the *podestà* at Viterbo, where the conclave was being held, removed the roof from the palace in which the cardinals were assembled. This had the desired effect; and on 1 September Teobaldo Visconti, Archdeacon of Liège, was elected to the pontifical throne. The news was brought to him in Palestine, whither he had accompanied Prince Edward of England, soon to become King Edward I. He embarked on the first available ship, and on arrival in Rome took the name of Gregory X.

Gregory's journey to the East had left an indelible impression on him. He was determined to recover Jerusalem. But since this was clearly impossible without Byzantine help, Church union was also of primary importance. Thus, in October 1271, he sent Michael Palaeologus a personal invitation to a General Council of the Church, to be held at Lyon in two years' time. Understanding Michael's difficulties, he did not demand unequivocal submission. Recognition of papal primacy by the bishops would, he suggested, be quite enough. Michael replied at once, assuring the Pope that he himself was putting the question of union before all others. His representatives would certainly attend the forthcoming council. He asked only for safe-conduct: the King of Sicily was perfectly capable of liquidating the Byzantine delegation as it passed through his dominions, and then accusing him of not having sent one at all.

The Pope, understanding his misgivings, instructed the Abbot of Monte Cassino to meet the envoys on their arrival in the Regno and to escort them as far as Rome. Meanwhile he continued to impress upon Charles his moral duty to work towards the proposed union. The King pointed out that he himself was committed to launch his campaign before May 1274; but Gregory begged him to accept a year's postponement and Charles, whose fleet had still not recovered from the Trapani disaster, none too reluctantly agreed.

The journey of the Greek delegates to Lyon was not a pleasant one. Leaving Constantinople in March 1274, they soon ran into a storm, in the course of which one of their two vessels was wrecked, with the loss of all on board, and all the Emperor's presents to the Pope. Thus, by the time the three remaining envoys reached Lyon in late June, the council had already been in session for seven weeks. It numbered all the leading ecclesiastics of Western Christendom, including the entire College of Cardinals – a total congregation of some fifteen hundred. On 24 June the envoys were escorted to the papal palace, where the Pope gave them the kiss of peace and they presented their letters. There were no discussions. Five days later Gregory presided at a special bilingual Mass to celebrate the forthcoming union, the Byzantines actively participating: gospel, epistle and creed were chanted in both Latin and Greek, including three somewhat pointed repetitions of the *Filioque*. Finally, on 6 July, the union was formally declared. The Emperor's letter was read in Latin translation. It included the 'confession of faith' – with the *Filioque* – and acknowledged papal primacy, asking only that the Byzantine Church might retain its creed (which pre-dated the schism) and such rites as did not conflict with the findings of the Ecumenical Councils. The Grand Logothete George Acropolites then took the oath in the Emperor's name. For the first time in 220 years, the Eastern and Western Churches were in communion one with the other.

Or so at least it seemed. Only with the return of the imperial envoys did Michael's subjects begin to understand the full significance of what had occurred. Papal primacy was bad enough; but the betrayal – for to many of them it was nothing less – went deeper. By what right had the Emperor attacked the very cornerstone of their religion, the creed itself? In riding roughshod over the canon law, he had grievously offended the Blessed Virgin, under whose special protection their city lay. What new tribulations must they now expect? For centuries they had despised the West as being not only heretical but also crude and boorish; and the fifty-seven-year occupation of their city had given them no reason to change their opinions. Now, after only thirteen years of freedom, they were harnessed once again to the Frankish yoke. Soon the demonstrators were on the streets; and feeling ran yet higher when the well-known unionist John Beccus was appointed Patriarch.

Had Michael Palaeologus for once misjudged the temper of his subjects?

Perhaps, to some degree. He could not, he believed, have acted otherwise than he did: union with Rome, by depriving the King of Sicily and the titular Latin Emperor, Philip of Courtenay – who had succeeded his father Baldwin in 1273 – of any moral justification for acting against it, had temporarily saved the Greek Empire; it legitimized Michael's claim to Constantinople in the eyes of the West; it even eliminated papal opposition to his programme for clearing the last few Latins from the Balkan peninsula. But the cost had been heavy indeed.

Long before the imperial envoys had reached Lyon, their master's latest campaign in the Balkans had begun; his troops had occupied Butrinto, driving the Angevin army back to the Adriatic. King Charles, fully occupied in Italy and Sicily, was obliged to accept severe losses in both men and territory. The following year the Emperor's brother, the Despot John Palaeologus, besieged John the Bastard in his castle of Neopatras; but the Bastard had been in tight corners before. One night he lowered himself by rope from the walls and passed unsuspected through the Byzantine camp. Three days later he reached Thebes whence, hurrying back with three hundred horsemen, he attacked the imperial army from behind. The Despot tried hard to rally his men, but panic seized them and they fled. A few months later he had his revenge; another battle near Demetrias on the Gulf of Volos resulted in the capture of nearly all the Frankish leaders. For Michael Palaeologus, that victory far outweighed the earlier defeat. For the Despot John, however, not even this triumph could atone for the humiliation of Neopatras. Once back in Constantinople, he immediately resigned his command.

On 10 January 1276 Pope Gregory died at Arezzo; and though his successor Innocent V was to maintain close contacts with Byzantium he was a good deal less eager for a Crusade. Innocent was, moreover, another Frenchman; and his election had been a triumph for Charles of Anjou, who had intrigued shamelessly on his behalf. But the Pope died in his turn after a pontificate of five months; his successor, Adrian V, after only five weeks; while Adrian's successor John XXI lasted just seven months before the ceiling of his new study fell on him and crushed him to death. Only in November 1277 did the Cardinals, after sitting for six months in their fourth conclave in a year and a half, finally succeed in defying Charles's machinations by electing a Pope capable of making a lasting mark.

Giovanni Gaetani Orsini, who took the name of Nicholas III, was a member of one of Rome's oldest and most powerful families. He had little patience with Charles's persistent interference in papal affairs, still less with his imperialist claims. For years Charles had used his title of Senator of Rome to sway papal elections, just as he had used the Imperial Vicariate of Tuscany to further his ambitions in the peninsula. Within weeks of his election, the new Pope had stripped him of both offices. He also absolutely forbade him to attack Constantinople. East and West were to him two opposing forces, the Papacy holding the balance between them. Michael had the satisfaction of seeing his enemy humbled, his Empire no longer under threat.

Pope Nicholas might have saved Byzantium; but he still had uneasy suspicions of the Eastern Church, and still needed proof that union was complete. Unfortunately he possessed little of Gregory X's patience and none of his diplomatic finesse. In the spring of 1279 he sent a new embassy to the Emperor, with a whole series of categorical demands. He specifically refused the Emperor's earlier requests that the Greeks should be allowed to preserve their ancient rites dating from before the schism: 'unity of faith,' he wrote, 'does not permit diversity in its confessors or in confession.' Finally, he announced his intention of appointing a cardinal-legate with a permanent residence in Constantinople.

Michael's whole position where Rome was concerned was becoming intolerable. His own Church made no secret of its anger, and he knew that he could press it no further. He could only try once again to temporize. Summoning all the senior churchmen to the palace, he spoke to them more frankly than ever before:

I am aware that I have used force against many of you and have offended many friends, including members of my own family ... I believed that the affair would be ended and that the Latins would demand nothing more ... but they are now demanding further proof of union.

As God is my witness, I shall not alter one accent, one iota of our faith. I promise to uphold the divine Creed of our fathers. If I receive the envoys cordially it will do you no harm. I believe that we should treat them kindly, lest we create new problems for ourselves.

His words had their effect. The Greek prelates listened to the envoys in silence and managed somehow to remain polite. But they refused adamantly to swear the required oaths. There was no more to be done. The envoys may or may not have been persuaded of the good faith of Michael and his son Andronicus; but with regard to the body of the Greek Church they can have only been confirmed in their previous suspicions. In Byzantine hearts, the schism still ruled as strongly as ever.

Pope Nicholas III had been no more successful in reconciling Charles of Anjou. His repeated efforts to make peace between the two rivals had been ignored by both of them – Charles because he still coveted Constantinople, and Michael because a treaty might have tied his hands in the Balkans, where his war against the princes of Achaia, Epirus and Thessaly was now yielding rich rewards. William of Achaia had died on 1 May 1278, a year after the death of his heir Philip of Anjou. Thus, by the terms of the Treaty of Viterbo, Charles himself had inherited the principality and with it the overlordship of all Eastern Europe still in Latin hands. The rapacity and corruption of his governors soon brought the local populations into a state of open revolt: and the imperial troops were able to continue the reconquest of the Morea even faster than before.

Charles hardly bothered. The death of Nicholas III in August 1280 had meant the end of the papal ban; and he was at last preparing his long-delayed attack on Constantinople. The Peloponnesian ports and harbours would have been useful in a naval expedition against the Empire; but his lack of an adequate fleet made this impossible. The attack would have to be made by land. In the autumn of 1280, an army of some eight thousand, including two thousand cavalry and a large force of Saracen archers, moved eastwards across Albania to the Byzantine fortress of Berat.

The town possessed a strong and well-equipped garrison; but the local commander sent messengers to Constantinople with an urgent appeal for reinforcements. They found Michael Palaeologus deeply worried. Tempers were still running high over ecclesiastical unity; many of his enemies might see in the Angevin expedition a means of getting rid of him once and for all. If Berat fell, Charles would be in Thessalonica in weeks; and what then would be the prospects for Constantinople? Entrusting his nephew Michael Tarchaneiotes with all the finest troops he could muster, he ordered a night-long vigil throughout the city. For that night at least, Church unity was forgotten: it was the old Byzantine liturgy that echoed from a hundred churches as the people prayed for their Empire.

The siege of Berat continued throughout the winter, until in March 1281 Tarchaneiotes appeared with his army. A pitched battle followed a day or two later. The heavily-armoured Latin cavalry were well protected from the imperial archers; but their horses were brought down one after the other, and by evening the greater part of the Angevin army had been killed or captured. For Michael Palaeologus, the victory was the greatest since the recovery of Constantinople. As a direct result, he was now in control of the whole interior of Albania and northern Epirus. To Charles of Anjou, on the other hand, the events of those few fateful hours brought humiliation and the indefinite postponement of his long-held dream of an empire in the East. But that dream was by no means abandoned. Despite his losses his situation was far from hopeless, and had been greatly improved by the papal election in

February 1281 of another Frenchman, who took the name of Martin IV. A fervent patriot who distrusted all Italians, Martin made no secret of his determination to submit the Papacy to the interests of France. Charles could henceforth pursue his expansionist policies unhindered.

His first objective was Venice, Berat having taught him that any new expedition must be sea-borne. Recent attempts by Charles to woo the Republic had always come to nothing, but by 1281 the Serenissima was ready to make her volte-face. The treaty signed on 3 July at Orvieto provided for a sea-borne expedition against Constantinople, in which all three sovereigns – Charles (or his eldest son), the 'Emperor' Philip of Courtenay and Doge Giovanni Dandolo – would participate in person, setting out in the spring of 1283. Just three months later, on 18 October, the Pope pronounced sentence of excommunication on the Byzantine Emperor.

Michael was outraged. No *basileus* had ever done so much for the Papacy. Now, instead of rewarding him, that same Church had put him under its ban, undoing the work of twenty years and leaving him naked to his enemies. He did not even now renounce the union; but he suspended all measures to impose the Latin rite and made every effort to restore good relations with the Greek Church. He would be needing its support more than ever in the trials to come.

Charles of Anjou was now the most powerful sovereign in Europe. Apart from his own Kingdoms of Sicily (which included all south Italy) and Albania, he was ruler of Achaia, Provence, Forcalquier, Anjou and Maine, overlord of Tunis and (once again) Senator of Rome. The King of France was his nephew, the King of Hungary and the titular Emperor of Constantinople his sons-in-law. He had treaties of alliance with Serbia, Bulgaria, the Greek Princes of Epirus and the Republic of Venice. The Pope was his puppet. He was now building three hundred ships in Naples, Provence and his Adriatic ports, while another hundred had been ordered from Sicily – a fleet massive enough to carry some twenty-seven thousand mounted knights and all the equipment necessary for the most ambitious campaign of his career.

Against him stood Michael Palaeologus, the Republic of Genoa and Peter III of Aragon, who, as son-in-law of Manfred, claimed to be the legitimate heir of the Hohenstaufen. His envoys had twice paid secret visits to Michael, continuing on each occasion to Sicily with quantities of Byzantine gold to fan the flames of discontent. Charles had always been hated in Sicily, bled white by his crippling taxation. By Easter 1282, with his vast armada lying at anchor at Messina while his bailiffs toured the island, requisitioning without compensation grain, fodder, horses, cattle and pigs to sustain the army on its long journey, anti-Angevin feeling was near flash-point. The fatal spark was lit on Easter Monday outside the Church of Santo Spirito in Palermo. The usual crowd thronged the square, awaiting the bell for evening Mass. Suddenly a group of drunken Angevin soldiers appeared and one of them began importuning a young Sicilian woman, whereupon her husband fell upon him and stabbed him to death. His friends, dashing forward to avenge him, were surrounded and quickly dispatched. And so, as the bells pealed for vespers, the people of Palermo ran through the city, calling on their fellow-citizens to rise against their oppressors. The following morning not a Frenchman was left alive in Palermo. By the end of April the revolt had reached Messina, where the seventy Angevin vessels in the harbour were set on fire. A furious Charles laid siege to the city; but on 30 August Peter of Aragon landed at Trapani and on 2 September entered Palermo, where he was proclaimed King. A fortnight later his ambassadors presented themselves at the Angevin camp outside Messina.

For Charles the situation was now desperate. His only sensible course was to return to the mainland while he could, reassemble his troops and plan a new invasion the following year. He told the ambassadors that, while he naturally rejected their master's claims to the island, he was prepared to make a temporary withdrawal. The evacuation continued at increasing speed as the Aragonese army approached; and on 2 October the Messinians opened their gates to their new King.

For Michael Palaeologus and his subjects, the almost miraculous war of the Sicilian Vespers was further proof that the Almighty was on their side; but Michael's anxieties were not over. The Turks were increasing their pressure; and no sooner had he returned from Anatolia than he was obliged to launch another expedition against John the Bastard – of which he ill-advisedly took personal command. He was now in his fifty-ninth year, and his exertions had taken their toll. By the time he reached the little Thracian village of Pachomios he could go no further. He died on Friday, 11 December 1282, proclaiming Andronicus, his son and co-Emperor, as his successor.

Andronicus had no delusions as to the late Emperor's unpopularity in the capital. On his orders his father's body was taken to a distant place, where it was covered with earth to protect it from wild animals. There was no grave, no ceremony. Since Michael had never formally renounced the Roman faith, in Orthodox eyes he had died a heretic; there could anyway be no question of a state funeral, and if the Church was resolved to refuse him a Christian burial, it would surely be better to deny it the opportunity. Years later, the remains were transferred to a nearby monastery; but the Emperor in whose reign Constantinople had been reconquered, and who had saved his Empire from almost certain annihilation, was rewarded by a posthumous sentence of exile and never returned, in life or in death, to his capital.

Michael Palaeologus is principally remembered today for the recovery of the capital, for which he deserves little of the credit. But then he was never really a soldier-Emperor; he was above all a diplomat, perhaps the most brilliant that Byzantium ever produced. To preserve the security of his Empire he was ready to make any sacrifice – even that of his Church; yet when he died he left the Empire safer than at any time for a century and the Church as free as it had ever been. It could be argued that he was lucky; but so are most great men, and Michael Palaeologus was a great Emperor. Like all great men, he also had his faults. He was devious and duplicitous; and when roused he could be pitiless and cruel. His treatment of the child-Emperor John Lascaris shocked all his contemporaries, including his own family. Yet few could have guided the Empire with so sure a hand through one of the most dangerous periods in all its history. Lucky he may have been; but his people, in having him when they needed him most, were luckier still.

Their immediate posterity was less fortunate. Economically, Michael left the Empire on the verge of bankruptcy; militarily, his continued preoccupation with Europe allowed the Turks and Mongols a free rein. He himself would have maintained that he could not fight simultaneously on two fronts and that the western represented the more immediate danger. But to most thinking Byzantines it was clear that the forces of Islam were a still more formidable enemy than the King of Anjou. If the capital had remained at Nicaea, the Byzantine presence in western Asia Minor would have held the balance; the return to Constantinople proved, in this respect, little short of disastrous.

There was nothing new in all this. Byzantium had always had to look in both directions, and every *basileus* worthy of his salt had found himself obliged to concentrate on one or the other. Michael could hardly have acted otherwise than he did. If there is blame to be apportioned, we must look elsewhere: to the nations of the West – and above all to the Greek princelings of the Balkan peninsula, so blinded by their own ambition that they could not see the threat, not just to themselves but to all Christendom, from which a strong and united Byzantium might yet have saved them.

25

The Two Andronici

[1282–1341]

The Emperor Andronicus II returned to Constantinople determined to proclaim once again the full independence of Orthodoxy. Although as co-Emperor he had been obliged to support his father's policies, he had always hated them. He could never forget that Michael had died under the ban of the Church, and was determined not to suffer the same fate; no sooner was he back in the capital than he made formal recantation of his earlier oaths of loyalty to Rome. The Patriarch John Beccus, the principal champion of unity, was stripped of his office; the former Patriarch Joseph, now in the last stages of decrepitude, was brought back on a stretcher and ceremonially reinstalled. But he did not last long; and after a longish interregnum Andronicus managed to secure the election of a former hermit from Mount Athos named Athanasius. To the pious Emperor, the new Patriarch's asceticism seemed just what was needed to divert the Church from political issues; to the ecclesiastics, on the other hand, the man was an unwashed fanatic in a hair shirt who seemed interested only in castigating them for their worldliness and wealth. In the summer of 1293 a delegation of leading churchmen demanded his removal, and in October Athanasius resigned – though not before pronouncing a formal anathema on his enemies.

In the following year the widowed Emperor took as his second wife the eleven-year-old Yolanda, daughter of William V, Marquis of Montferrat. William had therefore styled himself King of Thessalonica, a title which dated back to the Fourth Crusade but which he now surrendered to Andronicus: there must no longer be any ambiguity over the second city in the Empire. Andronicus knew too that if Thessalonica were attacked, he would be unable to come to its rescue; for he had decided to pare his armed forces to the bone.

With his Asiatic dominions shrinking almost daily, it seems hard to believe that he could have acted as he did. Byzantium had long relied on foreign mercenaries; Andronicus's mistake was to reduce these to almost suicidally low levels, disbanding the seasoned regiments in favour of groups of wanderers and refugees whose cheapness was no substitute for discipline or experience. The navy he abolished altogether – to the delight of the Genoese, who could now demand a far higher price for their support. Meanwhile the Turks, having reached the Mediterranean, had begun to build up a navy of their own and welcomed the expert guidance of the thousands of penniless sailors who now applied to them for employment.

The Turks were no longer the unified fighting force that they had been during the Seljuk heyday. The Sultan's defeat by the Mongols in 1243 had effectively put an end to his power in Anatolia; meanwhile a number of Turkish tribes, fleeing before the Mongol advance, had finally settled in the no-man's-land along the Byzantine frontier, whence they made regular incursions into imperial territory. These raids they soon began to justify as a form of the Islamic *jihad*, or Holy War against the infidel; and from there it was but a short step to see themselves as Ghazis, or Warriors of the Faith. By the first years of the fourteenth century only a few major Byzantine strongholds – Nicaea and Nicomedia, Sardis and Brusa, Philadelphia and Magnesia – and a few isolated ports like Ania and Heraclea on the Black Sea still held out; with these exceptions, all Anatolia had been engulfed in the Turkish tide.

In the West, too, the situation was deteriorating fast. Constantinople had rejoiced when Charles of Anjou had died in 1285, leaving the throne to his son Charles II; but the young King soon showed himself no friendlier than his father. In 1291 – the year of the fall of Acre, the last Crusader Kingdom of Outremer – he proposed an alliance with Nicephorus of Epirus, to be cemented by the marriage of the latter's daughter Thamar with his own son Philip; the groom was made overlord of all Charles's Greek possessions, with the title of Prince of Taranto. This second Angevin threat to Constantinople, still no bigger than a man's hand, was already unmistakable.

Meanwhile in Serbia a new ruler, Stephen Miliutin, had succeeded in 1282 under the name of Stephen Urosh II; he had declared his support for the Angevins, allied himself with Epirus, declared war on the Empire and made his capital at Skoplje, a strategic strong-point commanding the road south to Thessalonica and northern Greece. He had also gone through a form of marriage with a daughter of John Ducas of Thessaly. A Serbian–Thessalian alliance would threaten not only Thessalonica itself but the whole route across the Balkan peninsula to the Adriatic. In 1297 Andronicus decided on a diplomatic solution. Hearing that Miliutin's only legal wife (though he kept two full-time concubines, to say nothing of the Thessalian princess) had recently died, he proposed that she should be replaced by Simonis, his daughter by Yolanda. True, the girl was only five years old, her husband-to-be about forty; but the sacrifice had to be made. At Easter 1299 Andronicus personally escorted Simonis to Thessalonica, where her bridegroom was waiting.

For Byzantium the turn of the century was a time of unrelieved trouble, with Andronicus clearly incapable of halting the accelerating decline. Moreover, Constantinople had also become one of the principal battlefields on which Genoa and Venice settled their differences. In July 1296 a Venetian fleet sailed up to the mouth of the Bosphorus and made a vicious attack on the Genoese colony at Galata; when the imperial garrison intervened, the Venetians turned their fire on the city itself, burning all the Greek houses within range. In December the Genoese launched a counter-attack, destroying the principal Venetian buildings and massacring all the leading Venetians in the city. The following summer another Venetian fleet appeared, bearing a personal dispatch from the Doge. In it he accused the Emperor of encouraging the Genoese in their behaviour, held him responsible for the damage and demanded compensation. The fleet swept into the Golden Horn and set fire to one of the Emperor's galleys; it then returned, with a host of Genoese prisoners, to Venice.

In 1299 Venice and Genoa signed a separate peace; the Venetians, however, still insisted on their compensation and in the summer of 1302 raided Constantinople for the third time in seven years. Once again they entered the Golden Horn, setting fire to all Byzantine buildings in range; next they occupied the island of Prinkipo in the Marmara, then being used as a camp for Anatolian refugees, whom they now threatened to massacre if the Emperor did not pay them what he owed. Andronicus gave in, agreeing also to a ten-year treaty confirming all Venetian privileges in Constantinople.

That year of 1302 was an *annus horribilis* for Byzantium. In the early spring the Emperor's son and co-Emperor Michael IX had been defeated by the Turks near Magnesia and had narrowly escaped with his life. Next there had been the Venetian raid; and then, only a few weeks later on 27 July, just outside Nicomedia, a Byzantine force encountered a Turkish army more than twice its size, commanded by a local Ghazi Emir named Othman. The battle that followed was not particularly bloody; but Othman's way was now clear. He and his men surged southwestward along the Marmara until they reached the Aegean. Such is the first appearance in history of the man who, having begun his career as ruler of one of the smallest of the Ghazi emirates of Anatolia, lived to establish the dynasty which was to give its name to the Ottoman Empire. And it was in that same year of 1302 that Andronicus Palaeologus received a communication from Roger de Flor, leader of the Grand Company of Catalans.

The Grand Company was, in essence, a band of professional Spanish mercenaries – mostly but not exclusively from Catalonia – recruited in 1281 by Peter of Aragon for use in his North African and Sicilian campaigns. Roger de Flor is said to have been the son of Richard von der Blume, the German falconer of Frederick II. At the age of eight he had joined a Templar galley; later he had become a remarkably successful pirate, after which he offered his services to Peter's son Frederick, who immediately appointed him admiral. Roger soon proved as courageous a fighter on land as at sea, and quickly acquired a loyal following. So the Catalan Company was born.

Towards the end of 1302, Roger sent two envoys to Andronicus, offering his Company's services for nine months. In return his men were to be paid double the usual rate; he himself was to be appointed *megas dux* – at that time fifth in the whole Byzantine hierarchy – and to receive the hand in marriage of the Emperor's sixteen-year-old niece Maria. Andronicus rather surprisingly accepted; and in September 1302 the Catalan fleet sailed into the Golden Horn, carrying not only two and a half thousand fighting men – more than half of them cavalry – but also (to the Emperor's mild consternation) their wives, mistresses and children: a total of nearly seven thousand. Shortly afterwards Roger married his bride, and a few days later the entire Company crossed the Marmara to Cyzicus, at that very moment under siege by the Turks.

Now at last the Catalans proved their worth. By the spring of 1303 the Turks were everywhere in retreat. But Andronicus had unleashed forces which he could not control. The Catalans took their own decisions; when there was any plunder they kept it for themselves. Their overbearing arrogance caused constant disaffection among their allies; and by the time they reached the headquarters of the co-Emperor Michael IX at Pegae they had aroused such hostility that he closed the gates against them. But for Pegae they cared little; their eyes were on Philadelphia, which was under siege by the Karaman Turks. Despite a forced march of some 120 miles, the Catalans attacked at dawn the day after their arrival. By noon, some eighteen thousand Turks lay dead on the field; the remainder, including the Emir, had fled.

In less than two years the former pirate had become a member of the imperial family, had scored decisive victories over both the Ottomans and the Karamans and had secured much of south-western Asia Minor. There was little thought in his mind of fighting selflessly for Byzantium: the experience of the past few months had awoken hopes of an independent kingdom of his own, and at the beginning of 1304 he embarked on an ambitious expedition to the East. By the middle of August he and his men were besieging Magnesia when an urgent message reached them from the Emperor:

Theodore Svetoslav, the usurper who had united most of Bulgaria under his rule, had invaded Thrace and was already threatening Constantinople. Only with Catalan assistance could Andronicus hope to save his capital. Here was an appeal that could not be ignored: Magnesia must be left till later. Marching at full speed to the Hellespont, Roger de Flor led his men across the straits and pitched his camp in Gallipoli. At this point word came from the co-Emperor Michael that the Catalans were not after all required. No explanation was offered of how the Bulgar crisis had been settled so suddenly and with such apparent ease. Was the whole thing a trick to bring them back where the Byzantines could keep a proper eye on them?

It was fortunate at any rate for Roger that he was within reach of Constantinople when, early in 1305, nine Spanish galleys appeared in the Golden Horn, commanded by a certain Berenguer d'Entença, one of his old comrades-in-arms. The purpose of his visit remains a mystery; but he was warmly welcomed and was soon afterwards himself awarded the title of *megas dux*, Roger being simultaneously promoted to the rank of Caesar. This latter honour was admittedly deserved: but it was also intended as a palliative. Andronicus doubtless realized that his unnecessary recall of his allies at the time of the Bulgar scare had dangerously antagonized them. Moreover the Company had by now been a full year without pay – the imperial coffers were as usual empty – and its two commanders were adopting an increasingly threatening tone. Berenguer in particular made no secret of his indignation; he returned the gold and silver dinner service on which his meals had been provided, boarded his flagship and set sail for the Catalan camp at Gallipoli, ostentatiously hurling his ducal regalia overboard in full sight of the palace.

At last agreement was reached – though only after Andronicus had granted Roger's demand for the whole of Byzantine Anatolia in fief – and the Catalans began to prepare for their return to Asia. Before leaving for his new domains, however, Roger decided to make a formal visit to Michael IX at Adrianople. His pregnant wife Maria and her mother both implored him not to do so, but he ignored them and set off on 23 March 1305, with an escort of three hundred cavalry and a thousand infantry, for Michael's headquarters. He remained in Adrianople for over a week; then, on the eve of his departure for Gallipoli, he and his officers attended a farewell banquet given by Michael in his honour. Just as it was ending the doors were flung open and a fully-armed company of Alan mercenaries burst into the hall. The Catalans – unarmed, outnumbered and almost certainly drunk – stood no chance. Roger was killed with the rest. As soon as the report reached the camp at Gallipoli, the move to Asia stopped; those who had already crossed were summoned back, and the peninsula was declared Spanish territory. The Company then marched across Thrace taking a terrible vengeance. Michael IX did his utmost to check it, but his army was smashed near Rhaedestum and he himself was lucky to escape alive.

In the summer of 1308 the Catalans turned west towards Thessalonica, destroying countless towns and villages and even pillaging the monasteries of Mount Athos before descending into Thessaly and Boeotia, where they took service with Walter of Brienne, the French Duke of Athens. But Walter soon found, as the Byzantines had found, that the Catalans were easier to hire than to dismiss. On 15 March 1311 they annihilated him and his army; they then advanced to Athens, where they set up their own Duchy. It was to last another seventy-seven years. In less than a decade they had done the Empire almost as much harm as the Turks had done in a century, and had been paid by the Emperor to do it. Had they kept to the terms of their agreement, they might have turned back the Islamic tide and changed the whole future history of the Levant. Instead, almost exactly a century after the Fourth Crusade, they dealt the Empire that they had come to save yet another paralysing blow.

The Catalans were not the only problem with which Andronicus Palaeologus had to deal. To the west, Theodore Svetoslav continued to threaten – until Andronicus conceded to him the Black Sea ports that he had already occupied, together with the hand of Michael IX's daughter Theodora; and Charles II's son Philip of Taranto captured Durazzo. To the east the Turks continued their advance. In 1304 the tribe of Aydin took Ephesus; in 1307 Othman cut the line of communication between Nicomedia and Nicaea; and in 1308, by their capture of Iconium, the Karamans finally destroyed the long-moribund Seljuk Sultanate. In 1309 the island of Rhodes fell to the Knights of St John. With every day that passed, it seemed, the Empire was further diminished.

In 1310 Andronicus was faced with a new enemy – his own wife Irene, the former Yolanda of Montferrat. His eleven-year-old bride had turned into a formidably ambitious woman, and relations between the two had long been tense. The crisis came when Irene proposed that on her husband's death the Empire should not pass to Michael IX alone but should be divided among all his four sons – the younger three being of course her own. Andronicus refused, whereupon the Empress left with her three boys for Thessalonica which, besides being her childhood home, was closer to her daughter Simonis, now sixteen, at the Bulgar court. There she remained for the next seven years, constantly intriguing against her husband.

Another resident of Thessalonica was the co-Emperor Michael. Though still in his middle thirties, he was already disillusioned, having spent much of his life on campaign and losing every major battle he ever fought. Early in 1311 he had led an army against a huge band of Turkish freebooters in Thrace, with the usual catastrophic result. After this he had been relieved of his military command and had retired into private life. He had four children – the eldest of whom, Andronicus, was crowned co-Emperor at the age of nineteen in February 1316. There were now three Emperors sharing the throne, and the succession should have been assured for at least two generations. Young Andronicus, however, soon began to show signs of dangerous instability. He drank, he gambled and he was notoriously fond of women. In 1320, suspecting one of his mistresses of infidelity, he carefully laid an ambush for his unknown rival near her house. Whether that rival really was his own brother Manuel or whether Manuel just chanced to be passing is not certain; in any case he was set upon and killed. For Michael IX the shock was more than he could bear. He died on 12 October at Thessalonica. Andronicus furiously disowned his grandson and named his own younger son Constantine as heir to the throne of Byzantium. The result was civil war.

The Emperor was now sixty. He was fortunate to have as his chief adviser the scholar Theodore Metochites, who served him devotedly until the end of his reign; but the decline continued. Thrace was devastated, Asia Minor virtually lost. Taxes were constantly increased; the revenue was spent, however, not on rearmament but on protection money to the Catalans and Turks. No wonder that when young Andronicus III raised the flag of rebellion in Adrianople, there were many in the capital who rallied to his support.

At the young Emperor's right hand was John Cantacuzenus, one of the leading members of the military aristocracy. Though he was a year or two older than Andronicus, they had been close friends since childhood; and he was to dominate the Byzantine political scene for much of the century. Second only to him among the supporters of Andronicus III was a certain Syrgiannes Palaeologus. A minor member of the imperial family through his mother, he was to prove an unreliable ally; he and John, however, had both bought governorships for themselves in Thrace – the sale of offices was not the least of the abuses that had grown up under the Palaeologi – where they had immediately set to work fanning the flames of dissatisfaction among the local populace. At Easter 1321 the young Emperor joined them. Syrgiannes then marched on the capital where old Andronicus soon came to terms; and in July 1322 grandfather and grandson agreed to rule jointly, while Andronicus III was reconfirmed as sole heir.

The peace lasted a full five years, in the course of which the Ottoman Turks captured Brusa after a seven-year siege and made it their capital. But in 1327 civil war broke out again. On this occasion the two Emperors did not fight alone. Stephen Dechanski of Serbia declared his support for Andronicus II, while the Bulgar Tsar Michael Sisman – who had married Andronicus III's sister Theodora – was only too happy to conclude an alliance with his new brother-in-law. As before, there was little serious fighting; young Andronicus, however, was hailed wherever he appeared. In January 1328 he went with John Cantacuzenus to Thessalonica, where he was given a magnificent reception as *basileus*. Meanwhile, quietly and unhurriedly, he was making his preparations to march on the capital.

On the evening of 23 May 1328 he and John Cantacuzenus, followed by twenty-four men with siege ladders, crept up to the section of the great bastion opposite the Romanus Gate. Ropes were lowered by accomplices within, ladders were hoisted, and within minutes the first of the young Emperor's men were over the wall, opening the gate for their comrades. There was little looting; no one was hurt. Once old Andronicus had signed a deed of abdication he was allowed to keep his imperial title and his palace at Blachernae. Meanwhile a delegation was sent to free the Patriarch, Esaias by name, who in the previous year had been confined to the monastery of the Mangana. On his way back to his palace, we are told, he was escorted not by the usual ecclesiastics but by a troupe of musicians, dancing girls and comedians, one of whom had him so helpless with laughter that he almost fell off his horse.

The only serious sufferer was Theodore Metochites, who was universally blamed for all his master's failures. Much of his property was confiscated; his house was plundered and burnt. Initially exiled, he was later permitted to return to the monastery of St Saviour in Chora, which he had restored and embellished at his own expense some years before.[1] There he lived out his last years, dying in March 1332. He outlived Andronicus II by a month. The old Emperor remained in Constantinople for two years; then he too was packed off to a monastery, where he died on 13 February. He had reigned for almost exactly half a century. Had he possessed half the diplomatic skills of his father, the courage of his son or the energy of his grandson he might have arrested the Empire's decline. Instead, he had allowed it to drift from one catastrophe to the next until his grandson removed him.

---

1 The church of the Chora – more generally known today as Kariye Camii – still stands. Thanks to its dazzling mosaics and superb frescos, a visit there is one of the most memorable experiences that even Istanbul has to offer. The mosaics include a splendid representation of Theodore himself, offering his church to Christ; while the fresco of the *Anastasis*, or Harrowing of Hell, in the apse of the side chapel is perhaps the supreme masterpiece of all Christian art.

Andronicus III was now thirty-one. Though liable to sudden bouts of irresponsibility, he was to prove himself a fearless soldier and, normally, a conscientious ruler. He was certainly an immense improvement on his grandfather. Above all he was fortunate in having at his side John Cantacuzenus. Just as he had been the guiding force behind the rebellion, John now directed the affairs of the Empire. He held no titular office of state except that of Grand Domestic, or commander-in-chief; but few had any doubts as to where the real power lay.

On the international stage, the year 1331 brought palace revolutions to both the Slav states. The two new rulers – John Alexander in Bulgaria and Stephen Dushan in Serbia – then formed an alliance, which they cemented by a marriage between Stephen Dushan and John Alexander's sister Helena; together they then began to work towards the realization of their common dream – the overthrow of the *basileus* and the establishment of a great Slav Empire in Constantinople. As a result, a large part of Macedonia was soon lost for ever. In Asia Minor too the situation was grave. When, at the end of May 1329, the Ottoman Turks under Othman's son Orhan began blockading Nicaea, Andronicus and John crossed the straits with an army of some four thousand and advanced along the Marmara. On the third morning they spied the Turkish army encamped near the little village of Pelekanos, and on 10 June the battle began. By evening it seemed that the Byzantines had the advantage, but their casualties were severe; and Cantacuzenus advised that, as soon as possible after dawn, they should begin a discreet withdrawal.

So indeed they did; unfortunately some of the younger officers, harassed by the Turkish archers, broke ranks in order to drive them away. Cantacuzenus galloped off in their pursuit; and Andronicus, who had not seen him, did the same. They found the young hotheads surrounded, and in the fighting that followed the Emperor was struck in the thigh. He was returned the next day on a stretcher to Constantinople. The wound proved to be superficial; and all would have been well had not some of the soldiers, seeing him carried away, assumed that he had been killed. Panic resulted, and it was with the greatest difficulty that John Cantacuzenus managed to restore a semblance of order.

The battle of Pelekanos marked the first personal encounter between an Emperor of Byzantium and an Ottoman Emir. It had not been a disaster, but it had shown that the Turkish advance in Asia Minor was unstoppable. Nicaea fell on 2 March 1331, Nicomedia six years later. All that remained of the Empire in Asia were the occasional towns that the Turks had not yet bothered to conquer. Meanwhile Orhan could build up his sea power, with which he now began to subject the European shore of the Marmara to almost continuous attack.

For Andronicus, only three small shreds of comfort remained. First, diplomatic relations had been opened with the Turks. In August 1333 he had secretly met Orhan, whom he had agreed to pay tribute in return for leaving his possessions in Asia undisturbed. Second, Orhan had proved to be a reasonable and civilized man. He had not imposed Islam on the Christians he had conquered; his wish, like his father's, was to build a state dedicated to justice, learning and the Muslim faith, but embracing people of all races and creeds. Third was the strengthening of Byzantine power in the Aegean. Andronicus had begun to rebuild his navy, and Byzantine ships were once again making the Empire's presence felt among the islands. Thanks to them, Chios rebelled in 1329 against the Genoese family of Zaccaria and returned to the imperial fold. Of course Genoa was not the only Western power involved in the eastern Mediterranean: the Knights of St John from Rhodes, the Venetians, the Lusignans of Cyprus and other families who had ruled in individual islands since the Fourth Crusade, were all pursuing their own interests. All, however, were determined to deliver the archipelago from the depredations of the Turkish emirates along the coast.

Not surprisingly, therefore, the idea was proposed – and championed by Pope John XXII in Avignon[1] – of a great Christian league which would first deal with the Muslim pirates and then advance to the Holy Land in a full-blown Crusade. But what part would Byzantium play in such a league? The Pope was firm. For as long as the Empire remained schismatic, it could not be a member. It was the same old story, the same inability to understand that the schism could not be ended by a stroke of the pen. The Emperor himself would have had no objections to union; but he would not repeat his great-grandfather's mistake of imposing it from above. In any case, the Byzantines did not believe in Crusades; and history had proved them right. For Andronicus, the Genoese were far more troublesome than the Turks; only six years after their loss of Chios, they evened the score with the capture of Lesbos. In retaliation, he ordered the immediate destruction of the defences of Galata; then he and John Cantacuzenus sailed for the Aegean to negotiate a new alliance – with 'the Lion of God', Umur Pasha, Emir of Aydin. Umur, who hated the Genoese, welcomed the Byzantine proposals. The negotiations resulted in a life-long friendship between John and himself that was to prove more important than either could have suspected.

---

1 The Papacy had moved its seat to Avignon in 1307. It was to remain there for the next seventy years.

Early in 1341, in Thessalonica, Andronicus III celebrated the wedding of his cousin Irene to John Cantacuzenus's son Matthew. He and John then returned together to Constantinople and a new, characteristically Byzantine crisis. It concerned a small group of Orthodox hermits known as the hesychasts. Hesychasm – the Greek word means 'holy silence' – was nothing new; the Orthodox Church had always maintained a tradition of mysticism. But in the 1330s a monk named Gregory of Sinai had spread the word that through certain physical techniques it was possible to obtain a vision of the divine Light that had surrounded Jesus Christ at his Transfiguration. Inevitably, Gregory's teachings aroused the age-old Byzantine passion for disputation, particularly since the recommended techniques – which included the fixing of the eyes on the navel and the regulation of breathing, were obviously open to ridicule. By spring 1341 feelings on both sides were running so high that the Emperor was obliged to call a Council of the Church. It was held in St Sophia on 10 June, and resulted in an overwhelming victory for the hesychasts.

After the members of the council had returned to their homes, the Emperor complained of exhaustion and, on the following day, was stricken with a violent fever. Five days later he was dead. He had ruled wisely and well. His tragedy was to have come to the throne at a time when his Empire was already doomed: his gains in the Balkans were insignificant compared with the effective loss of Anatolia, which had brought the Ottoman Turks to within sight of Constantinople. None the less, he had achieved more than most people would have thought possible; and the partnership of himself and his Grand Domestic did much to prepare a sad and demoralized people for the still greater tribulations that lay ahead.

26

The Reluctant Emperor

[1341-54]

Andronicus III Palaeologus had made one disastrous mistake: he had left no instructions regarding his successor. The nine-year-old John, elder of his sons, was the heir-presumptive; but the monarchy was not necessarily hereditary and he had never been proclaimed or crowned co-Emperor. John Cantacuzenus had no imperial ambitions; his loyalty to the little prince and to his mother Anne of Savoy was unquestioned. On the other hand he had effectively governed the Empire for thirteen years. Almost without thinking he moved into the Imperial Palace, to ensure the maintenance of law and order and a smooth transfer of power. He soon found, however, that his closeness to Andronicus had aroused bitter jealousies. Most resentful of all was the Empress herself, whose husband had always preferred John's company to her own. Then there was the Patriarch, John Calecas. He owed his promotion entirely to Cantacuzenus, but ambition outweighed gratitude. Had not Andronicus, he demanded, twice already appointed him Regent, before leaving on campaign?

Cantacuzenus could easily have argued that, since he had himself always accompanied the Emperor on his campaigns, the present situation was entirely different; he was far more concerned, however, about another of his former protégés, Alexius Apocaucus. An upstart adventurer of obscure origin, Apocaucus had been one of the leading supporters of Andronicus III in his struggle with his grandfather. Since then he had attached himself to John, thanks to whom he was now High Admiral. On the death of Andronicus he had urged his patron to accept the crown; John however had been adamant. His duty was to the Palaeologi. And so Apocaucus began plotting his downfall, while Empress, Patriarch and Grand Domestic together evolved an uneasy *modus vivendi* for the conduct of affairs.

But the death of a *basileus* was always an invitation to make trouble; and before long Byzantium's three main enemies were all back on the offensive – the Serbs advancing on Thessalonica, the Bulgars massing on the northern frontier and the Ottoman Turks plundering the coast of Thrace. John was obliged to recruit troops at his own expense, but met with quite astonishing success: order was restored and treaties signed with Stephen Dushan, John Alexander and the Emir Orhan. Meanwhile a delegation had arrived from the Morea offering the surrender of the Principality of Achaia. During John's enforced absence from the capital, however, his enemies struck. Inspired by Apocaucus, the Empress Anne and the Patriarch, a mob marched on his palace, pillaged it and burnt it to the ground. His country estates, too, were destroyed. The Patriarch proclaimed himself Regent, while Apocaucus appointed himself Prefect of the City. Meanwhile John's family was placed under house arrest and he was instantly relieved of his command.

But the conspirators had gone too far. The army supported John to a man. Then and there, on 26 October 1341, they proclaimed him *basileus*. He himself continued to insist that the young John V – though still uncrowned – remained the rightful Emperor; and there is no reason to doubt his sincerity. But the fact remained that he had now been acclaimed in the traditional manner by the army; and since there was clearly no question of his recognition by the present regime in Constantinople, civil war was inevitable. Within days of his investiture came news of his excommunication by the Patriarch; and on 19 November, John V was duly crowned in St Sophia. The lines of battle were drawn.

Not, however, in favour of Cantacuzenus. For years the rift had been widening between proletariat and aristocracy. As the enemies of Byzantium had advanced and refugees had poured into the capital, the condition of the poor had grown ever more desperate: Alexius Apocaucus, grateful at last for his humble origins, could now pose as the champion of the dispossessed against the forces of privilege. The contagion spread rapidly. In Adrianople a people's commune took over in the name of the Regency and was duly recognized by Apocaucus, who sent his own son Manuel as his representative. Within a few weeks all Thrace was up in arms, the landowning classes either hiding or in headlong flight. In Thessalonica an extreme party known as the Zealots seized control, instituting a reign of terror for the next seven years. John Cantacuzenus must have been near despair – outlawed, excommunicated and condemned as a public enemy. His very name was being used as a symbol of the exploitation of the poor by the rich – an abuse against which he had struggled throughout his adult life.

More than anything, he needed allies. He sent an urgent message to his old friend Umur of Aydin; but Umur was far away, and so he turned, after long hesitation, to Stephen Dushan of Serbia. The two met in July 1342 near Skoplje. Stephen, happy to take advantage of the Empire's troubles, willingly agreed to give John his support. Thanks to him, Cantacuzenus was able to survive through the remainder of 1342. Then, shortly before Christmas, he heard that Umur was on his way. The tide was beginning to turn. In that same winter of 1342–3 the province of Thessaly declared for John, and the coming of spring saw a similar submission in Macedonia. Apocaucus, seriously alarmed, arrived in Thessalonica with a squadron, but left quickly enough when Umur appeared on the horizon with a fleet of some two hundred ships.

In Constantinople morale was now sinking fast. Moreover, the Turks were on the loose in the European provinces. Umur's troops were creating havoc; the Empress was terrified at the very thought of these pagan barbarians, now almost at the gates of the capital, and in the summer of 1343 she sent appeals to Venice and Genoa. Knowing, however, that neither republic would ever give anything for nothing, she took a fateful step: for 30,000 Venetian ducats, she pawned the Byzantine crown jewels to the Most Serene Republic. They were never to be redeemed.

The action did her no good. No help came. Now too, as John steadily consolidated his position, several of her closest adherents began to desert her. As for Apocaucus, his behaviour gave proof of his desperation. All those whose loyalties he suspected – they included virtually all the rich – were arrested. Part of the ruined Great Palace was converted into a prison to accommodate them, and it was here that he met his death. On 11 June 1345, during one of his regular tours of inspection, a group of prisoners fell upon him, seized an axe from one of the workmen and struck off their victim's head.

Nevertheless, for John Cantacuzenus there was much to be done before he could enter Constantinople in triumph. He knew that he could expect no more from Stephen Dushan. He still needed help on a large scale; and in the first weeks of 1345 he made contact with Orhan himself. Although John deplored the Turks as much as did the rest of his countrymen, on the personal level he had always got on with them remarkably well. With Orhan he quickly established a close friendship, which became yet closer when the Emir fell besottedly in love with Theodora, the second of his three daughters and, in 1346, married her. The bride was permitted to keep her Christian faith, and was later to work indefatigably on behalf of the Christian residents of her husband's emirate.

But that same year was marked by other, more sinister, developments. On Easter Sunday, in the Cathedral of Skoplje, Stephen Dushan was crowned by the Serbian Archbishop – whom he had promoted to Patriarch – with the title of Emperor of the Serbs and Greeks. It was probably as a deliberate response that, at Adrianople on 21 May, John had imperial crowns – hastily manufactured by a local goldsmith – laid on his own head and that of his wife by the Patriarch of Jerusalem. He refused, however, all suggestions that his eldest son Matthew should be crowned co-Emperor; that position was reserved for the fourteen-year-old John Palaeologus – still, so far as he was concerned, the senior legitimate monarch.

At last he was ready. Late at night on 2 February he slipped through a narrow gap in the bricked-up Golden Gate and entered Constantinople for the first time in five and a half years, a thousand men behind him. Six days later, agreement was reached. The two Emperors would reign jointly, with John VI Cantacuzenus occupying the senior position for the first decade. After that they would enjoy equal status. John's sentence of excommunication was lifted, and on 21 May 1347 he received his second coronation in the Church of the Virgin at Blachernae. A week later his youngest daughter, Helena, was married in the same church to his co-Emperor, John V. To both ceremonies, however, there was more than a touch of sadness. By tradition they should have been held at St Sophia; but the east end had collapsed in the previous year and it was no longer usable. They should also have made use of the Byzantine crown jewels; but these were now in pawn. Those present noted to their sorrow that the replacements were made of glass.

John Cantacuzenus was a man of integrity and a rare degree of political vision. Had he firmly asserted his claim to the throne in 1341, he might have checked the Empire's decline; six years later no real recovery was possible. It was his misfortune to inherit a divided and bankrupt Empire; and when at last he gained the supreme power, he lacked that last ounce of steel necessary to impose his will. Another misfortune was to be a contemporary of Stephen Dushan. By the time of his death in 1355 Stephen's Empire extended from the Adriatic to the Aegean and from the Danube to the Gulf of Corinth, making it far larger than the Byzantine. There can be no question but that he coveted the throne of Constantinople, and little doubt that he would have achieved it but for a single weakness: Serbia had always been a land-locked kingdom, and even after his maritime conquests he had no effective navy. Constantinople could be successfully attacked only from the seaward side, and without a fleet he was powerless to conquer it. Again and again he sought Venetian help, but the Venetians far preferred the weak Byzantine Empire to a powerful Serbian one.

Yet Stephen represented neither the beginning nor the end of John's misfortunes. In the spring of 1347 Constantinople was stricken by the Black Death. One contemporary chronicler claims that it eliminated eight-ninths of the entire population; to the Byzantines, it must have seemed the final proof that the Holy Virgin, their protectress, had at last deserted them. Their Empire was now limited to the former province of Thrace – with the two cities of Adrianople and Didymotichum – and a few Aegean islands. To this pathetic rump could be added Thessalonica, which finally rid itself of the Zealots in 1350; but Thessalonica was now a tiny Byzantine enclave within Stephen's dominions, accessible only by sea.

Economically, the position was still more catastrophic: war had reduced Thrace to a desert; the coast was under continual attack by Turkish pirates. Such food as was available was brought in by the Genoese, who named their prices and could cut off supplies whenever they liked. Trade was at a stand-still: the *hyperpyron* was losing value with every day that passed. Any major expenditure was made possible only by appeals for gifts or loans, which were all too often deflected from their stated purpose. When Symeon, Grand Duke of Muscovy, sent gold for the restoration of St Sophia, it was spent on the recruitment of Turkish mercenaries.

John's first care was to consolidate what remained of the Empire. His elder son Matthew was made responsible for an extensive area of Thrace along the Serbian frontier; the younger, Manuel, was given charge of the Morea, hence-forth an autonomous despotate. Next John looked towards Galata, where the annual customs dues received by the Genoese were nearly seven times those of Constantinople; he now decreed a dramatic reduction of import tariffs, to the point where foreign vessels were once again attracted to the western, rather than the eastern shore of the Golden Horn. Not surprisingly, the Genoese objected. In August 1348 a flotilla of their ships sailed across the Horn, burning the few Byzantine vessels they could find. But the Greeks fought back. The Genoese warehouses along the shore were set on fire; huge rocks and flaming bales were catapulted into Galata. It was weeks before peace was restored; but finally, when the plenipotentiaries arrived from Genoa, they proved remarkably accommodating. The Republic readily agreed to pay the Empire a war indemnity of more than 100,000 *hyperpyra*; it under-took to evacuate the land behind Galata which it had illegally occupied; finally, it promised never again to attack Constantinople. In return, Byzantium surrendered virtually nothing.

At the end of 1349 John Cantacuzenus might have been forgiven for think-ing that his difficulties with the two republics of Genoa and Venice were over. Alas, their rivalry soon turned again to open war, and the proximity of Galata to Constantinople made it impossible for Byzantium not to support one republic or the other. On 13 February 1352 they fought it out by themselves, beneath the walls of Galata. Soon fire broke out, which the high winds quickly spread through both fleets; but the battle continued far into the night, by the light of their own blazing ships. Finally it was the Venetians who had to yield; but when the dawn revealed the surface of the water to be almost invisible beneath the wrecks and the floating corpses, the Genoese losses were seen to have been almost as heavy. The Genoese victory had cost them more than many a defeat.

In May 1352, John V Palaeologus returned to the capital from Thessalonica. Now twenty years old, he was no longer content to submit unquestioningly to his father-in-law's bidding. The latter's sons were governing important areas of the Empire; his own mother Anne had recently been given control over Macedonia. It was time for him also to claim his due.

John VI, well aware of his son-in-law's ambitions, immediately allotted him the greater part of Thrace, strategically vital since it controlled the approaches to Constantinople itself. There was only one difficulty: the area included the city of Didymotichum and most of the appanage that he had already granted to his son Matthew. As a substitute Matthew was granted Adrianople and its surroundings, but he was left feeling resentful of his brother-in-law – who, to make matters worse, was now his immediate neighbour.

The first to break the uneasy peace was, surprisingly enough, John V, who crossed Matthew's frontier in 1352 and laid siege to Adrianople. Matthew appealed to his father, who hastened to his relief with a considerable force of Turkish troops, made available by the Emir Orhan and commanded by Oshan's son Süleyman. John for his part summoned help from the Serbs and Bulgars, an appeal to which Stephen Dushan responded with four thousand cavalry. In the event the city was saved, but far more significant was the fact that the Empire was once again at war with itself, and – more ominous still – that John Cantacuzenus had thrown an army of infidels against his own Christian subjects. He was not, the people reminded themselves, of the true imperial family: at best only a caretaker Emperor. Now that John Palaeologus had grown to manhood, must he still share his authority with a man who had brought the Empire little but disaster?

By this time John VI had lost all appetite for power. He had already bought himself a plot of land on Mount Athos, and often spoke wistfully of the attractions of the monastic life. From the first, too, he had supported the legitimate claims of John Palaeologus. But John had now shown that he was a ready tool of the Venetians, the Bulgars and Stephen Dushan. And so, in April 1353, John Cantacuzenus declared John Palaeologus formally deposed and named his own son Matthew co-Emperor in his stead – emphasizing, however, that the Palaeologi had not been disinherited and that John's son Andronicus remained heir apparent. He then exiled his son-in-law, with his family, to Tenedos.

Once again he had underestimated the opposition. The Patriarch flatly refused to perform Matthew's coronation, pronounced sentence of excommunication on Cantacuzenus and resigned his office. A few days later he slipped across to Galata and soon found his way to John V at Tenedos. Meanwhile a certain Philotheus, an enthusiastic Cantacuzenist, was elected as his successor; but it was not until February 1354 that Matthew and his wife Irene were finally crowned.

Less than a month later, on 2 March, a large part of Thrace was ravaged by a violent earthquake. Hundreds of towns and villages were destroyed; in Gallipoli scarcely a house was left standing. The disaster was made still more catastrophic by the conduct of the Turks. Süleyman Pasha set off at once for the stricken lands, taking with him as many Turkish families as he could find. The majority headed for the ruins of Gallipoli itself; and within a few months the restored city had an exclusively Turkish population where a Greek one had been before.

For the Empire, this first Turkish settlement on the European continent was a calamity greater than the earthquake itself. To John's demand for its restitution, Süleyman replied that it had fallen to him through the will of Allah; to return it would be an act of impious ingratitude. He had not taken it by force; his men had simply occupied a place abandoned by its former inhabitants.

On 21 November 1354 John V Palaeologus slipped out of Tenedos, up the Hellespont and into the Marmara; early on the 22nd he reached Constantinople; and by dawn the crowds were already gathering in the streets. Before long, inevitably, they went on the rampage. Again the Cantacuzenus family mansion was plundered and set on fire. Some of the rioters seized control of the arsenal; others marched on Blachernae, while John V installed himself in the old palace opposite St Sophia. His proposals were surprisingly moderate: the two should rule jointly as before, with Matthew continuing in Adrianople until his death. Cantacuzenus as senior Emperor would continue to live at Blachernae, while he himself would occupy the private palace of Theodore Metochites, one of the grandest in the city.

Several problems, however, remained unsolved. One was the continued presence of Süleyman's Turks in Thrace; another was the increasing unpopularity of John Cantacuzenus. For a week he bore the situation as best he could; then he finally took the decision that he had been long considering. On 4 December, at a ceremony in Blachernae, he and his wife Irene solemnly laid aside the diadem and regalia. Then, having adopted the simple robe of an Orthodox monk, he retired to a monastery.

John Cantacuzenus – known henceforth as the monk Joasaph – had reigned only seven years; but he had effectively governed the Empire for a quarter of a century, and guided it for ten years longer still. He was to live another twenty-nine, until 1383. The first years after his retirement were largely devoted to the completion of his *Histories*; when this was done he turned to a long defence of hesychasm. As we shall soon see, however, he did not, altogether withdraw from political life, much as he may have wished to do so.

It is hard not to feel sorry for him. Few Emperors had worked harder for the imperial good; few had possessed less personal ambition. He would never have deposed his son-in-law had he not believed that John Palaeologus, by resuming the war, was throwing the whole future of Byzantium into jeopardy. But luck was against him. John V 's foolishness, the hesychast controversy, the Black Death, the aggression of the Turks, the ambitions of the Genoese and the Venetians: without these he might have won through. But the greatest burden of all was the moral and financial bankruptcy of the Empire itself. The treasury was empty; the Byzantines themselves had lost heart. A charismatic personality might have galvanized them into action; but John Cantacuzenus was not ultimately an inspired leader of men, and succeeded only in alienating their trust. Thirty-five years of service had been ill repaid. As he and his wife exchanged the trappings of Empire for their coarse monastic habits, it is hard to believe that they can have done so with anything but relief.

27
The Sultan's Vassal

[1354–91]

With the departure of John Cantacuzenus, it was accepted throughout Christendom that Byzantium was on the verge of collapse. To what power, however, was it to fall? Four months before the abdication, the Venetian *bailo* in Constantinople had reported that the Byzantines were ready to submit to anyone who asked them to; four months after it, we find the Doge proposing the immediate annexation of the Empire, if only to save it from the Turkish tide.

One enemy, at least, left the stage: Stephen Dushan died in 1355, and his Empire disintegrated. The Ottomans, on the other hand, were spreading across Thrace. Süleyman's appropriation of Gallipoli had given them the bridgehead they needed and their advance had begun almost at once. Before long, too, other bands of freebooting Turks rallied to their standard. The rest of Thrace, already exhausted by civil war, proved an easy victim. In 1361 Didymotichum fell; in 1362, Adrianople. In every city and village that was captured, the bulk of the population was transported to Anatolia, its place being taken by Turkish colonists. That same year, 1362, saw the death of Orhan. He was succeeded as Emir by his son Murad, who soon proved himself a still more energetic and determined leader.

Once again John Palaeologus had to look for allies. Genoa and Venice were friendly but ineffectual. Pope Urban V and Peter of Cyprus had made an abortive sally against Egypt in 1365, but had succeeded only in making themselves look ridiculous. There remained Louis the Great, King of Hungary. Like so many of his co-religionists, he hated schismatics far more than infidels and had consequently decided on a holy war of his own against the heretic Bulgars. In 1365 the frontier province of Vidin was occupied by a Hungarian army, bringing in its wake quantities of Franciscan missionaries, who immediately set about the more or less forcible conversion of the local populations.

John now decided to go himself to Hungary. Such a step was without precedent. Emperors might travel outside their own frontiers at the head of an army; but never had a *basileus* left his capital as a petitioner to the

Christian West. Leaving the Empire in the hands of his son Andronicus, in the first weeks of 1366 John sailed along the Black Sea coast and thence up the Danube to Buda, his two younger sons Manuel and Michael accompanying him. King Louis took the old, all-too-familiar line: only after the Empire had submitted to Rome could there be any question of military assistance. John set off sadly homewards – to find himself effectively a prisoner of the Bulgars, who refused to allow him across their frontier.

The only previous Emperor to have been captured by a foreign power, Romanus Diogenes, had been taken by his Seljuk enemies, treated with consideration and courtesy and freed after a week. John was held by his Christian neighbours, utterly ignored by the Bulgar Tsar John Alexander – father-in-law of his prisoner's own first-born son Andronicus – and left in a small frontier town for some six months. There could be no more forcible illustration of the depths to which the Empire had sunk. When John's release came at last, he owed it not to the Tsar but, surprisingly enough, to his cousin Amadeus of Savoy.

In May 1366, with fifteen ships and some 1,700 men, Amadeus had sailed from Venice for Constantinople, determined to help his cousin against the Turks. On his arrival at the Hellespont he had recaptured Gallipoli, with an effect on Byzantine morale that can be easily imagined; but it was probably only when he reached Constantinople that he learned of John's captivity. Sailing up the Black Sea coast, he laid siege to Varna, whence he sent an ultimatum to the Tsar at Trnovo. John Alexander immediately gave his authority for the Emperor to cross his territory, and John V reached Amadeus's camp at Mesembria just before Christmas. In the spring of 1367 they returned together to Constantinople, where there was serious business to discuss. Amadeus had sworn to take up once again the cause of Church union and had actually brought with him a papal envoy in the person of Paul, the former Bishop of Smyrna who had recently been elevated to the titular rank of Latin Patriarch of Constantinople.

John's mind was quickly made up. He could not commit his subjects or his Church to union, but he could himself make a personal submission to Rome; and at the same time he could arrange for discussions between Paul and the Orthodox leaders. Patriarch Philotheus understandably refused to have any dealings with a pretender to his own title. He raised no objection, however, when John appointed his father-in-law, the monk Joasaph – formerly John VI – who was playing an increasingly important role in state affairs, to represent the Orthodox in his stead. Once again John explained the Byzantine position. Union could not be imposed from above; the Emperor had no authority over the souls of his subjects. The differences could be settled only by an ecumenical council – which had unfortunately never been acceptable to Rome. Paul finally agreed to such a council, to be held at Constantinople within two years. Meanwhile he himself would return to the West, together with Amadeus and representatives of the Orthodox clergy, both pastoral and monastic, on the understanding that the Emperor would himself visit the Pope before long.

Earlier that same year Pope Urban had attempted to move the Papacy back to Rome. The transfer was not a success, and he had soon afterwards returned to Avignon; but it was to Italy that the Byzantine delegation travelled that summer, where Urban welcomed them at Viterbo. Thence they accompanied him to Rome itself. But it was soon plain that he had no intention of calling the proposal council: of the twenty-three letters he signed on 6 November, all stressing the importance of the Byzantines' submission and of the Emperor's promised visit to Rome, not one even mentioned the possibility.

But John kept his promise. Once again leaving his eldest son – now crowned co-Emperor – as Regent, he set off in the early summer of 1369, accompanied by a suite including not one member of the violently-disapproving hierarchy. In Rome on 18 October he formally signed his submission to the Roman Church and its father the Pope, sealing it with his imperial seal; and the following Sunday he did obeisance to the Supreme Pontiff on the steps of St Peter's. The deed remained, however, an individual act, involving no one else. Apart from a dangerous weakening of his own position in Constantinople, John's public self-abasement achieved nothing.

Some time before, the Emperor had received a letter from Andrea Contarini, Doge of Venice, reminding him of the imperial crown jewels, pawned by the Empress Anne in 1343 against a loan of 30,000 ducats, the interest on which was rapidly increasing; would he perhaps like to call at Venice on his homeward journey? John arrived in early May. Normally, this first-ever visit to Venice by a Byzantine Emperor would have been celebrated with a degree of magnificence of which no other state was capable; but the Venetians had little respect for poverty. The atmosphere improved only when the Emperor offered the island of Tenedos at the entrance to the Hellespont, in return for a Venetian undertaking to return the jewels and to furnish six war galleys with 25,000 ducats in cash – 4,000 payable at once since, he was embarrassed to admit, he did not have enough money to get home.

The Doge willingly agreed; but the Regent Andronicus, under strong pressure from the Galata Genoese, refused to give up the island. No Tenedos, no ducats: John was now effectively a prisoner in Venice, Andronicus raising not a finger to help him. Deliverance finally came through his second son

Manuel, Governor of Thessalonica. Leaving the city in mid-winter, Manuel hastened along the snow-covered Via Egnatia with gold enough to secure his father's release. Thanks to him alone John was able to leave Venice in March 1371 with 30,000 ducats.

There was more bad news awaiting him. On 26 September 1371, on the bank of the river Maritsa, the Turks had utterly destroyed the Serbian army. No longer was there any barrier to keep them from overrunning Serbia, Macedonia and Greece. The Serbian nobles would henceforth be mere vassals, bound to pay tribute to the Ottoman Sultan (as Murad now styled himself), and to lend him military assistance on demand. In 1373 John V too was obliged to accept vassalage, as was the Bulgarian Tsar. His motive was probably sheer despair. With the Turks controlling both Serbia and Bulgaria, any effective Crusade was impossible; Byzantium, cut off from the West, could no longer make even a show of resistance. Only by joining forces with the Sultan could John perhaps hope to save something from the wreckage. Murad might at least check the bands of Turkish marauders in Macedonia and Thrace; he might also strengthen John's hand against his son Andronicus, who was causing him increasing anxiety.

Thus it was that in May 1373 John found himself in Anatolia, campaigning at the Sultan's side. Here was humiliation enough; still worse was the news that Andronicus had come out in open revolt against Emperor and Sultan together. The furious Murad demanded that John should have his son blinded, and John knew he could not refuse; he could, however, arrange for some mercy to be shown to the victim. Andronicus did not entirely lose his sight but was imprisoned in Constantinople, formally deprived of his right to the succession. The heir-apparent was now Manuel, who was summoned from Thessalonica and on 25 September crowned co-Emperor.

John soon had cause to regret his forbearance. In March 1376 a Venetian embassy arrived: with Andronicus eliminated, the Doge was eager to implement the agreement of six years before. In return for Tenedos, he now offered a further 30,000 ducats and the return of the crown jewels. The imperial standard, he promised, would fly over Tenedos alongside that of St Mark. But once again the plan was foiled by the Genoese; and once again their thoughts turned to Andronicus. In July they somehow organized his escape from prison. He went straight to Murad, promising him the immediate return of Gallipoli; and Murad provided him with a mixed force of cavalry and infantry with which he was able to enter the capital in strength. John and his family were soon forced to surrender; Andronicus had the satisfaction of consigning them to the Tower of Anemas that he himself had so recently left. He then formally granted Tenedos to Genoa. A year later, on 18 October

1377, he had himself crowned as Andronicus IV and his little son as his co-Emperor, John VII; but the Genoese never received their reward. The Byzantine Governor of Tenedos refused to surrender the island to them – though he was happy to yield it shortly afterwards to the Venetians. Sultan Murad was more fortunate. By the end of 1377 Gallipoli was once again in his possession.

How John and Manuel regained their liberty is unclear; but after three years they somehow managed to escape across the Bosphorus to the only refuge available to them, Murad's camp near Chrysopolis. Once there, Manuel promised the Sultan, in return for the reinstatement of himself and his father, an increased tribute, additional military assistance and, most humiliating of all, the city of Philadelphia, the last remaining Byzantine outpost in Asia Minor. Agreement was quickly reached. The Turks provided an army; the Venetians, eager to be rid of Andronicus, sent a small fleet; and on 1 July 1379 the two Emperors re-entered Constantinople, fleeing Andronicus to his Genoese friends in Galata. Not until April 1381 was peace restored. By its terms Andronicus was reinstated as heir to the throne, with his son John to succeed him, and meanwhile granted a small appanage on the northern coast of the Marmara. Manuel's reaction to this agreement is not recorded. He more than anyone had deserved well of his father; but he was no longer able to forgive John's defeatism, and he refused absolutely to accept the Turkish claim to the Balkan peninsula. In the autumn of 1382 he returned to Thessalonica. It was fortunate indeed for him that the insufferable Andronicus died in June 1385, leaving him once again the legitimate co-inheritor of what was left of Byzantium.

The year 1381 had also brought to a close the conflict between Venice and Genoa, when the two exhausted republics gratefully accepted the offer of Count Amadeus to mediate. After four years of bloodshed, both found themselves politically very much where they had been before. Tenedos, they agreed, would be neutral ground; both republics promised to do their utmost to bring about the conversion of the Roman Empire to the Catholic faith. But what was this Empire? No longer an Empire at all – simply a group of four small states, ruled by four so-called Emperors and a Despot. Although after 1383 each of these was a member of the house of Palaeologus, each remained effectively independent of the others, if not of his Turkish overlords. John V continued to reign in Constantinople; Andronicus IV with his son and co-Emperor John VII, both of them still more dependent on Turkish favour, ruled over the north shore of the Marmara; Manuel II governed Thessalonica; while Theodore I, John V's fourth son, held sway over the Despotate of the Morea, with his capital at Mistra. Theodore, who had succeeded John VI's son Manuel Cantacuzenus in 1380, was also obliged to accept Turkish vassalage; he was nevertheless to make the Morea the strongest and most prosperous bastion of a tottering Byzantium.

On all other fronts that Empire was disintegrating fast. The Turks had captured Ochrid and Prilep in 1380 before pushing north-west into Albania. Further to the east, another of Murad's armies overran Bulgaria, taking Sardica in 1385 and advancing in the following year as far as Nish. There remained only Thessalonica, now in grave danger. In October 1383 the Turkish general Khaireddin issued an ultimatum to the Thessalonians: surrender or massacre. Manuel Palaeologus acted at once. Summoning all his subjects to the main square, he exhorted them to resist the infidel with all the strength at their command; then he began work on the defences. Thessalonica had survived only because Murad, lacking naval power, could not set up an effective blockade. Nothing prevented the West from sending reinforcements and supplies by sea. Had they done so, Manuel and Theodore together might even have united northern Greece and saved it. But no help came, and after three and a half years morale had sunk to the point where surrender was imminent. Manuel still refused to submit; and on 6 April 1387, cursing the Thessalonians for their cowardice, he sailed away to Lesbos. Three days later they opened the gates, thereby escaping the bloodshed and pillage which they would inevitably have suffered had they fought on to the end.

The three years following the fall of Thessalonica were the saddest of Manuel's life. His father's policy of appeasement had been proved right. Clearly, the two Emperors must now settle their differences; but John V was determined that his son must do penance before there could be any formal reconciliation. He banished Manuel to the island of Lemnos; and Manuel was still there when the Serbs made their last stand. After the disaster on the Maritsa it had seemed impossible that they should ever fight again; but now a league of Serbian boyars gathered together under the leadership of a certain Prince Lazar Hrebelianovich. When in 1389 Sultan Murad advanced on to the plain of Kosovo, 'the field of blackbirds', they were there to meet him. The battle that followed on 15 June has entered Serbian folklore, and has inspired one of the greatest of all medieval epics; but the Serbs' defeat was total. For the few survivors, the only consolation was that Murad never lived to enjoy his victory. One of the captured boyars was brought before the Sultan and, before the guard could prevent him, plunged a dagger twice into his heart.

The report of the murder spread to the West, where it was initially interpreted as a major victory for Christendom: in Paris King Charles VI went so far as to order a service of thanksgiving in Notre-Dame. Gradually, however, the tragic truth became known. The Serbian nation was no more. The truth was that by now the Ottoman armies were unconquerable by anything less than a concerted Crusade; and such a Crusade was itself impossible.

Murad's elder son Bayezit was proclaimed Sultan on the field of Kosovo. A man of almost superhuman energy, impetuous and unpredictable, as quick in taking decisions as he was in implementing them and merciless to all who stood in his way, he well deserved his sobriquet of *Yildirim*, the Thunderbolt, though he himself now resurrected the old title Sultan of Rum, the ancient formula that had been adopted by the Seljuk Emirs to assert their dominion over 'Roman' Anatolia. To Bayezit however 'Rum' had a slightly different connotation: it now included the Second Rome itself – Constantinople.

Fortunately for the new Sultan, that city was still torn between rival factions. John V was still reigning from Blachernae, but the late Andronicus IV's detestation of his father was fully shared by his own son John VII who, on the night of 13 April 1390, with the aid of a small force put at his disposal by the Sultan, succeeded in overturning his grandfather for the second time. Once again John V – together with Manuel, whom he had summoned back from Lemnos just a fortnight before, and a number of loyal followers – barricaded himself into the fortress of the Golden Gate and, in an unwonted display of courage, settled down to withstand a siege. Manuel, however, slipped away to seek assistance, and on 25 August reappeared with nine borrowed galleys. On 17 September the old Emperor and his men made a sudden sally, taking his grandson off his guard and driving him out of the city.

Fully reconciled at last, John and Manuel returned triumphantly to Blachernae. There was, however, a price to be paid for their success. The furious Sultan now demanded that Manuel should immediately join him on campaign, sending a similar summons to John VII. The two men, despite their mutual detestation, could only obey; nor, that autumn, could they refuse Bayezit's orders to take part in the siege of Philadelphia.[1] And so it was that two Emperors found themselves directly instrumental in the capture of the last Byzantine stronghold in Asia Minor. Of all the many humiliations inflicted on the dying Empire, this was surely the most ironical.

John V died on 16 February 1391, aged fifty-eight. He had reigned as *basileus* a few months short of half a century, the longest reign of any Emperor in the

---

1 Had John and Manuel retracted their promise of 1378? Or had the Philadelphians simply refused to submit to the Sultan? We shall never know.

history of Byzantium. It was, by any standards, too long. We may deplore his passive obedience to his Turkish suzerains, but he had little choice. Of the Sultan's Christian enemies, Serbia and Bulgaria were gone. Only Byzantium remained; but it was a Byzantium so reduced and demoralized as to be scarcely identifiable as the glorious Empire it had once been. Yet it never gave up the struggle. Thanks to its last three determined Emperors it was to last another six decades – and, at the end, to go down fighting.

28

The Appeal to Europe

[1391–1448]

Within days of his accession, Manuel II showed his mettle. When the news of his father's death reached him he was still a hostage of the Sultan, and had returned with him to his capital at Brusa. There was now, he well knew, a serious danger that Bayezit, as Byzantium's suzerain, might appoint his nephew John VII as *basileus*. On the night of 7 March 1391, he slipped out of the camp and made his way secretly back to Constantinople, where he was welcomed with enthusiasm. Now forty, in appearance he was every inch an Emperor: Bayezit himself had once observed that his imperial blood was recognizable from his bearing alone. With his perfect health and boundless energy he seemed to be less the offspring of his father than of his grandfather, with whom he shared a love of literature and the traditional Byzantine passion for theology. He remained, however, a man of action. Twice, in 1371 and again in 1390, he had come to the rescue of his increasingly incapable father, on both occasions with complete success. In happier times he might have been a great ruler.

But the existing situation left little scope for greatness. Manuel was now but a vassal of the Sultan; and the Sultan had been outraged by his assumption of the throne without authority. His reaction was to inflict two more humiliations on the new Emperor. The first was to set aside a whole area of Constantinople for Turkish merchants, who would be no longer subject to imperial law but whose affairs would be regulated by a Muslim *qadi*, or judge; the second – in May 1391, only two months after Manuel's accession – was to summon him back to Anatolia to take part in yet another campaign, this time to the Black Sea.

The Emperor was back in Constantinople by the middle of January 1392, and on 10 February he took to himself a bride. She was Helena, daughter of Constantine Dragash, the Serbian Prince of Serres – like himself, a vassal of the Sultan. The marriage was followed the next day by a joint coronation. Manuel had already been crowned nineteen years before; but a new ceremony, performed with as much pomp and display as could be managed, would he believed be the best possible tonic for his subjects' morale. It would remind them, too, that whatever indignities he might be called upon to suffer he remained supreme among the princes of Christendom, Equal of the Apostles, God's own anointed Vice-Gerent on Earth. As the crowns were slowly lowered on to the heads of the imperial pair, it hardly seemed to matter that the true regalia were still in pawn to the Venetians; that the Emperor whose semi-divinity was being so loftily extolled had returned only a month before from a campaign on behalf of the infidel Sultan; or that that Sultan was even now at the gates of the capital.

For two years after his coronation Manuel was left in comparative peace; but in the winter of 1393–4 Bayezit called his principal Christian vassals to his camp at Serres. Apart from the Emperor himself, they included his brother Theodore, Despot of the Morea, his father-in-law Constantine Dragash, his nephew John VII and the Serbian Stephen Lazarevich. None of them knew that the others had been summoned also: only when they were all assembled did they realize how completely they had put themselves in the Sultan's power. Manuel himself shared the general view that a massacre had been intended, and that Bayezit had countermanded his own orders only at the last moment. What better proof was there that he was by now emotionally unstable, and consequently more dangerous than ever? Eventually, after giving his vassals grim warnings of the consequences of disobedience, the Sultan let them go. Manuel, shaken by what he believed till the end of his life to have been a narrow escape from death, returned with all speed to Constantinople.

Soon afterwards he received yet another summons from Bayezit. This time he refused. His experience at Serres had convinced him that the days of appeasement were over; the only hope lay in resistance. Meanwhile, however, he had no delusions: his defiance would be interpreted as a renunciation of his former vassalage – in effect, a declaration of war. He had taken the risk only because he still believed in the impregnability of Constantinople. On both occasions when the city had fallen to armed force during the Fourth Crusade, the attacks had been launched from the sea, against the inferior fortifications which ran along the shore of the Golden Horn. Such an operation would be impossible for Bayezit, who had no effective navy. Manuel was also encouraged by Sigismund of Hungary who, increasingly alarmed at the steady Turkish advance, in 1395 made a general appeal to the princes of Christendom.

This time they responded. So also did the two rival Popes, Boniface IX in Rome and Benedict XIII in Avignon. Ten thousand French knights, together with another six thousand from Germany, joined Sigismund's sixty thousand Hungarians and the ten thousand raised by the Prince of Wallachia. Another fifteen thousand came from Italy, Spain, England, Poland and Bohemia. The Genoese in Lesbos and Chios and the knights of Rhodes took responsibility for the mouth of the Danube and the Black Sea coast. Even Venice sent a fleet to patrol the Hellespont. This immense force – it almost certainly numbered over a hundred thousand men – set off in August 1396 down the valley of the Danube. But Sigismund's continued efforts to impose discipline and caution were in vain; the ardent young knights saw themselves as heroes of an earlier age of chivalry, driving all before them to the very doors of the Holy Sepulchre. A month or so after their departure they reached Nicopolis; and it was there that the Sultan caught up with them. What followed, on the morning of 25 September, was a massacre. Some ten thousand were beheaded in the Sultan's presence, many others taken prisoner. In its own way, the Crusade of Nicopolis was a milestone: it was the first trial of strength between the West and the Ottoman Sultan. As such, it hardly augured well for the future.

Early in 1397 the people of Constantinople watched with consternation as a great castle rose on the Asiatic shore of the Bosphorus: the castle known nowadays as Anadolu Hisar. Manuel was meanwhile redoubling his efforts to obtain aid from abroad. During 1397 and 1398, imperial embassies set forth once again – to the Pope, to the Kings of England, France and Aragon and to the Grand Duke of Muscovy, while further delegations were sent by Patriarch Antonius to the King of Poland and the Metropolitan of Kiev. In Rome Pope Boniface IX issued two bulls calling upon the nations of the West to partici-pate in a new Crusade or, failing that, to send financial contributions for the defence of Constantinople. Charles VI of France sent 12,000 gold francs with military aid, which actually appeared in 1399: a force of 1,200 men led by the greatest French soldier of his day, Jean le Maingre, Marshal Boucicault, who had fought at Nicopolis and longed for vengeance. Boucicault reached Constantinople in September, but immediately saw that any effective army would have to be organized on a far larger scale. The Emperor, he insisted, must himself make the journey to Paris and plead his cause in person before the French King.

And so, unwillingly entrusting the Empire to his nephew John VIII, Manuel left Constantinople for the West. In April 1400 he landed in Venice, whence he travelled slowly through north Italy, cheered and fêted in every town through which he passed. Italy had at last awoken to the danger, and in Italian eyes this tall, majestic figure was the principal defender of Christendom, the potential saviour of Europe. Finally on 3 June 1400, just before his fiftieth birthday, the Emperor arrived in Paris, where an entire wing of the old Louvre had been redecorated to receive him. But then came disappointment: King Charles, despite the warmth of his welcome, refused to contemplate a full-blown international Crusade.

Manuel next passed on to London, where King Henry IV treated him with the utmost reverence and respect: Henry's own position in the Kingdom was still uncertain – many of his subjects rightly considered him a usurper of the throne, and a probable murderer to boot – and he believed with good reason that to be seen playing host to the Emperor of Byzantium would do much to enhance his prestige. On Christmas Day he entertained his guest to a banquet in his palace at Eltham. Though he proved powerless to provide the military aid that he so cheerfully promised, he seems to have shown genuine sympathy with the Byzantine cause and presented Manuel with £4,000 contributed to the church collection boxes set up across the country specifically for the purpose.

After some seven weeks in England, Manuel was back in Paris early in 1401. He was to stay there for more than a year, continuing his negotiations with the Kings of Aragon and Portugal, with the Pope in Rome and the anti-Pope in Avignon. As autumn approached, however, his spirits began to sink. From every side there came only rejections and excuses. Most disappointing of all were the French, Charles VI being now hopelessly insane. The Emperor wrote to Venice, suggesting that Doge Michele Steno might take over the leadership where Charles had failed; but Steno refused.

Then, in September 1402, the Seigneur Jean de Chateaumorand – whom Boucicault had left in Constantinople with a token force of some three hundred French troops – arrived in Paris with news that instantly changed the entire situation. The Mongols under Tamburlaine had destroyed the Ottoman army. Bayezit himself had been taken prisoner. For Manuel Palaeologus, there was no longer any reason to remain in the West. He began to prepare for his journey home.

Tamburlaine had been born in 1336. He had seized the Mongol throne at Samarkand in 1369, and thirty years later his dominions extended from Afghanistan to the borders of Anatolia. His name was feared throughout Asia – the Mongol army was known to destroy everything in its path – and though now in his sixties he had lost none of his energy or his ambition. His ultimate trial of strength with the Ottoman Sultan occurred on Friday, 28 July 1402, just to the north of Ancyra. The Sultan had made the cardinal mistake of placing his Tartar cavalry in the front line; unwilling to fight men of their own race, they deserted and went over to the enemy. An hour or two later, fifteen thousand of the Ottoman army lay dead. Bayezit and his sons fought courageously for as long as they could. Prince Mustafa disappeared and was presumed dead. Prince Musa was captured. The others escaped, but their father, overtaken by Mongol archers, was taken prisoner and led in chains to the conqueror's tent. Tamburlaine, as he advanced through Anatolia, is said to have had the Sultan carried before him in an iron cage, occasionally using him as a footstool and a mounting-block. Soon he took over Bayezit's harem for his own personal use and forced the Sultan's Serbian wife to serve naked at his table. After eight months Bayezit's spirit was broken. In March 1403 he suffered a sudden apoplexy, and a few days later he was dead.

Descending on Brusa, the Ottoman capital, the Mongol hordes burned, pillaged and raped their way through the city; they then turned against Smyrna, where the Knights of St John fought valiantly; but the walls finally gave way and in December 1402 the last Christian enclave in Asia Minor was left a smouldering ruin. Had Tamburlaine lingered in the region for very much longer, he might well have dealt a fatal blow to the house of Othman; but in 1403 he left Asia Minor and led his horde back to Samarkand. It would be some years before the sons of Bayezit were able to re-establish themselves in their Anatolian heartland. In Europe it was a very different story. Rumelia – the Sultan's European dominions – remained as firmly as ever in the Ottoman grip. None the less, the great battle had divided the Ottoman Empire into two; no longer was there any regular communication between its European and its Asiatic provinces. The Sultan had shown that he too was human, and by no means invincible. His army had been beaten once; it could be beaten again.

Manuel Palaeologus was in no particular hurry to return to Constantinople. His return journey through Italy offered him the chance of discussions with several Italian states. The defeat of Bayezit had convinced him that there would never be a more appropriate time for a concerted onslaught by the European powers, and he had no intention of giving up his efforts. The Venetians in particular gave him a warm welcome, tempered only by their eagerness to get him home as soon as possible. The changed situation in the East would obviously have important diplomatic consequences; they therefore fitted out three warships for him and his suite, and eventually persuaded him to sail on 5 April 1403. On 9 June he stepped ashore in his capital, accompanied by John VII, who had ridden out to Gallipoli to meet him.

There was more good news waiting. Prince Süleyman, Bayezit's eldest surviving son, had arrived in Gallipoli to take over the European provinces. Tolerant and easy-going, he preferred the conference table to the battlefield, and a life of self-indulgence to either. Early in 1403 he had signed a treaty with Byzantium, Venice, Genoa and the knights of Rhodes, Stephen Lazarevich and the Latin Duke of Naxos; and Manuel heard its terms with astonishment. The Byzantines were released from their vassalage to the Sultan and from all obligation to pay tribute. Instead, Süleyman had freely undertaken to accept the Byzantine Emperor as his suzerain. He had returned to Byzantium the city of Thessalonica and its surroundings, including Mount Athos; the Black Sea coast, from the mouth of the Bosphorus to Varna; and a number of Aegean islands. All prisoners were released. Turkish vessels would enter neither the Hellespont nor the Bosphorus without prior permission. In return Süleyman asked only that he should be allowed to rule over Thrace from the palace at Adrianople.

Surprising as was the Prince's offer, his motives were not hard to understand. The Turks had no law of primogeniture, and no fewer than four of the sons of Bayezit were fighting for the Ottoman crown. If he were to succeed in his claim, Süleyman needed Byzantium every bit as much as Byzantium needed him. Clearly, too, there was no telling how long he might remain in power, and the Emperor was well aware that, whatever the immediate advantages of the 1403 treaty, he could not indefinitely rely on Turkish friendship even in Adrianople, let alone in Anatolia. Still less could he relax his efforts to alert the Christian nations of Europe.

The year 1407 saw the death after a long illness of Manuel's brother Theodore, Despot of the Morea. He had been a brilliant ruler who had maintained both the integrity of his dominion and the imperial prestige, but he left no legitimate male issue. In the summer of 1408, the Emperor travelled himself to Mistra to enthrone his own second son, another Theodore, in his place. He was still there in September, when the news came of the death of John VII in Thessalonica. This report he received with rather more equanimity; but John had also left no heir and the succession had to be provided for. The Emperor accordingly hurried to Thessalonica, where he installed his third son, the eight-year-old Andronicus. It was obviously his hope, when he returned to Constantinople early in 1409, to bring these two provinces directly under his own control; but before he could do more in this direction he found himself swept up once again in the struggle for the Ottoman Sultanate. Early in 1411 Süleyman's brother Musa captured Adrianople. Süleyman was taken prisoner and instantly strangled.

For Byzantium, this was serious news indeed. The Emperor had no delusions about Musa, who had inherited all the savagery of his father. One of the young man's first actions on assuming power was to abrogate the treaty of 1403 and to declare his brother's various concessions null and void. He then sent a number of regiments to besiege Thessalonica, while he himself led the main body of the army directly against Constantinople, leaving the usual trail of devastation behind him. Fortunately, the Land Walls proved as impregnable as ever. But Manuel knew that there was one chance only of eliminating Musa from the political scene: his brother Mehmet. Early in 1412 he dispatched a secret embassy to Mehmet's court at Brusa.

The fight for power among the sons of Bayezit had now polarized. To Mehmet, far more balanced than Musa, a Byzantine alliance seemed a small price to pay for the undisputed Ottoman throne. He led a huge army against his brother, who was finally defeated at Camurlu in Serbia on 5 July 1413 and strangled in his turn.

'Go and say to my father the Emperor of the Romans that from this day forth I am and shall be his subject, as a son to his father. Let him but command me to do his bidding, and I shall with the greatest of pleasure execute his wishes as his servant.' This was the message that Mehmet sent to Manuel Palaeologus after his victory. He freely admitted that he owed that victory largely to the Emperor, and lost no time in confirming all the concessions made by Süleyman. Manuel still had no delusions about long-term Turkish intentions, but the situation was certainly better now than in any of the twenty-two years since his accession. Perhaps there might be some hope for Byzantium after all.

Sultan Mehmet, as it happened, soon had to face a new crisis: a rebellion in the name of a pretender claiming to be Bayezit's eldest son Mustafa, presumed killed at the battle of Ancyra. The rising itself was quickly dealt with, but the Venetians engineered the claimant's escape to Europe. He eventually reached Thessalonica, where young Andronicus offered him refuge. Mehmet appealed to Manuel, who sentenced the pretender to life imprisonment on the island of Lemnos. Relations between Emperor and Sultan were scarcely ruffled; the fact remained that the Byzantines now had in their hands a claimant to the Ottoman throne. Genuine or not – and he almost certainly was not – he might, if properly handled, prove extremely useful in the future.

On 19 January 1421 Manuel's eldest son John married – with extreme reluctance – Sophia of Montferrat. His first wife had died of the plague just three years before, aged only fifteen; his second attempt was even more ill-starred. Poor Sophia was quite shatteringly plain: her figure, it was unkindly said, looked like Lent in front and Easter behind. John relegated her to a remote corner of the palace and made no attempt to consummate the marriage; she eventually escaped in 1426, entering a nunnery soon afterwards. But the real importance of this second wedding was that it provided a fitting occasion for John's coronation as co-Emperor. Remembering his own early difficulties, Manuel had already made it clear that he intended his eldest son to succeed him. He had also given John a thorough training in the art of government; the young man was now superbly prepared for the imperial throne. Henceforth he was to play an increasingly prominent part in the conduct of affairs, believing, like many of the younger generation, that a more aggressive policy was necessary. For as long as Manuel and Mehmet lived, there would probably have been little change in the status quo: but on 21 May 1421 Mehmet suddenly died, to be succeeded by his eldest son Murad II.

The war faction in Constantinople, which included John, now demanded that Murad's recognition should be withheld, and that the pretender Mustafa – still captive on Lemnos – should be played off against him. Manuel was horrified by the suggestion; but he was old and tired, and soon gave in. All too soon he was proved to have been right. Mustafa was released, and with Byzantine help quickly established himself in Rumelia; but in January 1422, when he attempted an invasion of Anatolia, he was decisively beaten and obliged to flee back to Europe. A week or two later Murad arrived from Asia Minor and put an end to all his hopes. But the furious Sultan was now bent on war. Sending a section of his army to blockade Thessalonica, he himself led the main body against Constantinople. On his arrival he built a huge rampart outside and parallel to the Land Walls, running all the way from the Marmara to the Golden Horn and enabling his catapults to hurl their missiles over the ramparts. The defenders, however, showed courage and determination, with John himself, working indefatigably, in supreme command.

Fortunately for the Byzantines, the Sultan was superstitious. A holy man had foretold that Constantinople would fall on 24 August, and on that day Murad concentrated all his efforts on a massive assault; but somehow the defences held. Disappointed and discouraged, the Sultan ordered the siege to be abandoned. There was, however, another reason for his decision. Few in either camp were aware that old Manuel had been secretly intriguing to place the late Sultan's youngest son, the thirteen-year-old Mustafa, on the Ottoman throne during his brother's absence; and that Murad, learning of this, had been obliged to leave in order to avoid a new outbreak of civil war.

Early in 1423 young Mustafa succumbed in his turn to the bowstring; meanwhile Thessalonica was still under siege. By spring, serious famine threatened. Manuel's son Andronicus, crippled at twenty-three with elephantiasis and manifestly unable to cope, now took an extraordinary step: with the consent of his father and brother, he offered the city to Venice. The Empire, he explained, could no longer afford to defend it, and he himself was too ill to bear the responsibility. If the Venetians were prepared to assume the burden, he asked only that they should preserve its political and religious institutions. After some hesitation they accepted; two representatives of the Doge sailed for Thessalonica, escorted by six transports laden with food and provisions, and on 14 September the banner of St Mark was proudly raised above the ramparts.

As the year drew to its close, John Palaeologus decided on one last appeal to the West. By now, he believed, all Europe must see the magnitude of the danger – for, once Constantinople had fallen, what was there to stop the Sultan continuing his westward advance? He sailed on 15 November and returned a year later, having visited Venice, Milan, Mantua and Hungary – all, however, without success. Back in the capital, he found the situation slightly easier. Peace had at last been made with the Sultan: once again the people of Constantinople could sleep securely in their beds. Old Manuel, who had suffered a severe stroke two years before, was by now permanently bed-ridden; but his mind remained clear. One day he turned to his old friend, the historian George Sphrantzes, and said: 'At other times in our history, my son might have been a great *basileus*; but today our Empire needs not a great *basileus* but a good manager. And I fear that his grandiose schemes and endeavours may bring ruin upon this house.'

Soon afterwards, the old Emperor took monastic vows and donned a monk's habit, adopting the name of Matthew. It was in this guise that he celebrated his seventy-fifth birthday on 27 June 1425. Just twenty-five days later the end came. Sphrantzes tells us that he was mourned more deeply and by more people than any of his predecessors. It was no more than he deserved.

The Empire of which, on 21 July 1425, the thirty-two-year-old John VIII Palaeologus became sole *basileus* was effectively bounded by the walls of Constantinople; and Constantinople now presented a dismal picture indeed. In the first quarter of the fifteenth century, after three sieges and several visitations of the plague, the population had declined dramatically. By 1425 the inhabitants are unlikely to have numbered more than fifty thousand – possibly even less. Economically, too, the Empire was in desperate straits. Once the richest and busiest commercial centre in the civilized world, Constantinople had seen her trade taken over by the Venetians and the Genoese; now their colonies too had suffered from the general instability, and a few paltry customs dues were all that ever trickled into the Byzantine exchequer. The coinage was repeatedly devalued; the system of food distribution frequently broke down altogether. The people were chronically undernourished, and their low resistance allowed one epidemic after another to rage unchecked.

The simultaneous lack of money and manpower was everywhere evident. Many of the churches were little more than empty shells. Constantine's great Hippodrome was used as a polo ground; even the Imperial Palace of Blachernae was crumbling. John must often have thought with envy of his younger brothers. Four of Manuel's sons were in the Morea, and for good reasons. The Morea could be defended; Constantinople could not. Its Land Walls, admittedly, were still intact; but every day saw a further decrease in the number of able-bodied men and women able to defend them. Few intelligent people any longer cherished a real hope of deliverance. Western Europe was obviously a broken reed. The Turks, after a brief setback, were now, under Murad II, as strong as they had ever been. It was all too likely that when the Sultan next attacked the city, its inhabitants might no longer have the spirit to resist.

The Morea, on the other hand, was relatively secure. True, it had been devastated as recently as 1423, when an army of Turks had swept down through Thessaly, seeming almost to ignore Manuel's much-vaunted Hexamilion – the wall which he had built a few years before across the Isthmus of Corinth. But they had not remained for long, the wall had since been strengthened, and Venice had promised to come to the rescue if the incident were repeated. Already Venetian ships patrolled the coasts, where they were more than a match for the still rudimentary Turkish navy. Compared to those in the capital, conditions in the Morea were pleasant indeed; and by 1425 few people, offered homes in Constantinople or in Mistra, would have hesitated at the choice.

The city of Mistra, lying on the slopes of the Taygetus range in the southern Peloponnese, had been founded by William of Villehardouin in 1249; but twelve years later, after the reconquest of Constantinople, he had been obliged to surrender it to Byzantium. By now, as the Latins gradually retreated, Mistra had grown steadily in size, until it was the obvious city to which John VI Cantacuzenus should send his son Manuel, first Despot of the Morea, in 1349 – exactly a hundred years after its foundation. By 1400 it had developed into something far more than a mere provincial capital. It was now an artistic, intellectual and religious centre comparable with what Constantinople had been a century before, attracting the greatest artists in the Byzantine world. John Cantacuzenus was a regular visitor, and had indeed died there in 1383. Among others were the famous Metropolitan Bessarion of Nicaea and the future Metropolitan Isidore of Kiev, both of whom were later to become cardinals in the Church of Rome; the philosopher and theologian George Scholarius, who under the name of Gennadius II would be the first Patriarch of Constantinople after its fall; and the most original of all Byzantine thinkers, George Gemistos Plethon.

During the first five years of the new reign, things went well for the Morea. Progress in the south, however, was outweighed by disaster further north; for in 1430 Thessalonica fell once again to the Sultan. The Turks had maintained their blockade; and before long the Venetians, far from turning the city into a second Venice as they had promised, were heartily regretting that they had ever accepted it at all. When Murad himself arrived on 26 March he captured it in a matter of hours. There was the usual frenzy of murder and pillage. All the churches were looted, many of them destroyed; the palaces of the nobility were ransacked and put to the torch. Then, after the statutory three days, Murad called a halt. Thessalonica was the second city of the Byzantine Empire; he had no wish to reduce it to ruins. A general amnesty was declared; the people were invited to return to their homes, with a guarantee that they would suffer no more ill-treatment. As for the Venetian governors of the city, they had somehow managed to make their way down to the harbour, where a ship had carried them off to the nearest Venetian soil, the colony of Euboea.

News of the fall of Thessalonica reached Constantinople at much the same time as a report that Pope Martin V had summoned a Council of the Church, to meet at Basel in 1431. To John Palaeologus, this seemed to offer a ray of hope. Representatives of all the Christian nations of the West would be present; at last, perhaps, a Byzantine appeal might fall on more receptive ears. For various reasons the Council was postponed another seven years and the venue changed to Ferrara, but the Emperor's determination to attend remained firm: thus it was that John once again left his brother Constantine as Regent and in November 1437 embarked on his historic journey, taking with him a party some seven hundred strong, including the most distinguished group of Eastern churchmen ever to visit the West. There was the Patriarch himself, Joseph II; eighteen Metropolitans, among them the brilliant young Bessarion of Nicaea and Isidore, Bishop of Kiev and All Russia. Among the laymen were George Scholarius, whose knowledge of Latin theology would, it was hoped, confound the scholars of the West; and, most revered of all, George Gemistos Plethon himself from Mistra. All these were pro-Western, to a greater or lesser degree. The leading light of the ultra-Orthodox camp was Mark Eugenicus, Metropolitan of Ephesus. The Emperor also took with him his brother Demetrius. He knew him for an intriguer, and preferred to have him where he could keep an eye on him.

The Council got off to a bad start. There were many painful problems of protocol and precedence; both Emperor and Pope were jealous of their dignity. The relative positions of their two thrones in the cathedral, for example, raised difficulties which at one moment seemed almost insuperable. If John's mission to the West were to succeed, it was essential that he should be seen not as a suppliant but as the monarch of a great Christian Empire. Whom, however, was he to impress? One of his principal reasons for attending the Council was to seek help from the other European princes, and he was determined that no important decisions should be taken before their arrival; but no princes appeared. The Latins grew ever more impatient, the Pope – who was responsible for the board and lodging of the entire Greek delegation – ever more concerned as his financial reserves steadily diminished. With August came the plague. The Greeks appeared immune, but there was heavy mortality among the Latin delegates. They grew even more irritated with their guests; but the Byzantines too were losing patience. After nearly a year's absence from their homes, they had so far achieved nothing. Moreover it was by now plain that none of the European princes had any intention of attending the Council at all. Deliberations began in earnest on 8 October; but the sessions ended on 13 December with agreement as far away as ever.

At this point the Pope managed to persuade the delegates to move to Florence. His motives were principally financial: in Florence, the Medici could be trusted to help out. But the move also proved beneficial in other ways. When the sessions were resumed towards the end of February 1439 the Greeks – tired, anxious, homesick and hungry – seemed readier now to compromise. By the end of March they had agreed that the Latin formula according to which the Holy Spirit proceeded from the Father *and* the Son meant the same as a recently-accepted Greek formula whereby it proceeded from the Father *through* the Son. With the *Filioque* at last out of the way, the other outstanding questions were quickly settled. By mid-summer agreement had been virtually reached, and on 5 July the official Decree of Union – little more than a statement of the Latin position – was signed by all the Orthodox churchmen except the Metropolitan of Ephesus, who had remained inflexible but was forbidden by the Emperor to exercise a veto. The Latins then added their own signatures; and on the following day the decree was publicly proclaimed in both Latin and Greek in Florence cathedral. The Latin version began with the words *Laetentur coeli* – 'let the heavens rejoice'. It soon became clear that they had little reason to do so.

It was February 1440 before John Palaeologus returned to Constantinople. He had a sad homecoming. His beloved third wife Maria of Trebizond had died a few weeks before; and already the Council of Florence was being almost universally condemned, its signatories reviled as outcasts and traitors to the Faith, and in several cases physically attacked. The Patriarchs of Jerusalem, Alexandria and Antioch disowned the delegates who had signed on their behalf. The Metropolitan of Ephesus was the hero of the hour. Such revulsion seriously weakened the Emperor's own position. In the summer of

1442 his ever-ambitious brother Demetrius tried to seize the throne in the name of Orthodoxy. He failed, but his attempted *coup* was only a symptom of a greater dissatisfaction.

Pope Eugenius IV chose to overlook these developments. With the Church theoretically reunited, he must now raise his promised Crusade against Byzantium's enemies. This was becoming more obviously necessary every day. Smederevo, the great Danubian fortress some twenty-five miles south-east of Belgrade, had surrendered in 1439 after a three-month siege; in 1441 the Sultan's army crossed into Transylvania; there could be no doubt that Hungary would be next. It was thus the Hungarians who formed the bulk of the Pope's Crusade, the Hungarian King Ladislas whom he named as its leader and a Hungarian general – the brilliant John Hunyadi – to whom he entrusted the supreme command. The necessary fleet was to be provided by the Venetians, the Duke of Burgundy and the Pope himself. It was to sail up the Bosphorus to the Black Sea, thence proceeding up the Danube to meet the army, which would advance simultaneously from the north-west.

The Crusade set off in the summer of 1443. Unopposed, it now marched into Bulgaria, where Sofia surrendered shortly before Christmas. January 1444 saw another major victory; and by late spring the Sultan was growing seriously alarmed. His armies were fully employed in Anatolia, Albania and the Morea. In June he made enough concessions to earn him a ten-year truce. When the news reached Rome, however, Pope Eugenius was horrified. Were all the gains that the Crusade had so far achieved to be thrown away? He immediately absolved King Ladislas from his oath to the Sultan and virtually ordered the Crusade on its way again. Ladislas should have refused; his forces were by now dangerously diminished. But he did as he was bidden, and in September he was back with the army. The Crusade started off again, and made its way across Bulgaria to the Black Sea near Varna, where Ladislas expected to find the fleet awaiting him. The fleet, however, was otherwise engaged: Murad had rushed back from Anatolia and the allied ships were desperately trying to prevent him from crossing the Bosphorus. They failed. Forcing his way across the strait, on 10 November 1444 the Sultan tore into the Crusading army. The Christians, outnumbered, had no chance. Ladislas fell; his army was annihilated; of its leaders, only John Hunyadi managed to escape with a few of his men. The last Crusade ever to be launched against the Turks in Europe had ended in catastrophe.

For John Palaeologus, the disaster meant the negation of all his work, the frustration of all his diplomacy, the end of all his hopes. It was for this, he now realized, that he had betrayed his Church and incurred the hatred and contempt of the vast majority of his own subjects. And the final humiliation was yet to come. When the victorious Sultan returned it was John, as his faithful vassal, who was obliged to congratulate him on his triumph.

Eleven days later, on 31 October 1448, he died in Constantinople. Though still only fifty-six, the disappointments of the past few years had left him a sad and broken man. There could be no more Crusades; no one now believed that the Empire could be saved, and there were now a good many who doubted whether it was worth saving. Of all the Byzantine Emperors John is the best known in appearance, thanks to his portrait in Benozzo Gozzoli's famous fresco of the Magi in the chapel of the Palazzo Medici-Riccardi in Florence. Perhaps he hardly merited his posthumous celebrity. Manuel II had remarked that the Empire needed not a great *basileus* but a good manager; John was neither. Nevertheless, he did his best; besides, the situation had long been hopeless: anything that he had attempted would have been doomed to failure. And perhaps it was just as well. Byzantium, devoured from within, threatened from without, reduced now to an almost invisible speck on the map of Europe, now needed the *coup de grâce*. It had been a long time coming. Now, finally, it was at hand.

29
The Fall

[1448–53]

John VIII Palaeologus died childless. Of his five brothers the first, Theodore, had predeceased him by four months and the second, Andronicus, had died young in Thessalonica. Of the three survivors – Constantine, Despot of the Morea Demetrius and Thomas – John had nominated Constantine as his heir. The ever-ambitious Demetrius immediately challenged him; but his mother the Empress Helena finally supported Constantine, simultaneously claiming the Regency until his arrival. Finding Thomas also against him, Demetrius was forced to submit.

Meanwhile two envoys had sailed for the Morea with powers to invest Constantine as Emperor. Clearly they could not perform a coronation and Mistra had no Patriarch; the ceremony which was held there on 6 January 1449 was a civil one. But Constantine XI Dragases – he always preferred to use this Greek form of his Serbian mother's name – could never be formally crowned. The Orthodox Church, since the Council of Florence, was in schism: the Patriarch Gregory III, a fervent unionist, was execrated as a traitor by well over half his flock. Constantine himself had never condemned the union; if by upholding it he could increase the chances of Western aid it was surely his duty to do so. But the price was high. The anti-unionists refused to pray for him. Without a coronation he had no moral claim on their loyalties, or on those of any of his subjects; with one, he could have triggered a civil war at a moment when Byzantium was faced by the most implacable of its enemies.

Surprisingly little was known about the inscrutable young prince who had recently succeeded to the Ottoman throne at Adrianople. Born in 1433, the third of Murad's sons, Mehmet had had an unhappy childhood. His mother had been a slave-girl – probably Christian – in the harem. His elder brother Ahmet had died in 1439; in 1444 his younger brother Ali had been strangled in his bed. Mehmet, now heir to the throne, was summoned back urgently to Adrianople, where he was entrusted to the leading scholars of the day – with whom he laid the foundations of the learning and culture for which he was soon to be famous. At the time of his accession he is said to have been fluent in Turkish, Arabic, Greek, Latin, Persian and Hebrew.

When Sultan Murad died of apoplexy on 13 February 1451, Mehmet was away in Anatolia. It took him just five days to reach Adrianople, where he confirmed his father's ministers in their places or appointed them elsewhere. Meanwhile Murad's widow arrived to congratulate him on his succession. Mehmet received her warmly; when she returned to the harem she found that her infant son had been murdered in his bath. The young Sultan was taking no chances.

But he was only nineteen, and in the West there was a feeling that he was still too immature to constitute the serious threat his father had done – a delusion that Mehmet did his best to encourage. To Constantine's ambassadors he cheerfully swore to live at peace with Byzantium, maintaining the traditional bonds of friendship. But Constantine remained on his guard; and his suspicions were confirmed when in April 1451 Mehmet began to build a fortress on the Bosphorus a few miles up from Constantinople where the great channel was at its narrowest, opposite Bayezit's castle of Anadolu Hisar. This not only gave him complete control of the Bosphorus; it provided the ideal base from which Constantinople could be attacked from the north-east, where the Golden Horn constituted virtually its only line of defence. In the capital, the reaction can well be imagined. Constantine sent two successive embassies, weighed down with presents, reminding the Sultan that he was breaking his oath and begging him at least to spare the neighbouring Byzantine villages. Both were sent back unheard. A week or two later Constantine made one last effort: his ambassadors were executed on the spot.

The castle of Rumeli Hisar still stands, essentially unchanged since it was completed after just twenty weeks, on Thursday, 31 August 1451. When it was ready the Sultan issued a proclamation that every passing ship, whatever its nationality or provenance, must stop for examination. Late in November a Venetian vessel coming from the Black Sea ignored the instruction. It was blasted out of the water; the crew were killed, the captain, Antonio Rizzo, impaled on a stake. In the West opinions were hastily revised. Mehmet II clearly meant business.

On Tuesday, 12 December 1452 Constantine XI and his court attended high mass in St Sophia, where the *Laetentur Coeli* was formally read out, as at Florence. In theory at any rate, the union was complete. And yet for the unionists it was an empty victory. The service had been poorly attended; the Emperor had seemed half-hearted and listless. Afterwards there was no rejoicing. It was noticed that the churches whose clergy had espoused the union – including of course the Great Church itself – were henceforth almost empty; the people had accepted the inevitable, but they worshipped only where the old liturgy remained unchanged.

Just one month later, in January 1453, Mehmet summoned his ministers to his presence in Adrianople. His Empire, he told them, could never be safe while Constantinople remained in Christian hands. The city must be taken, and now was the time to take it. Previous attempts had failed because no blockade had been possible. Now, for the first time, the Turks had naval superiority. If Constantinople could not be stormed, it must be starved. Two months later even his closest advisers were astonished at the size of the armada which assembled off Gallipoli; but their reactions were as nothing compared with those of the Byzantines when it approached across the Marmara and dropped anchor beneath the walls of their city.

The army, meanwhile, was gathering in Thrace. Mehmet had given it his personal attention throughout the previous winter. He had mobilized every regiment, stopped all leave and recruited hordes of mercenaries – in all some eighty thousand regular troops and up to twenty thousand *bashi-bazouks*, or irregulars. But there was something else of which he was prouder still. The previous year a German engineer named Urban had offered to build him a bronze cannon that would blast the walls of Babylon itself. Mehmet paid him well and was rewarded three months later by the fearsome weapon that had sunk Rizzo's ship. He then demanded another, twice the size of the first, which was completed in January 1453. It is said to have been nearly twenty-seven feet long and eight inches thick, with a muzzle two and a half feet across, capable of firing a ball weighing some thirteen hundredweight well over a mile. Two hundred men were sent out to organize the journey of this fearsome machine to Constantinople, smoothing the road and reinforcing the bridges; it was drawn by thirty pairs of oxen, with another two hundred men holding it steady.

On 5 April Mehmet pitched his tent before the walls of Constantinople, sending the Emperor the message required by Islamic law undertaking that all his subjects would be spared in return for immediate and voluntary surrender. If they refused, they would be given no quarter. He received no reply. Early in the morning of Friday, 6 April, the cannon opened fire. To the people of Constantinople, it came as no surprise. Throughout the previous winter they had worked – men, women and children, the Emperor at their head – on the city's defences. Although the main threat was clearly from the west, the sea walls along the Marmara and the Golden Horn had also been strengthened; no one had forgotten the Fourth Crusade. By the coming of spring preparations were complete. Easter fell on 1 April. Even on that day St Sophia with its Catholic rite was avoided by most Byzantines; they knew, however, that they had done everything possible to prepare for the coming onslaught.

Three months after the death of Antonio Rizzo, in February 1453, the

Venetian Senate had finally voted to send two transports, each carrying four hundred men, to Constantinople, with fifteen galleys following as soon as they were ready; but it was not till 20 April that even the first ships left the lagoon – by which time three Genoese vessels, chartered by Pope Nicholas V and filled with food and war provisions at his own personal expense, had already reached Constantinople. Fortunately for the honour of the Serenissima, however, the Venetian colony in the city had responded nobly. The *bailo*, Girolamo Minotto, had promised every support, assuring the Emperor that none of the Republic's vessels would leave the harbour without his permission. In all, the colony was able to provide nine merchantmen. Of the Genoese contingent, many predictably came from the colony at Galata; but there was also a group of determined young men from Genoa itself. Their leader, Giovanni Giustiniani Longo, a member of one of the Republic's leading families and a renowned expert in siege warfare, arrived on 29 January with a private army of seven hundred. All this must have given Constantine some encouragement, but a severe blow was in store for him; on the night of 26 February seven Venetian ships slipped out of the Golden Horn, carrying some seven hundred Italians. Only a few days before, their captains had sworn a solemn oath to remain in the city.

Now at last the Emperor could assess his available resources. Moored in the Golden Horn were eight other Venetian vessels, five Genoese and one each from Ancona, Catalonia and Provence, together with the ten which were all that remained of the Byzantine navy – a total of twenty-six, pitiable in comparison to the Ottoman armada. But the problem of manpower was more serious still: a census of all able-bodied men in the city, including monks and clerics, capable of manning the walls, amounted to just 4,983 Greeks and rather less than two thousand foreigners. To defend fourteen miles of wall against Mehmet's army of a hundred thousand, Constantine could muster less than seven thousand men.

By the morning of 6 April most of the defenders were in their places, the Emperor and Giustiniani in command of the most vulnerable section, crossing the valley of the little river Lycus about a mile from the northern end. The sea walls were less heavily manned, but their garrisons served also as look-outs, reporting on Turkish ship movements. The Sultan, meanwhile, was subjecting the Land Walls to a bombardment unprecedented in the history of siege warfare. By the evening of the first day he had pulverized a section near the Charisius Gate. His soldiers made repeated attempts to smash their way through, but again and again were forced to retreat until nightfall sent them back to their camp. Morning revealed the wall to have been rebuilt, and Mehmet decided to hold his fire until he could bring up reinforcements. On

11 April the bombardment resumed, to continue uninterruptedly for the next forty-eight days. Although the larger cannon could be fired only once every two or three hours, the damage they did was enormous; within a week the outer wall across the Lycus had collapsed in several places, and although the defenders worked ceaselessly to repair the damage they obviously could not continue indefinitely.

Shortly afterwards the Pope's three Genoese galleys finally arrived off the Hellespont. There they were joined by a heavy transport, made available by Alfonso of Aragon, with a cargo of corn from Sicily. Determined to mass the strongest possible naval force outside Constantinople, Mehmet had ill-advisedly left the straits unguarded, and the ships had been able to make their way unhindered into the Marmara. The moment they appeared on the morning of 20 April, the Sultan rode around the head of the Golden Horn to give his orders personally to his admiral, Süleyman Baltoğlu. On no account were they to reach the city.

Baltoğlu prepared to attack, but his sailing ships were powerless against the fresh southerly breeze while his biremes and triremes were unmanageable in the heavy swell. His captains, virtually defenceless against the deluge of arrows, javelins and other projectiles that greeted any approach, were forced to watch while the four galleys advanced serenely towards the Golden Horn. Suddenly the wind dropped; Baltoğlu gave the order to advance and board. His own flagship bore down upon the imperial transport, ramming it in the stern. But the Turkish ships road low in the water. Grappling and boarding a taller vessel was almost impossible; the Genoese sailors were equipped with huge axes with which to lop off the heads and hands of all who made the attempt. The Genoese captains now came alongside the transport and lashed all four vessels together, till they stood like a great sea-girt castle amid the chaos. Then, just as the sun was setting, the wind got up again. The Christian sails billowed out, and the great floating fortress began to move towards the entrance to the Horn, splintering all the Turkish ships in its path. A few hours later in the dead of night, the boom was opened and the four vessels slipped quietly into the Golden Horn.

The Sultan had watched every moment of the battle from the shore, occasionally in his excitement riding his horse out into the sea. Such now was his fury that his escort feared for his sanity. The next day he ordered Baltoğlu's immediate execution. The admiral gained a reprieve only after his subordinates testified to his courage; but he was bastinadoed and deprived alike of his public offices and his private possessions. He was never heard of again.

The Sultan's next objective was the Golden Horn. He had already set his engineers to work on a road running behind Galata, from the Marmara shore over the hill near what is now Taksim Square and down to the Horn itself. Iron wheels had been cast, and metal tracks; his carpenters, meanwhile, had fashioned wooden cradles large enough to accommodate the keels of moderate-sized vessels. It was a Herculean undertaking but, with Mehmet's resources, not an impossible one. On Sunday morning, 22 April, the Genoese colony in Galata watched astounded as some seventy Turkish ships were slowly hauled by innumerable teams of oxen over a two-hundred-foot hill and then lowered into the Horn beyond.

The Byzantines, ignorant of the Sultan's plan, were hard put to believe the evidence of their own eyes. Not only was their only major harbour no longer secure; they now had three and a half more miles of sea wall to defend, including the section breached by the Crusaders in 1204. By the beginning of May Constantine knew that he could not hold out much longer. Food was running short; more and more of the defenders along the walls were taking time off to find sustenance for their families. Only one hope – and that a faint one – remained: was a Venetian relief expedition on its way or not? If so, how big was it, and what was its cargo? When would it arrive, and how, with the enemy in possession of the Golden Horn, would it be received? On the answers to these questions the whole fate of Constantinople now depended. And so, just before midnight on 3 May, a Venetian brigantine flying the Turkish standard and carrying a crew of twelve volunteers in Turkish disguise, slipped out under the boom.

On the night of the 23rd it returned. The captain immediately sought an audience with the Emperor and Minotto. For three weeks, he reported, he had combed the Aegean, but nowhere had he seen a trace of the promised expedition. Finally he had called a meeting of his crew. One sailor had proposed a return to Venice, but he had been shouted down. To the rest, their duty was clear: they must report to the Emperor, as they had promised. And so they had returned, knowing full well that they were unlikely to leave the city alive. Constantine thanked each one personally, his voice choked with tears.

By now, too, the omens had begun. On 22 May there was a lunar eclipse; a day or two later, as the holiest icon of the Virgin was being carried through the streets in one last appeal for her intercession, it slipped from its platform. A few hundred yards further on, a violent thunderstorm caused the whole procession to be abandoned. The next morning the city was shrouded in fog, unheard-of at the end of May; the same night the dome of St Sophia was suffused with an unearthly red glow that crept slowly up from the base to the summit and then went out. This last phenomenon was also seen by the Turks in Galata; Mehmet himself was greatly disturbed, and was reassured only after his astrologers had interpreted it as a sign that the building would soon be illuminated by the True Faith. For the Byzantines, the meaning was clear: the Spirit of God itself had deserted their city.

Once again, as so often in the past, Constantine's ministers implored him to leave the capital while there was still time, to head a Byzantine government-in-exile in the Morea until he could recover the city, just as Michael Palaeologus had done nearly two centuries before. The exhausted Emperor fainted even as they spoke; but when he recovered he was as determined as ever. This was his city; these were his people. He could not leave them now.

On 26 May the Sultan held a council of war. The siege, he declared, had continued long enough; the time had come for the final assault. The following day would be occupied with preparations, the next to rest and prayer. The attack would begin in the early hours of Tuesday, 29 May. No attempt was made to conceal the plan from the defenders. For the next thirty-six hours the preparatory work continued without interruption; at night huge flares were lit to help the soldiers at their labours, while drums and trumpets encouraged them to still greater efforts. Then, at dawn on the 28th, a sudden silence fell. While his men prepared themselves for the morrow Mehmet set off on a day-long tour of inspection, returning only late in the evening to take his own rest.

Within the city, on that last Monday of the Empire's history, quarrels and differences were forgotten. Work on the walls continued as always, but elsewhere the people of Constantinople gathered for one last collective intercession. As the bells pealed, the most sacred icons and the most precious of relics were carried out to join the long, spontaneous procession that passed through the streets and along the whole length of the walls, pausing for special prayers where the Sultan's artillery might be expected to concentrate its fire on the following day. When it was finished the Emperor summoned his commanders for the last time. He spoke first to his Greek subjects, telling them that there were four great causes for which a man should be ready to die: his faith, his country, his family and his sovereign. They must now be prepared to give their lives for all four. He for his part was ready to sacrifice his own. Turning to the Italians, he thanked them for all that they had done and assured them of his love and trust. They and the Greeks were now one people; with God's help they would be victorious.

Dusk was falling. From all over the city the people were making their way to the Church of the Holy Wisdom. For the past five months it had been generally avoided by the Greeks, defiled as they believed it to be by the Latin usages that no honourable Byzantine could possibly accept. Now, liturgical differences were forgotten. St Sophia was, as no other church could ever be, the spiritual centre of Byzantium. In this moment of supreme crisis, there could be nowhere else to go.

That last service of vespers ever to be held in the Great Church was also the most inspiring. Those on duty remained once again at their posts along the walls; but virtually every other man, woman and child in the city crowded into St Sophia to take the Eucharist and to pray for deliverance. The service was still in progress when the Emperor arrived. He first asked forgiveness of his sins from every bishop present, Catholic and Orthodox alike; then he too took communion. Much later, when all but the few permanent candles had been put out and the Great Church was in darkness, he spent some time alone in prayer; then he returned to Blachernae for a last farewell to his household. Towards midnight, accompanied by Sphrantzes, he rode for the last time the length of the Land Walls to assure himself that all was ready.

At half-past one in the morning Mehmet gave the signal. Suddenly, the silence was shattered – the blasts of trumpets and the hammering of drums combining with the blood-curdling Turkish war-cries to produce a clamour fit to waken the dead. At once the church bells began to peal, a sign to the whole city that the final battle had begun.

The Sultan knew that if he were to take the city he must allow its defenders no rest. He first sent forward his irregulars, the *bashi-bazouks*. Badly armed and largely untrained, they had little staying power, but their initial onslaught could be terrifying indeed. For two hours they hurled themselves against the walls; then, shortly before four in the morning, came the second wave of the attack, by several regiments of Anatolian Turks, all superbly trained and disciplined. They came within an ace of forcing an entry; but the defenders, led by the Emperor himself, closed round them, killed as many as they could and drove the rest back across the ditch. The Sultan flew into his usual rage, but he was not unduly disturbed. Victory must be won not by the Anatolians but by his own élite regiment of Janissaries; and it was these whom he now threw into the fray.

The Christians had no time to recover themselves before this third attack began. In that steady, remorseless rhythm that struck terror into the hearts of all who heard it, the crack troops of the Ottoman Empire advanced across the plain at the double, their ranks unbroken despite the hail of missiles from the walls, the deafening military music that kept them in step almost a weapon in itself. In wave after wave they came, flinging themselves against the stockades, hacking away at the supports, throwing up scaling-ladders and then, at a given command, making way without fuss for the following wave, while they themselves waited and rested until their turn came round again. For the defenders, however, there could be no such alternation. The fighting had already continued for well over five hours; they could not last much longer.

Then disaster struck. Soon after dawn a bolt struck Giovanni Longo, pierced his breastplate and smashed through his chest. In excruciating pain, he was carried down to a Genoese ship in the harbour. Then, before the gate could be relocked, the Genoese streamed through it. The Sultan, seeing what had occurred, immediately launched yet another wave of Janissaries. Soon the Greeks were retreating back to the inner wall. Caught between the two rows of fortifications, they were easy prey to the advancing Turks. Many were slaughtered where they stood.

At this point a Turkish flag was seen flying from a tower a short distance away to the north. An hour or so earlier, a group of Turkish irregulars on patrol had found a small door, half-hidden at the foot of a tower. It was in fact a sally-port known as the Kerkoporta, through which the Genoese had organized several effective raids on the Turkish camp. The *bashi-bazouks* had managed to force it open, and had made their way to the top of the tower. In the confusion they were able to hoist their standard, leaving the door open for others to follow. It was almost certainly they, and not the Janissaries, who were the first to enter the city. By now, however, all the regiments were pouring through the open breaches; and Constantine, flinging off his imperial regalia, plunged into the fray where the fighting was thickest. He was never seen again.

It was early morning, with the waning moon high in the sky. The walls were strewn with the dead and dying; but of living defenders there was scarcely a trace. The surviving Greeks had hurried home to their families, hoping to save them from the rape and pillage that had already begun; the Venetians were making for the harbour, the Genoese for the comparative security of Galata. They found the Horn surprisingly quiet: most of the Turkish sailors had already gone ashore, lest the army beat them to the women and the plunder. The Venetian commander encountered no resistance when he set his sailors to break down the boom; his little fleet, accompanied by seven Genoese vessels and half a dozen Byzantine galleys, all packed to the gunwales with refugees, swung out into the Marmara and down the Hellespont to the open sea.

By noon the streets were running with blood. Houses were ransacked, women and children raped or impaled, churches razed, icons wrenched from their frames, books ripped from their bindings. The Imperial Palace at Blachernae was left an empty shell, the Empire's holiest icon, the Virgin Hodegetria, hacked into four pieces and destroyed. The most hideous scenes of all, however, were enacted in St Sophia. Matins were already in progress when the berserk conquerors were heard approaching. Immediately the great bronze doors were closed; but the Turks soon smashed their way in. The poorer and less attractive of the congregation were massacred on the spot; the remainder were led off to the Turkish camps to await their fate. The priests continued with the Mass until they were killed at the altar; but there are among the faithful those who still believe that one or two of them gathered up the patens and chalices and mysteriously disappeared into the southern wall of the sanctuary. There they will remain until Constantinople becomes once again a Christian city, when they will resume the service at the point at which it was interrupted.

Sultan Mehmet had promised his men the three traditional days of looting; but there were no protests when he brought it to a close the same evening. By then there was little left to plunder, and his soldiers were fully occupied sharing out the loot and enjoying their captives. In the late afternoon, accompanied by his chief ministers, his imams and his bodyguard of Janissaries, he rode slowly to St Sophia. Dismounting outside the central doors, he picked up a handful of earth which, in a gesture of humility, he sprinkled over his turban; then he entered the Great Church. As he walked towards the altar, he stopped one of his soldiers whom he saw hacking at the marble pavement; looting, he told him, did not include the destruction of public buildings. At his command the senior imam mounted the pulpit and proclaimed the name of Allah, the All-Merciful and Compassionate: there was no God but God and Mohammed was his Prophet. The Sultan touched his turbaned head to the ground in prayer and thanksgiving. St Sophia was now a mosque.

Leaving it, he crossed the square to the old, ruined Palace of the Emperors, founded by Constantine the Great eleven and a half centuries before; and as he wandered through its ancient halls, his slippers brushing the dust from the pebbled floor-mosaics – some of which have survived to this day – he is said to have murmured the lines of a Persian poet:

> The spider weaves the curtains in the palace of the Caesars;
> The owl calls the watches in the towers of Afrasiab.

He had achieved his ambition. Constantinople was his. He was just twenty-one years old.

Epilogue

The news of the conquest was received with horror throughout Christendom. The refugees carried the epic story with them; and their story lost nothing in the telling. The one point on which few could agree was the fate of the last Emperor of Byzantium. Inevitably, there were rumours that he had escaped; but the vast majority of sources – including Sphrantzes, his closest friend and with whom he would certainly have communicated had he survived – record with certainty that he perished in the fighting. According to one story, Turkish soldiers recognized the body by the imperial eagles embroidered on his boots. It seems unlikely that Mehmet would ever have allowed the Emperor a tomb, or even a simple grave, which would have become a place of pilgrimage and a focus for pro-Byzantine feeling; though there is still just a possibility that his body might have been concealed and buried secretly. But of all the stories relating the fate of Constantine XI, the most probable is also the simplest: that the corpse was never identified, and the last Emperor of Byzantium was buried anonymously with his fellow-soldiers in a common grave.

The Roman Empire of the East was founded by Constantine the Great on Monday, 11 May 330; it came to an end on Tuesday, 29 May 1453. During those one thousand, one hundred and twenty-three years and eighteen days, eighty-eight men and women occupied the imperial throne – excluding the seven who usurped it during the Latin occupation. Of those eighty-eight, a few – Constantine himself, Justinian, Heraclius, the two Basils, Alexius Comnenus – possessed true greatness; a few – Phocas, Michael III, Zoe and the Angeli – were contemptible; the vast majority were brave, upright, God-fearing men who did their best, with greater or lesser degrees of success. Byzantium may not have lived up to its highest ideals, but it certainly did not deserve the reputation which, thanks largely to Edward Gibbon, it acquired in the eighteenth and nineteenth centuries. The Byzantines were, on the contrary, a deeply religious society in which illiteracy – at least among the middle and upper classes – was virtually unknown, and in which one Emperor after another was renowned for his scholarship; a society which alone preserved much of the heritage of Greek and Latin antiquity, during these dark centuries in the West when the lights of learning were almost extinguished; a society, finally, which produced the astonishing phenomenon of Byzantine art. Restricted this art may have been, largely confined to the great mystery of the Christian faith; within this limitation, however, it achieved a degree of intensity and exaltation unparalleled before or since, qualities which entitle the masterpieces – the *deesis* in the south gallery of St Sophia, the *Anastasis* in the *parecclesion* of St Saviour in Chora in Constantinople – to be reckoned among the most sublime creations of the human spirit. The instructions given to the painters and mosaicists of Byzantium were simple enough: 'to represent the spirit of God'. It was a formidable challenge, and one which Western artists seldom even attempted; again and again, however, in the churches and monasteries of the Christian East, we see the task triumphantly accomplished.

One of the first and most brilliant of twentieth-century Philhellenes, Robert Byron, maintained that the greatness of Byzantium lay in what he described as 'the Triple Fusion': that of a Roman body, a Greek mind and an oriental, mystical soul. Certainly these three strands were always present, and were largely responsible for the Empire's unique character: at bottom, however, the Byzantines were human like the rest of us, victims of the same weaknesses and subject to the same temptations, deserving of praise and of blame much as we are ourselves. What they do not deserve is the obscurity to which for centuries we have condemned them. Their follies were many, as were their sins; but much should surely be forgiven for the beauty they left behind them and the heroism with which they and their last brave Emperor met their end, in one of those glorious epics of world history that has passed into legend and is remembered with equal pride by victors and vanquished alike. That is why five and a half centuries later, throughout the Greek world, Tuesday is still believed to be the unluckiest day of the week; why the Turkish flag still depicts not a crescent but a waning moon, reminding us that the moon was in its last quarter when Constantinople finally fell; and why, excepting only the Great Church of St Sophia itself, it is the Land Walls – broken, battered, but still marching from sea to sea – that stand as the city's grandest and most tragic monument.

List of Emperors

284–305	Diocletian	} *Joint Emperors*
286–305	Maximian	
305–6	Constantius I Chlorus	
305–11	Galerius	} *Joint Emperors*
306–12	Maxentius (replaced Constantius)	
306–24	Constantine I the Great	} *Joint Emperors*
312–24	Licinius	
324–37	Constantine I *Sole Emperor*	
337–40	Constantine II	
337–50	Constantius II	} *Joint Emperors*
337–50	Constans	
350–61	Constantius II *Sole Emperor*	
361–3	Julian	
363–4	Jovian	
364–75	Valentinian I	} *Joint Emperors*
364–78	Valens	
375–83	Gratian	
379–92	Theodosius I	} *Joint Emperors*
383–92	Valentinian II (replaced Gratian)	
392–5	Theodosius I	

EAST		WEST	
395–408	Arcadius	395–423	Honorius
408–50	Theodosius II	423	Constantius III
		423–5	Johannes
450–57	Marcian	425–55	Valentinian III
		455	Petronius Maximus
		455–6	Avitus
457–74	Leo I	457–61	Marjorian
		461–5	Libius Severus
		467–72	Anthemius
		472	Olybrius
		472–4	Glycerius

EAST		WEST	
474	Leo II	474	Julius Nepos
474–91	Zeno	474–476	Romulus Augustulus
[475–6	Basiliscus]		
491–518	Anastasius I		
518–27	Justin I		
527–65	Justinian I		
565–78	Justin II		
578–82	Tiberius II Constantine		
582–602	Maurice		
602–10	Phocas		
610–41	Heraclius		
641	Constantine III ⎱ *Joint*		
	Heraclonas ⎰ *Emperors*		
641–68	Constans II 'Pogonatus'		
668–85	Constantine IV		
685–95	Justinian II 'Rhinotmetus'		
695–8	Leontius		
698–705	Tiberius III		
705–11	Justinian II 'Rhinotmetus'		
711–13	Philippicus Bardanes		
713–15	Anastasius II		
715–17	Theodosius III		
717–41	Leo III		
741	Constantine V 'Copronymus'		
742	Artabasdus		
743–75	Constantine V 'Copronymus'		
775–80	Leo IV		
780–97	Constantine VI		
797–802	Irene	800–814	Charlemagne
802–11	Nicephorus I		
811	Stauracius		
811–13	Michael Rhangabe		
813–20	Leo V	814–40	Lewis the Pious
820–29	Michael II	817–31 ⎱ Lothair I	
829–42	Theophilus	840–55 ⎰	
842–67	Michael III	850–75	Lewis II
867–86	Basil I	875–7	Charles the Bald
		881–8	Charles the Fat
886–912	Leo VI	891–4	Guy
		894–8	Lambert
		896–9	Arnulf
		901–5	Lewis III
912–13	Alexander		

385

913–59	Constantine VII 'Porphyrogenitus'		915–22	Berengar
920–44	Romanus I Lecapenus			
959–63	Romanus II		962–73	Otto I
963–9	Nicephorus II Phocas			
969–76	John I Tzimisces		967–73	Otto II
976–1025	Basil II 'Bulgaroctonus'		996–1002	Otto III
			1014–24	Henry II
1025–8	Constantine VIII		1027–39	Conrad II
1028–34	Romanus III Argyrus			
1034–41	Michael IV the Paphlagonian			
1041–2	Michael V 'Calaphates'			
1042	Zoe and Theodora			
1042–55	Constantine IX Monomachus		1046–56	Henry III
1055–6	Theodora			
1056–7	Michael VI			
1057–9	Isaac I Comnenus			
1059–67	Constantine Ducas			
1068–71	Romanus IV Diogenes			
1071–8	Michael VII Ducas			
1078–81	Nicephorus III Botaneiates			
1081–1118	Alexius I Comnenus		1084–1105	Henry IV
1118–43	John II Comnenus			
1143–80	Manuel I Comnenus			
1180–83	Alexius II Comnenus			
1183–5	Andronicus I Comnenus			
1185–95	Isaac II Angelus			
1195–1203	Alexius III Angelus			
1203–4	Isaac II Angelus and Alexius IV			
1204	Alexius Murzuphlus			

THE LATIN EMPERORS OF CONSTANTINOPLE

1204–5	Baldwin I of Flanders
1206–16	Henry of Hainault
1217	Peter of Courtenay
1217–19	Yolanda
1221–28	Robert of Courtenay
1228–61	Baldwin II
[1231–7	John of Brienne]

1222–54	John III Ducas Vatatzes
1254–8	Theodore II Lascaris
1258–61	John IV Lascaris
1259–82	Michael VIII Palaeologus
1282–1328	Andronicus II Palaeologus
1328–41	Andronicus III Palaeologus
1341–91	John V Palaeologus
1347–54	John VI Cantacuzenus
1390	John VII Palaeologus

1391–1425 Manuel II Palaeologus
1425–48   John VIII Palaeologus
1449–53   Constantine XI Palaeologus

THE DESPOTATE OF EPIRUS

1204–c.1215 Michael I
c.1215–24   Theodore

Despots of Epirus
c.1237–71   Michael II
1271–96   Nicephorus
1296–1318   Thomas

Sebastocrators of Thessaly
1271–96   John I
1296–1303   Constantine
1303–18   John II

Emperors, then Despots of Thessalonica
1124–30   Theodore
1230–c.1240 Manuel
c.1240–44   John
1244–6   Demetrius

1318–23   Nicholas Orsini
1323–35   John Orsini
1335–40   Nicephorus II

List of Muslim Sultans

ABBASIDS OF BAGHDAD

786–809	Harun al-Rashid	902–8	Muktafi
809–13	Amin	912–32	Muqtadir
813–33	Mamun	932–4	Kahir
833–42	Mutasim	934–40	Radi
842–7	Wathik	940–43	Muttaki
847–61	Mutawakkil	943–6	Mustakfi
861–2	Muntasir	946–74	Muti
862–6	Mutazz	974–91	Tai
866–9	Muchtadi	991–1031	Kadir
869–92	Mutamid	1031–75	Kaim
892–902	Mutadid		

SELJUK SULTANS OF RUM

1063–72	Alp Arslan	1210–20	Kaikawus I
1072–92	Malik-Shah	1220–37	Kaikubad I
1077/8–1086	Süleyman I	1237–45	Kaikosru II
1092–1107	Kilij Arslan I	1246–57	Kaikawus II
1107–16	Malik-Shah	1248–65	Kilij Arslan IV
1116–56	Masud I	1249–57	Kaikubad II
1156–92	Kilij Arslan II	1265–82	Kaikosru III
1192–6	Kaikosru I	1282–1304	Masud II
1196–1204	Süleyman II	1284–1307	Kaikubad III
1204	Kilij Arslan III	1307–8	Masud III
1204–10	Kaikosru I		

THE OTTOMAN SULTANS TO THE FALL OF CONSTANTINOPLE

1288–1326	Othman	[1402–10	Süleyman]
1326–62	Orhan	[1411–13	Musa]
1362–89	Murad I	1421–51	Murad II
1389–1402	Bayezit I	1451–81	Mehmet II
1402–21	Mehmet I		

List of Popes

311–14	Melchiades	575–9	Benedict I
314–35	Sylvester I	579–90	Pelagius II
336	Mark	590–604	Gregory I
337–52	Julius I	604–6	Sabinianus
352–66	Liberius	607	Boniface III
355–65	*Felix II*	608–15	Boniface IV
366–84	Damasus I	615–18	Deusdedit *or* Adeodatus I
366–7	Ursinus	619–25	Boniface V
384–99	Siricius	625–38	Honorius I
399–401	Anastasius I	640	Severinus
402–17	Innocent I	640–42	John IV
417–18	Zosimus	642–9	Theodore I
418–22	Boniface I	649–55	Martin I
418–19	*Eulalius*	654–7	Eugenius I
422–32	Celestine I	657–72	Vitalian
432–40	Sixtus III	672–6	Adeodatus II
440–61	Leo I	676–8	Donus
461–8	Hilarus	678–81	Agatho
468–83	Simplicius	682–3	Leo II
483–92	Felix III(II)	684–5	Benedict II
492–6	Gelasius I	685–6	John V
496–8	Anastasius II	686–7	Cono
498–514	Symmachus	*687*	*Theodore*
498, 501–5	*Laurentius*	*687*	*Paschal*
514–23	Hormisdas	687–701	Sergius I
523–6	John I	701–5	John VI
526–30	Felix IV (III)	705–7	John VII
530–32	Boniface II	708	Sisinnius
530	*Dioscorus*	708–15	Constantine
533–5	John II	715–31	Gregory II
535–6	Agapetus I	731–41	Gregory III
536–7	Silverius	741–52	Zacharias
537–55	Vigilius	752	Stephen II
556–61	Pelagius I	752–7	Stephen II (III)
561–74	John III	757–67	Paul I

767–9	*Constantine*	973–4	Benedict VI
768	*Philip*	[974, 984–5	Boniface VII]
768–72	Stephen III (IV)	974–83	Benedict VII
772–95	Hadrian I	983–4	John XIV
795–816	Leo III	985–96	John XV
816–17	Stephen IV (V)	996–9	Gregory V
817–24	Paschal I	[997–8	John XVI]
824–7	Eugenius II	999–1003	Silvester II
827	Valentine	1003	John XVII
827–44	Gregory IV	1004–9	John XVIII
[844	John]	1009–12	Sergius IV
844–7	Sergius II	1012–24	Benedict VIII
847–55	Leo IV	[1012	Gregory]
855–8	Benedict III	1024–32	John XIX
[855	Athanasius]	1032–44	Benedict IX
858–67	Nicholas I	1045–6	Gregory VI
867–72	Hadrian I	1046–7	Clement II
872–82	John VIII	1047–8	Benedict IX
882–4	Marinus I	1048	Damasus II
884–5	Hadrian III	1049–54	Leo IX
885–91	Stephen V (VI)	1055–7	Victor II
891–6	Formosus	1057–8	Stephen IX (X)
896	Boniface VI	[1058–9	Benedict X]
896–7	Stephen VI (VII)	1059–61	Nicholas II
897	Romanus	1061–73	Alexander II
897	Theodore II	[1061–72	Honorius]
898–900	John IX	1073–85	Gregory VII
900–903	Benedict IV	*1080, 1084–1100*	*Clement III*
903	Leo V	1086–7	Victor III
903–4	Christopher	1088–99	Urban
904–11	Sergius III	1099–1118	Paschal II
911–13	Anastasius III	*1100–1102*	*Theodoric*
913–14	Lando	*1102*	*Albert*
914–28	John X	*1105*	*Sylvester IV*
928	Leo VI	1118–19	Gelasius II
928–31	Stephen VII (VIII)	*1118–21*	*Gregory VIII*
931–5	John XI	1119–24	Calixtus II
936–9	Leo VII	1124–30	Honorius II
939–42	Stephen VIII (IX)	*1124*	*Celestine*
942–6	Marinus II	1130–43	Innocent II
946–55	Agapetus II	1130–38	Anacletus II
955–64	John XII	*1138*	*Victor IV*
963–5	Leo VIII	*1143–4*	*Celestine II*
964–6	Benedict V	1144–5	Lucius II
965–72	John XIII	1145–53	Eugene III

1153–4	Anastasius IV	1288–92	Nicholas IV
1154–9	Hadrian IV	1294	Celestine V
1159–81	Alexander III	1294–1303	Boniface VIII
1159–64	*Victor IV*	1303–4	Benedict XI
1164–8	*Paschal III*	1305–14	Clement V
1168–78	*Calixtus III*	1316–34	John XXII
1179–80	*Innocent III*	*1328–30*	*Nicholas V*
1181–5	Lucius III	1334–42	Benedict XII
1185–7	Urban III	1342–52	Clement VI
1187	Gregory VIII	1352–62	Innocent VI
1187–91	Clement III	1362–70	Urban V
1191–8	Celestine III	1370–78	Gregory XI
1198–1216	Innocent III	1378–89	Urban VI
1216–1227	Honorius III	*1378–94*	*Clement VII*
1227–41	Gregory IX	1389–1404	Boniface IX
1241	Celestine IV	*1394–1423*	*Benedict XIII*
1243–54	Innocent IV	1404–6	Innocent VII
1254–61	Alexander IV	1406–15	Gregory XII
1261–4	Urban IV	*1409–10*	*Alexander V*
1265–8	Clement IV	*1410–15*	*John XXIII*
[1268–71	vacancy]	[1415–17	vacancy]
1271–6	Gregory X	1417–31	Martin V
1276	Innocent V	*1423–9*	*Clement VIII*
1276	Adrian V	*1424*	*Benedict XIV*
1276–7	John XXI	1431–47	Eugenius IV
1277–80	Nicholas III	*1439–49*	*Felix V*
1281–5	Martin IV	1447–55	Nicholas V
1285–7	Honorius IV		

Bibliography

1. Original Sources

COLLECTIONS OF SOURCES

Archivio Storico Italiano. 1st ser. Florence, various dates (A.S.I.).

BLOCKLEY, R. C. *The Fragmentary Classicising Historians of the Later Roman Empire.* Eng. trans. Vol. 2. Liverpool 1983 (B.F.C.H.).

Byzantinische Zeitschrift (B.Z.).

Byzantion. Revue Internationale des Etudes Byzantines. Paris and Liège 1924–9; Paris and Brussels 1930; Brussels etc. 1931– (B.).

Corpus Scriptorum Ecclesiasticorum Latinorum. 57 vols. Vienna 1866– (incomplete) (C.S.E.L.).

Corpus Scriptorum Historiae Byzantinae. Bonn 1828– (incomplete) (C.S.H.B.).

COUSIN, L. *Histoire de Constantinople.* Fr. trans. 8 vols. Paris 1685 (C.H.C.).

DE BOOR, C. (Ed.) *Opuscula Historica.* Leipzig 1880 (B.O.H.).

Dumbarton Oaks Papers. Cambridge, Mass. 1941– (D.O.P.).

GUIZOT, F. *Collection des Mémoires Relatifs à l'Histoire de France.* 29 vols. Paris 1823–7 (G.M.H.F.).

HAGENMEYER, H. *Die Kreuzzugsbriefe aus den Jahren 1088–1100.* Innsbruck 1902.

HOARE, F. R. *The Western Fathers.* Eng. trans. London 1954 (H.W.F.).

MAI, Cardinal A. (Ed.) *Novae Patrum Bibliothecae.* 10 vols. Rome 1844–1905 (M.N.P.B.).

MIGNE, J. P. *Patrologia Latina.* 221 vols. Paris 1844–55 (M.P.L.).

—— *Patrologia Graeca.* 161 vols. Paris 1857–66 (M.P.G.).

Monumenta Germaniae Historica. Eds. G. H. Pertz, T. Mommsen *et al.* Hanover 1826– (in progress) (M.G.H.).

MULLER, C. I. T. *Fragmenta Historicorum Graecorum.* 5 vols. Paris 1841–83 (M.F.H.G.).

MURATORI, L. A. *Rerum Italicarum Scriptores.* 25 vols. Milan 1723–51 (M.R.I.S.).

Nicene and Post-Nicene Fathers, Library of the. 2nd series. 14 vols. with trans. Oxford 1890–1900 (N.P.N.F.).

Recueil des Historiens des Croisades. Académie des Inscriptions et Belles Lettres. Paris 1841–1906.

—— *Historiens Occidentaux.* 5 vols. 1844–95 (R.H.C.Occ.).

—— *Historiens Grecs.* 2 vols. 1875–81 (R.H.C.G.).

Revue des Etudes Byzantines. Bucharest and Paris, 1946–   (R.E.B.).

Revue des Etudes Grecques. Paris 1888–   (R.E.G.).

Revue Historique (R.H.).

SANSOVINO, F. *Historia universale dell' origine et imperio de' Turchi.* 3 vols. Venice 1646. *Studies in Church History* (S.C.H.).

INDIVIDUAL SOURCES

ACROPOLITES, George. *Opera.* Ed. A. Heisenberg. Leipzig 1903.

ADAM of Usk. *Chronicon.* Ed. E. M. Thompson. London 1904.

AGATHIAS of Myrina. *The Histories.* Trans. J. D. Frendo. Berlin 1975.

AGNELLUS of Ravenna. *De Sancto Felice.* In *Liber Pontificalis Ecclesiae Ravennatis,* ed. O. Holder-Egger. In M.G.H., *Scriptores Rerum Langobardicarum et Italicarum, saec. VI–IX.* Hanover 1878.

AL-BALADHURI. *Kitab Futuh al-Buldan.* Trans. as *The Origins of the Islamic State* by Philip K. Hitti. New York 1916.

ALBERT of Aix (Albertus Aquensis). *Liber Christianae Expeditionis pro Ereptione Emundatione et Restitutione Sanctae Hierosolymitanae Ecclesiae.* R.H.C.Occ., Vol. 4.

Altino Chronicle. A.S.I. Vol. 8.

AMBROSE, Saint. *Opera.* In C.S.E.L., Vol. 73. 10 parts. Vienna 1955–64.

AMMIANUS MARCELLINUS. *Rerum Gestarum Libri.* Ed. V. Gardthausen. 2 vols. Leipzig 1874–5.

ANAGNOSTES, John. See SPHRANTZES.

ANASTASIUS, Bibliothecarius. In M.P.L., Vol. 80; M.P.G., Vol. 108.

ANNA COMNENA. *The Alexiad.* Ed. Ducange, R.H.C.G. Vol. 1. Eng. trans. E. A. S. Dawes. London 1928; another E. R. A. Sewter. London 1969.

ANONYMUS VALESII. Usually included with Ammianus Marcellinus, *q.v.*

Arab Historians of the Crusades. Select. and trans. from the Arabic sources F. Gabrieli. Eng. trans. E. J. Costello. London 1969.

ARISTAKES, of Lastivert. *History of Armenia.* Fr. trans. M. Canard and Haig Berberian. *Editions de Byzantion,* Brussels 1973.

ATTALEIATES, Michael. *Historia.* C.S.H.B. Vol. 50. Partial Fr. trans. H. Grégoire. *Byzantinische Zeitschrift.* Vol. 28 (1958) and E. Janssens. *Annuaire de l'Institut de Philologie et d'Histoire Orientales et Slaves.* Vol. 20. 1968–72.

AURELIUS VICTOR. *De Caesaribus.* Eds. F. Pichlmayr and R. Gruendal. Leipzig 1966.

BARBARO, N. *Giornale dell' Assedio di Constantinopoli.* Ed. E. Cornet. Vienna 1856. Eng. trans. J. R. Jones. New York 1969.

BRYENNIUS, Nicephorus. *Histories.* C.S.H.B. Vol. 26. Fr. trans. H. Grégoire. B., Vol. 23. 1953.

CANANUS, John. *De Constantinopoli oppugnata.* Ed. I. Bekker. C.S.H.B. 1838 (with Sphrantzes, *q.v.*).

CANDIDUS the Isaurian. *History.* Trans. in B.F.C.H.

CANTACUZENUS, John. *Historiae.* Ed. L. Schopen. 3 vols. C.S.H.B. 1838 (Fr. trans. in C.H.C. Vols. 7, 8. Ger. trans. G. Fatouros and T. Krischer, Stuttgart 1982).

CECAUMENUS. *Strategicon.* Ed. W. Wassiliewsky and V. Jernstedt. St Petersburg 1896.

CEDRENUS, Georgius. *Compendium Historiarum.* C.S.H.B.; M.P.G., Vols. 121–2.

—— *Synopsis Historiarum* (containing John Scylitzes and Scylitzes Continuatus). C.S.H.B.; M.P.G., Vols. 121–2.

CHALCOCONDYLAS, Laonicus. *De origine ac rebus gestis Turcorum.* C.S.H.B.

Chronicle of the Morea. Fr. version J. Longnon. *Livre de la Conqueste de la Princée de l'Amorée.* Paris 1911.

CINNAMUS, John. *Epitome Historiarum.* C.S.H.B. Eng. trans. C. M. Brand. New York 1976.

CLAUDIAN. *Carmina.* Ed. T. Birt. In M.G.H., Vol. 10 (Eng. verse trans. A. Hawkins. 2 vols. London 1817).

CLAVIJO, Ruy González de. *Embajada a Tamorlan.* Ed. F. López Estrada. Madrid 1943. Eng. trans. G. Le Strange. London 1928.

CONSTANTINE VII PORPHYROGENITUS. *De Administrando Imperio.* Gk. text with Eng. trans. R. J. H. Jenkins. Washington 1969.

—— Commentary, R. J. H. Jenkins. London 1962.

—— *De Ceremoniis Aulae Byzantinae.* Ed. and Ger. trans. J. J. Reiske. C.S.H.B.

—— *Narratio de Imagine Edessena.* M.P.G., Vol. 113.

CORIPPUS. *De Laudibus Justini Augusti Minoris.* In M.G.H., *Auctores Antiquissimi,* III, ii.

CYDONES, Demetrius. *Letters.* Ed. with Fr. trans. G. Cammelli. *Démétrius Cydonès, Correspondance.* Paris 1930.

DUCAS, Michael(?). *Historia Turco-Byzantina.* C.S.H.B. New edn. Ed. V. Grecu. Bucharest 1948.

EUNAPIUS. *History.* Trans. in B.F.C.H.

EUSEBIUS, Bishop of Caesarea. *A History of the Church from Christ to Constantine.* Trans. G. A. Williamson. London 1965.

—— *Life of Constantine.* Trans. A. C. McGiffert in N.P.N.F., Vol. 2.

EUSTATHIUS of Thessalonica. *De Thessalonica a Latinis capta, a. 1185.* Ed. I. Bekker. C.S.H.B. German trans. H. Hunger. Vienna 1955.

EUTROPIUS. *Breviarium ab Urbe Condita.* Ed. F. Ruehl. Leipzig 1887. Trans. J. S. Watson. London 1890.

EVAGRIUS. In M.F.H.G., Vol. 5.

GENESIUS, Joseph. *Regna.* Ed. C. Lachmann. C.S.H.B.

GEORGE of Pisidia. *The Heracliad, The Persian Expedition and the* Bellum Avaricum. In C.S.H.B., Vol. 19; also M.P.H., Vol. 92.

GERMANUS, Patriarch. *Letters.* In M.P.G., Vol. 98, 156ff.

GLYCAS, M. *Chronicon.* Ed. I. Bekker. C.S.H.B.

GREGORAS, Nicephorus. *Byzantina Historia.* Ed. L. Schopen and I. Bekker. In C.S.H.B. Ger. trans. J. L. van Dieten. *Nikephoros Gregoras, Rhomäische Geschichte,* 3 vols. Stuttgart 1973–88.

——*Letters. See* Guilland, R.

GREGORY of Cyprus. *Laudatio.* M.P.G. Vol. 142.

GREGORY of Nazianzus, St. *Selected Orations and Letters.* Trans. C. G. Browne and J. E. Swallow in N.P.N.F., Vol. 7.

IBN AL-ATHIR. *Sum of World History* (selection, with Fr. trans.) in R.H.C.Occ. Vol. 1.

IBN JUBAIR. *The Travels of Ibn Jubair.* Trans. R. J. C. Broadhurst. London 1952.

IGNATIUS the Deacon. *Vita Nicephori Patriarchae.* B.O.H.

IGNATIUS of Smolensk. *Pélérinage d'Ignace de Smolensk.* Ed. G. P. Majeska, *Russian Travelers to Constantinople in the 14th & 15th C,* Washington, DC 1984.

JEROME, Saint. *Letters.* Fr. trans. J. Labourt. 8 vols. Paris 1951–63.

JOANNES ANTIOCHENUS. In M.F.H.G., Vols. 4–5.

JOANNES LYDUS. *On Powers, or The Magistracies of the Roman State.* Ed. and trans. A. C. Bandy. Philadelphia 1983.

JOHN CHRYSOSTOM, Saint. *Oeuvres Complètes.* Fr. trans. Abbé Joly. 8 vols. Paris 1864–7.

JOHN of Damascus. *Orations.* In M.P.G., Vol. 94, 1232ff.

JOHN, Bishop of Ephesus. *Ecclesiastical History,* Pt. III. Ed. and trans. R. P. Smith. Oxford 1860.

JORDANES (JORNANDES). In M.R.I.S., Vol. 1.

JULIAN, Emperor. *Works.* Trans. W. C. Wright. 3 vols. London 1913.

LACTANTIUS. *On the Deaths of the Persecutors.* Trans. W. Fletcher. Ante-Nicene Library. Edinburgh 1871.

LEO the Deacon. *Historia.* C.S.H.B.; M.P.G., Vol. 117.

LEO the Grammarian. *Chronographia.* Ed. I. Bekker. C.S.H.B.; M.P.G., Vol. 108.

——— *Lives of the Emperors* (813–948). In C.H.C., Vol. 3.

LEONARD of Chios, Archbishop of Mitylene. *Epistola ad Papam Nicolaum V.* M.P.G. Vol. 159. 1866 (Italian version in Sansovino, *Historia Universale,* III).

LIBANIUS. *Selected Works.* Trans. A. F. Norman. 2 vols. London and Cambridge, Mass. 1969 and 1977.

Liber Pontificalis. De Gestis Romanorum Pontificum. Text, intr. and comm. L. Duchesne. 2 vols. Paris 1886–92 (reprint, Paris 1955).

LIUDPRAND, Bishop of Cremona. *Opera.* Ed. I. Bekker. Hanover 1915. Eng. trans. F. A. Wright. London 1930.

MALALAS, JOHN. In M.P.G., Vol. 97.

MALATERRA, Geoffrey. *Historia Sicula.* M.P.L. Vol. 149. M.R.I.S. Vol. 5.

MANASSES, Constantine. *Compendium Chronicum.* C.S.H.B.; M.P.G., Vol. 127.

MARTIN I, Pope. *Letters.* In M.P.L., Vol. 87.

MATTHEW of Edessa. *Chronicle.* Fr. trans. E. Delaurier. Paris 1858.

MENANDER, Protector. *Embassies.* In C.H.C., Vol. 3.

MICHAEL, Monk of the Studium. *Vita etc. S. Theodori abb. mon. Studii.* M.N.P.B., Vol. 6.

MICHAEL the Syrian (Patriarch). *Chronicle.* Ed. with Fr. trans. J. B. Chabot. Paris 1905–6.

MOUSKES, Philip, *Chronique rimée de Philippe Mouskès*. Ed. F. A. de Reiffenberg. *Collection de Chroniques Belges inédites*. II. Brussels 1838.

MUNTANER, Ramón. *Crónica*. Barcelona 1886 (Eng. trans. Lady Goodenough, in Hakluyt Society edn, London 1920).

NESTOR. *Chronique dite de Nestor*. Ed. and Fr. trans. L. Léger, Paris 1884.

NICEPHORUS, St, Patriarch. *Opuscula Historica* (602–770). Ed. C. de Boor. Leipzig 1880. Fr. trans. in C.H.C., Vol. III.

NICETAS CHONIATES. *Historia*. C.S.H.B. (Fr. trans. in C.H.C.).

NICHOLAS I, Pope. *Epistolae*. M.P.L., Vol. 119.

NICHOLAS MYSTICUS, Patriarch. *Epistolae*. M.P.G., Vol. 111.

OLYMPIODORUS. *History*. In B.F.C.H.

ORDERICUS VITALIS. *Historia Ecclesiastica*. (Ed. A. Le Prevost and L. Delisle.) In *Société de l'Histoire de France*. 5 vols. Paris 1838–55. Eng. trans. with notes T. Forester. 4 vols. London 1854.

OTTO of Freising. *Chronica, sive Historia de Duabus Civitatibus*. M.G.H. *Scriptores*. Vol. 20. Eng. trans. C. C. Mierow. New York 1953.

—— *Gesta Friderici Imperatoris, cum continuatione Rahewini*. Ed. Wilmans. M.G.H. *Scriptores*. Vol. 20. Eng. trans. C. C. Mierow. New York 1953.

PACHYMERES, George. *De Michaele et Andronico Palaeologis*. 2 vols. Ed. I. Bekker. C.S.H.B. (French trans. in C.H.C., Vol. 6).

—— *Georges Pachymérès: Relations historiques*. Ed. A. Failler. Vol. 1 (with Fr. trans. by V. Laurent). Paris 1984.

Paschal Chronicle. In M.P.G., Vol. 92.

PAUL the Deacon. *Historia Langobardorum*. In M.G.H., *Scriptores*, Vols. 2, 13. Eng. trans. W. C. Foulke. Philadelphia 1905.

PAULINUS. *Life of Ambrose*. In H.W.F.

PETER DAMIAN, St. *Opuscula*. M.P.L., Vol. 145.

PHILOSTORGIUS. *Historia Ecclesiae*. In M.P.G., Vol. 65. Partial trans. E. Walford. London 1851.

PHOTIUS, Patriarch of Constantinople. *Epistolae*. M.P.G., Vol. 102.

—— *Homilies. The Homilies of Photius*. Eng. trans., intro. and comm. C. Mango. Harvard 1958.

PRISCUS. *History*. Trans. in B.F.C.H.

PROCOPIUS of Caesarea. *Works*. Trans. H. B. Dewing. 7 vols. London 1914–40.

PRODROMUS, Theodore. *Poemata*. Selections in M.P.G. Vol. 133. R.H.C.G. Vol. 2.

PSELLUS, Michael. *Chronographia*. Eng. trans. E. R. A. Sewter. London 1953. Fr. trans. E. Renauld. 2 vols. Paris 1926.

ROBERT of Clary. *La Conquête de Constantinople*. Ed. Lauer. Paris 1924.

ROGER of Hoveden. *Annals*. Eng. trans. H. T. Riley. London 1853.

RUFINUS, TYRANNIUS. *Ecclesiastical History*. Trans. in N.P.N.F., Vol. 3.

SANUDO, Marino. *Istoria del regno di Romania*. Ed. C. Hopf. In *Chroniques gréco-romanes*. Berlin 1873.

SCRIPTOR INCERTUS. *De Leone Armenio*. C.S.H.B.

SCYLITZES, John. See CEDRENUS.

SEBEOS, Bishop. *Histoire d'Héraclius.* Trans. and ed. F. Macler. Paris 1904.

SIDONIUS, Apollinaris. *Poems and Letters.* Trans. W. C. Anderson. 2 vols. London 1936.

SIMEON, Magister, or Metaphrastes. *Chronicon.* M.P.G., Vols. 109, 113–16.

—— *Vita Theodori Grapti.* M.P.G., Vol. 116.

SIMEON LOGOTHETES. Survives in various forms, incl. Leo the Grammarian, *q.v.*

SOCRATES SCHOLASTICUS. *Ecclesiastical History.* Trans. in N.P.N.F., Vol. 2.

SOZOMEN. *Ecclesiastical History.* Trans. (anon.) in N.P.N.F., Vol. 2.

SPHRANTZES, George. *Chronicon Maius.* Ed. I. Bekker. C.S.H.B. (includes Anagnostes).

STEPHEN, Count of Blois. *Letters* Nos. IV and X, in Hagenmeyer, *Die Kreuzzugsbriefe.*

SYROPULUS, Silvester. *Memoirs.* Ed. R. Creyghton. *Vera historia unionis non verae inter Graecos et Latinos.* The Hague 1660 (See also Laurent, V. below).

THEODORE of the Studium, St. *Epistolae.* M.P.G., Vol. 99.

THEODORET. *History of the Church.* Trans. (anon.) London 1854.

THEODOSIUS, Melitenus. *Chronicon.* Ed. G. L. F. Tafel. Munich 1859.

THEOPHANES, Continuatus. *Chronographia.* Ed. I. Bekker. C.S.H.B.; M.P.G., Vol. 109.

THEOPHANES, St (called Isaacius). *Chronographia.* Ed. C. de Boor. 2 vols. Leipzig 1883 (reprinted Hildesheim 1963). Also in M.P.G., Vols. 108–9.

THEOPHYLACT, Archbishop of Ochrid. *Letters.* M.P.G. Vol. 126.

THEOPHYLACT, Simocatta. *History of the Emperor Maurice.* In C.S.H.B., 1924. Fr. trans. in C.H.C., Vol. III.

VILLEHARDOUIN, Geoffrey of. *La Conquête de Constantinople.* Ed. E. Faral. 2 vols. Paris 1938–9.

Vita Ignatii Patriarchae. M.P.G., Vol. 105.

Vita Nicholai Papae. M.P.L., Vol. 119.

Vita Sancti Euthymii. Ed. with Eng. trans. P. Karlin-Hayter. B., Vols. 25–7, 1955–7.

WILLIAM of Tyre. *Belli Sacri Historia* and *Historia Rerum in Partibus Transmarinis Gestarum.* R.H.C.Occ. Vol. 1. Also with French trans. G.M.H.F. Vols. 16–18.

YAHYA of Antioch. *History.* Partial Fr. trans. M. Canard, in Vasiliev, A. A., *Byzance et les Arabes (q.v.),* II, ii.

ZONARAS, Joannes. *Annales.* Ed. L. Dindorf. 6 vols. Leipzig 1868–75. Also in M.P.G., Vols. 134–5.

ZOSIMUS (Panopolitanus). *Historia.* Ed. with Latin trans. J. F. Reitemeyer. Leipzig 1784.

11. Modern Works

ADONTZ, N. *L'Age et l'Origine de l'Empereur Basile I.* B., Vols. 8–9, 1933–4.

AHRWEILER, H. *L'Expérience Nicéenne.* D.O.P. Vol. 29. (1975) pp. 23–40.

ALEXANDER, P. J. *The Patriarch Nicephorus of Constantinople.* Oxford 1958.

ALFOLDI, A. *The Conversion of Constantine and Pagan Rome*. Oxford 1948.

ALMEDINGEN, E. M. *Charlemagne*. London 1968.

ANDREOTTI, R. *Il Regno dell' Imperatore Giuliano*. Bologna 1936.

ANGOLD, M. *A Byzantine Government in Exile*. Oxford 1975.

—— *The Byzantine Empire, 1025–1204: A Political History*. London 1984.

BARKER, J. W. *Manuel II Palaeologus (1391–1425): A Study in Late Byzantine Statesmanship*. New Brunswick, N.J. 1969.

BAYNES, N. H. 'Constantine the Great and the Christian Church'. *Proceedings of the British Academy*. 1929.

—— *Byzantine Studies and Other Essays*. London 1955.

BAYNES, N. H. and MOSS, H. St L. B. (eds.) *Byzantium: an Introduction to East Roman Civilisation*. Oxford 1948.

BERGER de XIVREY, J. *Mémoire sur la Vie et les Ouvrages de l'Empereur Manuel Paléologue*. Paris 1853.

BERTELE, T. 'I gioielli della corona byzantina dati in pegno alla repubblica bveneta nel sec. XIV e Mastino della Scalla'. In *Studi in Onore di A. Fanfani, II: Medioevo*. Milan 1962, pp. 90–177.

BIBICOU, H. *Une Page d'Histoire Diplomatique de Byzance au XIe. Siècle: Michel VII Doukas, Robert Guiscard et la pension des dignitaires*. B. Vols. 29–30. 1959/60.

BIDEZ, J. *La Vie de l'Empereur Julien*. Paris 1930.

The Blue Guide to Istanbul. Ed. J. Freely. 2nd ed. London and New York 1987.

The Blue Guide to Turkey (The Aegean and Mediterranean Coasts). Ed. B. McDonagh. London and New York 1989.

BOWERSOCK, G. W. *Julian the Apostate*. London 1978.

BRÉHIER, L. *Le Monde Byzantin, I: Vie et Mort de Byzance*. Paris 1947.

BRÉHIER, L. *La Querelle des Images*. Paris 1904.

BROWNING, R. *Justinian and Theodora*. London 1971.

—— *The Emperor Julian*. London 1975.

—— *The Byzantine Empire*. London 1980.

BUCKLER, G. *Anna Comnena*. London 1929.

BURCKHARDT, J. *The Age of Constantine the Great*. Trans. M. Hadas. London 1849.

BURY, J. B. *History of the Later Roman Empire*. 2 vols. London 1889.

—— *The Roman Emperors from Basil II to Isaac Komnenos. English Historical Review*. Vol. 4. 1889.

—— *The Imperial Administrative System in the Ninth Century*. British Academy, Supplemental Papers. 1911.

—— *History of the Eastern Roman Empire*. London 1912.

BUTLER, A. J. *The Arab Conquest of Egypt and the Last Thirty Years of Roman Dominion*. Oxford 1902.

BYRON, R. *The Byzantine Achievement*. London 1929.

CAETANI, G. C. *Annali dell' Islam*. Vols. 1–8. Milan 1905–18.

CAHEN, C. *La Campagne de Manzikert d'après les Sources Musselmanes*. B., Vol. 9, 1934.

—— *La Première Pénétration Turque en Asie-Mineur.* B., Vol. 18, 1948.

—— 'Notes sur l'histoire des croisades et de l'orient latin'. *Bulletin de la Faculté des Lettres de l'Université de Strasbourg.* Vol. 29. 1950–51.

—— *Pre-Ottoman Turkey.* Eng. trans. J. Jones-Williams. New York 1968.

Cambridge Medieval History. Esp. Vol. IV, *The Byzantine Empire, 717–1453.* New edn, ed. J. M. Hussey. 2 vols. Cambridge 1966–7.

CANARD, M. 'La Campagne Arménienne du Sultan Salguqide [*sic*], Alp Arslan et la Prise d'Ani en 1064'. *Revue des Etudes Arméniennes,* II, Paris 1965.

CHALANDON, F. *Les Comnène: Etudes sur l'Empire Byzantin aux XIe and XIIe Siècles.* Vol. 1: *Essai sur le Règne d'Alexis Ier Comnène.* Paris 1900. Vol. 2: *Jean II Comnène et Manuel Comnène.* Paris 1913. (Both volumes reproduced New York 1960.)

—— *Histoire de la Première Croisade.* Paris 1925.

CHAPMAN, C. *Michel Paléologue, restaurateur de l'empire byzantin (1261–1282).* Paris 1926.

CHARLESWORTH, M. P. *The Roman Empire.* Oxford 1951.

COBHAM, C. D. *The Patriarchs of Constantinople.* Cambridge 1911.

DÉCARREAUX, J. 'L'arrivée des Grecs en Italie pour le Concile de l'Union, d'après les Mémoires de Syropoulos'. *Revue des études italiennes* 7. 1960. pp. 27–58.

DELEHAYE, H. *Les Saints Stylites.* Brussels and Paris 1923.

Dictionnaire d'Histoire et de Géographie Ecclésiastiques. Eds. A. Baudrillart, R. Aubert and others. Paris 1912–ㅤㅤ(in progress).

Dictionnaire de Théologie Catholique. 15 vols. in 30. Paris 1909–50 (with supplements).

DIEHL, C. *L'Afrique Byzantine.* 2 vols. Paris 1896.

—— *Etudes Byzantines.* Paris 1905.

—— *Figures Byzantines.* 2 ser. Paris 1906 and 1913.

—— *Histoire de l'Empire Byzantin.* Paris 1918.

—— *Choses et Gens de Byzance.* Paris 1926.

DOWNEY, G. *Constantinople in the Age of Justinian.* University of Oklahoma 1960.

DRAPEYRON, L. *L'Empereur Héraclius et l'Empire Byzantin.* Paris 1869.

DUDDEN, F. H. *The Life and Times of St Ambrose.* 2 vols. Oxford 1935.

DUNLOP, D. M. *The History of the Jewish Khazars.* Princeton 1954.

DVORNIK, F. *The Photian Schism: History and Legend.* Cambridge 1948.

EBERSOLT, J. *Le Grand Palais de Constantinople et le Livre des Cérémonies.* Paris 1910.

Enciclopedia Italiana. 36 vols. 1929–39 (with later appendices).

Encyclopaedia Britannica. 11th ed. 29 vols. Cambridge 1910–11.

—— 15th ed. 30 vols. University of Chicago 1974.

Encyclopaedia of Islam. 4 vols. Leiden, London 1913–34. (New edn in progress, 1960–ㅤ.)

FINLAY, G. *History of Greece, 146 BC to AD 1864.* New edn. Ed. H. F. Tozer. 8 vols. 1877.

FIRTH, J. B. *Constantine the Great.* New York 1905.

FISHER, H. A. L. *A History of Europe.* London 1935.

FLICHE, A. and MARTIN, V. *Histoire de l'Eglise, depuis les Origines jusqu'à nos Jours.* Paris 1934.

FRENCH, R. M. *The Eastern Orthodox Church*. London and New York 1951.

FRIENDLY, A. *The Dreadful Day: The Battle of Manzikert, 1071*. London 1981.

FULLER, J. F. C. *The Decisive Battles of the Western World*. Vol. 1. London 1954.

GARDNER, A. *Julian, Emperor and Philosopher, and the Last Struggle of Paganism against Christianity*. London 1895.

—— *Theodore of Studium*. London 1905.

GAY, J. *Le Pape Clément VI et les affaires d'Orient (1342–1352)*. Paris 1904.

GEANAKOPLOS, D. J. *Emperor Michael Palaeologus and the West, 1258–1282: A Study in Byzantine–Latin Relations*. Cambridge, Mass. 1959.

GFRORER, A. F. *Byzantinische Geschichten*. Ed. J. B. Weiss. 3 vols. Graz 1872–7.

GIBBON, E. *The History of the Decline and Fall of the Roman Empire*. 7 vols. Ed. J. B. Bury. London 1896.

GILL, J. *The Council of Florence*. Cambridge 1959.

—— *John VIII Palaeologus: A Character Study*. Originally published in *Studi byzantini e neoellenici*, Vol. 9. 1957. Reprinted in author's collection, *Personalities of the Council of Florence, and Other Essays*. New York 1964.

GIUSTINIANI, H. *The History of Chios*. Cambridge 1943.

GODFREY, J. *The Unholy Crusade*. Oxford 1980.

GORDON, C. D. *The Age of Attila* (trans. of contemporary sources). University of Michigan 1966.

GRANT, M. *The History of Rome*. London 1978.

GRÉGOIRE, H. *Etudes sur le 9ᵉ. Siècle*. B., Vol. 8. 1933.

—— *Etudes sur l'Epopée Byzantine*. R.E.G., Vol. 46. 1933.

GROSVENOR, E. A. *Constantinople*. 2 vols. Boston 1895.

GRUMEL, V. *La Chronologie*. Vol. 1 of *Traité des Etudes Byzantines*, ed. P. Lemerie. Paris 1958.

GUILLAND, R. *Correspondance de Nicéphore Grégoras*. Paris 1927.

GUIRAUD, J. *Les registres de Grégoire X*. Paris 1892–1906.

GWATKIN, H. M. *Eusebius of Caesarea*. London 1896.

HARNACK, T. G. A. *History of Dogma*. Eng. trans. London 1899.

HAUSSIG, H. W. *History of Byzantine Civilisation*. Trans. J. M. Hussey. London 1971.

HEAD, C. *Justinian II of Byzantium*. University of Wisconsin Press 1972.

HEFELE, C. J. von. *Histoire des Conciles d'après les Documents Originaux*. Fr. trans. from Ger. H. Leclercq. 5 vols. in 10. Paris 1907–13.

HEYD, W. *Geschichte des Levantehandels im Mittelalter*. Stuttgart 1879 (Fr. trans. by F. Raynaud, *Histoire du commerce du Levant au moyen âge*, 2 vols. Leipzig 1936).

HILL, Sir George. *A History of Cyprus*. 3 vols. Cambridge 1913.

HITTI, P. K. *History of the Arabs*. 3rd edn. New York 1951.

HODGKIN, T. *Italy and her Invaders*. 8 vols. Oxford 1880–99.

HOLMES, W. G. *The Age of Justinian and Theodora*. 2 vols. London 1907.

HOOKHAM, H. *Tamburlaine the Conqueror*. London 1962.

HUSSEY, J. M. *The Byzantine World*. London and New York 1957.

JANIN, R. *Constantinople Byzantine*. Paris 1950.

JENKINS, R. *The Byzantine Empire on the Eve of the Crusades.* London 1953.

—— *Byzantium: The Imperial Centuries, AD 610–1071.* London 1966.

JONES, A. H. M. *Constantine and the Conversion of Europe.* London 1948.

KARLIN-HAYTER, P. 'The Emperor Alexander's Bad Name'. *Speculum,* Vol. 44. 1969.

KEEGAN, J. *A History of Warfare.* London 1993.

KINROSS, Lord. *The Ottoman Centuries.* London 1977.

KNOLLES, R. *Turkish History.* 3 vols. London 1687–1700.

KRAUTHEIMER, R. *Early Christian and Byzantine Architecture* (Pelican History of Art). London 1965.

LAURENT, V. Les *'Mémoires' du grand ecclésiarque de l'Église de Constantinople Sylvestre Syropoulos sur le Concile de Florence (1438–1439).* Rome 1971.

LETHABY, W. R. and SWAINSON, H. *The Church of Sancta Sophia, Constantinople: a Study of Byzantine Building.* London 1894.

LOENERTZ, R. J. *Jean V Paléologue à Venise (1370–71).* R.E.B. Vol. 16. 1958.

—— *Byzantina et Franco-Graeca (Articles parus de 1935 à 1966, réédités avec la collaboration de Peter Schreiner)* [Storia e Letteratura: Raccolta di Studi e Testi 118]. Rome 1970.

LOWE, A. *The Catalan Vengeance.* London 1972.

MACLAGAN, M. *The City of Constantinople.* London 1968.

MACMULLEN, R. *Constantine.* London 1970.

MAGDALINO, P. *The Empire of Manuel I Komnenos, 1143–1180.* Cambridge 1993.

MAINSTONE, R. J. *Hagia Sophia: Architecture, Structure and Liturgy of Justinian's Great Church.* London 1988.

MANGO, C. *The Homilies of Photius, Patriarch of Constantinople.* Eng. trans., intro. and comm. Harvard 1958.

—— *The Mosaics of St Sophia at Istanbul.* Washington (Dumbarton Oaks) 1962.

MANN, H. K. *The Lives of the Popes in the Middle Ages.* 18 vols. London 1902–32.

MANZANO, R. *Los Grandes Capitanes Españoles.* Barcelona 1960.

MARIN, E. *Les Moines de Constantinople.* Paris 1897.

MARTIN, E. J. *A History of the Iconoclastic Controversy.* London 1930.

MILLER, W. *The Latins in the Levant: A History of Frankish Greece, 1204–1566.* London 1908.

—— *Essays on the Latin Orient.* Cambridge 1921.

MILMAN, H. H. *The History of Christianity from the Birth of Christ to the Abolition of Paganism in the Roman Empire.* 3 vols. Rev. edn. 1867.

MINNS, E. H. 'St Cyril Really Knew Hebrew'. In *Mélanges Publiés en l'Honneur de M. Paul Boyer.* Paris 1925. (London Library Pamphlets, Vol. 2859.)

NEANDER, A. *General History of the Christian Religion and Church.* 9 vols. Eng. trans. London 1876.

New Catholic Encyclopedia. Washington, DC 1967.

NICOL, D. M. *The Despotate of Epiros.* Oxford 1957.

—— *The Byzantine Family of Kantakouzenos [Cantacuzenus] ca. 1100–1460. A genealogical and prosopographical study.* Dumbarton Oaks Studies, 11. Washington, DC 1968.

—— 'The Byzantine Reaction to the Second Council of Lyons, 1274'. S.C.H. Vol. 7. 1971.

—— *The Last Centuries of Byzantium, 1261–1453.* London 1972.

—— *The Immortal Emperor.* Cambridge 1992.

NORWICH, J. J. *The Normans in the South.* London 1967.

—— *The Kingdom in the Sun.* London 1970.

(The above two volumes published in one, under the title *The Normans in Sicily*, London 1992.)

—— *A History of Venice: Vol. I, The Rise to Empire.* London 1977.

—— *A History of Venice: Vol. II, The Greatness and the Fall.* London 1981.

(The above two volumes published in one, under the title *A History of Venice*, London 1982.)

—— *Byzantium: The Early Centuries (330–800).* London 1988.

—— *Byzantium: The Apogee (800–1081).* London 1991.

—— *Byzantium: The Decline and Fall (1081–1453).* London 1995.

OBOLENSKY, D. *The Bogomils.* Oxford 1948.

—— *The Byzantine Commonwealth.* London 1971.

OCKLEY, S. *History of the Saracens.* 4th edn. London 1847.

OIKONOMIDES, N. 'Leo VI and the Narthex Mosaic at St Sophia'. *Dumbarton Oaks Papers,* Vol. 30. 1976.

OMAN, C. W. C. *The Byzantine Empire.* London 1897.

OSTROGORSKY, G. *History of the Byzantine State.* Trans. J. Hussey. 2nd edn. Oxford 1968.

Oxford Dictionary of Byzantium. Ed. A. P. Kazhdan *et al.* 3 vols. Oxford and New York 1991.

PEROWNE, S. *The End of the Roman World.* London 1966.

RAMBAUD, A. *L'Empire Grec au Dixième Siècle: Constantin Porphyrogénète.* Paris 1870.

RAMSAY, Sir William. *The Historical Geography of Asia Minor.* Royal Geographical Society, Supplementary Papers. Vol. 4. London 1890.

RIDLEY, F. A. *Julian the Apostate and the Rise of Christianity.* London 1937.

ROWE, J. G. *Paschal II, Bohemund of Antioch and the Byzantine Empire.* Bulletin of the John Rylands Library. Vol. 49 (1966–7), pp. 165–202.

RUNCIMAN, Sir Steven. *A History of the First Bulgarian Empire.* London 1930.

—— *The Medieval Manichee.* Cambridge 1946.

—— *A History of the Crusades.* 3 vols. Cambridge 1954.

—— *The Eastern Schism: A Study of the Papacy and the Eastern Churches during the 11th and 12th Centuries.* Oxford 1955.

—— *The Sicilian Vespers.* Cambridge 1958.

—— *The Emperor Romanus Lecapenus and his Reign.* 2nd edn. Cambridge 1963.

—— *The Great Church in Captivity.* Cambridge 1968.

—— *Mistra: Byzantine Capital of the Peloponnese.* London 1980.

SCHLUMBERGER, G. *Un Empereur Byzantin au Dixième Siècle: Nicéphore Phocas.* Paris 1890.

—— *L'Epopée Byzantine à la fin du Dixième Siècle.* Vol. I. Paris 1896.

—— *Expédition des Almugavares ou routiers catalans en orient de l'an 1302 à l'an 1311.* Paris 1902.

—— *Le siège, la prise et le sac de Constantinople en 1453.* Paris 1926.

SEGAL, J. B. *Edessa, 'The Blessed City'.* Oxford 1970.

SETTON, K. M. *Catalan Domination of Athens, 1311–1388.* Cambridge, Mass. 1948.

—— *The Byzantine Background to the Italian Renaissance.* Proceedings of the American Philosophical Society, Vol. 100, no. 1 (February 1956).

SETTON, K. M. (Editor-in-chief). *A History of the Crusades.* 2 vols. University of Wisconsin Press, Madison, Milwaukee and London 1969.

SKOULATOS, B. *Les Personages Byzantins de l'Alexiade.* Louvain 1980.

SMITH, J. H. *Constantine the Great.* London 1971.

SMITH, W. and WACE, H. *Dictionary of Christian Biography.* 4 vols. London 1877–87.

STEIN, E. *Histoire du Bas-Empire, II: de la Disparition de l'Empire de l'Occident à la Mort de Justinien (476–565).* Paris and Brussels 1949.

SUMNER-BOYD, H. and FREELY, J. *Strolling through Istanbul.* Istanbul 1972.

SWIFT, E. A. *Hagia Sophia.* New York 1940.

SYKES, Sir Percy. *A History of Persia.* 2 vols. 3rd edn. London 1930.

TAYLOR, J. *Imperial Istanbul: Iznik – Bursa – Edirne.* London 1989.

TEMPERLEY, H. W. V. *History of Serbia.* London 1919.

THOMPSON, E. A. *A History of Attila and the Huns.* London 1948.

TOYNBEE, A. *Constantine Porphyrogenitus and his World.* London 1973.

VAN DER MEER, F. *Atlas of Western Civilisation.* Trans. T. A. Birrell. Amsterdam 1954.

VAN DER MEER and MOHRMANN, C. *Atlas of the Early Christian World.* Trans. M. F. Hedlund and H. H. Rowley. London 1958.

VASILIEV, A. A. *Manuel Comnenus and Henry Plantagenet.* B.Z. Vol. 29. 1929–30. pp. 238–44.

—— *Byzance et les Arabes.* Fr. edn. prepared by H. Grégoire and M. Canard. Vol. 1: *La Dynastie d'Amorium, 820–867.* Brussels 1935. Vol. II: *La Dynastie Macédonienne, 867–959.* Brussels 1950.

—— *The Goths in the Crimea.* Cambridge, Mass. 1936.

—— *Justin the First: an Introduction to the Epoch of Justinian the Great.* Cambridge, Mass. 1950.

—— *History of the Byzantine Empire, 324–1453.* Madison, Wisconsin 1952.

VOGT, A. *Basile I⁰ʳ et la Civilisation Byzantine à la Fin du Onzième Siècle.* Paris 1908.

—— 'La Jeunesse de Léon VI le Sage.' *Revue Historique,* Vol. clxxiv. 1934.

VOGT, J. *The Decline of Rome: The Metamorphosis of Ancient Civilisation.* Trans. J. Sondheimer. London 1967.

VRYONIS, S. *Byzantium and Europe.* London 1967.

—— *The Decline of Medieval Hellenism in Asia Minor and the Process of Islamization from the Seventh through the Fifteenth Century.* Los Angeles 1971.

BIBLIOGRAPHY

WEST, Rebecca. *Black Lamb and Grey Falcon*. 2 vols. London 1944.
WHELER BUSH, R. *St Athanasias: His Life and Times*. London 1888.
ZAKYNTHOS, D. *Le Despotat grec de Morée, 1262–1460*. Vol. 1. Paris 1932.
ZIEGLER, P. *The Black Death*. London 1969.

Index

Aaron, magister, brother-in-law of
Emperor Isaac, 233
Abbasid Caliphate, 114, 179, 192, 236
Abdul-Malik, Caliph, 102, 192
Abelard de Hauteville, 253
Abu-Bakr, Caliph, 95
Abydos, battle of (989), 208–9
Acacius, Patriarch of Constantinople, 53,
57, 61, 63
Achaia, 321, 326, 343
Acre, 298, 332
Adata, 181
Adelaide, wife of Roger I of Sicily, then of
Baldwin I, 268–9
Adhemar, Bishop of Le Puy, 256, 258
Adrian, *for popes of this name see* Hadrian
Adrianople (*now* Edirne): battle of (323), 8;
Symeon recaptures (932), 174;
Nicephorus Bryennius at, 243;
Kalojan's victory and sacking of, 308;
and Catalans, 335; 1341 revolt, 343;
John VI crowned in, 344; remains in
Empire, 345; granted to Matthew
Cantacuzenus, 347; in Ottoman hands,
350, 363; Mehmet II in, 372–3
Agatha, daughter of Constantine VII, 183
Agnes (Anna), Princess of France, 289,
292, 296
Ahmet, son of Murad II, 372
Aistulf, Lombard King, 115
Alan tribesmen, 335
Alaric the Goth: supports Theodosius, 35;
leads revolt, 37; invades Italy, 38–41;
joined by disaffected barbarians, 40;
reported death, 40; demands agreement

from Rome, 41; death, 42; and sack of
Rome, 42
Albania, 354
Albano, Bishop of, 322
Alboin, King of the Lombards, 85
Aleppo (*formerly* Beroea), 27, 185–6, 192,
211–12, 278, 285
Alexander III, Pope, 288
Alexander IV, Pope, 315
Alexander, Archbishop of Alexandria, 8,
15
Alexander, Emperor, 158, 161, 166–7
Alexandria: importance, 12; Nicetas
captures, 90; captured by Saracens, 97
Alexis, son of Axuch, 284
Alexis of the Studium, Patriarch of
Constantinople, 219
Alexius I Comnenus, Emperor: pursues
Roussel, 243; accession, 244, 247–9;
adopted by Mary of Alania, 247, 249;
rebellion against Nicephorus, 247–8;
appearance and character, 248;
coronation, 249; married life, 249;
relations with Mary of Alania, 249; and
Norman offensive, 250–4; and defeat of
Pechenegs, 254–5; relations with Popes,
255–6; disapproves of First Crusade,
256; dealings with Crusaders, 257–60,
265; and occupation of Jerusalem, 260;
Bohemund accuses, 261; recaptures
fortresses, 261; rule criticized, 261;
subdues Bohemund, 261; fiscal and
economic policy, 262; military interests
and powers, 262–3; reforms, 262; and
East–West church differences, 263;